MW00637880

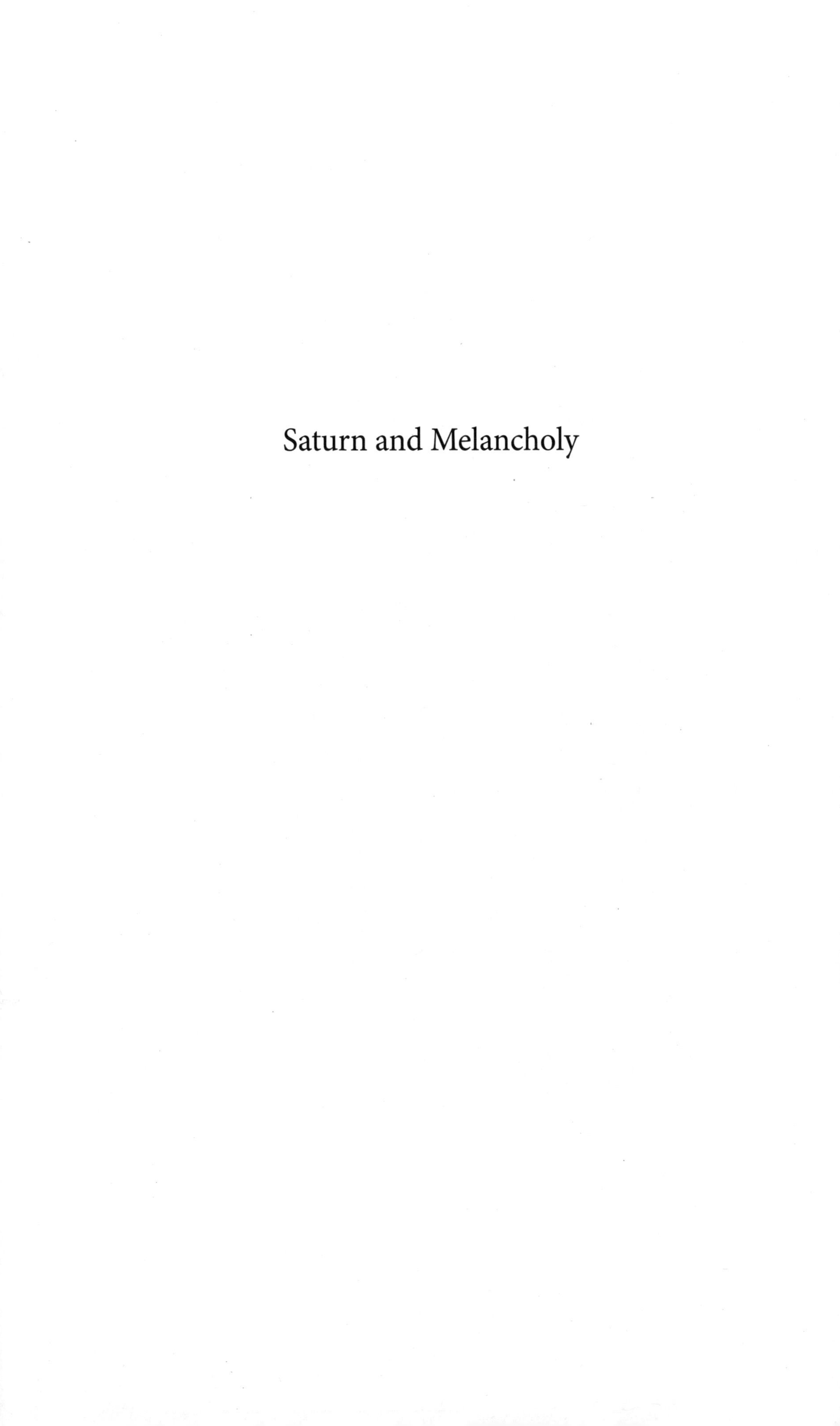

Saturn and Melancholy

Tomb of Robert Burton.
Christ Church Cathedral. Oxford

Saturn and Melancholy

Studies in the
History of Natural Philosophy,
Religion, and Art

NEW EDITION

Raymond Klibanksy,
Erwin Panofsky, and Fritz Saxl

Edited by Philippe Despoix and Georges Leroux
With a foreword by Bill Sherman

McGill-Queen's University Press
Montreal & Kingston • London • Chicago

ISBN 978-0-7735-5949-3 (cloth)
ISBN 978-0-7735-5952-3 (ePDF)

Legal deposit fourth quarter 2019
Bibliothèque nationale du Québec

Printed in Canada on acid-free paper that is 100% ancient forest free (100% post-consumer recycled), processed chlorine free

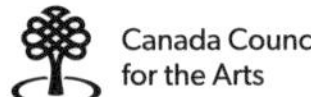

Funded by the Government of Canada | Financé par le gouvernement du Canada | Canada | Canada Council for the Arts | Conseil des arts du Canada

We acknowledge the support of the Canada Council for the Arts.
Nous remercions le Conseil des arts du Canada de son soutien.

Library and Archives Canada Cataloguing in Publication

Title: Saturn and melancholy: studies in the history of natural philosophy, religion, and art / Raymond Klibansky, Erwin Panofsky, and Fritz Saxl; edited by Philippe Despoix and Georges Leroux; with a foreword by Bill Sherman.

Names: Klibansky, Raymond, 1905–2005, author. | Panofsky, Erwin, 1892–1968, author. | Saxl, Fritz, 1890–1948, author. | Despoix, Philippe, editor. | Leroux, Georges, editor.

Description: New edition. | Includes bibliographical references and index.

Identifiers: Canadiana (print) 2019015019X | Canadiana (ebook) 20190150262 | ISBN 9780773559493 (cloth) | ISBN 9780773559523 (ePDF)

Subjects: LCSH: Melancholy. | LCSH: Human beings—Effect of Saturn on.

Classification: LCC BF798 .K5 2019 | DDC 155.2/6—dc23

Contents

Part III "Poetic Melancholy" and "Melancholia Generosa"

Chapter I Poetic Melancholy in post-Medieval Poetry

Chapter II "Melancholia Generosa"

Part IV Dürer

Chapter I Melancholy in Conrad Celtes

Chapter II The Engraving "Melencolia I"

Foreword

In my final year as an undergraduate at Columbia University, I wrote a senior thesis on "Hamlet and Melancholy". As an English major, I turned first to literary scholars such as Bridget Gellert Lyons, whose 1975 study *Voices of Melancholy* gave me my bearings in the Renaissance period's many textual treatments of the subject. But its cover led me to Albrecht Dürer's beguiling engraving *Melencolia I*, the image at the heart of the collaborative study that has been re-edited here and which introduced me, then, to a very different tradition of scholarship for which Art History was (and remains) far too narrow a description. I thus knew the names Saxl, Panofsky, and Klibansky before I knew that of Warburg—whose Institute provided the foundations for their work and whose library and research programmes I now have the privilege of directing. And my own study of the central role played by melancholy in sixteenth-century culture took me on the kind of journey to which Warburg's Institute was (and is) devoted, one moving between words and images and travelling from the Renaissance—in both directions—to antiquity and to modernity.

If *Saturn and Melancholy* served me (thirty years ago) as a guide to a new kind of intellectual history, it now looks like an iconic product—indeed perhaps *the* iconic output—of what the editors of this volume have come to call the Warburg Library Network. It is not just the subject matter (both analysed and experienced, in different ways, by all of these scholars); not just the method (which moves in ways which are increasingly rare between philology and iconology). It is also the conditions under which the book was produced and published, taking nearly seventy years to find its final form and suffering along the way from lost texts, broken relationships, and crossings of countries and languages. That makes its presentation in a new edition all the more precious.

May *Saturn and Melancholy* continue to introduce new students to this old subject and to the now legendary names of those who mastered it—Klibansky, Panofsky, Saxl, and Warburg.

Professor Bill Sherman
Director, Warburg Institute, London

Editors' Note

This volume is a new edition of *Saturn and Melancholy: Studies in the History of Natural Philosophy, Religion, and Art* (New York, Nelson, 1964), co-authored by Raymond Klibansky, Erwin Panofsky, and Fritz Saxl. It has been enlarged on the basis of the German edition (Frankfurt, Suhrkamp, 1990) of the same work, as prepared by Raymond Klibansky, the sole living author at the time. This was to be the last of the revised editions of the book, following the Italian (Turin, Einaudi, 1983) and the French (Paris, Gallimard, 1989) editions.

This new volume contains a reprint of the complete original text of the 1964 English edition with the following additions:

- a translation of Raymond Klibansky's Preface to the German edition (1990);
- a translation of Appendix III from the German edition (1990), introducing additional material on Lucas Cranach's depictions of Melancholy;
- a revised List of Illustrations, and four supplemental illustrations (PLATES 147–150).

The 155 illustrations in this edition have been supplied by the original plates of the Einaudi Italian edition.

Editors' additions include:

- additions to the notes based on the German edition, as well as several supplemental translations from Latin, Greek, Italian, French, Flemish and German quotations from the main text (1964); a manicule (☞) in the margin of the main text signals each instance for which augmented notes or new translations can be found in this section, which is organized by page number;
- the indication of PLATE numbers in page margins where illustrations are discussed in the main text or in footnotes without explicit plate references;
- an English revised version of the Supplemental Bibliography from the German edition;
- an Addendum on the text history of *Problem* XXX, 1, presenting a historical and philological complement to the Greek text, which is reproduced here unmodified from the 1964 edition but which had been revised and commented for the French and German editions;
- an Afterword on the long history of this Warburg Library and Institute publication project.

ACKNOWLEDGMENTS

This new augmented edition is the result of collaborative work spanning many years of study and discussion. We are deeply grateful to the team, whose assistance was invaluable to our efforts towards an edition designed to offer the public a book that is already a classic but which had long been unavailable. We wish to express the warmest thanks to Elisabeth Otto, who contributed to the translation and notes of the German edition; to Jillian Tomm, whose knowledge of the bibliography and the post-1964 history of the work was indispensable to the preparation of notes and translations and who collaborated closely with us on all editorial aspects; and to Maude Trottier, whose investigations and preparation of questions related to iconography were essential. Many thanks also to Miriam Sbih for her excellent help with additional bibliographical research.

This project was in the making for several years. While researching the necessary material for this enlarged edition, two meetings were organised (a preliminary workshop in Montreal in 2013 and a colloquium at the Warburg Institute in London in 2015) with scholars known for their expertise on the history of the Warburgian intellectual constellation. The *Saturn and Melancholy* project was among the central themes discussed, and the collective volume of these studies, now published under the title *Raymond Klibansky and the Warburg Library Network* (McGill-Queen's University Press, 2018) can be considered a companion to this enlarged edition. We are most grateful to all the scholars who contributed to these discussions and enriched our knowledge of the history leading to the publication of the first edition of the book in 1964, after years in waiting due to Nazism and to the Second World War and its aftermath.

This volume could not have reached completion without the generous cooperation of the Warburg Institute, and in particular of Claudia Wedepohl, archivist of the Warburg Institute. We are indebted also to the Deutsches Literaturarchiv Marbach and to McGill University Library's Rare Books and Special Collections for their invaluable help and the ready access to necessary documents that they offered. We are equally grateful for the support provided by the Centre of Intermedial Research in Arts, Literatures and Technologies at the Université de Montréal.

On the path to this new edition we received the constant support of Dr Ethel Groffier, widow of Raymond Klibansky, to whom we would like to express our deep gratitude for her assistance with innumerable consultations. We also wish to thank both Dr Groffier and Dr Gerda Panofsky for their kind permission and encouragement to proceed with this edition.

P. D. and G. L.

Raymond Klibansky's Preface to the German Edition (1990)

The volume at hand is the translation of *Saturn and Melancholy* published in 1964 in London and New York. The *Preface* to that English edition, which we have included in this volume, tells the history of the book, which spans six decades.

Interest in melancholy is today keener than ever. Does this topic not raise questions, apart from its historic importance, that particularly occupy our contemporaries? It is certainly not by chance that the number of studies published on the subject within the quarter century since the appearance of our book has seen a steady and constant increase that continues still; namely, in the fields of medicine and psychiatry, history and philosophy, religion and theology, astrology and alchemy, and literature and art. To do them justice, a separate book would be required.

Two of this volume's authors have now passed on: Fritz Saxl in 1948, Erwin Panofsky in 1968. I therefore considered it appropriate to remain here as faithful as possible to the original text. Modifications were found necessary only where errors required correction, or when readers should be directed to more recent and accessible editions of cited texts. To include new sources would, however, be beyond the scope of this book. In a few exceptions—for example, in the section on Babylonian astrology—it was found necessary to include the latest research. Also, after further review and re-examination of all earlier editions of the foundation text for the history of melancholy, the so-called Aristotelian *Problem* XXX, 1, a critical text was made.[1] The latest research on Lucas Cranach and the various versions of his *Melancholy* have also been summarised in a separate appendix; and finally, four illustrations have been added to the images section (PLATES 147–150), as well as a short selective bibliography.[2]

In what follows we shall also address a few points that could not be included in the English Edition [of 1964].

Few concepts in the history of Western thought compare, in ambiguity, to the word "melancholy". Tracing the word back to its Greek source, it could refer to a particular humour, the black bile, to a sick or abnormal condition, or to a temperament—in particular, to the peculiar temperament of exceptional people. For Martin Luther, "where there is a melancholy head, there the devil has made his bath,"[3] and following Luther, the Protestant tradition continued

---

Translated from the 1990 German edition by Elisabeth Otto and Jillian Tomm. Footnotes and translations are the editors' unless otherwise specified.

[1] See the Addendum on the text history of *Problem* XXX, 1, p. 443 sqq. of this edition.

[2] See Appendix III (Lucas Cranach's Depictions of Melancholy), p. 407 sqq.; and Supplemental Bibliography for the German edition, p. 429 sqq.

[3] M. LUTHER, *Tischreden*, vol. III (Weimarer Ausgabe), Weimar, 1912, No. 2889a and 2889b, p. 51: "Ubi est caput melancholicum, ibi habet Diabolus suum balneum."

to link melancholy to Satan. Jakob Böhme sees in the devil's special affinity for melancholics both the threatening danger of perdition and—equally because of this danger—an opportunity for salvation. In his reflections on the human spirit, Vauvenargues construes melancholy as "an all-encompassing disgust without hope" (*un dégoût universel sans espérance*).[4] Rousseau praises a sweet melancholy, "the friend of delight",[5] yet also refers to a dark melancholy (*mélancolie noire*) not unknown to himself. In the same period, the word signifies for Diderot "the familiar feeling of our own imperfection".[6] For Kant, who thought of himself as melancholic, "genuine virtue from principles therefore has something about it that seems to agree most with the melancholic frame of mind."[7] And, continues Kant, "all shackles, from the golden ones worn at court to the heavy irons of the galley slave, are abominable to [the melancholic]."[8] While Burton viewed melancholy as a chronic disease, other British authors saw in it a source of exquisite delights. For Steele, "that calm and elegant satisfaction which the vulgar call melancholy is the true and proper delight of men of knowledge and virtue";[9] and Addison admits that aesthetic "pleasure increases … and is still greater, if the beauty be softened with an air of melancholy or sorrow."[10] In "Les Amours de Psyché et de Cupidon", La Fontaine speaks of the dark pleasure of a melancholic heart.[11] Two centuries later, Musset confessed his love to Madame Jaubert with the words:

Un petit air de doute et de mélancolie,
Vous le savez, Ninon, vous rend bien plus jolie …

---

4 L. de Clapier, marquis de Vauvenargues, from the chapter "De la haine" of *Introduction à la connaissance de l'esprit humain* (1746), in *Œuvres complètes*, tome I, Paris, 1821, p. 71.

5 J. J. Rousseau, *Émile ou De l'éducation*, Livre IV, t.1, in *Collection complète des œuvres*, Genève, 1780–1789, vol. 4, p. 395: "Mais la mélancolie est amie de la volupté." English translation from *Emile, or On Education*, trans. A. Bloom, New York, 1979, p. 229.

6 D. Diderot, *Encyclopédie ou Dictionnaire raisonné des sciences, des arts et des métiers*, vol. 10, Paris, 1765, s.v. Art. Mélancolie [attrib. L. de Jaucourt and J.-F. de Saint-Lambert], pp. 307–311; here 307: "le sentiment habituel de nôtre imperfection".

7 I. Kant, *Beobachtungen über das Gefühl des Schönen und Erhabenen*, Königsberg 1766, p. 28: "[Die] echte Tugend [also] aus Grundsätzen [hat] etwas an sich, was am meisten mit der melancholischen Gemütsverfassung [im gemilderten Verstande] zusammenzustimmen scheint." English translation from Kant, *Observations on the Feeling of the Beautiful and Sublime and Other Writings*, ed. P. Frierson and P. Guyer, Cambridge, 2011, p. 26.

8 Kant, op. cit., p. 33: "Alle Ketten, von den vergoldeten an, die man am Hofe trägt, bis zu dem schweren Eisen des Galeerensclaven sind ihm abscheulich." English translation from Kant, *Observations on the Feeling of the Beautiful and Sublime and Other Writings*, ed. P. Frierson and P. Guyer, Cambridge, 2011, p. 28.

9 Originally published in *The Tatler* 89 (1709); quoted here from Johannes Harder, *Observations on Some Tendencies of Sentiment and Ethics: Chiefly in Minor Poetry and Essay in the Eighteenth Century Until the Execution of Dr. W. Dodd in 1777*, New York 1966, p. 51.

10 *The Spectator*, no 418, Monday, June 30, 1712.

11 J. de La Fontaine, "Les amours de Psyché et Cupidon" (1669), in *Œuvres complètes*, t. 5, ed., C.A. Walckenaer, Paris, 1821, p. 247: "jusqu'au sombre plaisir d'un cœur mélancolique."

A little air of doubt and melancholy,
You know, Ninon, makes you even more lovely ...[12]

And in *Les Travailleurs de la mer*, Victor Hugo phrased his famous paradox, if now banal due to frequent repetition: "Melancholy is the enjoyment of being sad."[13]

Of an entirely different disposition, Nicolas Chamfort reports the view that: "the melancholic temperament and the patriotic spirit must be purged. These are two unnatural diseases in the country that lies between the Rhine and the Pyrenees; and when a Frenchman falls victim to either of these evils, there is everything to fear for him."[14] In the following century we encounter again a different, more nuanced conception of melancholy with the *frères* Goncourt. In their *Journal*, 28 August 1855, we read: "Nobody has yet expressed in literature the contemporary French melancholia, not a *suiciding* melancholia, not blasphemous, not despairing, but good-humoured melancholia, a sadness which is not without sweetness and in which there is a slight smile of irony. The melancholias of Hamlet, of Lara, of Werther, even of Chateaubriand's René, are characteristic of more northerly peoples than the French."[15] Less than two months later Kierkegaard would die, he for whom melancholy—the form of melancholy that he calls *Tungsind*—was the deepest existential condition of human suffering, caused by separation from God.

What uniting thread holds these diverse meanings together—a multitude of which we have given just a few examples—if not the fact that in each case the word describes an unusual emotional state whose singular condition commands attention? Nonetheless, in this Babel, everyone believes that they understand, if only in their own terms, what it is the other is trying to say.

Likewise in contemporary medical literature, as in earlier centuries, the term is by no means clear. As Calmeil remarked in the *Dictionnaire encyclopédique des sciences médicales* of 1876, "even in the recent past, the word melancholy has nearly always been used to indicate a diseased state characterised by a

---

12 A. DE MUSSET, "À Ninon" (1850), in *Poésies complètes*, ed. M. Allem, Paris, 1962 (Gallimard, Bibliothèque de la Pléiade), p. 377.

13 V. HUGO, *Notre-Dame de Paris 1482—Les travailleurs de la mer*, ed. J. Seebacher, Paris, 1975 (Gallimard, Bibliothèque de la Pléiade), p. 961: "La mélancolie, c'est le bonheur d'être triste." English translation from *The Toilers of the Sea*, trans. J. Hogarth, New York, 2002 (Modern Library Paperback), p. 379.

14 N. de S.-R. CHAMFORT, *Maximes, Pensées, Caractères et Anecdotes* (1795), ed. P. L. Ginguené, London, 1796, p. 182: "[En France, disait M...,] il faut purger l'humeur mélancolique & l'esprit patriotique. Ce sont deux maladies contre nature dans le pays qui se trouve entre le Rhin & les Pyrénées; & quand un Français se trouve atteint de l'un de ces deux maux, il y a tout à craindre pour lui."

15 E. de GONCOURT and J. de GONCOURT, *Journal des Goncourt. Mémoires de la vie littéraire*, vol. 1: 1851–1861, Paris, 1891, p. 97: "Il reste à exprimer en littérature la mélancolie française contemporaine, une mélancolie non suicidante, non blasphématrice, non désespérée, mais la mélancolie humoristique: une tristesse qui n'est pas sans douceur et où rit un coin d'ironie. Les mélancolies d'Hamlet, de Lara, de Werther, de René même, sont des mélancolies de peuples plus septentrionaux que nous." English translation from *The Goncourt Journals, 1851-1870*, ed. and trans. L. Galantière, New York, 1968 [1937], p. 23.

persistence of fear, pessimism, and depression."[16] The melancholic type was assigned "all manner of partial deliriums" (*toutes les espèces de délires partiels*), regardless of the particular nature of the delirious ideas, and the psychiatrist Jean-Étienne Esquirol, regarded as an authority on the subject, objected to adopting the term for, in particular, delirium manifested as constant grief or depression. For him the word "melancholy" should be left to the language of poets, artists, and other "moralists" from whom the rigour of medical men was not expected.[17] He thus proposed to replace the word in the context of illness with the term "lypemania". In our own time, melancholy has been the topic of numerous studies by psychiatrists, especially in Germany, who believe they have found the key to the problem with recourse to contemporary philosophy—first Husserl, then Scheler and finally Heidegger. This approach has been dismissed at a scientific level by their British colleagues, however, who cite a lack of precision in the term, opting instead for distinguishing different levels of depression.

For the Marxist, the root of melancholy lies in the incapacity of the bourgeoisie to resolve in a positive manner the contradiction between the realm of possibility and the hard facts of historical reality. For example, at the first Soviet Writers' Congress it was decided that the goal of literature should be to work towards the abolition of social conditions such as melancholy, melancholy being considered a clear sign of bourgeois decadence. First feared as a disease, then condemned by the Church as the devil's work, now—by another orthodoxy—melancholy was denounced as a social evil.

The term, which up until the beginning of the modern era had been reserved for the *conditio humana*, begins in the Elizabethan age to be applied to a wider range of aspects of the natural world. This evolution would lead Schelling to write: "Thence the veil of sadness which is spread over all nature, the deep, unappeasable melancholy of all life."[18]

The ambivalence of the term had long since crept into the vocabulary of the Christian, who didn't always succeed in distinguishing clearly between melancholy and *acedia*, a conception of very different origin. *Acedia*, initially

---

[16] L.-F. Calmeil, "Lypémanie" in *Dictionnaire encyclopédique des sciences médicales,* t. III, 2nd ser., Paris, 1870, p. 542: "Même à une époque peu éloignée de nous, le mot de mélancolie a presque toujours été employé pour désigner un état maladif caractérisé par la persistance des idées de crainte, de découragement et de tristesse."

[17] J.-É. Esquirol, *Dictionnaire des sciences médicales*, vol. 32, Paris, 1819, s.v. Mélancolie; reprinted in Y. Hersant. *Mélancolies: de l'Antiquité au XXe siècle.* Paris, 2005, p. 714: "Le mot mélancolie, consacré dans le langage vulgaire, pour exprimer l'état habituel de tristesse de quelques individus, doit être laissé aux moralistes et aux poètes qui, dans leurs expressions, ne sont pas obligés à autant de sévérité que les médecins."

[18] F. W. J. Schelling, "Philosophische Untersuchungen über das Wesen der menschlichen Freiheit", in *Philosophische Schriften, erster Band*, Landshut, 1809, p. 399: "Daher der Schleier der Schwermut, der über die ganze Natur ausgebreitet ist, die tiefe unzerstörliche Melancholie alles Lebens." English translation from "Of Human Freedom: A Translation of F. W. J. Schelling's *Philosophische Untersuchungen über das Wesen der menschlichen Freiheit und die damit zusammenhängenden Gegenstände*; With a Critical Introduction and Notes" by James Gutmann, PhD Diss., Columbia University, 1936, p. 79.

identified with inertia, becomes one of the seven deadly sins, but the distinction later becomes blurred and the terms become mixed up, as, for example, in Petrarch.

In the modern era, the Germans and Danish, unlike the French and English, begin to differentiate between melancholy strictly speaking, meaning a temporary state, and notions like *Schwermut* or—for Kierkegaard—*Tungsind*, religious melancholy.

Significantly, in astrological literature since late antiquity, Kronos, like his Roman counterpart Saturn, was also recognised by many different faces; for Tycho Brahe as for Burton after him, he was still the ruler of melancholy. This god, punished by his own son, brings misfortune to the "children of Saturn", that is, those born under his sign. At the same time, in the Platonic tradition Saturn is—as the highest planet—the god of philosophers. Furthermore, because he was identified with Chronos, he is also "Time", who devours his children. Finally, in the astrological tradition that goes back to the end of Hellenism and is later strengthened by the Arabs, he becomes, because of his ominous characteristics, the patron of the infirm and of highwaymen, and yet sometimes also—and in the same texts, for example of Ptolemy and his followers—of the deep thinker (*bathyphrōn*).

In the languages of the Western world and in popular literature, the negative character of Saturn clearly prevails. Nonetheless, the duality appears again and again, both in the view that artists are born under the sign of Saturn and in general statements such as that of Battista da Crema, a Milanese Dominican from the first half of the sixteenth century: "The child of Saturn is either an angel or a devil."[19]

If one traces the history of the term "melancholy" or "black bile" in the texts of Greek antiquity, a pre-scientific element will be noticed which should not be disregarded: the great importance of the colour black and all that it evokes, from Homer onward. In Western history and also in parts of Asia, black is considered a sinister colour closely related to death and often also to diabolical forces. The humour of black bile possessed, then, from the beginning, a special meaning that distinguished it in affective tone from the others, something that remained, without being explicitly recognised, more or less unconsciously.

Without entering into discussion about the authenticity of the writings bearing Hippocrates's name, it is important to underline that we do not share the hypercritical tendencies according to which it would be impossible to attribute anything in the Hippocratic corpus. Good arguments have been put forward to link him to certain writings, such as the third book of the *Epidemics*. In that text, "melancholic" describes a disposition more than a pathological condition, establishing a connection between it and the book *On the Nature of Man*, a crucial work for the Four Humours theory that since the fourth century B.C. was attributed, if not as the work of Hippocrates, at least very

19 B. da Crema, *Opera utilissima della cognitione et vittoria di se stesso*, Venice, 1548, ch. VIII: "*Un saturnino ovvero è un angelo ovvero è un demonio.*" [Reference from the original German Preface.]

likely as that of his pupil Polybus. Its English translation was of the utmost importance for scholars and authors of Elizabethan England. Under the title "A Discourse of Humane Nature", it was published as part of the collection *The Key to Unknowne Knowledge. Or, a Shop of Five Windowes* (London 1599), from the French translation by the physician Jean de Bourges,[20] who also commented the text.

A variety of aspects of melancholy stand out in *Problem* XXX, 1, which is the most important document for the history of the concept and its later connection with the idea of genius. The new critical version presented in this book takes account of the literature published since [the 1964 edition]. At the same time, taking some distance from the text enabled an essential element of the *Problem* to better emerge—that is, the distinction between a state analogous to Plato's divine frenzy or the possession commented in Aristotle's famous phrase in the *Poetics*,[21] and a true illness, even if the former state can only too easily turn into a pathological one.

Among the various types of exceptional people (*perittoi*), the *Problem* mentions especially philosophers, upon whom, like tragic heroes, a punishment for their superiority must fall. This is the source of the tremendous interest that the *Problem* has attracted through the centuries. The history of this text and its transmission to the Occident is yet to be written. As far as the Western tradition is concerned, the text was first known to the Latin-speaking world of the Middle Ages through the philosopher David de Dinant, whose daring theses proclaiming the identity of God, spirit and matter were condemned in 1210 in Paris. This translation from the early thirteenth century precedes by half a century that by Bartholomew of Messina, which was previously thought to be the first.

Although during antiquity Aristotle's authorship of the *Problem* was not questioned, the attribution was put into doubt earlier than is often thought. Indeed, if German philologists of the nineteenth century suggested the name of Theophrastus, the Hessian scholar Friedrich Sylburg had already suggested this connection in his edition of 1585, citing the assessment of his Parisian mentor Henri Estienne.

It is unnecessary to emphasise that this presumed author of the *Problem* was an extremely independent mind. Although certainly a student of Aristotle's, this thinker did not hesitate to stray from the teacher. We have now only a small portion of the approximately two hundred works that are listed as those of Theophrastus in the catalogue made by Diogenes Laertius. Many are the areas in which he appears to have been an innovator. A comprehensive appraisal by historians of philosophy still awaits, but the scope of his interests and the force of his mind are easy to discern.[22]

---

20 Cf. HIPPOCRATES, *Le livre de la nature humaine*, trans. Jean de Bourges, Paris, 1548.

21 Cf. ARISTOTLE, *The Poetics of Aristotle*, ed. and trans. S. Halliwell, Chapel Hill, N.C., 1987, p. 89: "Hence poetry is the work of a gifted person, or of a manic."

22 See the Addendum on the text history of *Problem* XXX, 1, p. 443 sqq. of this edition.

For the logician, Theophrastus's treatment of the theory of modalities and of hypothetical syllogisms represents a remarkable evolution with respect to Aristotle. The historian of philosophy sees in his presentation of the Pre-Socratics the origin of the later doxography. Famous for his book *Characters*, Theophrastus is also author of the two earliest comprehensive works on plants, remarkable in their discussion of morphological concepts. His zoological texts surprise with their exploration of animal psychology. The extent to which he is cited by Hellenistic authors reveals a measure of his influence regarding the systematic application of specific aesthetic categories in moral philosophy. From his lost book on marriage, St Jerome recorded the dictum, much cited since the times of Abelard and Héloïse, that the wise man should not marry. As a follower of Aristotle, Theophrastus praised the life of contemplation and considered it the ideal; yet in various points he diverges from his teacher, for example in regard to the Prime Mover and the notion of place; even the theory of the intellect seems dubious to him. He also differs in his understanding of divinity and piety. Finally, he expresses reservations about Aristotle's fundamental teleological explanation, preferring, in his own arguments, empirical experience and material causes. We can credit him with being the first to have written a monograph on the idea of the individual of exceptional stature and to have searched for an explanation of this phenomenon in nature. Theophrastus is the first philosopher known to have written a treatise on melancholy. Furthermore, the catalogue of his works includes the title *On Drunkenness*, a subject discussed in the *Problem*, as well as a treatise *On Fire*, which—there being no known indication to the contrary—may be the text quoted in the *Problem*.

There is, then, reason to suppose that the *Urtext* of the *Problem* belongs in fact to a series of *Problems* that Diogenes Laertius attributes to Theophrastus, texts that in any case include content similar to that of his treatise on the topic. Shortly after Theophrastus's death, his text doubtless underwent revisions and corruptions through insertions: this would explain the obvious inconsistencies in both reasoning and style. The revised version was then included in a collection of disparate texts drawn from the writings of Aristotle and his school. This first collection of *Problems*, greatly augmented during the following centuries, was already known in Cicero's time under the name added by the compiler—that of Aristotle—and this attribution remained until recent editions.

To the works mentioned in the present volume, another document of great importance must be added—that is, the collection of letters that bear the name of Hippocrates. Among these, the letter to Damagetos, which contains the remarkable story of the encounter between Hippocrates and Democritus, stands out. The latter being considered insane, as he would laugh at everything, his fellow citizens, the Abderites, invited Hippocrates to come and heal him. When he arrived, he found Democritus busy dissecting animals in order to find the origin of melancholy. And when Hippocrates learned the reason for this laughter, he became convinced that it was Democritus who was sane in a world of madmen. From this context arose the observation that "it seems that the whole world is sick without knowing it" and that "we transform the earth our mother into an earth which is our enemy."[23] It is unfortunate that this beautiful text is only available in its original version in old editions of Hippocratic works by Littré and by Ermerins, and in an anthology of Greek epistolographs, all three over a hundred years old, and lately also in the annual report of a grammar school in a small Saxon town.[24] Though disdained by philologists, this fictional body of Hellenistic writing, which has its roots in the first century B.C., was widely appreciated during the Renaissance era, as the number of manuscripts and the two fifteenth-century translations attest, one made by Aurispa and the other by Rinutius of Arezzo. The latter was dedicated to Pope Nicolas V and was reprinted several times between 1479 and 1500. The Latin translations were followed by a French translation by I. Guichard, which can be found at the end of *Traité du ris, contenant son essance, ses causes et mervelheus effais, curieusemant recerchés, raisonnés & observés, par M. Laur. Ioubert, Conselier & Medecin ordinaire du Roy, & du Roy de Navarre* ... (Paris 1579). This translation, also made in 1579, is entitled "La cause morale du ris de l'excellant & tres-nommé Democrite, expliquee et temognee par le divin Hippocras an ses Epitres".

Robert Burton translated the letter to Damagetos in the Introduction to his *Anatomy of Melancholy* of 1621, and it was this very letter that inspired him to adopt the pseudonym Democritus Junior on the title page.

When it comes to Dürer's *Melencolia I*, the observation of Heinrich Wölfflin still holds: "The meaning of Melancholy is far from settled. Almost every year brings new explanations, which is unsurprising when authors fail to restrain themselves through more strict discipline from proclaiming every random idea regarding modern man to be Dürer's own."[25]

This statement from the famous art historian is more than ever true seventy years later. The number of publications about the engraving is so great that a bibliographer could hardly review them all. The diversity of interpretations equals the quantity of texts. Those signalled by Wölfflin tend to be characterised by a certain simplicity: for example, a reading of the central figure of Melancholy as "the spirit", "human reason" or "the angel of science and measurement". Today

---

23 HIPPOCRATES, *Œuvres complètes d'Hippocrate*, ed. E. Littré (grec-français), t. 9, Paris, 1861, p. 360–362: "... *mēpote gar dialanthanē hapas ho kosmos noseōn*" (360) and "... *poieontes ek gēs tēs mētros polemiēn gēn*..." (p. 362). Cf. Hippocrates, *Pseudepigraphic Writings*, ed. and transl. W. D. Smith, Leiden, 1990 (Brill Studies in Ancient Medicine, vol. 2), p. 81.

24 HIPPOCRATES, *Hippocratis quae ferunter Epistolae ad codicum fidem recensitae*, ed. Gualtharius Putzger, Wurzen, Königl. Gymnasium, Jahresbericht, 1914. [Reference from the original German Preface.]

25 H. WÖLFFLIN, *Die Kunst Albrecht Dürers*, 4th ed., Munich, 1920, p. 330 [= Anmerkung zu S. 211]: "Über den Sinn der Melancholie haben sich die Gemüter noch immer nicht ganz beruhigt. Fast jedes Jahr bringt neue Erklärungen, wie das selbstverständlich ist, solange keine strengere Selbstdisziplin die Schriftsteller abhält, jeden beliebigen Einfall eines modernen Menschen als Gedanken Dürers zu proklamieren."

one can choose among elaborate interpretations of astrological, theological, theosophical, freemason, numerological, magical or philosophical nature.

The history of these interpretations—beginning in the sixteenth century with the artist's contemporaries like Joachim Camerarius and passing through Vasari, continuing with Heinrich Conrad Arend, reverend in Goslar in the eighteenth century, and the readings of romantics like Carus, who saw in the Melancholy a representation of Faustian man; including poets like Victor Hugo, art historians such as Charles Blanc and Ruskin, connoisseurs like Oliver Wendell Holmes and painters like Odilon Redon, as well as the numerous interpretations of scholars of our time—is a history interesting in itself, revealing a wide variety of quite different ideas about and ways of understanding one and the same artwork. Such a history would constitute a model for the problem of art criticism generally.

We note also, as a remarkable symptom of its time, an interpretation founded in occult philosophy welcomed in certain circles in England. According to this interpretation, the woman with angel's wings is depicted in a state of visionary trance, expressing the connection between magic and the Cabbala. Moreover, some go as far as to say that the Elizabethan poet George Chapman drew his inspiration for *The Shadow of Night* from Dürer's *Melencolia II*, an image he is supposed to have seen beside *Melencolia I* and which is said to have been lost after serving as model for Gerung's painting (PLATE 123). It is but a small step from occult philosophy to occult history writing!

Certainly Dürer did share the ideas of his time regarding the influence of planets and the temperaments. The magic square is a talisman that invokes Jupiter's protection against menacing rays. But his numerous collected writings suggest no hint of demonology or Cabbala; they show only that Dürer was seeking precision in number and measure in his artistic process. What characterises Dürer is exactly this synthesis of inexhaustible creative imagination and the desire for clarity of structure based on a correct sense of proportion.

The history of interpretations demonstrates that, as in earlier times, painters today are fascinated by what the image reveals to them according to their own perspective. Oskar Kokoschka tells us, for example, at the end of his autobiography, that he considers Dürer's *Melencolia* the "most disturbing of all expressions of the profoundly human mood of fear and despair."[26]

Nor should one forget the reactions of poets, which bespeak at once the great attraction of the image and the personal manner in which it is interpreted. There are those like Théophile Gautier, whose beginnings as a painter prepared him particularly for a critical appreciation, and who saw in the figure the personification of the artist expressing his pain:

---

26 O. KOKOSCHKA, *Mein Leben*, Munich, 1971, p. 324: "[Zur selben Zeit hat Dürer die 'Melancholie' gestochen,] den beklemmendsten Ausdruck der Hoffnungslosigkeit, der Furcht, die ebenso tief menschlich ist." English translation from Kokoschka, *My Life*, trans. D. Britt, New York, 1974, p. 212.

Toi, le coude au genou, le menton dans la main,
Tu rêves tristement au pauvre sort humain:
Que pour durer si peu la vie est bien amère,
Que la science est vaine et que l'art est chimère.
Que le Christ à l'éponge a laissé bien du fiel,
Et que tout n'est pas fleurs dans le chemin du ciel.
Et, l'âme d'amertume et de dégoût remplie,
Tu t'es peint, ô Dürer! dans ta Mélancolie,
Et ton génie en pleurs, te prenant en pitié,
Dans sa création t'a personnifié.
Je ne sais rien qui soit plus admirable au monde,
Plus plein de rêverie et de douleur profonde,
Que ce grand ange assis, l'aile ployée au dos,
Dans l'immobilité du plus complet repos.
Son vêtement, drapé d'une façon austère,
Jusqu'au bout de son pied s'allonge avec mystère,
Son front est couronné d'ache et de nénufar;
...
Et convulsivement sa main presse sa tempe.
Sans ordre autour de lui mille objets sont épars,
...
Il a touché le fond de tout savoir humain;
...
Voilà comme Dürer, le grand maître allemand,
Philosophiquement et symboliquement,
Nous a représenté, dans ce dessin étrange,
Le rêve de son cœur sous une forme d'ange.

You, elbow on knee, chin resting on your hand,
You sadly ponder humanity's miserable lot:
That life is bitter for being so brief,
That science is vain and art an illusion,
That Christ left much gall on the sponge,
And that no flowers line the path to heaven,
And, your soul rife with bitterness and disgust,
You depicted yourself, O Dürer! in your Melencolia,
And your genius in tears, taking pity on you,
Personified you in its creation.
I know nothing more admirable in the world,
More steeped in reverie and profound pain,
Than the great seated angel, wings folded at her back,
In the immobility of absolute repose.
Her clothing, draped austerely,
Extends mysteriously to the tips of her toes,
Her head crowned with lovage and water lily;

...
And she forcefully presses her hand to her temple,
A thousand objects scattered chaotically around her,
...
She has touched upon the limits of human knowledge;
...
This is how Dürer, the great German master,
Philosophically and symbolically,
Portrayed for us in this mysterious drawing,
His heart's longing in the form of an angel.[27]

Others, like Henri Cazalis, see in Dürer's figure of Melancholy the futility of human action in the face of the void:

La Melencolia, songeant à ce mystère,
Qui fait que tout ici s'en retourne au néant,
Et qu'il n'est nulle part de ferme monument,
Et que partout nos pieds heurtent un cimetière
Se dit: Oh! puisque tout se doit anéantir,
Que sert donc de créer sans fin et de bâtir?

Melencolia, reflecting upon this mystery,
That everything returns to nothingness,
And that no monument is eternal,
And that everywhere our feet tread upon cemeteries,
Says to herself: Oh! since all must end in destruction,
What is the point of ceaselessly building and creating?[28]

Or James Thomson:

The sense that every struggle brings defeat
Because Fate holds no prize to crown success;
That all the oracles are dumb or cheat
Because they have no secret to express;
That none can pierce the vast black veil uncertain
Because there is no light beyond the curtain;
That all is vanity and nothingness.[29]

---

27 T. GAUTIER, "Melancholia", in *La comédie de la mort*, Paris, 1838, p. 141 sqq. English translation made by Éric Fontaine and Rachel Morgenstern-Clarren for this edition.

28 H. CAZALIS, "Devant la Melencolia d'Albert Dürer", in *Le Parnasse contemporain. Recueil de vers nouveaux,* Paris, 1866, p. 283. English translation made by Éric Fontaine and Rachel Morgenstern-Clarren for this edition.

29 J. THOMSON, "The 'Melencolia' of Albrecht Dürer", in *The City of Dreadful Night, and other Poems*, London, 1880.

Others, too, are susceptible to its mystery, like Sir William Watson in his "On Dürer's Melencolia":

What holds her fix'd far eyes nor lets them range?
Not the strange sea, strange earth, or heaven more strange;
But her own phantom dwarfing these great three,
More strange than all, more old than heaven, earth, sea.[30]

The number of contributions from art historians and other specialists aiming to explain the many details of the engraving is so great as to be difficult to manage. Some succeed in shedding light on the meaning of one or another element; but all too often we encounter the conviction that the whole can be grasped by understanding the entirety of its various details. The iconographical method is indeed indispensable and invaluable as an auxiliary discipline, but risks reducing the work of art to the sum of its details instead of considering the significance of its fundamental unity. According to a humanist teaching recounted by Dürer's friend Conrad Celtes in a speech to the professors and students of the University of Ingolstadt, the symbols of the poets serve to conceal the holy beneath a sacramental cover (*sacramentali quodam velamine*), protecting it from the common mob. Are not symbols—as the thought was continued by a student of Celtes—veils intended to spur one on to discover the secret? Ultimately, even the most comprehensive and erudite knowledge of its historical details and social context, which is so extensive, is not enough to properly interpret this work; it requires the will and the gift to grasp its uniqueness.

At the other extreme are those, among more recent interpreters in particular, who consider that they possess a special intuition. They have offered a number of hypotheses as ingenious as they are fantastic. For example, it has been argued that *Melencolia I* could embody the futility of human knowledge, ignoring the artist's constant interest in and insistence on the importance of the exact sciences. An interpretation is valid only if it considers both the context in which the work was created and the personal circumstances of the artist around 1514 and during the previous years. In terms of possible literary sources that may have inspired him, the artist's familiarity with them must also be verified, whether through first-hand knowledge or indirectly through those with whom he was associated.

There remain a few points to add to the picture of Dürer's Nuremberg milieu. The work of Ulrich Pinder, the city's physician from 1493 to 1519 and a friend of Conrad Celtes, has in particular been neglected. Pinder's writings, for example, published in his own printing shop, were illustrated by various artists connected with Dürer's circle. Especially rich in illustration, Pinder's

30 W. Watson, "Dürer's 'Melencolia'", in *The Poems of William Watson*, 2 vols. London, 1905 (John Lane, Bodley Head), vol. 2, p. 110.

comprehensive volume entitled *Der beschlossen gart des rosenkrantz marie* (1505), with which Dürer would doubtless have been familiar, integrates—and this is something that has thus far gone unnoticed—a multitude of teachings drawn from Nicholas of Cusa, unattributed and translated into German. Just a few years later, Pinder's deep knowledge of Cusanus's philosophical works was made plain in his *Speculum intellectuale humanae felicitatis* (1510), dedicated to Friedrich III, Elector of Saxony; no other contemporary German author had drawn so extensively from Nicholas's writings, in this case explicitly attributing them to their author. The extent to which they may have influenced Dürer, particularly in their emphasis on the unbreachable gap between human striving towards God and the goal of the infinite, remains uncertain.

Concerning his literary knowledge, Dürer owes much to his friend Willibald Pirckheimer, the author of several translations of Greek works. Dürer illustrated some of these, including a translation of Horapollo's *Hieroglyphica*, made for Emperor Maximilian, and an edition of the *Characters* of Theophrastus. The latter title was dedicated by the translator to the artist. It is through Pirckheimer that we know that Dürer became friends, during his Italian sojourn, with Giovanni Francesco, the nephew of Pico della Mirandola. Furthermore, Ficino's *De vita triplici*, in which the philosopher articulates his theories on melancholy, was accessible to Dürer in a German translation made by Johannes Adelphus Muelich. Trithemius, the abbot of St James's Abbey (Kloster St Jakob) in Würzburg, had, in addition, made known in Nuremberg the manuscript of the first version of Henricus Agrippa of Nettesheim's *Occulta philosophia*, which gives a plausible explanation for the numeral "I" in Dürer's *Melencolia*.

The circle of those who understood that the lowest of the three stages of melancholy as distinguished by Agrippa was actually Imagination, was limited to readers of his handwritten draft of the work that was only printed twenty years later as the *Occulta philosophia*. For those not familiar with this text, it doubtless seemed logical to assume that Dürer had two forms of melancholy in mind – the "natural" (the temperament) and the "unnatural" (pathological)—a view from teachings promoted for centuries in medical and scientific literature, and according to which therefore the numeral "I" would point to the first of these two forms of the *melancholia duplex*.

Dürer's notes emphasise the great importance he attached to the doctrine of temperaments; the different human types are explained exclusively by the four "complexes". He declares that to study and follow these is the student's first duty.[31] That Dürer was himself a melancholic is attested by Melanchthon, who knew him well and speaks of the "melancholia generosissima Dureri". Could this have been another reason for the choice of subject matter?

Dürer's notes also prove helpful in interpreting his engraving; most notably, they explain certain details; and on the basis of Dürer's conception of art, one

---

[31] Cf. A. Dürer, *Schriftlicher Nachlaß*, ed. H. Rupprich, Berlin, 1969, III, pp. 277–286. [Reference from the original German Preface.]

can conjecture as to the meaning of his composition. In the draft of the introduction to his *Four Books of Human Proportion* it says: "For, a good painter is inwardly full of figures (*inwendig voller Figur*), and if it were possible for him to live on forever he would always have to pour forth something new from the inner ideas of which Plato writes."[32]

These inner ideas are evidently very different from the Platonic concept of eternal ideas, which are independent of the people who behold them. They are, like the "inner images" (*inneren Bilde[r]*) spoken of by German mystics, situated in the human soul. As is so often the case, the "mystical" thinkers pick up on a teaching of Thomas Aquinas that, translated into German, takes on a new tone: "The name of the idea—as it says in his *Quaestiones quodlibetales*—means indeed that there exists a certain form, understood by the agent, of which he intends to realize a work that possesses an external similitude with it; for instance, when a builder first conceives in his mind the form of a building, which exists as the idea of the building to be realized materially."[33] But Dürer differs from his predecessors by comparing the artist with God, because—like God—he has the ability to create each day, from ideas in his soul, new human forms and other creatures. The artist is not merely an imitator of nature but a creator himself. However, this new conception of the artist's role is linked, as Dürer's notes show, to an acute awareness of the gap separating the vision of the artist from the finished work.

Thomas Venatorius, the editor of Leone Battista Alberti, commented in his Preface, written in 1540 in Nuremberg: "I remember my fellow townsman, Albrecht Dürer, perhaps the greatest painter of his time, who, when he created *protypa* or *ektypa* [images], as they are called by the Greeks, always satisfied those capable of judging; but (as he himself used to say), he remained always unsatisfied with his work as compared with the beauty of the *archetypos* previously conceived in his mind. What I am writing here, I—along with many other trustworthy and erudite men—have heard him say."[34]

That this attitude of Dürer's towards his own work caught the attention of his contemporaries is confirmed by Melanchthon. In a letter to Prince Georg von Anhalt (17 December 1546) written many years after Dürer's death,

---

32 A. Dürer, *Lehre von menschlicher Proportion, Schriftlicher Nachlaß*, Berlin, 1966, II, p. 109: "Dan ein guter maler ist jndwendig voller vigur. Vnd obs müglich wer, daz er ewiglich lebte, so het er aws den jnneren ideen, do van Plato schreibt, alberg etwes news durch die werck aws tzwgissen." English translation from E. Panofsky, *The Life and Art of Albrecht Dürer*, Princeton, 1955, p. 280.

33 T. Aquinas, *Quaestiones quodlibetales*, IV, I, I (Marietti edition), Roma, 1949, p. 71: "Hoc enim significat nomen ideae, ut sit scilicet quaedam forma intellecta ab agente, ad cuius similitudinem exterius opus producere intendit; sicut aedificator in mente sua praeconcipit formam domus, quae est quasi idea domus in materia fiendae."

34 From the "Epistola nuncupatoria" of Venatorius, in Alberti, *De pictura praestantissimae artis et nunquam satis laudatae*, Basel, 1540, pp. 2–3: "In memoriam venit mihi Albertus Durerus civis meus, pictorum seculi sui facile princeps, qui *protupa* aut *ektupa*, ut Graeci vocant, formans, aliis doctissimis quibusque satisfaciebat semper: at quod conatus fuisset tamen, pro concepti prius a sese in mente *archetupou* magnificentia, satisfecisse sibi nunquam. Nos, quod hic scribimus, ita loquentem, cum multis aliis & bonis & doctis viris, audivimus ..."

Melanchthon recalls the artist saying that in his youth he loved paintings full of colour and different forms, and that he took pleasure in such variety in his own paintings; but that later he began to look increasingly at nature and tried to grasp her unique character. This was when he realised that simplicity was the highest adornment of art; but, incapable of fully achieving it, Dürer could no longer appreciate his works; he would sigh with a sense of his powerlessness whenever he looked at them.

Dürer declared that he even sometimes felt ashamed when he looked at his works again after some time. And yet his records suggest that he did not reject his *Melencolia I*, as he made gifts of the print even long after making it. The fact that he would usually give *Melencolia* together with *Saint Jerome in His Study*, engraved in the same year, seems to indicate that he considered the works as two parts of a whole, likely on account of the contrast between the peace and serenity surrounding the man of faith, on the one hand, and, on the other, the conflicts that dominate a restless and frightening world, its negative aspects highlighted by the hostile character of the bat that flees the light.

It would therefore be justified to believe that Dürer, who was aware of the gulf between an idea and its realization, wanted to express, in this engraving full of symbols from a pagan world, the ultimate impotence of the artist who possesses, indeed, all the technical means necessary as well as knowledge of astral magic and Saturn's natural powers, but who is denied the comforting presence of God. This attitude has, however, nothing to do with a turn to "occult philosophy" or "Christian Cabbala" as has been lately attributed to him.[35]

We know of Dürer's strong interest in Luther's teachings and his close relationship with Melanchthon; but above all from his own writings we see the vital importance he attached to God. It is to God that the artist owes his creative power. Any interpretation—however profound—that leaves aside this deep conviction does justice neither to the artist nor to the work of art. If further proof of the intensity of Dürer's faith were needed, it would suffice to recall his *Man of Sorrows*, who, furthermore, is depicted in an attitude of melancholy.

Finally, even if one takes into account all the interpretations of scholars, artists and poets, it nonetheless must be emphasised that efforts to explain Dürer's intention can penetrate only to a certain extent the enigma of his work. Its magic retains an aspect irreducible to any historical interpretation.

The important books on melancholy that have been published in the last decades have the merit of deepening our knowledge in specific areas that are as diverse as its treatment over the centuries, or its role in French medieval poetry or the German Enlightenment. In his analysis of the symptoms of melancholy, Burton developed the hypothesis that melancholy is a social malady, and in the conclusion of his work proposed as a cure a change in the entire social constellation.

---

35 A reference to the interpretation to Frances YATES and her *The Occult Philosophy in the Elizabethan Age*, London, 1979.

Recently, the connection between melancholy and society has been the subject of another interesting study.[36] Still uncommon are studies that address melancholy across national borders and treat it as a European phenomenon; such an approach would provide an overview that takes over where our book ends.

The gulf that separates the psychiatrist's point of view from those of non-medical authors and artists goes back to the distinction made in the ancient tradition and emphasised in the later Middle Ages between melancholy as a sickness and melancholy as an emotional state rooted in human existence. To shed light on the latter is not the task of physicians; to teach us to interpret it we have, alike, the visions of artists, the creations of poets and the works of novelists. The task remains to present the ways in which melancholy was interpreted in the age of Reformation and Counter-Reformation in England, France, Italy and Germany, but also especially in the Spain of Cervantes and Tirso de Molina within the overall context; to explain why this theme played such a key role in the work of nineteenth-century poets such as Baudelaire and Verlaine, as well as authors like Flaubert; and to explore its significance in the modern novel, after Kierkegaard and Nietzsche, for the self-awareness of the thinking man.[37] The goal of our book is to clarify some of the pre-history of all of this.[38]

Raymond Klibansky
Montreal and Oxford, December 1988

---

36 A probable reference to Wolf LEPENIES and his *Melancholie und Gesellschaft* (Frankfurt am Main, 1972), now available in English translation by J. Gaines and D. Jones as *Melancholy and Society*, Cambridge, Mass., 1992.

37 There is no space nor time here to deliver a list, not even a selective one, of the works and essays published these last years. I will content myself by singling out—even if too cursorily—Jean STAROBINSKI, whose persistent and uniquely discerning attention is testified through numerous writings since his *Histoire du traitement de la mélancolie des origines à 1900* (Bâle, 1960) [reprinted in *L'Encre de la mélancolie*, Paris, Seuil, 2012, pp. 13–158]; English translation: *History of the Treatment of Melancholy from the Earliest Times to 1900*, Basel, Geigy, 1962. [From the French edition of 1989.]

38 I would like to thank the Hannah Foundation for the History of Medicine, Toronto, for their generous support, which made possible the work of re-examining manuscripts and rare books in European and American libraries.

My special thanks go to Dr Christa Buschendorf in Heidelberg, Lecturer at the University of Düsseldorf; she took pains to translate this difficult text, managed with a light touch the many problems that arose during printing, and made this collaboration a constant source of joy. I also gratefully thank Mr Friedhelm Herborth, Editor of the Suhrkamp publishing house, and his assistant, Ms Elke Habicht, for their helpful attention and assistance towards the completion of this book. And finally, we must mention the help of Silvia von Hase, PhD candidate, in translating the French, Italian and Latin text passages. [From the original German Preface.]

Preface to the First English Edition (1964)

From the remote times when events in the world of man were first held to be linked with the stars, Saturn was thought to retard any undertaking connected with him. No doubt the ancients would have found ample evidence of his sluggish influence in the fate of this book.

In 1923, Erwin Panofsky and Fritz Saxl published *Dürers 'Melencolia. I'. Eine quellen- und typengeschichtliche Untersuchung* (Studien der Bibliothek Warburg, B. G. Teubner, Leipzig). When this study was out of print, it was decided to prepare a new, revised and enlarged edition in which the development of the doctrine of the temperaments would be described in detail and the history of "Saturn, Lord of Melancholy" traced to the threshold of modern times. In due course, the broadened scope of the work made it necessary to abandon the framework of the monograph on Dürer's engraving. The plan of a new book on Saturn and Melancholy emerged, to be undertaken by the three authors whose names now appear on the title-page.

At every stage, the preparation of the book was beset by delay and adversity. After a lengthy interruption due to the political upheaval in Germany during the 'Thirties and to the authors' emigration from that country, work was resumed in Britain. In the summer of 1939, the final proofs were returned to the printers in Glückstadt near Hamburg; shortly after the Armistice, in 1945, it was learned that the standing type had been destroyed during the war. To resurrect the now defunct German book seemed out of the question. Instead, the authors agreed to publish an English translation, to be made from a surviving copy of the German proofs. Owing to the untimely death of Fritz Saxl in March 1948, the execution of this project suffered a long delay.

When eventually the work was taken in hand again, some rearrangements and several modifications were found necessary; however, the contents of the book were left substantially unaltered. During the last two decades much has been written concerning the various fields touched upon in this book; in particular, almost every year presents us with new interpretations of Dürer's engraving, a few of which are mentioned in E. Panofsky's *Albrecht Dürer* (4th edition, Princeton 1955). Any attempt to take account of all this literature would have swelled the present volume to an unmanageable size. Some further details might have been filled in, some controversial points more fully discussed; yet the authors feel confident that the argument as a whole would not have been affected.

At the same time, they are aware of some gaps in the treatment of their vast subject. There are many related themes which might have been followed up. To name only a few: The legend of Democritus, the melancholy philosopher, whom "the world's vanity, full of ridiculous contrariety," moves to laughter, could have been traced from its Hellenistic origins to its memorable appearance in the preface by 'Democritus Junior' to the *Anatomy of*

Melancholy. Much might have been added concerning the part played by melancholy in French literature of the later Middle Ages, e.g. in the poetry of Charles d'Orléans. In treating of astrology, the authors confined themselves to investigating the historical origins and the development of the belief in Saturn's influence; there remain the wider tasks of understanding the significance of any such belief in the power of the stars and of elucidating the reasons for which human beings have invested the planets with the very forces that rule their own microcosm.

The limits set to this book excluded any endeavour to do justice to the complex and enthralling topic of Elizabethan and Jacobean melancholy. Tempting as it was to delve into the riches of Burton, the authors had to content themselves with paying homage to the great 'melancholizer' by prefixing his effigy to the present volume.

Our warm thanks are due to Miss Frances Lobb who carried out the arduous task of preparing the first draft of the translation from the German. With particular gratitude we record the aid received from the staff of the Warburg Institute, University of London, above all in procuring the photographs for the illustrations and in rendering valuable assistance throughout the long period of preparation and in the earlier stages of the proofs. We are especially beholden to the late Hans Meier who first drew our attention to the original version of Agrippa's *De occulta philosophia*, discovered by him in a manuscript of the University Library of Würzburg.

We wish also to express our appreciation to the many institutes and libraries whose collections we were able to use: in particular, to the Johns Hopkins Institute of the History of Medicine, Baltimore, and to the Institut für Geschichte der Medizin, Johann Wolfgang Goethe-Universität, Frankfurt (Main); to the Courtauld Institute, University of London; to the British Museum, London; to the Bodleian Library, Oxford; to the Bayerische Staatsbibliothek, Munich, and to the Biblioteca Apostolica Vaticana; last, not least, to the librarians and the staff of the Redpath Library and the Osler Library of McGill University, Montreal.

We are obliged to the many scholars and collectors who answered our enquiries; and to Miss Désirée Park, M.A. (McGill), for sharing the burden of reading the proofs.

We are most grateful to all those who collaborated with us in revising the translation: Dr Gertrud Bing, London, Miss Rosemary Woolf, Fellow of Somerville College, Oxford and above all Dr Lotte Labowsky, Lady Carlisle Research Fellow of Somerville College, who by her valuable observations also helped in establishing the Greek text of the famous Problem XXX, I, attributed to Aristotle.

Finally, we are indebted to the publishers, Thomas Nelson & Sons, for their patience and assistance in seeing the book through the press.

R. K.
E. P.

List of Illustrations

FIGURES

List of Abbreviations

B or Bartsch	= A. BARTSCH, *Le peintre graveur*. Vols. I–XXI, nouvelle édition. Leipzig 1854–70.
BBC, *Sternglaube*	= F. BOLL, C. BEZOLD, W. GUNDEL, *Sternglaube und Sterndeutung*, 4th edn. Leipzig 1931.
BERNARDUS SILVESTRIS, *De univ. mundi*	= BERNARDUS SILVESTRIS, *De mundi universitate libri duo sive Megacosmus et Microcosmus*, edd. C. S. Barach and J. Wrobel. Innsbruck 1876.
Cat. astr. Gr.	= *Catalogus codicum astrologorum Graecorum*, tom. I–XII. Brussels 1898–1953 (continued).
Clm.	= *Codex latinus monacensis* = Munich, Bayerische Staatsbibliothek, MS lat.
Corp. med. Gr.	= *Corpus medicorum Graecorum*, edd. Academiae Berolinensis Havniensis Lipsiensis. Leipzig and Berlin (later, Berlin only) 1908–56 (continued).
Corpus Ss. Eccl. Lat.	= *Corpus Scriptorum Ecclesiasticorum Latinorum*, editum consilio et impensis Academiae Litterarum Caes. Vindobonensis (now Acad. Scientiarum Austriacae), Vienna 1866–1962 (continued).
DIELS, *Fragm.*	= *Fragmente der Vorsokratiker*, ed. H. Diels, revised by W. Kranz, Vols. I–III, 5th edn. Berlin 1934–37.
Dürers Melencolia I	= E. PANOFSKY and F. SAXL, *Dürers 'Melencolia I'*. (Studien der Bibliothek Warburg), Leipzig and Berlin 1923.
FICINO, *De v. tripl.*	= MARSILIUS FICINUS, *De vita triplici*, in: Marsilius Ficinus, *Opera omnia*. Basle 1576.
GALEN (KÜHN)	= CLAUDIUS GALENUS, *Opera omnia*, ed. C. G. Kühn, Vols. I–XX, Leipzig 1821–33.
GIEHLOW (1903)	= KARL GIEHLOW, "Dürers Stich 'Melencolia I' und der maximilianische Humanistenkreis", *Mitteilungen der Gesellschaft für vervielfältigende Kunst*. Vienna 1903, pp. 29–41.
GIEHLOW (1904)	= KARL GIEHLOW, "Dürers Stich 'Melencolia I' und der maximilianische Humanistenkreis", *Mitteilungen der Gesellschaft für vervielfältigende Kunst*. Vienna 1904, pp. 6–18; 57–58.
HARTLAUB, *Geheimnis*	= G. F. HARTLAUB, *Giorgiones Geheimnis*. Munich 1925.
HIPPOCRATES (Jones)	= HIPPOCRATES, with an English translation by W. H. S. Jones. Vols. I–IV. London and New York 1923–31.
H. d. G.	= C. HOFSTEDE DE GROOT, *Die Handzeichnungen Rembrandts*. Haarlem 1906.
ISIDORE, *Etym.*	= ISIDORUS, *Etymologiarum sive originum libri xx*, ed. W. M. Lindsay. Oxford 1911.
L or Lippmann	= F. LIPPMANN, *Dessins d'Albert Dürer–Zeichnungen von Albrecht Dürer*, Vols. I–VII. Berlin 1883–1929.
LF, *Nachlass*	= K. LANGE und F. FUHSE, *Dürers schriftlicher Nachlass*. Halle a. S. 1893.
LITTRÉ	= Oeuvres complètes d'Hippocrate, traduction nouvelle avec le texte grec en regard, par É. Littré. Vols. I–X. Paris 1839–61.
M. A. R. S.	= *Mediaeval and Renaissance Studies*, ed. R. Hunt and R. Klibansky, Vols. I–V, London, 1941–61.

MIGNE, P. Gr. = Patrologiae cursus completus . . . Series Graeca, accurante J. P. Migne. Paris 1857–66.

MIGNE, P. L. = Patrologiae cursus completus . . . Series Latina, . . . accurante J. P. Migne. Paris 1844–64.

PAULY-WISSOWA = *Paulys Real-Encyclopädie der Classischen Altertumswissenschaft*, neue Bearbeitung, begonnen von G. Wissowa, . . ., Vols. I–(continued) and Suppl. I–(continued). Stuttgart 1894 ff.

P or Passavant = J. D. PASSAVANT, *Le peintre-graveur*, Vols. I–VI, Leipzig 1860–64.

PRISCIAN, *Eupor.* = THEODORUS PRISCIANUS, *Euporiston libri III*, ed. V. Rose. Leipzig 1894.

RUFUS = RUFUS EPHESIUS, *Oeuvres*, edd. C. Daremberg and E. Ruelle. Paris 1879.

SAXL, *Verzeichnis* = F. SAXL, *Verzeichnis astrologischer und mythologischer illustrierter Handschriften des lateinischen Mittelalters*, Vol. I, Heidelberg 1915; Vol. II, Heidelberg 1927.

SCHREIBER = W. L. SCHREIBER, *Handbuch der Holz- und Metallschnitte des XV. Jahrhunderts*, Vols. I–VIII, Leipzig 1926–30.

T or Tietze = H. TIETZE und E. TIETZE-CONRAT, *Kritisches Verzeichnis der Werke Albrecht Dürers*, Vol. I, Augsburg 1928; Vol. II, i–ii, Basle and Leipzig 1937–38.

VINDICIANUS, *Epist.* = VINDICIANUS, *Epistula ad Pentadium nepotem suum*, in: THEODORUS PRISCIANUS, *Euporiston libri III*.—Accedunt Vindiciani Afri quae feruntur reliquiae. Ed. V. Rose. Leipzig 1894.

WEDEL, *M.A.A.* = T. O. WEDEL, *The Mediaeval Attitude towards Astrology, particularly in England* (Yale English Studies, Vol. LX). New Haven 1920.

PART I

The Notion of Melancholy and its Historical Development

In modern speech the word "melancholy" is used to denote any one of several somewhat different things. It can mean a mental illness characterised mainly by attacks of anxiety, deep depression and fatigue—though it is true that recently the medical concept has largely become disintegrated.[1] It may mean a type of character—generally associated with a certain type of physique—which together with the sanguine, the choleric and the phlegmatic, constituted the system of the "four humours", or the "four complexions" as the old expression was. It may mean a temporary state of mind, sometimes painful and depressing, sometimes merely mildly pensive or nostalgic. In this case it is a purely subjective mood which can then by transference be attributed to the objective world, so that one can legitimately speak of "the melancholy of evening", "the melancholy of autumn",[2] or even, like Shakespeare's Prince Hal, of "the melancholy of Moor-ditch".[3]

---

[1] See E. Kraepelin, *Manic-Depressive Insanity and Paranoia*. Transl. by R. M. Barclay, Edinburgh 1921; G. L. Dreyfus, *Die Melancholie*, with Preface by E. Kraepelin, Jena 1907; E. L. Hopewell-Ash, *Melancholie in Everyday Practice*, London 1934; E. Biermann's survey *Die Melancholiefrage in Literatur und Statistik*, MS. dissertation, Jena 1926; L. Binswanger, *Melancholie und Manie*, Pfullingen 1960.

[2] It is curious how these literary commonplaces in which 'melancholy' is used as a matter of course, as denoting a subjective mood, still echo the ancient medical and cosmological correlations (see below, p. 225).

[3] *Henry IV*, pt. i, i.ii, 88.

Chapter I

MELANCHOLY IN THE PHYSIOLOGICAL LITERATURE OF THE ANCIENTS

I. THE DOCTRINE OF THE FOUR HUMOURS

In the order stated above—not necessarily following one another, but often existing side by side—these various meanings evolved in the course of a development covering more than two thousand years. Although new meanings emerged, old meanings did not give way to them; in short, it was a case not of decay and metamorphosis, but of parallel survival. The original basis of the different meanings was the quite literal conception of a concrete, visible and tangible part of the body, the "black bile" (atra bilis, μέλαινα χολή, μελαγχολία), which, together with the phlegm, the yellow (or "red") bile, and the blood, constituted the Four Humours. These humours corresponded, it was held, to the cosmic elements and to the divisions of time; they controlled the whole existence and behaviour of mankind, and, according to the manner in which they were combined, determined the character of the individual.

> Sunt enim quattuor humores in homine, qui imitantur diversa elementa; crescunt in diversis temporibus, regnant in diversis aetatibus. Sanguis imitatur aerem, crescit in vere, regnat in pueritia. Cholera imitatur ignem, crescit in aestate, regnat in adolescentia. Melancholia imitatur terram, crescit in autumno, regnat in maturitate. Phlegma imitatur aquam, crescit in hieme, regnat in senectute. Hi cum nec plus nec minus iusto exuberant, viget homo.[4]

In these clear, terse sentences of an early medieval natural philosopher, we have the ancient doctrine of the Four Humours. This system was destined to dominate the whole trend of physiology and psychology almost until the present day; for what the

---

[4] Anon., *De mundi constitutione* (Migne, P. L., vol. xc, col. 881D). This cosmology, dating from before 1135, is printed among Bede's works. Though hitherto almost ignored (see below, p. 183, note 182), it is remarkable in many ways, and we shall deal with it elsewhere in greater detail.

"heterodox" schools of antiquity had opposed to humoral pathology was either forgotten or else merged into the orthodox doctrine by the second-century eclectics, especially Galen. In the same way, Paracelsus's objections went long unheard.

This system can be accounted for only by the combination of three very ancient (and, in part at least, specifically Greek) principles:

1. The search for simple primary elements or qualities, to which the complex and apparently irrational structure of both macrocosm and microcosm could be directly traced.

2. The urge to find a numerical expression for this complex structure of bodily and spiritual existence.

3. The theory of harmony, symmetry, isonomy, or whatever other name men may have chosen to express that perfect proportion in parts, in materials, or in faculties, which Greek thought down to Plotinus always regarded as essential to any value, moral, aesthetic or hygienic.

In seeking, then, to ascertain the origin of humoralism, we must go back to the Pythagoreans, not only because the veneration of number in general attained its highest expression in Pythagorean philosophy, but more particularly because the Pythagoreans regarded the number four as specially significant. They used to swear by four, "which holds the root and source of eternal nature"[5]; and not only nature in general, but rational man in particular, seemed to them governed by four principles, located in the brain, the heart, the navel and the phallus respectively.[6] Even the soul was later on envisaged as fourfold, enclosing intellect, understanding, opinion and perception (νοῦς, ἐπιστήμη, δόξα, αἴσθησις).[7]

The Pythagoreans themselves did not evolve a doctrine of four humours, but they prepared the ground by postulating a series of tetradic categories (such as, for instance, those already mentioned; earth, air, fire and water; spring, summer, autumn and winter).[8] In this system, once it was evolved, the four humours could easily be accommodated. Above all, they defined health as the equilibrium of different qualities, and sickness as the predominance of one—a concept truly decisive for humoralism proper.

---

[5] DIELS, *Fragm.*, Anonyme Pythagoreer, B15; cf. THEO SMYRNAEUS, ed. E. Hiller, Leipzig 1878, p. 97, 4.

[6] DIELS, *Fragm.*, Philolaus, B13.

[7] DIELS, *Fragm.*, Anonyme Pythagoreer, B15.

[8] THEO SMYRNAEUS, ed. cit., pp. 93 sqq.

Alcmaeon of Croton, a Pythagorean doctor who lived about 500 B.C., declared that "equality of rights (ἰσονομία) between the qualities (δυνάμεις) moist, dry, cold, hot, bitter, sweet, and the rest, preserved health, but the rule of one among them (μοναρχία) produces sickness"; and he condensed the notion of health into the formula "a well-balanced mixture of the qualities" (σύμμετρος τῶν ποιῶν κρᾶσις).[9] Whereas Alcmaeon left indefinite the number and nature of the qualities whose isonomy constituted health ("moist, dry, cold, hot, bitter, sweet, and the rest"), Philolaus took a step forward towards humoralism by describing the number four as "the principle of health" (ὑγιείας ἀρχή).[10]

The emergence of a thoroughgoing doctrine of humoralism required, however, the fulfilment of three further conditions. First, the Pythagoreans had venerated four as being a perfect number. It was now also given a physical content; this was achieved when the Pythagorean number symbolism was transformed into a doctrine of the cosmic elements. Secondly, each of these four elements had to be interpreted in terms of a quality which established, as it were, an apparent link between the original elements and the corresponding components of the human body which could not, in their empirical actuality, be regarded as pure earth, pure water, and so on. Thirdly, certain real substances which appeared to correspond to those elements and qualities had to be found in the human body, for only then could the speculations of natural philosophy be reconciled with the empirical evidence of medicine and physiology.

Thus from the Pythagoreans the road leads next to Empedocles, in whose doctrine the first of these conditions was fulfilled. He endeavoured to combine the speculations of the old natural philosophers, such as Thales or Anaximenes, who thought only in terms of matter and therefore traced all existence back to one primary element, with the precisely opposite tetradic doctrine of the Pythagoreans, which was based on the idea of pure number.

---

[9] DIELS, *Fragm.*, Alcmaeon, B4 (similarly PLATO, *Rep.*, 444D). Cf. here (and with what follows) C. FREDRICH'S valuable study "Hippokratische Untersuchungen", in *Philologische Untersuchungen*, XV (1899), pp. 33 sqq. (edd. A. Kiessling and U. von Wilamowitz-Moellendorff); K. SUDHOFF, *Kurzes Handbuch zur Geschichte der Medizin*, Berlin 1922; M. WELLMANN, "Die Fragmente der sikelischen Ärzte Akron, Philistion und Diokles von Karystos", in *Fragmentsammlung der Griechischen Ärzte*, ed. M. Wellmann, Berlin 1901, VOL. I, pp. 76 sqq.; O. TEMKIN, "Der systematische Zusammenhang im Corpus Hippocraticum", in *Kyklos* (*Jahrbuch des Instituts fur Geschichte der Medizin*), I, Leipzig 1928, pp. 9 sqq.; and L. EDELSTEIN, article "Hippokrates" in PAULY-WISSOWA, supplementary vol. VI, cols. 1290 sqq.

[10] DIELS, *Fragm.*, Philolaus, A11.

In this attempt he evolved the doctrine of the Four Elements, which paired the "four roots of the All" with four specific cosmic entities—the sun, the earth, the sky and the sea. These elements (called ῥιζώματα by Empedocles, but ever since Democritus στοιχεῖα) were of equal value and power, but each had its own particular task and its own particular nature. In the course of the seasons each in turn gained the ascendancy, and it was their combination (κρᾶσις), different in each single case, which brought into existence all individual things and which alone determined the characters of men. The perfect combination was, first, that in which all the elements were equally apportioned; secondly, that in which the elemental units—as we should say, the atoms—of the combination were neither too many nor too few in quantity, neither too coarse nor too fine in quality. This perfect combination produced the man with the largest understanding and the keenest wit. If all the elements were not equally apportioned, the man would be a fool. If the number of the apportioned atoms was either too great or too small, the man produced would be either gloomy and lethargic, or hot-blooded and enthusiastic, but incapable of sustained effort. And if the combination was more perfect in one part of the body than in another, this would produce individuals with a marked specific talent—orators, for instance, if the "crasis" of the tongue, artists if that of the hands, was especially good.[11]

From this it will be seen that Empedocles had firmly—almost too firmly—established the unity of macrocosm and microcosm (man and universe deriving from the same primary elements), and that he had already made an attempt to demonstrate a systematic connexion between physical and mental factors—in other words, to put forward a psychosomatic theory of character. But it will also be seen that this attempt was far too general and far too speculative to satisfy the requirements of a specifically anthropological theory, much less of a medical one. In so far as he held that human beings, as well as the physical universe, were composed only of earth, air, fire and water, Empedocles did indeed establish a common basis for the macrocosm and the microcosm: but he ignored what was proper to the microcosm as such. He reduced man to general, cosmic elements, without

---

[11] Cf. especially THEOPHRASTUS, *De sensu*, § 11 (DIELS, *Fragm.*, Empedokles, A86) and G. M. STRATTON, *Theophrastus and the Greek Physiological Psychology before Aristotle* (with text of Περὶ αἰσθήσεως), London 1917, pp. 74 sqq.

probing that which is specifically human; he gave us, as it were, the original matter, but not the materials of man's composition.

Those of a more anthropological turn of mind could not rest content with this, but were driven to search for specific substances (and faculties) in man, which should somehow correspond to the primary elements constituting the world as a whole, without being simply identical with them.

Empedocles's immediate successors had already felt the need of making his anthropological concepts rather more elastic, by partly depriving the elements composing man of their purely material nature and by attributing to them a more dynamic character. Philistion, the head of the Sicilian school of medicine founded by Empedocles, still, it is true, described man as a combination of the four elements earth, air, fire and water, just as his master had done; but he added the notion that each of these elements possessed a certain quality (δύναμις)—"to fire belongs heat, to air cold, to water the moist, to earth the dry".[12] In so doing he fulfilled the second of our conditions.

Thus Empedocles's theory of the elements was reconciled with Alcmaeon's theory of the qualities, with the result that the elements lost their uncompromisingly material nature, while the number of qualities, which Alcmaeon had left indefinite, was now reduced to a tetrad. It was therefore only logical that in answer to the question "When is the crasis of the qualities right and proper?", Philistion himself should reply simply with the words: "Illnesses arise from the predominance or defect of a quality".[13] While, regarding the primary particles of the elements, the Empedoclean theory of character (of Empedoclean medicine nothing certain is known[14]) had introduced the notion of "too coarse" and "too fine" side by side with the notion of "too much" and "too little", the new method, using only the ideas of superfluity and deficiency, made them stretch to cover a vast number of differentiations. For the qualities could not only form dual combinations (warm and moist, warm and dry, cold and moist, and cold and dry): they also, which was of more immediate importance, could free themselves from the Empedoclean primary elements and so be used as predicates of any other substances.

---

[12] Pap. Lond. xx, 25 (*The Medical Writings of Anon. Lond.*, ed. Jones, Cambr. 1947, p. 80).

[13] Cf. FREDRICH, op. cit., p. 47.

[14] This is the greater pity as Empedocles always thought of himself as a physician and was reckoned as such in antiquity: cf. DIELS, *Fragm.*, A3, B111.

Both theories reached their full maturity not long before 400, when humoralism really originated. It originated then for the very reason that the ideas discussed by us so far concerning the elements and qualities were now—not without violence—applied to the humours (χυμοί) as empirically demonstrated in the human body.[15] These humours had long been known in the specifically medical tradition, in the first instance as causes of illness, and, if they became visible (as in vomiting or the like), as symptoms of illness. Nourishment brought substances into the body which, thanks to the digestion, were partly made use of (that is, turned into bones, flesh and blood), but were partly ἄπεπτα—indigestible; and from the latter arose the "surplus humours" (περισσώματα), the notion of which had developed very similarly to that of the cosmic primary elements. Euryphon of Cnidus had assumed an indefinite number of such humours, which rose to the head and generated illnesses; Timotheus of Metapontus believed they were caused by a single acid salty fluid; and Herodicus of Cnidus distinguished two such fluids, one sour and one bitter.[16] These were the two humours which later received the names phlegm (φλέγμα) and bile (χολή)—phlegm because it caused inflammation, although not a few writers attributed to it the qualities of cold and moisture. Such a correlation is presupposed in the very important treatise *Of the Nature of Man* (Περὶ φύσιος ἀνθρώπου),[17] attributed by the ancients, as we know from Galen, either to Hippocrates or to his son-in-law Polybus,[18] and written in any case not later than 400 B.C. What gave this document its unique value for posterity was its attempt to combine in one system humoral pathology proper with general cosmological speculation, more particularly that of Empedocles.[19]

---

[15] Such an attempt was made in the work *Περὶ ἀρχαίης ἰητρικῆς* (before 400), which transformed Alcmaeon's doctrine so as to apply primarily to substances actually present in the body (salt, bitter, sweet, sour, sharp and insipid stuffs), while representing the qualities warm, cold, wet and dry as mere accidents: cf. FREDRICH, op. cit., p. 33. This attempt, however, deviates from the trend under investigation, in so far as it increases the number of these substances even more indefinitely than the original Alcmaeic doctrine had increased the number of qualities: *ἔνι γὰρ ἐν ἀνθρώπῳ καὶ ἁλμυρὸν καὶ πικρὸν καὶ γλυκὺ καὶ ὀξὺ καὶ στρυφνὸν καὶ πλαδαρὸν καὶ ἄλλα μυρία* . . . (c. 14; *Corp. med. Gr.*, I, i, 45).

[16] FREDRICH, op. cit., pp. 34 sqq.

[17] We are concerned only with the first part of this composite work.

[18] FREDRICH, op. cit., pp. 51 sqq.; HIPPOCRATES, ed. W. H. S. Jones, VOL. IV, p. xxvi, London 1931.

[19] FREDRICH, op. cit., pp. 28 sqq.; cf. also R. O. MOON, *Hippocrates and his Successors in Relation to the Philosophy of their Time*, London 1923, especially pp. 67 sqq. Also O. VILLARET's dissertation *Hippocratis de natura hominis liber*, Berlin 1911; GALEN, *In Hippocratis de nat. hom. comm.*, in *Corp. med. Gr.*, V, ix, I.

Guided by this desire, the author's first step was to reject the view of those who held that the human body originated from, and subsisted in virtue of, a single element only. He was moreover, as far as we know, the first writer who put forward a theory of the four humours. At the outset—though later it was to become almost canonical—it could only be established with the help of two quite arbitrary assumptions. The blood had to be included in the system, although it was not in fact a surplus humour; and in the bile, which hitherto had been regarded as a single fluid, or else split down into innumerable sub-species, it was necessary to distinguish two independent "humours", the yellow bile (χολὴ νξαθή), and the black (μέλαινα χολή = μελαγχολία).[20] These four humours were always present in the human body and determined its nature; but according to the season sometimes one and sometimes another gained the ascendancy—the black bile, for instance, in the autumn, whereas the winter was unfavourable to it and the spring inimical, so that autumn-engendered pains would be relieved by the spring. The four humours, then, caused both illness and health, since their right combination was health, but the predominance or defect of one or another, illness: ὑγιαίνει μὲν οὖν μάλιστα, ὅταν μετρίως ἔχῃ ταῦτα τῆς πρὸς ἄλληλα δυνάμεως καὶ τοῦ πλήθεος καὶ μάλιστα, ἢν μεμιγμένα ᾖ.[21]

These are all ideas of which the origin can now be established. The notion of the humours as such comes from empirical medicine. The notion of the tetrad, the definition of health as the equilibrium of the different parts, and of sickness as the disturbance of this equilibrium, are Pythagorean contributions (which were taken up by Empedocles). The notion that in the course of the seasons each of the four substances in turn gains the ascendancy seems to be purely Empedoclean. But the credit for combining all these notions in one system, and thereby creating the doctrine of

---

[20] Admittedly, already Philolaus (DIELS, *Fragm.*, A27) considered blood a cause of illness, while the division of bile into τὰ χολώδη and μέλαινα χολή (as in Dexippus of Cos) or into χολώδεα ξανθά and χολώδεα μέλανα (as in *Epidemics* I, case 5, HIPPOCRATES, VOL. I, p. 196, ed. W. H. S. Jones, London 1923) seems to have been known to some 'Hippocrateans'. These references are isolated, however—those in Dexippus and in *Epidemics* are definitely not older than the work Περὶ φύσιος ἀνθρώπου—and here too there is a tendency to include them in the cosmological system. In any case, that the doctrine contained in Περὶ φύσιος ἀνθρώπου rather than any other gained the day (cf. WELLMANN, op. cit., pp. 75 sqq.) was due to the fact that it was the one to make this inclusion complete and to present the system with impressive simplicity.

[21] *De nat. hom.*, cap. 4; we follow GALEN, *Comment.* I, 20, *Corp. med. Gr.*, V, ix, I, p. 33.

humoralism which was to dominate the future, is no doubt due to the powerful writer who composed the first part of Περὶ φύσιος ἀνθρώπου.[22] This system included not only the Pythagorean and Empedoclean tetrad but also the doctrine of the qualities that Philistion handed down to us—first, in groups of two, forming a link between the humours and the seasons, later also appearing singly and connecting the humours with the Empedoclean primary elements. From this the author of the Περι φύσιος ἀνθρώπου evolved the following schema, which was to remain in force for more than two thousand years[23]:

Humour	*Season*	*Qualities*
Blood	Spring	Warm and Moist
Yellow Bile	Summer	Warm and Dry
Black Bile	Autumn	Cold and Dry
Phlegm	Winter	Cold and Moist

Probably as early as with the Pythagoreans, the four seasons had been matched with the Four Ages of Man, the latter being counted either as boyhood, youth, manhood and old age; or, alternatively, as youth till twenty, prime till about forty, decline till about sixty, and after that old age. A connexion could therefore be established without more ado between the Four Humours (and later the Four Temperaments) and the Four Ages of Man—a connexion which held good for all time and which was to be of fundamental significance in the future development of both speculation and imagery.

Through the whole of the Middle Ages and the Renaissance this cycle remained virtually unchanged, apart from some controversy over its starting point: it could begin with "phlegmatic" childhood, passing through "sanguine" youth and "choleric" prime to "melancholic" old age (in certain circumstances returning to a "second childhood"); or else it could begin with "sanguine" youth, pass through a "choleric" period between twenty and

---

[22] Many ancient writers believed in the genuinely 'Hippocratean' origin of Περὶ φύσιος ἀνθρώπου: see above, p. 8 and note 18; in any case the author of this work appears to have been the first to put this doctrine in writing. Cf. FREDRICH, op. cit., pp. 49, 51 sqq.

[23] FREDRICH, op. cit., p. 45. Cf. GALEN, *De placitis Hippocratis et Platonis libri novem*, ed. I. Mueller, Leipzig 1874, VOL. I, pp. 679 sqq. (*κοινὸς ὁ λόγος ἐστὶν ἐπί τε τῶν χυμῶν καὶ τῶν στοιχείων*). If Boll is right, the series in 'Antiochus of Athens' would be roughly contemporary with Galen (*Cat. astr. Gr.*, VOL. VII, p. 104; BBG, *Sternglaube*, p. 54), whence, however, the rubric 'temperaments' should be omitted.

forty and a "melancholic" period between forty and sixty, and end in a "phlegmatic" old age.[24]

But this combination of the purely medical doctrine of humours with a system of natural philosophy gave rise to a curious difficulty of which earlier writers were quite unconscious but which was later to come very much to the fore and which was never wholly resolved. On the one hand, with the exception of blood, the humours taken over from medicine were quite useless substances, not to say harmful.[25] They were excretions, "humores vitiosi", causing illness, first observed primarily in vomiting and other symptoms[26]; the adjectives derived from them, φλεγματικός (φλεγματώδης), χολερικός (χολώδης), and especially μελαγχολικός, were in origin merely descriptive of illness; and one could only speak of true health when all the humours were present in the right combination, so that each harmful influence neutralised the other.

On the other hand, these very substances, though regarded as in themselves causes of illness, or at least as predisposing factors, were paired with the universal (and hygienically neutral) qualities, cold, moist, warm and dry. Each gained the ascendancy once a year without necessarily causing acute illnesses; and since the absolutely healthy man was one who was never ill at all (so that he must be as like every other absolutely healthy man as two peas in a pod, the right combination of the humours being one alone and permitting no divergencies), the physician, of all people, could not avoid the conclusion that this absolutely healthy man represented an ideal hardly ever met with in reality.[27]

---

[24] For these correlations, cf. F. Boll, "Die Lebensalter", in *Neue Jahrbücher für das klassische Altertum*, XXXI (Leipzig 1913), pp. 101 sqq., with numerous references; also below, pp. 112 sqq. and pp. 369 sqq. While some post-classical authors extend the cycle of the four seasons so as to apply to each of the ages of man (this view also found its way into rabbinical writings), others narrowed it so as to apply to the different times of day. Thus, blood reigned from the ninth hour of the night until the third hour of the day, i.e. from 3 a.m. to 9 a.m., and thereafter the others reigned in six-hourly shifts, red bile, black bile and phlegm; cf. Pseudo-Soranus (*Medici antiqui*, Venice 1547, fol. 159v) and Vindician (Priscian, *Eupor.*, p. 487). The distribution of the humours among the four ages of man differs slightly from the ordinary in these two authors: phlegm "cum sanguine" reigned from birth till the fifteenth year, red bile "cum parte sanguinis" till the twenty-sixth year, black bile "cum maxima parte sanguinis" till the forty-second year, and lastly, "sicut in pueris", phlegm once more. Cf. the comments on Pseudo-Soranus and Vindician below, pp. 63 sqq. and pp. 108 sqq.

[25] See the familar passage in Plato, *Timaeus*, 82A–83E.

[26] Fredrich, op. cit. (see above, p. 5, note 9), p. 34.

[27] Cf. Sudhoff, op. cit., p. 120: "Everyone [sc. according to Galen] lives in a certain distemper; temperament is already the beginning of a painful and disordered condition; in every individual one of the four humours predominates against nature."

Thus, in such a tradition, what had of old been symptoms of illness came gradually to be regarded, at first unconsciously, as types of disposition. Complete health was only an ideal, approximated, but never in fact attained. It was logical enough, if one said of someone in whose body the humours were perfectly combined that he was "in the very best of health" (μάλιστα ὑγιαίνει), for it was thereby implicitly admitted that someone in whom one or other humour predominated could nevertheless enjoy good health, though not in the highest possible degree. And thus it had to be conceded that in fact it was usually a predominance of one or other humour which determined a man's constitution and that such an individual, though predisposed to certain quite definite illnesses, normally seemed quite healthy. The words "phlegmatic" and so on came to be used for peculiar but (within the limits of this peculiarity) not necessarily morbid aspects of human nature; and once the doctrine of four humours had been systematised in the form described, it was bound gradually to become a doctrine of four temperaments.

As 'Hippocrates' says at one point, "too dry a summer or autumn suits phlegmatics but does the greatest harm to cholerics, who are in danger of being dried up completely, for their eyes run dry, they are feverish, and some fall into melancholy sicknesses"[28]—which shows that the Hippocrateans themselves envisaged men with constitutions determined by a permanent predominance of either phlegm or yellow bile, who were not as a rule actually ill but merely predisposed to certain illnesses, and who were in certain circumstances even susceptible to illnesses other than those deriving from their predominant humour. From this time onward the expressions "choleric", "phlegmatic", and "melancholy", were capable of two fundamentally quite different meanings. They could denote either pathological states or constitutional aptitudes. It is true, however, that the two were closely linked, since it was usually one and the same humour which adverse circumstances permitted to develop from mere predisposition into actual illness. As Isidore says, "the healthy are governed by these four humours, and the sick suffer from them".[29]

The system into which humoralism developed brought with it, however, another complication, in that two of the four humours,

---

[28] Περὶ ἀέρων, ὑδάτων, τόπων, cap. 10. (LITTRÉ, II, p. 50; *Corp. med. Gr.*, I, I, p. 66).

[29] ISIDORE, *Etym.*, IV, 5, 7.

blood, and black bile, clearly occupied an exceptional position, arising out of the system's historical development; and this distinction makes itself felt in the terms used.

As to the blood, from the very beginning it had (so to speak) got in only by the back door, for not only was it *not* a surplus humour, it was the noblest and most essential part of the body.[30] Though it remained a recognised principle that the blood too caused illnesses (mainly acute, like those caused by the yellow bile, the two cold humours generating more chronic ones), and though the *Corpus Hippocraticum* ranged excess of blood alongside phlegmatic, choleric, and melancholy sickness,[31] yet constitutional predominance of the blood was generally regarded, not as a morbid disposition, but rather as the healthy one *par excellence*, and therefore the best,[32] so that medical texts often replace the usual wording "complexio sanguinea" simply by the term "complexio temperata".[33]

Greek physiology, in which humoralism meant primarily humoral pathology, apparently lacked an adjective to describe a constitution determined by the blood,[34] as the choleric is determined by the yellow bile, or the phlegmatic by the phlegm. And it is significant that in the later doctrine of the four temperaments (in which, as in modern speech, the terms were applied to the habitus and character of the healthy) the "sanguine" temperament, and only that, bore a Latin name.[35]

The opposite was the case with the "humor melancholicus". The blood fitted into the series of humours (conceived as waste) so little that it was difficult to make a purely pathological diagnosis of the condition caused by an excess of blood; for that very reason, the sanguine temperament stood out from the others in much

---

[30] Fredrich, op. cit., p. 45; Galen, Περὶ κράσεων, ed. Helmreich, Leipzig 1904, II, 603, p. 59, where, for instance, blood is called τῶν χυμῶν ὁ μὲν χρηστότατός τε καὶ οἰκειότατος).

[31] Fredrich, op. cit., p. 45.

[32] See below pp. 58 sqq., 98 sqq. (esp. 102) and passim.

[33] See below, p. 128, note 5.

[34] The expression ὕφαιμος had indeed lost its morbid meaning among the Physiognomists, but as far as we know it was not equated with χολώδης etc., but meant either "full-blooded" (as in 'Aristotle', in *Scriptores physiognomici graeci et latini*, ed. R. Förster, Leipzig 1893, vol. I, p. 18, 8) or, more generally, was used for the ruddy or bloodshot appearance of individual features (*Script. phys. gr. et lat.*, I, 30, 17; II, 225, 16). The Physiognomists seem to have used the word αἱματώδης only in the latter sense (*Script. phys. gr. et lat.*, I, 388, 5; 331, 3).

[35] Significantly enough, it took the form "sanguineus", whereas the three other adjectives had been formed with "-icus".

the same way as the beautiful but vacant "normal profile" stands out from the ugly but striking "character profiles" in Dürer's physiognomic drawings. The black bile, on the contrary, had long been considered a noxious degeneration of the yellow bile, or, alternatively, of the blood.[36] It presented such a well-known and characteristic picture of morbidity (dating possibly even from pre-Hippocratean times) that the disease as such was denoted by one noun. Against the compound expressions χολερικαὶ or φλεγματικαὶ νόσοι, χολερικὰ or φλεγματικὰ παθήματα, were set the simple μελαγχολία, μελαγχολίαι.[37] So, too, later conceptions of the melancholy temperament were coloured far more by the notion of a melancholy illness than was the case with the other three temperaments. It is also significant that melancholy as an illness became the subject of monographs particularly early and often.[38]

Thus it is understandable that the special problem of melancholy should have furnished, as it were, the leaven for the further development of humoralism. For the more striking and terrifying the morbid manifestations that came to be associated with the notion of a certain humour, the greater became its power to create a character type; and it is only by an apparent paradox that this very melancholy, which of all the "crases" bore the most markedly pathological connotation, came to be the one in which a difference was earliest and most clearly discerned between actual disease and mere predisposition, between pathological states and divergencies of character, in short between disease and temperament; whereas an analogous development of the other humoral conceptions followed only much later.[39]

There is, however, a further consideration. Unlike the others, the illness called "melancholia" was one mainly characterised by symptoms of mental change, ranging from fear, misanthropy and depression, to madness in its most frightful forms. Later, melancholia could equally well be defined as a bodily illness with mental repercussions or as a "permixtio rationis" of physical origin; a peculiarity which must have considerably facilitated

---

[36] See below, p. 103.

[37] Cf. *Scriptores physiognomici graeci et latini*, ed. R. FÖRSTER, Leipzig 1893, VOL. II, p. 274, 25 and p. 282, 21.

[38] Cf. Rufus, and Galen's review of older works, cited below, pp. 44 sqq.

[39] As far as we know, the complete system of the doctrine of the four temperaments, correlating habitual physical and mental qualities with the four humours, was not fully developed until A.D. 200 or a little later (see below, p. 58).

the process of separating the merely melancholic temperament from melancholic illness. For the ambiguity of psychological symptoms blurred the borderline between illness and normality and compelled recognition of a habitude which, though being melancholy, did not make it necessary to describe the subject as one who was really a sick man all the time. This peculiarity was bound to shift the whole conception of melancholy into the realm of psychology and physiognomy, thereby making way for a transformation of the doctrine of the four humours into a theory of characters and mental types. In fact we can see how even the medical writers had begun to conceive the melancholic in decidedly physiognomic and psychological terms: the lisping, the bald, the stuttering, and the hirsute are afflicted with strongly melancholic diseases,[40] emotional disturbances were described as an indication of "mental melancholy,"[41] and finally—a constantly repeated diagnosis—the symptoms were summarised in the phrase: "Constant anxiety and depression are signs of melancholy."[42]

2. THE NOTION OF MELANCHOLY AS REVOLUTIONISED BY THE PERIPATETICS: PROBLEM XXX, I

We are now in a position to understand the great transformation which the notion of melancholy underwent during the fourth century B.C., owing to the irruption of two great cultural influences: the notion of madness in the great tragedies, and the notion of frenzy in Platonic philosophy. The clouding of consciousness, depression, fear and delusions, and finally the dread lycanthropy, which drove its victims through the night as howling, ravening wolves,[43] were all regarded as effects of the sinister substance

---

[40] *Epidem.*, II, 5, I (Ps. Hippocr.), in *Scriptores physiognomici graeci et latini*, VOL. II, p. 246, 18; and p. 247, 14, from *Epidem.*, II, 6, I: *οἱ τραυλοί, ταχύγλωσσοι, μελαγχολικοί, κατακορέες, ἀσκαρδαμύκται, ὀξύθυμοι.*

[41] *Epidem.*, III, 17β; HIPPOCR. VOL. I, p. 262 Jones. A somewhat later addition to *Epidem.*, VI, 8, 31, points out the close connexion between melancholy and epilepsy, and actually states that the only difference between them is that while the illness is one and the same, it attacks the body in the case of epilepsy, but the mind in the case of melancholy.

[42] *Aphorismata*, VI, 23. Even Galen, though already possessing a highly developed system of psychological semiology, wrote with regard to this passage that "Hippocrates was right in summing up all melancholy symptoms in the two following: Fear and Depression". (*De locis affectis* III, 10, in GALEN (KÜHN), VOL. VIII, p. 190).

[43] MARCELLUS SIDETES, transmitted by Oribasius and others; *Scriptores physiognomici graeci et latini*, ed. R. FÖRSTER, Leipzig 1893, VOL. II, p. 282, 10. Also in the collection of excerpts Περὶ *μελαγχολίας* in Ps-GALEN (KÜHN), VOL. XIX, pp. 719 sqq. For Marcellus Sidetes see U. v. WILAMOWITZ-MOELLENDORFF, *Sb. d. Preuss. Akademie d. Wissensch.*, 1928, II, 3 sq.; M. WELLMANN, "Marcellus von Side als Arzt", in *Philologus*, SUPPL. VOL. XXVII, 2 (1934).

whose very name (μέλας = black) conjured up the idea of all that was evil and nocturnal.[44] This substance was so generally accepted as the source of insanity that the verb μελαγχολᾶν (with which cf. χολεριᾶν) was used from the end of the fifth century B.C. synonymously with μαίνεσθαι (to be mad). "Ὦ μοχθηρέ, μελαγχολᾷς,"[45] meant "Poor man, you are mad;" Demosthenes' words concerning Olympiodorus, "οὐ μόνον ἄδικος ἀλλὰ καὶ μελαγχολᾶν δοκῶν,"[46] might be translated as "one who seems not only an offender but a madman". In the fourth century B.C., the religious intuition of an earlier age was giving way to discursive scientific reasoning, and symbolic interpretations of myths are found side by side with rationalist explanations; hence it is not surprising that traits of pathological melancholy now began to be discerned in the great figures of those accursed heroes punished with madness by an insulted godhead—Heracles, Ajax and Bellerophon—whom Euripides had represented in their mythical superhuman greatness.[47] But even for the fourth century the spell of those great figures was strong enough to give the notion of melancholy now associated with them a nimbus of sinister sublimity. It became, as Gellius later ironically said, "a disease of heroes".[48] Thus it came about that, associated with the myths, the melancholic disposition began to be regarded as, in some degree, heroic; it was idealised still further when equated with "frenzy", inasmuch as the "humor melancholicus" began to figure as a source, however dangerous, of the highest spiritual exaltation, as soon as the notion of frenzy itself was interpreted (or rather, re-interpreted) in this way. As is well known, this transvaluation was effected by Plato. As Socrates says in the *Phaedrus*, "if it were simply that frenzy were an evil", Lysias would be right; "but in fact we receive the greatest benefits through frenzy, that is, in so far as

---

[44] The word *μέλας*, as its equivalent in most other languages, means far more than a colour; *μέλανες ἄνθρωποι* for instance, are ruthless men, *μέλαιναι ὀδύναι* are horrible pains. Hence we have no difficulty in understanding Galen's words: "Just as outward darkness fills nearly all men with fear, unless they are very brave or very enlightened, so the dark colour of black bile generates fear, in that it darkens the seat of reason." (*De locis affectis*, III, 10, in GALEN (KÜHN), VOL. VIII, p. 191.) There are countless parallels in later literature.

[45] *Phaedrus* 268E.

[46] DEMOSTHENES, *Or.* 48, *In Olympiod.* 56.

[47] Cf. 'ARISTOTLE', Problem XXX, I (below, pp. 18–29), where the previously mentioned heroes "and many others" are quoted as melancholics. See also E. D. BAUMANN, *Psyche's Lijden*, Rotterdam 1927, pp. 178 sqq.

[48] *Noctes Atticae*, XVIII, 7, 4, p. 229. Quoted below, p. 42, note 100.

it is sent as a divine gift".[49] In the beginning, however, there was nothing in Plato's thought to connect the notion of melancholy with that of the ecstasy which elevated philosopher, lover, and poet alike, to the suprarational apprehension of pure ideas. For him, melancholy meant primarily, if not actual madness, at least moral insanity, clouding and weakening will and reason; for he regarded it as a symptom of what he describes in the *Phaedrus* as the worst soul of all—that of the tyrant.[50] As we read in the *Republic*, "a man becomes a tyrant when, whether by nature or by manner of life, or both, he is a drunkard, a voluptuary and a melancholic."[51]

It was Aristotelian natural philosophy which first brought about the union between the purely medical notion of melancholy and the Platonic conception of frenzy. This union found expression in what for the Greeks was the paradoxical thesis[52] that not only the tragic heroes, like Ajax, Heracles and Bellerophon, but all really outstanding men, whether in the realm of the arts or in those of poetry, philosophy or statesmanship—even Socrates and Plato—, were melancholics.[53]

---

[49] *Phaedrus*, 244A. This is not the place to enlarge on the historical antecedents of Plato's doctrine of frenzy. Nevertheless we may point out that Empedocles had already distinguished between a "furor" emanating "ex animi purgamento" and an "alienatio mentis ex corporis causa sive iniquitate" (DIELS, *Fragm.*, A98), and that a similar distinction seems to be implied in Democritus's doctrine of poetic madness (Περὶ ποιήσιος, DIELS, *Fragm.*, B17–18, 21), as is evident from his choice of words. It was an essentially Platonic thought, however, that θεία μανία in its "fourth" (erotic) form transcends the prophetic, religious and poetic forms, and becomes the universal power which raises souls to the vision of ideas.

[50] *Phaedrus*, 248E. In the *Timaeus* (71A sqq.) only the unconscious side of the prophetic state seems to be linked in some complicated way with the function of the liver and the "bitter" bile.

[51] *Republic*, 573C.

[52] The notion of melancholy generally held by educated men of the late fourth century B.C. is admirably illustrated by some lines of MENANDER (ed. C. Jensen, Berlin 1929), Ἐπιτρέποντες, lines 494 sqq., in which the slave Onesimus expresses his opinion of his master:

ὑπομαίνεθ' οὗτος, νὴ τὸν Ἀπόλλω, μαίνεται,
μεμάνητ' ἀληθῶς, μαίνεται, νὴ τοὺς θεούς.
τὸν δεσπότην λέγω Χαρίσιον. χολὴ
μέλαινα προσπέπτωκεν ἢ τοιοῦτό τι.
τί γὰρ ἂν τις εἰκάσειεν ἄλλο γεγονέναι;

In F. G. Allinson's rendering (MENANDER, *The Principal Fragments*, London and New York 1921):

He's going crazy, by Apollo; yes, he's crazed!
Clean crazed he is, in truth; he's crazy, by the gods!
Charisius I mean, my master. Taken with
An atrabilious fit he is, or some such thing.
Nay, what else would one fancy has befallen him?

[53] See below, pp. 18–19.

The theory is explained in the most famous of the "Problems" attributed to Aristotle, which shall be rendered in full.

PROBLEM XXX, 1[54]

Διὰ τί πάντες ὅσοι περιττοὶ γεγόνασιν ἄνδρες ἢ κατὰ φιλοσοφίαν ἢ πολιτικὴν ἢ ποίησιν ἢ τέχνας φαίνονται μελαγχολικοὶ ὄντες, καὶ οἱ μὲν οὕτως ὥστε καί λαμβάνεσθαι τοῖς ἀπὸ μελαίνης χολῆς ἀρρωστήμασιν, οἷον λέγεται τῶν τε ἡρωϊκῶν τὰ περὶ τὸν Ἡρακλέα; καὶ γὰρ ἐκεῖνος ἔοικε γενέσθαι ταύτης τῆς φύσεως, διὸ καὶ τὰ ἀρρωστήματα τῶν ἐπιληπτικῶν ἀπ' ἐκείνου προσηγόρευον οἱ ἀρχαῖοι ἱερὰν νόσον. καὶ ἡ περὶ τοὺς παῖδας ἔκστασις καὶ ἡ πρὸ τῆς ἀφανίσεως ἐν Οἴτῃ τῶν ἑλκῶν ἔκφυσις γενομένη τοῦτο δηλοῖ· καὶ γὰρ τοῦτο γίνεται πολλοῖς ἀπὸ μελαίνης χολῆς. συνέβη δὲ καί Λυσάνδρῳ τῷ Λάκωνι πρὸ τῆς τελευτῆς γενέσθαι τὰ ἕλκη ταῦτα. ἔτι δὲ τὰ περὶ Αἴαντα καὶ Βελλεροφόντην, ὧν ὁ μὲν ἐκστατικὸς ἐγένετο παντε-

Why is it that all those who have become eminent in philosophy or politics or poetry or the arts are clearly melancholics, and some of them to such an extent as to be affected by diseases caused by black bile? An example from heroic mythology is Heracles. For he apparently had this constitution, and therefore epileptic afflictions were called after him "the sacred disease" by the ancients.[55] His mad fit in the incident with the children points to this, as well as the eruption of sores which happened before his disappearance on Mount Oeta; for this is with many people a symptom of black bile. Lysander the Lacedaemonian too suffered from such sores before his death. There are also the stories of Ajax and Bellerophon: the one went completely out of his mind, while the other sought out desert

---

[54] Editions, translations, critical works: ARISTOTELES, *Problemata physica* edd. Ruelle, Knoellinger, Klek, Leipzig 1922 = Ruelle; *Aristotelis, Alexandri et Cassii Problemata cum Theophrasteorum quorundam collectaneis*, cum praefatione Frid. Sylburgii, Francof. 1585 = Sylburg; H. P. Richards, *Aristotelica*, London 1915 = Richards; *The Works of Aristotle transl. into English*, ed. W. D. Ross, vol. VII: Problemata, tr. E. S. Forster, Oxford 1927 = Forster.—Except where stated in the apparatus, we follow the text of Ruelle.

[55] The close connexion between melancholy and epilepsy was pointed out by the Hippocrateans; see p. 15, note 41.

λῶς, ὁ δὲ τὰς ἐρημίας ἐδίωκεν, διὸ οὕτως ἐποίησεν Ὅμηρος

> "αὐτὰρ ἐπεὶ καὶ κεῖνος ἀπήχθετο πᾶσι θεοῖσιν,
> ἤτοι ὁ καππεδίον τὸ Ἀλήϊον οἶος ἀλᾶτο,
> ὃν θυμὸν κατέδων, πάτον ἀνθρώπων ἀλεείνων".

καὶ ἄλλοι δὲ πολλοὶ τῶν ἡρώων ὁμοιοπαθεῖς φαίνονται τούτοις. τῶν δὲ ὕστερον Ἐμπεδοκλῆς καὶ Πλάτων καὶ Σωκράτης καὶ ἕτεροι συχνοὶ τῶν γνωρίμων· ἔτι δὲ τῶν περὶ τὴν ποίησιν οἱ πλεῖστοι. πολλοῖς μὲν γὰρ τῶν τοιούτων γίνεται νοσήματα ἀπὸ τῆς τοιαύτης κράσεως τῷ σώματι, τοῖς δὲ ἡ φύσις δήλη ῥέπουσα πρὸς τὰ πάθη. πάντες δ' οὖν ὡς εἰπεῖν ἁπλῶς εἰσί, καθάπερ ἐλέχθη, τοιοῦτοι τὴν φύσιν.

δεῖ δὴ λαβεῖν τὴν αἰτίαν πρῶτον ἐπὶ παραδείγματος προχειρισαμένους. ὁ γὰρ οἶνος ὁ πολὺς μάλιστα φαίνεται παρασκευάζειν τοιούτους οἵους λέγομεν τοὺς μελαγχολικοὺς εἶναι, καὶ πλεῖστα ἤθη ποιεῖν πινόμενος, οἷον ὀργίλους, φιλανθρώπους, ἐλεήμονας, ἰταμούς· ἀλλ' οὐχὶ τὸ μέλι οὐδὲ τὸ γάλα οὐδὲ τὸ ὕδωρ οὐδ' ἄλλο τῶν τοιούτων οὐδέν. ἴδοι δ' ἄν τις ὅτι

places for his habitation; wherefore Homer says:

> "And since of all the Gods he was hated,
> Verily o'er the Aleian plain alone he would wander,
> Eating his own heart out, avoiding the pathway of mortals;"

Among the heroes many others evidently suffered in the same way, and among men of recent times Empedocles, Plato, and Socrates, and numerous other well-known men, and also most of the poets. For many such people have bodily diseases as the result of this kind of temperament; some of them have only a clear constitutional tendency towards such afflictions, but to put it briefly, all of them are, as has been said before, melancholics by constitution.

In order to find out the reason, we must begin by making use of an analogy: Wine in large quantity manifestly produces in men much the same characteristics which we attribute to the melancholic, and as it is being drunk it fashions various characters, for instance irritable, benevolent, compassionate or reckless ones; whereas honey or milk or water, or anything else of this kind, do not have this effect. One can see that wine makes the most varied characters, by observing how it

παντοδαποὺς ἀπεργάζεται, θεωρῶν ὡς μεταβάλλει τοὺς πίνοντας ἐκ προσαγωγῆς· παραλαβὼν γὰρ ἀπεψυγμένους ἐν τῷ νήφειν καὶ σιωπηλοὺς μικρῷ μὲν πλείων ποθεὶς λαλιστέρους ποιεῖ, ἔτι δὲ πλείων ῥητορικοὺς καὶ θαρραλέους, προϊόντας δὲ πρὸς τὸ πράττειν ἰταμούς, ἔτι δὲ μᾶλλον πινόμενος ὑβριστάς, ἔπειτα μανικούς, λίαν δὲ πολὺς ἐκλύει καὶ ποιεῖ μωρούς, ὥσπερ τοὺς ἐκ παίδων ἐπιλήπτους ἢ καὶ ἐχομένους τοῖς μελαγχολικοῖς ἄγαν. ὥσπερ οὖν ὁ εἷς ἄνθρωπος μεταβάλλει τὸ ἦθος πίνων καὶ χρώμενος τῷ οἴνῳ ποσῷ τινί, οὕτω καθ' ἕκαστον τὸ ἦθος εἰσί τινες ἄνθρωποι. οἷος γὰρ οὗτος μεθύων νῦν ἐστίν, ἄλλος τις τοιοῦτος φύσει ἐστίν, ὁ μὲν λάλος, ὁ δὲ κεκινημένος, ὁ δὲ ἀρίδακρυς· ποιεῖ γάρ τινας καὶ τοιούτους, διὸ καὶ Ὅμηρος ἐποίησε

"καί μέ φησι δακρυπλώειν βεβαρημένον οἴνῳ".

καὶ γὰρ ἐλεήμονές ποτε γίνονται καὶ ἄγριοι καὶ σιωπηλοί· ἔνιοι γὰρ αὖ ἀποσιωπῶσι, καὶ μάλιστα τῶν μελαγχολικῶν ὅσοι ἐκστατικοί. ποιεῖ δὲ καὶ φιλητικοὺς ὁ οἶνος· σημεῖον

gradually changes those who drink it; for those who, to begin with, when sober, are cool and taciturn become more talkative when they have drunk just a little too much; if they drink a little more it makes them grandiloquent and boisterous and, when they proceed to action, reckless; if they drink still more it makes them insolent, and then frenzied; while very great excess enfeebles them completely and makes them as stupid as those who have been epileptic from childhood or as those who are a prey to excessive melancholy. Now, even as one individual who is drinking changes his character according to the quantity of wine he consumes, so there is for each character a class of men who represent it. For as one man is momentarily, while drunk, another is by nature: one man is loquacious, another emotional, another easily moved to tears; for this effect, too, wine has on some people. Hence Homer said in the poem:

"He says that I swim in tears
like a man that is heavy
with drinking."

Sometimes they also become compassionate or savage or taciturn—for some relapse into complete silence, especially those melancholics who are out of their minds. Wine also makes

δὲ ὅτι προάγεται ὁ πίνων καὶ τῷ στόματι φιλεῖν, οὓς νήφων οὐδ' ἂν εἷς φιλήσειεν ἢ διὰ τὸ εἶδος ἢ διὰ τὴν ἡλικίαν. ὁ μὲν οὖν οἶνος οὐ πολὺν χρόνον ποιεῖ περιττόν, ἀλλ' ὀλίγον, ἡ δὲ φύσις ἀεί, ἕως τις ἂν ᾖ· οἱ μὲν γὰρ θρασεῖς, οἱ δὲ σιωπηλοί, οἱ δὲ ἐλεήμονες, οἱ δὲ δειλοὶ γίνονται φύσει. ὥστε δῆλον ὅτι διὰ τοῦ αὐτοῦ[(a)] ποιεῖ ὅ τε οἶνος καὶ ἡ φύσις ἑκάστου[(b)] τὸ ἦθος· πάντα γὰρ κατεργάζεται τῇ θερμότητι ταμιευόμενα. ὅ τε δὴ χυμὸς καὶ ἡ κρᾶσις ἡ τῆς μελαίνης χολῆς πνευματικά ἐστιν· διὸ καὶ τὰ πνευματώδη πάθη καὶ τὰ ὑποχονδριακὰ μελαγχολικὰ οἱ ἰατροί φασιν εἶναι. καὶ ὁ οἶνος δὲ πνευματώδης τὴν δύναμιν. διὸ δή ἐστι τὴν φύσιν ὅμοια ὅ τε οἶνος καὶ ἡ κρᾶσις. δηλοῖ δὲ ὅτι πνευματώδης ὁ οἶνός ἐστιν ὁ ἀφρός· τὸ μὲν γὰρ ἔλαιον θερμὸν ὂν οὐ ποιεῖ ἀφρόν, ὁ δὲ οἶνος πολύν, καὶ μᾶλλον ὁ μέλας τοῦ λευκοῦ, ὅτι θερμότερος καὶ σωματωδέστερος.

καὶ διὰ τοῦτο ὅ τε οἶνος ἀφροδισιαστικοὺς ἀπεργάζεται, καὶ ὀρθῶς Διόνυσος καὶ Ἀφροδίτη λέγονται μετ' ἀλλήλων εἶναι, καὶ οἱ μελαγχολικοὶ οἱ πλεῖστοι λάγνοι εἰσίν. ὅ τε γὰρ ἀφροδισιασμὸς πνευματώδης. σημεῖον δὲ τὸ αἰδοῖον,

(a) διὰ τοῦ αὐτοῦ Richards] διὰ τὸ αὐτὸ *codd.*

(b) ἕκαστον Richards.

men amorous; this is shown by the fact that a man in his cups may even be induced to kiss persons whom, because of their appearance or age, nobody at all would kiss when sober. Wine makes a man abnormal not for long, but for a short time only, but a man's natural constitution does it permanently, for his whole lifetime; for some are bold, others taciturn, others compassionate and others cowardly by nature. It is therefore clear that it is the same agent that produces character both in the case of wine and of the individual nature, for all processes are governed by heat. Now melancholy, both the humour and the temperament, produce air[56]; wherefore the physicians say that flatulence and abdominal disorders are due to black bile. Now wine too has the quality of generating air, so wine and the melancholy temperament are of a similar nature. The froth which forms on wine shows that it generates air; for oil does not produce froth, even when it is hot, but wine produces it in large quantities, and dark wine more than white because it is warmer and has more body.

It is for this reason that wine excites sexual desire, and Dionysus and Aphrodite are rightly said to belong together,

[56] Cf. the passages cited on p. 34, note 71.

ὡς ἐκ μικροῦ ταχεῖαν ποιεῖται τὴν αὔξησιν διὰ τὸ ἐμφυσᾶσθαι. καὶ ἔτι πρὶν δύνασθαι προΐεσθαι σπέρμα, γίνεταί τις ἡδονὴ ἔτι[(c)] παισὶν οὖσιν, ὅταν ἐγγὺς ὄντες τοῦ ἡβᾶν ξύωνται τὰ αἰδοῖα δι' ἀκολασίαν· γίνεται δὲ δῆλον διὰ τὸ πνεῦμα διεξιέναι διὰ τῶν πόρων, δι' ὧν ὕστερον τὸ ὑγρὸν φέρεται. ἥ τε ἔκχυσις τοῦ σπέρματος ἐν ταῖς ὁμιλίαις καὶ ἡ ῥῖψις ὑπὸ τοῦ πνεύματος ὠθοῦντος φανερὸν ὅτι γίνεται.[(d)] ὥστε καὶ τῶν ἐδεσμάτων καὶ ποτῶν εὐλόγως ταῦτ' ἐστὶν ἀφροδισιαστικά, ὅσα πνευματώδη τὸν περὶ τὰ αἰδοῖα ποιεῖ τόπον. διὸ καὶ ὁ μέλας οἶνος οὐδενὸς ἧττον τοιούτους ἀπεργάζεται, οἷοι καὶ οἱ μελαγχολικοὶ ⟨πνευματώδεις⟩.[(e)] δῆλοι δ' εἰσὶν ἐπ' ἐνίων· σκληροὶ γὰρ οἱ πλείους τῶν μελαγχολικῶν, καὶ αἱ φλέβες ἐξέχουσιν· τούτου δ' αἴτιον οὐ τὸ τοῦ αἵματος πλῆθος, ἀλλὰ τοῦ πνεύματος· διότι δὲ οὐδὲ πάντες οἱ μελαγχολικοὶ σκληροὶ οὐδὲ [οἱ][(f)] μέλανες, ἀλλ' οἱ μᾶλλον κακόχυμοι, ἄλλος λόγος.

περὶ οὗ δὲ ἐξ ἀρχῆς προειλόμεθα διελθεῖν, ὅτι ἐν τῇ φύσει εὐθὺς ὁ τοιοῦτος χυμὸς ὁ μελαγχολικὸς κεράννυται·

(c) ἔτι Bonitz, Richards] ἐπὶ *codd.*

(d) ὅτι γίνεται Richards] γίνεσθαι *codd.*

(e) πνευματώδεις *secl.* Forster.

(f) οἱ *secl.* Bekker.

and most melancholy persons are lustful. For the sexual act is connected with the generation of air, as is shown by the fact that the virile organ quickly increases from a small size by inflation. Even before they are capable of emitting semen, boys approaching puberty already find a certain pleasure in rubbing their sexual organs from wantonness, the manifest reason being that the air escapes through the passage through which the fluid flows later on. Also the effusion and impetus of the semen in sexual intercourse is clearly due to propulsion by air. Accordingly those foods and liquids which fill the region of the sexual organs with air have an aphrodisiac effect. Thus dark wine more than anything else makes men such as the melancholics are. That they contain air is obvious in some cases; for most melancholy persons have firm flesh and their veins stand out, the reason being the abundance not of blood but of air. However, the reason why not all melancholics have hard flesh and why not all of them are dark but only those who contain particularly unhealthy humours, is another question.

But to return to our original subject: the atrabilious humour in the natural constitution is already something mixed as it

θερμοῦ γὰρ καὶ ψυχροῦ κρᾶσίς ἐστιν· ἐκ τούτων γὰρ τῶν δυοῖν ἡ φύσις συνέστηκεν. διὸ καὶ ἡ μέλαινα χολὴ καὶ θερμότατον καὶ ψυχρότατον γίνεται. τὸ γὰρ αὐτὸ πάσχειν πέφυκε ταῦτ' ἄμφω, οἷον καὶ τὸ ὕδωρ ὂν ψυχρόν, ὅμως ἐὰν ἱκανῶς θερμανθῇ, οἷον τὸ ȝέον, τῆς φλογὸς αὐτῆς θερμότερόν ἐστι, καὶ λίθος καὶ σίδηρος διάπυρα γενόμενα μᾶλλον θερμὰ γίνεται ἄνθρακος, ψυχρὰ ὄντα φύσει. εἴρηται δὲ σαφέστερον περὶ τούτων ἐν τοῖς περὶ πυρός.

καὶ ἡ χολὴ δὲ ἡ μέλαινα φύσει ψυχρὰ καὶ οὐκ ἐπιπολαίως[(g)] οὖσα, ὅταν μὲν οὕτως ἔχῃ ὡς εἴρηται, ἐὰν ὑπερβάλλῃ ἐν τῷ σώματι, ἀποπληξίας ἢ νάρκας ἢ ἀθυμίας ποιεῖ ἢ φόβους, ἐὰν δὲ ὑπερθερμανθῇ, τὰς μετ' ᾠδῆς εὐθυμίας καὶ ἐκστάσεις καὶ ἐκȝέσεις ἑλκῶν καὶ ἄλλα τοιαῦτα. τοῖς μὲν οὖν πολλοῖς ἀπὸ τῆς καθ' ἡμέραν τροφῆς ἐγγινομένη οὐδὲν τὸ ἦθος ποιεῖ διαφόρους, ἀλλὰ μόνον νόσημά τι μελαγχολικὸν

(g) ἐπιπόλαιος Sylburg.

is a mixture of heat and cold, for of these two things nature is composed. Black bile can therefore become both very hot and very cold, for one and the same substance can naturally undergo both: for example water, which although in itself cold, yet when sufficiently heated (for example, when boiling) is hotter than the flame itself. And stone and iron when red-hot become hotter than charcoal, though they are cold by nature. This subject is dealt with in more detail in the book concerning fire.[57]

Now, if black bile, being cold by nature and not superficially so, is in the stated condition, it can induce paralysis or torpor or depression or anxiety when it prevails in the body; but if it is overheated it produces cheerfulness, bursting into song, and ecstasies and the eruption of sores and the like. To most people the bile engendered from their daily nutriment does not give a distinctive character but merely results in some atrabilious disease. But among those who constitutionally possess this temperament there is

[57] It has been observed (C. Prantl, *Abh. d. bayer. Akad.*, VI, 2, 353) that this reference clearly points to a connexion of our Problem with Theophrastus. It evidently refers to Theophrastus *Περὶ πυρός* (ed. A. Gercke, Greifswald 1896), ch. 35 which deals with materials like iron and stone which, though 'naturally cold', get very hot. As we know from the list of his writings given in Diogenes Laertius (v, 44) that Theophrastus wrote a book *On Melancholy*, the inference that our Problem is connected with this book seems safe. Cf. also below, p. 41, and O. Regenbogen, Art. 'Theophrastos', Pauly-Wissowa, *Realenz. d. Kl. Altertumswissenschaft*, Suppl. 7, cols. 1402, 1406.

ἀπειργάσατο. ὅσοις δὲ ἐν τῇ φύσει συνέστη κρᾶσις τοιαύτη, εὐθὺς οὗτοι τὰ ἤθη γίνονται παντοδαποί, ἄλλος κατ' ἄλλην κρᾶσιν· οἷον ὅσοις μὲν πολλὴ καὶ ψυχρὰ ἐνυπάρχει, νωθροὶ καὶ μωροί, ὅσοις δὲ λίαν πολλὴ καὶ θερμή, μανικοὶ καὶ εὐφυεῖς καὶ ἐρωτικοὶ καὶ εὐκίνητοι πρὸς τοὺς θυμοὺς καὶ τὰς ἐπιθυμίας, ἔνιοι δὲ καὶ λάλοι μᾶλλον. πολλοὶ δὲ καὶ διὰ τὸ ἐγγὺς εἶναι τοῦ νοεροῦ τόπου τὴν θερμότητα ταύτην νοσήμασιν ἁλίσκονται μανικοῖς ἢ ἐνθουσιαστικοῖς· ὅθεν Σίβυλλαι καὶ Βάκιδες καὶ οἱ ἔνθεοι γίνονται πάντες, ὅταν μὴ νοσήματι γένωνται ἀλλὰ φυσικῇ κράσει.—Μαρακὸς δὲ ὁ Συρακούσιος καὶ ἀμείνων ἦν ποιητής, ὅτ' ἐκσταίη.—ὅσοις δ' ἂν ἐπανεθῇ[h] τὴν ἄγαν θερμότητα πρὸς τὸ μέσον, οὗτοι μελαγχολικοὶ μέν εἰσι, φρονιμώτεροι

[h] ἐπανεθῇ Bywater] ἐπανθῇ *codd.*

straight away the greatest variety of characters, each according to his individual mixture. For example, those who possess much cold black bile become dull and stupid, whereas those who possess much hot bile are elated and brilliant or erotic or easily moved to anger and desire, while some become more loquacious. Many too are subject to fits of exaltation and ecstasy, because this heat is located near the seat of the intellect; and this is how Sibyls and soothsayers arise and all that are divinely inspired, when they become such not by illness but by natural temperament.—Maracus, the Syracusan, was actually a better poet when he was out of his mind.—Those, however, in whom the black bile's excessive heat is relaxed towards a mean,[58] are melancholy, but they are more rational

[58] The sentence *ὅσοις δ' ἂν ἐπανθῇ τὴν ἄγαν θερμότητα πρὸς τὸ μέσον* is unintelligible as it stands (H. Bonitz in his admirable *Index Aristotelicus*, p. 265, also cites the verb *ἐπανθῇ* as corrupt), and has given rise to several emendations, none entirely satisfactory; the best, perhaps, is Bywater's *ἐπανεθῇ ἡ ἄγαν θερμότης*. According to the context the meaning must be that reasonable (and therefore highly gifted) melancholics are protected both from over-heating (as occurs among *μανικοί*, and especially among Bakides, Sibyls, etc.) and from chill (as occurs among *νωθροὶ καὶ μῶροι*), thus, to that extent, achieving a "*μέσον*". It might be suggested to replace "*ἐπανθῇ*" by "*ἐπανισωθῇ*", thus not only making the sentence correct grammatically, and giving it a meaning, but making it accord with Aristotle's usage elsewhere: cf. *Περὶ ἀναπνοῆς* 14, 478 a 3: . . . *ἐπανισοῖ γὰρ εἰς τὸ μέτριον ὁ τόπος τὴν τῆς ἕξεως ὑπερβολήν*. However, we prefer to read *ἐπανεθῇ τὴν ἄγαν θερμότητα* (understood as "accusative of respect"). Earlier translators were also agreed as to the necessity for emending this passage. Theodorus of Gaza translates it: "at quibus minus [*sic* for 'nimius'] ille calor remissus ad mediocritatem sit"; the Venice edition of 1501 (*Aristotelis Problemata*, fol. 244r) has "quibuscunque autem valde caliditatem reducit ad medium", and the edition with excellent commentary of LUDOVICUS SEPTALIUS (*In Aristotelis Problemata commentaria*, Lyons 1632, VOL. III, p. 346) has "At quibus caliditas magna ad mediocritatem reducitur".

δέ, καὶ ἧττον μὲν ἔκτοποι, πρὸς πολλὰ δὲ διαφέροντες τῶν ἄλλων, οἱ μὲν πρὸς παιδείαν, οἱ δὲ πρὸς τέχνας, οἱ δὲ πρὸς πολιτείαν. πολλὴν δὲ καὶ εἰς τοὺς κινδύνους ποιεῖ διαφορὰν ἡ τοιαύτη ἕξις τῷ[i] ἐνίοτε ἀνωμάλους εἶναι ἐν[k] τοῖς φόβοις πολλοὺς τῶν ἀνδρῶν. ὡς γὰρ ἂν τύχωσι τὸ σῶμα ἔχοντες πρὸς τὴν τοιαύτην κρᾶσιν, διαφέρουσιν αὐτοὶ αὑτῶν. ἡ δὲ μελαγχολικὴ κρᾶσις, ὥσπερ καὶ ἐν ταῖς νόσοις ἀνωμάλους ποιεῖ, οὕτω καὶ αὐτὴ ἀνώμαλός ἐστιν· ὁτὲ μὲν γὰρ ψυχρά ἐστιν ὥσπερ ὕδωρ, ὁτὲ δὲ θερμή. ὥστε φοβερόν τι ὅταν εἰσαγγελθῇ, ἐὰν μὲν ψυχροτέρας οὔσης τῆς κράσεως τύχῃ, δειλὸν ποιεῖ· προωδοπεποίηκε γὰρ τῷ φόβῳ, καὶ ὁ φόβος καταψύχει. δηλοῦσι δὲ οἱ περίφοβοι· τρέμουσι γάρ. ἐὰν δὲ μᾶλλον θερμή, εἰς τὸ μέτριον κατέστησεν ὁ φόβος, καὶ ἐν αὑτῷ καὶ ἀπαθῆ.

ὁμοίως δὲ καὶ πρὸς τὰς καθ' ἡμέραν ἀθυμίας· πολλάκις γὰρ οὕτως ἔχομεν ὥστε λυπεῖσθαι, ἐφ' ὅτῳ δέ, οὐκ ἂν ἔχοιμεν εἰπεῖν· ὁτὲ δὲ εὐθύμως, ἐφ' ᾧ δ' οὐ δῆλον. τὰ δὴ τοιαῦτα

[i] τῷ Richards] τοῦ *codd.*
[k] ἐν Richards] μὲν *codd.*

and less eccentric and in many respects superior to others either in culture or in the arts or in statesmanship. Such a constitution also makes for great differences in behaviour in dangerous situations in that many of these people react inconsistently in frightening circumstances; for according to the condition of their bodies at a given time in relation to their temperament, they behave now one way now another: the melancholy temperament, just as it produces illnesses with a variety of symptoms, is itself variable, for like water it is sometimes cold and sometimes hot. Therefore if it so happens that something alarming is announced at a time when the admixture is rather cold, then it makes a man cowardly;—for it has prepared a way for the fear, and fear makes one cold, as is shown by the fact that those who are frightened tremble.—If however the mixture is rather warm, fear reduces it to a moderate temperature and so he is self-possessed and unmoved.

So too with the despondency which occurs in everyday life, for we are often in a state of grieving, but could not say why, while at other times we feel cheerful without apparent reason. To such affections and

πάθη καὶ τὰ πάλαι(1) λεχθέντα κατὰ μέν τι μικρὸν πᾶσι γίνεται· πᾶσι γὰρ μέμικταί τι τῆς δυνάμεως· ὅσοις δ' εἰς βάθος, οὗτοι δ' ἤδη ποιοί τινές εἰσι τὰ ἤθη. ὥσπερ γὰρ τὸ εἶδος ἕτεροι γίνονται οὐ τῷ πρόσωπον ἔχειν, ἀλλὰ τῷ ποιόν τι τὸ πρόσωπον, οἱ μὲν καλόν, οἱ δὲ αἰσχρόν, οἱ δὲ μηθὲν ἔχοντες περιττόν, οὗτοι δὲ μέσοι τὴν φύσιν, οὕτω καί οἱ μὲν μικρὰ μετέχοντες τῆς τοιαύτης κράσεως μέσοι εἰσίν, οἱ δὲ πλήθους ἤδη ἀνόμοιοι τοῖς πολλοῖς. ἐὰν μὲν γὰρ σφόδρα κατακορὴς ᾖ ἡ ἕξις, μελαγχολικοί εἰσι λίαν, ἐὰν δέ πως κραθῶσι, περιττοί. ῥέπουσι δ', ἂν ἀμελῶσιν, ἐπὶ τὰ μελαγχολικὰ νοσήματα, ἄλλοι περὶ ἄλλο μέρος τοῦ σώματος· καὶ τοῖς μὲν ἐπιληπτικὰ ἀποσημαίνει, τοῖς δὲ ἀποπληκτικά, ἄλλοις δὲ ἀθυμίαι ἰσχυραὶ ἢ φόβοι, τοῖς δὲ θάρρη λίαν, οἷον καὶ Ἀρχελάῳ συνέβαινε τῷ Μακεδονίας βασιλεῖ.

αἴτιον δὲ τῆς τοιαύτης δυνάμεως ἡ κρᾶσις, ὅπως ἂν ἔχῃ ψύξεώς τε καὶ θερμότητος. ψυχροτέρα μὲν γὰρ οὖσα

(1) πάλαι Sylburg (*superius* Theodorus Gaza)] παλαιὰ *codd.*

to those mentioned before[59] we are all subject in some small degree, for a little of the stuff which causes them is mixed in with everybody. But with people in whom this quality goes deep, it determines the character. For as men differ in appearance not because they possess a face but because they possess such and such a face, some handsome, others ugly, others with nothing extraordinary about it (those whose looks are ordinary); so those who have a little of this temperament are ordinary, but those who have much of it are unlike the majority of people. For if their melancholy habitus is quite undiluted they are too melancholy; but if it is somewhat tempered they are outstanding. If they are not careful they tend to melancholy sicknesses, different individuals being affected in different parts of the body: some people suffer from epileptic symptoms, others from paralytic ones, others from violent despondency or terrors, others from over-confidence, as happened to Archelaus, King of Macedonia.

Such tendencies are caused by the temperament, according to whether it is hot or cold. If it is

[59] Sylburg's conjecture seems necessary and restores an expression frequently used by Aristotle when referring to something 'said above', cf. *Polit.* B4, 1262 b 29; and Γ11, 1282 a 15. The reference here is to the melancholy symptoms described before. There is, however, the possibility, that the reference as such has been lifted from the original source of the Problema, just as the one above (see note 57), and refers to a passage in Theophrastus's work now lost.

τοῦ καιροῦ δυσθυμίας ποιεῖ ἀλόγους· διὸ αἵ τ' ἀγχόναι μάλιστα τοῖς νέοις, ἐνίοτε δὲ καὶ πρεσβυτέροις. πολλοὶ δὲ καὶ μετὰ τὰς μέθας διαφθείρουσιν ἑαυτούς· ἔνιοι δὲ τῶν μελαγχολικῶν ἐκ τῶν πότων ἀθύμως διάγουσιν, σβέννυσι γὰρ ἡ τοῦ οἴνου θερμότης τὴν φυσικὴν θερμότητα. τὸ δὲ θερμὸν τὸ περὶ τὸν τόπον ᾧ φρονοῦμεν καὶ ἐλπίζομεν ποιεῖ εὐθύμους· καὶ διὰ τοῦτο πρὸς τὸ πίνειν εἰς μέθην πάντες ἔχουσι προθύμως, ὅτι πάντας ὁ οἶνος ὁ πολὺς εὐέλπιδας ποιεῖ, καθάπερ ἡ νεότης τοὺς παῖδας· τὸ μὲν γὰρ γῆρας δύσελπί ἐστιν, ἡ δὲ νεότης ἐλπίδος πλήρης. εἰσὶ δέ τινες ὀλίγοι οὓς πίνοντας δυσθυμίαι λαμβάνουσι, διὰ τὴν αὐτὴν αἰτίαν δι' ἣν καί μετὰ τοὺς πότους ἐνίους. ὅσοις μὲν οὖν μαραινομένου τοῦ θερμοῦ αἱ ἀθυμίαι γίνονται, μᾶλλον ἀπάγχονται. διὸ καὶ οἱ νέοι [ἢ] καὶ οἱ πρεσβῦται μᾶλλον ἀπάγχονται· τὸ μὲν γὰρ γῆρας μαραίνει τὸ θερμόν, τῶν δὲ τὸ πάθος, φυσικὸν ὂν καὶ αὐτό [τὸ μαραινόμενον θερμόν].[m] ὅσοις δὲ σβεννυμένου ἐξαίφνης, οἱ πλεῖστοι διαχρῶνται ἑαυτούς, ὥστε θαυμάζειν πάντας διὰ τὸ μηθὲν ποιῆσαι σημεῖον πρότερον.

[m] τὸ μαραινόμενον θερμόν *secl.* Forster.

unduly cold, considering the circumstances, it produces irrational despondency; hence suicide by hanging occurs most frequently among the young, and sometimes also among elderly men. Many men, also, put an end to themselves after drunkenness, and some melancholics continue in a state of despondency after drinking; for the heat of the wine quenches their natural heat. (Heat in the region in which we think and hope makes us cheerful; and therefore all men are keen on drinking to the point of intoxication, for wine makes everybody hopeful, even as youth does children; for old age is pessimistic, but youth is full of hope.) There are a few who are seized with despondency while actually drinking, for the same reason as makes others despondent after drinking. Now those who become despondent as the heat in them dies down are inclined to hang themselves. Hence the young and the old are more likely to hang themselves; for in one case old age itself makes the heat die down, in the other, passion, which is something physical too. Most of those men in whom the heat is extinguished suddenly make away with themselves unexpectedly, to the astonishment of all, since they have given no previous sign of any such intention.

ψυχροτέρα μὲν οὖν γινομένη ἡ κρᾶσις ἡ ἀπὸ τῆς μελαίνης χολῆς, ὥσπερ εἴρηται, ποιεῖ ἀθυμίας παντοδαπάς, θερμοτέρα δὲ οὖσα εὐθυμίας. διὸ καὶ οἱ μὲν παῖδες εὐθυμότεροι, οἱ δὲ γέροντες δυσθυμότεροι. οἱ μὲν γὰρ θερμοί, οἱ δὲ ψυχροί· τὸ γὰρ γῆρας κατάψυξίς τις. συμβαίνει δὲ σβέννυσθαι ἐξαίφνης ὑπό τε τῶν ἐκτὸς αἰτιῶν, ὡς καὶ παρὰ φύσιν τὰ πυρωθέντα, οἷον ἄνθρακα ὕδατος ἐπιχυθέντος. διὸ καὶ ἐκ μέθης ἔνιοι ἑαυτοὺς διαχρῶνται· ἡ γὰρ ἀπὸ τοῦ οἴνου θερμότης ἐπείσακτός ἐστιν, ἧς σβεννυμένης συμβαίνει τὸ πάθος. καὶ μετὰ τὰ ἀφροδίσια οἱ πλεῖστοι ἀθυμότεροι γίνονται, ὅσοι δὲ περίττωμα πολὺ προΐενται μετὰ τοῦ σπέρματος, οὗτοι εὐθυμότεροι· κουφίζονται γὰρ περιττώματός τε καὶ πνεύματος καὶ θερμοῦ ὑπερβολῆς. ἐκεῖνοι δὲ ἀθυμότεροι πολλάκις· καταψύχονται γὰρ ἀφροδισιάσαντες διὰ τὸ τῶν ἱκανῶν τι ἀφαιρεθῆναι· δηλοῖ δὲ τοῦτο τὸ μὴ πολλὴν τὴν ἀπορροὴν γεγονέναι.

ὡς οὖν ἐν κεφαλαίῳ εἰπεῖν, διὰ μὲν τὸ ἀνώμαλον εἶναι τὴν δύναμιν τῆς μελαίνης χολῆς ἀνώμαλοί εἰσιν οἱ μελαγχολικοί· καὶ γὰρ ψυχρὰ σφόδρα

When the mixture dominated by black bile is colder it gives rise, as has already been remarked, to despondency of various kinds, but when it is hotter, to states of cheerfulness. Hence children are more cheerful and the old more despondent, the former being hot and the latter cold; for old age is a process of cooling. Sometimes the heat is extinguished suddenly from external causes, just as red-hot objects being quenched against their natural tendency (i.e. artificially), for example, coal when water is poured on. Hence men sometimes commit suicide after drunkenness; for the heat of the wine is introduced from outside, and when it is quenched suddenly this condition is set up. Also after sexual intercourse most men become despondent; those however who emit abundant secretion with the semen become more cheerful, for they are relieved of superfluous liquid, of air, and of excessive heat. But the others often become rather despondent, for they become cooled by the sexual act, because they lose necessary constituents, as is shown by the fact that the amount of fluid emitted is not great.

To sum up: The action of black bile being variable, melancholics are variable, for the black bile becomes very hot and

γίνεται καὶ θερμή. διὰ δὲ τὸ ἠθοποιὸς εἶναι (ἠθοποιὸν γὰρ τὸ θερμὸν καὶ ψυχρὸν μάλιστα τῶν ἐν ἡμῖν ἐστιν) ὥσπερ ὁ οἶνος πλείων καὶ ἐλάττων κεραννύμενος τῷ σώματι ποιεῖ τὸ ἦθος ποιούς τινας ἡμᾶς. ἄμφω δὲ πνευματικά, καὶ ὁ οἶνος καὶ ἡ μέλαινα χολή. ἐπεὶ δ' ἔστι καὶ εὔκρατον εἶναι τὴν ἀνωμαλίαν καὶ καλῶς πως ἔχειν, καὶ ὅπου δεῖ θερμοτέραν εἶναι τὴν διάθεσιν καί πάλιν ψυχρὰν ἢ τοὐναντίον διὰ τὸ ὑπερβολὴν ἔχειν, περιττοὶ μέν εἰσι πάντες οἱ μελαγχολικοί, οὐ διὰ νόσον ⟨δέ⟩,[n] ἀλλὰ διὰ φύσιν.

very cold. And as it determines the character (for heat and cold are the factors in our bodies most important for determining our character): like wine introduced in a larger or smaller quantity into the body, it makes us persons of such and such a character. And both wine and bile contain air. Since it is possible for this variable mixture to be well tempered and well adjusted in a certain respect—that is to say, to be now in a warmer and then again a colder condition, or vice versa, just as required, owing to its tendency to extremes—therefore all melancholy persons are out of the ordinary, not owing to illness, but from their natural constitution.

[n] δὲ *add.* Richards.

Black bile—so runs the argument in the preceding Problem XXX, I, which has been called "a monograph on black bile"—is a humour present in every man without necessarily manifesting itself either in a low bodily condition or in peculiarities of character. These latter depend rather, either on a temporary and qualitative alteration of the melancholy humour as caused by digestive disturbances or by immoderate heat or cold, or on a constitutional and quantitative preponderance of the melancholy humour over the others. The first generates "melancholic diseases" (among them epilepsy, paralysis, depression, phobias, and, if immoderate heat be the cause, recklessness, ulcers and frenzy); the second makes a man a melancholic by nature (μελαγχολικὸς διὰ φύσιν)—and here for the first time the difference, present in the theories of medical writers as a tacit presupposition of which they were at most only partially aware, was clearly shown and expressed. Evidently the second possibility did not exclude the first, for it was obvious that the natural melancholic would be particularly subject to melancholy diseases, and in a particularly virulent form. On the other hand, men normal by nature—οἱ πολλοί—could never acquire the qualities proper to the natural melancholic thanks to his habitual disposition. The normal man certainly was liable to melancholy diseases, but these diseases would then be merely temporary disturbances with no psychical significance, having no lasting effect on his mental constitution. The natural melancholic, however, even when perfectly well, possessed a quite special "ethos", which, however it chose to manifest itself, made him fundamentally and permanently different from "ordinary" men; he was, as it were, normally abnormal.

This spiritual singularity of the natural melancholic was due to the fact that the black bile possessed one quality lacking in the other humours, namely that it affected the disposition (ἠθοποιόν). The basic idea was that there were some substances—water, milk or honey, for instance—whose absorption into the body did not influence the condition of the soul at all; but there were others which worked immediately and powerfully upon the mind and also threw the victim into all sorts of spiritual conditions which normally were foreign to him. Wine was a good example of this, and black bile produced comparable effects (an idea often repeated in later authors).[60] Just as wine, according to its temperature and the amount drunk, produced the most varied emotional effects, making men cheerful or sad, or garrulous or taciturn, or raving or apathetic, so black bile too produced the most varied mental conditions. The main difference from the effects of wine was that the effects of black bile were not always temporary, but became permanent characteristics wherever the black bile had a natural ascendancy and was not merely morbidly chilled or inflamed. "Wine then makes a man abnormal (περιττόν), but for a short time only, while nature (that is to say, in this case, the melancholy disposition) does so permanently, for his whole lifetime." The reason, however, was the same in both cases—black bile, like wine, was of an airy nature (πνευματώδης), the proof lying, on the one hand, in the froth of wine; on the other, in the tightly-stretched skin and distended veins of the melancholic. In this "pneuma" there dwells a singularly stimulating driving-force which sets the whole organism in a state of tension (ὄρεξις), strongly affects the mind and tries, above all in sexual intercourse, literally to "vent itself"; hence both the aphrodisiac effect of wine and the lack of sexual restraint, proper, in the author's view, to the man of melancholic temperament.[61]

---

60 Ficino, *De v. tripl.*, I, 5 in *Opera omnia*, Basle 1576, vol. I, p. 498.

61 See below, p. 34.

There was also the very important fact that the black bile, like stone or iron, could be powerfully affected by heat and cold. Naturally cold, it could become immoderately so, as well as immoderately hot (διὸ καὶ ἡ μέλαινα χολὴ καὶ θερμότατον καὶ ψυχρότατον γίνεται). Marsilio Ficino, whose ideas decisively influenced the notion of melancholy in the Renaissance, was later to say:

Bilis enim atra ferri instar, quando multum ad frigus intenditur, friget ad summum, quando contra ad calidum valde declinat, calet ad summum.[62]

And as character was primarily determined by heat and cold (ἠθοποιὸν γὰρ τὸ θερμὸν καὶ ψυχρὸν μάλιστα τῶν ἐν ἡμῖν ἐστιν) it was clear that those men in whose bodies black bile played a predominant role were bound to be also mentally "abnormal" in one way or another.

Once this was established, it formed a basis of argument for the main thesis that all outstanding men were melancholics. Admittedly only a basis, for to follow the argument to the end it was necessary to show that (and also, in what circumstances) the "abnormality" of the melancholics could consist in abnormal *talent*. Even in our text, the notion "περιττός" (which we have translated "abnormal") is a neutral conception, implying no more than a deviation from normal conditions or behaviour in one direction or another, so that either a beautiful or an ugly face—and even drunkenness—could be called an "abnormality". Only in a context where it is clear that the word is used in a favourable sense (as in the introduction to the Problem, "concerning philosophers, statesmen, poets and artists"), or where the one word "περιττός" is opposed to an unworthy characteristic (as in the sentence "ἐὰν μὲν γὰρ σφόδρα κατακορὴς ᾖ ἡ ἕξις, μελαγχολικοί εἰσι λίαν, ἐὰν δέ πως κραθῶσι, περιττοί"), would we be justified in replacing "abnormal" by "outstanding". The deviation from the normal, distinguishing every melancholic, does not of itself include a capacity for outstanding intellectual achievements. Indeed, the prevalence of black bile—and it does prevail in every natural melancholic—is directly detrimental to character and ability as long as its "anomaly" operates unchecked. With too overwhelming a predominance of black bile men become "all too melancholy", but with too small a proportion they are hardly distinguishable from the many. If the black bile is entirely cold it produces lethargic weaklings or dull fools (νωθροὶ καὶ μωροί),

---

[62] Ficino, *De v. tripl.*, I, 5.

if entirely hot it produces mad, lively, erotic, and otherwise excitable people, who (since the seat of the black bile lies near the seat of reason) are prone to trances and ecstasies like the Sibyls and soothsayers, or those poets who only produce good work when in an ecstasy. Really "outstanding" talent, as shown in objective achievement, presupposes a double limitation of the effects emanating from the black bile. The final answer to the question put at the beginning reads that the amount of melancholy humour must be great enough to raise the character above the average, but not so great as to generate a melancholy "all too deep",[63] and that it must maintain an average temperature, between "too hot" and "too cold". Then and only then is the melancholic not a freak but a genius; for then and only then, as the admirable conclusion runs, is it "possible that this anomalous admixture is well attempered and in a certain sense well adjusted" (ἐπεὶ δ' ἔστι καὶ εὔκρατον εἶναι τὴν ἀνωμαλίαν καὶ καλῶς πως ἔχειν). It was not always easy, however, for Aristotle's followers to draw the line between natural melancholy and melancholy sickness, for it need hardly be said that even a well-attempered melancholy was constantly in danger of turning into an actual illness, either through a temporary increase in the quantity of bile already present, or above all through the influence of heat or cold on the temperature of the bile. Even the gifted melancholic walked a narrow path between two abysses; it was expressly stated that if he did not take care he would easily fall into melancholy sickness, would be afflicted with overwhelming depression (ἀθυμίαι ἰσχυραί) and fits of terror or else of recklessness.

Melancholy, then, within the limits of "natural melancholy" (μελαγχολία διὰ φύσιν) could be regarded in two ways, each with a double aspect. One concerned the formation of character, in that the "humor melancholicus", if *permanently* present in abnormal quantity or condition, produced exaggerated types of one sort or another, known as freaks or "ἔκτοποι". The other concerned the outlining of particular states of mind in that the "humor melancholicus", if *temporarily* present in abnormal quantity or condition, could plunge people who in themselves were not pathological cases into either illness or at least unhealthy

---

[63] Ficino even gives the formula for the "best" combination in figures: 8 parts blood, 2 parts yellow bile, 2 parts black bile (*De v. tripl.*, I, 5). AGRIPPA OF NETTESHEIM (*De occulta philosophia*, II, 27, in *H. Cornelii Agrippae ab Nettesheym Opera*, Lyons [?] s.d. [1630]), p. 247, makes the proportion of black bile in the "homo sanus et bene compositus" even smaller; blood, phlegm, yellow bile and black bile are in the proportion 8:4:2:1.

moods, hurling them back and forth between creative excitement and gloomy dullness. A penetrating phrase—coined, it is true, only in the fifteenth century A.D.—applies to both:

> Ad utrumque extremum melancholia vim habet, unitate quadam stabilis fixaeque naturae. Quae quidem extremitas ceteris humoribus non contingit.[64]

Problem XXX, I, whose content Melanchthon described as a "dulcissima doctrina", and which has seldom been equalled and still more rarely surpassed in psychological subtlety, was considered a genuine Aristotelian work by both Cicero and Plutarch, who cite it independently of each other.[65] From this it is clear at least that it bore Aristotle's name even before the edition of his complete works, which appeared probably not earlier than the first or second century A.D.[66] But had it any right to bear that name?

It is typically Aristotelian not only to try to show a connexion between mental and physical processes (as the Hippocrateans had begun to do)[67] but to try to prove it down to the last detail. The conceptions, too, made use of to prove the case are typically Aristotelian. There is the notion of heat, which here, as in Aristotle generally, signifies the foremost dynamic principle of organic nature and which (an important point) was thought to be independent of physical substances, so that the same black bile could as easily become very hot as very cold; and thanks to this "thermodynamic ambivalence" it achieved its effects in the formation of character.[68] Then, too, there is the notion of the "mean"

---

[64] FICINO, *De v. tripl.*, I, 5.

[65] CICERO, *Tusculanae disputationes*, I, 80: "Aristoteles quidem ait omnes ingeniosos melancholicos esse, ut ego me tardiorem esse non moleste feram." Cf. also SENECA, *De tranquillitate*, 17, 10: "nam sive Graeco poetae credimus 'aliquando et insanire iucundum est,' sive Platoni 'frustra poeticas fores compos sui pepulit', sive Aristoteli 'nullum magnum ingenium sine mixtura dementiae fuit': non potest grande aliquid et super ceteros loqui nisi mota mens." Cf. PLUTARCH, *Life of Lysander* II, 3: 'Αριστοτέλης δὲ τὰς μεγάλας φύσεις ἀποφαίνων μελαγχολικάς, ὡς τὴν Σωκράτους καὶ Πλάτωνος καὶ Ἡρακλέους, ἱστορεῖ καὶ Λύσανδρον οὐκ εὐθὺς ἀλλὰ πρεσβύτερον ὄντα τῇ μελαγχολίᾳ περιπεσεῖν. Lysander himself was always described by Plutarch as μεγάλη φύσις.

[66] Cf. E. S. FORSTER's introduction to VOL. VII of *The Works of Aristotle translated into English under the editorship of W. D. Ross*, Oxford 1927.

[67] Cf. esp. Περὶ διαίτης, chapter 35, which describes the conditioning of the φρόνησις by a mixture of the four elements (HIPPOCR. VOL. IV, p. 280 sq. Jones). See also above, p. 14.

[68] Although Archelaus and Diogenes derived the affections from the relationship between heat and cold, they still considered heat and cold as elemental powers bound up with matter, and not as mere states of an in itself indifferent ὕλη, which Aristotle was the first to contrast with the determining factors, as a constant *determinandum*. Cf. FREDRICH, op. cit., pp. 134, 137 and 140. Περὶ νουσῶν, I, 2 (LITTRÉ, VI, p. 142) is particularly informative, for it tells us that illnesses may come ὑπὸ τοῦ θερμοῦ ὑπερθερμαίνοντος καὶ τοῦ ψυχροῦ ὑπερψύχοντος; only the essentially warm can become inordinately hot, and the essentially cold inordinately cold. For Rufus's even more materialistic conception, see below, p. 52 (text).

(μεσότης), which determines the ideal melancholic in the same way as it determines the ideal mental and physical performance in the genuine Aristotelian writings. For even if (say) courage seems to be the mean between cowardice and recklessness, it is not a fixed point between two other fixed points, but a varying equilibrium between two vital, constantly opposed forces, which is preserved not by a weakening of the opposed energies but by their controlled interaction. Finally, also the notion of σφοδρότης which is used to characterise the melancholic is typically Aristotelian.[69]

The constant high tension of the melancholic's spiritual life, which originated from the body and was therefore independent of the will, made it as impossible for him to act reasonably as it was for the choleric; except that in the latter case it was rashness (ταχυτής) which prevented calm reflection, in the former, vehemence (σφοδρότης). Melancholics followed their fancy entirely, were uncontrolled in every respect,[70] and were driven by ungovernable lust.[71] (Plato had already classed the melancholic with the lover and the drunkard—a connexion which may have inspired the comparison, brilliantly traced in the Problem, of black bile with wine.) They were greedy,[72] and had no command over their memory, which refused to recall things when wanted, only to bring them to mind later and unseasonably.[73] All these weaknesses, to which Problem XI, 38, adds stuttering (supposed to result from speech lagging behind thought),[74] came from the immoderate irritability of their physical constitution, so that neither

---

[69] *De divinatione per somnum*, II (464 b 5): διὰ τὴν σφοδρότητα οὐκ ἐκκρούεται αὐτῶν ἡ κίνησις ὑφ' ἑτέρας κινήσεως. Cf. *Eth. Nic.*, 1154 b 11: οἱ δὲ μελαγχολικοὶ τὴν φύσιν ἀεὶ δέονται ἰατρείας. καὶ γὰρ τὸ σῶμα δακνόμενον διατελεῖ διὰ τὴν κρᾶσιν, καὶ ἀεὶ ἐν ὀρέξει σφοδρᾷ εἰσίν. ἐξελαύνει δὲ ἡδονὴ λύπην ἥ τε ἐναντία καὶ ἡ τυχοῦσα, ἐὰν ᾖ ἰσχυρά. καὶ διὰ ταῦτα ἀκόλαστοι καὶ φαῦλοι γίνονται.

[70] *Eth. Nic.*, 1150 b 25: μάλιστα δ' οἱ ὀξεῖς καὶ μελαγχολικοὶ τὴν προπετῆ ἀκρασίαν εἰσὶν ἀκρατεῖς. οἱ μὲν γὰρ διὰ τὴν ταχυτῆτα, οἱ δὲ διὰ τὴν σφοδρότητα οὐκ ἀναμένουσι τὸν λόγον, διὰ τὸ ἀκολουθητικοὶ εἶναι τῇ φαντασίᾳ.

[71] Cf. *Problema* IV,30 (880 a), where the melancholic's "libido" is attributed, just as in *Problema* XXX,1, to an excess of "pneuma". This view, too, is based on genuinely Aristotelian presuppositions: cf. *De generatione animalium*, 728 a 9, and elsewhere.

[72] *De somno et vigilia*, III (457 a 29).

[73] *De memoria et reminiscentia*, II (453 a 19).

[74] Διὰ τί οἱ ἰσχνόφωνοι μελαγχολικοί; ἢ ὅτι τὸ τῇ φαντασίᾳ ἀκολουθεῖν ταχέως τὸ μελαγχολικόν εἶναί ἐστιν . . . προτερεῖ γὰρ ἡ ὁρμὴ τοῦ λέγειν τῆς δυνάμεως αὐτοῖς . . . καὶ οἱ τραυλοὶ δὲ ὡσαύτως. This close agreement with the passage from Pseudo-Hippocrates's *Epidem. libri*, II, 5, 1, cited on p. 15 (text) was already observed by FRANZ POSCHENRIEDER, "Die naturwissenschaftlichen Schriften des Aristoteles in ihrem Verhältnis zu den Büchern der Hippokratischen Sammlung", in *Programm der kgl. Studienanstalt zu Bamberg*, 1887, p. 63.

could love give them lasting satisfaction nor gluttony alter their congenital leanness. In both cases they sought enjoyment not for its own sake but simply as a necessary protection against an organic failing; for just as their sexual craving came from excessive tension, so did their greed spring from a metabolic deficiency—the latter having the virtue of protecting them from normal after-lunch sleepiness.[75] The melancholic's capricious memory,[76] however, was the effect of another peculiarity derived from his vehemence, which was to prepare the way for the conception of the melancholic as a man of genius. This peculiarity lay in his capacity to react just as easily and violently to all physical and psychical influences—especially to visual images—as the melancholy humour in Problem XXX, I, reacted to heat and cold. If the melancholic was more liable than other men to be seized with a recollection too late or unseasonably, after he had tried and failed to conjure it up by an effort of will, it was due to the very fact that this exertion of his memory had produced in him mental pictures or images (φαντάσματα) which affected his mind more strongly and were more compelling than was the case with other people; and this agitated and crowded memory, once it had been awakened, could as little be arrested in its automatic course as an archer could recall an arrow once shot.[77]

It would seem that the expression ἀκολουθητικοὶ τῇ φαντασίᾳ is meant to characterise this exaggerated irritability of the "vis

---

[75] *De somno et vigilia*, III (457 a 29). This indifference to sleep was later reckoned as one of the few favourable traits in the melancholy disposition—"Hi vigilant studiis, nec mens est dedita somno." In view of all this, Aristotle as a moralist cannot really condemn the melancholic's lack of control, for since his organic constitution excludes the possibility of free will, he is morally less to be blamed (and, in fact, easier to cure since the treatment is purely medical) than those who resolve to do evil, or those who have the capacity to make good resolutions but lack the strength to keep them. For the latter can control themselves more easily in the same way as a person who knows he is going to be tickled can take himself in hand (*Eth. Nic.*, 1150 b 25 sqq., esp. 1152 a 19 and 1152 b 22). The passage in the *Magna Moralia* (II, 1203 b 7 sqq.) which treats the melancholic's lack of self-control as more blameworthy, on the ground that, being by nature cold, he is uncontrolled only from a certain weakness (ἀσθενική τις), is in contradiction with all other passages, and can be explained as a mistaken attempt to reconcile Aristotle's notions with the simple doctrine of the qualities held by school medicine. In any case it might be argued that the author of the *Magna Moralia* falls into many errors as soon as he attempts to go forward on his own; and the contradiction just pointed out is fresh evidence that, despite H. von Arnim's attempt to rescue it, the work should be regarded more or less as an abridgment of the two Aristotelian *Ethics*. Cf. E. KAPP in *Gnomon*, VOL. III (1927), pp. 19 sqq., and 73 sqq.

[76] In later literature, especially after a connexion had been established between temperaments and planets, the "constant" Saturn became patron of melancholics, and the latter were thought to have particularly good memories.

[77] *De memoria et reminiscentia*, II, 453 a 18 sqq.

imaginativa", which was later believed to produce hallucinations, or to enhance the power of visual imagination.[78] It was this faculty which sent the melancholic true dreams, as described in the *Eudemian Ethics*,[79] and which even enabled him to prophesy the future with astonishing accuracy (εὔστοχοί εἰσιν). Just by virtue of the vehemence of his imagination the melancholic was in a position—in fact he was bound—to associate every given idea with the next, and became like those "possessed ones" (ἐμμανεῖς) who continually wrote and recited songs like those composed by Philainis[80]; it was no coincidence that later the Arabic expression for "black" or "melancholic" became synonymous with "passion".[81]

Nevertheless, a fundamental contradiction exists between the picture of the melancholic as a complete and expressive whole, shown in Problem XXX, I, and that which we can piece together, mosaic-wise, from statements made by Aristotle elsewhere. (Albertus Magnus, in the chapter of his *Ethics* in which he collected all the Aristotelian statements concerning the melancholic, showed this in a significant "quamvis—tamen".[82]) Elsewhere, melancholy

---

[78] For the morbid perversions of the "vis imaginativa," which, of course, are best described in medical literature, cf. pp. 47, 50, 55, 93. The notion of a melancholic as a man with enhanced powers of inward vision occurs in the thirteenth-century scholastics, and we shall deal with this below in greater detail; see pp. 337 sqq. (text).

[79] *Eth. Eud.*, VIII, 2 (1248 a 40).

[80] *De divinatione per somnum*, II, 464 a 32 sqq. The traditional text has *τὰ Φιλαιγίδου ποήματα*, but the old emendation *Φιλαινίδος* is obviously right, as the context applies to poems treating of love, the characteristic of these poems being the way they dragged in every possible association; and this might well be said of the works of the notorious Philainis of Leucadia.

[81] Arabic *saudâ'u* = black (fem.); Arabic *saudāwī al-mizăǧ* = black by admixture, melancholy; Turkish and Persian *sewdā* = passion (information kindly supplied by Dr. Björkmann).

[82] *Ethics*, VII, 2, 5 (*B. Alberti Magni opera omnia*, ed. A. Borgnet, Paris 1890–99, VOL. VII, p. 511). The young man as well as the old "multis laborat defectibus", the young because he wastes too much energy, the old because "in senectute, quae frigida et sicca est ad modum melancholiae", he, like a building fallen into ruins, is in constant need of repair: "Nec hoc dicimus tantum de melancholicis melancholia innaturali, quae combusta cholera est et nigra, sed de melancholicis generaliter. *Quamvis* enim melancholici de melancholia accidentali ex acumine humoris morsa habeant corpora, *tamen* dicit Aristoteles in Problematibus, quod omnes hi, qui fuerunt heroicarum virtutum, Hector et Priamus et alii, in hac melancholia laborabant: eo quod haec melancholia rubei vini, quod vaporosum est, habet similitudinem; et quia gravitatem habet, constantiam facit; quia vero vaporosa, virtutem erigit ad operationem. Melancholia enim naturalis, ut dicit Galenus, frigida est et sicca. Per frigiditatem abscidens motum et evaporationem, per siccitatem autem gravitate propria decidit; propter quod stomachus melancholicorum et senum superius vacuus est, omni evaporatione destitutus, et semper suam sentiens inanitionem ex nutrimenti defectu; propter quod continue cibum desiderant . . . . Cuius signum est, quod tales multum et continue comedunt, multi stercoris sunt et parvi nutrimenti. Appetunt continue et supplens defectum et expellens tristitiam, quae est ex defectu. Delectatio autem si fortis sit, facit expulsionem, sive illa delectatio sit contraria sive etiam conveniens quaecumque. Vehemens enim

is treated throughout as a pathological abnormality always needing medical aid, with virtues that are merely the reverse side of its failings (true dreams, for instance, come not from good sense—φρόνησις—but, to put it in modern language, from the unchecked activity of the "unconscious"). The Problem, however, considers a melancholy disposition essential for just those achievements which require conscious aim and deliberate action—those in fact which correspond to the essentially intellectual virtues, that is to say achievements in the realm of art, poetry, philosophy or politics. Such a conception is not "un-Aristotelian", but to a certain extent it does go beyond Aristotle's own range of interests. In the *Parva naturalia* it is the physiologist who speaks, for whom the "abnormal" means merely a "modus deficiens"; in the *Ethics* the speaker is the moralist, who considers the individual in his relation to the community, and who to that extent sees the existence and behaviour of men from the standpoint of decorum and responsibility. In both cases the melancholic is conceived as "melancholic through illness", whose physical suffering results either in quite clear deviations from the normal, or in a smaller degree of moral responsibility. The author of Problem XXX, I, however, sets himself the task of doing justice to a type of character which evades judgement from the medical as well as from the moral point of view—the "exceptional" type (περιττός).

This concept really denoted the fatal lack of moderation characteristic of the heroes and victims in the great tragedies, shown in Electra's grief[83] or Antigone's work of charity; these seemed insolent and pointless to the reasonable Ismene or the rigidly autocratic Creon, but they meant the fulfilment of a higher moral law to poet and audience.[84] The epithet "exceptional" carried a certain sinister pathos because of the suspicion of ὕβρις which any attempted departure from the recognised human norm seemed to imply. To this popular religious feeling Aristotle alludes in the beginning of the *Metaphysics*[85]: "If there is

delectatio in quocumque sit, ad se trahit animam, et non sinit avertere tristitias, quae ex aliis contingunt defectibus. Propter hoc ergo, quod tam senes quam iuvenes superabundantias prosequuntur delectationum, fiunt intemperati et pravi: quia intemperatus circa tales est delectationes." The derivation from Aristotle is obvious almost everywhere.

[83] SOPHOCLES, *Electra* line 155.

[84] *Antigone*, lines 68, 780. When Creon calls Antigone's burial of her brother *πόνος περισσός* it includes the notions both of "excess" (because the act is contrary to woman's nature or a citizen's duty) and of "superfluity" (cf. the frequently quoted medical expression *περισσώματα*).

[85] *Metaphysics*, I, 2 (982 b 32 sqq.).

something in what the poets say and the godhead is by nature jealous, then all exceptional (outstanding) men are bound to be unfortunate."

Again, in passages where Aristotle uses his favourite method of analysing popular assumptions in order to arrive at a clearer distinction between ethical terms, the word "περιττόν" is sometimes used in the colloquial sense, in which it had become one of the slightly ambiguous expressions of exaggerated admiration used by the philistine concerning things which are above his head and therefore suspect.[86] But if this concept eventually came to have a mainly positive connotation, and the "mean" sank to denote "mediocrity", this development can after all be traced back to Aristotle, who extended the notion of the "exceptional" beyond the realm of emotion and action, and used it in such a way as to cover rational behaviour and even that highest of human achievements, the contemplative thought of the philosopher.

In his *Ethics* the "greatness of soul" (μεγαλοψυχία) of the outstanding man is considered as a value over and above the simple equilibrium of forces achieved by lesser natures. The magnanimous is described as "in respect to greatness an extreme, in respect to ⟨right⟩ proportion a mean".[87]

With the same feeling for greatness as an absolute value, the contemplation of the First Principles, which is the object of the philosopher, is characterised as a περιττόν in the popular as well as the more profound sense. For it does not only go beyond any knowledge of immediately utilitarian or even moral and political value,[88] but, being an end in itself, might be thought to transcend human nature and to be a privilege of the gods. But it is just because of the "transcending" value of this wisdom that Aristotle, rejecting the old superstition of the jealous deity, claims it to be the true aim and perfect felicity of man.[89]

Whoever he was, the author of Problem XXX, I, tried to understand and to a certain extent to justify the man who was

---

[86] Cf. e.g. *Eth. Nic.*, VI (1141 b 6): "Therefore they say that Anaxagoras, Thales and men like that are wise, but not sensible, when it appears that they do not know what is useful to themselves, and they say that [these men] know out-of-the-way-things, things wonderful, difficult and marvellous, but useless".

[87] Or: "absolutely speaking an extreme, relatively a mean" (*Eth. Nic.*, IV, 7, 1123 b 13: *τῷ μὲν μεγέθει ἄκρος, τῷ δὲ ὡς δεῖ μέσος*). The resemblance of the thought to the phrase in the Problem, "since it is possible for an abnormal admixture to be well attempered . . ," is striking.

[88] Cf. *Politics*, VIII, 2 (1337 a 42): . . . disciplines useful in life or those tending to virtue or to the *περιττά*.

[89] *Metaphysics*, I, 2 (983 a 2 sqq.); *Eth. Nic.*, X, 7 (1177 b 26 sqq.).

great because his passions were more violent than those of ordinary men and because he was strong enough, in spite of this, to achieve a balance out of excess; not only Ajax and Bellerophon, but Plato and Socrates belonged to this type. And so the Problem links up with genuine Aristotelian themes. The notions of creative frenzy and of enthusiasm were not unacceptable to the young Aristotle,[90] nor did he abandon them in the course of his development; they remained operative in his thought and feelings, though they were not always explicitly stated. For the same thinker who sometimes used the words μανικός and ἐνθουσιαστικός in an entirely derogatory sense[91] was also the man who described the art of poetry itself as inspired,[92] and who said in the *Poetics*[93] that, because the poet must have a clear picture of every moment of the drama and must in himself directly experience all the emotions experienced by his heroes, he must either be a talented man (εὐφυής) or inspired by frenzy, for the one has an impressionable (εὔπλαστος) nature, the other is ecstatic.[94]

---

[90] Cf. WERNER JAEGER, *Aristotle*, Oxford 1934, *passim*. Here the notion of μανία is too much considered as having been taken over from Plato and as having become less important to Aristotle as he became more independent; whereas in our opinion it is something quite consonant with Aristotelian thought, which in the course of his development was not so much pushed aside as assimilated, and thus, of course, modified.

[91] See for instance *Eth. Eud.*, 1230 a 32: μὴ καλὸν ἀλλὰ μανικόν.

[92] *Rhetoric*, III, 7 (1408 b 19).

[93] *Poetics*, 17 (1455 a 33); cf. J. VAHLEN, *Beiträge zu Aristoteles Poetik*, new edn. prepared by R. Schöne, Leipzig 1914 (from *Sitzungsberichte der Akademie der Wissenschaften, Phil.-hist. Kl.*, LII, Vienna 1866, p. 129). The εὐφυής is the man equipped with intellectual gifts by nature (the opposite of γεγυμνασμένος), especially he who knows and chooses truth thanks to his native powers of judgement (*Eth. Nic.*, 1114 b 7, *Topica*, 163 b 13), and may therefore be described as εὔπλαστος (pliant, easily sympathetic to other people's ideas). Vahlen and others read ἐξεταστικοί instead of ἐκστατικοί, but pairing εὐφυής with εὔπλαστοι and μανικός with ἐξεταστικοί would not make such good sense, since "judgement" applies to the εὐφυής much sooner than to the μανικός. Cf. also the Arabic text, JAROSLAUS TKATSCH, *Die arabische Uebersetzung der Poetik des Aristoteles*, I (*Akademie der Wissenschaften in Wien, Phil.-hist. Kl., Kommission für die Herausgabe der arabischen Aristoteles-Uebersetzungen*) Vienna 1928, pp. 256 sqq.

[94] The fragment from SEXTUS EMPIRICUS, *Adversus dogmaticos*, III, 20–22, (*Aristotelis Fragmenta*, ed. V. Rose, frag. 10) is important for Aristotle's attitude to enthusiasm and prophecy. We cannot say whether Aristotle himself was a melancholic. (If he was, it would of course be a very illuminating circumstance with regard to the presuppositions of Problem XXX,1.) In any case it is curious that a malicious satire should give a list of the very traits which appear in the genuine writings of Aristotle as signs of the melancholic:

σμικρός, φαλακρός, τραυλὸς ὁ Σταγειρίτης,/λάγνος, προγάστωρ, παλλακαῖς συνημμένος.

(*Aristotelis Fragmenta*, ed. V. Rose, p. 10, at the end of a short life of Aristotle which also names some of the traits here ridiculed.) On the other hand, there is no doubt that the conception of the melancholic set forth in Problem XXX,1 was realised in the persons of *other* great philosophers. For Heraclitus, see below p. 41; and Socrates is convincingly described as completely "uncontrolled", irascible and sensual by nature, attaining the status of a philosopher only by deliberate effort.

Admittedly Aristotle could not concede this frenzy to be "godlike" in the sense that it could be traced back to a non-natural origin. One might say that he would have accepted it only when it had lost its transcendental character, and when it had acquired legitimate status by being drawn into the natural nexus of cause and effect.

This indeed was precisely the task undertaken by Problem XXX, I. The mythical notion of frenzy was replaced by the scientific notion of melancholy, a task made the easier as "melancholic" and "mad"—in the purely pathological sense—had long been synonymous, and as the peculiar gift of true dreams and prophecies belonging to the diseased melancholic corresponded to the Platonic equation of "mantic" and "manic".

In this way the notion of melancholy acquired in its turn a new and positive content, and thanks to this it was possible at once to recognise and to explain the phenomenon of the "man of genius". Plato described how an abnormal condition which when seen from without looked like madness and made a deep thinker appear a fool in the eyes of the world[95] might be the source of all great intellectual achievements; and only this idea could have enabled a type of mind more scientific than metaphysical to conceive the notion that even the dread melancholy could furnish its victims with gifts of the spirit surpassing reason. Only the distinction between divine frenzy and frenzy as a human disease that is established in the *Phaedrus*[96] could have made possible the differentiation between natural and pathological melancholy (μελαγχολία διὰ φύσιν ἢ διὰ νόσον) set forth in Problem XXX, I. But only the Aristotelian notion of matter coupled with the Aristotelian theory of heat made it possible to bring systematic order into the many forms of "vehemence" ascribed to the melancholic in the clear terms of a theory of opposites; only the Aristotelian conception of the "mean" made it possible to conceive an effective equilibrium between the poles of this antithesis, a "eucrasia within an anomaly" which justified the apparently paradoxical statement that only the abnormal was great. The miracle of the man of genius remained; but it was conceived (thereby perhaps becoming even more miraculous) no longer as an irruption of mythical forces into reality, but as nature

---

[95] A German author of the sixteenth century, JOHANNES ADELPHUS MULICHIUS, uses the word "schellig" in his translation of Ficino, Strassburg, about 1505 (quoted p. 282).

[96] *Phaedrus*, 265A.

surpassing herself by following her own immanent laws, making man, though necessarily very seldom, a superman.

Problem XXX, I, stands therefore at a point in the history of thought where Platonism and Aristotelianism interpenetrate and balance one another. The conception of frenzy as the sole basis for the highest creative gifts was Platonic. The attempt to bring this recognised mysterious relationship between genius and madness, which Plato had expressed only in a myth, into the bright light of rational science was Aristotelian, as was likewise the attempt to resolve the contradictions between the world of physical objects and the world of ideas by a new interpretation of nature. This union led to a shift of values through which the "many" were equated with the "average", and which stressed the emotional "Be different!" rather than the ethical "Be virtuous!"; and this subjectivism is characteristically hellenistic—which perhaps accounts for its peculiarly modern flavour. Divine frenzy came to be regarded as a sensibility of soul, and a man's spiritual greatness was measured by his capacity for experience and, above all, for suffering. In fine, the conception of Problem XXX, I, points to Theophrastus, the philosopher who was the first to write a whole book on melancholy, and who said of Heraclitus that owing to melancholy he left most of his work unfinished or lost himself in contradictions.[97]

For the first time the dark source of genius—already implicit in the word "melancholy"—was uncovered. Plato's divine frenzy was the recollection of an otherworldly realm of supracelestial light, now recaptured only in moments of ecstasy: in Peripatetic thought melancholy was a form of experience in which light was a mere correlative of darkness, and in which the way to the light, as later times understood, was exposed to daemonic perils.[98]

3. THE DEVELOPMENT OF THE NOTION OF MELANCHOLY AFTER THE PERIPATETICS

It was only natural that this conception should not have been capable at once of satisfactory development; a true understanding of Problem XXX, I, could not begin to emerge until something which was here anticipated had become a reality for men's

---

[97] DIOGENES LAERTIUS, *Lives of the philosophers*, V, 2, 44 and IX, I, 6. H. Usener, *Analecta Theophrastea* (Kl. Schriften I, 54), Leipzig 1912–14, traces the whole Problem back to Theophrastus. See also above, p. 23, note 57.

[98] See below, pp. 250 sqq. (text).

self-consciousness, namely, the phenomenon of "genius". One may say that the Italian Renaissance of the fifteenth century was the first age that grasped the full significance of the Problem. (It was no sooner grasped than transformed.) Ancient writers record its main thesis, that all great men are melancholics, with either a certain remote astonishment[99] or else with frank irony,[100] but in any case with dwindling sympathy for the tragic anomaly of the outstanding man hurled back and forth between exaltation and overwhelming depression. Lost too was the basis of this sympathy, the manner of regarding the melancholy humour itself like a highly sensitive precision instrument which could be thrown out of equilibrium by any outside or inner influence. According to a doctrine of elements and qualities which took no account of the "thermodynamic ambivalence", the black bile was a cold, dry, earthy substance[101] and nothing more.

Apart from the complex of symptoms described in Problem XXX, I, and in the corpus of indubitably Aristotelian writings, all that survived of the new conception was a feeling that there was some special connexion between melancholy and the intellectual life; and that a sharp distinction must be drawn between what was "natural" and what was "diseased", which led to the conclusion that the humours, envisaged in terms of "natural" predominance, also determined a man's mental condition. Both thoughts were pregnant enough, the first for the further development of the notion of pathological melancholy, the second for the creation of a type of character—an idea which, before the end of antiquity, was to merge with the doctrine of the four temperaments as four types of disposition.

(*a*) Melancholy as an Illness

With regard to the further development of a pathological notion of melancholy, a distinction must be drawn between the moral judgment of the philosophers and the purely curative approach of the physicians. The former was represented by the Stoics,

---

[99] CICERO, loc. cit. (cf. *De divinatione*, I, 81), PLUTARCH, loc. cit., see above p. 33, note 65.

[100] AULUS GELLIUS, *Noctium Atticarum libri* 20, XVIII, 7, 4: "Cumque digressi essemus, 'Non tempestive,' inquit Favorinus, 'hunc hominem accessimus. Videtur enim mihi *ἐπισήμως μαίνεσθαι*. Scitote,' inquit, 'tamen intemperiem istam, quae *μελαγχολία* dicitur non parvis nec abiectis ingeniis accidere, *ἀλλὰ εἶναι σχεδόν τι τὸ πάθος τοῦτο ἡρωϊκόν* et veritates plerumque fortiter dicere, sed respectum non habere *μήτε καιροῦ μήτε μέτρου*'."

[101] See esp. RUFUS, p. 355, 2: *ψυχρὸς γὰρ καὶ ξηρὸς ὁ μελαγχολικὸς χυμός*; also Galen's commentary on the Περὶ *φύσιος ἀνθρώπου* I, 40–I (*Corp. med. Gr.*, V, ix, I, p. 51), quoted, for instance by Albertus Magnus: see above, p. 36, note 82.

the latter mainly by Rufus of Ephesus (*c.* A.D. 200), who played as great a part in the history of the medical conception of melancholy as the author of Problem XXX, 1, in the history of the philosophical and psychological conception of genius.

(i) *The Stoic View*

The Stoics affirmed that a wise man can never be overtaken by madness because the notions of wisdom and madness were mutually exclusive—so much so that anyone who was not wise could be described as "a madman" (μαίνεσθαι ὁμοίως πάντας, ὅσοι μὴ σοφοί).[102] But though the Wise Man of the Stoics was safe from mania he could, curiously enough, be occasionally overtaken by melancholy. "The Wise Man cannot become mad, but he may occasionally be subject to delusions owing to melancholy or delirium."[103] He could even lose his virtue, which the Stoics normally considered imperishable: according to Diogenes Laertius, Chrysippus declared that the Sage could forfeit his excellence through melancholy[104]; and that was apparently the usual Stoic teaching. Cicero also adopted it, declaring with a certain patriotic pride that the Latin word "furor" (as he translated the Greek "melancholia") was more appropriate because it directly and clearly described a convulsion of the soul which could not be gathered from the mere concept of "atrabiliousness".[105] The opponents of Stoic ethics seized on the Sage's concession to human weakness with eagerness and with a certain malicious pleasure.[106]

What concerns us in the Stoic doctrine is that in it the notion of melancholy reverted to that of pure illness, and a very severe one at that, in the pre-Aristotelian sense. Cicero calls it a

---

[102] *Stoicorum veterum fragmenta*, ed. I. AB ARNIM, VOL. III, frags. 658, 662, 663, 668. With frag. 664: *πάντας τοὺς ἄφρονας μαίνεσθαι . . . ἀλλὰ κατὰ τὴν ἴσην τῇ ἀφροσύνῃ μανίαν πάντα πράττειν*, cf. frag. 665 (= CICERO, *Tusc. Disp.*, IV, 54): "Stoici, qui omnes insipientes insanos esse dicunt." Cf. also frag. 666: "Stoici omnes homines insanos et stultos esse dicunt, excepto sapiente." Accordingly, the statement that the wise man can never be overtaken by madness is logical; whosoever is *μὴ σοφός* (insipiens) is a *μαινόμενος* (insanus), and as the *σοφός* cannot be *μὴ σοφός*, neither can he be a *μαινόμενος*.

[103] DIOGENES LAERTIUS, *Lives of the philosophers*, VII, 118 = I AB ARNIM (ed.), op. cit., VOL. III, frag. 644.

[104] I. AB ARNIM (ed.), op. cit., VOL. III, frag. 237; the *διὰ μέθην* is probably an addition by Diogenes Laertius, as the notion of stoic virtue comprises the view that the "Sage" can never be the victim of drunkenness.

[105] *Tusc. disp.*, III, 5, 2.

[106] I. AB ARNIM (ed.), op. cit., VOL. III, frag. 238 (cf. also frag. 239).

"mentis ad omnia caecitas", contrasting it with "insania", which arose from mere dullness and whose victims might still be equal to managing their lives and affairs moderately well. But on the other hand, this illness was treated throughout as a negative privilege of the Sage. Melancholy as a disposition ceased to be the main requisite for outstanding gifts, but as a disease it remained the main danger for the outstandingly gifted; it alone had the right to take away from a man what in the opinion of the Peripatetics it had had the power to confer. Posidonius seems to have been the first to acknowledge again the prophetic gift of the diseased melancholic, and thence to have rediscovered a scientific basis for the phenomenon of prophecy—so important in the eyes of the Stoic.[107] It was this basis to which a mystic like Iamblichus was bound to take violent exception just because of its scientific nature.[108]

(ii) *Asclepiades, Archigenes and Soranus*

In the introduction to his monograph on black bile, Galenus passed in review the older writings on this subject; and in so doing he seemed, somewhat maliciously, to take exception to those who had opposed the true doctrine from a spirit of pure contradiction, particularly those who "called themselves Erasistratians, Asclepiadians and Methodics".[109] The common vice in all these heretics was that, following the example of the medical school of Cnidus, they had made a more or less decisive break with the humoralism of Cos; and that in so far as they concerned themselves at all with melancholy, which Erasistratus

---

[107] SEXTUS EMPIRICUS, *Adversus dogmaticos*, I, 247. Among true conceits, a distinction is drawn between "cataleptic" ones, i.e. those based on evident perceptions, and those occurring in a state of πάθος. To these latter belong the admittedly true, but not "cataleptic" and therefore subjectively uncertain φαντασίαι of the φρενιτίζοντες καὶ μελαγχολῶντες. Along these lines, which correspond to the notion of the prophetic melancholic contained in the *Eudemian Ethics* rather than to the theory of genius contained in Problem XXX,1, there are statements such as Cicero's in *De divinatione*, I, 81 (that Aristotle had credited melancholics with "aliquid praesagiens atque divinum"), or Plutarch's, who opposed the prevailing opinion as to the melancholic's true dreams: dreaming a lot, and imagining a lot, they often hit on the truth by chance (*De defectu oraculorum*, 50).

[108] IAMBLICHUS, *De mysteriis*, III, 8, 25, ed. G. Parthey, Berlin 1857, pp. 116 sq.; 158. Melancholy frenzy belongs to those ecstasies which, like drunkenness or hydrophobia, degrade us ἐπὶ τὸ χεῖρον; the true prophetic frenzy, on the other hand, raises us ἐπὶ τὸ βέλτιον, and is a predisposition neither of the body nor of the soul nor yet of the "natural" man resulting from the combination of the two, but is something entirely supernatural, namely, τὰ καθήκοντα ἀπὸ τῶν θεῶν φῶτα, or, as he says elsewhere (ed. cit., p. 100) ὁρμωμένη οὔτε ἀπὸ τῶν περὶ τοῖς σώμασι παθημάτων. Thus he considers melancholy frenzy in express contrast to θεία μανία.

[109] GALEN (KÜHN), VOL. V, p. 105 (= *Corp. med. Gr.* V 4, 1.1, p. 71), printed in part in RUFUS, p. 291.

himself, according to Galen, "did not dare to do", they had defined it in a new manner.

Asclepiades of Bithynia, who came to Rome in 91 B.C. and became the friend of Cicero and other noble Romans, was the first to bring Greek medicine into repute on Italian soil[110]; and his teachings have been transmitted to us mainly by Aulus Cornelius Celsus, who flourished under Tiberius.[111] It is from Celsus's writings that we first learn of a systematic division of mental illness into three categories: (1) frenzy ("phrenesis"), which came on suddenly and was accompanied by fever; (2) the more lasting and generally feverless "tristitia quam videtur atra bilis contrahere"; and (3) an absolutely chronic form, which arose either from a disorder of the imagination, sometimes sad and sometimes cheerful, or else from a disorder of the understanding. Thus not merely the second but also the third type came under what in earlier—and again later—authors was described as "melancholy". This is clear from the fact that it was exemplified in Ajax, among others, whom Problem XXX, 1, had explicitly represented as a melancholic. Celsus barely mentions symptoms and causes but confines himself mainly to therapeutic prescriptions; and in accordance with the general principles of Asclepiades, the treatment of all these illnesses was based far less on the use of medicaments and surgery[112] than on dietary and, most important of all, on psychological remedies. These remedies were: living in rooms full of light (as opposed to the old view that darkness was soothing); avoidance of heavy food; moderation in the drinking of wine, especially of strong wines; massage, baths, exercises, and (if the patient was strong enough) gymnastics; fighting insomnia (not with medicaments but by gentle rocking to-and-fro, or by the sound of running water); change of surroundings, and long journeys[113]; especially, strict avoidance of all frightening ideas; cheering conversation and amusements; gentle admonition;

---

[110] K. SUDHOFF, *Kurzes Handbuch zur Geschichte der Medizin*, Berlin 1922, pp. 93 sqq.

[111] *A. Cornelii Celsi quae supersunt*, ed. F. Marx (*Corpus medicorum Latinorum*, VOL. I, Leipzig 1915, pp. 122 sqq.). For this and the following, cf. M. WELLMANN, *A. Cornelius Celsus, eine Quellenuntersuchung*, Berlin 1913, pp. 105 sqq., and J. L. HEIBERG, *Geisteskrankheiten im klassischen Altertum*, Berlin 1927, offprint from *Allgemeine Zeitschrift für Psychiatrie*, VOL. LXXXVI.

[112] Prescribing (among other things) hellebore, proverbial in ancient and modern times as an aid to the understanding.

[113] Prescribing travel as a means of distraction is typical: Porphyry says in chapter XI of his *Life of Plotinus* that he himself was once near suicide; Plotinus, diagnosing it as arising *ἐκ μελαγχολικῆς τινος νόσου*, advised him to travel, and this saved him.

sympathetic treatment of any fixed ideas; discussions in which the patient should be brought into a different frame of mind more by unobtrusive suggestion than by open contradiction; and, most important of all, music, whose psychiatric use, first suggested by Theophrastus,[114] had finally been systematised by Asclepiades[115] —we even know which modes he recommended for the various forms of mental illness.[116] Thus one of the earliest conceptions of humanity, expressed not only in the teachings of the Pythagoreans, but also in the myths of Orpheus and in the biblical story of Saul and David, was linked with Plato's theory of the moral effects of the different keys[117] to form a "musical therapy" which was held to be valid almost until to-day,[118] and even seems to be reviving after a fashion at this moment. On the other hand, Asclepiades's pupil Titus (unlike Asclepiades himself) recommended shock therapy (as it is called) for certain cases and, for violent madmen, overtly forcible measures, ranging from compulsory memorising to fettering, flogging (also much employed in the Middle Ages—see plate 71), deprivation of food and drink, artificial intoxication and inducement to sexual indulgence.[119]

Almost at the opposite pole to the Asclepiadian doctrine was that of Archigenes of Apamea, who lived under Trajan and was one of the last and most important representatives of the "pneumatic" school.[120] Asclepiades had attempted to separate the illness "which probably originated from the black bile" both from acute mania and from the chronic form of madness; Archigenes recognised only "melancholy" and "mania", and

---

[114] THEOPHRASTUS, fragm. 87, *Opera omnia*, ed. F. Wimmer, Paris 1931, p. 436 (= ATHENAEUS, *Deipnosophistae*, XIV, 624a); fragm. 88, ibid.

[115] CENSORINUS, *De die natali*, XII, 4; CAELIUS AURELIANUS, *De morbis acutis et chronicis*, Amsterdam 1709, chron. I, 5, pp. 338 sqq.: "Asclepiades secundo libro adhibendam praecepit cantilenam."

[116] CAELIUS AURELIANUS, op. cit., p. 337: The sad are to be cheered by airs in the Phrygian mode, the frivolous sobered by those in the Dorian.

[117] *Republic*, 398D sqq. For the Phrygian and Dorian modes see esp. 399A–C; further, cf. ARISTOTLE, *Politics*, VIII, 4–9 (1339b sqq.); PLUTARCH, Περὶ μουσικῆς, 17; in Christian times, *Cassiodori Senatoris Variae*, II, 40, ed. Th. Mommsen, Berlin 1894, in *Monumenta Germaniae Historica, Auctores Antiquissimi*, VOL. XII, pp. 70–2.

[118] See below, pp. 85, 267 sqq. and passim (text).

[119] Besides Celsus, cf. CAELIUS AURELIANUS, *De morbis acutis et chronicis*, cap. cit., p. 339; M. WELLMANN, *A. Cornelius Celsus, eine Quellenuntersuchung*, p. 65.

[120] Transmitted by ARETAEUS, III, 5 (*Opera omnia*, ed. C. G. Kühn, Leipzig 1828, p. 74; ☞ ed. C. Hude, in *Corp. med. Gr.*, II, p. 39, whose text we follow).

further limited this distinction by making melancholy independent in principle of the "atra bilis"[121] and treating it as merely an "early form or symptom of mania"—although he admitted that irascible, cheerful and violent natures tended more to a manic illness, and the dull, gloomy and slow to a melancholy one, which he described as a depression without fever, due to an obsession (ἔστι δὲ ⟨ἡ μελαγχολίη⟩ ἀθυμίη ἐπὶ μιῇ φαντασίῃ ἄνευθε πυρετοῦ· δοκέει δέ μοι μανίης γε ἔμμεναι ἀρχὴ καὶ μέρος ἡ μελαγχολίη).[122] And while in Asclepiades semeiology was somewhat neglected and attention concentrated on psychological remedies, the contrary was the case in Archigenes. His analysis of symptoms was sometimes of a penetration and subtlety which is unsurpassed even to-day; his therapy, on the contrary—in general not unlike the Asclepiadean—ignored all psychological methods, except that those used against insomnia were to be suited to the patient's type of mind, the musician being lulled to sleep by music, the schoolmaster by the prattle of children. According to him, the conspicuous symptoms of melancholy were: dark skin,[123] puffiness, bad odour,[124] greed coupled with permanent leanness, depression, misanthropy, suicidal tendencies, true dreams, fears, visions, and abrupt transitions from hostility, pettiness and avarice, to sociability and generosity. If mere melancholy turned to downright madness, the symptoms were: various hallucinations, fear of "daimones", delusions (the educated launching into fantastic astronomical or philosophical theories or artistic activities supposedly inspired by the Muses, the uneducated, however, believing themselves extraordinarily gifted in other fields), religious ecstasy, and curious obsessions such as the compulsive belief that one was an earthenware jar. Archigenes mentions only heat or dryness as basic factors, the immediate causes being overeating, immoderate fulness, drunkenness, lust, sexual indulgence, or disturbance of the normal excretions.

The school of the "Methodics"—much despised by Galen—was influenced by Themison, a pupil of Asclepiades. To this

---

[121] *Μετεξετέροισι δὲ οὔτε φῦσα οὔτε μέλαινα χολὴ ἐγγίγνεται, ὀργὴ δὲ ἄκρητος καὶ λύπη καὶ κατηφείη δεινή. καὶ τούσδε ὦν μελαγχολικοὺς καλέομεν, χολῇ μὲν τῆς ὀργῆς ξυμφραζομένης, μελαίνῃ δὲ πολλῆς καὶ θηριώδεος* (ARETAEUS, III, 5, 2).

[122] ARETAEUS, III, 5, 3.

[123] ARETAEUS, III, 5, 7: *χροιὴ μελάγχλωρος.*

[124] ARETAEUS, III, 5, 1: *φῦσάν τε νὰρ ἐμποιέει καὶ ἐρυγὰς κακώδεας, ἰχθυώδεας*; III, 5, 7: *ἐρυγαὶ κακώδεες, βρωμώδεες.*

school belonged Soranus of Ephesus,[125] who lived in the first half of the second century and who, though he invented little that was new in diagnosis, yet sharply criticised the therapeutic teachings of his predecessors. In general he supported a milder treatment of the sick, thereby bringing psychological remedies very much to the fore again. He enriched therapy in many ways, some very subtle[126]: for instance, the bed of a sick man was to be placed so that he should not be upset by his visitors' changing expressions; in conversation he should be given an opportunity of triumphing in argument, so as to strengthen his self-respect; in musical therapy the flute was to be avoided as too stimulating, and so on. For us Soranus's main importance lies in his attempt to draw a sharper distinction again between madness and melancholy (the first located in the head, the second in the body), and in his formal and explicit denial of the opinion (held "by most people" and queried only within certain limits even by Archigenes) that the origin of melancholy lay in the black bile:

☞ Melancholia dicta, quod nigra fella aegrotantibus saepe per vomitum veniant . . . et non, ut plerique existimant, quod passionis causa vel generatio nigra sint fella; hoc enim est aestimantium magis quam videntium veritatem, vel potius falsum, sicut in aliis ostendimus.[127]

(iii) *Rufus of Ephesus*

The teachings of the physicians so far mentioned could exert only a partial and indirect influence on future development. The future, indeed, did not belong to the opponents of the "School of Cos" and its humoral pathology. Through its great representative Galen, eclecticism was now to attain almost unchallenged supremacy, and Galen made it his supreme task to re-establish ancient humoralism, as modified by the spirit of the age. Electicism did sometimes take advantage of the diagnostic and therapeutic discoveries of the "Asclepiadians and Methodics"; but it could not accept their aetiological concepts as authoritative, and we have already heard how bitterly Galen expressed himself with regard to their idea of melancholy. All the more, however, did he appreciate Rufus of Ephesus, who flourished in the first

125 Transmitted by CAELIUS AURELIANUS, op. cit., I, 5 and 6 (pp. 325 sqq.).

126 The emphasis on sea voyages, also recommended by Vindician, was important for the future.

127 CAELIUS AURELIANUS, op. cit., I, 6, p. 339.

half of the second century A.D. His work *On Melancholy* can be partly reconstructed from citations, acknowledged or unacknowledged, in other authors, and it is this work which Galen declared the best—and in fact an unexceptionable—presentation of the subject.[128]

It was Rufus of Ephesus's teaching, too, which was to govern the views of medical schools up to the threshold of the present time, for not only did Galen associate himself unreservedly with it but it was embraced also by the great ninth-century Arabic writers. One of them, Isḥâq ibn Amrân, called Rufus's writing "the one ancient work which gave one satisfaction"; and his treatment of melancholy, based as it was mainly on Rufus, seems to have been the direct source of Constantinus Africanus's monograph. Constantinus, closely connected with the medical school of Salerno, had in turn a decisive influence on the development of medicine in the west during the Middle Ages; it may therefore be said that Rufus of Ephesus led the way with regard to the medical conception of melancholy for more than fifteen hundred years.[129]

The first and most important thing that Rufus did was to re-forge the link made in Problem XXX, I, between melancholy and intellect, which the other physicians had broken; but in so doing he approached the Stoic view, and made the link a perilous snare. He too saw primarily the intellectual man, the "man of large understanding and keen wit", as threatened with melancholy, for—just as in Aristotle—

> illi qui sunt subtilis ingenii et multae perspicationis, de facili incidunt in melancolias, eo quod sunt velocis motus et multae praemeditationis et imaginationis.[130]

---

[128] The main passages are: the fragment transmitted by Rhazes (RUFUS, p. 454, 18 sqq.); the excerpt from Aetius (RUFUS, p. 354, 7 sqq.); and the fragment in RUFUS, p. 320, 8 sqq., also from Aetius. Cf. J. ILBERG, *Rufus von Ephesos*, Leipzig 1930 (*Abhandlungen der Sächsischen Akademie der Wissenschaften, Phil.-hist. Klasse*, VOL. XLI, p. 35).

[129] Cf. A. BUMM, *Über die Identität der Abhandlungen des Ishâk ibn Amrân und des Constantinus Africanus über Melancholie*, Munich, privately printed, no date. R. CREUTZ and W. CREUTZ, in *Archiv für Psychiatrie*, XCVII (1932), pp. 244 sqq., attempt to prove that Constantine owed his knowledge not to Isḥâq but to Rufus direct, but their proof (which, incidentally, is put forward without reference to Isḥâq's original text) is mainly based on the fact that Constantine named Rufus and not the Arabic author as his authority; but this, of course, means little in view of the medieval habits of quoting. For us, the question whether Constantine made use of Rufus's treatise on melancholy directly or indirectly makes hardly any difference.

[130] RUFUS, p. 457, 18.

But the physician went one step further than the natural philosophers: for the author of Problem XXX, I, intellectual pre-eminence was a direct consequence of natural melancholy; for the Stoics it had become merely a predisposition to pathological melancholy; but for Rufus activity of the mind became the direct cause of melancholy illness:

☞ dixit, quod multa cogitatio et tristitia faciunt accidere melancoliam.[131]

This turn of phrase reverses completely the relation established in Problem XXX, I, between cause and effect, and the tragic destiny of the man of genius became merely the "spleen" of an overworked scholar. It also reveals an antithesis which was to determine the development of men's conception of melancholy for a long time to come, that is to say, the antithesis between specifically medical views and aims and those of natural or moral philosophers.

In diagnosis as well as in aetiology, then, Rufus reinstated the observations and discoveries of the Peripatetics, which the heterodox physicians had neglected. The symptoms of the melancholic were by now established. He was bloated and swarthy; plagued by all manner of desires, depressed (κατηφής, i.e. "looking at the ground", a symptom later to be cited particularly often, but in its literal sense); cowardly and misanthropic; generally sad without cause but sometimes immoderately cheerful[132]; given over to various eccentricities, phobias and obsessions.[133] Among these, like some of his predecessors, Rufus of Ephesus accounted stuttering and lisping,[134] as well as the gift of prophecy;

---

[131] RUFUS, p. 455, 31. Of the three physicians previously mentioned, only Soranus cites the "intentio nimia sensuum et intellectus ob cupiditatem disciplinarum", and then as cause only of mania, not of melancholy, and not as anything very remarkable; it is ranged alongside "quaestus pecunialis" and "gloria" (CAELIUS AURELIANUS, *De morbis acutis et chronicis*, chron. I, 5, p. 326).

[132] According to ISIDORE (*Etym.*, XI, 127), who is certainly following older sources, the spleen, which is the organ generating black bile, is also the seat of laughter: "nam splene ridemus, felle irascimur, corde sapimus, iecore amamus." A curious witness for the longevity of such notions is a dialogue from CASANOVA's *Memoirs* (I, 9): "What! The hypochondriac affections, which make all who suffer from them sad, make you cheerful?" "Yes, because without doubt my 'flati' do not affect the diaphragm but the spleen, which, in the opinion of my doctor, is the organ of laughter. It is his discovery." "Not at all. This idea is very ancient"—in which we fully agree with the author.

[133] Among compulsive ideas he mentions not only the delusion of being an earthenware jar (already cited by Archigenes) but also the belief that one had no head, an example frequently quoted in later times; as remedy some physicians suggested a leaden headpiece!

[134] Here, too, *ταχύγλωσσοι, ἰσχνόφωνοι, τραυλοί.* Rhazes (RUFUS, p. 454, 18 sqq.) says explicitly that they cannot pronounce S, and say T instead.

above all, he returned with full conviction to the Hippocratean and Peripatetic opinion as to the cause of all these symptoms; the root of the evil was partly an excess of "pneuma", which caused the puffiness, stuttering, and lust; partly the predominance of black bile, the earthy dryness and coldness of which produced, for instance, the obsession of being an earthenware jar, and also explained the dull depression, the reserve, the sudden maniacal outbursts of the man in a state of melancholy. It is true, however, that at the very point where it concerned method and principle, Rufus of Ephesus gave to the main thesis of Problem XXX, 1, a medical turn, with significant and far-reaching results.

The 'Aristotelian' Problem had declared that the melancholy humour could either attain a temporary preponderance as a consequence of daily nutriment, without influencing the character, or could from the beginning possess a permanent preponderance in certain people, determining the formation of character: in this latter case, the black bile, if too cold, resulted in fear and depression; if too hot, in inflammations, ecstasies, and maniacal states; but if at a moderate temperature, in important intellectual qualities. Among these statements, Rufus first adopted the differentiation between the melancholy deriving from the taking in of daily nutriment and that deriving from a constitutional preponderance.[135] But what for the natural philosopher had signified a difference between acute illness and habitual disposition, as also between purely physical suffering and moral character, acquired an aetiological, and thereby a therapeutic, shade of meaning for the physician:

> In treatment it makes a not unimportant difference where the illness comes from, for you must know that melancholy is of two kinds: some of them (that is: of melancholics) have it naturally, thanks to an inborn combination of humours, but others have acquired this combination of humours later, through bad diet.[136]

Thus, temporary illness was not divorced from natural constitution, but within the limits of the disease a distinction was made between an innate and an acquired form.[137] Next, however—and this was perhaps still more enlightening and more important

---

[135] Problem XXX,1, 954 a 26 sqq.

[136] RUFUS, p. 357, 12.

[137] Only in certain circumstances ("quando residet melancholia") can a man, despite "multiplicatio" of the black bile, be safe from melancholy disease: RUFUS, p. 456, 38.

for future development—Rufus of Ephesus took over the conceptions of excessive heat and cold but applied them in an entirely new way. According to 'Aristotle' it was the property of black bile to manifest both great heat and great cold without altering its material nature; according to Rufus, its property was to originate from the immoderate heating or cooling of other elements of the body. Rufus declared that either the blood could change into black bile by being chilled, or yellow bile could change into black by overheating (ὑπερόπτησις), for the black colour could result both from cooling (as in quenched coals) and from heating (as shown by fruit dried up by the sun).[138]

The physician tried to combine the medical humoralism with the Peripatetic ambivalence of melancholia. He thought in terms not of function but of matter, and rather than attribute two different symptoms and effects to one and the same substance, he preferred to recognise two different substances. In so doing he distinguished the black bile deriving from the cooling of the blood from a far more noxious "melancholia combusta" or "adusta" arising from "burning" of the yellow bile, a difference which from then onwards was never forgotten. In Rufus's text, which has been handed down to us only indirectly, this does not emerge quite as distinctly as we have put it here; but Galen (especially in his work *De locis affectis*), put it in so clear a form that we can certainly deduce Rufus's opinion from him.[139]

According to its composition, black bile manifests distinct differences. One is like the dregs of the blood,[140] very thick and not unlike the dregs of wine. The other is much thinner and so acid that it eats into the ground . . . and produces bubbles. The one I have compared with dregs . . . I call "melancholy humour" or "melancholy blood" (μελαγχολικὸς χυμός or μελαγχολικὸν αἷμα), for it cannot really be described as black bile. In some it predominates, whether as the result of the original combination, or as the result of nourishment. . . . If it establishes itself in the passages of a brain ventricle, it usually generates epilepsy: but if it predominates in

---

138 RUFUS, p. 356, 14 sqq.: *Μελαίνεται δὲ ὁ χυμὸς οὕτως ποτὲ μὲν ὑπερθερμαινόμενος, ποτὲ δὲ ὑπερψυχόμενος, οἷον πάσχουσι γάρ τι οἱ καιόμενοι ἄνθρακες, διαυγέστατοι μὲν ὄντες τῇ φλογί, σβεννυμένης δὲ τῆς φλογὸς ἀπομελαίνονται, τοιοῦτόν τι καὶ ἡ ψῦξις περὶ τὸ φαιδρὸν χρῶμα τοῦ αἵματος ἐργάζεται . . . ἡ δὲ ὑπερβολὴ τοῦ θερμοῦ πάλιν ξηράνασα καὶ δαπανήσασα τὰς ὑγρότητας . . . μελαίνει τοὺς χυμούς, ὥσπερ καὶ ὁ ἥλιος τοὺς καρπούς . . . ὅτι δὲ ἐξ ὑπεροπτήσεως τῆς ξανθῆς χολῆς τῇ παραφροσύνῃ παραπίπτουσι* . . . The foundation of this theory of adustion can be seen in the *Timaeus* 83A–C, 85D, where, it is true, the bile is attributed to adustion of the body in general.

139 *De locis affectis*, III, 9, in GALEN (KÜHN), VOL. VIII, pp. 176 sqq.

140 Here *τρύξ*, Latin "faex": in another passage where the cold quality of the fluid thus produced is emphasised, it is called *ὑπόστασις*, Latin "residuum," and *ἰλύς*, Latin also "faex". GALEN, *De temperamentis*, II, 603 (ed. G. Helmreich, Leipzig 1904, p. 59).

the substance of the brain itself, it causes that sort of madness which we call melancholy. . . . But as for the other atrabilious humour, which arises from overheated yellow bile (ὁ κατωπτημένης τῆς ξανθῆς χολῆς γενόμενος), if it predominates in the substance of the brain, it causes bestial raving both with and without fever.

One cannot say that the notion of melancholy was much simplified by this transformation. The melancholy humour, as one of the four primary humours, no longer had anything to do with the bile but was thickened and chilled blood; what was really black bile was a corruption through burning of the yellow bile—and therefore no longer belonged to the four humours. But one advantage of this complicated theory was that it provided a firm basis for the different types of mental disturbances and linked up the distinction drawn in Problem XXX, 1, between "natural" and "diseased" melancholy with a difference in tangible substances. Thereafter those physicians who admitted this distinction at all (popular scientific literature generally ignored it) understood thus first, under "natural black bile", one of the four humours always present in the body—essentially nothing but a thick and cold residuum of the blood, and (as such) still tainted with the stigma of dross and dregs, capable of generating illness, even if it was not actually harmful in a small quantity. And secondly, under "melancholia adusta" or "incensa" they understood *diseased* black bile, which (as such) did not belong to the four humours but arose from "superassatio", "combustio", or whatever expressions were later used, of the yellow bile; it therefore not only always caused illness, even when present in the smallest quantity, but owed its very existence to a process of corruption. This laid the foundations for the medical theory of melancholy. Neither Galen[141] nor the later Romans such as

[141] A particularly simple description is in the *Isagoge in Tegni* (*τέχνη*) *Galeni* by Johannitius (Honein ibn Ishâq), a text much used in the West before the Greek originals were known. "Cholera nigra duobus modis constat: uno modo est naturalis in modo fecis sanguinis et eiusdem perturbationis . . . et iste modus est veraciter frigidus et siccus. Est et alius modus extra naturalem cursum; et origo eius est de ustione cholerici commixtionis et hic veraciter appellatur niger; et est calidior et levior ac superior modus, habens in se impetum pernecabilem et qualitatem perniciosam." (Isidore, *Etym.*, IV, 5 tries to combine both viewpoints: "Melancholia dicta eo quod sit ex nigri sanguinis faece admixta abundantia fellis").

Apart from the fundamentally important distinction between the various morbid stuffs, Rufus also established an equally important one between the various seats of illness. He distinguished (1) infiltration of all the blood, resulting, among other things, in a darkening of the skin; (2) an affection of the brain, which was the cause particularly of mental disturbances; and (3) a "hypochondriac" form of illness, in which the black bile established itself in the "os stomachi," primarily generating flatulence and digestive disturbances, but secondarily affecting consciousness to a considerable degree as well (this threefold division

Theodore Priscian,[142] the early Byzantines such as Aetius,[143] Paul of Aegina[144] and Alexander of Tralles,[145] nor the first of the Arabic writers added much that was new; in many ways they even simplified. The last trace of the melancholic's heroic nimbus vanished; in particular, his connexion with "profunda cogitatio" was more and more lost sight of, not to be emphasised again till Isḥâq ibn Amrân[146]; and it is also very significant that the melancholic's gift of prophecy, which was observed by Aristotle and which Rufus still considered a reality despite its pathological origin, now began to be regarded merely as a sick man's illusion. Rufus's words, "Et contingit quod . . . prognosticantur futura, et eveniunt ea, quae ipsi praedicunt,"[147] were juxtaposed with those of Paul of Aegina: "Some men give the impression of being visited by higher powers and of foretelling the future as if by divine inspiration, so that they are called ἐνθεαστικοί (that is to say, god-possessed) in the proper sense."[148]

In the practical field many new features were added by later writers. Alexander of Tralles mentioned an additional symptom of melancholy—allegedly observed by himself—which, as we shall see, was to play a certain role in later pictorial tradition, namely a spasm of the fingers. By this, according to the Greek text, he seems to have meant a morbid stiffening of the middle finger,[149] but later authors, perhaps owing to an ambiguity in the

---

can be found in GALEN (KÜHN), VOL. VIII, p. 185; ALEXANDER OF TRALLES, *Originaltext und Übersetzung*, ed. T. Puschmann, Vienna 1878, I, pp. 591 sqq.; and many others). Rufus was also naturally interested in clinical questions proper, and provided a thorough system of therapy which collated all the previous information and handed it down to posterity. He combined Asclepiades's dietetic and gymnastic measures with the prescription of drugs, including the long famous *ἱερὰ Ῥούφου πρὸς μελαγχολίας* (p. 323, 7), recommended—in opposition to Soranus—intercourse with women as the best remedy for the non-manic form of the disease, and, unlike Archigenes, praised the enlivening effects of dramatic poetry and music (p. 583). Rufus also deals with the treatment for melancholy in a treatise on morbid disturbances (Περὶ ἀποσκημμάτων), cf. J. ILBERG, *Rufus von Ephesos*, pp. 31 sqq. His cure for melancholy by "quartary fever" (obviously malaria), recalling as it does the modern fever-therapy, is particularly interesting.

142 PRISCIAN, *Eupor.*, II, 18, p. 152.

143 J. L. HEIBERG, *Geisteskrankheiten im klassischen Altertum*, Berlin 1927 (offprint from *Allgemeine Zeitschrift für Psychiatrie*, VOL. LXXXVI), pp. 37 sqq.

144 PAULUS AEGINETA, ed. I. L. Heiberg, Leipzig 1921 (*Corp. med. Gr.*, IX, 1), pp. 156 ff.

145 Edited by T. Puschmann, Vienna 1878, I, pp. 591 sqq.; HEIBERG, op cit., pp. 40 sqq.

146 For this man, and his successors in the later Middle Ages, see below, pp. 83 sqq. (text).

147 RUFUS, p. 456, 1.

148 *Corp. med. Gr.*, IX, 1, p. 156, 20.

149 ALEXANDER OF TRALLES, ed. T. Puschmann, p. 506.

Latin translation, took it to mean an involuntary clenching of the fist:

> Novimus quippe foeminam ipsi eiusmodi phantasia obrutam, quae pollicem tam arctissime constringebat, ut nemo digitum facile posset corrigere, affirmans se universum orbem sustinere. . . .[150]

It is further remarkable that Paul of Aegina advised treating melancholy by cautery—a practice to which we owe the inclusion of the melancholic's portrait in the medieval series of zodiacal diagrams of cauterisation.[151]

(*b*) Melancholy in the System of the Four Temperaments

'Hippocrates' had already tried to relate physical characteristics to mental behaviour—he was even said to have reckoned the pulse-beat a sign of the moral disposition; and in the course of a development involving close co-operation between medical, biological and ethnological observations and the speculations of natural philosophy, it is understandable that a special science called "physiognomy" should have emerged, dealing with the idiosyncrasies of healthy people, as a counterpart of the medical semeiology of invalids.[152] The earliest text treating it as an independent science was attributed to Aristotle himself; and it certainly started in his circle. Indeed, these efforts received their confirmation and impulse from the Aristotelian doctrine that the soul is the "entelechy" of the body, and from the highly developed analysis of emotions and character in Aristotelian ethics. To this was added in the fourth century the specifically Hellenistic taste

---

150 ALEXANDER OF TRALLES, *De singularum corporis partium . . . vitiis, etc.* (tr. by Albanus Torinus), Basle 1533, p. 50. Obviously in connexion with this tradition, M. PLATEARIUS, *Practica, de aegrit. capitis*, chap. v, in the Venice edition of 1497, p. 173: "Alii tenent pugnum clausum, quod non potest aperiri: credunt enim se tenere thesaurum in manu vel totum mundum" (for the meaning of the "thesaurus" interpolated in Alexander's text, see below, p. 303, note 2). Earlier, GUILLELMUS BRIXIENSIS (Guglielmo de Corvi, d. 1326), *Practica,* Venice 1508, fol. 20v: "quidam putant se mundum tenere in manu: et ideo ipsi manum claudunt." See our PLATE 72. The constant motif of "the whole universe", which the unfortunate creatures think they hold, makes the connexion of these later passages with Alexander's passage clear.

151 Cf. K. SUDHOFF, *Beiträge zur Geschichte der Chirurgie im Mittelalter* (*Studien zur Geschichte der Medizin*, VOL. X), Leipzig 1914, pp. 76 sqq. In Paul of Aegina, however, it seems to be a question of cauterising the region of the spleen, and not yet the "media vertex" as described in medieval sources (see below, p. 291).

152 The relative texts and passages are collected in *Scriptores physiognomici graeci et latini*, ed. R. FÖRSTER, Leipzig 1893.

for close observation of individual details. It appears particularly clearly in the *Characters* of Theophrastus, where thousands of psychological peculiarities were observed, as it were, in close view, and then embodied in main types. The same trait appears in Hellenistic poetry and art, which enriched certain recurrent genres with a wealth of realistically observed details. Finally there was the fact that philosophy inclined more and more decisively to the view that "et morum varietates mixtura elementorum facit".[153] It was perhaps Posidonius who gave the final impetus; he himself was exceedingly interested in physiognomic and ethnological questions; and he emphasised so strongly the dynamic function of the cosmic elements and of the powers abiding in them, that the elements themselves became in his philosophy intermediaries, as it were, between what is usually termed matter and spirit.[154]

On the other hand, as we have already seen, the opinion had steadily persisted that the humours with their warm, cold, dry and moist qualities were not only sources of illness but also factors in determining men's constitutions. Sextus Empiricus took it simply for granted that the natural constitution of every living thing was determined by one of the four humours; for those governed by the blood and the phlegm he already used the adjectives "sanguine" and "phlegmatic" (πολύαιμος and φλεγματώδης), while he still described the two other types by the periphrasis "those who are governed by, and have a superfluity of, yellow or black bile".[155] With the growth of interest in physiognomic and characterological theory it was now inevitable that all the humours should be held to possess that power of informing the character which Problem XXX, I, had attributed only to the black bile. In other words, in the new psychology of types the paths of humoral pathology converged with those of physiognomy and characterology—Problem XXX, I, standing at the crossing of the roads like a signpost.

---

[153] SENECA, *De ira*, II, 19, obviously following older Stoic sources. He says further: "iracundos fervida animi natura faciet . . . frigidi mixtura timidos facit."

[154] K. REINHARDT, *Poseidonios*, Munich 1921, esp. pp. 225 sqq., 317 sqq. and 385 sqq.

[155] SEXTUS EMPIRICUS, *Πυῤῥώνειοι Ὑποτυπώσεις* A51 (ed. H. Mutschmann, Leipzig 1912, p. 16). He was merely interested in proving the subjectivity and individual differences of sensory perception, and he thought he could do this most easily by referring to the humoral "crases", which by their very nature involved a difference in sensory impressions. The reason why Sextus did not yet use the expressions *χολερικός* and *μελαγχολικός* for men governed respectively by yellow and black bile is perhaps that, to him, these were still specifically pathological terms.

We can see from the above-mentioned works of the physicians how greatly this interest grew even among purely medical circles, where, besides frankly morbid symptoms, purely physiognomic characteristics were also described, such as emaciated limbs,[156] a relatively large torso, and quick movements[157]; and, in addition, psychological symptoms were pictured with the same feeling for detail as we see in Hellenistic minor arts. The more the 'Coan' doctrine of the four humours displaced the heterodox opinions, the clearer became the necessity of including physiognomic and "characterological" observations in a definite system. Galen himself, especially in his commentary on the Περὶ φύσιος ἀνθρώπου and in his book Περὶ κράσεων, systematically classified the visible signs of each particular "combination", though always with the empiricist's regard to the variety of the symptoms.[158] Of importance to us is the principle that heat made a man tall, cold short, moisture fat, and dryness thin, and such a statement as that the soft, fair and fat possessed least melancholy humour, the thin, dark, hirsute and prominently-veined the most.[159] Galen emphasised more clearly than anyone else the direct causal connexion between bodily constitution and character, and maintained in a special monograph that "spiritual disposition depends on the "crasis" in the body"[160]; it is therefore not surprising that he pressed on to a systematic presentation of mental characteristics determined by the humours, though admittedly his system was not yet complete, for the phlegm was still denied any power to form character:

There is also another theory . . . according to which the four humours are shown to contribute to the formation of moral characteristics and

---

[156] RUFUS, p. 456, 6.

[157] RUFUS, p. 456, 21.

[158] Cf. for instance GALEN, *De temperamentis*, III, 646 sqq. (ed. G. Helmreich, Leipzig 1904, pp. 86 sqq.), who distinguishes between natural and acquired qualities; or *ibid.*, II, 641 (ed. G. Helmreich, pp. 82 sqq.), where it is recommended that attention be paid to age: thick hair, for instance, is an indication of melancholy in the prime of life, but neither in youth nor in old age. Statements as to the melancholic's outward appearance are also found in Galen's commentary (surviving only in Arabic; German translation in *Corp. med. Gr.*, V, X, I, p. 355) on the second book of Ps.-Hippocrates's *Epidemics*. For the "characterological" side of the doctrine of "crases" see below, p. 100 (text).

[159] GALEN, *De locis affectis*, III, 10 (KÜHN, VOL. VIII, p. 182) = *Scriptores physiognomic graeci et latini*, ed. R. FÖRSTER, VOL. II, p. 293, frag. 100.

[160] Galen quotes this work among others in the passage of his commentary on Περὶ φύσιος ἀνθρώπου, quoted in text below. The work is edited by I. MÜLLER (GALENUS, *Scripta Minora*, VOL. II, Leipzig 1891, pp. 32–79): Ὅτι ταῖς τοῦ σώματος κράσεσιν αἱ τῆς ψυχῆς δυνάμεις ἕπονται.

aptitudes. But one would have to start by demonstrating first that the mental characteristics depend on the bodily constitution. About this we have written elsewhere. Assuming it, therefore, as proved, it follows that acuteness and intelligence of the mind come from the bilious humours, steadiness and solidity from the atrabilious, but from the blood simplicity bordering on foolishness. But phlegm by its nature does not contribute to the formation of character, as it evidently is always a by-product at the first stage of the metabolic process.[161]

Blood, then, made a man simple and foolish, yellow bile keen-witted and adroit, black bile firm and constant; and we can see at a glance how much ancient cosmological speculation lies behind this statement. But as thought progressed in this direction—that is, as the new theory of character wove itself more and more into the old system of the four elements, and was enriched by fresh properties and relations corresponding to the humours and elements—there arose, in the course of the second, or at latest the third century A.D., a complete schema of the four *temperaments* as types of physical and mental constitutions. This revival of the old cosmological tenets was carried farthest in a short work entitled Περὶ τῆς τοῦ κόσμου κατασκευῆς ⟨καὶ τῆς⟩ τοῦ ἀνθρώπου (*Of the Constitution of the Universe and of Man*).[162] Air was warm and moist, fire warm and dry, earth cold and dry, and water cold and moist. Each of these elements "was like" (ἔοικεν) one of the substances composing the human organism, air like blood, fire like yellow bile, earth like black bile, water like phlegm. Each of these humours gained the ascendancy (πληθύνεται) in one of the seasons and governed (κυριεύει) one of the Four Ages of Man: blood was proper to spring and childhood, yellow bile to summer and youth, black bile to autumn and prime, phlegm to winter and old age. With the exception of the blood, which here as elsewhere showed its special position by being located only in the heart, each of the humours was now located in two bodily organs (black bile in the liver and—owing to a gap in the text—in some part now unknown), and had its own means of exit: blood through the nose, yellow bile through the ears, phlegm through the mouth, and black bile through the eyes. And now

---

[161] Commentary on Περὶ φύσιος ἀνθρώπου, ed. G. C. Kühn, XV, p. 97; ed. J. Mewaldt, *Corp. med. Gr.*, V, 9, i, Leipzig 1914; p. 51. also printed in Förster (ed.), op. cit., VOL. II, p. 295, frag. 103 (cf. *ibid.*, p. 296, frag. 105).

[162] Published by J. L. IDELER, *Physici et medici graeci minores*, Berlin 1841, I, p. 303 (not II, p. 303, as Fredrich says, op. cit., p. 49).

the humours caused differences of character also:

Why is it that some people are amiable and laugh and jest, others are peevish, sullen and depressed, some again are irritable, violent and given to rages, while others are indolent, irresolute and timid? The cause lies in the four humours. For those governed by the purest blood (οἱ ἐξ αἵματος καθαρωτάτου τυγχάνοντες) are agreeable, laugh, joke and have rosy, well-coloured bodies; those governed by yellow bile are irritable, violent, bold, and have fair, yellowish bodies; those governed by black bile are indolent, timid, ailing, and, with regard to body, swarthy and black-haired; but those governed by phlegm are sad, forgetful, and, with regard to the body, very pale.[163]

In this detailed and schematic example of late antiquity, the factors composing the new doctrine of the four temperaments emerge very distinctly; the cosmological train of thought had become bound up with the discoveries of therapy proper and with the observations of physiognomy. Thus, for instance, the signs distinguishing a man "governed by the blood" (whom we are now justified in calling "sanguine" and whose disposition was later almost always considered the best or noblest) became largely identical with those of the εὐφυής, the "bene natus", whose pink and white complexion and amiable nature the sanguine shared.[164] The characteristics of the melancholic, on the contrary, corresponded mainly to those of the πικρός, who is distinguished by black hair and swarthy skin[165]; we have already come across this latter peculiarity as a symptom of illness in Archigenes and Rufus. A bent head (τὸ πρόσωπον σεσηρός), and leanness, were also among the symptoms of gall, and when, according to other physiognomers, all these signs came to be regarded as

[163] Some of these peculiarities appear not only permanently in those men whose dispositions are governed by one or other of the four humours, but also temporarily in everyone, since each humour temporarily gains the upper hand in one of the four ages of man; so that apart from those who are by nature sanguinics, cholerics, melancholics or phlegmatics, children, youths, men in their prime and old men each share in the nature of the different temperaments (and so say Pseudo-Soranus, Vindician and the medieval authors who follow them). How deliberately the characters drawn in Περὶ κατασκευῆς were distinguished from actual pathological portraits is clear from the fact that each normal type was credited with a particular form of disorder: when (sanguine) children cry, they soon cheer up; when (choleric) youths get angry, they take longer to recover (ἀλλάσσονται), but do so of their own accord. When (melancholy) men go mad, it is difficult to bring them to another frame of mind, and, to do so, the influence of others is needed (δυσμετάβλητοι, the passive voice is used); and when in (phlegmatic) old age the same thing occurs, change is no longer possible (ἀμετάβλητοι διαμείνουσι).

[164] "Aristotle", in *Scriptores physiognomici graeci et latini*, ed. R. Förster, vol. I, p. 28, line 10; Anonymus, Förster (ed.), op. cit., vol. II, p. 232, line 15.

[165] "Aristotle", in Förster (ed.), op. cit., vol. I, p. 34, line 7.

characteristic of misers and cowards,[166] yet another contact was made with the picture of a melancholic in whom "timor" and "avaritia" had been constant features.

The work which for brevity's sake we will call Περὶ κατασκευῆς cannot be assigned a precise date; however, there is no reason to suppose it an early medieval product affected by Islamic notions.[167] The equivalents to "melancholicus", "cholericus", "sanguineus", "phlegmaticus" seem already to have been firmly established among ninth-century Arabic astrologers. But when these expressions became common parlance is quite irrelevant beside the question whether the ancients had already conceived the notion of the four types; that is to say, whether they had succeeded in dividing healthy people systematically into four physical and mental categories and in attributing the differences between them to the predominance of one or another humour. The answer is unreservedly "Yes". Luckily the Περὶ κατασκευῆς is by no means the only work which contains a complete schema of the four temperaments, for we can produce a whole series of further testimonies, some later, some certainly more ancient, which clearly show the further development of Galen's still incomplete schema. They are as follows:

(1) The pseudo-Galenian work Περὶ χυμῶν.[168]

(2) A treatise falsely attributed to Soranus, but possibly dating from the third century A.D.[169]

(3) Closely related with No. 2 above, Vindician's *Letter to Pentadius*. Vindician was a friend of St Augustine and lived in North Africa in the latter half of the fourth

---

[166] POLEMON in Förster (ed.), op. cit., VOL. I, p. 278, line 14 (the "colligendae pecuniae amans" is of mean stature, dark-haired and with a rapid gait, "in quo aliquid inclinationis est"); p. 270, line 13 (the bowed attitude and dark colouring as a sign of "vir timidus ignavus"); p. 244, line 5 the dark skin means "timiditatem et diuturnam sollicitudinem et maestitiam"). In the anonymous text, Förster (ed.), op. cit. VOL. II, p. 92, line 7, black hair means "timidum nimium et avarum"; in PSEUDO-POLEMON, Förster (ed.), op. cit., VOL. II, p. 160, line 6, the "timidus" is distinguished by, among other things, "flexio staturae," dark skin, and "tristis obtutus."

[167] This alone undermines J. van Wageningen's theory that we owe the formulation of the doctrine of the four temperaments as character types to 'Honorius of Autun' (that is, William of Conches). Cf. J. VAN WAGENINGEN's article "De quattuor temperamentis", in *Mnemosyne*, new series, XLVI, 4 (1918), pp. 374 sqq. Also F. Boll, "Vita contemplativa", in *Sitzungsberichte der HeidelbergerA kademie der Wissenschaften, Phil.-hist. Klasse*, VIII (Heidelberg 1920), p. 20.

[168] GALEN (KÜHN), VOL. XIX, pp. 485 sqq., esp. p. 492.

[169] *Medici antiqui*, Venice 1547, fol. 159^v sq.

century. This short treatise of his was to exert a determining influence on the medieval notion of the temperaments which began to take shape in the twelfth century.[170]

It is certain that the pseudo-Galenian work Περὶ χυμῶν cannot have been composed under Arabic influence but must have been written not later than the sixth or seventh century, because some of its statements—combined with the genuine commentary on the Περὶ φύσιος ἀνθρώπου, and more particularly with the letter to Pentadius—found their way into Bede's *De temporum ratione*.[171]

We will now tabulate the statements met with in all these works, in so far as they are of importance to us.[172]

What makes the development shown in this table so particularly interesting is the growing acceptance of the idea that the humours possessed the power of determining types of men. In the commentary on the Περὶ φύσιος ἀνθρώπου it is still stated in a neutral manner—"keen wit arises or increases through the yellow bile." In fact, it is very doubtful whether Galen ever believed that the predominance of one or other humour could determine the whole being of a specific type of man. But later the theory is expressed by a transitive verb—"yellow bile produces quick-tempered men," to which the expression used in the Περὶ χυμῶν, "yellow bile makes the soul more irritable," provides a kind of stepping stone. Moreover, amid all the vacillations and irrelevancies, there appears a clear shifting of values which decisively determines—and, in fact, anticipates—both medieval and modern conceptions of the temperaments. The sanguine person, who in the genuine Galenian writings was still merely the simpleton, gradually became what he was always to remain—a merry, light-hearted, good-tempered, handsome person of an altogether good

170 Printed in Priscian, *Eupor.*, pp. 484 sqq. For Pseudo-Soranus's and Vindician's distribution of the humours among the ages of man and the hours of the day, see above, pp. 10 sqq. (text). Distribution among the seasons is customary: Vindician's distribution among the orifices of the body, which Pseudo-Soranus does not mention, agrees with the statements in the work Περὶ κατασκευῆς. For the revival of Vindician's doctrine in the twelfth century, see below, pp. 102 sqq., esp. pp. 112 sqq. (text).

171 Ch. xxxv (Migne, P. L., vol. xc, col. 459). Among points of similarity with Περὶ χυμῶν we may mention the application of the term "hilares" to the sanguinic, and of "audaces" to the choleric. It can also be shown that the work Περὶ χυμῶν must have been known to the Byzantine monk Meletius who wrote in the ninth century (see below, p. 99, note 98).

172 We include the statements in Isidore and in the short work, probably early sixth-century, *Sapientia artis medicinae* (ed. by M. Wlaschky in *Kyklos. Jahrbuch des Instituts für die Geschichte der Medizin*, I, Leipzig 1928, pp. 103 sqq.), though here it is merely a question of traditional elements which are embedded in statements on pathology.

	Galen Commentary Περὶ φύσιος ἀνθρώπου	pseudo-Galen Περὶ χυμῶν	Pseudo-Soranus	Vindician, Letter to Pentadius	Περὶ κατασκευῆς . . .
Blood	τὸ ἁπλοῦν καὶ ἠλιθιώτερον (sc. ἔσται διὰ τὸ αἷμα)	ἱλαρωτέραν (sc. ἀπεργάζεται τὴν ψυχήν)	moderatos, blandos, formosos (sc. facit)	boni voti (= benivolos) simplices, moderatos, blandos, euchymos (sc. facit)	χαρίεις, παίζουσι, γελῶσι, ῥόδινοι, ὑπόπυρροι, καλλίχροοι
Yellow bile	τὸ ὀξὺ καὶ συνετόν	ὀργιλωτέραν ἢ θρασυτέραν ἢ γοργοτέραν ἢ καὶ ἀμφότερα	iracundos, acutos, ingeniosos et leves, macilentos et multum comedentes, cito digerentes	iracundos, ingeniosos, acutos, leves, macilentos, plurimum comedentes et cito digerentes	ὀργίλοι, πικροί, εὔτολμοι, μανιώδεις, ὕπωχροι, ξανθόχροοι
Black bile	τὸ ἑδραῖον καὶ βέβαιον	ὀργιλωτέραν καὶ ἰταμωτέραν (ferociorem et impudentiorem)	subdolos, avaros et perfidos, tristes, somniculosos, invidiosos et timidos	subdolos cum iracundia, avaros, timidos, tristes, somniculosos, invidiosos	ῥάθυμοι, ὀλιγόψυχοι, φιλάσθενοι, (ὀκνηροί), μελανόψιοι, μελάντριχοι
Phlegm	τοῦ δὲ φλέγματος ἡ φύσις εἰς μὲν ἠθοποιίαν ἄχρηστος, ἀναγκαίαν δὲ φαίνεται τὴν γένεσιν ἔχον ἐν τῇ πρώτῃ μεταβολῇ τῶν σιτίων	ἀργοτέραν καὶ ἠλιθιωτέραν (pigriorem et stupidiorem)	corpora composita, vigilantes et intra se cogitantes, canos cito producentes	corpore compositos, vigilantes, intra se cogitantes, cito adferentes canos in capite, minus audaces	λυπηροί, ἀμνήμονες, (πολυπηροί, στυγνοί), λευκόχροοι

disposition; and although in the strictly Galenian system the predominance of the blood too was accounted a "dyscrasis", it advanced in status so far beyond the others that in the twelfth century the other three temperaments could actually be described as degenerate forms of the sanguine.[173]

[173] In William of Conches, *Philosophia*, printed under the name of Honorius of Autun in Migne, *P. L.*, vol. clxxii, col. 93, and quoted under this wrong name by J. van Wageningen, in *Mnemosyne*, new series, vol. xlvi (1918), pp. 374 sqq. See also below, p. 102 (text).

Sapientia Artis Medicinae	Isidore	Bede	Galen *τέχνη ἰατρική* (Remarks on the compound 'dyscrasiae')	
—	(unde et homines, in quibus dominatur sanguis) dulces et blandi (sunt)	hilares, laetos, misericordes, multum ridentes et loquentes (sc. facit)	*οὐ μὴν οὐδ' ἐγρηγορέναι δύνανται μέχρι πλείονος, ὕπνῳ τ' ἐπιτρέψαντες ἑαυτούς, ἅμα τε κωματώδεις εἰσὶ καὶ ἄγρυπνοι, καὶ φαντασιώδεις τοῖς ὀνείρασιν, καὶ αἱ ὄψεις ἀχλυώδεις καὶ αἱ αἰσθήσεις οὐκ ἀκριβεῖς* (KÜHN i, p. 327), *ἕτοιμοι δὲ εἰς τὰς πράξεις οὐδὲν ἧττον* [sc. than the warm and dry ones], *οὐ μὴν ἄγριος ὁ θυμός ἀλλ' εἰς ὀργὴν μόνον ἕτοιμοι* (KÜHN i, p. 335).	warm and moist
Faciem rotundam habent et robustam, oculos acutos, gulam asperam . . . Fervidi erunt in ira et celerius declinant . . .	—	macilentos, multum tamen comedentes, veloces, audaces, iracundos, agiles	*ἀκριβεῖς ταῖς αἰσθήσεσι, καὶ ἀγρυπνητικώτατοι, καὶ φαλακροῦνται ταχέως* (KÜHN i, p. 326). *εἰς δὲ τὰς πράξεις ἕτοιμοι καὶ θυμικοὶ καὶ ταχεῖς, ἄγριοι καὶ ἀνήμεροι καὶ ἰταμοὶ καὶ ἀναίσχυντοι καὶ τυραννικοὶ τοῖς ἤθεσι καὶ γὰρ ὀξύθυμοι καὶ δύσπαυστοι* (KÜHN i, p. 335).	warm and dry
Faciem sublongam habent, supercilia obducta oculos obscuros reddent, gravitatem patiuntur et in somno intenti erunt. Corpora reumatica habent, melancholici erunt . . . et multas aegritudines corporis patiuntur	(melancholici dicuntur) homines, qui et conversationem humanam refugiunt et amicorum carorum suspecti sunt	stabiles, graves, compositos moribus, dolosos	*αἱ δ' αἰσθήσεις αὐτῶν ἐν νεότητι μὲν ἀκριβεῖς τέ εἰσι καὶ ἄμεμπτοι τὰ πάντα, προϊοῦσι δὲ ἀπομαραίνονται ταχέως, καὶ . . . . ταχύγηροι τὰ περὶ τὴν κεφαλὴν ἅπαντές εἰσι, διὸ καὶ πολιοῦνται ταχέως* (quocirca cito canescunt; KÜHN i, p. 328), *ἀοργητότατοι πάντων οὗτοι· βιασθέντες μέντοι τισὶν ὀργισθῆναι, φυλάττουσι τὴν μῆνιν* (KÜHN i, p. 336).	cold and dry
—	—	tardos, somnolentos, obliviosos	*ἐγκεφάλου κωματώδεις . . . . καὶ ὑπνηλοὺς καὶ φαύλους ταῖς αἰσθήσεσι . . . . οὐ μὴν οὐδὲ φαλακροῦνται οἱ τοιοῦτοι* (KÜHN i, p. 329). *τὸ δὲ ἦθος ἄτολμόν τε καὶ δειλὸν καὶ ὀκνηρόν . . . . καὶ ἥκιστα μηνιῶσιν, ὥσπερ καὶ εἰς ὀργὴν οὐχ ἕτοιμοι* (KÜHN i, p. 336).	cold and moist

On the other hand, the choleric, whose predominant humour (according to Galen) produced keen perceptions and wit, now became merely violent, abrupt, and hot-tempered. With regard to the melancholic there are two points: first, that in course of time his "earthy" humour, which Galen considered the source of firmness and constancy, was endowed more and more with unfavourable properties, and secondly, that his characteristics began to merge into those of the phlegmatic; in the end they became interchangeable, so that in the fifteenth- and sixteenth-century illustrations the portrait of the melancholic frequently changed places with the portrait of the phlegmatic, sometimes one and sometimes the other occupying the third place, whereas the sanguine regularly appeared first and the choleric second (see PLATES 77, 78, 81, 119–122, 124–7). According to the Περὶ χυμῶν, the phlegm, to which Galen had expressly denied any power of character-formation, inherited the inanity which Galen had traced to the blood; in pseudo-Soranus and Vindician the phlegmatic is described as constant, wakeful, and thoughtful, while according to Bede constancy belongs to the melancholic; and finally in the Περὶ κατασκευῆς and in Bede he is sad, sleepy, and forgetful—which qualities are again attributed to the melancholic by pseudo-Soranus and Vindician. One can see that the notions "phlegmatic" and "melancholic" were intermixed and that this confusion lowered the status of the melancholy disposition until at length there was scarcely anything good to be said of it.

We believe that this shift in values was due to two factors: (1) the inclination, quite understandable from an historical point of view, to attribute to the blood, which did not belong to the surplus humours, a more and more favourable influence on the formation of character—at the expense of the other three humours, especially of the black bile; and (2) the effect of Galen's doctrine of the "crases".

Galen, without prejudice to the great significance which he attributed to the four primary humours, really reckoned not them but the simple qualities of warm, cold, dry, and moist, as the authentic principles of division in his doctrine of the different constitutions. Against the one perfect combination, which could never be attained, he set eight imperfect combinations in which either one of the four qualities, or one of the combinations of two qualities, predominated. He therefore envisaged four simple and four compound temperaments (δυσκρασίαι ἁπλαῖ and δυσκρασίαι σύνθετοι), which, however—and this is the important thing—were not originally humoral but determined purely by qualities.[174] On the other hand, of these eight, or really nine, "temperaments"—and we must always put the word in inverted commas when

[174] For Galen's doctrine of "crases", cf. J. VAN WAGENINGEN, loc. cit., and below, p. 100 (text). Also the very instructive work by WERNER SEYFERT, "Ein Komplexionentext einer Leipziger Inkunabel und seine handschriftliche Herleitung", in *Archiv für Geschichte der Medizin*, XX (Leipzig 1928), pp. 272 sqq., which provides much valuable material for the history of the doctrine of temperaments.

speaking of Galen or orthodox Galenists, to avoid confusing it with the complexions as determined by the humours—the four compound ones were connected with the humours in so far as the latter were also invested with the corresponding compound qualities. Black bile was cold and dry, phlegm was cold and wet, and so on. It was therefore inevitable that what Galen had said of the compound "temperaments" should later be quite automatically transferred to the humours.[175] There is, as far as we know, no overt statement by the master himself affirming the equivalence, and in our table his compounds are therefore shown separately as not strictly referring to the humours. But when his successors, as already mentioned, applied to the humours the definitions of character which Galen had only coupled with the "crases", they did so all the more readily because they had no other for phlegm. They created some confusion,[176] but one has only to glance at the texts to see that even pseudo-Soranus and Vindician could not have drawn up their tables of the humoral dispositions without using Galen's doctrine of the dispositions determined by "crases".[177]

The most important point, however, is that after pseudo-Soranus the picture even of the melancholic by temperament was generally coloured by the idea of the disease which bore the same name, and disfigured by traits of character directly taken over from psychiatric treatises. Even as a type the melancholic was crafty, avaricious, despondent, misanthropic and timid—all qualities constantly met with in writings on mental illness. Traces of this are found in Isidore of Seville, in whose writings two contradictory notions exist side by side without being reconciled. One is the old physiological theory that health means the equilibrium of the four humours, sickness the preponderance of one of them[178]; the other is the new theory of the four character-types.

---

[175] Esp. in Τέχνη ἰατρική, ch. 7–11; GALEN (KÜHN), VOL. I., pp. 324 sqq.

[176] In Pseudo-Soranus and Vindician, for instance, one can hardly escape the thought that certain "cold and moist" and "warm and dry" qualities were attributed to the black bile purely by mistake, since the latter is both cold and dry. Were it not for such a mistake, the attribution to the melancholic of such untraditional attributes as "sleepiness" and "irascibility", or, to the phlegmatic, of "wakefulness" and "reflexion", could hardly be explained. Bede restores the traditional order.

[177] The statement that the phlegmatic man "goes grey early" is so specific that its agreement with the πολιοῦνται ταχέως in Galen's "cold and dry crasis" can hardly be a pure coincidence.

[178] ISIDORE, *Etym.*, IV, 5, 7.

Therefore, while coupling the word "sanguis" with "suavis", so that people in whom the blood predominates are for him "dulces et blandi",[179] he links the word "melancholia" with "malus", and even endeavours to derive "malus" from the Greek name for the black bile:

☞ malus appellatur a nigro felle, quod Graeci μέλαν dicunt; unde et melancholici appellantur homines, qui et conversationem humanam refugiunt, et amicorum carorum suspecti sunt.[180]

[179] Isidore, *Etym.*, iv, 5, 6.

[180] Isidore, *Etym.*, x, 176.

Chapter II

MELANCHOLY IN MEDIEVAL MEDICINE, SCIENCE AND PHILOSOPHY

We have now traced the development of the notion of melancholy among the ancients in two, or even three directions. Its starting point was an idea of illness, traced originally to an immoderate increase or unnatural alteration in the "humor melancholicus," later to an "adustio" of the yellow bile. As well as this idea of a purely morbid melancholy, however, there arose that of a melancholy constitution, which in turn was interpreted in two ways: either as the condition, exceptional in every way, of "great men", as described in Problem XXX, I; or else as one of the "types of disposition" which constituted the doctrine of the four temperaments, systematised after the time of Galen. In this context the melancholy type depreciated more and more and in future times it was to mean, unambiguously, a bad disposition in which unpleasant traits of mind and character were combined with poor physique and with unattractiveness; not unnaturally, this notion remained always conditioned by the original idea of illness.

I. THE SURVIVAL OF THE ARISTOTELIAN NOTION OF MELANCHOLY IN THE MIDDLE AGES

We have seen how already in post-Aristotelian antiquity the thought expressed in Problem XXX, I, could no longer find full acceptance. In the Middle Ages, which assessed the worth of an individual not according to his intellectual gifts and capacities but according to his virtues in which God's grace enabled him to persevere, such an idea was even less acceptable; indeed, whenever it raised its head, it came into conflict with certain basic principles. During the first twelve hundred years after Christ the idea of the highly gifted melancholic had apparently been completely forgotten. The great scholastic rehabilitation of Aristotle had brought the *Problemata* as well as the other scientific works within the horizon of the west—their first complete translation, by Bartholomeus of Messina, must have been finished between 1258 and 1266, for it was dedicated to King Manfred of Sicily.[1] But even after this, the thesis in Problem XXX, 1, though respectfully mentioned here and there, was chiefly a matter for erudite quotation; references to the Aristotelian theory—generally made more for completeness' sake than from conviction—barely influenced the general view and tended, moreover, partly to weaken the ancient author's true meaning and always to modify it more and more. Except for a lost work of Albertus Magnus, the *Liber super Problemata*,[2] only Pietro d'Abano's commentary on the *Problemata* (1310)[3] dealt exhaustively with the contents of the Peripatetic doctrine; but only the men of the Quattrocento, with their new conception of humanity, drew from it conclusions amounting to a basic revaluation of the notion of melancholy and to the creation of a modern doctrine of genius.

Famous for the important role he played in the revival of antiquity,[4] Alexander Neckham (who died in 1217) is (as far as we know) the first medieval writer to mention the Aristotelian thesis. His reference, based perhaps on Cicero's, was made with considerable reservations and with a certain diffidence. In agreement with the view most widely held in scholastic psychology, Neckham declared that the human intellect comprised three distinct functions, each located in a different part of the brain: (1) Imagination ("vis imaginativa"), located in the warm and dry ventricle of the fore-brain, generally described as the "cellula phantastica"; (2) Reason ("vis rationalis" or "cogitativa"),

[1] Cf. e.g. C. MARCHESI, *L'Etica Nicomachea nella tradizione latina medievale*, Messina 1904, pp. 9 sqq. and R. SELIGSOHN, *Die Übersetzung der pseudo-aristotelischen Problemata durch Bartholomaeus von Messina*, dissertation, Berlin 1933. On the other hand, excerpts must have already been translated earlier, for Albertus Magnus says in *De somno et vigilia*, lib. I, tract. II, ch. v (*Opera*, ed. A. Borgnet, Paris 1890–99, VOL. IX, p. 145): "dictum est in libro de problematibus ab Aristotele, qui liber non ad me pervenit licet viderim quaedam excerpta de ipso". It would be interesting to know if Albertus's remarks on melancholy were based on knowledge of the complete translation or only of the "excerpta", in which case his mention of Hector and Priam could be particularly easily accounted for.

[2] J. QUETIF and J. ECHARD, *Scriptores Ordinis Praedicatorum*, Paris 1719, VOL. I, p. 180.

[3] PETRUS DE APONO, *Expositio Problematum Aristotelis*, Mantua 1475, Padua 1482. In the postscript to the Mantuan edition, Pietro's commentary is expressly described as the first attempt of its kind, and the date of its completion is given as 1310. For printed editions and manuscripts, see L. NORPOTH, "Zur Bio-, Bibliographie und Wissenschaftslehre des Pietro d'Abano," in *Kyklos*, VOL. III, Leipzig 1930, p. 303.

[4] Cf. esp. H. LIEBESCHÜTZ, *Fulgentius Metaforalis* (Studien der Bibliothek Warburg IV), Leipzig 1926, esp. pp. 16 sqq.

located in the warm and moist "cellula logistica" in the middle-brain; and (3) Memory, located in the cold and dry ventricle of the back part of the head.[5] For this reason the sanguine natures, whose warm and moist complexions (already regarded as indisputably the most favourable) corresponded to the "cellula logistica", were most inclined towards learning:

> Videtur autem nobis contrarius esse Aristoteles, qui dicit solos melancholicos ingeniosos esse. Sed hoc dictum est ab Aristotele propter felicitatem memoriae, quae frigida est et sicca, aut propter eorum astutiam.[6]

Whereas here the outstanding qualities of the Aristotelian melancholic were somewhat arbitrarily limited to a good memory and astuteness, Albertus Magnus attempted to restore the thesis of Problem XXX, 1, to its full stature, but in order to harmonise it with the general opinion he was obliged to take refuge in an almost reckless reconstruction of the whole doctrine. The expressive "tamen" in his introduction to the *Ethics* (cited above, p. 36) suggests that he was not quite happy about the 'Aristotelian' Problem; and in the fuller statements contained in certain passages of the *Liber de animalibus*[7] he attempted to resolve the contradiction as follows: natural melancholy was (as in Rufus and Galen)

[5] This theory of localisation, occasionally attributed to Aristotle in the Middle Ages (thus Adelard of Bath, *Quaestiones naturales*, ed. M. Müller, Münster 1934, ch. xviii) presupposes Galen's anatomy of the brain and the division (probably Stoic, but transmitted by Galen) of the faculties into φαντασία, μνήμη and νόησις, an analysis which Galen himself had not fully developed; for the early history of this theory see the remarks of H. Liebeschütz, *Vorträge der Bibliothek Warburg*, vol. iii, 1923–24, p. 127; this should be supplemented by Walther Sudhoff's very thorough-going research, tracing the notion back to the fourth century A.D. and down to Leonardo and Vesalius: "Die Lehre von den Hirnventrikeln", in *Archiv für Geschichte der Medizin*, vii (Leipzig 1913), pp. 149 sqq. According to Liebeschütz the classification of the various brain ventricles as "warm and moist," etc., as taught by Neckam as well as by the professional anatomists (Richardus Salernitanus, Lanfranc, etc). is to be attributed to William of Conches (see, however, below, text, pp. 104 sqq.)—an easily explicable by-product of his urge to scientific systematisation—and also W. Sudhoff does not place this conception any earlier (op. cit. p. 170).

[6] Alexander Neckam, *De naturis rerum libri duo*, ed. T. Wright, London 1863 (*Rerum Britannicarum medii aevi Scriptores*, vol. xxiv), p. 42. According to the view held there Neckam is bound to give the planet Venus (which he also regards as "warm and moist") the patronage of science: "Quintus autem planeta propter effectus, quos exercet in inferioribus, calidus dicitur et humidus, ideoque scientia ei aptatur, quae in sanguineis vigere solet . . ." though—a very significant distinction—he puts wisdom under the influence of Saturn. The view that melancholy, as corresponding to the heavy and impressionable elements water and earth, favoured memory, was everywhere widely held; cf. the passage from Raimundus Lullus, *Principia philosophiae*, quoted by L. Volkmann, in *Jahrbuch der kunsthistorischen Sammlungen in Wien*, n.f. iii (1929), p. 117: "Rursus ait Memoria, 'effective mea natura est melancholia, quoniam per frigiditatem restringo species et conservo metaphorice loquendo, quoniam aqua habet naturam restringendi, et quia terra habet naturam vacuativam, habeo loca, in quibus possum ponere ipsas species.' " (See also below, text pp. 337 sqq.).

[7] Quoted in Giehlow (1904), p. 61.

a "faex sanguinis"[8] as opposed to the "melancholia non naturalis" arising from the "adustio" of the natural humours and thus divided into four sub-species.[9] It might now have been expected that the 'Aristotelian' notion of the outstandingly gifted melancholic would, in accordance with the division between natural and pathological melancholy, be coupled with the notion of a naturally melancholic temperament. But that was impossible for Albertus, because he conceived the "natural" melancholic (that is to say, the representative of the "complexio sicca et frigida") as the unamiable, gloomy, dirty, misanthropic, suspicious and occasionally kleptomaniac creature that the doctrine of the temperaments had made him.[10] For Albertus Magnus, too, the predisposition to intellectual ability was bound up with the qualities of warm and moist, with which the coldness and dryness of "melancholia naturalis" compared unfavourably. There was therefore nothing left for him but to make the gifted melancholic of the 'Aristotelian' Problem into a sort of optimal special form of the inherently morbid "melancholia adusta". When the process of "adustio" to which this owed its origin was not carried too far, and when the blood for its part was warm and powerful enough to bear the admixture of "melancholia adusta", then there arose that worthy melancholic who did not really, for Albertus, represent a type of temperament at all but was simply an exceptionally favourable example of the "melancholia non naturalis".

If that melancholy be not violently affected by "adustio", it will generate vital spirits which are abundant, constant and strong. For this reason such peo, le have firm convictions and very well regulated passions; and they will be industrious and possess the highest virtues. Therefore Aristotle says in his book of *Problems* that all the great philosophers such

---

[8] Albertus Magnus, *De animalibus libri xxvi*, ed. H. Stadler, Münster i.W. 1916–21, vol i, p. 329, § 119 (Beiträge zur Geschichte der Philosophie des Mittelalters, vol. xv).

[9] See op. cit., vol. i, p. 329, § 120 for the division of "melancholia non naturalis" into four sub-species, which we call the "doctrine of the four forms," see below, pp. 86 sqq. (text).

[10] See op. cit., vol. ii, p. 1305, § 61: "Nihil delectationis apud se invenientes et malae suspicionis etiam existentes ad alios, occidunt se ipsos, et sunt nec diligentes nec diligibiles, solitudinem, quae malitia vitae humanae est, amantes, et in sordibus esse delectabile est eis, et alia multa mala contingunt eis et sunt frequenter fures etiam quando non indigent de re quam furantur, et multum sunt insomnes propter complexionis siccitatem et frigiditatem." Here, perhaps in unconscious regard for Aristotle, the melancholic is not so called by name, but, quite apart from the traditional sameness of the predicates and the expression "complexionis siccitas et frigiditas," the description is so obviously connected with the doctrine of temperaments contained in §§ 59–62 (for this see below, text p. 119) that there can be no doubt of the author's intention. Moreover in the same work, vol. i, p. 47, § 129, it has been stated that the melancholic is sad and gloomy, and suffers from terrifying delusions.

as Anaxagoras and Thales of Miletus, and all those who distinguished themselves by heroic virtue, such as Hector, Aeneas, Priam, and others, were in this sense melancholics. He says that such a melancholy is of the nature of red wine, which is airy and strong, and possesses the power of generating constant vital spirits.[11]

In the short sentences at the end Albertus once more summarised the physiognomic signs of the different temperaments. But even here he felt obliged, for the sake of the 'Aristotelian' doctrine, to introduce a special category for the "melancolicus de melancolia adusta calida", who combined the mobility of a warm-blooded temperament with the "stabilitas" of earth, and owing to his "melancholia adusta" shared a number of characteristics with the choleric, such as being "longus et gracilis".

Sanguine persons are of good flesh and good general condition, cholerics are tall and slender, phlegmatics short and stout. Melancholics are thin, short and swarthy. But those who are of that sort of melancholy which is warm and affected by "adustio" [that is to say, the Aristotelian great men] are very tall and slender and dark, and have firm flesh.[12]

---

[11] Op. cit., VOL. I, p. 330, § 121: "Quoniam si non sit multum adusta, . . . tunc illa melancolia erit habens multos et stabiles et confirmatos spiritus: quia calidum eius bene movet et humidum eius cum ypostasi terrestri non incinerata optime movetur propter quod tales habent stabilitos conceptus et ordinatissimos affectus, et efficiuntur studiosi et virtutum optimarum. Et ideo dicit Aristoteles in libro de Problematibus, quod omnes maiores philosophi sicut Anaxagoras et Tales Mylesius, et omnes illi qui virtutibus praecellebant heroycis, sicut Hector et Eneas et Priamus et alii [the replacing of Greek heroes by Trojans is typically medieval], de tali erant melancolia. Dicit enim, quod talis melancolya habet naturam vini rubei, quod fumosum est et confirmatorum et stabilium spirituum generativum". Cf. also VOL. II, p. 1304, § 60: "Quaecumque autem ⟨scil. animalia⟩ grossi sunt sanguinis et calidi, immixtam in sanguine habent coleram adustam vel aduri incipientem, quae est quoddam genus melancoliae: et haec satis sunt stabilia et constantis audaciae et multorum spirituum mediorum inter grossos et subtiles: propter quod etiam talis complexionis existentes homines stabilis sunt animi et fortis, et non praecipites. Talis enim melancolia est quasi de complexione vini rubei, sicut dixit Aristoteles in libro de Problematibus . . . . Et quia fumosa [πνευματώδης] est huiusmodi colera, multiplicat spiritum stabilem qui bene tenet formas [i.e. because of dryness: in water, everything flows away, hence the phlegmatic's weak memory] . . . et resultant conceptus mentis stabiles et operationes ordinatae: et per huiusmodi calorem ascendentem . . . non desperant seipsos semper et confortant, sicut fecit Eneas alloquens socios in periculis existentes et dicens, 'O passi graviora, dabit Deus hiis quoque finem.' Et ideo dicit Aristoteles, quod omnes viri in philosophia et heroycis virtutibus praecipui de huiusmodi fuerunt melancolya, sicut Hector et Eneas et Priamus et alii. Propter quod et leo et alia quaedam huiusmodi complexionis animalia magis sunt aliis liberalia et communicativa."

[12] See op. cit., VOL. II, p. 1305, § 62: " . . . sanguinei sunt bonae carnis et bonae habitudinis. Colerici autem longi et graciles, fleumatici breves et pingues et melancolici sunt tenues et breves et nigri. Hii autem, qui sunt de melancolia adusta calida, sunt valde longi et graciles et nigri et durae carnis." See also the attribution of the lion, mentioned in the previous note, which is otherwise always a typical choleric beast, to the special form of melancholy complexion here in question. The attempt of F. M. BARBADO (*Revue Thomiste*, new series, XIV (1931), pp. 314 sqq.) to bring Albertus Magnus's doctrine of temperaments into harmony both with the findings of modern psychology and the doctrine of glandular secretions is interesting, though perhaps not from an historical point of view.

Albertus's attempt to relegate the melancholy of "exceptional" men to the realm of "melancholia non naturalis" remained a relatively isolated instance. In general, the Middle Ages took little interest in the interpretation of Problem XXX, I, while writers of the Renaissance, realising very soon the true meaning of the distinction between natural and pathological melancholy, were to apply it regardless of its divergences from the then already vulgarised doctrine of the complexions.

Only Pietro d'Abano, in his somewhat obscure commentary on the *Problems*,[13] seems to have made an attempt in the same direction as Albertus, but this was either ignored by later writers,[14] or else explicitly and even passionately rebutted.[15] In the

---

[13] The clearest are the following passages: (1) col. 3 of the Commentary (the beautiful edition of 1475 has no page numbers; in the edition of 1482, fol. N2^r): "Notandum quod melancolici sunt duplices; quidam enim sunt natura frigidi et sicci, maxime in quibus materia dominans secundum G⟨alenum⟩ est humor niger; de quibus non est sermo; non enim fuerit in predictis illustribus aut patiuntur pretacta. Sunt autem et alii ex adustione colere ac sanguis [*sic*]. . . ." (2) The final passage (ed. cit., fol. N4^r): "Dicendum igitur, quod melancolici, sive per se sive qualitercumque contingat, precellunt alios in premissis consequenter temperati, licet per se magis, deinde colerici et qui deinceps; melancolia enim est duplex, ut visum est: secundum enim primam coleram nigram sive humorem magis nigrum obiectam [*sic!*] non sunt huiusmodi, verum propter secundam, colere permixtam rubee vel adustam." Pietro d'Abano seems in fact, therefore, like Albertus Magnus (whom he may have known) to have been reluctant to include the highly-gifted among natural melancholics, and to have preferred identifying them with the representatives of "cholera nigra mixed with, or adust with, red bile", because such people possessed particularly "subtle and shining vital spirits," as well as a good memory (penultimate column of the Commentary).

[14] Cf. FICINO, *De v. tripl.*, I, 5, p. 497: "Sola igitur atra bilis illa quam diximus naturalem, ad iudicium nobis et sapientiam conducit; neque tamen semper."

[15] Especially MELANCHTHON, *De anima*, II (*Corpus Reformatorum*, XIII), col. 85: "Hic quaeritur de atra bile: an et quomodo praestantiores motus in ingeniis efficiat? Aponensis non recte iudicat, qui existimat hos motus in magnis viris ab adusta bile esse, non a naturali. Nam adusta efficit furores et amentias, non parit motus, qui reguntur consilio. Deceptus est Aponensis, cum putavit Aristotelem hoc interrogare, an paulatim aetate heroici viri fiant melancholici. Id enim non proponit Aristoteles, sed ipsas naturas et temperamenta eorum sentit esse melancholica. Ac deinde satis ostendit, se non de vicioso humore loqui, sed de naturali." The fact that Pietro d'Abano's view was not able to prevail in the special case of the problem of melancholy does not of course alter the fact that the general effect of his Commentary was very considerable. As early as 1315, JOHANNES DE JANDUNO (Jean de Jandun), head of the Parisian Averroists, made a commentary on Pietro's commentary (E. RENAN, *Averroès*, 3rd edn., Paris 1866, p. 340); he had received the manuscript from Marsilius of Padua, and it appears that the Averroist trend in North Italy, which Petrarch frequently denounced, and which was partly based on Aristotle's *Problems*, was due, to a considerable extent, to Pietro d'Abano's activities. RICHARD OF MEDIAVILLA (*Omnes Questiones quodlibetales fundatissimi doctoris Ricardi de Mediavilla*, quaestio XVIII, Venice 1509, fol. 19^r et sqq.) makes a similar attempt, though admittedly without direct reference to Problem XXX,I The question as to which temperament was the best for scholarship was generally answered in favour of the choleric and the sanguine, and the objection that melancholics too were often particularly gifted scholars was brushed aside by the hypothesis that such people were really cholerics and had only become melancholics "accidenter propter adustionem cholerae": "sed intellexi hoc [i.e. that the melancholy temperament was by nature not favourable to scholarship] de melancholicis naturaliter . . . illi enim sunt minime apti per se ad scientiam."

thirteenth century, William of Auvergne, another great scholastic who had adopted Aristotle's teaching, arrived once more at interpreting the melancholy of great men in terms of natural disposition, and in contrasting it, as particularly favourable for a man's salvation, with the phlegmatic complexion which (according to Galen!) "benefits none of the faculties of the soul". He was, however, speaking entirely as a theologian, concerned far less with the scientific basis of the Aristotelian thesis than he was with its interpretation in terms of Christian moral philosophy. He could therefore simply ignore the difficulties which Albertus Magnus and Neckham had found so considerable. In his eyes, the immense advantage of the melancholy disposition, and the real reason for its glorification in Aristotle, lay in the fact that it withdrew men from physical pleasures and worldly turmoil, prepared the mind for the direct influx of divine grace, and elevated it, in cases of special holiness, to mystic and prophetic visions.

There is no doubt that many are hindered from direct illumination by the stench of their vices and sins, but many are hindered by their complexions. For some complexions gorge the soul and hinder its noble powers, for which reason Galen, the great physician, says that the phlegmatic complexion benefits none of the faculties of the soul. . . . The reason is that they (that is to say, the relevant humours) bend the soul and take possession of it; for which reason they keep it far from the attainment of sublime and hidden matters, even as a vessel filled with liquid can receive no other liquid, or a tablet or parchment covered with writing can receive no other writing. This accords with the words of the sage, when he says "Non recipit stultus verba prudentiae, nisi ea dixeris, quae versantur in corde eius. . . ." [Prov., XVIII.2]. For these reasons Aristotle was of the opinion that all highly-gifted men were melancholics; and he even believed that melancholics were fitted for inspirations of this kind in a higher degree than men of other complexions—namely, because this complexion withdraws men more from bodily pleasures and wordly turmoil. Nevertheless, though nature affords these aids to illumination and revelation, they are achieved far more abundantly through the grace of the Creator, integrity of living, and holiness and purity.[16]

---

[16] WILLIAM OF AUVERGNE, Bishop of Paris, *De universo*, II, 3, 20 (*Opera omnia*, Venice 1591, p. 993: *Opera*, Orleans 1674, VOL. I, p. 1054): "Et in multis indubitanter prohibet irradiationem mmediatam ipsa vitiorum et peccatorum faetulentia . . . , in multis autem complexio; quaedam enim complexiones incrassant animas et impediunt vires earum nobiles, propter quod dicit Galenus summus medicus, quia flegmatica complexio nullam virtutem animae iuvat . . . . Causa in hoc est, quoniam incurvant et occupant animas humanas, propter hoc prohibent eas a perfectione rerum sublimium et rerum occultarum, quemadmodum plenitudo vasis de uno liquore prohibet ipsum a receptione liquoris alterius, sic et inscriptio tabulae

William of Auvergne, therefore, interpreted the 'Aristotelian' conception in a typically medieval sense, and attributed to the ancients his own medieval approach ("propter huiusmodi causas visum fuit Aristoteli . . ."). He considered the excellence of the melancholy temperament (as opposed to the particular worthlessness of the phlegmatic) as fitting for the ideal life of ascetic contemplation. However, nature could admittedly contribute no more than a favourable condition; it would be of no avail without individual free will, and, above all, divine grace. This ideal naturally required not so much a capacity for great achievements as security from temptation. William, of course, was not unaware of the danger that too deep an immersion in supernatural matters and too glowing a fervour might cause a melancholic complexion to develop into a melancholic disease—that is to say, into manifest insanity[17]; but even this real madness, he argues, was no more an evil than were the sufferings which God inflicted on the holy martyrs. Even in manifestly morbid melancholy the victims retained the gift of inspired revelation, though this was intermittent[18]; and even complete alienation was earnestly desired by the holiest of men, because it ensured once and for all the salvation of the soul; for either a man was just and good before his illness, in which case he could not lose merit, since he could not sin when mad, or else he was a sinner, in which case his guilt, at least, could not grow any greater.[19]

---

vel pellis prohibet aliam inscriptionem ab illa iuxta sermonem Sapientis, quo dixit: 'Quia non recipit stultus verba prudentiae nisi ea dixeris, quae versantur in corde eius.' Propter huiusmodi causas visum fuit Aristoteli omnes ingeniosos melancholicos esse et videri eidem potuit melancholicos ad irradiationes huiusmodi magis idoneos esse quam homines alterius complexionis, propter hoc quia complexio ista magis abstrahit a delectationibus corporalibus et a tumultibus mundanis. Licet autem adiumenta praenominata natura praestet ad illuminationes et revelationes, gratia tamen creatoris munditiaque conversationis et sanctitas et puritas multo abundantius ipsas impetrant . . . ."

[17] "Inveniuntur tamen animae aliquae, quibus istae irradiationes superveniunt ex fortitudine cogitationum in rebus divinalibus et ex vehementia devotionis in orationibus suis, similiter ex ardore piorum ac sanctorum desideriorum, quibus pulchritudinem iucundissimam creatoris concupiscunt. Galenus autem in libro de melancholia dicit ex huiusmodi desideriis interdum aliquos incurrere morbum melancholicum, qui procul dubio desipientia magna est et abalienatio a rectitudine intellectus et discretione rationis."

[18] "Scire tamen debes, quia huiusmodi homines, videlicet morbo melancholico laborantes, irradiationes recipiunt, verum particulatas et detruncatas. Quapropter ad instar prophetarum de rebus divinalibus naturaliter loqui incipiunt. Sed loquelam huiusmodi non continuant, nisi ad modicum. Et propter hoc statim recidunt in verba desipientiae consuetae, tanquam si fumus melancholicus ascendens ad virtutem intellectivam in illis fulgorem ipsius intercipiens illam offuscet, et propter hoc ab altitudine tanti luminis mentem in aliena deiiciat."

[19] *De universo*, I, 3, 7 (*Opera omnia*, Venice 1591, p. 725; *Opera*, Orleans 1674, VOL. I, p. 769): "De ipso etiam malo furoris dico, quod plerumque, immo semper, valde utile est furiosis:

2. MELANCHOLY AS AN ILLNESS

(*a*) Melancholy in Theology and Moral Philosophy

These remarks of William of Auvergne lead us straight from 'Aristotle's' notion of melancholy to that of the psychopathologists, for whom it was nothing but a mental illness. Other theologians had also dealt with the question of melancholy from this point of view, and it is natural that the existence of a mental illness which overtook the pious and unworldly, not in spite of their piety and unworldliness, but because of it, should have appeared a particularly burning problem for Christian moral philosophy. Hardly anyone, admittedly, rose to the height of William's hymn in praise of melancholy; but then, only someone who like him was both a thorough-going Christian and a thorough-going Aristotelian could have felt as he did.

Here we shall quote only a few of the disquisitions on the problem of pathological melancholy in moral theology. First came Chrysostom's exhortation to the monk Stagirius, the Λόγος παραινετικὸς πρὸς Σταγείριον ἀσκητὴν δαιμονῶντα, written in A.D. 380 or 381.[20] It is true that the condition from which the saint hoped to beguile his protégé was described neither in title nor in text explicitly as "melancholy", but was called despondency (ἀθυμία); but quite apart from the fact that despondency had always been the main symptom of melancholy illness, both the aetiology and semeiology in this case (which gives us a deep insight into early Christian asceticism) agree so completely with the definitions in medical literature on melancholy that Johannes Trithemius was fully justified in rendering the expression ἀθυμία as it occurs in

sive enim boni et iusti sint, cum in furorem incidunt, in tuto ponitur per furorem sanctitas eorum sive bonitas, cum tempore furoris peccare non possint . . . , sive mali et iniusti sint, in hoc eis per furorem consulitur, ut malitia eorundem eo tempore non augeatur . . . . Quod si creditur Galeno, adiuvat hunc sermonem id quod dicit in libro de Melancholia, videlicet quia quidam ex nimio desiderio videndi Deum nimiaque sollicitudine circa hoc incidere in melancholiam, quod non esset possibile apud creatoris bonitatem . . . nisi eisdem ipsum praenosceret utilem fore multipliciter et salubre. Debes autem scire, quia tempore meo multi fuerunt viri sanctissimi ac religiosissimi, quibus desiderio magno erat morbus melancholiae propter securitatem antedictam. Unde et cum inter eos esset quidam melancholicus et statum eius non mediocriter affectarent, aperte dicebant Deum inaestimabilem gratiam illi melancholico contulisse . . . ."

[20] MIGNE, P. Gr., VOL. XLVII, cols. 423 sqq. Ed. separately, as *De providentia Dei ad Stagirium*, Alost 1487.

the epistle to Stagirius by "melancolische Traurigkeit".[21] Nor is there any lack of contemporary witnesses who describe what happened to Stagirius expressly as "melancholy", with pity or censure thrown in according to the author's viewpoint.[22] But of all the descriptions of this typical "monastic melancholy", Chrysostom's letter is the most detailed and penetrating.[23] The unfortunate Stagirius suffered from terrifying nightmares, disorders of speech, fits and swooning; he despaired of his salvation, and was tormented by an irresistible urge to commit suicide; and what rendered him completely desperate was the fact—a very natural one, the physicians would have said—that none of this had come upon him until his entrance into monastic life, and that he could see some of his fellow sufferers immediately cured of their illness when they came out into the world again and married.

What Chrysostom held out to him as consolation was mainly an appeal to God's providence. God allowed the devil to continue his work simply for the good of mankind, for in giving the devil

---

[21] *Antwort Herrn Johan Abts zu Spanhaim auff acht Fragstuck*, Ingolstadt 1555, fol. N2v. The sentence quoted by Trithemius is in MIGNE, P. Gr. VOL. XLVII, col. 491.

TRITHEMIUS:

"Die grösse oder vile ainer Melancolischen traurigkait ist krefftiger vnnd schadt auch mer dann alle Teüflische würckung, dann wöllichen der böß gaist vberwindt, den vberwindt er mit aigner traurigkait des menschen. So du nun solche Melancolische traurigkait auß deinem sinn schlechst, so mag dir der Teüffel gar nichts schaden."

CHRYSOSTOMUS:

πάσης γὰρ δαιμονικῆς ἐνεργείας βλαβερώτερον ἡ τῆς ἀθυμίας ὑπερβολή, ἐπεὶ καὶ ὁ δαίμων ἐν οἷς ἂν κρατῇ διὰ ταύτης κρατεῖ. κἂν ταύτην ἀφέλῃς, οὐδὲν παρ' ἐκείνου πείσεταί τις δεινόν.

[22] Two examples may be quoted. First, a passage from ST JEROME's *Epistula* CXXV, 16 (MIGNE, P. L., VOL. XXII, col. 1082): "Sunt qui humore cellarum immoderatisque ieiuniis, taedio solitudinis ac nimia lectione, dum diebus ac noctibus auribus suis personant, vertuntur in melancholiam, et Hippocratis magis fomentis quam nostris monitis indigent." Second, from the opposite point of view, some lines by Augustine's contemporary, RUTILIUS CLAUDIUS NAMATIANUS, *De reditu suo*, V, 439 sqq., edd. CH. H. KEENE & G. F. SAVAGE, London 1907.

"Ipsi se monachos Graio cognomine dicunt,
Quod soli nullo vivere teste volunt . . .
Sive suas repetunt factorum ergastula poenas,
Tristia seu nigro viscera felle tument.
Sic nimiae bilis morbum assignavit Homerus
Bellerephonteis sollicitudinibus:
Nam iuveni offenso saevi post tela doloris
Dicitur humanum displicuisse genus."

[23] See also CASSIAN, *Collationes*, chapter "De spiritu acediae", or arguments on the same theme by JOHANNES CLIMACUS and ISIDORE OF SEVILLE (jointly dealt with by F. PAGET, *The Spirit of Discipline*, 7th edn., London 1896, pp. 8 sqq.).

the power of temptation and man the power of resistance He guides the soul through the necessity of self-defence to virtue; and just as, like an umpire in the arena, he sets the strong greater tasks than the weak, in order to reward them more richly on the Day of Judgement, so too He had sent these temptations to Stagirius (who by adopting a religious life had stepped out of the audience and down into the arena) at a time when He knew him to be strong enough to overcome them. Stagirius's torments were really gain, and the devil, whom holiness always provoked to do battle, could only attain real power over an ascetic man when the latter yielded to temptation. Admittedly, "melancholy sadness" made the devil's victory easier,[24] in fact it could be said that he overcame men by their own ἀθυμία: but this despondency in turn could be overcome by the thought that it was one of those sufferings inflicted on men not by their own guilt but by divine providence. "Thou canst overcome thy despondency if thou sayest thou hast done nought that might justify it."

William of Auvergne therefore considered melancholy illness as a grace, while Chrysostom interpreted it as a trial which reasonable reflection could make comprehensible and tolerable. (Incidentally, the great rationalist Maimonides attempted to combat attacks of melancholic despair with similar consolations,[25] though these were addressed less to a religious hope of the next

[24] In the sixteenth century this notion still—or again—appears, treated now from the angle of humoral pathology rather than of moral psychology. Cornelius a Lapide (*Cornelii a Lapide . . . commentarii in scripturam sacram*, Lyons-Paris 1865, says (on I Reg. 16.23): "Nullus enim humor magis quam hic melancholicus (sc. opportunus est diabolo, ut homines vexet.) Quare daemon, qui agit per causas naturales, maxime utitur humore melancholico."

[25] Rabbi Moysis, *Tractatus de regimine sanitatis*, 1477 and after; chapter III (in the edition available to us, Augsburg 1518, fols. b 4^{v} sq.): "Et causa totius huius [sc. the condition of disordered melancholy, and fear] est mollities animae et ipsius ignorantia rerum veritatis. Docti vero et acquirentes mores philosophiae . . . acquirunt animabus suis fortitudinem . . . et quantumcunque aliquis magis suscipit de doctrina, minus patietur ex ambobus accidentibus aequaliter, videlicet ex die boni vel mali. Donec si pervenerit ad aliquid magnum bonum ex bonis mundi, quae quidem vocantur a philosophis bona phantastica, non magnificatur illud apud ipsum . . . et cum pervenerit ad eum magnum damnum, et angustia magna ex tempore adversitatis . . . non stupescit neque timet, sed eas tolerat bono modo . . . . Merito namque philosophi appellaverunt bona huius saeculi et huius mala bona et mala phantastica. Plura etenim suorum bonorum imaginatur homo bona esse, quae quidem in veritate mala sunt, similiter et plura mala malorum suorum existimat esse mala, quae quidem bona sunt . . . ." Nevertheless, Maimonides also prescribes purely medical remedies, especially medicines which are particularly adapted to the disposition of the august addressee. Naturally reasoned reflection—with specifically Christian overtones, of course—as a remedy against melancholy continued to be recommended in western literature as well, until far into modern times. As well as medical, scientific and characterological literature, there is a whole series of writings which might be grouped under the title "Anti-melancholy hortations"; a very

world than to a stoical contempt of the present.) Melancholy, however, could also be envisaged as a vice of one's own incurring as soon as it was identified with the sinful "acedia" which was sister—or mother—to "tristitia",[26] and this identification was made the easier by the fact that the outward symptoms of these sins—"timor", "taedium cordis", "instabilitas loci", "amaritudo animi" and "spei de salute aut venia obtinenda abiectio"—built up a picture very like melancholy,[27] and were sometimes even expressly linked with the "atra bilis".[28] But on the other hand—and this interpretation must have met the spiritual desires of the devout most adequately—melancholy might be considered as a chastisement from heaven which divine providence inflicted both on men in general and on individuals in particular, partly to punish past sins, partly, by painful experience, to avert future ones.

St Hildegard of Bingen was particularly fond of relating the origin of the "humor melancholicus" to the Fall of Man, but

---

typical example is the Jesuit FRANZ NEUMAYR's *Curatio melancholiae* or *Gedult in Trübsalen*, 1757 and later, while, on the other hand, there also appeared collections of jocular and witty poems and stories under titles such as *Exilium melancholiae* or *Recreations for the Melancholic* (numerous quotations in A. FARINELLI, *La vita è un sogno*, Turin 1916, pp. 151 and 283). Cf. also *The Mad Pranks and Merry Jests of Robin Goodfellow*, reprinted from the edition of 1628, with an Introduction by J. Payne Collier, London 1841 (Percy Society, *Early English Poetry*, VOL. IX).

[26] The complexity of the notion of "acedia" poses a problem which cannot be dealt with here. Cf. the (unfortunately unpublished) dissertation by M. A. CONNELL of Cornell University, Ithaca, entitled *A Study of Accidia and some of its Literary Phases*, 1932, kindly pointed out to us by Mr Herbert Stone, New York.

[27] Cf. the definitions in RABANUS MAURUS (MIGNE, P. L., VOL. CXII, cols. 1250 sqq.), where "study and good works" are recommended as antidotes, and in PS.-HUGO OF ST VICTOR (MIGNE, P. L., VOL. CLXXVI, cols. 1000 sq.). How nearly the theological definitions of "acedia" or "tristitia" coincide with medical descriptions of melancholy can be seen from the brilliant description of "tristitia" by Theodulf of Orleans (printed in C. PASCAL, *Poesia latina medievale*, Catania 1907, p. 120):

"Est et ei sine clade dolor, sine nomine moeror,
  Intima sed cordis nubilus error habet.
Hanc modo somnus habet, modo tarda silentia prensant,
  Ambulat et stertit, murmurat atque tacet.
Somniat hic oculis residens ignavus apertis,
  Nilque loquens sese dicere multa putat.
Actus hebes, secessus iners, oblivia pigra
  Sunt, et nil fixum mente vel ore vehit . . . ."

[28] 'Hugo of St Victor' (loc. cit.) considered "tristitia" as the master notion to which "desperatio, rancor, torpor, timor, acidia, querela, pusillanimitas" are subordinated as "comites". "Rancor", however, is defined as "ex atra bili aut nimia pigritia virium animi et corporis enervatio et corruptio." To name a Greek author as well, JOHN DAMASCENE, in his *Vices of the Soul*, lists, *inter alia*, μισανθρωπία, λύπη ἄλογος ("tristitia absque causa"!), φόβος, δειλία, ἀκηδία, μικροψυχία (*De virtutibus et vitiis*, MIGNE, P. Gr., VOL. XCV, col. 88).

in so doing she admittedly had in mind not only real melancholy illness and the melancholy temperament itself, which she adjudged particularly unfavourable, but in the last resort every deviation from the perfect and harmonious state of man in paradise. Combining an eye for realistic detail with a taste for bold symbolism in a manner characteristic of many mystics, but particularly marked in her own work, St Hildegard described the symptoms of melancholy in her *Causae et curae*[29] with clinical precision, in order to interpret them theologically; she remarks, for example:

> Cum autem Adam transgressus est . . . fel immutatum est in amaritudinem et melancolia in nigredinem impietatis.[30]

Picturing the physical quality of the melancholy humour ("qui tenax est et qui se ut gummi in longum protrahit"),[31] she paints a graphic picture of how this humour originated in Adam's body as the result of the Fall (and to that extent "de flatu serpentis" and "suggestione diaboli"). Had man remained in paradise he would have been free from all harmful humours; but as it was, men became "sad and timid and inconstant in mind, so that there is no right constitution or bearing in them. But they are like a high wind which is good for neither herbs nor fruit. For a humour springs in them . . . generating the melancholy which was born in the first fruit of Adam's seed out of the breath of the serpent when Adam followed its advice by devouring the apple."[32] For at the same moment that Adam sinned in taking the apple, melancholy "curdled in his blood" (as St Hildegard expressively interpreted the medical doctrine of "hypostasis"); "as when a lamp is quenched, the smouldering and smoking wick remains

---

[29] *Hildegardis "Causae et curae"*, ed. P. Kaiser, Leipzig 1903, esp. pp. 38, 18 sqq.; 145, 18 sqq. (many corrections by P. VON WINTERFELD, in *Anzeiger für deutsches Altertum*, XXIX (1904), pp. 292 sqq.). For St Hildegard's remarks applying only to melancholy as a temperament (since they are contained in a consistent doctrine of the four complexions), see below pp. 110 sqq.

[30] Kaiser (ed.), op. cit., p. 145, 35.

[31] Kaiser (ed.), op. cit., p. 38, 24.

[32] Kaiser (ed.), op. cit., p. 38, 27. "Et haec melancolia nigra est", says the following section (entitled "De melancoliae morbo"), "et amara et omne malum efflat ac interdum etiam infirmitatem ad cerebrum et ad cor quasi venas ebullire facit, atque tristitiam et dubietatem totius consolationis parat, ita quod homo nullum gaudium habere potest, quod ad supernam vitam et ad consolationem praesentis vitae pertinet. Haec autem melancolia naturalis est omni homini de prima suggestione diaboli, quando homo praeceptum dei transgressus est in cibo pomi. Et de hoc cibo eadem melancolia in Adam et in omni genere eius crevit atque omnem pestem in hominibus excitat."

reeking behind."[33] Before Adam fell, "what is now gall in him sparkled like crystal, and bore the taste of good works, and what is now melancholy in man shone in him like the dawn and contained in itself the wisdom and perfection of good works; but when Adam broke the law, the sparkle of innocence was dulled in him, and his eyes, which had formerly beheld heaven, were blinded, and his gall was changed to bitterness, and his melancholy to blackness."[34]

This tragic conception of melancholy to a certain extent reintroduced the ancient notion of a blasphemer stricken with madness, except that it replaced a single offence by original sin and thus transformed an individual tragedy into the tragedy of all mankind; no wonder, then, that it could not admit of moral extenuation or consolation. Melancholy was once and for all the "poena Adae" and had to be borne by the whole race, and only a physician (and the saint herself spoke in *Causae et curae* no less as a physician than as a theologian) could ease the worst symptoms of this essentially incurable hereditary evil.[35]

It was reserved for the hypocritical malice of Gaspar Offhuys, to whom we owe a remarkable account of the illness of his fellow-novice Hugo van der Goes,[36] to interpret melancholy madness as a punishment for the spiritual pride of a highly gifted man, which should serve as a corrective to the victim and a warning to others. He relates how, on deciding to enter the monastery in 1475, the famous painter had at first been granted all sorts of privileges which shocked the other brothers. After describing the noble visitors with whom Hugo was allowed to eat and drink, he gave an account of the "curious mental illness" which overtook him on a journey:

☞ quo incessanter dicebat se esse dampnatum et dampnationi eterne adiudicatum, quo etiam ipsi corporaliter et letaliter (nisi violenter impeditus fuisset auxilio astantium) nocere volebat.

---

[33] Kaiser (ed.), op. cit., p. 143, 22: "Nam cum Adam bonum scivit et pomum comedendo malum fecit, in vicissitudine mutationis illius melancolia in eo surrexit . . . . Cum enim Adam divinum praeceptum praevaricatus est, in ipso momento melancolia in sanguine eius coagulata est, ut splendor recedit cum lumen extinguitur, et ut stuppa ardens et fumigans foetendo remanet; et sic factum est in Adam, quia cum splendor in eo extinctus est, melancolia in sanguine eius coagulata est, de qua tristitia et desperatio in eo surrexerunt . . . ."

[34] Kaiser (ed.), op. cit., p. 145, 27.

[35] Cf. the dietary, Kaiser (ed.), op. cit., p. 146, 32, or the remedies for a melancholy headache, *ibid.*, p. 166, 7.

[36] Best edition by Hjalmar G. Sander, in *Repertorium für Kunstwissenschaft*, XXXV (1912), pp. 519 sqq.

As they finally reached Brussels, the abbot was hastily summoned, and being of the opinion that Hugo's illness was like King Saul's, he ordered music to be played diligently to Hugo—thus recalling the prescription, still valid, of ancient psychiatry[37]—and also recommended other "spectacula recreativa" to drive away his fancies. But it was not until long after his return to the monastery that he recovered.

Then follows a discussion as to the causes. Hugo's illness could be regarded either as a "natural" one, such as tended to originate "ex cibis melancolicis, aliquando ex potatione fortis vini, ex animi passionibus, scilicet solicitudine, tristitia, nimio studio et timore"—and the artist really did frequently lose himself in gloomy thoughts because he despaired of the fulfilment of his artistic aims,[38] and the drinking of wine may have made his condition worse; or else it might be traced to the providence of God, who wished to save the artist from the sin of vanity into which too much admiration had led him, and to recall him, by a "humiliativa infirmitas", to modesty, which, from all accounts, Hugo did display after his recovery by renouncing all his privileges. In either case, however, his fate should serve as a wholesome warning, for one should not only avoid the natural causes of such an illness (that is to say, set a limit to "fantasiis nostris et ymaginationibus, suspicionibus et aliis vanis cogitationibus") but also try to shun moral situations which might force Providence to step in. "If thou art proud, humble thyself greatly . . . for if thou dost not thyself amend thyself . . . then God himself, who puts down the proud and who desires not that thou shouldst be destroyed, will humble thee so greatly . . . that thou wilt become a warning example to others."[39]

---

[37] On pilgrimages, too, people with mental disorders were calmed by music, which, how ever, had to be of an elevating nature. Cf. ALFRED MAURY, *La magie et l'astrologie dans l'antiquité et au moyen âge*, 4th edn., Paris 1877, p. 333.

[38] A German physician, Hieronymus Münzer, travelling in the Netherlands in 1495, was obviously referring to Hugo van der Goes when, in speaking of the Ghent altarpiece by the brothers van Eyck, he said that "another great painter" "supervenit volens imitari . . . hanc picturam, et factus est melancolicus et insipiens" (W. H. WEALE, *H. and J. van Eyck*, London 1908, p. lxxv). See E. P. GOLDSCHMIDT, *Hieronymus Münzer und seine Bibliothek*, Studies of the Warburg Institute IV, London 1938.

[39] "Si superbus es, humilia te ipsum valde, . . . quia nisi te emendaveris, . . . ipse deus, qui superbis resistit, nolens quod pereas, adeo te humiliabit . . . quod exemplum aliis eris."

(*b*) Melancholy in Scholastic Medicine

(i) *Early Arabic Medicine and its Translation to the West: Constantinus Africanus*

In contrast to the blendings of theological and medical conceptions such as we may observe in the writings of St Hildegard and in many other medieval works, especially of the twelfth century,[40] Gaspar Offhuys drew a sharp line between the "ex accidenti naturali" view, and the "ex dei providentia". But what did he cite as "natural" causes of melancholy illness? The partaking of "melancholy foods" and "strong wine", the "animi passiones, scilicet solicitudo, tristitia, nimium studium et timor", and in general "malicia humoris corrupti dominantis in corpore hominis"—in other words, exactly the same as appeared in the writings of Rufus of Ephesus and his followers in later antiquity.

The account given by this monastic chronicler, who later rose to various honours, thus reveals the remarkable stability of views in clinical psychiatry, which really had changed only in minor points since the days of later Hellenism. The reason for this remarkable stability lay mainly in the fact that, as we have said, Constantinus Africanus's monograph on melancholy, which became of great importance to the western world, was based either directly or indirectly on Galen and particularly on his account of the doctrine of Rufus.[41] But, in addition, the early Arabic treatises on melancholy, which were absorbed into the culture of the school of Salerno and therefore of the whole west, made use of the later Greek conceptions, yet they adopted a considerably less theoretical, and, regarding the subject matter, much more practical point of view. Both "Serapion", whose writings were sometimes circulated under the name of "Janus Damascenus",[42] and the great "Rhazes",[43]

---

[40] Cf. for instance Hugues de Fouilloi, below, pp. 107 sqq. (text).

[41] Cf. A. BUMM, *Über die Identität der Abhandlungen des Isḥâk ibn Amrân und des Constantinus Africanus über Melancholie*, Munich, privately printed, no date. The parts of Isḥâq's work not given in Bumm can therefore be completed from CONSTANTINUS AFRICANUS (*Opera*, VOL. I, Basle 1536, pp. 280 sqq.).

[42] Really YUHANNÂ IBN SARÂBIYÛN, of Damascus (later half of ninth century): *Jani Damasceni . . . curandi artis libri*, VOL. III, 22: in the Basle edition (1543), pp. 123 sqq.; in the edition which was published under the name of SERAPION (Venice 1550), fols. 7v sqq.

[43] Really Abû Bekr Muḥammad ibn Zakarîyâ al-Râzî, d. 925: *Almansoris liber nonus*, ch. 13, frequently reprinted with various commentaries. For western commentaries see H. ILLGEN, *Die abendländischen Rhazes-Kommentatoren des XIV. bis XVII. Jahrhunderts*, dissertation, Leipzig 1921.

strove less for a deeper psychological understanding or a refinement of theoretic distinctions, than for the perfection and usefulness of semeiology and therapy as achieved in the prescribing of medicines, dietetic measures, and, in certain cases, the letting of blood. The author whom Constantinus copied, however, was Isḥâq ben 'Amrân (said to have been executed at the beginning of the tenth century) whose work on melancholy a thirteenth-century Arabic medical historian already extols as "incomparable". He went deeper; and it is largely thanks to him that in both the aetiological and in the therapeutic field, spiritual factors once more came into the foreground of the medical picture. Isḥâq described melancholy illness as "notions disturbed by black bile with fear, anxiety, and nervousness", that is to say, as a physically-conditioned sickness of the soul which could attack all three "virtutes ordinativae"—imagination, reason, and memory—and thence, reacting on the body, cause sleeplessness, loss of weight, and disorder of all the natural functions. The author never tired of picturing the boundless variety of the symptoms and, most important, their obvious contradictoriness in many cases. Men loquacious and quick-tempered by nature could become silent and pacific, the shy and quiet could become bold and eloquent; some became greedy, others refused nourishment; very many went from one extreme to the other in their whole behaviour.

> Some . . . love solitude and the dark and living apart from mankind, others love spaciousness, light, and meadowy surroundings, and gardens rich in fruits and streams. Some love riding, listening to different sorts of music, or conversing with wise or amiable people. . . . Some sleep too much, some weep, some laugh.[44]

Added to this there were the various obsessions, "timor de re non timenda", "cogitatio de re non cogitanda", "sensus rei quae non est".[45] And this variety and contradictoriness of the symptoms corresponded to the variety and contradictoriness of the causes. "The astonishing thing is that in our experience melancholy can always arise from opposite causes," as, for instance, both from

[44] Thus CONSTANTINUS AFRICANUS (*Opera*, VOL. I, Basle 1536, p. 288): "Alii . . . amant solitudinem et obscuritatem et ab hominibus remotionem. Alii spatiosa loca amant et lucida atque pratosa, hortos fructiferos, aquosos. Alii amant equitare, diversa musicorum genera audire, loqui quoque cum sapientibus vel amabilibus . . . Alii habent nimium somnum, alii plorant, alii rident."

[45] After CONSTANTINUS AFRICANUS (*Opera*, VOL. I, p. 287).

every sort of voluptuousness and from a too exaggerated asceticism.[46]

As well as these physical causes, however, there were the spiritual ones, and this idea (which, as we know, originated from Rufus) was traced in beautiful language acknowledging the burden of intellectual achievement, recalling the Hippocratean definition of thought as a "labour of the soul", and even bringing in the Platonic doctrine of recollection. It ran as follows:

We say that their moods constantly fluctuate between irascible excitement and a peaceable frame of mind, recklessness and timidity, between sadness and frivolity, and so on. The conditions [incidents] cited apply to the animal soul; but the activities of the rational soul are strenuous thinking, remembering, studying, investigating, imagining, seeking the meaning of things, and fantasies and judgements, whether apt [founded on fact] or mere suspicions. And all these conditions—which are partly permanent forces [mental faculties], partly accidental symptoms [passions] —can turn the soul within a short time to melancholy if it immerses itself too deeply in them. There are very many holy and pious men who become melancholy owing to their great piety and from fear of God's anger or owing to their great longing for God until this longing masters and overpowers the soul; their whole feeling and thoughts are only of God, the contemplation of God, His greatness and the example of His perfection. They fall into melancholy as do lovers and voluptuaries, whereby the abilities of both soul and body are harmed, since the one depends on the other. And all those will fall into melancholy who overexert themselves in reading philosophical books, or books on medicine and logic, or books which permit a view [theory] of all things; as well as books on the origin of numbers, on the science which the Greeks call arithmetic; on the origin of the heavenly spheres and the stars, that is, the science of the stars, which the Greeks call astronomy; on geometry, which bears the name of "science of lines" among the Arabians, but which the Greeks call geometry; and finally the science of composition, namely of songs and notes, which means the same as the Greek word "music". These sciences are products of the soul, for the soul isolates and explores them; knowledge [recognition] of them is innate to the soul, as Galen says, in recalling the philosopher Plato. . . . Such men—Allah knows—assimilate melancholy . . . in the consciousness of their intellectual weakness, and in their distress thereat they fall into melancholy. The reason why their soul falls sick [disorders of the understanding and the memory, and other disorders which affect the soul] lies in fatigue and overexertion, as Hippocrates says in Book VI of the *Epidemics*: "Fatigue of the soul comes from the soul's thinking."

---

[46] CONSTANTINUS AFRICANUS (*Opera*, VOL. I, p. 283 sq.): Also climatic conditions favourable to it can arise from too great heat and dryness as well as from too great moisture ("air as there is in autumn" is of course particularly harmful); lack of physical exercise is always harmful, and so is the habitual partaking of foods and drinks which thicken the blood and favour the birth of the "humor melancholicus."

Just as bodily overexertion leads to severe illnesses of which fatigue is the least, so does mental overexertion lead to severe illnesses of which the worst is melancholy.[46a]

Treatment, too, which was always difficult and wearisome, had to be suited to the variety of symptoms and causes. As well as the regulation of the six "vital things" (air, food, drink, sleeping and waking, evacuation and retention, rest and movement) for which precise orders were given,[47] and the prescribing of medicine, spiritual measures played a particularly important rôle. The physician was indeed expected to combat and overcome the substance of the evil ("materia infirmitatis") in every illness; but if the accompanying symptoms ("accidentia") were particularly burdensome, dangerous, or shocking, they were to be dealt with first, and since this was the case in melancholy mental illness, it was the symptoms which had primarily to be overcome.

But the physician must fight against the melancholics' suspicions, grant them what they used to like before . . . reasonable and pleasant discourse should be employed . . . with various kinds of music, and aromatic, clear, and very light wine.[48]

Mental exertion was naturally to be avoided, but—and here he quotes Rufus—moderate sexual intercourse was desirable: "Coitus, inquit, pacificat, austeriorem superbiam refrenat, melancholicos adiuvat."[49] If we remember that Rabanus Maurus recommended

---

[46a] A. Bumm, op. cit., p. 24 sq.—Constantinus Africanus, *Opera*, vol. i, p. 283 sq.

[47] Constantinus Africanus (*Opera*, vol. i, pp. 291 sqq.): The melancholic's dwelling should face the east and lie open to it; to counteract the dry nature of the "atra bilis", preference should be given to moist things in his diet, such as fresh fish, honey, all manner of fruit, and, with regard to meat, the flesh of very young and, if possible, female, animals, like yearling lambs, young hens and female partridges (vegetables, on the contrary, are to be avoided, because of wind); above all, his digestion is to be aided by means of this diet, as well as of early morning walks in cheerful dry surroundings, massage with warm and moist ointments, and daily infusions of lukewarm (or cold, in summer) water: "Studium nostrum maxime adhibendum est in digestione. Ordinetur dieta humida et simpla, quia ille cibus facile digeritur, qui in substantia simplex est et humidus . . . . Melancholici assuescant ad pedum exercitia aliquantulum, apparente aurora, per loca spatiosa ac plana, arenosa et saporosa . . . . Post exercitia infundantur aqua calida et dulci."

[48] Constantinus Africanus (*Opera*, vol. i, pp. 294 and 290: "Oportet autem medicum meliorare suspicionem melancholicorum, mitigare furorem eorum et gratificare quod prius habuerint charum . . . . Adhibenda rationabilia et grata verba, cum perfecto ingenio et sufficienti memoria, tollendo quae in anima sunt plantata cum diversa musica et vino odorifero claro et subtilissimo."

[49] Constantinus Africanus (*Opera*, vol. i, p. 293). Cf. also his *Liber de coitu* (*Opera*, vol. i, p. 303): "Rufus vero ait: Quod coitus solvit malum habitum corporis et furorem mitigat. Prodest melancholicis et amentes revocat ad notitiam, et solvit amorem concupiscentis, licet concumbat cum alia quam concupivit". Platearius's *Practica* (*De aegritudine capitis*, v, Venice 1497, fol. 173), summarising the views current in Salerno at the

a more energetic preoccupation with intellectual studies to combat the "acedia" of the pious, and Chrysostom constant perseverance in abstinence to combat the despondency of the ascetic, it is at this point that we encounter the main, insoluble contradiction between medical and theological or ethical psychopathology—a contradiction which, with minor exceptions,[50] continued in later times and even to-day governs discussions on such themes. Shorter, and no less derivative, than the monograph *De melancholia*, are the chapters on melancholy in the Constantinian *Theorica* and *Practica Pantegni*[51] (παντέχνης); but their influence was nearly as great. They are based on the *Liber regius* by 'Alî ibn Abbâs ("Haly Abbas", who died in 994),[52] and thus represented the attitude of Arabic scholarship shortly before the appearance of Avicenna. Considerably inferior in erudition and breadth of vision to Isḥâq ibn 'Amrân's monograph, these short extracts served mainly as convenient summaries or "schemata" for essays, as nearly all later medical "practices" and the like began their chapter on melancholy with similar words—"melancholia est alienatio mentis sine febre"—and also followed the *Pantegni* in linking love (generally called "hereos" and coupled with the notion of the heroic) with melancholy: in fact, they treated passion as a "species melancholiae", which was of decisive importance for the development of the "melancholy lover" as a literary type.[53]

(ii) *Attempts at Systematisation on the Basis of Humoral Pathology: Avicenna's Doctrine of the Four Forms*

The early Salernitans were as yet unfamiliar with the writings of the great Avicenna (who died in 1037). We know that the

height of its development, says: "Adsint soni musicorum instrumentorum, cantilene iocunde . . . et formose mulieres, quibus quandoque utantur, quia moderatus coitus spiritum mundificat et malas suspiciones removet."

[50] E. g. UGO SENENSIS, *Consilia*, XIV, Venice 1518, fol. 14v: "Caveat a venereis". Not till Marsilio Ficino, who otherwise accords entirely with medical tradition with regard to therapeutical practice, do we see—in connexion with his Neoplatonic attitude—the ascetic ideal again applied to empirical dietetics, admittedly those designed especially for intellectual men.

[51] *Theorica Pantegni*, IX, 8 (*Opera*, VOL. II, Basle 1539, pp. 249 sqq.); *Practica Pantegni*, I, 20 (*Opera*, VOL. I, pp. 18 sq.).

[52] HALY FILIUS ABBAS, *Liber totius medicinae*, Lyons 1523, *Theor.*, IX, 7, fol. 104r; *Practica*, V, 23, fol. 217r. Whether 'Alî ibn 'Abbâs for his part was familiar with Isḥâq ibn 'Amrân's work, it is difficult to decide. It is fairly certain that Abûlqâsim knew it (ALSAHARAVIUS, *Liber theoricae necnon practicae*, pract. 26/27, Augsburg edition of 1519, fols. 32v sqq.).

[53] Cf. I. L. LOWES, "The Loveres Maladye of Heroes", in *Modern Philology*, XI (1914), pp. 491 sqq.

distinction (deriving apparently from Rufus) between the substance of a "succus melancholicus" as a deposit of the blood and that of a "melancholia adusta" originating from the scorching of the yellow bile had to some extent disrupted the cogency of the scheme of the four humours; and we can see how later times took advantage of this loophole, in classifying and accounting for the endless variety of symptoms of melancholy. If red bile could turn to "melancholia adusta", why should the same not be possible for other humours? 'Alî ibn 'Abbâs (and of course Constantinus) admitted that non-natural melancholy might originate both in burnt red bile and in burnt black bile,[54] and later added yet a third form originating in "adust blood", so that the difference between the more depressive, more euphoric and more manic symptoms seemed to repose on a genetic foundation.[55] All that was lacking was its logical completion by a fourth form originating from the scorching of the phlegm, the possibility of which, however, had been expressly denied by the earlier school of Salerno.[56] Avicenna's orderly mind adopted one principle of division which the authors so far cited had either not accepted or not known, and which brought melancholy completely into the system of the four humours.[57]

---

[54] HALY, *Theor.*, I, 25, fol. 19^{v}; following him, CONSTANTINUS AFRICANUS, *Theorica Pantegni*, I, 25 (*Opera*, VOL. II, p. 22 sq.), "Colera nigra non naturalis ex incensa colera nigra est naturali. Estque calida et a acut. . . . Alia nascitur ex incensione colerae < rubrae, et > acutior et calidior priore. Haec habet pessimas qualitates destruendi." This melancholy from burnt red bile may be identical with the "melancholia leonina" also mentioned by Constantinus (cf. R. and W. CREUTZ, in *Archiv für Psychiatrie*, XCIV (1932), pp. 244 sqq.), symptoms of which include "insolence, foolhardiness and indifference to correction," all things to remain characteristic of the choleric melancholic.

[55] HALY, *Theor.*, IX, 7, fol. 104^{r}, according to CONSTANTINUS AFRICANUS, *Theorica Pantegni*, IX, 8 (*Opera*, VOL. II, p. 249): "Significatio uniuscuiusque speciei propria. Quae enim de humoribus est melancholicis in cerebro incensis, nimiam habet alienationem, angustias, tristitias, timores, dubitationes, malas imaginationes, suspiciones & similia . . . . Quae ex sanguine est ardente, alienationem, cum risu & laetitia. Corpus infirmi macidum, color rubeus. Pili in corpore sunt nimii, nisi in pectore, uenae latae, oculi rubei, pulsus magnus, parum uelox, ... In humoribus ex colera rubea, habent alienationem, clamorem, instabilitatem, uigilias, non quiescunt, multum irascuntur, calidum habent tactum sine febri, maciditatem, et corporis siccitatem, oculorum instabilitatem, aspectum quasi leonis, citrinitatem coloris."

[56] PLATEARIUS's *Practica* further defines the Haly-Constantinus doctrine of the three forms, and, recalling the old correspondence with the seasons, states that adustion of the "cholera rubra" occurs mainly in summer, of the "cholera nigra" in autumn, and of the blood in spring, adding (fol. 173): "quod non habentur fieri [sc. melancholicae passiones] ex phlegmate, quia phlegma, cum sit album, albedinem cerebri non immutat." Instead of this, Haly and the Salernitans took "melancholia ex stomacho", i.e. the hypochondriac form, not really at all suitable, for the fourth form of melancholy.

[57] This principle appears in PSEUDO-GALEN, *Ὅροι ἰατρικοί*, GALEN (KÜHN), VOL. XIX, p. 364. According to M. WELLMANN, *Die pneumatische Schule*, Philologische Untersuchungen, XIV, Berlin, 1895, p. 65, this work is based on a "a follower of the pneumatic school inclining to syncretism, who lived in the third century at the earliest."

Melancholy is either natural, or secretious and unnatural. . . . Of secretious [unnatural] melancholy, one sort originates from the bile when burnt to ashes . . . another originates from the phlegm when burnt to ashes . . . another is generated from the blood when burnt to ashes . . . a fourth finally comes from natural melancholy when this has become ashes.[58]

From now on, therefore, melancholy illness could have a sanguine, choleric, phlegmatic or "natural melancholic" basis, which last might be described as, so to say, "melancholy squared". This system had the advantage of coupling the variety of symptoms with a variety of causes. At the same time, it logically and satisfactorily combined Galen's canonical theory of combustion with the doctrine of the four humours. It remained operative until the seventeenth or eighteenth century, which was not surprising in view of the fact that later medieval medicine largely limited itself to annotating Avicenna,[59] and even the later Salernitans could not do without the doctrine of the four forms for long.[60] The thirteenth-century encyclopaedists,[61] the physicians from Gordonius[62] and Guglielmo de Corvi[63] to Giovanni da Concorreggio[64] and Antonio Guainerio,[65] and the humanists from Ficino[66] and Melanchthon[67] to Burton,[68] all grasped the possibility of tracing

---

[58] AVICENNA, *Liber canonis*, Venice 1555, I, I, 4, ch. I, fol. 7^v.

[59] For these commentators, cf. H. ECKLEBEN's Leipzig dissertation, *Die abendländischen Avicenna-Kommentare*, 1921.

[60] *De conservanda valetudine . . . cum Arnoldi Novicomensis* [Arnaldus de Villanova] *enarrationibus*, frequently printed and translated; in the Frankfurt edn., 1551, fols. 111 sqq.; cf. also ARNALDUS DE VILLANOVA, *De morbis curandis*, I, 26, in the Strasbourg edn., 1541, fols. 87^r sqq.

[61] ALBERTUS MAGNUS, *Liber de animalibus*, ed. H. Stadler, Münster i.W. 1916–21, VOL. I, p. 329, § 120, almost word for word like Avicenna, except that he adds a discourse on Problem XXX,1. (cf. above, text pp. 69 sqq.). Also Bartholomeus de Glanvilla (that is, BARTHOLOMEUS ANGLICUS), *De proprietatibus rerum*, IV, 11 (in the Strasbourg ed., 1485, no page numbers).

[62] B. GORDONIUS (1282–1318), *Practica, lilium medicinae nuncupata*, Venice 1498, VOL. II fol. 30^v sqq. He would also like treatment to be differentiated according to the four forms respectively.

[63] GUILLELMUS BRIXIENSIS (d. 1326), *Practica*, Venice 1508, ch. 22, fol. 20^r.

[64] Died about 1440. *Practica nova*, Pavia 1509, VOL. I, ch. 23, fol. 16^r.

[65] *Practica*, Venice 1517, tract. 15, fol. 23^r. For GUAINERIO (d. 1440) see below, pp. 95 sqq. (text).

[66] FICINO, *De v. tripl.*, I, 5: "Melancholia, id est atra bilis, est duplex; altera quidem naturalis a medicis appellatur, altera vero adustione contingit. Naturalis illa nihil aliud est quam densior quaedam sicciorque pars sanguinis. Adusta vero in species quattuor distribuitur, aut enim naturalis melancholiae, aut sanguinis purioris aut bilis [sc. flavae] aut salsae pituitae combustione concipitur."

[67] *De anima*, II; *Corpus Reformatorum*, XIII, cols. 83 ff.

the different varieties of "adust" melancholy back to the character of the four primary humours. We read in Avicenna:

> If the black bile which causes melancholy be mixed with blood it will appear coupled with joy and laughter and not accompanied by deep sadness; but if it be mixed with phlegm, it is coupled with inertia, lack of movement, and quiet; if it be mixed with yellow bile its symptoms will be unrest, violence, and obsessions, and it is like frenzy. And if it be pure black bile, then there is very great thoughtfulness and less agitation and frenzy except when the patient is provoked and quarrels, or nourishes a hatred which he cannot forget.[69]

We can see how these few though clear-cut traits were built up into a more and more vivid picture; until at length, deeply imbued as he was with the heroic conception of Problem XXX, I, Melanchthon finally ennobled even the four forms of melancholy disease as far as possible by classical and mythological examples, and, by including Democritus, even anticipated the romantic type of melancholy humorist:

> When melancholy originates from the blood and is tempered with the blood, it gives rise to the insanity of the fatuously happy, just as the cheerful madness of Democritus is said to have been, who used to laugh at the foolishness of mankind and by his unruffled mind prolonged his life to the hundred-and-ninth year.
>
> But when melancholy originates from the red bile or is tempered with much red bile, there arise horrible ravings and frenzies; of this sort was the madness of Heracles and of Ajax. As Virgil says of Heracles's rage: "Hic vero Alcidae furiis exarserat atro Felle dolor." For although in anger the red bile is irritated, Virgil calls it black because the red is mixed with a larger quantity of black, indeed it is burnt up together with the black, and together with it becomes like ashes.

---

[68] *Anatomy of Melancholy*, London 1621. G. A. Bieber (*Der Melancholikertypus Shakespeares und sein Ursprung*, Anglistische Arbeiten, III, Heidelberg 1913, p. 12) makes a curious mistake when he draws the conclusion, from the completely traditional distinction between sanguine, choleric, phlegmatic and melancholic melancholy, that Burton sometimes used the word 'melancholy' only as a synonym for temperament.

[69] Avicenna, *Liber canonis*, Venice 1555, III, I, 4, ch. 19, fol. 205r: "Et dicimus quod cholera nigra faciens melancholiam, cum est cum sanguine, est cum gaudio et risu et non concomitatur ipsam tristitia vehemens. Si autem est cum phlegmate est cum pigritia et paucitate motus et quiete. Et si est cum cholera, vel ex cholera est cum agitatione et aliquali daemonio et est similis maniae. Et si fuerit cholera nigra pura, tunc cogitatio in ipsa erit plurima et agitatio seu furiositas erit minus: nisi moveatur et rixetur et habeat odium cuius non obliviscitur." The characteristics of these four forms of melancholy, with the exception of the phlegmatic, which is transformed into the complete opposite, correspond to those given in Περὶ χυμῶν for the general pathological states deriving from the four humours: *ὅσαι γὰρ αὐτῶν [sc. τῶν νόσων] εἰσιν ἐφ' αἵματος, μετ' ᾠδῆς προσπίπτουσί τε καὶ γέλωτος, ὅσαι δ' ἀπὸ ξανθῆς ⟨χολῆς⟩, θρασύτεραι καὶ πικρότεραι. . . . Ὅσαι δ' αὖ ἀπὸ μελαίνης, σκυθρωπότεραι καὶ σιωπηλότεραι καὶ ἀστειότεραι. ὅσαι δ' αὖ ἀπὸ φλέγματος ληρώδεις καὶ ἀσταταίνουσαι* (Pseudo-Galen, (Kühn), vol. XIX, p. 493).

When it is tempered with much phlegm, it causes unusual apathy, and we ourselves have seen a mentally deranged person who slept almost constantly, spoke without expression, and could not be moved at all, save by the sound of the lute; when he heard that, he raised his head, began to smile, and answered questions moderately cheerfully.

When the black bile, already present in preponderance, is inflamed, it causes deep depression and misanthropy; of this sort was Bellerophon's grief:

☞ "Qui miser in campis errabat solus Aleis,
Ipse suum cor edens, hominum vestigia vitans,"

as Homer says.[70]

(iii) *Attempts at Classification on a Psychological Basis: Averroes and Scholastic Medicine*

This doctrine of the four forms made many important distinctions possible; even the difference between melancholy and frenzy,[71] always problematic, and sometimes confused even in antiquity, could now be reduced to the relatively clear formula: "si ex colera [scilicet melancholia], tunc vocatur proprie mania."[72]

---

[70] MELANCHTHON, loc. cit.: "Atra bilis viciosa est, cum vel coeteri humores, vel ipsa atra bilis ita aduritur, ut humor cineris naturam crassiorem et mordacem referat . . . . Cum melancholia est ex sanguine et diluitur modico sanguine, efficit amentias ridicule laetantium, quale aiunt fuisse delirium Democriti hilarius, qui ridere solebat hominum stulticiam, eaque animi tranquillitate vitam produxit usque ad annum centesimum nonum suae aetatis.

"Cum vero melancholia est ex rubra bile, aut diluitur multa rubra bile, fiunt atroces furores et maniae, qualis fuit Herculis et Aiacis furor. Ut Virgilius de ira Herculis inquit:

'Hic vero Alcidae furiis exarserat atro
Felle dolor.'

Etsi enim rubra bilis in ira cietur, tamen Virgilius atram nominat, quia rubra mixta est atrae copiosiori, imo et uritur, ac velut cinerea est simul cum atra.

"Si diluitur copioso phlegmate, fit inusitata segnicies, sicut ipse vidimus mente errantem, qui fere perpetuo dormiebat, summisse loquebatur, nec excitabatur, nisi citharae sono, quem cum audiret, attollens caput, arridere incipiebat, et interrogatus hilariuscule respondebat.

"Si ipsa per sese atra bilis redundans aduritur, fiunt tristiciae maiores, fugae hominum, qualis fuit Bellerophontis moesticia:

'Qui miser in campis errabat solus Aleis,
Ipse suum cor edens, hominum vestigia vitans.'

ut inquit Homerus."

It is remarkable that no mythological example exists of phlegmatic melancholy. Phlegm is *εἰς μὲν ἠθοποιίαν ἄχρηστος* also in relation to morbid exaggeration of the heroic. For the significance of the doctrine of the four forms in interpreting Dürer's steel engraving B70, see below, p. 404 (text).

[71] See above, pp. 16 sqq., 46 (text). ALEXANDER OF TRALLES's remark (*Originaltext und Übersetzung*, ed. J. Puschmann, Vienna 1878, VOL. I, pp. 591 sqq.) is significant: *οὐδὲν γάρ ἐστιν ἄλλο μανία ἢ ἐπίτασις τῆς μελαγχολίας ἐπὶ τὸ ἀγριώτερον.*

[72] Similarly in PLATEARIUS, op. cit., fol. 173. In the passage quoted on page 93, AVICENNA had already said that the choleric form of melancholy resembled "mania", and elsewhere (*Liber canonis*, Venice 1555, III, I, 4, cap. XVIII, fol. 204v) he even declared that the "ultima adustio" of yellow bile generated not melancholy but mania.

But as well as this there was also another opinion which attributed the variety of mental disorders to an alteration not in the noxious humours but in the damaged faculties of the mind. According to Averroes, in a chapter entitled "Quod est de accidentibus trium virtutum, scilicet imaginativae, cogitativae et memorativae", melancholy could either attack the whole brain and paralyse all three faculties, or else cause only partial damage, according to its field of action.

Quando fuerit causa in prora cerebri, tunc erit laesa imaginatio; et quando fuerit in parte media, tunc erit laesa ratio et cogitatio; et quando fuerit in parte posteriori, tunc erit laesa memoria et conservatio.[73]

This theory was not by any means entirely new; Asclepiades had already distinguished between a melancholy disorder of the imagination and one of the understanding,[74] and Isḥâq ibn 'Amrân (and hence Constantinus Africanus) wrote that this disorder could refer to all three "virtutes ordinativas, id est imaginationem, memoriam, rationem".[75] It was then only a step to combining these views with the theory of localisation which assigned the "virtutes ordinativas" to the three brain ventricles respectively.[76] The physician Posidonius (fourth century A.D.) had already completed this classification in associating disorders of the imagination with damage to the forebrain, disorders of the understanding with damage to the mid ventricle of the brain, and disorders of the memory with damage to the back part of the brain[77]; and 'Alî ibn 'Abbâs and Constantinus even reinforced this view with examples from Galen.[78] Nevertheless, an explicit connexion between melancholy (as distinct from damage in general) and the cells of the brain does not seem to have been generally current before Averroes. This doctrine was at first rather overshadowed by pure humoral pathology, and later did not so much supersede as supplement it[79]; at all events we can see how the doctrine

[73] *Colliget Averroys*, III, 40. We quote from *Abhomeron Abynzohar, Colliget Averroys*, Venice 1514, fol. 65ᵛ.

[74] See above, text p. 45 (Asclepiades).

[75] See above, text p. 83.

[76] See above, text p. 68 sq.

[77] Cf. AETIUS, VI, 2 (printed by KARL SUDHOFF, in *Archiv für Geschichte der Medizin*, VII, Leipzig 1913, p. 157).

[78] *Theorica Pantegni*, VI, 11 (*Opera*, VOL. II, p. 152). Printed in KARL SUDHOFF, op. cit., p. 166; HALY, *Theor.*, VI, 10 (fol. 72ᵛ), not mentioned in Sudhoff.

[79] Even Averroes himself mentions the old humoral divisions as well as the divisions according to mental function: "Sed corruptio, quae accidit his virtutibus propter complexionem melancholicam, est cum timore, quae fit sine causa .... Et quando uritur melancholia et fiunt accidentia cholerae in ipsa, tunc convertitur homo ad ferinos mores."

gained in importance after the twelfth and thirteenth centuries, in proportion as medicine proper began to yield to the influence of scholastic philosophy both in form and in substance; how also, not in opposition to this process of assimilation, but in close alliance with it, the need grew for a systematic description of the functions and disorders of the soul. This doctrine played its part in giving future discussions on melancholy a new scholastic stamp. Sometimes diseases of the memory continued to be included in the main notion of melancholy[80]; but much more commonly, it seems, melancholy was equated only with the "laesio virtutis imaginativae seu aestimativae [or cogitativae] aut utriusque", while disorder of the memory was regarded as a special form of illness ("lithargia").[81] In either case, discussion almost always centred round the "diversitas laesionis operationum", to use a contemporary expression.[82] Not only was the doctrine of the three faculties of the mind[83] used to differentiate between the various forms of melancholy disorder, but from this angle an attempt was made to elucidate the old argument of "frenzy or melancholy",[84] and to attribute the examples of "frenzy", constantly quoted in literature or occasionally taken from experience'

[80] Thus, among others, GIOVANNI DA CONCORREGGIO, *Practica nova*, Pavia 1509, fol. 15ᵛ; VALESCUS DE TARANTA, *Aureum ac perutile opus . . . Philonium*, I, 13, Venice 1521, fol. 12ʳ; and, with the slight difference that melancholy is defined as an unnatural alteration of the "virtus rationalis" and its subordinate faculties (namely, the "virtutes sensibiles", the "virtus imaginativa" and "memoria"), GUILLELMUS BRIXIENSIS (Guglielmo de Corvi), *Practica*, Venice 1508, fol. 20ʳ.

[81] Thus A. GUAINERIUS, *Practica*, Venice 1517, tract. 15, fol. 22ᵛ, and JOHN OF GADDESDEN (Johannes Anglicus), *Rosa anglica, practica medicine a capite ad pedes*, completed in 1314, Pavia 1492, fols. 131ᵛ sqq.—who, however, also mentions disorders of the memory in his chapter on melancholy; and most clearly of all Giovanni d'Arcole (Johannes Arculanus, d. 1458) who says: "Dicitur [sc. melancholia] mutatio existimationum et cogitationum et, suppletive, etiam imaginationum . . . non autem corrumpitur memoria, cum sit in cerebro posteriori, sed virtutes iam dictae sunt in anteriori" (GIOVANNI D'ARCOLE, *Practica*, Venice 1560, pp. 50 sqq.).

[82] PLATEARIUS, loc. cit.

[83] Two important medieval authors admittedly adopted a very different standpoint, linking the notion of melancholy (in one case as illness, in the other as temperament) with the notion of the faculties of the soul, not in order to pursue the pathological disturbances threatening the three faculties from the side of melancholy, but, on the contrary, in order to confirm the fact that men in whose mental disposition one of the three "virtutes", i.e., the imaginative, predominated over the other two, were at the same time, indeed for this very reason, either melancholics already or bound to become such. But these two authors, HENRICUS DE GANDAVO and RAIMUNDUS LULLUS, will be dealt with later (see below, text pp. 337 sqq.).

[84] Cf. PLATEARIUS, loc. cit.: "Mania est infectio anterioris cellulae capitis cum privatione imaginationis. Melancolia est infectio mediae cellulae cum privatione rationis"; similarly ARNALDUS DE VILLANOVA, *De morbis curandis*, Strasbourg 1541, fol. 87, and, almost word for word, BERNHARD VON WAGING, *Remediarius contra pusillanimos et scrupulosos*, clm. 18600,

to disturbance of one or other of the three faculties. In those who thought they had no head, or that they saw black men, the "imaginatio" was disturbed, while understanding and memory remained intact. Those who during a plague forgot the names of their kinsmen still thought correctly on the whole and also imagined correctly. Finally, the sick man who threw glass vessels and a child out of the window was affected neither in imagination nor memory, but in his power of thought and judgement, "because he did not know that the vessels were fragile and the child vulnerable, and because he thought it correct and useful to throw such things out of the window as though they were harmful in the house."[85]

For the rest, later medieval medicine added little to the traditional notion. On the one hand, the stream of medical knowledge trickled into the channels of popular medical literature, preserved for us in the shape of countless calendars, pharmacopoeias and herbals[86]; on the other hand, though the medical practitioners emphasised that they were speaking not as philosophers or theologians but as "physici", they attempted more and more to adopt the later scholastic way of thinking. Thus the ancient problem, whether melancholy was possibly caused by evil demons, was elaborated with ever greater abundance of subtle distinctions, without progressing beyond Avicenna's consciously sceptical attitude.[87] "Substantial" and "accidental"

---

printed in PEZ, *Bibliotheca Ascetica*, VOL. VII, pp. 496 sqq.; and JOHN OF GADDESDEN (Johannes Anglicus), *Rosa anglica, practica medicine a capite ad pedes*, completed in 1314, Pavia 1492, fol. 132ʳ; here however, only as an addition to Averroes's tripartite division, and therefore introduced with a "tamen proprie loquendo." VALESCUS DE TARANTA even approved of a division which located "lythargia" as usual in the "cellula posterior", but put melancholy and "mania" together in the "media cellula," and (feverish) frenzy in the "prima cellula" (op. cit., fol. 12ᵛ). Guainerius repeats Platearius's division, but uses it only as a convenient system of nomenclature and ultimately falls back on purely symptomatic distinctions: melancholy proper is always "sine rixa," "mania" never (op. cit., fol. 22ʳ).

[85] Thus Giovanni da Concorreggio's version of the frequently repeated story (*Practica nova*, Pavia 1509, fol. 15ᵛ). The distribution of Galen's examples among the three faculties of the soul (though without special mention of melancholy) occurs already in 'Alî ibn 'Abbâs and Constantinus Africanus. See p. 91 (text).

[86] Examples in GIEHLOW (1903).

[87] AVICENNA, *Liber canonis*, Venice 1555, III, I, 4, ch. 18, fol. 204ᵛ: "Et quibusdam medicorum visum est, quod melancholia contingat a daemonio: sed nos non curamus, cum physicam docemus, si illud contingat a daemonio aut non contingat, . . . quod si contingat a daemonio tunc contingit ita ut convertat complexionem ad choleram nigram et sit causa eius propinqua [prob. "proxima"] cholera nigra: deinde sit causa illius daemonium aut non daemonium." On the other hand the question becomes important in PIETRO D'ABANO'S *Conciliator*, differentia XXXII (*Eminentissimi philosophi ac medici Petri Aponensis liber Conciliator differentiarum philosophorum et medicorum appellatus*, Florence 1526, fol. 46ᵛ).

causes, "general" and "special" symptoms, as well as therapeutic measures, were more and more subtly differentiated, though in theoretical expositions far less attention was paid to the barbarous method of chaining up, flogging and branding the patient, than seems to have been the case in practice[88]; and certain controversies on method which had arisen between physician and philosopher were discussed with ever greater enthusiasm.[89] But the inner core of the conception remained untouched by all this; earnest study and deep thinking, still constantly mentioned, were reckoned, now as before, only as causes or symptoms of the disease, and the "higher inspiration" (to quote Dürer), which, whatever form it took, always seemed mere "alienation" to the physician, was also accounted nothing but a symptom of illness. To the physician, the "prophetici divinatores" were just as ill as the prostrated creatures who despaired of their salvation, those who thought they spoke with angels, or the woman who said that the devil lay with her every night and who yet could be cured by God's grace.[90] Even in those days the true physician recognised neither saints nor witches.

One event, however, was a revolution of fundamental significance: the permeation of medical thought—naturally rational and concerned with the human microcosm—with astrological and magical notions issuing from speculations on the universe. In other words, medicine was transformed into iatromathematics.[91] But this process, though already begun in the thirteenth and fourteenth centuries by such men as Michael

---

[88] Treatment by cauterisation and trepanning, so often mentioned in surgical works and directions for cautery (cf. text pp. 55, 291, and PLATE 72) is only very rarely mentioned in specifically psychiatric texts, as, for instance in JOHN OF GADDESDEN, op. cit., fol. 132[v], and in GUAINERIUS, op. cit., fol. 26[r] where "verberationes" (cf. PLATE 71) are also mentioned.

[89] The most characteristic point of discussion is perhaps the following: as against medical (and especially Galenic) opinion, according to which melancholic anxiety was derived from the blackness of the "cholera nigra"—which put the reason in as much of a fright as natural darkness did—Averroes stated that the colour of a χυμός was quite irrelevant to its pathogenic effect. This argument is dealt with by GIOVANNI D'ARCOLE, *Practica*, Venice 1560, pp. 50 sqq., in a discourse of two folio columns' length containing seven "instantiae" and "solutiones", and reaches the conclusion "nos autem, cum medici simus, sequamur medicos; licet rationes medicorum suprascriptae non sint demonstrationes".

[90] VALESCUS, op. cit., fol. 12[r]: "et sciendum . . . quod istius alienationis . . . multae sunt species. Nam quidam faciunt se divinatores, alii praescientes omnia, alii credunt se loqui cum angelis . . . . Et tenui mulierem in cura, quae dicebat, quod diabolus coierat cum eà qualibet nocte, et tamen curata fuit cum adiutorio dei."

[91] Cf. K. SUDHOFF, *Iatromathematiker, vornehmlich im* 15. *und* 16. *Jahrhundert* (Abhandlungen zur Geschichte der Medizin, II), Breslau 1902; moreover see below, pp. 266 sqq. (text).

Scot, Pietro d'Abano and Arnold of Villanova, was essentially a product of the Renaissance, intimately connected with the revival of orientalised late classical learning and (to keep strictly to our subject) the 'Aristotelian' notion of melancholy. It reached maturity in Ficino and Gioviano Pontano on Italian, in Agrippa of Nettesheim and Paracelsus on German soil.

The speculations of the iatromathematicians were related to medieval notions in much the same way as, say, the principles of fifteenth- and sixteenth-century art were related to the Gothic. This is not the place to discuss them in detail, but one typical example of the transition may be briefly mentioned. Like all examples of transition it reveals both the historical connexion of the phenomena and the basic differences between them. Antonio Guainerio was a professor at Padua who died in 1440.[92] He was on the whole a typical representative of scholastic medicine, or medical scholasticism; for this reason indeed we have already had occasion to mention his views. Nevertheless, he may be regarded as Ficino's predecessor, for it is in his treatise on melancholy that a transformation becomes clearly visible. In his fourth chapter, having previously discussed the notion, the causes and the outward symptoms of melancholy illness in the first three chapters, he poses the questions, "Quare illiterati quidam melancolici literati facti sunt, et qualiter etiam ex his aliqui futura praedicunt?"[93] The mere fact that these questions are allotted a complete, long chapter is something new and shows a revival of interest in divination in general and once again a serious consideration of melancholy inspiration in particular. In fact, Guainerio treats the promptings of these sick people no longer as mere delusions but as facts; he himself knew a simple peasant who, though quite illiterate, wrote poems during his periodic attacks of melancholy, and Guainerio (the first physician, in the strict sense of the term, to refer to Problem XXX, 1) compares him with "Marcus" (Maracus), the poet mentioned by Aristotle, "qui factus melancolicus poeta quoque factus est."[94]

[92] Incidentally, he was honoured with a mention in HARTMANN SCHEDEL's *World Chronicle* (Nuremberg 1493, fol. ccxlvi^r).

[93] GUAINERIUS, op. cit., fol. 23^v.

[94] In fact, 'Aristotle' merely says that Maracus wrote better poetry when in ecstasy. Just as Guainerius brings in Aristotle to lend authority to his story of the peasant who wrote poetry, so, vice versa, Pietro d'Abano reinforced Aristotle's statement by the evidence of a "reliable physician" from whom he had heard "quod mulier quae⟨dam⟩ illitterata, dum esset melancoli⟨c⟩a, latinum loquebatur congruum, quae sanata evanuit". *Expositio problematum Aristotelis*, col. J, in the Mantua edition of 1475; fol. N.3^r in the Padua edition of 1482.

Guainerio completely denies the 'Aristotelian' explanation of this symptom, namely, the peculiar quality of the melancholy "humour" itself, and he also refuses to admit (on the grounds that it was "heathenish") the view, sanctioned, as he maintains, by Avicenna, that such exceptional achievements were due to "demoniac" influences. But what he himself substitutes for it in his attempts at explanation reveals an essentially new interpretation of the traditional heritage. All intellective souls, he says, were equally perfect in the beginning and were born with all the knowledge that they could ever attain. If in later life some souls achieve more or less than others, that is due merely to their better or worse physical constitutions, which, in contrast to the soul, are dissimilar and of unequal value, and thus to a greater or lesser extent restrict the intellect. The "embodied" soul is doomed to forget its innate ideas in a greater or lesser degree and recollects only through learning part of what has been forgotten. "Et ex istis sequitur, quod nostrum scire est quoddam reminisci, ut voluit Plato." Apart from this, the moment of the soul's incarnation is governed by a special constellation which endows the soul with its qualities and adapts it to special forms of activity; but these "influentiae", too, can work only to a limited extent in later life, because the soul, chained as it is to the body and dependent on the help of bodily organs, can recognise things only "discursively", that is to say, not by immediate insight, but only through the combination of reasoning and sense impressions. But if, owing to a state of ecstasy, the senses are put out of action ("bound"), then the soul is left to itself and is enabled for a short time to re-experience (as it were) its pre-natal state; it then perceives "sine discursu", by direct intuition, and can receive the influence of its presiding star without adulteration or diminution. And since the melancholic was liable to this ecstatic state which put the senses out of action, it was understandable that even without any education he should then become "literatissimus", "absque eo, quod ab aliquo . . . didicerit vel addiscat, sed per influxum solum."

One can see how the ideas which in Florence a few years later were to be built into a doctrinal structure of imposing size and solidity—namely, the theme of Problem XXX, I, the Platonist epistemology, and finally, above all, the belief in an astral "influxus"—had already come together here, though for the time being merely coincidentally; they began gradually but inevitably to transform the contemporary notion of nature, and compelled even medicine, bound by tradition though it was, to take up a position for or against them. But this is still, as it were, an advance guard. It was significant that although he expressly referred to Aristotle, Guainerio denied the essential part of the 'Aristotelian' conception ("rationem hanc nullus acceptat"); he took the melancholic's prodigious intellectual qualities quite seriously, but considered them as nothing more than prodigies: that is, they were for him symptoms of disease requiring explanation and not achievements of genius determined by natural melancholy. He asked why people suffering from a melancholy disease should sometimes develop remarkable gifts, but ignored the real 'Aristotelian' question, why men who were, innately, specially gifted, should always be melancholic by nature. In Ficino and his successors, the notions based on astral influences grew to encompass so comprehensive a picture of the world that the whole art of healing was considered as nothing but a particular method of employing the general cosmic forces; and like the other sciences, it merged in the last resort with magic, which in turn was a kind of "applied cosmology".[95] But Guainerio's iatro-mathematical disquisition remained an isolated and somewhat menacing foreign body in the structure of a school of medicine simply and solely concerned with the practical and the mundane. It was no mere flower of speech when at the outset the Paduan physician declared:

> Although the solution of the problems mentioned in this work in which we had thought only to treat of practical healing, is not entirely relevant, yet we would like to provide a fairly probable explanation in order not to remain silent in face of those laymen who very frequently enquire after the origin of such symptoms, and in order not to appear ignorant of the causes of the accidents which befall mankind.

And he concluded his exposition with a sigh of relief:

> et hoc de problemate, cuius assignatae causae post se non leves difficultates trahunt, quas theoretizantibus dimitto. Et ad practicam gloriosam transiens huic capiti finem impono.

3. MELANCHOLY IN THE SYSTEM OF THE FOUR TEMPERAMENTS

The overwhelming majority of treatises on melancholy written

---

[95] See below, p. 262 (text). The phrase "magic is applied cosmology" was coined by A. Warburg.

in the Middle Ages began with a remark such as the following:

☞ Nota primo, quod melancolia potest sumi dupliciter. Uno modo pro humore distincto ab aliis humoribus: et sic non accipitur hic. Alio modo pro quadam passione cerebri: et sic accipitur hic.[96]

Or:

☞ Melancholia est nomen humoris unius de quattuor, qui sunt in nostro corpore: et est nomen aegritudinis provenientis ex dicto humore.[97]

Such stereotyped phrases clearly point to a distinction between the disease itself and its identically named "causa materialis"; but their sudden and frequent appearance can be taken indirectly as a sign that men were beginning to emphasise that the notion "humor" was entirely independent of "aegritudo" and "passio"; in other words, non-pathological humoralism, which until then had played a relatively modest part compared with the other kind, had now risen to equal if not greater significance in popular opinion; the four humours were now the material causes not of certain illnesses, but of certain physical and mental types of constitution.

(*a*) The Galenic Tradition, particularly among the Arabians and Constantinus Africanus

While the ancient doctrine of melancholy as an illness had been handed down to the Middle Ages as a firmly-cemented whole and transmitted exclusively by the Arabs, the doctrine of temperaments (by which, whenever we use the expression without limiting context, we mean the definition of humorally-determined types of men) had to be built up of two different elements from two different sources.

We can now say with some certainty that the basic idea of the system was not transmitted by Arabic physicians, for the Arabs, in so far as they may have been responsible for its transmission to the early and later school of Salerno, were generally such orthodox adherents of Galen's doctrine of the "crases" that they could not accept, let alone develop, the fundamental principle of the humoral doctrine of temperaments, that is to say, the idea that the preponderance of one or other primary humour determined

---

[96] Thus the commentary on Rhazes by Geraldo de Solo (d. 1371). We quote from *Almansori liber nonus cum expositione Geraldi de Solo*, Lyons 1504, ch. 13, fol. 34ᵛ.

[97] Thus VALESCUS, op. cit., fol. 12ʳ.

the characteristic qualities of the various types of men.[98] Ḥunain ibn Isḥâq (whom the west quoted as Johannitius or simply as "Physicus", because until independent translations of Galen were made, his *Isagoge in artem parvam Galeni* represented the most important source of general physiological knowledge),[99] 'Alî ibn 'Abbâs, and Avicenna,[100] all adhered to Galen's doctrine,[101] which

---

[98] The "Pure Brothers" were something of an exception, for by their Platonist syncretism they linked in a remarkable manner the humoral standpoint with the doctrine based on the qualities alone. In their view, physiognomical and psychological types were intrinsically based on the (simple) qualities of warmth, cold, etc. Dry people, for instance, were "generally patient in their dealings, constant in opinion, unreceptive; predominant in them is patience, hatred, avarice, tenacity, caution [or memory?]". The qualities for their part were closely linked with the four humours. God says of the creation of Adam: "I composed his body of moisture, dryness, heat and cold, and indeed I made him from dust and water and breathed breath and spirit into him. Thus the dryness comes from dust, moisture from water, heat from breath, and cold from spirit. Thereupon, after these, I set in his body four other kinds which hold the bodily dispositions together. Without them the body cannot exist, and not even one of them can exist without the others. These are the black bile, yellow bile, blood and phlegm. And then I let them reside with one another, and gave dryness its seat in the black bile, heat in the yellow bile, moisture in the blood, and cold in the phlegm. Now the body in which the four admixtures, which I gave it as a wall and protection, are of equal strength, so that each is in the proportion of one quarter, neither more nor less—that body is completely healthy, and constituted equally. But when one of them exceeds its brothers, oppressing them and departing from them, then sickness overtakes the body . . . ." (in the *Rasā'il iḫwān aṣ-ṣafā'wa-hillān al-wafā'*, Cairo 1347/1928, VOL. I, pp. 229 sqq.; see also VOL. II, p. 321).

Middle Byzantine literature shows a certain split. On the one hand, writers remained faithful to Oribasios and Aetius and the orthodox doctrine of the "crases"; on the other hand, the humoral doctrine of temperaments survived, such as it had been transmitted also in Greek, in Περὶ *κατασκευῆς*, and, more especially, in Περὶ *χυμῶν*. Thus the monk MELETIUS in his (probably ninth-century) work Περὶ *τῆς τοῦ ἀνθρώπου κατασκευῆς* (MIGNE, P. Gr., VOL. LXIV, cols. 1075 sqq., esp. 1272 sqq.) repeats the traditional correlation of the humours with the elements, qualities, seasons and ages of man (though he qualifies the usual comparison of *αἷμα* = youth, *χολή* = manhood, *μελαγχολία* = middle age, *φλέγμα* = old age, by the remark that physicians had also mentioned infancy and senility as two special phases); but he also transmits a humoral "characterology" which was essentially based on Περὶ *χυμῶν*, as the use of otherwise rare expressions in both works shows: *ἱλαρωτέραν δὲ τὴν ψυχὴν τοῦτο* [*sc. αἷμα*] *ἐργάζεται, ἐν οἷς πλεονάζει· ἡ δὲ ξανθὴ χολὴ γοργοτέραν ἢ θρασυτέραν· ἡ δὲ μέλαινα σεμνοτέραν καὶ εὐσθενεστέραν* [!]*· τὸ δὲ φλέγμα ἀργωδεστέραν καὶ σκληρωδεστέραν.*

The author adds that also outward appearance (proportion and colouring) is due to the mixture of humours.

[99] For the notion of melancholy in particular, the important division into the natural and unnatural kind, given at the beginning of his *Isagoge*, remained definitive: see J. VAN WAGENINGEN, in *Mnemosyne*, new series, VOL. XLVI, 4 (1918), pp. 374 sqq. In fact Johannitius's summary recommended itself by its unequalled brevity and clarity: "Commixtiones sunt novem, octo inaequales et una aequalis. De inaequalibus vero quattuor sunt simplices, hoc est cal., frig., hum., sicc. Et quattuor ex his compositae, scil. cal. et hum., cal. et sicc., frig. et hum., frig. et sicc. Aequalis vero est, quando cum moderatione corpus incolume ducitur."

[100] Cf. W. SEYFERT, "Ein Komplexionentext einer Leipziger Inkunabel und seine handschriftliche Herleitung", in *Archiv für Geschichte der Medizin*, XX (1928), p. 280.

[101] See above, pp. 57 sqq. (text). Averroes was the first to do away with the four simple "crases" and to recognise only the four compound ones. Cf. SEYFERT, op. cit., p. 281.

was of course accepted completely by Constantinus Africanus as well. Thus the various types of men, considered if not as ideal, at least as normal in the framework of their dispositions, were distinguished by their proportions, by the colour of their skin and hair, by the quality of their flesh, by their way of moving, and, partially at least, by their mental characteristics.[102] But these distinctions derived exclusively from the qualities warm, dry, cold, and moist, and although the characteristic dual qualities, "cold-and-moist", and so on, proper to the four "compound crases", were also applicable to the four humours, and although, for instance, what Constantinus said of the representatives of the "warm-and-dry crasis" was almost word for word what Vindician and Bede described as the effects of "cholera rubra",[103] yet it cannot have crossed the minds of the orthodox Galenists themselves expressly to identify the "warm-and-dry" type of man of the doctrine of "crases" with the "choleric" type of the doctrine of humoral temperaments, or to refer to the "cold-and-moist" type expressly as the "phlegmatic". This was precluded partly by the fundmental principle of the Galenic doctrine of "crases", which measured every empirically-observed "combination" against an ideal state, whereas the humoral doctrine regarded the "sanguine" complexion, the equivalent of the warm-and-moist combination, as the absolute optimum, frequently described as the "complexio temperata". It was also precluded by the fact that,

---

[102] We quote as example Constantinus Africanus, *Theorica Pantegni*, I, 15 (*Opera*, vol. II, p. 16), after Haly, *Theor.*, I, 17, fol. 15:

Simple "Crases":
- Warm: "intellectus bonus, homo multum facundus, mobilissimus, audax, iracundus, libidinosus, multum appetens et cito digerens."
- Cold: "contraria e contrario."
- Dry: (only physiological characteristics).
- Moist: (only physiological characteristics).

Compound "Crases":
- Warm and Dry: "homo intellectualis, audax, appetibilis et digestibilis, maxime tamen grossi cibi, libidinosus."
- Warm and moist: (only physiological characteristics).
- Cold and moist: "intellectus durus, homo obliviosus, animosus, neque multum appetens neque cito digerens, non libidinosus."
- Cold and dry: (only physiological characteristics).

[103] The role which the four compound "crases" play in the course of man's life is also determined by a law of succession corresponding exactly to that governing the four humours:

Pueritia (till 30) *calidior et humidior.*
Juventus (30–40) *calida et sicca.*
Senectus (till 60) *frigida et sicca.*
Aetas decrepita—according to some, very cold and dry, to others, cold and moist.

Thus Constantinus Africanus, *Theorica Pantegni*, I, 21 (*Opera*, vol. II, p. 17); cf. Haly, *Theor.*, I, 21, fols. 15ᵛ sqq.

while according to the humoralists the simple preponderance of one or other primary humour was merely a factor in determining the constitution, leading to disorders only in the case of abnormal increase ("superexcessio"), yet for the orthodox Galenists it signified in any case a pathological condition. In strict Galenism expressions such as "cholericus" and "phlegmaticus" never became descriptive of constitutional types but remained tainted with the meaning given to the χολώδης or φλεγματώδης by the Hippocrateans. It was no coincidence that Constantinus Africanus and 'Alî ibn 'Abbâs, who described the eight Galenic "dyscrases" merely as "complexiones extra temperantiam" or "intemperatae"[104] (that is, simply distinguished them from the ideal combination as less well balanced), should without more ado describe a man governed by the predominance of a single humour as sick, "quia quicumque humores in quantitate sive in qualitate praevalent ex necessitate morbidum corpus facient."[105]

So, too, in attempting to describe the "signa cuiusque humoris redundantis", Avicenna painted not so much types of character as frankly morbid states, distinguished by various disorders and even affecting the victim's dreams[106]—states which could indeed be favoured by the "temperamenta" (that is, presumably, the "crases") as well as by age, climate and mode of living,[107] but which, as is clear from the very distinction drawn between an actual condition and a mere predisposition, were in no way dependent on these "temperamenta", let alone identical with them.[108] The main assumption of the doctrine of humoral

---

[104] CONSTANTINUS AFRICANUS, *Theorica Pantegni*, I, 18 (*Opera*, VOL. II, p. 16); cf. HALY, *Theor.*, I, 18, fol. 15v.

[105] CONSTANTINUS AFRICANUS, *Theorica Pantegni*, I, 25 (*Opera*, VOL. II, p. 23); cf. HALY, *Theor.*, I, 25, fol. 18v.

[106] AVICENNA, *Liber canonis*, Venice 1555, I, 2, 3, 7, fol. 45v. The man suffering from a superfluity of black bile is not only lean and discoloured (as the melancholic is in the real complexion doctrine), but also labours under "immodica sollicitudo et cogitatio," heartburn, "falsa appetentia," bad ulcers, and spleen, and has nightmares about dark abysses, tortures, and black and terrifying matters. We must therefore disagree with Seyfert when he relates such descriptions of frankly morbid states simply with sanguinics, melancholics, etc., in the temperamental sense.

[107] Cf. the passage cited in note 106 from Avicenna.

[108] In a chapter designed mainly for the requirements of slave buyers, and therefore differentiating between white, brown and black races, CONSTANTINUS AFRICANUS—cf. also GALEN, *De temperamentis*, II, 5 (KÜHN, I, 618)—considers the preponderance of one or other humour as essentially a disturbance of health: "Si quis . . . servos vel ancillas emat aliquando, ad medicum causa consilii, sani ne sint, recurrit. . . . Quod si sit citrinus color corporis, ex abundantia colerae rubeae designatur. Si lividus vel plumbeus, mala complexio significatur. Aut de epatis frigiditate aut de abundantia colerae . . . aut ex splenis defectione.

temperaments, therefore, could not be transmitted to the Middle Ages by the Arabians, but was taken over directly from the writings of the later Empire, which, as we have seen, had presented themselves at the outset in Latin guise, and by the sixth or seventh century had already passed into the general fund of knowledge of north-west Europe.[109]

(*b*) The Revival of Humoral Characterology in Western Natural Philosophy during the first half of the Twelfth Century

In view of all this, it is natural that it should have been not the preponderantly Galenist clinical medicine but rather scholastic philosophy which, in the course of a comprehensive revival of learning,[110] revived and codified anew the real doctrine of temperaments.

One vivid and highly significant exposition was that of William of Conches, in whose *Philosophia* the doctrine seems to have been incorporated into a vast framework of Christian cosmology.[111] When the earth was freed from the water, he says, moisture prevailed in one place, fire in another, earth in another, whence resulted the various substances for the creation of the animal kingdom; there arose choleric animals like the lion, phlegmatic ones like the pig, and melancholic ones like the ox and the ass; and only where the mixture was equally proportioned could man

---

Sanum ergo corpus ex perfectione coloris . . . cognoscitur" (*Theorica Pantegni*, I, 24, in *Opera*, VOL. II, p. 19); cf. also HALY, *Theor.*, I, 24, fol. 17ʳ. On the other hand, the Galenic doctrine, too, connects the "crases", determined solely by the qualities, so intimately with the disorders determined by the preponderance of one of the humours that, despite all attempts to effect a clear division, a certain confusion was inevitable. Thus, for instance, the content of Avicenna's chapter mentioned in the previous note, as well as of other corresponding passages, was taken over in MICHAEL SCOT's *Liber phisionomiae*; and this work became very important for the future development of this branch of knowledge (chs. 162–171, in the Breslau manuscript available to us, Cod. F. 21, fols. 61ʳ sqq.).

[109] See our abstracts from Isidore and Bede (text pp. 61 sqq.). A rhymed version of Isidore's statements, of uncertain date, perhaps Carolingian, occurs in the pseudepigraphic *Ovidius de quattuor humoribus*, for which cf. esp. C. PASCAL, *Poesia latina medievale*, Catania 1907, pp. 107 sqq.

[110] Cf. e.g. C. H. HASKINS, *The Renaissance of the Twelfth Century*, Cambridge 1927.

[111] This work was printed under three different names (Bede, William of Hirsau and Honorius of Autun) until CHARLES JOURDAIN discovered the real author (cf. *Dissertation sur l'état de la philosophie naturelle, en Occident et principalement en France, pendant la première moitié du XIIe siècle*, thèse, Paris 1838). We quote from MIGNE, P. L., VOL. CLXXII, cols. 39 sqq. A discussion of William of Conches's sources by R. Klibansky will appear in connexion with his studies on the mediaeval commentaries on Plato.

be created. But man too lost his correct temperament owing to the Fall; through the privations imposed on him by life outside paradise, man, naturally warm and moist, lost either heat, or moisture, or both; and so there arose three degenerate forms, namely, the warm-and-dry, the cold-and-moist, and the cold-and-dry temperaments, which are called respectively the choleric, the phlegmatic and the melancholic. Only where the two original qualities preserve something approaching their "aequalitas", in being equally but only slightly reduced, could there arise a type of man who at least resembled the sinless Adam, without being exactly like him. This was the "homo sanguineus".

Man is by nature warm and moist, and [harmoniously] conditioned by the four qualities. But since his original nature is corrupted, it happens that in certain individuals certain qualities increase or diminish. When warmth increases and moisture diminishes in a man, he is called choleric, that is, warm and dry. When on the contrary moisture increases and warmth diminishes, he is called phlegmatic. When dryness increases and warmth diminishes he is called melancholic. But when the qualities are present in equal strength he is called sanguine.[112]

It is true that these four types were not yet distinguished "characterologically" but only physiognomically[113]; yet it was important for future development that in so influential a philosopher as William of Conches the representatives of the four temperaments should have appeared with the designations still current to-day—"sanguine", "choleric", and so on.[114] Vindician had stated the relation between humour and character in terms of cause and effect; he could say, for example, "cholera facit homines iracundos"; but a choleric was still simply a sick man suffering from a superfluity of red bile.[115]

[112] *Philosophia*, IV, 20, in MIGNE, P. L., VOL. CLXXII, col. 93: "Homo naturaliter calidus et humidus, et inter quattuor qualitates temperatus; sed quia corrumpitur natura, contingit illas in aliquo intendi et remitti. Si vero in aliquo intendatur calor et remittatur humiditas, dicitur cholericus, id est calidus et siccus . . . Sin vero in aliquo intensus sit humor, calor vero remissus, dicitur phlegmaticus. Sin autem intensa sit siccitas, remissus calor, melancholicus. Sin vero aequaliter insunt, dicitur sanguineus."

[113] Environment can alter the original constitution.

[114] William of Conches was also acquainted with the correspondence between temperaments seasons, and ages of man: according to *Philosophia*, II, 26 (MIGNE, P. L., VOL. CLXXII, col. 67), and IV, 35/36 (MIGNE, P. L., VOL. CLXXII, col. 99), children are sanguine, men choleric, middle-aged men melancholy, and old men phlegmatic.

[115] Taken over by William of Conches (see below), this terminology made rapid headway. A twelfth-century pseudo-Augustinian tract (*De spiritu et anima*, XXV, MIGNE, P. L., VOL. XL, col. 798) considers in a section dealing with the meaning of dreams their different effect on the four temperaments: "Alia namque vident sanguinei, alia cholerici, alia phlegmatici, alia melancholici." Another early piece of evidence for the adjectival form of the names of the

William of Conches gives Johannitius as his source. The latter was far from conceiving a doctrine of temperaments, but this difficulty can be resolved when we think of the numerous commentaries on Johannitius made in the schools at the beginning of the twelfth century. It is among these commentaries that we must look for the origin of the system of "types" adopted by William. Whether the four types were systematically established as early as the late eleventh century, at Salerno, or not until the French schools of the early twelfth century, is a question that cannot yet be decided. At all events, in the *Glosae super Johannitium*[116] (of which we possess two twelfth-century manuscripts), and in the commentary on Theophilus's *Liber de urinis*,[117] probably by the same author (both works being certainly independent of William of Conches), we find the names of the temperaments as well as a whole series of characteristics overlapping from the physiognomic to the psychological.

Among men too there are some who are of a moderate temperament and of a better complexion. They may be recognised by the fact that they are more reasonable than the rest, more eloquent, more amiable, more cheerful and more ingenious—the sanguine and the choleric.[118]

Whenever the orthodox list of names of the four temperaments was first laid down, it is obvious that it only represented the terminological fixation of a doctrine hundreds of years old, of which the essential form had been transmitted to the western world of the early Middle Ages by Vindician's letter. Inasmuch as it emphasised the power of character-determination inherent in the four humours, that letter contained, as we have seen, the core of a system later developed in detail. It was copied more than once even in Carolingian times, but does not seem to have become the basis of a comprehensive system until the time of the school of Salerno,[119] or to have influenced the development of western European medicine decisively before 1050–1150.

---

temperaments appears in a text in Cod. Dresd. Dc. 185, 12th cent., published by R. Fuchs, "Anecdota Hippocratica", in *Philologus*, vol. LVIII (1899), p. 413.

[116] Oxford, Bodl., Digby MS 108, fols. 4–26; Berne, Cod. A 52, fols. 1–20; inc. "Cum inter omnia animalia".

[117] Oxford, Bodl., Digby MS 108, fol. 76r–91r; see fol. 79v.

[118] Oxford, Bodl., Digby MS 108, fol. 6v.

[119] Cf. the piece *De quattuor humoribus* printed in S. de Renzi, *Collectio Salernitana*, vol. II (Naples 1853), pp. 411–12, which, according to the editor (but on unconvincing evidence), might originate from Johannes Monachus, a pupil of Constantinus Africanus; the text is Vindician's epistle enlarged by various additions.

In this connexion the effect of clinical medical doctrine on philosophy can also be noted in Adelard of Bath,[120] who, prior to William of Conches, talks of "melancholy animals", giving the "physici" as his authority, and applies the expression "melancholic" to human beings in a way no longer descriptive of illness.

The close connexion of William of Conches with the medical scientific literature of his time is thus proved. In future development the form which William of Conches had given to medical typology held good. One important feature of this development was that he assigned the special place of a perfect type to the warm-and-moist of sanguine complexion which in Galenic doctrine was merely one of the "dyscrases"; so much so that he considered it not only the basis of a natural intelligence which the representatives of other temperaments had to replace by wearisome diligence,[121] but also the exclusive privilege of man compared with the beasts; for William of Conches there were melancholy, choleric, and phlegmatic beasts, but none sanguine; whereas men, on the contrary, were originally created sanguine, and had only degenerated into melancholic, choleric, and phlegmatic types after the expulsion from paradise.

It can be seen how William of Conches set himself the task not only of bringing the views of physiology and cosmology (both inseparably linked by the doctrine of elements and qualities) into line with divine revelation, but of actually deducing them from the Bible. The account of the creation of man just alluded to was to him nothing but an elaboration of the words "formavit Deus hominem ex limo terrae et inspiravit in faciem eius spiraculum vitae". He found the medical tenet that woman was colder and moister (that is to say, more phlegmatic) than man[122] expressed in the myth of Eve's creation out of Adam's rib.[123]

---

[120] ADELARD OF BATH, *Quaestiones naturales*, ch. 7, ed. M. Müller, Münster 1934.

[121] *Philosophia*, IV, 39 (MIGNE, P. L., VOL. CLXXII, col. 100): "quamvis vero sanguinea complexio sit habilis ad doctrinam, in omni tamen aliquis perfectus potest esse cum labore, quia labor omnia vincit."

[122] For this view, particularly well expressed by William of Conches ("calidissima ⟨mulier⟩ frigidior est frigidissimo viro")—which survived until well into the eighteenth century—cf. GALEN, *De usu partium*, VII, 22, ed. G. Helmreich, VOL. I (Leipzig 1907), p. 440 = KÜHN, VOL. III, p. 606; CONSTANTINUS AFRICANUS, *Theorica Pantegni*, I, 22, "De mutatione ⟨complexionis⟩ propter sexum" (*Opera*, VOL. II, p. 19); and ADELARD OF BATH's *Quaestiones naturales*, ch. 41. For the significance of this axiom in interpreting Dürer's steel engraving B70, see below, p. 404 sq.

[123] *Philosophia*, I, 23 (MIGNE, P. L., VOL. CLXXII, col. 56).

His new doctrine of the temperaments, then, served a double purpose: first, to trace the variety and inequality of men back to the Fall, which had destroyed the original perfection and unity; secondly, to establish and account for the inalienable nobility of human nature.

While for this reason various beasts were created melancholic, and innumerable ones phlegmatic and choleric, only man was created as a creature by himself, because, as Boethius says in the *Arithmetic*, every equality is confined to a small and limited number of cases, but inequality knows countless different forms.[124]

Perhaps it was precisely this concern with the Christian dogma which caused, or at least favoured, after the first half of the twelfth century,[125] the revival and expansion of the doctrine that the temperaments were conditioned by the humours. At all events we can trace how throughout the century the tendency to interpret the temperaments theologically grew at the same rate as the tendency to develop the doctrine in other ways, and how the attempt to differentiate them characterologically was even expressly justified by reference to the claims of moral philosophy and education. We might fairly speak of a revival of the ancient characterological doctrine within the framework of Christian moral theology.[126] Perhaps the best witness for this process in which the elaboration of the moral system advanced simultaneously with the deepening of psychological insight is a treatise

---

[124] *Philosophia*, I, 23 (MIGNE, P. L., VOL. CLXXII, col. 55): "Unde, cum diversa animalia melancholica creata sunt, et infinita phlegmatica et cholerica, unus solus homo creatus est, quia, ut ait Boethius in Arithmetica, omnis aequalitas pauca est et finita, inaequalitas numerosa et multiplex . . . ." CONSTANTINUS AFRICANUS too, *Theorica Pantegni*, I, 5 (*Opera*, VOL. II, p. 8) has the sentence "Homo . . . omnibus temperatior est animalis [sic] speciebus." But, quite apart from the material difference that Constantinus did not yet consider "temperatus" a synonym for "warm and moist", let alone for "sanguine", the emphasis is quite different.

[125] Bernardus Silvestris modifies the doctrine transmitted by William of Conches only in so far as he introduces sanguine animals as well, while proclaiming the right of all men by nature to an equilibrium of the four humours. Whereas in William of Conches man's special place was due to the fact that he alone could be sanguine, animals being limited to the three other temperaments, in Bernardus Silvestris it is due to the fact that man alone is immune from the disharmony of the humours. "Ceterum non ea, quae in homine est, et in ceteris animantibus Naturae diligentia reperitur. Intemperans enim humorum cohaerentia brutorum conplexionem saepius assolet depravare. Asinus hebes est ex phlegmate, leo iracundus ex cholera, canis aerio totus inficitur odoratu. Sola et singularis hominum conditio; de humorum complexu facta est in qualitatibus et quantitatibus temperatio . . . . Futurum enim intelligentiae et rationis habitaculum non oportuit inaequalitatem aut turbatricem consilii diffidentiam pateretur" (BERNARDUS SILVESTRIS, *De universitate mundi*, II, 13).

[126] For a similar development in the typology of the vices, and its influence on portrayals of the temperaments, see below, pp. 300 sqq.

formerly attributed to the great Hugh of St Victor, but probably written by the Picard Hugues de Fouilloi (Hugo de Folieto, who died about A.D. 1174). Essentially scientific and sometimes even specifically medical matters (for example, remedies for baldness) are here treated in such a moralising manner that the treatise rightly bears the title *De medicina animae.* After a prologue which begins by declaring the necessity of interpreting all natural events "spiritually", and an introductory chapter expounding the familiar parallel between macrocosm and microcosm theologically,[127] there follows a general doctrine of the elements and humours. Here, as usual, the four humours correspond to the elements and seasons; but as fire also signifies intellectual subtlety, air purity, earth stability, and water mobility; and as, moreover, there has to be the same harmony between the faculties of the mind as between the elements, so the four humours and their mutual relationships have also a moral significance.

Similarly, the mind also makes use of the four humours. In place of blood it has sweetness, in place of red bile bitterness, in place of black bile grief, in place of phlegm equanimity. For the doctors say that the sanguine are sweet, cholerics bitter, melancholics sad, and phlegmatics equable [corpore compositos].[128] Thus in contemplation lies sweetness, from remembrance of sin comes bitterness, from its commission grief, from its atonement equanimity. And one must keep watch lest spiritual sweetness be tainted by worldly bitterness or the bitterness arising from sin corrupted by fleshly sweetness, lest wholesome grief be troubled by idleness or weariness or the equable spirit brought into confusion by unlawfulness.[129]

We need only glance at our former table to discover the source of Hugo's attributes.[130] The sweetness of the sanguine nature comes from Isidore, the grief of the melancholic and equanimity of the phlegmatic from Vindician: only the bitterness of the

---

[127] Cf. SAXL, *Verzeichnis*, VOL. II, pp. 40 sqq.

[128] See above, p. 62: VINDICIAN, *Ep. ad Pentadium.*

[129] HUGO DE FOLIETO, in MIGNE, P. L., VOL. CLXXVI, col. 1185: "Similiter et animus utitur quatuor humoribus; pro sanguine utitur dulcedine; pro cholera rubra amaritudine; pro cholera nigra tristitia; pro phlegmate mentis compositione. Dicunt enim physici sanguineos esse dulces, cholericos amaros, melancholicos tristes, phlegmaticos corpore compositos. Ut sit dulcedo in contemplatione, amaritudo de peccati recordatione, tristitia de perpetratione, compositio de emendatione. Est enim attendendum, ne dulcedo spiritalis turbetur amaritudine temporali, vel amaritudo habita de peccato corrumpatur dulcedine carnali; ne utilis tristitia turbetur otio vel inertia, vel mens composita dissolvatur per illicita." Cf. also the approximately contemporary remarks by WILLIAM OF ST THIERRY (MIGNE, P. L., VOL. CLXXX, col. 698): "Eodem . . . modo elementa operantur in mundo maiori, quo operantur quattuor humores in mundo minori, qui est homo . . . ex sua sibi diversitate concordantia et per concordem diversitatem facientia pulcherrimam ordinis sui unitatem."

[130] See above, table on p. 62 sq. (text).

cholerics is new; no doubt he deduced it from the generally recognised bitterness of the bile. Against the humoral pathology which, coupled with the doctrine of the "crases", then prevailed in clinical medicine, the natural philosophy of the twelfth century established a new interpretation of humoral characterology. From its beginnings in the later Empire onwards this doctrine had always had a slightly popular character, and in the early Middle Ages it had already found its way into the encyclopaedias; it could therefore be accommodated far more comfortably in a cosmology with a moral and theological bias than could the less equivocal science of the specialists. Science, including astrology, had continued to flourish only among the Arabians; and when it found its way back to the west it still preserved a far more esoteric character.

Hugues de Fouilloi especially emphasised that he wrote only for "edification"—it is a word of which he was particularly fond—and that the examples in the following four chapters aimed only at showing the "diversitates morum" resulting from the "effectibus humorum". At every point in those chapters he reveals his familiarity with Bede, Isidore, and Vindician[131]; but here too all the physiological and characterological data were essentially a basis for theological interpretations which, with the help of numerous Biblical quotations, completely obscured pure science. We restrict ourselves here to an abbreviated version of the chapter on melancholics:

We must now say something in brief of the nature of black bile. It reigns in the left side of the body; its seat is in the spleen; it is cold and dry. It makes men irascible, timid, sleepy or sometimes wakeful. It issues from the eyes. Its quantity increases in autumn. . . . By black bile we may, as we have said elsewhere, mean grief, which we should feel for our evil actions. But one may also speak of a different sort of grief, when the spirit is tormented by the longing to be united with the Lord. The black bile reigns in the left side because it is subject to the vices which are on the left. It has its seat in the spleen because, in its sadness over the delay in returning to its heavenly home, it rejoices in the spleen as in hope ["splen"—"spes"]. As I think I have read, the physicians declare

[131] HUGO DE FOLIETO, in MIGNE, P. L., VOL. CLXXVI, cols. 1185 sqq. As evidence of this familiarity we may quote the following: "Phlegma habet sedem in pulmone. . . . , purgationem habet per os" from Vindician (practically identical with Περὶ κατασκευῆς); "Unde fiunt homines tardi et obliviosi atque somnolenti" from Bede (though the previous traits given in chapter II had included Vindician's "corpore compositi"). The remark that "cholera rubra" "habet sedem in felle . . . respirationem habet per aures" comes from Vindician, and so does "unde fiunt homines iracundi, ingeniosi, acuti, et leves." Statements regarding the melancholic also come from Vindician, even the addition of "aliquando vigilantes" mentioned in the text.

that laughter comes from the spleen; from this proximity it seems to me very understandable that melancholics both laugh and cry. . . . It makes men irascible, according to the words of the Bible, "irascimini et nolite peccare." It makes them timid, because "beatus homo, qui semper est pavidus." Sometimes sleepy and sometimes wakeful means sometimes bowed down by cares, sometimes wakefully directed to heavenly aims. It is like autumn, earth and old age, because in the shape of the earth, it imitates earth's constancy, in the shape of old age, it imitates the worthiness of the old, in the shape of autumn, it imitates the ripeness of fruit. Its exit is from the eyes, for if we free ourselves by confession of the sins that sadden us we are purified ["purgamur"] by tears. . . . Its quantity increases in autumn . . . for the more thou waitest upon ripeness of understanding and age, the more must grow the agony of pain for the commission of sin. . . . Through blood thou hadst the sweetness of love—now, through black bile or "melancholia", hast thou grief for sin.[132]

Though such a "moralised" text, relating every natural fact with a certain element of the doctrine of salvation, was by no means an exception, it has nevertheless a special interest for us, firstly, because it confirms the suspicion that the moralising tendencies of the twelfth century played a large part in the new acceptance of the late classical doctrine of the temperaments, and secondly, because it shows that this urge itself could affect even factual understanding of the traditional data. The characteristics which the basic text (a version of Vindician's treatise) attributed to the melancholic were the most unfavourable possible and were not greatly improved by the addition, to "somniculos", of the qualifying remark "aliquando vigilantes". The allegorical exposition, however, emphasised with the utmost clarity that it was entirely a matter for men's will-power to turn the conditions even of this complexion to advantage. In that case, melancholy could signify retirement from the world and a concentration on heavenly matters; sadness might not only be a punishment for past sins but might also arise from longing for union with God—a very illuminating interpretation of the melancholic's suicidal tendencies; and even the autumnal signs of the zodiac, which corresponded to the melancholy complexion, were to reveal to the soul the possibility of choosing between "bestial" and "rational" life. By "moralising" his text, the author therefore interpreted its purely negative statements in such a way that—with the help of quite un-Aristotelian assumptions—the old ambivalence of the notion of melancholy seemed for an instant to reappear.

[132] Hugo de Folieto, op. cit., col. 1190.

A very different spirit informs St Hildegard's work. She too adopted the contemporary view of the four humoral temperaments,[133] and she too "moralised" this doctrine; that is to say, she moralised it in so far as she considered not only the melancholy humour but all the humours other than the sanguine (and for these she used the general term "flegmata") as the direct consequence of the forbidden apple; in other words, she condensed William of Conches's theory of corruption into a vivid aetiological myth.[134] Only in describing the various types, among which the sanguine now occupied the place of honour unopposed,[135] did this theological conception give way to a more scientific one. But everywhere St Hildegard's descriptions, agreeing, in the main, with those of Isidore, Vindician and Bede, were merged not only with the physiognomic definitions of the medical doctrine of "crases", but also, as far as the three non-sanguine temperaments are concerned, with the complex of symptoms in clinical pathology. Thus there emerged exceptionally vivid full-length portraits, among which that of the melancholic stands out, owing to the especially sinister, in fact almost diabolical, glow emanating from him. That these pictures, though built up from such varied components, should nevertheless possess an unsurpassed and absolutely convincing inner unity can be explained mainly by the fact that their composition centres throughout on one point; they are stated invariably in terms of sexual behaviour. In older literature, in which melancholics had been endowed sometimes with unusual incontinence, sometimes with marked indifference, sexual behaviour had certainly been mentioned, and later treatises habitually devoted a special heading to it.[136] But whereas generally

---

[133] *Causae et curae*, ed. P. Kaiser, Leipzig 1903, pp. 72,8–76,8 (males) and pp. 87,11–89,37 (females).

[134] *Ibid.*, p. 36, 15: "Si enim homo in paradiso permansisset, flegmata in corpore suo non haberet".

[135] *Ibid.*, p. 72, 16 sqq. (*de sanguineis*) " . . . Sed et delectabilem humorem in se habent, qui nec tristitia nec acerbitate oppressus est, et quem acerbitas melancoliae fugit et devitat . . . . Sed cum mulieribus in honestate et fertilitate esse possunt et se etiam ab eis abstinere valent et pulchris et sobriis oculis eas inspiciunt, quoniam, ubi oculi aliorum ad eas velut sagittae sunt, ibi oculi istorum ad ipsas honeste symphonizant, et ubi auditus aliorum quasi validissimus ventus ad ipsas sunt, ibi auditus istorum velut sonum citharae habent . . . , et etiam intelligibilem intellectum habent. Sed qui de his nascuntur, continentes et felices ac utiles et probi in omnibus operibus sunt et sine invidia manent . . . . Et quia in visu, in auditu et in cogitationibus suaves sunt, saepius quam alii aquosam spumam et non coctam de se emittunt . . . . Atque facilius quam quidam alii seu cum semet ipsis seu cum aliis rebus a calore libidinis solvuntur".

[136] See below, pp. 117 sqq. (text).

it was simply a question of different types of temperament distinguishable, among other things, by their sexual behaviour, St Hildegard's account, painted in the liveliest turns of phrase, could really be described as a picture of sexual types conditioned by the temperaments underlying them; and perhaps this very singular and entirely individual viewpoint also accounts for the fact that St Hildegard was the first, and for a long time the only, writer to treat of male and female types separately.[137] Thus, in the *Causae et curae*, we find the various traits whose origin we have described always referred in the last resort to sex, and the temperate and cheerful sanguine persons who "omnia officia sua in honore et sobrio more perficiunt" are contrasted in particular with the melancholy person, a type described with horrible clarity as a sadist driven by hellish desire: one who runs mad if he cannot sate his lust, and, simultaneously hating the women he loves, would kill them by his "wolfish" embraces if he could; and whose children, "absque caritate emissi", are just as unfortunate, warped, shunned and misanthropic as himself, although sometimes, like him, "utiles et prudentes sunt in operibus manuum suarum et libenter operantur."[138]

---

[137] Hitherto no-one had got beyond the already mentioned statement that women in general were "colder and moister" than men, and that therefore men should only be compared with men, women with women. This peculiarity alone of *Causae et curae* must surely silence any doubt as to its authenticity. Against C. SINGER's isolated doubt (*Studies in the History and Method of Science*, Oxford 1917, VOL. I, pp. I sqq.), cf. H. LIEBESCHÜTZ, *Das allegorische Weltbild der Hl. Hildegard v. Bingen* (Studien der Bibliothek Warburg XVII), Leipzig 1930, *passim*.

[138] *Causae et curae*, p. 73,20 sqq. (*de melancholicis*): "Alii autem viri sunt, quorum cerebrum pingue est . . . atque austerum colorem faciei habent, ita quod etiam oculi eorum aliquantum ignei et viperei sunt, et duras et fortes venas habent, quae nigrum et spissum sanguinem in se continent, et grossas et duras carnes habent atque grossa ossa, quae modicam medullam in se tenent, quae tamen tam fortiter ardet, quod cum mulieribus velut animalia et ut viperae incontinentes sunt . . .; sed amari et avari et insipientes sunt et superflui in libidine ac sine moderatione cum mulieribus velut asini; unde si de hac libidine interdum cessaverint, facile insaniam capitis incurrunt, ita quod frenetici erunt. Et cum hanc libidinem in coniunctione mulierum exercent, insaniam capitis non patiuntur; sed tamen amplexio . . . tortuosa atque odiosa et mortifera est velut rapidorum luporum. Quidam autem ex istis . . . libenter cum feminis secundum humanam naturam sunt, sed tamen eas odio habent. Quidam autem femineum sexum devitare possunt, quia feminas non diligunt nec eas habere volunt, sed in cordibus suis tam acres sunt ut leones, et mores ursorum habent; sed tamen utiles et prudentes sunt in operibus manuum suarum atque libenter operantur. Ventus autem delectationis, qui in duo tabernacula praedictorum virorum cadit, tanta immoderatione et tam repentino motu venit, quemadmodum ventus, qui totam domum repente et fortiter movet, et stirpem in tanta tyrannide erigit, quod eadem stirps, quae in florem florere debebat, in acerbitatem vipereorum morum se intorquet . . . , quia suggestio diaboli in libidine virorum istorum ita furit, ut, si possent, feminam in coniunctione hac mortificarent, quoniam nulla opera caritatis et amplexionis in eis sunt. Unde filii aut filiae, quos sic de se producunt, multotiens diabolicam insaniam in vitiis et in moribus suis habent,

(c) The Popular Doctrine of Temperaments in the Later Middle Ages, and its Effects

Roughly at the same time as the composition of the *Medicina animae* and the *Causae et curae* we can again find mention of humoral "characterology" in the school of Salerno (the time given by medical historians varies between about 1160 and about 1180 A.D.), but it is significant that the treatise in which it occurs, the *Flores diaetarum*, attributed to the Frenchman Jean de St Paul (Johannes de Sancto Paulo), was intended merely to provide a somewhat popularly conceived collection of dietetic prescriptions. The section devoted to the doctrine of temperaments served only as a short explanatory introduction[139]; and this section was nothing but an almost literal copy of Vindician's text,[140] a fact which eluded the first editor despite an "eager search".[141] The distribution of the humours among the seasons, hours of the day and ages of man; the account of the exits of the various humours[142]; the principle that the predominance of one humour determines the character, but that its "too great predominance" causes illnesses, which then have to be combated according to the principle "contraria contrariis"—

☞ nam si aegritudo fuerit nata ex sanguine, qui est dulcis, humidus et calidus, ex amaris, siccis et frigidis curabitur[143];

---

quoniam absque caritate emissi sunt. Nam qui de his nascuntur, saepe infelices erunt et tortuosi in omnibus moribus suis, et ideo ab hominibus amari non possunt, nec ipsi mansionem cum hominibus libenter habent, quoniam multis fantasmatibus fatigantur. Si autem cum hominibus manent, odio et invidia et perversis moribus cum eis sunt, et nullum gaudium cum eis habent. Quidam tamen ex his nati prudentes et utiles interdum fiunt, sed tamen in eadem utilitate tam graves et contrarios mores ostendunt, quod inde nec diligi nec honorari possunt, velut ignobiles lapides, qui sine nitore iacent . . . ."

"Melancholica" (p. 89, 7) is the female counterpart of this revolting and pitiable creature. She is of inconstant mind, joyless, shunned by men, sterile (only sanguine and strong men can sometimes get her with child at an advanced age), prone to many diseases, especially melancholy madness, and threatened with death even in otherwise harmless circumstances.

[139] H. J. OSTERMUTH, *Flores diaetarum, eine Salernitanische Nahrungsmitteldiätetik aus dem 12. Jahrhundert, verfasst vermutlich von Johannes de Sancto Paulo*, dissertation, Leipzig 1919.

[140] This had frequently been copied in the eighth, ninth and tenth centuries. (Cf. VINDICIAN, *Epist.*, p. 484, and C. PASCAL, *Poesia latina medievale*, Catania 1907, pp. 117 sqq.). An extract quite independent of Salerno (and with partly different readings) exists in an English manuscript (Oxford, St John's College, Cod. 17), which can be dated 1110–1112 with some certainty. (Cf. C. SINGER, "A Review of the Medical Literature of the Dark Ages, with a New Text of about 1110", in *Proceedings of the Royal Society of Medicine*, VOL. X (1917), pp. 107 sqq.).

[141] OSTERMUTH, op. cit., p. 54; Seyfert has meanwhile seen the connexion.

[142] Cf. p. 58 (text). Pseudo-Soranus has no statements as to the orifices of exit; they first appear in Vindician and in Περὶ κατασκευῆς.

[143] Hence also the emphasis on the qualities of the different foodstuffs and delicacies.

—all this came out of the letter to Pentadius; and the characterological statements (except for the admittedly not unimportant deletion of "somniculosus" in the description of the melancholic) are taken over literally from this text, as they were also in the somewhat earlier *De quattuor humoribus* (see above, p. 104, note 119).

There are no significant additions, and so our interest in these Salernitan texts (the only ones known to us) is limited to two questions. The first is the problem of their historical position—that is to say, whether they were connected at all with any of the scholastic treatises mentioned above, in particular with Hugues de Fouilloi's *Medicina animae*; the second is the problem of their historical consequences. Inasmuch as the excellent researches of the medical historians have unfortunately not yet dealt with scholastic writings,[144] the first question cannot yet be decided; the answer to the second is that these modest Salernitan treatises may be regarded, if not as the basis, nevertheless as the starting point, of a development which was to determine the commonly accepted notion of the nature of the four temperaments in general and of the "complexio melancholica" in particular.

The echoes of Aristotle among the learned scholastics, St Hildegard's visionary descriptions, highly subjective and often horrifying, Hugues de Fouilloi's interpretations expressly designed "ad aedificationem claustralium", the subtle doctrine of the medical schools, always sceptical of, or downright inimical to, a schematic adaptation of pure humoralism—all this was not calculated to become part of the common stock of knowledge or to serve as a guide to medieval man, overshadowed as his existence was by fear of diseases of all kinds. What was needed was

[144] All we know is that both Jean de St Paul and Hugues de Fouilloi must have made direct use of Vindician's text, as each of them includes statements from it which the other omits. Only an edition of the commentaries on Johannitius surviving in several manuscripts but hitherto ignored by scholars (see above, text p. 104) can answer the question as to whether the doctrine of temperaments was not evolved in Salerno in the eleventh century and spread from there. Also deserving of mention is a close accord between one of Hugues de Fouilloi's sentences and a Salernitan fragment rather difficult to place, but probably also dating from the twelfth century (P. GIACOSA, *Magistri Salernitani* . . . , Turin 1901, p. 172). With both passages cf. WILLIAM OF CONCHES, *Philosophia*, IV, 35–36 (MIGNE, P. L., VOL. CLXXII, col. 99); no doubt both are derived from a common source.

Salernitan Fragment	*Medicina animae* (MIGNE, P. L., VOL. CLXXVI, col. 1195):
". . . videmus enim quod colera sui calidi et sicci iuvat appetitivam; melencolia sui frigiditate et sic retentionem; flegma frigida et humida expulsiva; sanguis calidus et humidus digestiva."	" . . . cum ignis calidus et siccus sit virtutis appetitivae, terra frigida et sicca retentivae, aer calidus et humidus digestivae, aqua humida et frigida expulsivae, necessario contingit, ut . . . ."

not so much a full or even a profound picture as one that was clearly defined. Men wished to know how the choleric, the sanguine or the melancholy type could infallibly be recognised, at what times each had to be particularly careful, and in what manner he had to combat the dangers of his particular disposition; and in its original form Vindician's doctrine met this need so thoroughly that it is not surprising that it should have formed a considerable proportion of those easily memorised rules of health that were destined to win great popularity among the wider public.

The mnemonic verses "Largus, amans, hilaris . . .", quoted almost ad nauseam until relatively modern times, must have originated in the thirteenth century, and probably in Salerno. As well as predications of character, these mnemonics contain a number of physiognomic statements concerning hair, colour of skin, and general physical constitution. The lines on the melancholic ran as follows[145]:

> Invidus et tristis, cupidus, dextraeque tenacis,
> non expers fraudis, timidus, luteique coloris.

In the course of the century they were expanded to six lines, and the very widely circulated *Regimen Salernitanum*, which was early translated into the vernacular, incorporated them. These six lines are remarkable for their readmission of two relatively

---

[145] For completeness's sake we include the other couplets, which appear with small and unimportant variations:

Sang. Largus, amans, hilaris, ridens rubeique coloris,
Cantans, carnosus, satis audax atque benignus.

Chol. Hirsutus, fallax, iracundus, prodigus, audax,
Astutus, gracilis, siccus croceique coloris.

Phlegm. Hic somnolentus, piger, in sputamine multus,
Huic hebes est sensus, pinguis facies, color albus.

Cf. also C. PASCAL, *Poesia latina medievale*, Catania 1907, p. 114, and K. SUDHOFF in *Archiv für Geschichte der Medizin*, XII (1920), p. 152. Sudhoff also found the verses in a thirteenth century manuscript with the following additions:

Sang. Consona sunt aer, sanguis, puericia verque.
(calida et humida appetit et petit rubea et turbida)

Chol. Conveniunt estas, ignis coleraque iuventus.
(calida et sicca appetit et non petit rubea et clara)

Mel. Autumpnus, terra, melancholia, senectus.
(frigida et sicca non appetit et non petit alba et clara)

Phlegm. Flecma latex (not "later") et hyemps, senium sibi consociantur
(frigida et humida non appetit et petit alba et turbida)

favourable characteristics of the melancholic, namely, strength of will and capacity for ceaseless study:

> Restat adhuc tristis colerae substantia nigra,
> quae reddit pravos, pertristes, pauca loquentes.
> Hi vigilant studiis, nec mens est dedita somno.
> Servant propositum, sibi nil reputant fore tutum.
> Invidus et tristis, cupidus dextraeque tenacis,
> non expers fraudis, timidus, luteique coloris.[146]

The *Tractatus de complexionibus*, attributed to one Johann von Neuhaus, seems to have been written at the same time or a little later. It combined the now established (and in the melancholic's case unfavourable) character-traits in a detailed and systematic way with physiological and physiognomic observations, as well as with advice about diet. In this way the ideal of a comprehensive and independent compendium of the medieval doctrine of temperaments was realised for the first time.[147] What still remained to be done was to translate this codified doctrine into the vulgar tongue, and this task was tackled with considerable alacrity in

---

[146] Cf. K. Sudhoff, *Geschichte der Medizin*, Leipzig 1922, p. 185, with bibliography.

[147] Werner Seyfert, "Ein Komplexionentext einer Leipziger Inkunabel und seine handschriftliche Herleitung", in *Archiv für Geschichte der Medizin*, XX (1928), pp. 286 sqq. The "complexio melancholica" is described as follows: "Et ideo sicut iste humor est frigidus et siccus, sic ista complexio est frigida et sicca et assimilatur terrae et autumno. Signa huiusmodi complexionis sunt per oppositum signis sanguineae complexionis. Qui est semper tristis et non iocundus, parcus, corporis niger sicut lutum, male digerit, invidus, infidelis, malus, fallax, inconstans animo, tardus in omnibus factis suis, inordinatum habet appetitum, semper diligit esse solus, et claudit oculos semper sicut lepus, quando debet inspicere homines, timidus, non diligit honorabilia, ebes est in ingenio, duras habet carnes, multum bibit, parum comedit, quia non potest digerere ratione frigidi et sicci. Parum appetit quia frigidus, parum vel nihil potest ratione sicci, quia a sicco humidum spermaticum vix vel difficile potest separari. Ideo nota unam doctrinam: si melancholicus vult bene appetere, bona cibaria humida et pulverosa, sive bene piperata comedat, bonum vinum vel potum calidum bibat. Tunc ratione caloris in speciebus augmentatur calor naturalis in ipsis et per consequens appetit. Sed ratione humiditatis humidum incipiet augmentari . . . . Haec sunt signa melancholici. Unde versus:

> Invidus et tristis,
> Cupidus, dextraeque tenacis,
> Non expers fraudis,
> Timidus, luteique coloris.

The concluding statements as to the "immutatio" of the humours by the way of life, by climate and heredity, are also important, especially the introduction of combined types of temperament (Seyfert, op. cit., pp. 296 sqq.). Complexions which have one quality in common can be combined in one and the same individual, so that beside the four pure types there are four mixed types, namely, the sanguine-phlegmatic, the melancholic-choleric, the sanguine-choleric and the melancholic-phlegmatic. This view, complicating an agreeably simple system again, did not at once influence the popular doctrine of temperaments, but reappeared in the popular philosophy of later centuries; cf. among others J. H. Becker, *Kurtzer doch gründlicher Unterricht von den Temperamenten*. Bremen 1739, ch. 6: "Von denen zusammengesetzten oder vermischten Temperamenten."

the fourteenth and fifteenth centuries. Apart from the mere translation of the *Regimen Salernitanum* and other verses, some of which described the melancholic as even more repulsive,[148] there is the rhyming jingle (1325) by the Low German Everhard of Wampen, which describes the melancholy complexion expressly as the "snodeste"[149]; and this was followed by a vast number of cheap manuscripts, broadsheets, almanacs, and popular pamphlets on the subject of the complexions. Generally based on Johann von Neuhaus's treatise, they bring to the humblest cottage not merely those definitions (handed down from late antiquity) of the types of temperament, but the still more venerable conception of that mysterious correspondence between elements, humours, seasons and ages of man, in a rough and often somewhat garbled form. Even the last great transformation in the medieval notion of nature, which expressed itself in the medical field as a recourse to iatromathematics, was reflected in these coarsely but powerfully illustrated productions; for they included the

---

148 We quote two Italian stanzas:

(a) LIONARDO DATI, *Sfera* (London, Brit. Mus., Add. MS 23329, fol. 5r; New York, Pierpont Morgan Library, MS 721; and Cod. Vat. Chis., M. VII. 148, fol. 12r):

"Malinconia è di tucte peggiore,
palidi et magri son sanza letitia
color chabbondan in cotale homore,
disposti a tucte larte dauaritia
et a molti pensieri sempre hanno il core,
son solitari et di poca amicitia,
quartane so le febbri malinconiche,
che piu che tucte l'altre sono croniche."

(b) F. GIOVANNI M. TOLOSANI, *La Nuova Sfera*, Florence 1514:

"Il maninconico è freddo ed asciutto
Come la terra, e sempre ha il core amaro,
Resta pallido e magro e par distrutto
Ed e tenace, cupido ed avaro:
E vive in pianto, pena, doglia e lutto,
Ed a sua infermita non è riparo:
È solitario e pare un uom monastico,
Senz' amicizia, ed ha ingegno fantastico."

These texts were reprinted together, Florence 1859. See also the Carnival Song published by ERNST STEINMANN (*Das Geheimnis der Medicigräber Michel Angelos*, Leipzig 1906, p. 79):

"Il quarto loco tien Maninconia
A cui Saturno eccelso è conjugato.
La terra in compagnia
Coll' Autunno Natura gli ha dato:
Chi è di sua Signoria,
Son magri, avari, timidi e sdegnosi,
Pallidi, solitar, gravi e pensosi."

149 EVERHARD VON WAMPEN, *Spiegel der Natur*, ed. Erik Björkman, Upsala Universitets Årsskrift, Upsala 1902, p. 12.

connexion between earthly life and the course of the stars, so that each temperament appeared both in word and picture under the dominion of certain constellations or planets (see PLATES 78, 144): PL. 52

God has given me unduly
In my nature melancholy.
Like the earth both cold and dry,
Black of skin with gait awry,
Hostile, mean, ambitious, sly,
Sullen, crafty, false and shy.
No love for fame or woman have I;
In Saturn and autumn the fault doth lie.[150]

Another description reads:

The ingredients which men have in their nature are four. Some have two, some three, some four, but the one which a man has most of takes the upper hand, and no man has only one. But let us first write of the melancholic. He resembles the earth, for the earth is cold and dry; and his signs are the Bull, the Ram, and the Virgin, and though cold and dry predominate in him, yet he inclines to those same signs in all things. He is also like to the autumn, for that is cold and dry. He is also like to age, for when a man grows old the labour of his days of sickness begins, and thus it is when a man becomes seventy years old. But if a man is in good health when he is seventy years old, yet has he still to labour and suffer pain. Secondly, note and perceive that the melancholic is timid and not thirsty, for he lacks something belonging to thirst, and that is warmth. And that warmth is a property of thirst can be seen in the hot beasts, such as the lion. Thirdly, it should be observed that the melancholic is lazy and of slow movement, for he is of a cold nature: for the cold which is in him makes the limbs slow and halts the limbs so that they become no longer supple, just as warmth causes men's limbs to run swiftly. Fourthly, it should be observed that the melancholic, because of his property of coldness, is hostile, sad, forgetful, indolent and clumsy. Fifthly, the melancholic, owing to his properties has but rare and weak desires, and is not much

---

[150] Thus the caption to the Zürich broadsheet reproduced in PLATE 78 reads:

"Gott hat gegeben vngehure
mir melancholicus eyn nature
glich der erden kalt vnd druge
ertuar haut swartz vnd ungefuge
karch hessig girich vnd bose
unmudig falsch lois vnd blode
Ich enachten eren noch frowen hulde
Saturnus vnd herbst habent die schulde."

In the Munich manuscript, clm. 4394, which shows the four complexions as riders (like our PLATE 81), the various temperaments are subordinated not to the planets but only to the zodiacal signs of the Ram, the Bull, and the Virgin (similarly, among others, in MS lat. 14068 of the Bibl. Nationale, dating from about 1450).

given to liking. He desires little owing to his sadness, and likes little owing to his coldness. He also resembles the planet Mars and the sun.[151]

But not only was the opinion of the readers of such almanacs and pamphlets determined by this overwhelmingly negative presentation of the melancholic's nature, only softened here and there by recognition of his good memory, penitence, and love of study, but so powerful was the influence of the new trend inspired by Vindician, reinforced as it was by popular scientific literature

---

[151] *Teutscher Kalender*, Augsburg 1495 (H. SCHÖNSPERGER), fol. g.5^{r-v}. The mention of Mars and the sun instead of Saturn as the melancholic's planets may be due to a misunderstanding. Among other texts of this type, we may mention (1) the relevant sections in the yearly *Königspergerschen Kalender* which, according to Giehlow, can be traced back in manuscript form to 1471 (Vienna, Nationalbibliothek, MS 5486, GIEHLOW (1903), p. 32); (2) the very similar *In diesem biechlein wirt erfunden von complexion der menschen . . .* , Augsburg, H. Schönsperger, 1512, ch. II, fol. a. 3^{v} ("Melancolici seind kalt vnnd trucken gleich der Erden vnd dem herbst. vnnd ist die vnedelst complexion. Welicher mensch der natur ⟨ist⟩, ist karg, geytzig, traurig, aschenfar, träg, vntrew, forchtsam, böszbegierig, eerliche ding nit liebhabend, blöd seinn, vnweiss, hert flaisch, trinckt vil vnnd iszt wenig, mag nit vil vnkeusch sein, hatt ain bösen magen"); approximately the same in English, Oxford, Bodl., Ashmol. MS 396, fol. 90^{r-v} (melancholy as "the worst complexion of all"); and finally (3) the frequently reprinted *Compost et kalendrier des bergiers*, Paris 1493, fol. l 2^{v} ("Le melencolique a nature de terre sec et froit; si est triste, pesant, conuoiteux, eschers, mesdisant, suspicionneux, malicieux, paresseux. A vin de porceau cest a dire quant a bien beu ne quiert qua dormir ou sommeiller. Naturellement ayme robe de noire couleur") translated word for word in the *Calendar of Shepherdes*, Paris 1503 (ed. H. O. Sommer, London 1892, fol. K7^{r}). Clm. 4394 repeats, *inter alia*, the Salernitan verses, while the broadsheet corresponding to its illustrations in the Gotha Museum (our PLATE 81) contains the following lines:

"Dabey kent melancolicus
Vnd der hat kainen lust alsus;
Vor zeytlich sorg zu kayner freud
Mit seinem gut mag er nit geud;
Klainhait von silber vnd das golt
Vnd schon geticht, das hat er holt.
Darzu ist er neydig vnd kargk
Vnd geitzikait er nye verbargk,
Doch ist er dechtig vnd auch weys,
Wie er sein sach it furt zu preys.
Der erden art sagt sein natur
Vnd plod ist er, ein plaich figur.
Gros lieb hat er zu schatz vnd kunst,
Wem er das givt des hat er gunst.
Trucken vnd kalt ist sein natur,
Er ist gern allein in seiner maur,
Vnd ist sorckfeltig seines guts,
Darumb ist er eins schwern mutz.
Sein harm der ist rot gefar
Sagen die maister vns für war."

The fact that the melancholic is credited sometimes with indifference to sleep, sometimes, on the contrary, with a liking for much sleep, has its medical origins in the dual function ascribed to the black bile with regard to sleeping and waking (cf. CONSTANTINUS AFRICANUS, *Opera*, VOL. I, p. 288: "Cholera autem nigra in actione sua duplex est circa somnum et vigilias. Quae enim dominatur essentialiter, cerebrum deprimens, ex fumi multitudine nimium facit dormire. Quod si cum suis qualitatibus faciat, vel cum qualitate faciet fere incensa, unde

afterwards, that even poets[152] and thinkers of a high order were unable to rid themselves of it. We already know that ideas of the melancholic held by Albertus Magnus and Pietro d'Abano were in full accord with that which governed the literature on temperaments as first set out in the *Flores diaetarum*, and that they could only rescue the main thesis in Problem XXX, I, by postulating a special type of melancholy derived from "melancholia adusta".[153] The greatest fifteenth-century philosopher, Nicholas of Cusa, may be cited, too, as witness to the general acceptance of this notion. In his early work *De concordantia catholica*, which he prepared for the Council of Basle in 1433, he paints a powerful picture: the state is conceived as a being with a soul, a living body whose limbs, in a comparison traced down to the last detail, correspond to the limbs of men. The end of this work runs:

> The king therefore must be a luteplayer, who well understands . . . how to preserve harmony . . . and how to tune the string neither too high nor too low, so that through the combined tone of them all a companionable harmony sounds. . . . For that reason it is the business of the ruler, like a wise doctor, duly to keep the body of the state healthy, so that the vital

---

naturaliter fit nigra, vel cum iam fere incensa. Nigra autem naturaliter somnum facit. Fere incensa qualitas facit vigilias, quia pungit cerebrum et desiccat"). Thus EOBANUS HESSUS (*Farragines*, Schwäb. Hall 1539, VOL. II, fol. 82^v) writes in full accordance with the calender texts:

"Anxius et niger est, timet omnia tristia, dormit,
Mole sua bilis quem nimis atra premit."

At the same time, this existence of contraries expresses the polarity inherent in melancholy.

152 MATFRE ERMENGAUD, *Le Breviari d'Amor*, ed. G. Azaïs, Béziers 1862, lines 7779–7854. The poet (almost as in Aristotle's doctrine of self-control, see above, p. 35, note 75) considers avarice and irritability relatively more pardonable in the melancholic than in the sanguinic, though he maintains that the former, too, can control his passions by the exercise of his free will:

v. 7836 "Que non es tan grans lo peccatz
D'un home malincolios,
Si es avars o es iros,
Que d'un sanguini seria; . . . ."
v. 7852 "Pero excusatz non es ges,
Quar Dieus a dat poder e sen
De restrenger lo movemen."

153 See above, p. 70 sq. (text). As is well known, Albertus Magnus deals with the doctrine of temperaments (*Liber de animalibus*, ed. H. Stadler, Münster i.W. 1916–20, VOL. II, p. 1304, §§ 59 sqq.) as a universal law governing man and beast, so that his remarks always apply both to certain kinds of animals and to certain human types (for which reason he attributes great influence to the quality of the blood). Here one can see a synthesis of Aristotle's comprehensive idea of nature, and the "zoological" doctrine of temperaments brought to the fore by William of Conches. With regard to physiognomics, too, (short or tall, fat or thin), Albertus's characteristics correspond exactly with William of Conches's statements quoted above, pp. 102 sqq. (text).

spirit, "per proportionabile medium", can be at one with it. He may observe that one of the four vital humours goes beyond or lags behind right proportion in the combination, and that thereby the body is estranged from its proper combination. This may occur through an excess of covetous melancholy, which gives rise to the most varied pestilences in the body—usury, fraud, deceit, theft, pillage, and all the arts by which great riches are won not by work but only by a certain deceitful craftiness, which can never exist without doing harm to the State; or again it may occur through choleric dissensions, wars, factions and schisms, or through sanguine ostentation, excess, debauchery and suchlike, or through phlegmatic sloth in all good works, in the daily toil for existence and in the defence of the fatherland. Then the body becomes paralysed, feverish, swollen up or bled dry; then must he seek a remedy, consult books, and give ear to the wisest State physicians; and when he has found a remedy he must bring it forth and test it by means of taste, sight and smell . . . .[154]

Here we must certainly take account of the fact that the context requires an elaborately worked-out exposition of the unfavourable characteristics of all the temperaments alike. Yet not only the expressions used, but the whole construction of Nicholas of Cusa's sentences, make it plain that the indolence of the phlegmatic, the contentiousness of the choleric and the ostentation and voluptuousness of the sanguine were in his view far less weighty matters than the "pestilential" vices of the avaricious, thievish, usurious, pillaging melancholic with his ill-gotten gains, whose picture seems to have been drawn with the most lively repugnance.

The doctrine of temperaments may be described as one of the longest-lived and in some respects one of the most conservative parts of modern culture. Though superficially affected, it was not fundamentally altered either by the renascence of the 'Aristotelian' notion of genius, which we shall describe in Part III

---

[154] Nicholas of Cusa, *Opera*, Paris 1514, vol. iii, fol. 75ᵛ: "Debet itaque citharoedus rex esse, et qui bene sciat . . . concordiam observare . . . nec nimis nec minus extendere, ut communis concordantia per omnium harmoniam resonet. Sit itaque cura imperatori, ut recte ad modum experti medici corpus in sanitate servet, ut vitalis spiritus recte per proportionabile medium sibi iungi possit. Nam dum viderit aliquam ex quattuor complexionibus excedere a temperamento vel deficere, et propterea corpus distemperatum, vel propter abundantem avaritiosam melancoliam, quae pestes in corpus seminavit varias, usuram, fraudes, deceptiones, furta, rapinas et omnes eas artes, quibus absque labore cum quadam calliditate deceptoria divitiae magnae quaeruntur, quod absque laesione Reipublicae fieri nequit, vel si ex colericis dissidiis, bellis, discisionibus et divisionibus, aut sanguineis pompositatibus, luxuriis, comessationibus et similibus, aut flegmaticis acediositatibus in cunctis bonis operibus, et lucrandi victus causa, et ob patriae tutelam laboribus corpus torpescere, febrescere, tumescere vel exinaniri: quaerat medelam et audiat libros et consilia peritissimorum quorundam Reipublicae medicorum. Receptam conficiat, tentet per gustum, visum, et odoratum . . ."

of this work, nor by the fact that the humoral explanation of the temperaments was ultimately reduced to a mere outline of characters and emotions. In a commentary on the *Regimen Salernitanum*[155] printed in 1559, for instance, the words "Hi vigilant studiis" were made the point of departure for a long and enthusiastic description of the contemplative life. Ovid, Quintilian,[156] Cicero and, of course, Aristotle, were cited, and the advantages of the melancholic disposition were highly praised, while the other purely negative statements in the text were no less eagerly defended and substantiated. This attitude remained typical of even the most scholarly treatises on the temperaments.[157]

In the popular philosophic writings of the eighteenth century the character portraits first painted in later antiquity still preserve a stability which they have not entirely lost even to-day. Buddeus,[158] J. H. Becker,[159] G. E. Stahl,[160] Appelius,[161] and the rest, were all content merely to fill in the old contours with new colours; while elaborating the familiar traits with regard to the "inclinations of the human mind, manners, and dispositions", they laid a stronger emphasis on the psychology of races, and, as we should expect, devoted more space to what they called "moral and historical" aspects. They were hardly affected at all by the great process of transformation which the picture of the melancholic had undergone during the Renaissance, and which had had such a significant effect in other realms of life and literature[162]; all of them continued immovably to maintain the fundamental inferiority of the melancholy temperament, the most obstinate being, perhaps, Appelius, who blamed it for the avarice, betrayal and suicide of Judas, as well as for the "despicable timidity" of the Jews as a race; and all of them adopted the view

155 ANON., *Conservandae sanitatis praecepta saluberrima*, Frankfurt 1559, fol. 248.

156 Quintilian's remarks as to the favourable effects of silence and solitude on mental work (*Inst. Or.* X, 3, 22 sqq.) have been frequently quoted in this connexion.

157 Cf. among many other examples: LEVINUS LEMNIUS, *De habitu et constitutione corporis quam Graeci κρᾶσιν, triviales complexionem vocant*, Antwerp 1561, and T. WALKINGTON, *The Optick Glasse of Humors*, London, 1607.

158 *Elementa philosophiae practicae*, editio novissima auctior et correctior, Halle 1727, ch. II, sect. III, §§ 9–14, pp. 66–68.

159 J. H. BECKER, *Kurtzer doch gründlicher Unterricht von den Temperamenten*, Bremen 1739.

160 *Neu-verbesserte Lehre von den Temperamenten*, translated by G. H. Ulau, Leipzig 1716; new and enlarged edition, Leipzig 1734.

161 J. W. APPELIUS, *Historisch-moralischer Entwurff der Temperamenten*, 2nd edition, 1737.

162 See below, pp. 249 sqq. (text).

that each temperament in turn governed the stages of man's life.[163]

Even the magnificent description in Kant's *Observations on the Sense of the Beautiful and the Sublime*[164] may be included in this category. In material matters, Kant follows tradition entirely. When he says, "As in the phlegmatic combination no ingredients of the sublime or the beautiful generally appear in a particularly noticeable degree, this type of temperament does not belong to the context of our reflections", Kant still echoes the Galenic "no power to determine character". But just as Vindician's text had once received a theological interpretation by Hugues de Fouilloi, so does Kant now give an aesthetic and ethical interpretation to the traditional doctrine of temperaments. He does even more; for through his attitude to the question with which we are here concerned he breaks down the rigid scheme at a decisive point. Kant was not untouched, perhaps, by the Renaissance view, but it was rather, in all probability, a deep feeling of sympathy which led him to endow the melancholy character, limited though its traits were by tradition, with the stamp of the "sublime", and, point by point, to interpret every trait of melancholy as the expression of a great moral consciousness. The melancholic and no other represented Kant's notion of virtue ("True virtue based on principle has something in it which seems to accord best with the melancholy disposition in its more moderate sense"). The melancholic became in this way the possessor of an ideal of freedom, and the chains with which the sick melancholic used to be bound became the symbol of all the chains which free men abhor,[165] no matter whether they shackle the slave, or decorate the courtier. The "sadness without cause" was based on his possession of a moral scale which destroyed personal happiness by the merciless revelation of his own and others' worthlessness.

---

[163] Generally in the following order: Phlegma, Sanguis, Cholera rubra, Melancholia (and, possibly, again Phlegma). Casanova, too, at 72 years of age, writes in the preface to his *Memoirs*: "I have had every temperament one after the other, the phlegmatic in childhood, the sanguine in youth, and later the choleric, and now I have the melancholic which will probably not leave me any more."

A diet for the different temperaments even survived in the fashionable beauty magazines of the early nineteenth century, about which Erica Strauss wrote in *Querschnitt*, Sept. 1928.

[164] Part II, pp. 27 sqq. of the 2nd edn., Königsberg 1766; *Werke*, ed. E. Cassirer, VOL. II, Berlin 1912, pp. 258–64.

[165] With this, cf. WALTER BENJAMIN, *Ursprung des deutschen Trauerspiels*, Berlin 1928, p. 141.

He whose emotions incline him to melancholy does not have that name because he is afflicted with gloomy depression as being robbed of life's joys, but because his sensibilities, when strung above a certain pitch, or when for some reason given a wrong direction, attain to this condition more easily than to any other. In particular, he has a sense of the sublime. . . . All the sensations of the sublime possess for him a greater fascination than the transient charms of the beautiful. . . . He is constant. For that reason he subjects his sensibilities to principles. . . . The man of melancholic disposition cares little for the opinions of others . . . for that reason he depends solely on his own judgment. Because impulses assume in him the nature of principles, he is not easily distracted; his constancy, too, turns sometimes into obstinacy. . . . Friendship is sublime and he is therefore susceptible to it. He may lose a fickle friend, but the latter will not lose him as quickly. Even the remembrance of a severed friendship remains precious to him. . . . He is a good guardian of his own and others' secrets. Truth is sublime, and he hates lies or deceit. He has a deep conviction of the nobility of human nature. . . . He will not suffer base subjection: instead, he breathes freedom in a noble breast. From the courtier's golden chains to the heavy irons of the galley-slave, all fetters are abhorrent to him. He is a stern judge of himself and of others; and is not seldom weary both of himself and of the world.[166]

[166] Kant describes the well-known darker aspects of the melancholy temperament too quite in accord with tradition. He considers them as "degenerate forms" and dissociates them from what he considers the essentially significant characteristics.

PART II

Saturn, Star of Melancholy

Les sages d'autrefois, qui valaient bien ceux-ci,
Crurent—et c'est un point encor mal éclairci—
Lire au ciel les bonheurs ainsi que les désastres,
Et que chaque âme était liée à l'un des astres.
(On a beaucoup raillé, sans penser que souvent
Le rire est ridicule autant que décevant,
Cette explication du mystère nocturne.)
Or ceux-là qui sont nés sous le signe Saturne,
Fauve planète, chère aux nécromanciens,
Ont entre tous, d'après les grimoires anciens,
Bonne part de malheur et bonne part de bile.
L'imagination, inquiète et débile,
Vient rendre nul en eux l'effort de la Raison.
Dans leurs veines, le sang, subtile comme un poison,
Brûlant comme une lave, et rare, coule et roule
En dévorant leur triste idéal qui s'écroule.
Tels les saturniens doivent souffrir et tels
Mourir—en admettant que nous soyons mortels—,
Leur plan de vie étant dessiné ligne à ligne
Par la logique d'une influence maligne.

PAUL VERLAINE

Chapter I

SATURN IN THE LITERARY TRADITION

I. THE NOTION OF SATURN IN ARABIC ASTROLOGY

Nearly all the writers of the later Middle Ages and the Renaissance considered it an incontestable fact that melancholy, whether morbid or natural, stood in some special relationship to Saturn, and that the latter was really to blame for the melancholic's unfortunate character and destiny.[1] To-day, a sombre and melancholy disposition is still described as "Saturnine"[2]; and, as Karl Giehlow has incontrovertibly proved, for a sixteenth-century artist the task of drawing a melancholic was equivalent to drawing a child of Saturn.[3]

This close and fundamental connexion between melancholy and Saturn, together with the corresponding connexions between the sanguine disposition and Jupiter, the choleric and Mars, and the phlegmatic and the moon or Venus, seems to have been definitely established for the first time by certain Arab writers of the ninth century. In Book IV of his *Introduction to Astrology*, Abû-Ma'šar (who died in 885) inveighs against a certain primitive "analysis of the spectrum," which he attributes not to one author[4] but to the "universitas astrologorum" and which endeavoured to relate the planets to the humours. According to this doctrine, stars, elements and humours could and must be linked with their corresponding colours. The colour of black bile is dark and black;

---

[1] Thus the rhymed caption (quoted above, text p. 117) to the woodcut in PLATE 78.

[2] Cf. also the Portuguese "soturno," dark, unfriendly, and the group of words of Romance origin collected by G. KÖRTING, *Lateinisch-romanisches Wörterbuch*, 2nd edn., Paderborn 1901.

[3] GIEHLOW (1904), p. 67.

[4] Abû Ma'šar, indeed, occasionally quotes Apollonius in this connexion: "De saporibus. Secundum Appollinem [!] humiditas in natura sua est suavis saporis, siccitas vero amari" (from the manuscript quoted in the following note, fol. 32 v). The Latin translation of the so-called Apollonius in Cod. Paris, Bibl. Nat., MS lat. 13951 does contain this statement (cf. fol. 15r and fol. 27r), but we could not find the planet-spectrum theory there. For Apollonius, see J. RUSKA, *Tabula Smaragdina* (Heidelberger Akten der v. Portheim-Stiftung, XVI), Heidelberg 1926, *passim*; for planet-spectrum theories cf. BBG, 44 sq.

its nature, like that of the earth, is cold and dry. But the colour of Saturn also is dark and black, so that Saturn too must be cold and dry by nature. Similarly red Mars is coupled with red bile, Jupiter with blood, and the moon with phlegm.[5] As we learn from Abû Ma'šar's detailed polemics, this hypothesis of the colours and correlation of planets with humours must have been regarded as a proven theory in certain circles in the middle of the ninth century. Abû Ma'šar himself attributes to the various planets the qualities corresponding to the temperaments (cold and moist, and so forth), and credits them with an influence on physique, emotions and character largely corresponding to the effects of the humours; but he does not relate them systematically to the four humours.[6] How widespread this correlation must have been in the east among Abû Ma'šar's predecessors and immediate successors, however, can be seen even from the medieval Latin translations which are our only source of information. Abû Ma'šar's master, Al-Kindî (born in the early part of the ninth century), distinguishes the four parts of the circle of the day according to the four humours. Men born in the first quadrant from the east point to the centre of the sky are sanguine, in the

[5] Here, as always, Johannes Hispalensis's translation is more detailed than Dalmata's. We quote from the manuscript in Corpus Christi College, Oxford, No. 248, fol. 33ra: "colere nigre color est fuscus, id est grisius, et eius sapor acredo. Natura quoque eius frigida sicca, proprietas vero eius est siccitas et opus eius retentio rerum; et hoc congruit nature terre et proprietati eius. Hoc est quod narraverunt ex naturis elementorum et commixtionum . . . . Percipiuntur enim nature eorum [i.e. planetarum] atque colores per concordiam caloris eorum cum colore harum IIII commixtionum, quia cuius planete colorem videmus concordare cum colore harum commixtionum, scimus quod natura eiusdem planete sit concors nature eiusdem elementi, cui ipsa commixtio concordat per naturam ac proprietatem. Et si fuerit color planete diversus a colore IIII commixtionum, commiscemus ei, id est querimus ei (33rb) complexionem et ponemus natura [!] eius, secundum quod congruit eius colori, dum sit commixtio. Dixerunt itaque, cum sit color ⟨colere⟩ nigre fuscus et niger, natura quoque eius ut natura terre frigida et sicca. Color uero Saturni est fuscus et niger; novimus quod esset ei concors per naturam frigoris et siccitatis et per proprietatem eius atque opus . . . ; colorem colere rufe similem colori ignis . . . colorque Martis similis colori eorum . . . natura eius [i.e. Solis] sit calida sicca, quemadmodum indicauimus de natura Martis . . . propter croceum colorem, qui est in ea [i. e. Venere], qui est similis colori colere rufe, retulimus eam ad calorem, et ob albedinem . . . assimilatur colori flegmatis . . . natura Iouis sit calida humida temperata et hoc congruit nature sanguinis et aeris; . . . quod natura lune sit frigida humida, et hoc congruit nature flegmatis . . ."

[6] Johannes Hispalensis's Latin translation of Abû Ma'šar, which is generally more faithful than Hermannus Dalmata's, differs from the latter in introducing the word "melancholica" into the description of Saturn's nature, but this interpretation, though understandable for the twelfth century, is not justified by the original Arabic text. Abû Bakr (*Albubatris Liber Genethliacus*, Nuremberg 1540; cf. George Sarton, *Introduction to the History of Science*, vol. I, Baltimore 1927, p. 603), who flourished probably in the third quarter of the ninth century, countenanced a systematic correlation between humours and planets as little as did Abû Ma'šar.

second choleric, in the third melancholic, in the fourth phlegmatic.[7] The very remarkable *Liber Aristotelis de cclv Indorum voluminibus*, translated by Hugo Sanctallensis, contains a similar account; it actually names the four planets corresponding to the humours, Venus, Mars, Saturn and the moon,[8] and gives a detailed theoretic justification of these correlations.

Moreover, even outside the strictly astrological field, we find this relationship established in principle at the end of the tenth century among the so-called "Faithful of Basra", or "Pure Brothers". Admittedly the phlegm is not yet included in the system as it is here described. Of Saturn they say:

> The spleen occupies the same position in the body as Saturn in the world. For Saturn with its rays sends forth transcendent powers which penetrate into every part of the world. Through these, forms adhere to, and remain in, matter. Even so goes forth from the spleen the power of the black bile, which is cold and dry and it flows with the blood through the

---

[7] "Alkyndus", Oxford, Bodl., Ashm. MS 369, fol. 86[rb]: "Super omnem item horam . . . circulus quadripartite secernitur . . . prima ab horientis gradu ad celi medium nascens, sanguinea, uernalis et mascula dicitur. Secunda quidem pars a celi medio ad occidentis gradum crescens, ignea, estivalis, colerica atqua feminea. Tercius quidem quadrans a VII. gradu ad quartum procensus [!] . . . melancolicus, decrepitus et masculus et autumnalis. Quartus autem quadrans spacium a quarto in orientem optinens, senilis, flegmaticus, finiens, hyemalis, femineus existit."

[8] Oxford, Bodl., Digby MS 159, fol. 5[v]: "Nunquam enim ipsum sperma in orificium descendit matricis, nec planta terre inseritur, nisi iuxta ipsius stelle ortus [*suprascr.* uel ascensus] vel naturam, que ipsius hore temperanciam et proprietatem deo cooperante vendicauit. Nam quociens in prima trium diurnalium horarum et sub vernali signo sperma matrici commendatur et sub stellarum eiusdem generis ac proprietatis de trigono vel opposicione ad ipsum respectu nascitur vir precipue sub Veneris potencia, in propria lege summus ac excellens, honeste forme, omni utilitate despecta, risibus, iocis deditus et ocio incestus [!]. Cuius tandem natura mens atque uoluntas et operacio, ad eius complexionis et temperantie modum necessario referuntur. Cuius enim conceptus sive plantatio in sequentibus tribus horis et sub signis igneis, sub Martis precipue potestate facta erit, dum stelle (prout supradictum est) ipsum respiciant, nascetur vir colericus, audax, strenuus, promtus, impacabilis [fol. 6[r]] iracundie: Huius rursum doctrinam, naturam, salutem, morbum, animos atque negocia Marti necessario similari oportet. Si vero in his, que secuntur, tribus quid conceptum uel plantatum sit, sub Saturni potissimum potestate et in signo terreo, melancolicus erit, corpulentus, iracundus, fraudulentus deoque in actibus suis contrarius. Sicque color, natura, salus atque infirmitas, animus et operacio ab eiusdem ordine non recedunt. In reliquis demum tribus, que videlicet diem terminant, plantacio sive conceptio facta maxime luna dominante et signo aquatico magnum, carneum, corpulentum exibent atque flegmaticum, Sed et color ac natura, salus atque egritudo, et quicquid ex eo est ad lune temperantiam necessario accedunt . . . . Deus enim sub prime creacionis ortu, dum ea indissolubili nature nexu attributo ad esse produxit, VII stellarum [Glossa: id est planetarum] atque XII signorum [Glossa: id est signorum] nature ac proprietati omni similitudine relata placuit subiugari . . . [fol. 6[v]] bonum porro atque malum, laudem, vituperium, fortunam utramque, sponsalicia, sobolem filiorum, servos, itinera, que mortis sit occasio, legem, colores, naturas, operationes, humores IIII—sanguinem dico, melancoliam, coleram et flegma—et quicquid ex his procreatur, mundane molis conditor deus VII planetarum et signorum XII nature sua providencia naturaliter subdidit."

veins into every part of the body, and through it the blood coagulates and the parts adhere to one another.[9]

So far as they reached the west at all, the works of these authors and the theses of those masters against whom Abû Ma'šar's polemics were directed, did not have any considerable influence in Europe. For the west, the decisive event was the translation of Alcabitius. In his widely known *Introductorium maius*, with its full commentary, we find a connexion traced between the humours and Saturn, Jupiter, Mars and the moon respectively.[10] Living two generations after Abû Ma'šar, Alcabitius in general agrees closely with him, but he transmits the account of the planets' effects in a somewhat richer and more systematically arranged form. We give here the texts on Saturn of Abû Ma'šar and Alcabitius from the Leiden[11] and Oxford[12] manuscripts.

ABÛ MA'ŠAR (Leiden, Cod. or. 47):

With regard to Saturn, his nature is cold, dry, bitter, black, dark, violent and harsh. Sometimes too it is cold, moist, heavy, and of stinking wind. He eats much and is honest in friendship. He presides over works of moisture, husbandry, and farming; over owners of land, works of construction on estates, lakes and rivers; over measuring things, division of estates, land and much property, and estates with their wealth; over avarice and bitter poverty; over domiciles, sea travel and long sojourn abroad; over far, evil journeys; over blindness, corruption, hatred, guile, craftiness, fraud, disloyalty, harmfulness (or harm); over being withdrawn into one's self; over loneliness and unsociability; over ostentation, lust for power, pride, haughtiness and boastfulness; over those who enslave men and rule,

---

[9] Thus in F. DIETERICI's version, *Die Anthropologie der Araber*, Leipzig 1871, p. 61; very similarly in the same writer's *Die Philosophie der Araber im 10. Jahrhundert*, PT. II (*Mikrokosmos*), Leipzig 1879, p. 74. Corresponding connexions exist between Jupiter and the liver from which the blood flows harmonising all the elements of the body, between Mars and the yellow bile, the moon and the lungs, Mercury and the brain, the sun and the heart, Venus and the stomach.

[10] In the prints of Alcabitius of 1485, 1491 and 1521 "flegma" is misprinted as "falsa". Abenragel, who wrote during the first half of the eleventh century (ALBOHAZEN HALY FILIUS ABENRAGELIS, *Preclarissimus liber completus in judiciis astrorum*, Venice 1503, fol. 3v) mentions only (in describing the nature of Saturn): "assimilatur melancolie que gubernatur de omnibus humoribus et nullus de ea." The express inclusion of the phlegm, which is needed to complete the classification, is also found in a Byzantine treatise, based on a Persian or Arabic source of unknown date; cf. *Cat. astr. Gr.*, VOL. VII, p. 96; here, however, the phlegm belongs to the moon as well as to Venus. In western sources (cf. below, text pp. 188 sqq.) this complete classification is the rule rather than the exception.

[11] Leiden, University Library, Cod. or. 47, fol. 255r.

[12] Oxford, Bodl., Marsh MS 663, fol. 16r.

as well as over every deed of wickedness, force, tyranny and rage; over fighters (?); over bondage, imprisonment, distraint, fettering, honest speech, caution, reflection, understanding, testing, pondering . . . over much thinking, aversion from speech and importunity, over persistence in a course. He is scarcely ever angry, but when he becomes angry he is not master of himself; he wishes no one well; he further presides over old men and surly people; over fear, reverses of fortune, cares, fits of sadness, writing, confusion, . . . affliction, hard life, straits, loss, deaths, inheritances, dirges and orphanage; over old things, grandfathers, fathers, elder brothers, servants, grooms, misers and people whose attention women require (?); over those covered with shame, thieves, gravediggers, corpse robbers, tanners and over people who count things; over magic and rebels; over low-born people and eunuchs; over long reflection and little speech; over secrets, while no one knows what is in him and neither does he show it, though he knows of every dark occasion. He presides over self-destruction and matters of boredom.

ALCABITIUS (Bodl. Marsh 663):

He is bad, masculine, in daytime cold, dry, melancholy (literally: blackish of mixture), presides over fathers . . . over old age and dotage and over elder brothers and ancestors, and over honesty in speech and in love, and absence of impulses . . . , and over experience of things, keeping of a secret and its concealment, much eating and silence, deliberate dealings, over understanding and the faculty of distinguishing; he presides over lasting, permanent things, like land, husbandry, farming, tilling the land, and over respectable professions which have to do with water like the commanding of ships and their management, and the administration of work, and shrewdness and fatigue, pride, kings' servants, the pious among the peoples, the weak, slaves, the worried, the low born, the heavy, the dead, magicians, demons, devils and people of ill-fame—all this when his condition is good. But when he is evil he presides over hatred, obstinacy, care, grief, lamenting, weeping, evil opinion, suspicion between men; and he is timid, easily confused, obdurate, fearful, given to anger, wishes no one well; further, he presides over miserly gains, over old and impossible things, far travels, long absence, great poverty, avarice towards himself and others, employment of deceit, want, astonishment, preference for solitude, wishes that kill by cruelty, prison, difficulties, guile, inheritances, causes of death. He also presides over vulgar trades like those of tanners, blood-letters, bath attendants, sailors, grave-diggers, the sale of ironware and objects of lead and bones, as well as working in leather. All this when he is unfortunate. To him belong hearing, comprehension, the viscous, sticky, blackish (melancholy) thick humours, and of the parts of the body, the right ear, the back, the knees . . . the bladder, the spleen, the bones . . . and of diseases, gout, elephantiasis, dropsy, hypochondria, and all chronic illnesses which come from cold and dryness. In the human form he presides over the circumstances that a new-born child has black and curly hair, thick hair on the breast, medium eyes inclining from black to yellow with meeting eyebrows, well-proportioned bones, thick lips; he is easily overcome by cold and dryness. It is also said of him that he is lean, timid, thin, strict, with large head and small body, wide mouth, large hands, bandy legs, but pleasant to see when he walks, bending his head, walking heavily, shuffling his feet, a friend to guile and deceit. He has the faith of Judaism, black clothing; of days Saturday, and the night of Wednesday. . . . To him belong iron, remedies, the oak, gallnuts, latrines, sacks and old coarse stuffs, the bark of wood, pepper, qust (a herb), the onyx, olives, medlars, sour pomegranates . . . lentils, myrobalans, barley, . . . the terebinth and everything whatsoever that is black, and goats and bullocks, waterfowl, black snakes and mountains.

Jupiter is auspicious, masculine, in daytime warm, moist, temperate, bringing temperate blood like that of the heart; of the ages of man, youth belongs to him . . .

On receiving the full force of this wealth of characteristics and correspondences, derived mainly from post-classical sources (especially Ptolemy and Vettius Valens),[13] one's immediate impression is of utter madness. Saturn is said to be dry, but sometimes moist too. He "presides over" the utmost poverty, but also over great wealth (admittedly always coupled with avarice and ill-will towards others), over treachery but also over uprightness, over domiciles but also over long sea journeys and exile. Men born under him are members of "vulgar" trades, slaves, felons, prisoners and eunuchs, but they are also powerful commanders and silent people with mysterious wisdom and deep thoughts.

But order emerges from the chaos as soon as the origins are traced. For Abû Ma'šar and Alcabitius, Saturn was one of the seven planets endowed with demoniac powers, to which definite classes of entities, men, beasts, plants, minerals, professions, biological or meteorological events, constitutions, characters and dealings in everyday life essentially "belonged", and which exercised a decisive influence on the fate of men and the course of all earthly events, the effect of these planets being strengthened or weakened according to their position in the firmament at any given time and their relations towards one another.[14] But the nature of these planets was determined not only by the astronomical and physical properties which ancient natural

---

[13] Cf. below, text p. 142 sq. A very instructive and detailed table of the attributes of Saturn according to ancient writers appears in G. SEYFFARTH, *Beiträge zur Kenntnis der Literatur . . . des alten Ägypten*, VOL. II, Leipzig 1833, pp. 58–60.

[14] For the technique of reading the stars, cf. BBG, *Sternglaube*, pp. 58 sqq.

science had attributed to the *stars* Saturn, Jupiter, and the rest, but also by the tradition which ancient mythology had handed down concerning the *gods* Saturn, Jupiter, and so on. In astrology generally, but especially in astrological notions of planetary rulers who had inherited the names and qualities of the great Olympic gods, ancient piety had been preserved in an apparently profane form; and it was to remain so much alive in the future that the very gods who had been turned into stars—that is to say, apparently stripped of divinity—were an object of pious veneration and even of formal cults for hundreds of years afterwards,[15] while those not turned into stars—Hephaestus, Poseidon and Athena—continued to exist merely in learned compendiums and allegorical moral tracts; even their re-awakening in the humanism of the Renaissance, was to a certain extent a matter of literary convention.

Even in the sources from which the Arabic astrological notion of Saturn had arisen, the characteristics of the primeval Latin god of crops Saturn had been merged with those of Kronos, the son of Uranus, whom Zeus had dethroned and castrated, as well as with Chronos the god of time, who in turn had been equated with the two former even in antiquity; to say nothing of ancient oriental influences, whose significance we can only roughly estimate. When one considers further that all these mythological definitions were in turn mixed with astronomical and scientific definitions, and that astrological (that is, fundamentally magical) speculation, by reasoning from analogy, derived a mass of further more or less indirect associations from every given predicate, the apparently chaotic nature of a text such as Abû Ma'šar's or Alcabitius's seems perfectly intelligible.

2. SATURN IN ANCIENT LITERATURE

(*a*) Kronos–Saturn as a Mythical Figure

From the beginning, the notion of the god Kronos, a divinity apparently venerated before the days of classical Greece, and

---

[15] Cf. e.g. H. RITTER, "Picatrix, ein arabisches Handbuch hellenistischer Magie," in: *Vorträge der Bibliothek Warburg*, VOL. I (1921–22), pp. 94 sqq. and A. WARBURG, *Gesammelte Schriften*, Leipzig 1932, VOL. II, pp. 459 sqq.

of whose original character we know virtually nothing,[16] was distinguished by a marked internal contradiction or ambivalence. It is true that the other Greek gods, too, nearly all appear under a dual aspect, in the sense that they both chastise and bless, destroy and aid. But in none of them is this dual aspect so real and fundamental as in Kronos. His nature is a dual one not only with regard to his effect on the outer world, but with regard to his own—as it were, personal—destiny, and this dualism is so sharply marked that Kronos might fairly be described as god of opposites. The Homeric epithets, repeated by Hesiod, described the father of the three rulers of the world, Zeus, Poseidon and Hades (as he appears in the *Iliad*) as "great" and "of crooked counsel".[17] On the one hand he was the benevolent god of agriculture, whose harvest festival was celebrated by free men and slaves together,[18] the ruler of the Golden Age when men had abundance of all things and enjoyed the innocent happiness of Rousseau's natural man,[19] the lord of the Islands of the Blessed,[20] and the inventor of agriculture[21] and of the building of cities.[22] On the other hand he was the gloomy, dethroned and solitary god conceived as "dwelling at the uttermost end of land and sea",[23] "exiled beneath the earth and the flood of the seas"[24]; he was "a ruler of the nether gods"[25]; he lived as a

---

[16] For this and the following cf. the articles "Saturn", "Kronos" and "Planeten" in W. ROSCHER, *Ausführliches Lexikon der griechischen und römischen Mythologie*, Leipzig 1890–97, and in PAULY-WISSOWA. U. VON WILAMOWITZ-MÖLLENDORFF's suggestion that the figure of Kronos is a sort of hypostatisation of the Homeric epithet for Zeus, Κρονίδης ("Kronos und die Titanen", in *Sitzungsberichte der Preussischen Akademie der Wissenschaften, phil.-hist. Klasse*, IV (1929), pp. 35 sqq.) has met with little support.

[17] *Iliad* IV, 59; V, 721; HESIOD, *Theogony*, line 168, etc.

[18] L. DEUBNER, *Attische Feste*, Berlin 1932, pp. 152 sqq.

[19] HESIOD, *Works and Days*, lines 111 sqq. Hence Kronos appears in the comedy as lord of Utopia (CRATINUS, Πλοῦτοι, according to ATHENAEUS, *Deipnosophistae*, 267 e). PHILO mentions τὸν παρὰ ποιηταῖς ἀναγραφέντα Κρονικὸν βίον somewhat in the sense of "bliss" (*Legatio ad Caium*, 13, in *Opera*, ed. L. Cohn and P. Wendland, VOL. VI, Berlin 1915, p. 158, 3).

[20] HESIOD, *Works and Days*, addition to line 169. PINDAR, *Olympics* 2, 68 sqq. Cf. U. VON WILAMOWITZ-MÖLLENDORFF, op. cit., p. 36.

[21] According to MACROBIUS, *Saturnalia*, I, 7, 25, the Cyreneans venerated Cronus as "fructuum repertorem."

[22] Cf. e.g. DIODORUS SICULUS, *Bibliotheca*, III, 61: JOHANNES LYDUS, *De mensibus*, ed. R. Wuensch, Leipzig 1898, p. 170,6 sqq.

[23] *Iliad*, VIII, 479.

[24] *Iliad*, XIV, 204.

[25] *Iliad*, XV, 225; XIV, 274.

prisoner[26] or bondsman[27] in, or even beneath, Tartarus, and later he actually passed for the god of death and the dead. On the one hand he was the father of gods and men,[28] on the other hand the devourer of children,[29] eater of raw flesh (ὠμηστήρ), the consumer of all, who "swallowed up all the gods",[30] and exacted human sacrifice from the barbarians[31]; he castrated his father Uranus with the very sickle which, in the hand of his son, repaid measure for measure and made the procreator of all things for ever infertile—a sickle which, prepared by Gaea,[32] was both an instrument of the most horrible outrage and at the same time of harvesting.

The equation of the Greek Kronos with Saturn, the Roman god of fields and crops, confirmed the latent contradiction without particularly accentuating it. The Roman Saturn was originally not ambivalent but definitely good. In the general picture of the hybrid Kronos-Saturn, the fusion of the Greek god with the Roman produced an increase of positive traits by adding the attributes of guardian of wealth, overseer of a system of counting by weight and measure and inventor of coin-minting,[33] and of negative traits by adding those of the hunted fugitive.[34] Against this, however, the Greek Kronos's ambivalence was increased when the notion of the mythical god was linked, and soon merged, with that of the star that is still called Saturn to-day.

---

[26] HESIOD, *Theogony*, lines 729 sqq.

[27] AESCHYLUS, *Eumenides*, e.g. line 641. Cf. also the woollen bonds of the Roman Saturn (MACROBIUS, *Saturnalia*, I, 8, 5), and the "Saturniacae catenae" in AUGUSTINE, *Contra Faustum Manich.*, XX, 13 (MIGNE, P. L., VOL. XLII, col. 379).

[28] *Iliad*, and HESIOD, *Theogony*, *passim*.

[29] HESIOD, *Theogony*, line 467.

[30] *Orphicorum Fragmenta*, Pars post. 80, ed. O. Kern, Berlin 1922: ὁ πάντας καταπίνων θεούς. Cf. NONNUS, *Dionysiaca*, II, line 337: Κρόνον ὠμηστῆρα; or E. ABEL (ed.), *Orphica*, Leipzig 1885, Hymnus XIII, 3: ὃς δαπανᾷς μὲν ἅπαντα.

[31] SOPHOCLES, *Andromeda*, frag. 122. Here and elsewhere, Kronos represents Moloch.

[32] HESIOD, *Theogony*, lines 161 sqq.

[33] Cf. MACROBIUS, *Saturnalia*, I, 7, 24 ("vitae melioris auctor"), DIONYSIUS OF HALICARNASSUS, I, 38, I (πάσης εὐδαιμονίας δοτῆρα καὶ πληρωτήν). For Saturn as guardian of the aerarium, cf. TERTULLIAN, *Apologetic.* 10 (MIGNE, P. L., VOL. I, cols. 330 sq.), and *Thesaurus linguae latinae*, VOL. I, pp. 1055 sqq. For Saturn as patron of the monetary system, cf. VARRO, *De lingua latina*, V, 183: "Per trutinam solvi solitum: vestigium etiam nunc manet in aede Saturni, quod ea etiam nunc propter pensuram trutinam habet positam." ISIDORE, *Etym.* XVI, 18, 3: "Postea a Saturno aereus nummus inventus."

[34] LACTANTIUS, *Divin. inst.*, I, 13, MIGNE, P. L., VOL. VI, col. 188 ("fugit igitur, et in Italiam navigio venit, . . . cum errasset diu"). SIDONIUS APOLLINARIS, *Carmina*, VII, 32 ("profugus"). MINUCIUS FELIX, quoted below, p. 160 (text).

(b) Kronos–Saturn as a Planet

How the god Kronos came to be linked with the star Saturn has been explained by Franz Cumont, in so far as explanation has been possible.[35] The Greeks, whose primitive religion contained hardly any elements of star-worship, at first knew only the planets Φωσφόρος and Ἕσπερος, which seemed to precede the sun in its rising and setting; the one seems not to have been identified with the other until the time of the Pythagoreans or even of Parmenides. The fact that in addition to this most obvious of the planets, four others pursued their courses through the zodiac, was communicated to the Greeks by the Babylonians, who from time immemorial had clearly recognised the planets as such, and worshipped them as gods of destiny—Mercury as Nebu, the god of writing and wisdom, Venus as Ishtar, the great goddess of love and fertility, Mars as Nergal, the grim god of war and hell, Jupiter as Marduk, the kingly ruler, and Saturn as the strange god Ninib, of whom little more is known than that he was sometimes regarded as the nightly representative of the sun and was therefore, in spite of Marduk, considered the "mightiest" of the five planets.

Thus, with the single exception of Phosphorus–Hesperus, the planets appeared to the Greeks from the beginning in the guise not only of stars but of divinities, with which indigenous Greek gods were almost inevitably equated. Nebu must be Hermes, Ishtar Aphrodite, Nergal Ares, and Marduk Zeus; and Ninib must be Kronos, with his cruelty and his great age; (his age corresponded to the length of his revolution, in marked contrast to the steady pace of his "son" and the swift movement of his "grandchildren") and his peculiar powers were overshadowed but by no means lessened by his dethronement.

This original set of equations, however, which first appeared in complete form in the late Platonic *Epinomis*,[36] was brought into confusion by the growing influx of eastern elements in the Hellenistic period. According to the country in which the process took place, the planets Zeus or Aphrodite were associated with Bel and Baltis, or else with the Great Mother, or with Osiris and

---

[35] Franz Cumont, "Les noms des planètes et l'astrolatrie chez les Grecs," in *L'Antiquité classique*, vol. iv (1935), pp. 6 sqq. See also the articles on the planets quoted above (p. 134 n. 16); BBG, *Sternglaube*, p. 5 and passim; and A. Bouché-Leclercq, *L'astrologie grecque*, Paris 1899, esp. pp. 93 sqq.

[36] *Epin.*, 987b, c. The fifth-century Pythagoreans (e.g. Philolaus) seem to have been the first to establish the equation with the Babylonian gods (Cumont, op. cit., p.8).

Isis; the planet Ares with Heracles; the planet Kronos with the Egyptian Nemesis; and so on. The astronomers attempted to stem this confusion by seeking to replace the multiplicity of mythological terms by a uniform system of nomenclature on a purely phenomenal basis. Mercury became Στίλβων the twinkler, Venus Φωσφόρος the bringer of light, Mars Πυρόεις the fiery one, Jupiter Φαέθων the brilliant one, and Saturn Φαίνων the shining one. But owing to its non-personal character, this terminology, which itself very probably came from Babylonian sources of a more scientific type, was as little able to make headway against the old mythological terms as, say, the artificially chosen names of the months in the French Revolution were able to supplant the traditional ones. The Romans never attempted to translate the Στίλβων-Φαίνων series (Isidore of Seville still continued to use the Greek words), and the growth of astrology as a "religion", which characterises the later Empire, weighted the scales decisively in favour of the "mythological" nomenclature. Towards the end of the Republic we find the periphrasis "the star of Kronos", replaced by the simple "Kronos", and "star of Saturn" replaced by the simple "Saturn".[37] Thus, the mythical identification of the planets with what the western world had hitherto considered only their "corresponding" divinities was completed once and for all.

(i) *Kronos–Saturn in Ancient Astrophysics*

The Greeks at first developed the planetary doctrine transmitted to them in classical times in a purely scientific direction. In this, an astrophysical viewpoint seems from the beginning to have been adopted simultaneously with the purely astronomical.

Epigenes of Byzantium, who is thought to have lived in early Alexandrian times and therefore to have been one of the oldest mediators between Babylon and Hellas, classified Saturn as "cold and windy".[38] The epithet "cold", according both with the planet's great distance from the sun and with the god's great age, adhered to Saturn throughout the years and was never

---

[37] Thus Cicero, *De natura deorum*, II, 119, in the case of Mars. First Greek instance in a papyrus of A.D. 200, the text of which is older (Cumont, op. cit., pp. 35 and 37).

[38] Seneca, *Naturales quaestiones*, VII, 4, 2 "natura ventosa et frigida." Cf. also Cicero, *De natura deorum*, II, 119, according to whom the cold Saturn fills the highest spheres of the universe with icy frost. Both passages explicitly emphasise that the doctrine is of "Chaldean" origin.

questioned. The property of dryness, implied by "windy", on the other hand, came into conflict with the fact that Pythagorean and Orphic texts described the mythical Kronos as just the opposite, namely, as the god of rain or of the sea[39]; and this accounts for the fact that in later, especially in astrological literature, we so often encounter the singular definition "natura frigida et sicca, sed accidentaliter humida", or something of the sort—a contradiction which can only be explained, if at all, with the help of laborious argumentation.[40]

Whether it was really Posidonius who reduced the elemental qualities of the planets to an orderly system,[41] we would not venture to decide, but it would be safe to say that it was within the framework of the Stoic system that the doctrine was endowed with its full meaning.[42] Not till the formation of a cosmological system in which the opposites heat and cold determined the basic structure of the universe, did the qualities hitherto more or less arbitrarily attributed to the stars reveal a general and universally applicable law of nature, valid for both heavenly and earthly things and therefore establishing for the first time a rationally comprehensible connexion between the one set and the other. To Saturn, which was cold because of its distance from the sun (whether the Stoics thought it moist or dry we do not know), everything cold on earth was first related and finally subordinated; and it is clear that this embodying of planetary qualities in a universal framework of natural laws must have brought the basic tenet of astrology, namely, the dependence of all earthly things and events upon the "influence" of the heavenly bodies, considerably nearer to Greek thought.

---

[39] PHILOLAUS, DIELS, *Fragm.*, A14: ὁ μὲν γὰρ Κρόνος πᾶσαν ὑφίστησι τὴν ὑγρὰν καὶ ψυχρὰν οὐσίαν (almost word for word also SERVIUS, *Comment. in Georg.*, I, 12). Cf. PHILODEMUS, DIELS, *Doxogr. Graeci*, 546B (Κρόνον μὲν τὸν τοῦ ῥεύματος ῥόον); PLATO, *Cratylus*, 402B (Rhea and Cronus as ῥευμάτων ὀνόματα); NONNUS, *Dionysiaca*, VI, line 178 (Κρόνος ὄμβρον ἰάλλων); PORPHYRY (in connexion with the etymology Κρόνος—κρουνός) in *Schol. Homer.*, O 21. For the sea as Κρόνου δάκρυον among the Pythagoreans, cf. PORPHYRY, *Life of Pythagoras*, § 41; and the parallel passages given in the apparatus.

[40] Cf. PLINY, *Nat. Hist.*, II, 106: Saturn brings rain when he passes from one zodiacal sign to the next. PTOLEMY, *Tetrabiblos*, III (Περὶ μορφῆς), Basle 1553, pp. 142 sqq.: Saturn produces men of cold and moist disposition when he is in the east, cold and dry when in the west. Later astrologers did not find this moist-dry contradiction incomprehensible since it seemed to agree more or less with Saturn's two "houses", the Goat and the Water-carrier.

[41] Thus K. REINHARDT, *Kosmos und Sympathie*, Munich 1926, pp. 343 sqq., esp. pp. 345 sqq.

[42] SENECA, *De ira*, II, 19: "refert quantum quisque humidi in se calidique contineat: cuius in illo elementi portio praevalebit, inde mores erunt."

Stoic philosophy, however, had prepared the ground for recognition of astrological belief in two further directions. In the first place, there was the Stoic acceptance of the notion of "Moira", which was conceived both as a law of nature and as Fate,[43] and was bound, in view of this dual significance, to favour astrological fatalism. Secondly, there was the rationalistic disintegration of the religious myths, enabling later times to identify the properties of the stars, considered as physical bodies, that is, as natural phenomena, with those of the divinities whose names they bore. The Stoics did not complete this fusion themselves, but the effect of reducing the myths to a rationalistic and allegorical significance was to deprive the gods of their status as "persons",[44] so that their characteristics and destinies, separated from their mythical context and surviving only as single traits, were no longer contrasted with the properties which men attributed to the stars as natural phenomena, but could be merged with them as soon as the moment was ripe.

The moment was ripe when the question, prompted by an age-old psychological urge, as to the destiny of the individual, could find as little answer in the various philosophical systems as in the official religion which these very systems had displaced, and when it sought a new answer which should satisfy faith rather than reason. With regard to the fate of the individual in the next world, the answer was given in the ever more widespread mystery cults, among which Christianity was ultimately to triumph. But with regard to the fate of the individual in this world, the answer was afforded by the astrology of later antiquity, whose development and recognition took place at the same time as the adoption of the mystery religions. Through this astrology the old mythological motives which Stoicism had secularised—thereby ensuring their survival—once more became "mythically

---

[43] Note the Stoic reference to the *Iliad,* VI, 488: *Μοῖραν δ' οὔτινά φημι πεφυγμένον ἔμμεναι ἀνδρῶν.* Cf. *Stoicorum veterum fragmenta,* ed. J. von Arnim, VOL. II, Leipzig 1923, frag. 925.

[44] The "physica ratio" of the old myths in Cleanthes and Chrysippus. Cf. Arnim (ed.), op. cit., frags. 528 sqq. and 1008 sqq. In these Kronos was identified with Chronos by the Stoics (hence "Saturnus quod saturaretur annis"). He devours his children like Time, who brings forth the ages and swallows them up again, and he is chained by Jupiter so that the flight of time should not be measureless but should be "bound" by the course of the stars. CICERO, *De natura deorum,* II, 64; Arnim (ed.), op. cit., frag. 1091. The other interpretation accepted by Varro (transmitted by AUGUSTINE, *De Civitate Dei,* VI, 8 and VII, 19) takes the word "sata" as the derivation of Saturn's name; he devours his children as the earth devours the seeds she herself generates, and he was given a clod instead of the infant Zeus to eat because, before the plough was discovered, clods used to be thrown on the seed corn.

active". Combined with the original scientific conceptions, they provide the background of the picture drawn by Abû Ma'šar and Alcabitius.

(ii) *Kronos–Saturn in Ancient Astrology*

The astrological elements of ancient oriental astronomy were made known to the Greeks at the same time as the astronomical, but it is significant that it was a Chaldean rather than a Greek who systematically developed and summarised them. This was Berossus, born about 350–340 B.C. and originally a priest of the Temple of Bel in Babylon, who is said to have founded a school of astrology on Cos; he dedicated a work to the Seleucidian Antiochus I, entitled *Babyloniaca*[45]; this summary of all Babylonian knowledge of the stars seems to have been the main source for writers of the later Empire. For the Greeks themselves, the astrological side of this knowledge was so much overshadowed by the astronomical that we know very little about the actual content of "older", that is to say, pre-Augustan, astrology, and least of all about its definitions concerning the nature and effect of the planets.[46] One thing, however, may be said with some certainty, that the division of the planets into "good" and "evil", which was generally known at any rate by the first century B.C. and is usually described as "Chaldean", must have been imported considerably earlier. According to this system of division, which formed the basis of all Roman writers' statements on astrology and also represented the days of the week named after the planets as "auspicious" or "inauspicious", two of the planets, Jupiter and Venus, were consistently "good" by nature, one, namely Mercury, was "neutral", and two, Mars and Saturn, were "evil".[47] And it

---

[45] Cf. P. SCHNABEL, *Berossos und die babylonisch-hellenistische Literatur*, Leipzig 1923. Berossus's great influence, and the reputation he enjoyed throughout antiquity, can be seen from PLINY (*Nat. hist.*, VII, 123) and FLAVIUS JOSEPHUS (*Contra Apionem*, I, § 129) ("Testimonia", Schnabel, op. cit., p. 250). According to Pliny the Athenians even erected a statue to Berossus, which because of his marvellous prophecies had a gilded tongue.

[46] For the astrology of the constellations and "decans" cf. F. BOLL, *Sphaera*, Leipzig 1903, and W. GUNDEL, *Dekane und Dekan-Sternbilder* (Studien der Bibliothek Warburg, XIX, 1936).

[47] CICERO, *De divinatione*, I, 85; PLUTARCH, *De Iside et Osiride*, 18. Corresponding passages in poetry are: HORACE, *Odes*, II. 17 ("Te Iovis impio tutela/Saturno refulgens/Eripuit volucrisque fati/Tardavit alas . . . ."); TIBULLUS, I, 3, 17 ("sacra dies Saturni" as a bad day for travel); OVID, *Ibis*, lines 209 sqq. ("Te fera nec quicquam placidum spondentia Martis/Sidera presserunt falciferique senis"); JUVENAL, *Sat.*, VI, 569 ("quid sidus triste minetur/Saturni . . . ."); PROPERTIUS, IV, I, 83 (". . . Felicesque Jovis stellas Martisque rapaces/Et grave Saturni sidus"); LUCAN, *Bellum civile*, I, 651 ("Summo si frigida caelo/ Stella nocens nigros Saturni accenderet ignis"). Further, *Schol. in Luc.*, I, 660. In FILOCALUS's calendar of 354, Tuesday and Saturday are described as "dies nefasti", Thursday ☞ and Friday as lucky days, and the remainder as neutral ("communes").

is clear that this doctrine, which showed the complicated nature of Saturn in a markedly sinister and baleful light,[48] was of great significance with regard to the later apportionment of melancholy to his sphere.

Thus, in Manilius's few lines—one of the earliest extant astrological statements about the nature of Saturn—we encounter a heavenly ruler of strangely sombre character. Hurled from his throne and expelled from the threshold of the gods, Saturn exerted his powers on "the opposite end of the world's axis" and ruled the "foundations" of the universe, that is, the lowest part of the heavens, called the "imum coeli", with the result that he also saw the world from the opposite perspective, from an essentially inimical standpoint. And just as his own mythical destiny had been determined by his fatherhood, so now as a planetary power he held the fate of all fathers and old men in his hands.[49]

The significant part of this sketchy description—apart from the sombre colouring of Saturn's portrait—lies in the fusion of scientific and, especially, Stoic doctrine with mythology, as well as in the emergence of an ever more authoritative type of speculation distinguished by the classification of sets of relationships with little rational or logical connexion between them. The astrological view, as seen in Manilius, has something in common with the Stoic; both are interested in the old myths only in so far as single elements of them can be interpreted so as to apply to the definition of a natural phenomenon. It differs from the Stoic view, however, firstly in that the notion of the divinity is no longer kept separate from that of the star known by the same name, but is identified with it; secondly, in that the nature of this stellar force now comprising both god and heavenly body is of importance to the astrologers only in so far as it may exert

---

[48] Cf. for instance the passage from Lucan quoted in the previous note, where "frigida" stands immediately next to "nocens". Later we find Saturn's coldness (as well as his dryness) actually described as "qualitas mortifera" (see below, text p. 187).

[49] MANILIUS, *Astronomica*, II, lines 929 sqq.:

at qua subsidit converso cardine mundus
fundamenta tenens adversum et suspicit orbem
ac media sub nocte iacet, Saturnus in illa
parte suas agitat vires, deiectus et ipse
imperio quondam mundi solioque deorum,
et pater in patrios exercet numina casus
fortunamque senum; priva est tutela duorum,
[nascentum atque patrum, quae tali condita pars est.]
asper erit templis titulus, quem Graecia fecit
daemonium, signatque suas pro nomine uires.

a directly ascertainable influence on man and his destiny; and thirdly, in that the method of interpreting the myths is no longer that of abstract allegory, but a method of concrete analogy. They no longer say: "Saturn signifies Time because Time devours temporal events as Saturn did his children"; but: "Saturn, cast out from Olympus into Hades, rules the lowest region of the celestial globe"; or: "Saturn, himself an old man and a father, determines the fate of old men and fathers".

Later astrologers continued to expand these relationships founded in "structural" analogies, so that Manilius's still very sketchy account of the planetary gods and their powers attained an ever richer, more definite and at the same time more complicated form, while on the other hand the original mythological attributes of the gods which Manilius still mentioned ("deiectus et ipse Imperio quondam mundi solioque deorum", and so on) seem gradually to have faded from the recollection of authors and readers, and can now be recaptured only by retrospective analysis.

A relatively early exponent of this fully developed astrological characterisation was the second-century writer Vettius Valens,[50] whose work begins with a detailed description of the nature and influence of the planets and, as far as this description is concerned, has very much in common with early Arabic literature.[51] In his account, Saturn, to whom in Greco-Egyptian fashion he also refers as "the Star of Nemesis", governs a vast number of different types of men, and in fact not only governs but even generates them: to him are subordinated also a series of substances (like lead, wood and stone), parts of the body, diseases (especially

[50] Vettius Valens, *Anthologiarum libri*, ed. W. Kroll, Berlin 1908, p. 2: ⟨ὁ⟩ δὲ τοῦ Κρόνου ποιεῖ μὲν τοὺς ὑπ' αὐτὸν γεννωμένους μικρολόγους, βασκάνους, πολυμερίμνους, ἑαυτοὺς καταῤῥίπτοντας, μονοτρόπους, τυφώδεις, ἀποκρύπτοντας τὴν δολιότητα, αὐστηρούς, κατανενευκότας, ὑποκρινομένην τὴν ὅρασιν ἔχοντας, αὐχμηρούς, μελανοείμονας, προσαιτητικούς, καταστύγνους, κακοπαθεῖς, πλαστικούς [read: πλευστικούς], πάρυγρα πράσσοντας. ποιεῖ δὲ καὶ ταπεινότητας, νωχελίας, ἀπραξίας, ἐγκοπὰς τῶν πρασσομένων, πολυχρονίους δίκας, ἀνασκευὰς πραγμάτων, κρυβάς, συνοχάς, δεσμά, πένθη, καταιτιασμούς, δάκρυα, ὀρφανίας, αἰχμαλωσίας, ἐκθέσεις· γεηπόνους δὲ καὶ γεωργοὺς ποιεῖ διὰ τὸ τῆς γῆς αὐτὸν κυριεύειν, μισθωτάς τε κτημάτων καὶ τελώνας καὶ βιαίους πράξεις ἀποτελεῖ, δόξας περιποιεῖ μεγάλας καὶ τάξεις ἐπισήμους καὶ ἐπιτροπείας καὶ ἀλλοτρίων διοικητὰς καὶ ἀλλοτρίων τέκνων πατέρας. οὐσίας δὲ κυριεύει μολύβδου, ξύλων καὶ λίθων· τῶν δὲ τοῦ σώματος μελῶν κυριεύει σκελῶν, γονάτων, νεύρων, ἰχώρων, φλέγματος, κύστεως, νεφρῶν καὶ τῶν ἐντὸς ἀποκρύφων. σινῶν δὲ δηλωτικὸς ὅσα συνίσταται ἐκ ψύξεως καὶ ὑγρότητος, οἷον ὑδρωπικῶν, νεύρων ἀλγηδόνων, ποδάγρας, βηχός, δυσεντερίας, κηλῶν, σπασμῶν, παθῶν δὲ δαιμονισμοῦ, κιναιδίας, ἀκαθαρσίας. ποιεῖ δὲ καὶ ἀγάμους καὶ χηρείας, ὀρφανίας, ἀτεκνίας. τοὺς δὲ θανάτους ἀποτελεῖ βιαίους ἐν ὕδατι ἢ δι' ἀγχόνης ἢ δεσμῶν ἢ δυσεντερίας. ποιεῖ δὲ καὶ πτώσεις ἐπὶ στόμα. ἐστὶ δὲ Νεμέσεως ἀστὴρ καὶ τῆς ἡμερινῆς αἱρέσεως, τῇ μὲν χρόᾳ καστορίζων, τῇ δὲ γεύσει στυφός.

[51] For the wide diffusion of Vettius Valens' astrology see Kroll (ed.), op. cit., pp. vii sqq.

those caused by cold or moisture), and manners of death (especially drowning, hanging, chaining-up and dysentery).

Some of these correlations, which have quite clearly been incorporated in the Arabic texts, can be traced without difficulty to the true mythological core of the conception. Vettius Valens himself informs us that agriculture and husbandry belong to Saturn, διὰ τὸ τῆς γῆς αὐτὸν κυριεύειν. His association with celibacy and childlessness, widowhood, child-exposure, orphanhood, violence and hidden malice can be explained by the unfortunate experiences of the Greek Kronos in his family life; his association with the sad, the worried, and misused, beggars, chains, captivity, and concealment, derives from his dethronement and imprisonment in Tartarus; the attribution to him of "authority", "guardianship", great fame and high rank is due to his original position as ruler of the world and king of the gods. Patronage of the earth, wood, stone, agriculture and husbandry clearly derives from the qualities of the Italian god of crops Saturn[52]; and patronage of voyagers from his long, perilous flight to Latium.[53] Further, the assignment to him of tears, of those working with moist objects, of damage and illnesses caused by cold and wet, of the bladder, of glands, of death by drowning, and so on, is based on the Pythagorean and Orphic interpretation of Kronos as a sea and river god.[54] But now something was done that Manilius had only modestly attempted. All these mythical traits were reinterpreted as types of terrestrial things and events; the various experiences and qualities of the god materialised, so to speak, into categories of earthly substances, and, above all, into categories of human character and destiny.

It was now possible, therefore, for the astrologers to connect the categories of men and substances deriving from the myth with others deriving from purely natural conceptions. Firstly,

---

[52] The fact that Saturn was accorded the firmest parts of the human body (bones, tendons, knees, etc.) was no doubt due to his "earthy" nature: the parallel between the earth and the human body (earth as flesh, water as blood, etc.), present still in Nicholas of Cusa and Leonardo da Vinci, goes back to oriental and classical thought (cf. R. REITZENSTEIN and H. H. SCHAEDER, *Aus Iran und Griechenland* (Studien der Bibliothek Warburg, VII), Leipzig 1926, pp. 136 sqq.; SAXL, *Verzeichnis*, VOL. II, pp. 40 sqq.; cf. also CHARLES DE TOLNAY, *Pierre Bruegel l'Ancien*, Brussels 1935, pp. 7 and 60, who, however, leaves out evidence from the high Middle Ages, e.g. Honorius of Autun and Hildegard of Bingen. For the whole, cf. R. Klibansky (ed.) in NICHOLAS OF CUSA, *De docta ignorantia*, II, 13, Leipzig 1932, p. 111 (list of sources).

[53] That in Vettius Valens *πλευστικούς* should be read instead of *πλαστικούς* is clear from the parallel passage in RHETORIUS (*Cat. astr. Gr.*, VOL. VII, p. 215).

[54] See above, p. 138 (text).

as in Manilius, the astronomical and physical properties of Saturn as a heavenly body could be condensed into types of nature and destiny. The slowness of his revolution conferred on those born under him the character of indolence, and caused him to be regarded as the ruler of lead (we still speak of "leaden feet" and "leaden dullness"), and as the cause of prolonged litigation. The quality of cold, universally attributed to him, generated certain diseases, such as dropsy and rheumatism, especially if in combination with moisture—this again was of mythological origin. One can see how some of these statements derive from a kind of analogy not hitherto encountered; the formula underlying them is no longer "Just as Kronos himself lay bound in Tartarus, so the children of Saturn are often imprisoned"; but rather "As Saturn is cold and moist, and as dropsy and rheumatism are caused by cold and moisture, so dropsy and rheumatism are proper to Saturn". By this means of indirect analogy the astrological notion of Saturn could now include a third group of predicates which in themselves were associated neither with mythical nor with astrophysical attributes, but were, if one may say so, of secular origin, and possessed a quite special significance in our context. This was the whole area of knowledge gained by physiognomy, characterology and popular ethics, themselves quite independent of the lore of the stars.[55]

The mythical Kronos was distinguished by a quite definite physiognomy—by a sad or thoughtful old age,[56] and above all by certain, often negative, features. These human qualities, as we have just seen, could first be applied by direct analogy to the nature and destiny of the sad, the old, the childless, the malevolent and so on.[57] But since the special characteristic of a god had become a general type of human character, those sciences were now involved which from Aristotle onwards had aimed at exploring the physical and mental structure of man. The purely "natural" types evolved by them had much in common with the "planetary" types of beings and destinies evolved indirectly from the nature of the planetary gods, just as the illnesses said

---

[55] See above, pp. 56 sqq. (text).

[56] Cf. also representations of Saturn such as our PLATE 13.

[57] Astrologers, of course, endow children of the Goat, which is the house of Saturn, with the same qualities as the children of the planet. Thus they are described (*Cat. astr. Gr.*, VOL. X, pp. 238 sqq.): *πολλὰ μοχθήσας, γυνὴ μικρή*; HEPHAEST., II, 2 (*Cat. astr. Gr.*, VOL. VIII, 2, p. 59) has *μικροφυεῖς κάτω κύπτοντας*, etc. Especially clear connexions appear in VETTIUS VALENS, *Anthologiarum libri*, I, 2, ed. W. Kroll, Berlin 1908, p. 11.

to be caused by the stars agreed with the notions of medicine. This agreement was so complete that a further "indirect" analogy, the inclusion in astrology of "related" types from the store of physiognomy and characterology, could not fail to follow. Thus the churlish, the petty, the selfish, misers, slanderers and the like came to be included among "Saturnine" people, and thus Saturnine people came to be identified with melancholics. The same procedure, that of Hellenistic physiognomy and characterology, was used, as we saw, by the humoralists of the later Empire in constructing the "four temperaments"; and we now see it being used by the astrology of the later Empire in constructing its "planetary" types.

As far as concerns the melancholy character in the doctrine of temperaments, we have already remarked that it had acquired the important attributes of bitterness, despondency, money-hoarding and small-mindedness.[58] These physiognomic and characterological types with their essential qualities were now used in descriptions of the equally pessimistic, lonely and cold-natured Saturnine character, and reinforced (through further analogy) by descriptions derived from the pathological study of melancholy.[59] A table based exclusively on Vettius Valens (see p. 146) will show the general outlines of this connexion.

By recourse to further astrological sources of the same or only slightly later date, the number of these analogies can be considerably increased. The quality of greed, for instance, the mythical origin of which is plain, and which was postulated by almost all astrologers, found its analogy as early as Aristotle in the semeiotics of the melancholic[60]; the poem *Aetna* described Saturn as a "stella tenax",[61] corresponding to the description of the melancholic as steadfast and firm (ἑδραῖον καὶ βέβαιον), and also as "stabilis"; Julian of Laodicea credited Saturn with autocracy,[62] corresponding to the "tyrannic" nature of the melancholic in Plato[63]; Rhetorius called him silent and attributed to his influence the tendency to be superstitious[64]; and Ptolemy in his list of men

---

[58] See the passages cited above, pp. 62 sqq.; esp. R. FÖRSTER, *Script. phys. gr. et lat.*, I, pp. 32–6.

[59] See above, pp. 44 sqq. (text).

[60] See above, pp. 34 sqq. (text).

[61] *Aetna*, II, 244 (ed. S. Sudhaus, Leipzig 1898, p. 18).

[62] *Cat. astr. Gr.*, VOL. IV, p. 105.

[63] See above, p. 17 (text).

[64] *Cat. astr. Gr.*, VOL. VII, p. 215. Cf. also *Cat. astr. Gr.*, VOL. VII, p. 96: μοναχικὸν σχῆμα καὶ ἐρημικὸς βίος.

governed only by Saturn, such as misers, the avaricious, and hoarders, also added deep thinkers.[65]

Postulates of Saturn (after Vettius Valens)	Physiognomical and characterological postulates				Postulates of Melancholy
	(*a*) Πικρός (cf. Vettius Valens: τῇ δὲ γεύσει στυφός)	(*b*) Ἄθυμος (cf. Vettius Valens: κατάστυγνοι, πολυμέριμνοι, κακοπαθεῖς, πένθη, δάκρυα)	(*c*) Μικρόψυχος (cf. Vettius Valens: μικρολόγοι)	(*d*) Miser (Colligendae pecuniae amans, cf. Vettius Valens: μισθωταί τε κτημάτων καὶ τελῶναι)	
ἑαυτοὺς καταρρίπτοντες					The melancholic's suicidal tendencies
μονότροποι					Conversationem humanam fugiunt, πάτον ἀνθρώπων ἀλεείνων
τυφώδεις					νωθροὶ καὶ μωροί
ἀποκρύπτοντες τὴν δολιότητα					subdoli, perfidi
κατανενευκότες, ὑποκρινομένην τὴν ὅρασιν ἔχοντες	τὸ πρόσωπον σεσηρός	ὄμματα κατακεκλασμένα		in quo aliquid inclinationis est	κατηφεῖς, aspectu assiduo in terram
αὐχμηροί	ἰσχνός	ἰσχνός	ἰσχνός	Leanness	Leanness in spite of much food, thin limbs
μελανοείμονες	μελανόχρως, μελάνθριξ			Black hair as sign of the miser	μελανόψιοι, μελάντριχοι
ταπεινότης		ταπεινός		poor figure	
νωχελία		ταῖς κινήσεσιν ἀπηγορευκῶς			somniculosi
τῇ χρόᾳ καστορίζων					The melancholic's bad smell[66]

[65] PTOLEMY, *Tetrabiblos*, III (Basle 1553, p. 158). In an iatromathematical work entitled *Liber ad Ammonem* (J. L. IDELER (ed.), *Physici et medici graeci minores*, Berlin 1841, VOL. I, p. 389), patients who fell sick under Saturn (and, it is true, Mercury) were given a prognosis some symptoms of which were word for word like those of melancholy: Οἱ μὲν γὰρ ὑπὸ ♄ καὶ ☿ κατακλινόμενοι, νωχελεῖς ἔσονται καὶ δυσκίνητοι (καὶ ἀναλγεῖς) τοῖς τε ἄρθροις καὶ παντὶ τῷ σώματι ἀπὸ ψύξεων καὶ ῥευματισμοῦ κατὰ μικρὸν ἐμφαίνοντος τὴν νόσον καὶ βραδέως διεγειρόμενοι μικρόφωνοί τε καὶ δεδιότες καὶ φοβούμενοι καὶ ἑαυτοὺς θάλποντες τοῖς ἱματίοις καὶ τὸ φῶς φεύγοντες καὶ πυκνῶς ἀναστενάζοντες καὶ βραδέως ἀναπνέοντες καὶ μικρόσφυγμοι καὶ τὴν βοήθειαν θερμασίαν ἔχοντες, καὶ διὰ τῶν σφυγμῶν δεικνύμενοι ἐνδεεῖς καὶ ἄτονοι καὶ τὴν ἐπιφάνειαν τοῦ σώματος κατεψυγμένοι. χρῆσθαι οὖν ἐπὶ τούτων δεῖ τοῖς θερμαίνουσι καὶ ἀναχαλῶσιν ἐστεγνωμένως.

What was admittedly still lacking in all this astrology of the later Empire was a definite and constant distribution of the four humours among certain planets, in particular the definite and constant association of black bile with Saturn. Vettius Valens and his successors in the late Empire did indeed mention Saturn in connexion with black bile, with the spleen and with the corresponding physical and mental conditions, but it was then a question of a relationship either not yet universal or not yet specific. Either they said, in general terms, "The spleen is governed by Saturn"—in which case this was not a specific patronage, for the spleen was ranged alongside the bones, the bladder, the right ear and so on[67]; or else they spoke of some specific effect of Saturn upon black bile and conditions connected with it—in which case this effect was neither permanent nor exclusive to Saturn, but conditioned by Saturn's momentary position in the firmament or even by the joint action of Saturn and other planets.[68] As an example we may take an extract from the astrologer Dorotheus (not later than the beginning of the second century), whose work now survives only in fragments, or in Greek and Latin prose paraphrases, though it was still known in complete form to the

---

[66] Incidentally the predicate of "evil smell" (generally described as "foetidus", and qualified by Guido Bonatti—quoted below, text p. 189—as "goatlike smell") has a basis in myth as well; in Rome there was a particular "Saturnus Stercutius" or "Sterculius", the god of manure (cf. Macrobius, *Saturnalia*, I, 7, 25 and W. H. Roscher, *Ausführliches Lexikon der griechischen und römischen Mythologie*, Leipzig 1884, s.v. "Saturnus", col. 428).

[67] Thus Ptolemy, *Tetrabiblos*, III (Basle 1553, p. 148). This classification was subject to considerable fluctuations; cf. e.g. the work attributed to Porphyry, *Introductio in Ptolemaei opus de effectibus astrorum*, Basle 1559, p. 198: "Saturnus ex interioribus phlegmaticum humorem, tussim et solutionem intestinorum." Among the dangerous illnesses caused by Saturn were ranged disorders of the spleen, as well as giddiness, slow fever and other serious diseases due to cold (Ptolemy, *Tetrabiblos*, IV, Basle 1553, p. 198).

[68] For instance, according to the doctrine of the twelve "loci", Saturn caused in the sixth place ἐξ ὑγρῶν καὶ ψυγμῶν καὶ μελαίνης χολῆς . . . τὸ σῖνος κτλ. (Rhetorius, in *Cat. astr. Gr.*, VOL. VIII, 4, p. 155). According to Vettius Valens (*Anthologiarum libri*, ed. W. Kroll, Berlin 1908, p. 17), the "termini" of the Scorpion belonged to Saturn and engendered melancholics as well as other undesirable types of men. According to Firmicus, when Saturn is in a certain point of the firmament, and when the moon, retreating from him, comes into conjunction with Mars, he generates "insanos, lunaticos, melancholicos, languidos" (Firmicus Maternus, *Matheseos libri VIII*, edd. W. Kroll and F. Skutsch, Leipzig 1897–1913, BK III, 2, 24; p. 104, 4). Cf. also the passage IV, 9, 9: p. 211, 11, which says that under certain even more complicated conditions Saturn's influence helps to generate "melancholici, icterici, splenetici, thisici, hydropici, pleumatici, etc." The passage in Firmicus, III, 2, is obviously connected with a passage in Manetho, *Apotelesmata*, III, 593 sqq.: "But when the horned Selene comes into conjunction with Helios, and Ares shines in their midst, and Kronos is seen together with them in a constellation of four, then the black bile seething in the breast confuses the understanding of men and rouses them to madness."

Arabs of the tenth century.[69] In his poem he declared that when cold Saturn and hot Mars were in conjunction work was hampered, and the black bile was brought into activity.[70]

It is understandable that in the later Empire no lasting connexion was established between Saturn and melancholy as an illness, let alone between Saturn and melancholy as a temperament. At the time when the astrology of the later Empire developed, the system of the four temperaments was still in the making, and it did not reach anything like a stable form until the fourth century.[71] The Galenic "crases" could be embodied in the astrological doctrine of the planets more easily than the four humours, and this was in fact attempted by so strictly scientific an astrologer as Ptolemy.[72] Moreover, by the time the theory of the four humours had been firmly established, the western world had temporarily lost all interest in the further development of astrology.[73] The problem of how to bring the four humours into harmony with the seven planets was raised again only by the eastern scholars of the Middle Ages. But the conditions for such a connexion were implicit in the astrology of the late Empire, and this connexion was so far prefigured in all essentials that all it required was explicit formulation and codification.

Even the preponderantly negative picture of Saturn painted by Vettius Valens was not altogether lacking in positive traits ("great fame and high degree"), and one can see how these positive traits later increased in number and became more sharply defined by being made dependent on a definite position of the planet, and by thus becoming more clearly distinguishable from its generally inauspicious influences.

Saturn's children were generally the unhappiest of mortals, and when it came to the distribution of the seven ages of man

---

[69] Cf. Kuhnert in PAULY-WISSOWA, s.v. "Dorotheus"; and A. ENGELBRECHT, *Hephaestion von Theben*, Vienna 1887, pp. 29 sqq.

[70] *Cat. astr. Gr.*, VOL. V, 3, p. 125. The sentence *κωλύσεις ἔργων καὶ χολῆς μελαίνης κίνησιν ποιεῖ* is linked by an *εἶτα προστίθησιν ὅτι* . . . to six verses in Dorotheus referring to the effect of Saturn in conjunction with Mars. For this passage cf. J. HAEG in *Hermes*, VOL. XLV (1910), pp. 315–19, and *Cat. astr. Gr.*, VOL. II, pp. 159 sqq., esp. p. 162, 3 sqq. Also W. Kroll in the critical apparatus to FIRMICUS MATERNUS, op. cit., VOL. II, p. 115. For Dorotheus cf. now V. STEGEMANN, in *Beiträge zur Geschichte der Astrologie*, I, Heidelberg 1935.

[71] See above, pp. 60 sqq. (text).

[72] Admittedly Saturn with his dual, moist-dry nature was thus bound to be credited not only with the "cold and dry" crasis of the melancholic—which in itself was important enough—but also with the "cold and damp" crasis of the phlegmatic. PTOLEMY, *Tetrabiblos*, III (Basle 1553, p. 143).

[73] See below, pp. 178 sqq. (text).

among the seven planets, Saturn was allotted the last and saddest phase of human existence, that is to say, old age with its loneliness, its physical and mental decay, and its hopelessness.[74] And yet this same Saturn, according to Manetho, "in peculiaribus suis domibus", might not only signify riches and luxury, but also produce men who were happy, versatile, and sociable as long as they lived.[75] Elsewhere we read that in certain constellations he generated physicians, geometricians,[76] and those who could prophesy from hidden books and knew many esoteric rites of the mysteries.[77] Firmicus and the writer of another, closely related, Greek text credit Saturn with the power to produce "in the fifth place, kings, rulers, and founders of cities", and "in the ninth

---

[74] Cf. F. Boll, "Die Lebensalter", in *Neue Jahrbücher für das klassische Altertum*, xvi (1913), pp. 117 sqq. There is little to be added to his masterly account which traces the evolution of the idea that each of the seven ages of man is governed by one of the seven planets, best expressed by Ptolemy, *Tetrabiblos*, iv (Basle 1553, p. 204), from its first appearance down to modern times. We may, however, remark that this system, too, was bound to prepare the way for an association between Saturn and melancholy, which also governed the later phase of man's life. Also, the "sixth act" of man's life as described by the melancholy Jaques (Boll, op. cit., p. 131) belongs beyond doubt to Saturn, and not, as Boll thought, to Jupiter. Jupiter is allotted the fifth act, while the age corresponding to the sun is omitted as too similar to the "jovial". The slippered pantaloon's "youthful hose" can hardly in this connexion be interpreted as the rudiments of the εὔσχημον characteristic of the age ascribed to Jupiter, while the purse denotes not the joyous wealth of the "Jovial" period of life but the miserly riches of the Saturnine period (cf. below, text pp. 284 sqq.).

[75] Manetho, *Apotelesmata*, iv, 15 sqq.:

"Stella, quam Phaenonta dei hominesque appellant.
Haec quando in peculiaribus suis apparet domibus,
Nascentibus mortalibus ad inspectorem horae vitae,
Locupletes ostendit & opulentia plurima potiri
Felices, & in vita etiam ad finem usque semper faciles."

If, however, Saturn shines "in non domesticis locis" (iv, 31 sqq.):

"Prorsus calamitosos facit, & cassos opibus & gloria
Indigos vitae & quotidiani victus;
Et omnes tristitiae experientes, lugentes in aedibus
Facit & tristem errantemque vitam subeuntes."

This splitting of the effects of Saturn into good and evil also appears in Arabic writings. Cf. e.g. Albohali (Abû 'Ali Al-Khaiyât, who died about 835), *De iudiciis nativitatum liber*, Nuremberg 1546, fol. C3r: "Quando autem Saturnus fuerit dominus ascendentis, et fuerit in bono loco, liber a malis, significat magni precii hominem, profunditatem atque singularitatem consilii, et paucitatem interrogationis. At si fuerit in malo loco impeditus, significat servile, ac parvi precii ingenium, ignobilitatem animi atque versutiam."

[76] Thus Palchus, *Cat. astr. Gr.*, vol. v, 1, p. 189. It is also noteworthy that in a town laid out in accordance with astrological requirements which is described in the Persian book *Dabistân*, "mathematicians, prophets and astronomers," among others, are said to have lived round about Saturn's temple, while in the temple itself "the sciences were transmitted and taught" (cf. Sheik Mohamed Fani's *Dabistân*, translated by Francis Gladwin and F. von Dalberg, Bamberg and Würzburg 1817, p. 52).

[77] *Cat. astr. Gr.*, vol. i, p. 115.

place, even famous magicians and philosophers, as well as excellent soothsayers and mathematicians (that is to say, astrologers), who always prophesy correctly, and whose words possess, as it were, divine authority".[78]

The positive evaluation of Saturn's influence as it appears in these and similar passages and as it was partly adopted by the Arabic astrologers (whose conception therefore appears considerably less homogeneous than that of Vettius Valens) can in turn be partly derived from certain features of Saturnian myths. For instance, riches, the founding of cities, association with geometry, knowledge of everything secret or hidden, can be traced immediately to the myths of the Golden Age, of the colonisation of Italy and of the sojourn in "Latium", or perhaps of Saturn's banishment to the hidden underworld.[79] With regard, however, to the purely mental qualities attributed to some specially fortunate children of Saturn, namely the capacity for deep philosophical reflexion, and for prophecy and priesthood, one must reckon with the influence of one notion of Saturn which had no connexion with astrology but had used the same mythical and astrophysical raw material to form a very different picture. This notion of Saturn, which astrology, of course, could only

---

[78] Thus FIRMICUS MATERNUS, op. cit., BK III, 2, pp. 97 sqq. Thieves born under Saturn, incidentally, are those "quos in furto numquam prosper sequatur eventus". A parallel passage from RHETORIUS is in *Cat. astr. Gr.*, VOL. VIII, 4, pp. 152 sqq.; Saturn when in the fifth place generated the *πολυκτήμονας, ἐγγείων ἄρχοντας, θεμελίων κτίστας ἢ χωρῶν ἢ πόλεων*; in the ninth place, other conditions being favourable, the *μύστας, ἀρχιμάγους, φιλοσόφους, τὸ μέλλον προλέγοντας, τινὰς δὲ καὶ ἐν ἱερατικαῖς ἀσχολίαις ἢ ἱερῶν προεστῶτας.* Another important passage is in FIRMICUS MATERNUS, op. cit., BK IV, 19, pp. 244 sqq.: "Si Saturnus dominus genituræ fuerit effectus et sit oportune in genitura positus et ei dominium crescens Luna decreverit, faciet homines inflatos, spiritu sublevatos, honoratos bonos graves, boni consilii et quorum fides recto semper iudicio comprobetur et qui negotia omnia recti iudicii rationibus compleant, sed circa uxores et filios erunt alieno semper affectu; erunt sane semoti et sibi vacantes, modicum sumentes cibum et multa potatione gaudentes. Corpore erunt modici pallidi languidi, frigido ventri et qui adsidue reiectare consueverint et quos semper malignus humor inpugnet et quos intrinsecus collectus dolor adsidua ratione discruciet. Vita vero eorum erit malitiosa laboriosa sollicita et adsiduis doloribus animi implicata, circa aquam vel in aquoso loco habentes vitae subsidium." This passage (cf. also *Cat. astr. Gr.*, VOL. VII, p. 239, 20 sqq.) is repeated almost word for word in Johannes Engel (JOHANNES ANGELUS, *Astrolabium planum*, Augsburg 1488 and Venice 1494, fol. t1^r, as a sixteenth-century reader has noted in his copy of the Venice edition, now at the Warburg Institute, London. GUIDO COLONNA's *Historia Troiana* still bases the fact that Saturn foresaw the evil threatened him by his son on his being "in mathematica arte peritissimus" (ch. "De initio idolatrie", Strasbourg 1494, fol. e5^r).

[79] For the Latin etymology "Latium = latere", see below, text pp. 160; 162. For the Greek expressions *ἀπόκρυφα βιβλία* (*Cat. astr. Gr.*, VOL. I, p. 115) and *κρυβαί* (Vettius Valens) see HESIOD, *Theogony*, lines 729 sqq.:

ἔνθα θεοὶ Τιτῆνες ὑπὸ ζόφῳ ἠερόεντι
κεκρύφαται. . . .

gradually assimilate, was that of the Neoplatonists, and its uniformity, its roundness, its essential positivity stood out in as clear a contrast with the complex and preponderantly negative astrological notion of Saturn as did 'Aristotle's' notion of melancholy with respect to that of the schools of medicine.

(iii) *Kronos–Saturn in Neoplatonism*

When Neoplatonism made use of the same mythical and scientific data as astrology, it did so not in order to subordinate this world as a whole to the determinative influence of the stars, but in order to find a metaphysical unity which could give meaning to all physical existence. While this supreme unity gradually descends and branches out into the multiplicity of earthly things, phenomena are ranged in vertical series (σειραί) which by degrees reach down to the motionless minerals.[80] The principle governing these "chains of being" was now symbolised by the heavenly bodies, which occupied a position midway between this world and "the place above the heavens". Hence the Neoplatonic series were comparable with the astrological categories, since both associated certain groups of earthly phenomena with certain planets, as well as with certain signs of the zodiac. But the Neoplatonic categories did not at first imply any causal relationship in the sense of astral predestination.[81] The heavenly bodies were envisaged, on the one hand, as metaphysical symbols through which the various degrees in the structure of the All became visible, and, on the other, as cosmological principles according to which were ordered the emanations of the All-One into the material world, and, vice versa, the ascent from the material world into the realm of the All-One. Thus the phenomena composing the vertical series were connected with one another not because they were determined, let alone generated, by Saturn, Jupiter or Mars, but only because, in a form transmitted by Saturn, Jupiter or Mars, and therefore modified to a certain extent, they had a part in the nature of the All-One.

---

[80] PROCLUS, *Comm. in Tim.*, I, p. 210, 19 sqq. (ed. E. Diehl, Leipzig 1903–06) and *passim*. A very characteristic passage is VOL. II, 268, 29 sqq.: *συγχωρήσειε δ' ἂν καὶ Πλάτων καὶ ἀπὸ τῆς ἀπλανοῦς καὶ ἀπὸ τῆς πλανωμένης [sc. σφαίρας] διατείνειν τὰς σειρὰς μέχρι τῶν χθονίων . . . , ὅπου γε καὶ τῶν ἀπολύτων ἡγεμόνων τῶν δώδεκα τὰς σειρὰς ἄνωθεν καθήκειν ἐθέλει μέχρι τῶν ἐσχάτων.*

[81] Heavenly phenomena are, however, admitted as 'signs' of the future (PLOTINUS, *Enneads*, II, 3, 7) for that which is enacted only slowly and confusedly on earth is bound to be recognised earlier and more clearly in the sky.

From this[82] it is clear that in Neoplatonism it was not possible for any star to have an essentially evil influence. Even the meanest of the planets was still nearer to the divine than the material world. Even the planet mythically or physically regarded as the most evil and noxious was a transmitter of forces which by their very nature could only be good. This principle was expressed most clearly by Iamblichus[83]:

> In this manner all the visible gods in heaven [i.e. the stars] are in a certain sense incorporeal. The further question is in doubt as to how some of these can work good, others evil. This notion is taken from the astrologers, but misses completely the real state of affairs. For, in truth, all the astral divinities are good and are the cause of good, since they all equally gaze upon the good and complete their courses according to the good and the beautiful alone. . . . The world of becoming, however, since it is itself multiform and composed of different parts, can because of its own inconsistency and fragmentation, absorb these uniform and homogeneous forces only in a contradictory and fragmentary way.

This positive interpretation of astral influence benefited Saturn relatively more than any of the other planets. Mars, too, of course, which was also formerly "evil", now became a no less positive principle in Neoplatonism than Saturn. But Saturn possessed the double property of being the forefather of all the other planetary gods, and of having his seat in the highest heaven. These two qualities, which must originally have been connected,[84] assured him of unopposed supremacy in the Neoplatonic system, which here as elsewhere endeavoured to reconcile Platonic with

---

[82] How powerfully these cosmological constructions affected Arab philosophers, mystics and ultimately even magicians, is now general knowledge. A particularly characteristic account of the Neoplatonic doctrine of emanation is found, e.g., in Avicenna (cf. B. CARRA DE VAUX, *Avicenne*, Paris 1900, p. 247). In other, preponderantly magical, works, on the other hand, there is a very interesting encounter between Neoplatonism and astrology, the former envisaging the gifts of the planets as purely beneficial, the latter considering Saturn's influence in particular as preponderantly harmful. In the essentially Neoplatonic metaphysics of Picatrix, the planets have the task of transmitting the emanations of the *νοῦς* to the *ὕλη*, and, in so doing, to differentiate them according to their own natures (for this, cf. H. RITTER, "Picatrix, ein arabisches Handbuch hellenistischer Magie," in *Vorträge der Bibliothek Warburg*, VOL. I, 1921–22). Therefore, since these emanations are by nature good, the planets can
PL. 149 only work good, though that does not prevent Picatrix, any more than the Pure Brothers (who were also influenced by Neoplatonism) from painting the influence of Saturn or Mars as preponderantly baleful. One can see that at bottom the very complicated astrological system could not be reconciled with the essentially optimistic views of Neoplatonism.

[83] IAMBLICHUS, *De mysteriis*, ed. G. Parthey, Berlin 1857, I, 18, pp. 52 and 54. The notion, which also re-emerged occasionally in the Middle Ages, that the influence of the stars was conditioned by the nature of the substance receiving it and not merely by their own dynamism (see below, text pp. 162, 169 sqq.) is dealt with in greater detail in the following sections, particularly with reference to Saturn and Mars, whose metaphysical sublimity is contrasted with the malevolence attributed to them by the astrologers.

[84] See above, p. 136 (text).

Aristotelian views. The hierarchy of metaphysical principles going back to Plato according to which the genitor took precedence over the generated,[85] was linked with Aristotle's principle of "topological" thinking, according to which a higher position in space signified greater metaphysical worth.

Thus, in Neoplatonism, Kronos became the most exalted figure in the philosophically interpreted pantheon. According to Plotinus he symbolised Intellect (Νοῦς), as opposed to Zeus, who represented Soul.[86] The myth of his devouring his children could be interpreted so as to mean that the intellect, until it brings forth the soul, retains its offspring within itself[87]; and even the castration of Uranus by Kronos followed by the dethronement of Kronos by Zeus could on this basis acquire a metaphysical explanation.[88]

This glorification of Saturn as the representative not of earthly power and riches but of the purest and highest power of thought could invoke Plato himself, who, just as he had interpreted madness as "divine frenzy", now became the authority for the new nobility with which Saturn was endowed. Not only had he placed the notion of the Golden Age formed by Hesiod in the foreground of his political observations, but also he had prepared the ground for the equation of Kronos with Νοῦς. The etymologies in the *Cratylus* are to a certain extent ironical. But a name was essentially a condensation of myth, and the etymology of a name its magical explication by means of images. It is therefore understandable that the Neoplatonists should have taken Plato's ironical words literally when he said:

> At first sight it might seem an irreverence to call Zeus the son of Kronos, but it is quite apt to say that he must be the offspring of a mighty intellect.

---

[85] Cf. PLATO's well-known tripartite division of the principles often interpreted as a model for the Christian doctrine of the Trinity: *Letter VI*, 323cd (genuine) and *Letter II*, 312e (apocryphal). On this, see R. KLIBANSKY, *Ein Proklos-Fund und seine Bedeutung*, Heidelberg 1929, pp. 10 sqq., esp. p. 11, note 1.

[86] PLOTINUS, *Enneads*, V, 1, 4: Κρόνου . . . *θεοῦ κόρου καὶ νοῦ ὄντος.*

[87] PLOTINUS, *Enneads*, V, 1, 7: Κρόνον *μὲν θεὸν σοφώτατον πρὸ τοῦ Διὸς γενέσθαι ἃ γεννᾷ πάλιν ἐν ἑαυτῷ ἔχειν, ᾗ καὶ πλήρης καὶ νοῦς ἐν κόρῳ.*

[88] PLOTINUS, Enneads, V, 8, 13: *ὁ οὖν θεὸς ὁ εἰς τὸ μένειν ὡσαύτως δεδεμένος καὶ συγχωρήσας τῷ παιδὶ τοῦδε τοῦ παντὸς ἄρχειν (οὐ γὰρ ἦν αὐτῷ πρὸς τρόπου τὴν ἐκεῖ ἀρχὴν ἀφέντι νεωτέραν αὐτοῦ καὶ ὑστέραν μεθέπειν κόρον ἔχοντι τῶν καλῶν) ταῦτ' ἀφεὶς ἔστησέ τε τὸν αὐτοῦ πατέρα εἰς ἑαυτὸν καὶ μέχρις αὐτοῦ πρὸς τὸ ἄνω. . . . 'Αλλ' ἐπειδὴ ὁ πατὴρ αὐτῷ* [*sc.* Zeus] *μείζων ἢ κατὰ κάλλος ἦν, πρώτως αὐτὸς ἔμεινε καλός, καίτοι καλῆς καὶ τῆς ψυχῆς οὔσης.*

For the word κόρος does not mean "son" but signifies the pure and unadulterated mind itself.[89]

Moreover, in the passages where Plato deals in mythical form with the birth of the State, Kronos is mentioned as a god friendly to mankind, under whose rule contentment, modesty, law, and ungrudging righteousness prevailed, so that men of the present day are advised in every way to strive after life as it was under Kronos, and in this sense to call the rule of Νοῦς their law.[90] One can also discover Orphic sources, transmitted mainly by the Neoplatonists themselves. In Orphism, Kronos—his bonds sometimes interpreted as a cosmological principle of unity[91]—passed for the architect of the world, who, as the father of all, while still in Tartarus, transmitted to his son the basic principles of the universe.[92] He was also regarded as a seer, and described as a πρόμαντις or προμηθεύς.[93] The foundation of this lay in the equation, expressly recognised by the Neoplatonists, of Kronos with Chronos—that is to say, with Time, the fundamental principle of the Orphic theology[94]; and this equation, based not only on the apparent kinship of name,[95] led Macrobius (or rather, Porphyry, whom he follows) to say that Kronos–Chronos was regarded as the

---

[89] PLATO, *Cratylus*, 396b. Particularly interesting is the connexion *κορόνους, ὡς νοῦς ἄυλος καὶ καθαρός*: PROCLUS, *Scholia in Cratylum*, ed. G. Pasquali, Leipzig 1908, p. 59, 5; similarly in *In theol. Platon.*, ed. A. Portus, Hamburg 1618, v, 5, p. 258 (and elsewhere); the same, in *Schol. ad Hesiod. Erga*, line III, (*Poetae minores graeci*, ed. T. Gaisford, new edn., VOL. II, Leipzig 1823, p. 112, 20); and EUSTATHIUS, *In Iliad.*, p. 203, 20. Cf. also PROCLUS, *In Tim.*, I, 34, 25 sq., (Diehl): *τὸ δὲ φιλόσοφον τῷ Κρόνῳ, καθόσον ἐστὶ νοερὸν καὶ ἄνεισι μεχρὶ τῆς πρωτίστης αἰτίας*. For the understanding of Greek etymology in general, and especially in the *Cratylus*, cf. MAX A. WARBURG, *Zwei Fragen zum Kratylos*, Berlin 1929.

[90] PLATO, *Laws*, IV, 713c–714a; cf. also *Statesman*, 269a sqq. The notion of a cruel and wicked Kronos, on the other hand, occurs in Plato only once, and then only in connexion with a general polemic against the notions of the gods in the old myths (*Republic*, II, 378a).

[91] Cf. E. ABEL (ed.), *Orphica*, Leipzig 1885, XIII, 4: *δεσμοὺς ἀρρήκτους ὃς ἔχεις κατ' ἀπείρονα κόσμον.*

[92] Cf. E. ABEL (ed.), loc. cit.; also *Orphicorum fragmenta*, ed. O. Kern, Berlin 1922, 129.

[93] Cf. E. ABEL (ed.), loc. cit.: *σεμνὲ προμηθεῦ*; also LYCOPHRON, *Alexandra*, line 202: *τοῦ προμάντιος Κρόνου*, with scholion: *πρόμαντις οὖν ὁ Κρόνος, ὁ πρὸ τοῦ δράκοντος μαντευσάμενος* (p. 84, 19, in G. Kinkel's edition, Leipzig 1880).

[94] "Orpheus calls the very first principle *Χρόνος*, i.e. almost homonymously with *Κρόνος*," says PROCLUS, *Scholia in Cratylum*, ed. G. Pasquali, Leipzig 1908, p. 59, 17; the *Κρόνος-νοῦς* connexion is also described as Orphic: DAMASCIUS, *De primis principiis*, 67; O. Kern (ed.), *Orphicorum fragmenta*, 131: *ἔοικε δὲ καὶ 'Ορφεὺς τὸν Κρόνον εἰδὼς νοῦν*; and PROCLUS in *Schol. ad Hesiod. Erga*, line 126 (Gaisford (ed.) op. cit., p. 121, 17): *ὁ μὲν 'Ορφεὺς τοῦ ἀργύρου γένους βασιλεύειν φησὶ τὸν Κρόνον, τοὺς κατὰ τὸν καθαρὸν λόγον ζῶντας ἀργυροὺς λέγων, ὥσπερ τοὺς κατὰ νοῦν μόνον χρυσοῦς.*

[95] *Χρόνος*, for instance, is called *τέκτων σοφός*, which brings the concept of him close to that of the old and wise founder of a city (cf. CRATES, *Fragm.* 39, and the parallels quoted in this connexion by T. KOCK, *Comicorum Atticorum fragmenta*, VOL. I, Leipzig 1880, p. 142).

sun, whose course established the "ordo elementorum" by measure and by number.[96]

Into Neoplatonism too, however, an astrological trend found its way. While Proclus, recollecting Plato's *Phaedrus*, describes all the Olympic gods as regents of those "series" connecting all "related" things and beings with one another, other Neoplatonists attribute this power only to the planetary rulers.[97] What for Plotinus had been essentially a mythical allegory, and for Proclus a cosmological relationship, becomes for Macrobius (or his source) a genuine astrological doctrine of planetary influence. Proclus and Macrobius are in agreement, however, in so far as they associate the power of the stars with the physical and mental capacity of the individual in an almost identical formula, and maintain that the highest faculties of the human soul, namely rational and speculative thought, correspond to Saturn, or even (according to Macrobius) originate in Saturn's sphere.

In Macrobius's account, which was ever afterwards of fundamental importance, the equation Kronos = Νοῦς became fused with a peculiar myth, the history of which reveals plainly the essentially optimistic trend of Neoplatonic interpretation—namely, the doctrine of the soul's journey. The soul, strongly attracted by the corporeal world, more and more oblivious of her pure and divine nature, and "befuddled"—so we are told in the commentary on the *Somnium Scipionis*[98]—in the constellation of

---

[96] MACROBIUS, *Saturnalia*, I, 22, 8: "Saturnus ipse, qui auctor est temporum et ideo a Graecis inmutata littera Κρόνος quasi χρόνος vocatur, quid aliud nisi sol intellegendus est, cum tradatur ordo elementorum numerositate distinctus, luce patefactus, nexus aeternitate conductus, visione discretus, quae omnia actum solis ostendunt?" For the connexion between Saturn and Sol, dating from the Babylonians, see p. 136 (text).

[97] Gods who were not identified with stars, on the other hand, were either ignored or else absorbed by the planetary gods, thereby losing their identity (cf. H. RITTER, "Picatrix, ein arabisches Handbuch hellenistischer Magie," in *Vorträge der Bibliothek Warburg*, VOL. I, 1921–22, p. 101).

[98] MACROBIUS, *In somnium Scipionis*, I, 12, 13–14 (p. 533 in F. Eyssenhardt's edition, Leipzig 1893): "Hoc ergo primo pondere de zodiaco et lacteo ad subiectas usque sphaeras anima delapsa, dum et per illas labitur, in singulis non solum, ut iam diximus, luminosi corporis amicitur accessu, sed et singulos motus, quos in exercitio est habitura, producit:

In Saturni ratiocinationem et intelligentiam, quod λογιστικόν et θεωρητικόν vocant:
in Iovis vim agendi, quod πρακτικόν dicitur:
in Martis animositatis ardorem, quod θυμικόν nuncupatur:
in Solis sentiendi opinandique naturam, quod αἰσθητικόν et φανταστικόν appellant:
desiderii vero motum, quod ἐπιθυμητικόν vocatur, in Veneris:
pronuntiandi et interpretandi quae sentiat, quod ἑρμηνευτικόν dicitur, in orbe Mercurii:
φυτικόν vero, id est naturam plantandi et augendi corpora, in ingressu globi lunaris exercet."

This text, which like the similar one in PROCLUS (*In Tim.*, I, 34, 25 sq. Diehl) admirably summarises the Neoplatonic doctrine, was known throughout the Middle Ages, and its survival

the Wine-Bowl ("Crater") by a draught as of the waters of Lethe, sinks from the heights of the starry firmament (de zodiaco et lacteo) down to the nether spheres (that is, those of the planets); and even while she is gliding down through the spheres she not only becomes clothed in each of them, as she approaches the luminous body, but also learns to produce the particular motions which she is to exercise. In the sphere of Saturn, she develops the faculty of reasoned thought and understanding, "which they call λογιστικόν and θεωρητικόν"; in Jupiter's, she acquires the power to act, "which is spoken of as πρακτικόν"; in that of Mars, a fervour of spirit, "which is well known as θυμικόν"; in that of the sun, she becomes capable of feeling and imagining, "which are named αἰσθητικόν and φανταστικόν"; the motion, however, of desire ("desiderii"), "which they call ἐπιθυμητικόν", she acquires in the sphere of Venus; that of expressing and interpreting her sense-experience, which is referred to as "ἑρμηνευτικόν", in the sphere of Mercury; and finally that which is called φυτικόν, in other words the power of planting and nourishing organic bodies, when she enters the lunar orbit.

This view can scarcely be accounted for save by the Neoplatonic doctrine of the "series", which was connected with a theory more religious than philosophic, according to which individual human souls passed through the heavens before their earthly birth and in so doing received a gift from each of the astral powers in turn, which they returned in the same manner on their ascension after death. This notion seems in fact to have originated in the religious system of Gnosticism, and as this system was governed by a radically world-abnegating dualism dividing (as in ancient Persia) a sinless other world from an impure and guilty present world, it is not surprising that the soul's journey from heaven to earth should originally be conceived only as a "Fall".[99] The fullest and best account of the soul's journeyings is that of Servius,

can be traced (admittedly along a very specialised line) down to the fifteenth and sixteenth centuries (see below, text pp. 192 sqq., 253 sqq.). For its significance in regard to NICHOLAS OF CUSA (*De doct. ign.*, I, 25), cf. R. Klibansky's list of sources, ed. cit., Leipzig 1932, p. 52.

[99] Cf. F. BOLL, "Die Lebensalter", in *Neue Jahrbücher für das klassische Altertum*, XVI (1913), pp. 125 sqq. A passage indicative of the spirit of radical world negation underlying this doctrine can be found, for instance, in the *Corpus hermeticum*, libellus VI, 4a, ed. W. Scott, Oxford 1924, p. 168: ὁ γὰρ κόσμος πλήρωμά ἐστι τῆς κακίας, ὁ δὲ θεὸς τοῦ ἀγαθοῦ. For the derivation of the seven deadly sins in Christian theology from the fatal gifts of the seven planets, cf. T. ZIELINSKI, in *Philologus*, VOL. LXIV (1905), pp. 21 sqq. W. BOUSSET (*Hauptprobleme der Gnosis*, Göttingen 1907, pp. 91 sqq.) is inclined to attribute to Persian influence the metaphysical dualism of Gnosticism, to which we might add that Persian sources describe the seven planets as "leaders on the side of Ahriman," while the twelve signs of

though even here it appears in a form already rationalised in astronomical terms. This runs as follows:

> The philosophers teach us what the soul loses in its descent through the various spheres. For that reason the astrologers say that our souls and bodies are connected by the agency of the divinities in those various spheres; for when souls descend they drag with them the lethargy of Saturn, the irascibility of Mars, the sensuality of Venus, the greed for gain of Mercury and the lust for power of Jupiter.[100]

Correspondingly, Poimandres says that on the soul's ascension after death it frees itself of the bad qualities of its earthly existence, leaving in the sphere of Saturn its "lurking lies".[101]

This account of the soul's journeyings largely retained its essentially Gnostic character, that is, the "endowment" of the soul descending through the spheres with specific properties, all of them fatal gifts; but this basic character was lost as soon as a connexion was formed with a purely cosmological theory, that is to say, one directed not so much to the problem of sin as to the problem of the essential unity of man and universe. When this essential unity began to be sought more generally in the biological rather than in the psychological realm, the original idea of "journeying" faded into the background, while the planetary gifts, now not so much acquired on a journey as received at birth, become neutral, constructive elements, some mental, some physical. It so happens that Servius is again the writer who passes on this version of the old doctrine, this time appealing not to the philosophers and astrologers, but to the "physici". At birth, human nature receives "a Sole spiritum, a Luna corpus, a Marte sanguinem, a Mercurio ingenium, a Iove bonorum desiderium, a Venere cupiditatem, a Saturno humorem".[102]

---

the Zodiac, on the other hand, are called "leaders on the side of Ormuzd" (cf. H. JUNKER, "Über iranische Quellen des hellenistischen Aionbegriffs", in *Vorträge der Bibliothek Warburg*, 1922, pp. 141 sqq.). Cf. also T. ZIELINSKI, "Hermes und die Hermetik", in *Archiv für Religionswissenschaft*, VIII (1905), pp. 325 sqq., esp. 330 sqq.

[100] SERVIUS, *Comm. in Aeneid.*, VI, 714.

[101] Cf. BOLL, BOUSSET, and ZIELINSKI, loc. cit.; ZIELINSKI, op. cit., pp. 321 sqq.; F. CUMONT, *After-Life in Roman Paganism*, New Haven 1922, pp. 106 sqq.

[102] SERVIUS, *Comm. in Aeneid.*, XI, 51. This physico-biological conception of the gifts of the planets side by side with a more Neoplatonic one was accepted also by Isidore (ISIDORE, *Etym.*, V, 30, 8, largely agreeing with Servius, but put forward, significantly enough, as "stultitia gentilium"); this Servius series is reproduced word for word in *Mythographus* III (cf. below, text pp. 172 sqq.), in the chapter on Mercury (G. H. BODE, *Scriptores rerum mythicarum latini tres*, Celle 1834, pp. 217, line 33). On the other hand, the real notion of the soul's journeyings survived in many forms in a large number of Platonist writings and poems, e.g. in BERNARDUS SILVESTRIS, *De univ. mundi*, II, 3; ALANUS AB INSULIS (see below, pp. 186 sqq., text); and later in MATTEO PALMIERI (see below pp. 251 sqq., text); CARDANUS, ATHANASIUS KIRCHER, etc.

When, however, the relationship between macrocosm and microcosm was so conceived that planetary influences were supposed to be of a physical as well as of an ethical nature, and when at the same time the ideas of emanation and reascension were linked with the journeyings of the soul, all this gave rise to a transformation such as we have encountered in the Neoplatonists Proclus and Macrobius. Whether classified according to "series" as in Proclus, or regarded as acquired in different planetary spheres, as in Macrobius, the planetary gifts became faculties of the soul, and these faculties were without exception beneficial. Neoplatonism, too, considered the soul's incarnation in the material world as a descent, but one in which the soul's endowments, brought with her from her higher home, could only be good; and among these innate goods the noblest, as we have seen, was Saturn's gift.[103]

Thus, in this double interpretation of the myth of the soul's journeyings—and between those extremes there existed many mixed forms[104]—the polarity of the notion of Kronos led to two opposing basic attitudes. The pregnant antithesis "dullness, sadness, fraud *vs.* reasoned or even inspired thought" was to dominate the future too, though the bald "either/or" was soon softened to "both/and". The Saturn to whom the lethargic and vulgar belonged was at the same time venerated as the planet of high contemplation, the star of anchorets and philosophers.

Nevertheless, the nature and destiny of the man born under Saturn, even when, within the limits of his condition, his lot was the most fortunate, still retained a basis of the sinister; and it is on the idea of a contrast, born of darkness, between the greatest possibilities of good and evil, that the most profound analogy between Saturn and melancholy was founded. It was not only the combination of cold and dryness that linked black bile with the apparently similar nature of the star; nor was it only the tendency to depression, loneliness and visions, which the melancholic

[103] See above, p. 155 (text).

[104] Cf. the literature quoted on page 157, notes 101 sq. In this type of mixed series (as e.g. in
Pl. 150 Isidore, *De natura rerum*, ed. G. Becker, Berlin 1857, III, p. 10; Bede, *De temporum ratione*, ch. 8 (Migne, P. L., vol. XC, col. 328 sq.); Andalus de Nigro, Brit. Mus., MS Add. 23770, fols. 36^{v}–37^{r}), Saturn generally belongs to the evil side; he bestows or signifies δάκρυ, νωχελία, ψεῦδος, "merores, tristitiam, vilitatem et malum" and "tarditatem". Only in the Κόρη Κόσμου (T. Zielinski, "Hermes und die Hermetik," in *Archiv für Religionswissenschaft*, VIII (1905), p. 365) does Saturn play a good part; as ὁ τῆς Νεμέσεως ἀστήρ he bestows Δίκη and Ἀνάγκη on the soul. This at first sight singular exception can be explained by the influence of Platonist literature, traceable also elsewhere in the *Corpus Hermeticum*.

shared with the planet of tears, of solitary life and of soothsayers; above all, there was an analogy of action. Like melancholy, Saturn, that demon of the opposites, endowed the soul both with slowness and stupidity and with the power of intelligence and contemplation. Like melancholy, Saturn menaced those in his power, illustrious though they might be, with depression, or even madness. To quote Ficino, Saturn "seldom denotes ordinary characters and destinies, but rather people set apart from the rest, divine or bestial, blissful, or bowed down by the deepest sorrow".[105]

3. SATURN IN MEDIEVAL LITERATURE

(*a*) Saturn in the Controversies of the Church Fathers

Early Christianity was bound to declare war on the astrological view of the universe, as well as on the veneration of the ancient pagan gods.[106] From the very beginning, therefore, it was the task of the Church Fathers to weaken belief in astral predestination[107] and to reveal the emptiness of faith in the ancient gods. In the case of gods who were also planetary rulers, a battle was fought on two fronts against one and the same enemy, during which, as always happens in the combating of heresies, the very refutation of the heterodox views helped to preserve them.

The weapons employed by an early and relatively straightforward group of apologists could be taken from the arsenal of

---

[105] FICINO, *De v. tripl.*, III, 2 (*Opera*, p. 533): "Saturnus non facile communem significat humani generis qualitatem atque sortem, sed hominem ab aliis segregatum, divinum aut brutum, beatum aut extrema miseria pressum." The connexion between the Neoplatonic notion of Saturn and the birth of the modern notion of genius (see below, text pp. 241 sqq.) can here be seen already from the choice of words, for "divinus" became the typical description of modern philosophical, poetic and (since Michelangelo) artistic men of genius.

Sometimes the contrast inherent in the notion of Saturn already appears in older texts, as in HERMIPPUS, *Anonymi Christiani Hermippus de astrologia dialogus*, XIII, 86, edd. W. Kroll and P. Viereck, Leipzig 1895, p. 19 (fourteenth century): *εἴληχε μὲν ὡς εἴρηται ὁ τοῦ Κρόνου, οἷον φαντασίαν, μνήμην, ἔτι δὲ καὶ τὴν ἐναντίαν αὐτῇ λήθην καὶ γονὴν σπέρματος.* For ALANUS AB INSULIS, see below, p. 186 (text).

[106] A history of medieval astrology does not yet exist. For the moment, cf. WEDEL, M. A. A.

[107] TERTULLIAN, *De idolatria*, 9, however, tells us in referring to the star which led the Three Kings: "at enim scientia ista [i.e. astrology] usque ad evangelium fuit concessa." For his attitude to astrology, cf. F. W. C. L. SCHULTE, *Het Heidendom bij Tertullianus*, Nijkerk 1923, ch. 7. ISIDORE, *Etym.*, VIII, 9, 26 follows Tertullian word for word (cf. WEDEL, M. A. A., p. 18).

the ancients themselves. The notion of Saturn, with its many contradictions, was a particularly suitable object of attack. Thus Minucius Felix, Tertullian, and Lactantius, the latter almost word for word the same as Minucius, took their stand on the Euhemeristic view, according to which the gods had been mere men, and Saturn, said to be the chief of the gods, a man particularly hard pressed by fate:

> Saturn, the prince of this race and horde, was described by all writers in antiquity, both Greek and Roman, as a man. . . . When he fled Crete for fear of his son's wrath, came to Italy and was hospitably received by Janus, he instructed those wild and savage men in many things, like the cultured Greek that he was, in writing, in minting coin, and in the making of tools. For that reason he wanted the asylum where he had safely hidden himself to be called Latium (from "latere") . . . so he was altogether a man who fled, altogether a man who hid himself.[108]

This is not the place to describe in detail the way in which other themes in heathen or Jewish polemics against the gods were taken over by the apologists and employed in Christian speculation.[109] Throughout this battle the Kronos–Saturn myth played a not unimportant part, whether because its primitive and violent theme shocked the sensibilities of the time,[110] or because its Stoic and physiological interpretation seemed so profound as especially to warrant rebuttal. Whether Kronos's madness was interpreted as the metamorphosis of the "Kairos", or whether Kronos was time, darkness, frost or moisture, he certainly was not a god, for divinity is essentially unchanging. Thus argued Athenagoras, taking his argument from the older Stoic

---

[108] MINUCIUS FELIX, *Octavius*, XXI, 4–7; TERTULLIAN, *Apologetic.*, X; LACTANTIUS, *Divin. inst.*, I, 13, 6–8, is based on the quotation from VIRGIL (*Aen.*, VIII, lines 320 sqq.: see below, text p. 162) later taken over by Augustine. The passage on Saturn is frequently mentioned in critical literature in connexion with the question, discussed in numerous articles, of the interdependence of Minucius Felix and Tertullian. See the bibliographies in H. J. BAYLIS, *Minucius Felix*, London 1928, and in G. A. JOHANNA SCHMIDT, *Minucius Felix oder Tertullian* (dissertation, Munich 1932), pp. 89 sqq. For the star of the Magi, cf. A. BOUCHÉ-LECLERCQ, *L'astrologie grecque*, Paris 1899, p. 611, and L. DE VREESE, *Augustinus en de Astrologie* (dissertation, Amsterdam 1933), pp. 71 sqq.

[109] The passages on Saturn in the Church Fathers are conveniently collected in VOL. II of the index to MIGNE, P. L., VOL. CCXIX, pp. 388 sqq. For the early history of the criticism of pagan gods with a detailed commentary on two of the earliest Greek works, cf. J. GEFFCKEN, *Zwei griechische Apologeten* (Aristides and Athenagoras), Leipzig 1907. JOSEF LORTZ, *Tertullian als Apologet*, VOLS. I–II, 1927–28 (Münster. Beiträge zur Theologie, IX–X) discusses the problem of early Roman attacks on paganism. Cf. esp. pp. 128–179.

[110] For the distaste with which the myth of the birth of Zeus and Kronos's devouring of the stone was regarded, we may mention a later text, GREGORY OF NAZIANZUS, *Oratio in sancta lumina* (MIGNE, P. Gr., VOL. XXXVI, col. 337) see below, text p. 199, and PLATE 14.

controversialists whom he may have known from Jewish–Hellenistic sources.[111] Tertullian, too, dealt particularly thoroughly with Saturn, because in him lay the origin of the gods: "Heaven and Earth gave birth to him, the patriarch of the gods, and the poets were the midwives".[112] Different though Tertullian was in origin and in temperament and character from an average Greek such as Athenagoras, Greeks and Romans in these early Christian times fought the common enemy with roughly the same methods and ideas; in some places this resulted in such similarity of text that even to-day philologists cannot be certain which was the source of which.[113]

St Augustine, however, whose opposition to astrology was based as much on his concern for free will as on his faith in divine predestination,[114] was not content with such arguments. Not only did he completely refute, in *De civitate Dei*, all the learned interpretations of the ancient pantheon,[115] but he also devoted to Saturn in particular a detailed examination. This systematically contrasted the Euhemeristic humanising of originally divine figures with the allegorical treatment in natural philosophy and etymology, and then compared both interpretations with that of

---

[111] *Apologia pro Christianis*, 22 (J. GEFFCKEN, *Zwei griechische Apologeten*, Leipzig 1907 pp. 139 sqq., 205 sqq.).

[112] *Ad nationes*, II, 12 (Corp. Ss. Eccl. Lat., VOL. XX, p. 118). Tertullian contradicts the Stoic doctrine developed by CICERO, *De natura deorum*, II, 24–25, equating Κρόνος with Χρόνος: "Sed eleganter quidam sibi videntur physiologice per allegoricam argumentationem de Saturno interpretari tempus esse. . . . Nominis quoque testimonium compellant: Κρόνον dictum Graece ut Χρόνον. Aeque latini vocabuli a sationibus rationem deducunt, qui eum procreatorem coniectantur, per eum seminalia caeli in terram deferri." The later derivation of the name Saturn "a satu", based on VARRO, *De lingua latina*, v, 64, edd. G. Goetz and F. Schoell, Leipzig 1910, p. 20 (see also the parallel passages given in the appendix) is also mentioned several times by AUGUSTINE, *De Civitate Dei*, VI, 8; VII, 2; VII, 3 ("Saturnus seminis dator vel sator"); VII, 13; VII, 15. How Varro attempted to combine this derivation with that from the notion of Time can be seen in *De Civitate Dei*, VII, 19: "Chronon appellatum dicit [sc. Varro], quod Graeco vocabulo significat temporis spatium, sine quo semen, inquit, non potest esse fecundum." Cf. E. SCHWARTZ, "De M. T. Varronis apud sanctos patres vestigiis" in *Jahrbuch für klassische Philologie*, SUPPL. VOL. XVI (1888), pp. 424 sqq., 439, 482 sqq.

[113] E.g. JOSEF LORTZ, *Tertullian als Apologet*, I, p. 134.

[114] Cf. L. DE VREESE, *Augustinus en de Astrologie* (dissertation, Amsterdam 1933), and J. A. DAVIS, *De Orosio et sancto Augustino Priscillianistarum adversariis commentaria historica et philologica* (dissertation, Nimwegen 1930), pp. 189 sqq.

[115] *De Civitate Dei*, VII, 19. The remaining passages on Saturn in *De Civitate Dei* are easily available in the index to E. Hoffmann's edition, Vienna 1899–1900 (Saturn as unlucky planet, god of the Jews, lord of the Sabbath, etc.). For Saturn in Augustine's other works see SISTER MARY DANIEL MADDEN, *The Pagan Divinities and their Worship . . . in the works of St Augustine exclusive of the City of God* (The Catholic University of America, Patristic Studies, VOL. XXIV, 1930), pp. 46–53. For Augustine's transmitting and perfecting of early Christian, apologetics in general, see GEFFCKEN, op. cit., pp. 318 sqq.

the Neoplatonists, who recognised that the earlier doctrines were untenable. In Neoplatonism, Saturn represented the highest intellect. But, logically, should not these philosophers alter their faith with the alteration in their interpretation, and either not erect any images to the gods, or else erect them only to Saturn and not to Jupiter Capitolinus? But the world ignored these doctrines and continued to worship Jupiter as the highest god, and common opinion was at one with the astrologers in regarding Saturn not as a wise creator, but as a wicked old man. Thus his polemic reaches a climax in a magnificently built-up contrast between the Neoplatonic metaphysical and affirmative notion of Saturn and the astrological superstitious and negative notion; and the malicious acumen of this contrast brought out the inner ambivalence of Saturn with a clarity not attained again save by the subtle intuition of the Renaissance.

What do they say of Saturn? What being do they worship as Saturn? Is it not he who first came down from Olympus—

"Fleeing the war of Jupiter and kingdom overthrown,
He laid in peace the rugged folk amid the mountains steep
Scattered about, and gave them laws and wished them well to keep
The name of Latium since he lay safe hidden on that shore."[116]

Does not his own portrait distinguish him, which shows him with covered head like one that hides himself? Was it not he who showed the Italians agriculture, as is shown by his sickle? No, say they. . . . For we interpret Saturn as the "fullness of time", which his Greek name suggests: for he is called Kronos, which, when aspirated, is also the name of Time. For this reason he is also called Saturnus in Latin, as it were, full of years ["quasi saturetur annis"]. I really do not know what to do with people who, in attempting to interpret the names and portraits of their gods in a better sense, admit that their greatest god, the father of all others, is Time. For what else do they betray but that all their gods are temporal, since they make Time itself the father of them?

And so their later Platonic philosophers, who lived in Christian times, blushed thereat. They therefore attempted to interpret Saturn in another fashion, by saying that he was called Kronos because, as it were, of the fullness of his intellect ["velut a satietate intellectus"] because in Greek fullness is called κόρος, and understanding or intellect is νοῦς. This notion seems also to be reinforced by the Latin name which is, as it were, compounded of a Latin first part and Greek second part, so that he was called Saturnus in the sense of "abundant intellect" (satur-νοῦς). They saw how absurd it would be if Jupiter, whom they considered or wished to be considered as an eternal divinity, were regarded as a son of Time.

---

[116] "His quoniam latuisset tutus in oris"; VIRGIL, *Aen.*, VIII, 320–324.

According to this modern interpretation . . . they call Jupiter the son of Saturn more in the sense as it were of spirit ["spiritus"] emanating from that highest intellect ["mens"], and considered as the soul of the world filling all heavenly and earthly bodies. . . . The Romans, however, who dedicated the Capitol not to Saturn but to Jupiter, and also other peoples who believed that they owed worship to Jupiter before all other gods, were not of the same opinion as the Platonists. The latter in their new theory, if only they had had any power in such matters, would have preferred to dedicate their chief sanctuaries to Saturn, and also, above all, to extirpate the astrologers and horoscope-makers who had relegated Saturn (described by the Romans as the "wise creator"),[117] to the position of an evil god among other stars.[118]

The Neoplatonic interpretation of Saturn was here treated with unmistakable irony, it is true, but not altogether without respect. It is therefore the more remarkable that Augustine, who elsewhere frequently made use of middle and later Platonic notions,[119] should not have employed this pagan heritage in the service of the Christian viewpoint. His radical aversion applied as much to pagan theology as to pagan astrology.[120]

St Ambrose blazed another trail important for posterity when, instead of attacking, as Tertullian, Athenagoras, Augustine and their contemporaries had done, he associated himself with Philonian and Pythagorean speculation. He took his point of departure not from the planetary gods but from their number,

---

[117] According to another reading: "creator of wise men".

[118] AUGUSTINE, *De consensu evangelistarum*, I, 34 sqq. (Corp. Ss. Eccl. Lat., VOL. XLIII, ed. F. Weihrich, Vienna 1904, pp. 32 sqq.). Some of the polemics accord with Lactantius's statements mentioned above (see the notes to the edition cited). The concluding passage, of great pregnancy, may be given in the original: "Romani tamen, qui non Saturno, sed Iovi Capitolium condiderunt, vel aliae nationes, quae Iovem praecipue supra ceteros deos colendum esse putaverunt, non hoc quod isti [sc. philosophi recentiores Platonici] senserunt, qui secundum istam suam novam opinionem et summas arces, si quicquam in his rebus potestatis habuissent, Saturno potius dedicarent et mathematicos uel genethliacos maxime delerent, qui Saturnum, quem sapientem [another reading: sapientum] effectorem isti dicerent, maleficum deum inter alia sidera constituerent."

[119] A striking example of this is Augustine's doctrine of ideas (e.g. MIGNE, P. L., VOL. XL, col. 29 sq.); cf. also E. PANOFSKY, *Idea* (Studien der Bibliothek Warburg, VOL. V, 1924), pp. 18 sqq. and 81 sqq.

[120] This radically hostile attitude is well illustrated by a passage from MARTIN OF BRACARA's sermon to the peasants. Martin of Bracara regards the gods of the days of the week as fallen angels or demons, who observe the wickedness of men and give themselves out as godless men of earlier times (Saturn, Jupiter, etc.). These demons persuade the people to worship them under the names of these supposed persons. Hence Martin heartily disapproves of naming the days of the week after the planets. "Non tamen sine permissione dei nocent, quia deum habent iratum et non ex toto corde in fide Christi credunt. Sed sunt dubii in tantum, ut nomina ipsa daemoniorum in singulos dies nominent, et appellent diem Martis et Mercuri et Iovis et Veneris et Saturni, qui nullum diem fecerunt, sed fuerunt homines pessimi et scelerati in gente Graecorum" (*De correctione rusticorum*, 8, ed. K. P. Caspari, Christiania 1883, pp. 11 and lxxviii.) This work was written between A.D. 572 and 574. See Caspari (ed.), op. cit., pp. cvii sqq., for its survival in the Middle Ages.

seven. In a certain sense Ambrose had a predecessor in this, Victorinus of Pettau, who in a magnificent survey had distributed the seven gifts of the Holy Spirit among the seven heavenly spheres. The seven heavens, according to Victorinus, corresponded to the seven days of the creation. As witness thereof he quotes the words of Psalm XXXIII. 6: "By the word of the Lord were the heavens made: and all the host of them by the breath of his mouth." The heavens are seven spirits. Their names are the names of those spirits which rested upon Christ, according to the prophet Isaiah. The highest heaven is therefore the heaven of wisdom, the second that of understanding, the third of counsel. From them too the thunder roars and the lightning flashes, and so on.[121] Here, therefore, we encounter cosmological speculation about the seven gifts. But it is characteristic of Victorinus not to take any interest in fixing more precisely the position of these spheres in the cosmos.

Ambrose rightly says that his treatise is written from a viewpoint other than that of the Pythagoreans and the rest of the philosophers. The comparison with Philo, used by him, shows the boldness of Ambrosian symbolism, which did not hesitate with the help of mystic numbers[122] to relate the cosmic system to the gifts of the Holy Spirit. Ambrose says: "The number seven is good."[123] Isaiah numbered seven main virtues of the Holy Spirit. The Hebdomad, like the Trinity, is outside time or measure; it is the author of numbers, not subject to their laws.

> According to this sevenfold circle of spiritual virtues . . . we see created a sevenfold ministration of the planets, by which this world is illumined.[124]

---

[121] VICTORINUS OF PETTAU, *Tractatus de fabrica mundi*, ch. 7 (ed. J. Haussleiter, Corp. Ss. Eccl. Lat., VOL. XLIX, Vienna, 1916, pp. 6 sqq.). For this passage see W. MACHOLZ, *Spuren binitarischer Denkweise* (dissertation, Halle-Wittenberg 1902), pp. 16 sqq. Victorinus of Pettau follows Origen in the main. For Victorinus's attitude to Origen, cf. HIERONYMUS, Epist. 61, 2, 4, and Vigilius. (*Sancti E. Hieronymi epistulae*, ed. J. Hilberg, Corp. Ss. Eccl. Lat., VOL. LIV, Vienna 1910–12, pp. 557–8): "Taceo de Uictorino Petobionensi et ceteris, qui Origenem in explanatione dumtaxat scripturarum secuti sunt et expresserunt"; also Epist. 84, 7, *ad Pammachium et Oceanum* (Hilberg (ed.), ibid., VOL. LV, pp. 130, sqq.): "Nec disertiores sumus Hilario nec fideliores Victorino, qui tractatus eius [scil. Origenis] non ut interpretes sed ut auctores proprii operis transtulerunt. Nuper Ambrosius sic Exaemeron illius [scil. Origenis] conpilavit, ut magis Hippolyti sententias Basiliique sequeretur"; also HIERONYMUS, *Adversus libros Rufini*, 3, 14 (MIGNE, P. L., VOL. XXIII, col. 467).

[122] F. BOLL ("Die Lebensalter", in *Neue Jahrbücher für das klassische Altertum*, XVI (1913), p. 126, note 3) was the first to point out the passage in Ambrose in this connexion. For Philo, cf. K. STAEHLE, *Die Zahlenmystik bei Philon von Alexandria*, Leipzig 1931.

[123] Cf. εἶναι τελεσφόρον ὄντως τὸν ἕβδομον ἀριθμόν in PHILO, *De opificio mundi*, 106 (*Opera*, I, 38, ed. L. Cohn, Berlin 1896).

[124] AMBROSE, *Epist. ad Horontianum*, 44, 3 (MIGNE, P. L., VOL. XVI, cols. 1136 sqq.): "Bonus septimus numerus, quem non Pythagorico et ceterorum philosophorum more

This viewpoint opened the way to Christian speculation concerning the stars: the planets, at least to begin with, were not regarded as distributors of spiritual gifts as in the Neoplatonic doctrine of the soul's journeyings, but were nevertheless brought into direct relation with Christian ethics.

(*b*) Saturn in Later Medieval Speculation

(i) *Saturn in Moral Theology*

The doctrine of the seven gifts of the Holy Spirit had a particularly profound significance in the Middle Ages.[125] After St Augustine had interpreted the seven gifts as a ladder, the highest rung of which was wisdom, this doctrine had become merged with the Neoplatonic notion of the soul's ascension, and towards the end of the twelfth century it was further developed along cosmological lines.

Alexander Neckam, living at the time of the revival of astrology, gave to Ambrose's doctrine a specifically astrological tinge. While, in Ambrose, the notion of a relationship between the planets and the seven gifts had arisen in connexion with a disquisition on the Hebdomad, not concerned with astrology, in Alexander Neckam the same notion appears in a chapter beginning with the words[126]: "Seven are the planets which not only adorn the world but exert their influence on things below, an influence transmitted to them by the highest nature, which is God." Even with regard to the seven gifts he makes use of a purely astrological turn of phrase when he speaks of the seven gifts "which adorn the microcosm with bright ornament and exert their influence on the natural faculties of the soul".

It is therefore understandable that Neckam was not content with general analogies but explored them in detail, bringing in

tractamus, sed secundum formam et divisiones gratiae spiritalis; septem enim virtutes principales sancti spiritus propheta Esaias complexus est (*Isaiah*, XI, 2). Haec hebdomas ... sine tempore, sine ordine, auctor numeri, non sub numeri lege devincta. Itaque sicut ad aeternae Trinitatis gratiam caelum, terra, maria formata, sicut sol, luna et stellae: ita etiam ad illum septenarium virtutum spiritalium circuitum atque orbem operationis divinae vigore praestantem, septenarium quoddam ministerium planetarum creatum advertimus, quo hic mundus illuminatur." According to J. A. DAVIS, op. cit., p. 187, Ambrose was here under Origen's influence. In *Hexaem. lib.*, 4, § 17 (MIGNE, P. L., VOL. XIV, col. 153) Ambrose adopted another view.

125 Cf. K. BOECKL, *Die sieben Gaben des heiligen Geistes in ihrer Bedeutung für die Mystik nach der Theologie des* 13. *und* 14. *Jahrhunderts* (Freiburg i.B. 1931), and the article "Dons du Saint-Esprit" in *Dictionnaire de Théologie Catholique*, VOL. IV (A. Gardeil).

126 *De naturis rerum*, ed. T. Wright, London 1863, pp. 39 sqq.

astrological and astronomical elements.[127] He describes the mode of operation of the seven gifts in terms corresponding to the Neoplatonic doctrine, transmitted by Macrobius, of the beneficent gifts of the planets. For us, the main interest lies in the effects this had on the notion of Saturn. The series of the seven gifts in Isaiah begins with wisdom and ends with the fear of the Lord. Saturn, as the highest planet, could therefore be credited with either the first or the last gift. Neckam credited him with wisdom and gave the following reason for so doing: "As the planet Saturn takes a considerable time to complete his revolution, so wisdom generates maturity from itself. Saturn is rightly described as an old man by the philosophers for old men are of mature judgment."[128]

This description of Saturn, like the general notion of beneficent planetary gifts, is Neoplatonic, for it was Neoplatonism which celebrated Saturn as an old and wise god. In other words, the very view which St Augustine had derided[129] was now resuscitated by Neckam and used in the development of his Christian speculative system.

A friar, a popular preacher, as he described himself, Berthold of Regensburg, who lived at a time of widespread astrological belief, could hardly help including the planets and their influence in his system of moral exhortation. "There are seven stars in the sky. Thereby shall ye read and learn virtue, for if ye have not virtue ye shall never enter into the promised land, and therefore God hath shown forth the seven virtues in the seven planets, so that they shall show you the way to heaven."[130] Berthold

---

[127] Here one must bear in mind the significant fact that Neckam, when introducing astrological doctrines, always emphasises strongly that these are not to be considered as in any way limiting free will; cf. *De naturis rerum* ed. Wright, op. cit.), pp. 40–41. See also below, p. 178, note 161.

[128] *De naturis rerum* (ed. Wright), p. 41. The soul also acquires the following faculties: from Jupiter "intellectus, qui providentiam creat et hebetudinem expellit"; from Mars "donum consilii, quod praecipitationem renuit et cautelam procreat" (this, no doubt, because of discretion being the better part of the soldierly virtue of valour); from Sol on the other hand, "donum fortitudinis, quia . . . creat perseverantiam et fiduciam et magnanimitatem"; from Venus "scientia . . . quae in sanguineis vigere solet." Mercury's gift is connected with the "pietatis donum," as "hominibus dulcis conversationis spirituale augmentum gratiae ministrat"; Luna's gift is connected with "timor qui negligentiam expellit . . . et . . . humilitatem generat." In Abailard we find a similar conception, namely that the planets are spiritually illumined by God's grace which is described as sevenfold. (*Opera*, ed. V. Cousin, Paris 1859, VOL. II, p. 42).

[129] See above, pp. 161 sqq. (text).

[130] BERTHOLD VON REGENSBURG, *Sermons* IV and LXI (F. Pfeiffer's edition, VOL. I, Vienna 1862, pp. 48 sqq., VOL. II, Vienna 1880, pp. 233 sqq.).

was no systematiser. He did not compare the seven gifts or any other ready-made set of virtues with the planets, but based his selection of virtues partly upon theological considerations, and partly upon what seemed appropriate to him as a result of his familiarity with cosmological and astrological doctrine. His set of virtues bears some resemblance to a set which St Thomas Aquinas had listed in quite another connexion.[131] The latter attempted systematically to apportion the influence of the planets. Accordingly, the influence of the three highest planets was concerned with the existence of things. The four lesser planets determined not so much the existence as the motions of things. For this reason Saturn bestowed the highest gift, namely the stability of existence itself ("ipsa stabilitas esse rei"), Jupiter its completion, and Mars the power of survival and the strength to keep existence from harm. Berthold adopted the attributes of Saturn, and perhaps of Mars as well, from a series related to that of St Thomas. Saturn bestowed "continuity", Mars "combating of sin". The Thomist system, however, was of no importance for Berthold's purpose, which was to influence the plain man's morals. Somewhat banal in comparison with that of St Thomas, his attribution of continuity to Saturn is founded on the fact (known to the least educated of his audience) that the planet was so slow that it took thirty years to complete a single revolution—in other words, on the same fact which had induced Neckam to connect Saturn with wisdom. But while the latter attribute is specifically Neoplatonic, the connexion of Saturn with continuity was obviously established on the basis of those astrological sources which had described the planet by the adjective "tenax" and had considered it primarily as the ruler of earthly heaviness, slowness and tenacity.[132]

From the same reservoir of Saturn's good qualities comes the text of a German sermon which passed for Master Eckhart's and gave Ambrose's notion a strongly mystical sense.[133] The influences of divine grace and consolation were to be bestowed on the spiritual heaven of the soul. When the soul becomes a blessed

[131] Thomas Aquinas, *In Metaphysicam Aristotelis Commentaria*, ed. M.-R. Cathala, Turin 1926, p. 123, §§ 2560 sqq.

[132] Cf. for instance the above (p. 145 text) mentioned correlation of *βέβαιον* and "tenacitas"; and below, p. 190 (text), Saturn's characteristics according to Guido Bonatti.

[133] Master Eckhart, *Sermon* LXVII (ed. F. Pfeiffer, Leipzig 1857, pp. 212 sqq.). For this tradition cf. A. Spamer in *Beiträge zur Geschichte der deutschen Literatur und Sprache*, XXXIV (1909), p. 324 n.2.

spiritual heaven the Lord adorns her with spiritual stars. In contrast to Berthold of Regensburg, the preacher returns to the Ambrosian theme, though with a variant. He compares the seven planets with the seven Beatitudes which theology had closely associated with the seven gifts of the Holy Spirit. "So in the heaven of the soul Saturn is a cleanser giving angelic purity and brings about a vision of the godhead: as our Lord said, 'blessed are the pure in heart, for they shall see God'."[134] The Beatitudes begin with praise of the poor in spirit and end with praise of those who suffer. The preacher had therefore altered their biblical order so as to link Saturn, the first of the planets, with the blessedness of angelic purity which occupied the sixth place in the Gospel. In the preceding sentences he gives a brief account of the astrological powers of the planets; for example, "Jupiter is auspicious, Mars wrathful, Venus a lover, Mercury a gainer, the moon a runner"—the usual characteristics of the planets in Arabic and Latin authors. But he begins his series with this—"the first star, Saturn, is a cleanser ('ein fürber')." In accordance with this characteristic, the author links Saturn with the purity of the angels in the spiritual heaven of the soul. Where can we find a parallel to this characteristic, which, in contrast to those of all the other planets, is quite exceptional? We have indeed encountered it in pagan authors, in Proclus and the Neoplatonists, for whom Saturn signified purity of intellect.[135] The Neoplatonic doctrine of the soul's journeyings was, in the form given it by Ambrose, adopted by writers as essentially different as Neckam, Thomas Aquinas, Berthold of Regensburg, and the author of the sermon attributed to Master Eckhart; and it is quite striking to observe the way in which the figure of the Greek father of the gods in his Neoplatonic, idealised form, is robbed of his divinity and yet recognised throughout as an active force.

---

[134] *Loc. cit.* "Alsô wirt an dem himel der sêle Saturnus [der fürber] der engelischen reinekeit unde bringet zu lône anschouwunge der gotheit . . . ."

[135] The passages quoted above, pp. 153 sqq., can be adduced only as parallels, not as sources. The other correspondences are: Jupiter: "Blessed are the meek, for they shall inherit the earth" (cf. BERTHOLD VON REGENSBURG, ed. cit. I, p. 58: "miltekeit"; II, p. 236, also referring to etymology: "iuvans pater"); Mars (with a curious inversion of his nature): "Blessed are those who are persecuted for righteousness' sake"; Sol (with a play on "Sol Iustitiae"); "Blessed are they that hunger and thirst after righteousness"; Venus (the train of thought leading to love, weeping, longing and consolation): "Blessed are they that mourn, for they shall be comforted"; Mercury (because of "des himelriches richeit"): "Blessed are the poor in spirit, for theirs is the kingdom of Heaven."

A remarkable position was taken up also by William of Auvergne, who insisted so decidedly, it will be remembered, on the advantages of a melancholy temperament.[136] It is hardly surprising that he too should have known of the series of beneficial planetary gifts enumerated by Macrobius. When William declared that according to the doctrine of the astronomers Saturn determined the "virtus intellectiva animae humanae", and Mercury directed and favoured the "virtus interpretiva", he, too, referred to the teaching transmitted by Macrobius.

Though William of Auvergne used the same material as the moralists previously mentioned, his aim was a different one. What he passionately sought to combat with all the power of his scholarship was the idea that there could be stars which were naturally evil. For a theologian following Ambrose such a notion was *a priori* inconceivable, but by William of Auvergne's time astrology had again been practised for several generations, and he took a keen interest in it. He therefore disputed with the astrologers on their own ground. If earthly things depended on the stars, how did evil arise? Through the evil influence of Saturn and Mars? William replied to this in the spirit of Neoplatonism. For him, as for Iamblichus, the influence of the stars was entirely good, and could turn to the opposite only through the incapacity or perversion of the vessel receiving it. Besides this, however, William discussed the influence of Saturn with an unmistakable personal bias until, just as in the case of melancholy, he ended with a panegyric on the allegedly evil planet. Saturn, too, as he accomplishes the divine will, is good in himself and can have an evil effect only through men's misusing his gifts ("ad intentionem abusionis"), in the same way as even the blessed sunlight could blind the careless. Saturn taken on his own merits had the power to supply and direct intelligence, and if he led to fraud, deceit, and the disease of melancholy, that was due only to the unworthiness which belonged to the human mind "a parte materiae". Saturn's true purpose was directed to "enlightening and guiding the 'virtus intellectiva' and leading it to knowledge of what was right and useful, sometimes as far as the light of prophecy". Here the echo of Saturn's old ambivalence clearly rings, but in true Neoplatonic and yet true theological style, the negative side is transferred from the realm of the active substance

---

[136] See above, pp. 73 sqq. (text).

to that of the recipient. Saturn's true nature, as in Proclus and Macrobius, was speculative thought.[137]

(ii) *Saturn in Medieval Mythography*

Another legitimate way in which the planetary gods could come within the realm of medieval speculation—legitimate, that is, in so far as it left the realm of faith quite untouched—was broader and trodden more often than that indicated by the Ambrosian interpretation. This was the recourse to the collections and glosses made by scholars which dealt with the ancient gods and heroes purely as objects of learning; and such procedure had the double purpose of facilitating practical understanding of classical authors and of bringing the ancient myths more into line with the altered spirit of the age. The names of the gods and heroes were explained etymologically, while their portraits represented them with all their attributes and were interpreted just as allegorically as their actions and destinies; and finally, an attempt was made to interpret each feature of the pagan myths on the lines of entirely Christian conceptions.

The history of this tradition, always conscious of its origin in the writings of Varro, Cicero, Virgil, Ovid, Pliny and other pagan authors, has recently been clarified in several important respects.[138] We can see how the quantity of traditional material was first collected and allegorised in Servius's commentary on the *Aeneid*, the *Narrationes* of pseudo-Lactantius, Fulgentius's *Mythologiae*, Hyginus's *Fabulae*, Macrobius's *Saturnalia* and Martianus Capella's encyclopaedic didactic novel; and how during this process the Fathers of the Church unwittingly acted as

---

[137] WILLIAM OF AUVERGNE, *De universo*, I, I, ch. 46, p. 619 in the Venice edn. of 1591, VOL. I, p. 655 in the Orleans edn. of 1674: "sed qui ponunt Saturno vel vim vel potentiam adiuvandi et dirigendi vim intellectivam humanam, nullo modo debent ei attribuere corruptiones aut perversitates ipsius, neque inclinationem sive extorsionem eiusdem ad fraudes, dolos, astutias, simulationes atque mendacia, sed haec omnia fieri in vi intellectiva per ineptitudinem . . . et haec ineptitudo est ei a parte materiae, hoc est corporis . . . cum Saturnus secundum eos [i.e. astronomos] intendat dirigere et illuminare virtutem intellectivam humanam ad ea cognoscenda, quae recta et utilia, et interdum usque ad splendorem prophetiae: impeditur haec intentio eius et operatio a parte corporis, quod animae illi coniunctum est." With this passage cf. K. WERNER "Die Kosmologie und Naturlehre des scholastischen Mittelalters mit specieller Beziehung auf Wilhelm von Conches", in *Sitzungsberichte der kaiserlichen Akademie der Wissenschaften, Phil.-hist. Klasse*, LXXV (1873), pp. 334 sqq.

[138] Both the older and the recent literature has lately been admirably dealt with by F. GHISALBERTI, "L' 'Ovidius moralizatus' di Pierre Bersuire," in *Studi romanzi*, VOL. XXIII (1933), pp. 5–136.

intermediaries by their polemics.[139] We can see, too, how the tradition penetrated into the medieval encyclopaedias of Isidore and Rabanus Maurus and into the late medieval *Catholica, Repertoria, Thesauri* and *Specula,* while at the same time it began to form an independent species of literature of a purely mythological character.

It appears that some idea of the nature of Saturn himself survived in northern countries even during the first thousand years after Christ. The author of the Old English dialogue *Solomon and Saturn* was certainly no humanist. Nevertheless, his work is at bottom not so unclassical, for Saturn is made to begin the debate with the words:

"Lo! of all the islands
I the books
have tasted,
have thoroughly turned over the letters,
the wisdom have unlocked
of Libya and Greece,
also the history
of the Indian realm.
To me the teachers
showed the stories
in the great book."[140]

There we have before us Saturn the omniscient, just as we have encountered him in numerous sources; and the fact that he appears in the dialogue as King of the Chaldees is not at all unclassical either. This is clearly an echo of the Euhemeristic tradition, according to which Saturn was a king who came out of the east.

But we encounter this popular tradition of Saturn far less often than the learned tradition taught continuously from Carolingian times onward. Knowledge of it was transmitted to the Middle Ages mainly by the fifth-century allegorical writers, who had already divested the classical gods of their religious character. From these authors the way obviously leads straight to Petrarch

---

[139] A particularly interesting example of this kind (a corrupt passage from St Augustine, as source of a pictorial motif in the Cybele fresco in the Palazzo Schifanoja, Ferrara) has been brought to light by F. ROUGEMONT (A. Warburg, *Ges. Schriften,* VOL. II, Leipzig 1932, p. 641.

[140] We correct J. M. KEMBLE's translation, *The Dialogue of Salomon and Saturnus,* London 1848, p. 134. For the sources of the notion of Saturn in the O. E. dialogue, cf. A. VON VINCENTS' "Die alt-englischen Dialoge von Solomon und Saturn", in *Münchner Beiträge zur romanischen und englischen Philologie,* XXXI (1904), pp. 87–105.

and Boccaccio. In the ninth century the most important philosopher of the time, Johannes Scotus, had written a commentary on Martianus Capella. He was followed by Remigius of Auxerre who based his work on Scotus and other predecessors, some of whom we do not know, as unfortunately he described them only by their initials[141]; and Remigius's commentary became of first-class importance for the Middle Ages.[142] Together with the usual ancient authors, Servius, Macrobius, Martianus Capella, Fulgentius, Juvenal, Lucan, Cicero, and others, Remigius represents the main source for the account of Saturn which was still accepted by the great forerunners of the Italian humanists—that is to say, the account of Saturn in the so-called Mythographus III.

A typical protagonist of that proto-humanism which is a worthy counterpart of the early Italian and Provençal Renaissance movement,[143] this author collected all the available material with great scholarship and in a clear genealogical arrangement. He praises the philosophers who took the view that all the various pagan gods were only "varia vocabula", different descriptions of the different manifestations of God's influence on the world.[144] He relates the myths and describes the portraits with all their etymological and allegorical interpretations, and, in so far as certain gods were also planetary rulers, added astrophysical and (though with visible scepticism) astrological observations as

---

[141] DOM M. CAPPUYNS, *Jean Scot Erigène*, Louvain 1933, pp. 75 sqq., and M. L. W. LAISTNER, "Martianus Capella and his Ninth-Century Commentators", in *Bulletin of the John Rylands Library*, IX (1925), pp. 130–8. Cf. R. KLIBANSKY, "The Rock of Parmenides," *M.A.R.S.* I, 2 (1943), pp. 181–3.

[142] For the commentary by Remigius, see DOM CAPPUYNS, op. cit.; also M. MANITIUS, "Zwei Remigiuskommentare", in *Neues Archiv für ältere deutsche Geschichtskunde*, VOL. XLIX (1932), pp. 173–83. Substantial portions of the commentary were even translated into German (by Notker Labeo); see KARL SCHULTE, *Das Verhältnis von Notkers Nuptiae Philologiae et Mercurii zum Kommentar des Remigius Antissiodorensis*, Münster i.W. 1911.

[143] For Neckam, see H. LIEBESCHÜTZ, *Fulgentius Metaforalis* (Studien der Bibliothek Warburg, VOL. IV, 1926), pp. 16 sqq., and MARIO ESPOSITO, in *English Historical Review*, VOL. XXX (1915), p. 466. Mr R. W. Hunt's researches have shown that Neckam made extensive use of *Mythographus III* for his commentary on Martianus Capella, but for this very reason there is no question of his being himself the author. The true author, as Miss E. Rathbone has shown, is Magister Albericus Londinensis, c. 1170; see *Mediaeval and Renaissance Studies*, I, I (1943), pp. 35 sqq. and pp. 39 sqq.

[144] *Proemium*; G. H. BODE, *Scriptores rerum mythicarum latini tres*, Celle 1834, pp. 152, 16 sqq. He takes this Stoic doctrine from SERVIUS's *Comm. in Aeneid.*, IV, 638, and REMIGIUS's *Comm. in Mart.*, ch. V; cf. R. RASCHKE, *De Alberico Mythologo*, *Breslauer philologische Abhandlungen*, XLV (1913), p. 13. Even NICHOLAS OF CUSA devoted the whole of ch. XXV of his *De docta ignorantia* to the idea that "Gentiles Deum varie nominabant creaturarum respectu" (edd. E. Hoffmann and R. Klibansky, Leipzig 1932, pp. 52 sqq., and the list of sources for that chapter).

well.[145] He states, for instance, that the rising of Saturn always signified sadness, and that he caused harm and was called a "malicious god"; but he does not present arguments of his own, and merely repeats the views of the "mathematici", as well as those of many others. He does not range the planetary gods according to their sequence in the cosmic system but according to a purely genealogical scheme, and he is still far from moralising them along specifically Christian lines.

Both these things were done, however, in a mythographical preface to the Latin *Ovide moralisé*, printed under the name of Thomas Waleys but really written by the French theologian Petrus Berchorius (Pierre Bersuire), the *Metamorphosis Ovidiana moraliter a magistro Thomas Waleys . . . explanata*, an outstanding example of the art of Christianising explanation ("literaliter", "naturaliter", "historialiter", "spiritualiter"). Its tendency, later sharply rebutted by the Counter-Reformation,[146] was to liberate the pagan myths from the remoteness of the study, to reconcile them with the Christian view, and even to make use of them in sermons, a tendency shared by Robert Holcot's approximately contemporary *Moralitates* and John Ridewall's more ancient *Fulgentius metaforalis*, used by Berchorius. This new tendency naturally did not prevent Berchorius from also taking parts of his interpretation, often word for word, from the tradition going back to the early medieval commentary on Martianus, transmitted to him by Mythographus III.

Petrarch had already used some of the statements in Mythographus III, together with various echoes of original Roman poetry, for his descriptions of the gods in his *Africa*; his borrowings were dictated by purely artistic motives and moulded into classical hexameters[147]; and if it is significant that a great fourteenth-century Italian poet should have pictured the gods of his Roman forefathers with the aid of a compendium put together entirely from works of the early Eastern Empire

---

[145] Cf. for instance the account of Servius quoted on p. 157, note 100, introducing which the Mythographer says "Neu abhorreas, quod iuxta stellarum status prospera nobis vel adversa dicantur destinari; et fides catholica quod sane sentit, firmissime amplectatur. Gentilium tamen opinio habet . . ." (*Mythographus, III, 9, 7*).

[146] As is well known, it was not Ovid's text, but the moralisations of Ovid which were placed on the Tridentine Index (cf. *Metropolitan Museum Studies*, IV (1933), pp. 276 sqq.).

[147] Cf. H. Liebeschütz, *Fulgentius Metaforalis* (Studien der Bibliothek Warburg, vol. IV, Leipzig 1926), pp. 16 and 41; and, for Petrarch's principles of transformation, E. Panofsky, *Hercules am Scheidewege* (Studien der Bibliothek Warburg, vol. XVIII, Leipzig 1930).

and from Carolingian sources, it is no less significant that a contemporary French theologian who by his own admission knew these magnificent, straightforward and in no way allegorical lines, should yet have taken over the old elements from Mythographus III and garbed them in the laborious prose of a Christian allegory; for Berchorius borrowed various traits from Petrarch's descriptions, now scarcely recognisable among the chaos of allegory.[148]

About 1400 the pictorial content was sifted from the rubble and enriched with some fresh elements, whence emerged the *Libellus de imaginibus deorum*,[149] often quoted as "Albricus"—an unpretentious, but for that very reason unusually popular, handbook for "educated laymen", and, more especially, for creative artists. The text laid special emphasis on the astronomical sequence of the planetary gods introduced by Berchorius. Boccaccio's *Genealogia deorum*, begun about 1350, retained the genealogical arrangement of Mythographus III; but it is significant that despite all its associations with the medieval tradition and attitude of mind, it was the first to put forward scientific claims.[150] The material was "collated" and deliberately evaluated, rather than merely collected; later sources were compared with one another and, if possible, measured against a "genuine ancient core"—Boccaccio, not without pride, counted five authentic Venuses and thirty-one authentic labours of Hercules, and he at least aimed at re-establishing the link with Greek sources.[151] The chapter on Saturn was based mainly on such ancient sources as we have already quoted (Lactantius, Virgil and the rest) and on the medieval tradition, that is to say, on Mythographus III. As well as these, he quoted a statement of Hermes Trismegistus, that Saturn belonged to the completely wise, and he put forward the highly peculiar theory of "Theodontius" concerning the stone which was given to Saturn instead of Jupiter to devour. These

[148] Cf. F. GHISALBERTI, "L' 'Ovidius moralizatus' di Pierre Bersuire", in *Studi romanzi*, XXIII (1933), pp. 30 sqq. and 65.

[149] Cf. the literature cited on p. 172, note 143.

[150] Cf. the introductory chapter quoted by LIEBESCHÜTZ, op. cit., p. 21, note 33: "Qui primus apud gentiles deus habitus sit . . ." Boccaccio deals with Saturn in ch. I of Book VIII (pp. 197 sqq. in the Basle edition of 1532). For Boccaccio's method of interpreting the myths, see C. G. OSGOOD, *Boccaccio on Poetry*, Princeton 1930, pp. xvii sqq., and the excellent monograph by CARLO LANDI, *Demogorgone*, Palermo 1930.

[151] Cf. E. H. WILKINS, *The University of Chicago MS of the Genealogia deorum* (The Modern Philology Monographs), Chicago 1927, ch. II, "The Greek quotations in the *Genealogia*"; also LANDI, op. cit., pp. 22 sqq.

pseudo-classical citations alone gave the chapter a new character. But the decisive thing is that Boccaccio endeavoured to identify with one another the two worlds which we have already observed approaching one another to a certain extent. As far as we know, Boccaccio was the first mythographer to declare that astrological statements were worthy to be placed beside mythological statements concerning Saturn. "But the fact that he is sad, aged, with covered head, slow, dirty, and armed with a sickle, all applies to the planet as well as to the person" (Saturn is here a "person" in the Euhemeristic sense).[152] The features which, as we saw, originally came from mythology and, with others, formed the astrological picture, now reverted again to mythology. Thus it is that Boccaccio comments on the predicates of Saturn taken from Mythographus III (that is, from the Martianus tradition) with sentences taken from Abû Ma'šar describing the nature of the children of Saturn.

With the emergence of critical scholarship, the colourful world of the Middle Ages vanished, though not in a moment. The excellent studies of Schoell and Seznec have drawn attention to the great importance of mythological handbooks such as the mythologies by Natale Conti and Vincenzo Cartari,[153] which are inconceivable without their medieval predecessors. The old material still survived, too, in emblems and collections of allegories.[154] But from the moment L. G. Gyraldus's mythological handbook appeared (in which "Albricus" was still quoted, though stigmatised as "auctor proletarius"),[155] a model of serious scholarship was set, compared with which all previous efforts seemed fantastic and unscientific. Gyraldus was certainly conscious of his new attitude, as is clearly shown in the polemic against Boccaccio in his preface.

---

[152] Similarly (but leading from astrology to mythology, and not vice versa), the passage quoted in extenso on p. 187 (text) from Bartholomaeus Anglicus: "planeta malivolus . . . ponderosus, et ideo in fabulis senex depingitur."

[153] V. CARTARI, *Le Imagini de i dei degli antichi*, Venice 1556. Later editions mentioned by J. SEZNEC, "Les manuels mythologiques italiens et leur diffusion en Angleterre", in *Mélanges d'Archéologie et d'Histoire*, L (1933), p. 281. The Latin translation of Verderius was unscrupulously used in JOACHIM SANDRART's *Iconologia deorum*, Nuremberg 1680. For mythological handbooks, cf. F. L. SCHOELL, "Les mythologistes italiens de la Renaissance et la poésie Elisabéthaine", in *Revue de littérature comparée*, IV (1924), pp. 5–25, and the same author's *Études sur l'humanisme continental en Angleterre à la fin de la Renaissance*, Paris 1926 (Bibliothèque de la Revue de littérature comparée, VOL. XXIX).

[154] Cf. MARIO PRAZ, *Studies in Seventeenth-Century Imagery*, VOL. I, London 1939, and E. MANDOWSKY, *Ricerche intorno all' Iconologia di Cesare Ripa* (La Bibliofilia, XLI), Florence 1939.

[155] L. G. GYRALDUS, *De deis gentilium varia et multiplex historia*, Basle 1548. The passage from "Albricus" in L. G. GYRALDUS, *Opera*, Lyons 1696, VOL. I, col. 153.

There Gyraldus speaks of Boccaccio with great respect as a man of diligence, intelligence and culture, a man of letters far ahead of all other Italian prose writers. But Boccaccio was no Latin scholar, let alone a Greek one. He, Gyraldus, could not understand how some people valued Boccaccio's *Genealogia* so highly as to quote it as an authority or even to write commentaries on it. On scientific grounds he disapproved of Boccaccio's profound speculations over the primeval god Demogorgon, whose name must not be known. Widely though he had sought, this Demogorgon was nowhere to be found, "nowhere, I say, did he appear" ("nusquam Demogorgon iste, nusquam, inquam, apparuit"). Gyraldus discovered the solution: 'Demogorgon' was only a corruption of 'Demiurgos'.[156]

This example is typical of the critical turn which Gyraldus gave to the history of mythography. It is true that his work was fundamentally no more than an assembly of views from a great variety of ancient authors concerning different gods, their portraits, and their type of worship. Nowhere was an attempt made to build up these views into a general picture or to give a consecutive account of their development from the earliest authors onwards. According to Cicero, for instance, Saturn was the son of Coelus, but according to Fulgentius[157] he was the son of Pollux; and both statements appear side by side with no connexion. But this very fact reveals Gyraldus as an author on the threshold of a new, philological and critical epoch in the history of classical studies. Men sought to avoid the short-circuits of earlier combinations and to limit themselves to collecting only classical material—Latin and, above all, Greek texts, or occasionally inscriptions—ignoring "Albricus" and the uncritical blunderings of medieval commentators such as Berchorius.

This mythographical literature is particularly important for the history of the notion of Saturn; in the first place because it provided scholarly material for the rest of literature, and a basic form for pictorial art; secondly, in that, being uncontroversial, unsuperstitious, conservative and devoted to etymology, it represented Saturn without bias of any kind, handing down to posterity a complete and variegated portrait.

---

[156] Cf. CARLO LANDI, *Demogorgone*, Palermo, 1930; also M. CASTELAIN, "Démogorgon ou le barbarisme déifié" in *Bulletin de l'Association Guillaume Budé*, 36, July 1932, pp. 22 sqq.; BOCCACCIO, *Opera*, pp. 118 sqq. in the 1565 edn.

[157] FULGENTIUS, *Mythologiae*, I, 34, ed. R. Helm, Leipzig 1898, pp. 17 sqq.

In Fulgentius, Saturn was already the god of fruit and seed, and his covered head, for instance, was explained by the fact that fruits were shadowed by their leaves; he was also the god of time devouring his children (as "all-devouring" Time), while the question was left open whether the sickle, too, because of its circular shape, was a symbol of time or only a harvesting implement; and finally he was the Neoplatonic universal spirit which made all things (in accordance with the later oft-repeated etymology, "Saturnus quasi *sacer-nus*"). So it went on, with the inclusion of more and more sources. In Mythographus III[158] Saturn is still the god of sowing, and of time; but as we have seen, he was also represented as a planet bringing cold and moisture, and acting, "according to the 'mathematici'," as a "malicious god": the attribution to him of a sickle meant that he, like a sickle, could cause harm only by a backward movement. In fourteenth-century Christian interpretations the ancient rural god could appear as "Prudentia" (as in Ridewall),[159] and as the personification of a higher ecclesiastic grown grey in sin (as in Berchorius); as well as this, a typical example of his polarity, he could be taken as the model of a pious and upright prelate who busied himself on the one hand with feeding the poor, on the other with devouring his wicked children "by way of correcting them". Furthermore, still according to Berchorius, he was an example of the tyrant who subjugated the state by guile or force, a personification of the sin of greed, and finally a shocking example of the inevitability of divine providence, since not even the devouring of his children could shield him from the fate that threatened him.[160] These were merely the "spiritual" interpretations, interpretations envisaging a strictly moral application·

---

[158] *Mythographus III*, I, 3 sqq., in G. H. Bode, *Scriptores rerum mythicarum latini tres*, Celle 1834, pp. 153 sqq.

[159] Cf. H. Liebeschütz, *Fulgentius Metaforalis* (Studien der Bibliothek Warburg, vol. iv, 1926), pp. 71 sqq.; cf. also F. Saxl in *Festschrift für Julius Schlosser*, Zürich 1926, pp. 104 sqq. Hence, the covered head of the ancient sages is interpreted here as a sign of the honour they pay to intellect, and the sickle is intellect's sceptre, being curved back upon itself to show how the intelligent man "omnes ad se possit attrahere et panem potumque sapientiae cunctis largissime ministrare," etc.

[160] *Metamorphosis Ovidiana, moraliter a Magistro Thoma Waleys . . . explanata*, fols. ii^r sqq. in the Paris edn. of 1515. In all these cases, of course, each individual trait has a corresponding interpretation, castration, for instance, proving in the case of the "evil pastor" that "tota voluptas eius in amaritudinem convertitur"; in the case of the "good pastor" that "tales boni prelati solent . . . ambitiosis subditis infestari"; in the case of the "tyrant" that like shall be rendered for like, and in the case of gluttony that this generates lust as Saturn's castrated member generated Venus, etc.

Besides these, Berchorius, still interpreting every trait, dealt with Saturn "literaliter" as a star, "naturaliter" as time, and "historialiter" as the exiled Cretan king of Euhemeristic belief. In Gyraldus all this has vanished, with the exception of the contradictory but untainted tradition which could be substantiated from the classical authors.

(iii) *Saturn in Medieval Astrology: Astrological Elements adopted by Scholastic Natural Philosophy*

If, as we have seen, it was not till about 1200 that we again come across Ambrose's idea of associating the seven planets with the gifts of the Holy Spirit, this is mainly due to the fact that not until this time did a situation again arise comparable with that of the Patristic epoch. Just as the Fathers had had to settle accounts with a still virulent astrology, so the theologians of the twelfth and thirteenth centuries had to take their stand against a revival of it; and both Alexander Neckam and Berthold of Regensburg make this position clear. Both protest with polemical clarity against the view that the stars can determine the human will and therefore human destiny (in the ethical sense), and they restrict this influence to the world of natural phenomena. As Berthold of Regensburg says:

> They [the stars] have power over trees and over vineyards, over foliage and grass, over plants and roots, over corn and all things that bear seed, over the birds of the air and over the beasts of the field, and over the fish of the sea and over the worms of the earth; over all this and over everything which is under the sun, hath our Lord given the stars dominion, save over one thing only; thereover hath no man dominion or power, neither star nor root nor stock nor stone nor angel nor devil nor none save God alone; He Himself will not either, He will have no power over it. That is, the free will of man: thereover hath none power, save thee thyself.[161]

Apart from a few exceptions,[162] the warfare of the early Church had actually succeeded in reducing astrology for hundreds of

---

[161] Berthold von Regensburg, *Sermons*, ed. F. Pfeiffer, vol. I, Vienna 1862, p. 50. Similarly in Neckam, *De naturis rerum*, ed. cit., pp. 39 sqq: "Absit autem, ut ipsos aliquam inevitabilis necessitatis legem in inferiora sortiri censeamus . . . Voluntas enim divina certissima est rerum causa et primitiva, cui non solum planetae parent, sed et omnis natura creata. Sciendum etiam est quod, licet superiora corpora effectus quosdam compleant in inferioribus, liberum tamen arbitrium animae non impellunt in ullam necessitatem hoc vel illud exequendi . . . ." See above, p. 166, note 127.

[162] Cf. the decrees of Bishops Burchard of Worms and Ivo of Chartres (quoted in Wedel, *M.A.A.*, pp. 30 sqq.) against astrological practices on occasions like marriages, agricultural undertakings, etc.

years to a state of complete unimportance in practical Church politics, so that it merely formed a theme for theoretical discussions.

Between 1120 and 1180 a comprehensive body of astrological doctrine of the later Empire and of the east became available to the west through translations from the Arabic. But even earlier, in the tenth century, there existed a copy—now in Paris—of the *Liber Alchandri philosophi*, which brought later Greek doctrines back to the Latin west via the orient and was copied continually until the fifteenth century, and later went into print.[163]

In the tenth century at the latest, therefore, the notion of children of Saturn came back to Europe with "Alchandrinus". Those born under Saturn were dark, broad-shouldered, round-headed and sparsely bearded. They were thieves; they were loquacious; they were persons who said one thing with their mouth but thought another in their heart; they nourished resentment, they were sons of the devil, they were miserly on their own soil, rapacious abroad,[164] and so on. Admittedly there were few people in the early Middle Ages capable of making the observations necessary for casting a horoscope ("cumque tamen a paucis hoc iugiter possit observari", says our author).[165] For that reason the early medieval doctrine was based on ascertaining the star of birth from the numerical value of a person's name—the name was divided by seven, and if five remained the person was a child of Saturn.

The revival of mythological elements had taken place early, then, and astrological practice had become so simplified that these elements could be used in foretelling the future. The theological compromise with astrology, however, did not take place until the twelfth century, when Spain and Southern Italy had familiarised the west with the works of the great masters Ptolemy and Abû Ma'šar. For men such as Adelard of Bath, who were in Spain during the full bloom of this translating activity, "those higher and divine beings [the planets] are both 'principium' and 'causae' of lower beings."[166] This thoroughgoing adoption of astrological

---

[163] Cf. A. VAN DE VYVER, "Les plus anciennes traductions latines médiévales (X^e et XIe siècles) de traités d'astronomie et d'astrologie," in *Osiris* I (1936), pp. 689–691. R. Klibansky discovered Nicholas of Cusa's copy of the *Liber Alchandri philosophi* in London, Brit. Mus., Harleian MS 5402.

[164] Paris, Bibl. Nat. MS lat. 17868 fol. 10^v.

[165] Paris, Bibl. Nat. MS. lat. 17868 fol. 5^v.

[166] H. WILLNER, "Des Adelard von Bath Traktat 'De eodem et diverso' ", in *Beiträge zur Geschichte der Philosophie des Mittelalters*, IV, 1, Münster 1903, p. 32, 10: "Superiora quippe illa divinaque animalia inferiorum naturarum et principium et causae sunt."

belief was criticised by Abailard and William of Conches. Abailard's criticism starts from the notion of the "accidental", the "contingens" of Boethius's commentary on Aristotle.[167] Anyone who promised by means of astrology to acquire knowledge of future contingent events, which were unknown even to Nature herself, should be regarded not as an astronomer but as a servant of the devil.[168] And it was not merely the logical consequence of Abailard's clearly-drawn distinction when Hugo of St Victor distinguished between two types of astrology in his *Didascaleion*. One, the natural kind, was concerned with the constitution of earthly bodies which changed according to the heavenly bodies—with (for example) health, sickness, good and bad weather, fertility and barrenness. The other kind of astrology was concerned with future contingent events and with matters of free will, and this last type was superstitious.[169]

William of Conches's treatment of astrology was similar in tendency but fundamentally different in method.[170] He distinguished three ways of regarding the heavenly bodies: one mythological ("fabulosa"), concerning the names of the stars and the fables associated with them; one astrological, concerned with the motions of the heavenly bodies as they appear to the eye; and one astronomical, which inquired not into the apparent, but into the real motions of the heavenly bodies.[171] Without expressly emphasising it, William of Conches made it clear in the course of his exposition that these three methods were not mutually exclusive, but might, properly understood, each express the same truth in their several ways. Saturn, for instance, who was discussed at greater length than the other planets, was characterised from the astronomical point of view as the planet furthest away and with the longest course—"for that reason he is

---

[167] "Contingens autem secundum Aristotelicam sententiam est, quodcumque aut casus fert aut ex libero cuiuslibet arbitrio et propria voluntate venit aut facilitate naturae in utramque partem redire possibile est, ut fiat scilicet et non fiat." BOETHIUS, *Commentarii in librum Aristotelis* Περὶ ἑρμηνείας, 2nd edn., III, 9, ed. C. Meiser, Leipzig 1880, p. 190, 1 sqq.

[168] ABAILARD, *Expositio in Hexaemeron, Opera*, ed. V. Cousin, Paris 1849–59, VOL. I, p. 649 sq.

[169] ABAILARD, loc. cit.

[170] The historical context of William of Conches's natural philosophy will be more clearly understood when his commentary on Plato's Timaeus will be available in the *Corpus Platonicum Medii Aevi*.

[171] *Philosophia*, II, 5 (MIGNE, P. L., VOL. CLXXII, col. 59A-B); *Dragmaticon*, III ("Dialogus de substantiis physicis a Vuilhelmo Aneponymo," Strasbourg 1567, pp. 70–71).

represented in the myths as an old man."[172] The quality of cold attributed to him by the astrologers was based on their observations, according to which the sun lost warmth when in a certain conjunction with Saturn. From the cold resulted the quality of harmfulness, especially prominent when he reversed his course, and this discovery again had found mythical expression in the image of his carrying a sickle.[173] Here, as elsewhere, William endeavoured, in a manner reminiscent of the Stoic interpretation of the myths,[174] to sift the core of physical truth from both the "fables" and the doctrines of the astrologers.

In connexion with the discussion on Saturn, William propounded a series of questions whose treatment was particularly characteristic of his attitude to astrology. In his *Philosophia* as well as in the *Dragmaticon* written some twenty years later, he raised the objection: "If stars are of a fiery nature how is it possible that some can engender coldness?" In the earlier work he puts forward at this point a theory of physics by means of which men had previously attempted to resolve this difficulty. The nature of fire comprehended two qualities, light and heat, of which the second could manifest itself only through a medium, namely "density and moisture". As evidence of this, the sun gives more heat in valleys than on tops of mountains, where snow does not melt—although the mountain-tops are nearer to the sun. William does not immediately accept this explanation, but endeavours to resolve the doubt by making a logical distinction between different meanings of the statement. Saturn is called cold not because he is inherently cold himself but because he causes cold. As to the second question, how it was possible that a hot, or at any rate not-cold, star could generate cold, William leaves that unanswered in the *Philosophia*, as transcending the bounds

---

[172] "Unde in fabulis senex fingitur," *Philosophia* II, 17 (MIGNE, P. L., VOL. CLXXII, col. 62 B emended according to Oxford, Bodleian Library, MS Bodley 679); *Dragmaticon*, IV (Strasbourg edn. of 1567, p. 99).

[173] "Haec eadem stella ex frigiditate dicitur nociva, et maxime quando est retrograda: unde in fabulis dicitur falcem deferre", *Philosophia*, II, 17 (MIGNE, P. L., VOL. CLXXII, col. 63B); cf. *Dragmaticon*, IV (ed. cit., p. 102). In L. THORNDIKE, *A History of Magic and Experimental Science*, VOL. II, London 1923, p. 57, the meaning of the sentence "Dicitur Jupiter patrem Saturnum expulisse, quia Saturno vicinior factus naturalem nocivitatem ei aufert" is inadvertently reversed. For the special role which this astrological interpretation of the Saturn-Jupiter myth played in the Renaissance, see below, pp. 271 sq., 326 sqq. (text).

[174] Cf. esp. SERVIUS, *Comment. in Vergil. Georgica*, I, 336 (*Commentarii in Vergilii carmina*, VOL. III, edd. G. Thilo and H. Hagen, Leipzig 1878, p. 201), whose doctrine William modified in a characteristic manner.

of his knowledge.[175] In his later work, however, he attempts to solve this problem with the help of the physical theory, merely mentioned in the *Philosophia*, of fire's two qualities; but even here his critical mind will not allow him to see more than a possible hypothesis in this explanation. He now puts forward yet another possible solution, also derived from the logical distinction between the meanings of this statement: Saturn is credited with cold not because he is cold in himself or because he causes cold, but because he signifies cold.[176]

By this suggestion, even if so far only tentatively, another factor was introduced, or rather revived, in medieval expositions of astrology: as in Neoplatonism, the stars were not active forces but symbols.

This view of the planets as symbols was forcibly expressed in a recently discovered commentary on Macrobius's explanation of Cicero's *Somnium Scipionis*,[177] based on William of Conches. Quoting Plotinus, the writer states that the planets do not bring men either good or ill fortune, but indicate that good or ill fortune will come to them.[178] His real intention is to distinguish between the domain of planetary influence and that of human free will. He parts company with Ptolemy, who had acknowledged the dependence of some human actions on the stars, and he emphasises strongly that though men's predispositions come under the influence of the stars, yet their various actions do not, for it is left to their own free will to develop these predispositions for good or evil.[179] The view "inclinant astra, non necessitant" is

---

[175] *Philosophia*, II, 17 (MIGNE, P. L., VOL. CLXXII, col. 63A).

[176] *Dragmaticon*, IV (Strasbourg edn., pp. 99–102). "Saturnus igitur, etsi non sit frigidus, frigus tamen generat. Vel si Saturnum nec frigidum esse nec frigus facere contendis; dic, quod frigus non facit sed significat. Unde propter illud quod significat, frigidus dicitur" (ed. cit., pp. 101–2, emended according to Oxford, Bodleian Library, Digby MS I, fol. 25v).

[177] This commentary, which appears in a series of MSS of the twelfth to fourteenth centuries (e.g. Copenhagen, Gl. Kgl. S. 1910; Bamberg J IV 21 = class. 40; Berne 266), will be the subject of a special paper. R.K.

[178] MS Berne 226 fol. 11rb: ". . . ut appareat, qualis est ratio Plotini, ponit eam; quae talis est, quod planetae non conferunt hominibus prospera vel adversa, sed significant prospera vel adversa hominibus eventura. Unde, quia utraque stella, Solis scilicet et Lunae, signum est boni eventus, dicitur salutaris; stellae vero Saturni et Martis terribiles dicuntur, ideo quia Soli coniunctae in aliquo signo sunt signum mali eventus."

[179] Ibid.: "sic Ptolomaeus et eius sequaces volebant actus hominum provenire ex effectu planetarum, non tamen omnes, quia actuum alii naturales, alii voluntarii, alii casuales . . . . Volumus tamen actus hominum non provenire ex effectu planetarum, sed aptitudines actuum et humanorum officiorum . . . . Nam minime volumus quod planetae conferant hominibus scientiam, divitias, et huiusmodi, sed aptitudines ipsas."

here clearly anticipated. The stars have dominion only over the physical realm, the actions of men are outside their power.[180]

William of Conches provides the metaphysical basis for this division of spheres of influence by adopting Plato's explanation, according to which the formation of the body is left to the spirits and stars "created" by God, the soul, on the contrary, being a direct "creation" of God.[181]

This drew a new theological boundary, and though the intention with which it was drawn was certainly hostile to astrology,[182] the result meant a decisive victory for the new doctrine.

For all the scientific and astrological knowledge that reached the west between Abailard and the later scholastics, theology had altered very little in its attitude towards astrological fatalism. Naturally the data were better differentiated than in the old days; a whole fresh arsenal lacking to their predecessors was available to thirteenth-century theologians for discussion *pro* and *contra*. St Thomas Aquinas, for instance, considers it a possible result of stellar influence that one doctor is more gifted than another, one peasant better at growing things than another, or one warrior better adapted to fighting (though the perfection of any such aptitude was due to Grace).[183] But though Thomas Aquinas himself thought he could go so far as to consider that the stars might exert an indirect influence on the intellect,[184] yet he, like his

---

[180] Ibid.: "Namque planetae in terris et in aquis vi vel potestate operantur, sed in actibus hominum neque vi neque potestate aliquid operantur."

[181] "Unde Plato . . . dicit Deum creatorem stellis et spiritibus a se creatis curam formandi hominis iniecisse, ipsum vero animam fecisse"; *Philosophia*, IV, 32 (MIGNE, P. L., VOL. CLXXII, col. 98C, emended according to MS Bodley 679, and the Basle edn. of 1531. "Philosophicarum et astronomicarum institutionum Guilielmi Hirsaugiensis olim abbatis libri tres," fol. a.3 v).

[182] This trend is particularly noticeable if one compares William's writings with the *De mundi constitutione.* This cosmology, printed among Bede's works but really written by one of William's immediate predecessors (MIGNE, P. L., VOL. XC, cols. 881 sqq., falsely attributed to the ninth century by P. DUHEM (*Le système du monde*, VOL. III, Paris 1915, p. 81, and mistaken for an astrological extract from Martianus Capella by L. THORNDIKE and P. KIBRE, *A Catalogue of Incipits* . . . , Cambridge, Mass., 1937, col. 421) adopts astrological doctrines unreservedly.

[183] The main references to stellar influences are: *Summa Theol.*, BK I, qu. 115, art. 3 and 4: *Summa contra gentiles*, BK III, 82 sqq.: "In quibus homo potest licite uti iudicio astrorum" (*Opusculum XVII*, ed. P. Mandonnet, Paris 1927, VOL. III, pp. 142 sq.). Cf. P. CHOISNARD, *S. Thomas d'Aquin et l'influence des astres*, Paris 1926; G. GUSNELLI, "S.T. d'A. e l'influsso genetliaco delle stelle", in *Civiltà Cattolica*, IV (1927), p. 303–316; W. SCHÖLLGEN, "Der anthropologische Sinn der astrologischen Schicksalsdeutung . . . im Weltbild des Thomas von Aquino", in *Philosophisches Jahrbuch der Görres-Gesellschaft*, XLIX (1936), pp. 124–37. The passages quoted here are taken from book III, § 92 of the *Summa contra gentiles.*

[184] *Summa contra gentiles*, BK III, 84.

successors, eventually comes to the conclusion that man's will is not subject to the stars. "For that reason," St Thomas remarks, "the astrologers themselves say that the wise man commands the stars, in so far as he commands his passions," and he exhorts every Christian to regard it as quite certain that what depends on man's will is not subject to the exigencies of the stars.[185]

We must now return once more to the development of the idea of nature in the twelfth century, and introduce another group of thinkers for the completion of our picture—namely, admirers of astrology like Adelard of Bath. We have already mentioned his doctrine, according to which the upper and divine beings, that is, the stars, are both the principle and the cause of lesser natures. The enthusiastic tone in which Adelard speaks of the stars shows that he and his contemporaries have already found a way back to the belief in the power of the stellar spirits. Adelard's English successor, Daniel of Morley, succumbs almost completely to fatalism. He considers those who deny the power and activity of the heavenly motions as impudent fools. Man can foretell future adversity but cannot entirely escape it; nevertheless, he will bear his burden more easily if he knows of it in advance.[186] Daniel of Morley and others linked the remains of Latin tradition with the new Arabic doctrine,[187] and so we find

---

[185] *Summa Theol.*, BK I, qu. 115, art. 4; *Opusculum XVII* (cited above, note 183). The sentence quoted e.g. in the *Roman de la Rose:* "Sapiens homo dominatur astris" is probably based ultimately on a passage in Pseudo-Ptolemy (cf. PSEUDO-PTOLEMY, *Centiloquium*, 8: "anima sapiens adiuvat opus stellarum"), according to which the learned astrologer can perceive whether the stellar influences permit human counter-action or not (BBG, *Sternglaube*, p. 169). But for St Thomas the "homo sapiens" was no longer the astrologer but the Christian endowed with free will, who can therefore oppose any stellar influence with regard to matters affecting his soul. In Gower (see below, p. 194, note 207) he becomes the humble and devout person who attempts to save himself by prayer, and in Renaissance authors, like Pico della Mirandola, he becomes the man who, thanks to his inherent dignity, and independently of his religious attitude, is above the power of the stars.

[186] DANIEL OF MORLEY, *Liber de naturis inferiorum et superiorum*, ed. K. Sudhoff (Archiv für die Geschichte der Naturwissenschaft und der Technik, VIII), Leipzig 1917, p. 34. For the Ptolemaic background, cf. BBG, *Sternglaube*, p. 168.

[187] Adelard of Bath was certainly one of the first to be familiar with the new material in Arabic astrology; he himself worked on two astrological treatises by Arabic authors (cf. C. H. HASKINS, *Studies in the History of Medieval Science*, 2nd edn. Cambridge 1927, pp. 22 and 30). In his own works, however, we have so far found no trace of the use of Arabic astrological doctrines. Abû Ma'šar was used in the south of France from about 1140 onwards (e.g. RAYMOND OF MARSEILLE, *De cursu planetarum*, Corpus Christi College, Oxford, Cod. 243 fol. 59v); and extensive use both of this author and of other great astrologers like Messahalā is found in the main work written by Abû Ma'šar's translator, HERMANNUS DALMATA, *De essentiis* (for Saturn cf. Corpus Christi College, Oxford, Codex 243, fol. 105r).

in Daniel of Morley the familiar series of gifts: from Saturn men receive slowness, from Jupiter moderation, from Mars anger, and so on.[188] But he also describes, "according to the Arabs", the nature which those born under Saturn receive: corresponding to the nature of the god, it is dark, coarse and heavy, and so we again come face to face with the familiar picture of Saturn's children, who are melancholy and miserly, and speak one thing with their tongue and another with their heart; they are solitary; they work the inheritance of their fathers and forefathers; they are silent and dull, and when they know something they do not forget it easily—and so on.[189]

In the main work of one of the most important writers a generation before Daniel of Morley, Bernardus Silvestris's treatise on Macrocosm and Microcosm, the vivid picturing of the planetary divinities is carried still further. He goes so far in his belief in the power of the stars that he includes not only the rule of Pope Eugenius but even the Incarnation in the list of events announced by the stars.[190] Bernardus's description of Saturn is perhaps the most vivid of all. Here Saturn appears as the wicked old man, cruel and despicable, constantly watching over women in labour so as mercilessly to devour the new-born infant. How powerful the demoniac notion was can be seen by the fact that the poet was able to give it a new image without in any way departing from tradition. Saturn is here the reaper, whose sharp sickle destroys all that is lovely and bears blossom: he lets no roses or lilies flower, and cannot bear fructification. In only one respect is he worthy of veneration, in that he is the son of eternity, the father of time.[191]

Gilson has attempted to prove in a lucid and instructive essay that Bernardus Silvestris's cosmology conformed essentially to tradition.[192] Bernardus certainly was not an arbitrary thinker, and the originality of his statements lay more in manner than

---

[188] DANIEL OF MORLEY, op. cit., p. 38.

[189] Ibid.

[190] BERNARDUS SILVESTRIS, *De univ. mundi*, edd. Barach and Wrobel, p. 16.

[191] BERNARDUS SILVESTRIS, *De univ. mundi*, ed. cit., pp. 41 sqq.

[192] E. GILSON, *La cosmologie de Bernardus Silvestris* (Archives d'histoire doctrinale et littéraire du moyen âge, VOL. III, Paris 1928), pp. 5–24. In his endeavour to present Bernard's work as essentially in the Christian tradition Gilson misunderstands its peculiarities just as much as previous scholars did when they emphasised the unchristian character of the *De mundi universitate*. The peculiarity of this work (as a detailed analysis shows) lies rather in the continual use of Hermetic doctrines combined with those of Plato-Chalcidius, and in the attempt to incorporate them in the structure of Christian cosmology.

in matter. It was a powerful religious and poetic imagination which could regard Saturn as Death the Reaper, and transform an antiquated demon into a medieval figure of dread.

For that reason Bernardus's work long retained its power of direct suggestion. Towards the end of the century Alanus ab Insulis painted a picture of Saturn similar to Bernardus's; and though determined mainly by the negative characteristics given in astrological texts (cold, dryness, age, avarice, darkness, silence, pain, tears, injustice, horror and sorrow), it is remarkable and impressive for the antithetical language in which it is rendered, such language as is not found in the description of the other planetary spheres. Consciously or not, the old contradictions implicit in the notion of Saturn find poetic expression:

☞ Ulterius progressa suos Prudentia gressus
dirigit ad superos, superans Iovis atria cursu,
Saturnique domos tractu maiore iacentes
intrat et algores hiemis brumaeque pruinas
horret et ignavum frigus miratur in aestu.
Illic fervet hiems, aestas algescit et aestus
friget, delirat splendor dum flamma tepescit.
Hic tenebrae lucent, hic lux tenebrescit, et illic
nox cum luce viget, et lux cum nocte diescit.
Illic Saturnus spatium percurrit avaro
motu, progessuque gravi, longaque diaeta.
Hic algore suo praedatur gaudia veris,
furaturque decus pratis, et sidera florum,
algescitque calens, frigens fervescit, inundat
aridus, obscurus lucet, iuvenisque senescit.
Nec tamen a cantu sonus eius degener errat,
sed comitum voces vox praevenit huius adulto
concentu, quem non cantus obtusio reddit
insipidum, cui dat vocis dulcedo saporem.
Hic dolor et gemitus, lacrimae, discordia, terror,
tristities, pallor, planctus, iniuria regnant.[193]

In the course of the twelfth century, then, astrological belief was gradually introduced into certain systems of scholastic natural philosophy, and from then onwards it could develop both within and outside the sphere of philosophy proper. Even among the mainly encyclopaedic authors we find a growing tendency to include what is really astrological material. For thirteenth-century writers such as Arnoldus Saxo, Vincent of Beauvais or

---

[193] ALANUS AB INSULIS, *Anticlaudianus*, IV, 8 (MIGNE, P. L., VOL. CCX, col. 528).

Bartholomeus Anglicus, who quoted Ptolemy and made no further attempt at moral or cosmological interpretation, it was no longer risky to put forward the view that life, architecture and doctrine were proper to Saturn, or that he signified trouble, sorrow, lowliness and evil.[194] Vincent of Beauvais, too, considered him cold and dry, occasionally moist and earthy, melancholy, leaden, dark, a lover of black clothing, tenacious, pious and a countryman.[195] Bartholomeus Anglicus describes Saturn as follows:

> Saturnus est a saturando dictus. Cuius uxor Ops est dicta ab opulentia, quam tribuit mortalibus, ut dicunt Isidorus et Martianus. De quo dicunt fabulae quod ideo depingitur maestissimus, quia a filio suo fingitur castratus fuisse, cuius virilia in mare proiecta Venerem creaverunt. Est autem secundum Misael Saturnus planeta malivolus, frigidus et siccus, nocturnus et ponderosus, et ideo in fabulis senex depingitur. Iste circulus a terra est remotissimus, et tamen terrae est maxime nocivus. . . . In colore etiam pallidus aut lividus sicut plumbum, quia duas habet qualitates mortiferas, scilicet frigiditatem et siccitatem. Et ideo foetus sub ipsius dominio natus et conceptus vel moritur vel pessimas consequitur qualitates. Nam secundum Ptolomaeum in libro de iudiciis astrorum dat hominem esse fuscum, turpem, iniqua operantem, pigrum, gravem, tristem, raro hilarem seu ridentem. Unde dicit idem Ptolomaeus: "Subiecti Saturno . . . glauci sunt coloris et lividi in capillis, et in toto corpore asperi et inculti, turpia et fetida non abhorrent vestimenta, animalia diligunt fetida et immunda, res diligunt acidas et stipticas, quia in eorum complexione humor melancolicus dominatur."[196]

Texts such as these, especially that of Bartholomeus Anglicus, show at a glance how a source of material strange to older writers but familiar to us has erupted into the current mythographical and scientific tradition and brought about a fundamental change of attitude. Throughout, the descriptions are detailed, and they encompass man's destiny, length of life, sickness, health, constitution and character; they associate Saturn on principle with "melancholica complexio", just as they say that Jupiter "praeest sanguini et sanguineae complexioni" and that Mars "disponit ad iram et animositatem et alias colericas passiones"; and they are

---

[194] The encyclopaedia of ARNOLDUS SAXO, I, 'De coelo et mundo' (ed. E. Stange, Beilage zum Jahresbericht des Kgl. Gymnasiums zu Erfurt, 1904–05, p. 18): "In libro de motibus planetarum Ptolomeus . . . . Sub eo [sc. Saturno] continetur vita, edificium, doctrina et locus. Frigidus est et siccus, et significat merorem, vilitatem, malum . . . ."

[195] VINCENTIUS BELLOVACENSIS, *Speculum naturae*, 15, 44 sqq. (Bibl. mundi, I, Douai 1624, col. 1119).

[196] BARTHOLOMEUS ANGLICUS, *De proprietatibus rerum*, VIII, 23, Strasbourg 1485, fol. o 2v.

overwhelmingly unfavourable. We find in fact that "Misael" is quoted as an authority as well as Ptolemy, Isidore, and Martianus Capella—and "Misael" is none other than Messahalā. In other words, we can see here a complete acceptance of Arabic texts, and, based on them, a western professional astrology whose robust characteristics were bound to exert a far greater influence on the general notion of the stars than could the idealising interpretations of the mystics and moral philosophers, the moralising descriptions of the mythographers, or the speculative reflections of the natural philosophers. The popularity of this professional astrology enabled the idea of Saturn as a malevolent figure of menace to gain as decisive a victory over all other interpretations as had been the case with melancholy, thanks to the medical tracts and books on the four complexions.

Professional astrology, as it developed in the west after the discovery of Arabic sources, had, like contemporary medicine, an unusually conservative, not to say stationary character.

The Arabic astrologers, whose notion of Saturn we described at the beginning of this chapter, did little more than collect and classify the material available from later antiquity. Only two facts have any real importance for our subject. Firstly, the equation of certain planets with the four temperaments, and, in particular, of Saturn with the melancholic—prepared but not completed in late antiquity—was now explicitly formulated and henceforward became a firm doctrine. Secondly, Saturn's favourable characteristics, sporadically cited in the later Empire, such as riches, might, talent for geometry and architecture, knowledge of hidden things, and, above all, "deep reflection" (this last perhaps taken over from Neoplatonism), became stereotyped distinctions constantly, though not always logically, incorporated in the general picture, and handed down with it. Thus it is the exhaustiveness of the data and the solidity of the system rather than any originality of conception which gives importance to Arabic astrology, the main works of which were available in Latin translation by about 1200. Combined with the application of scholastic speculation to science, and the reception of Aristotle and of Galen's medicine—also transmitted mainly by the Arabs—, what really influenced both medieval and even modern thought above all was the basic tenet of Arabic astrology that every earthly event, and, in particular, human destiny, was "written in the stars".

In this respect, the Arabs of the ninth, tenth and eleventh centuries had a significance for the Middle Ages similar to that of the "Chaldeans" for the Hellenistic world. In both cases one can see how the general influence of astrology increased more and more as a variety of "mystical" trends emerged alongside the official creeds, and, in both cases, provided a parallel to belief in the stars. This increase of fatalism was naturally accompanied by sharp protests from philosophical, astronomical and, especially, religious quarters, until finally the Renaissance made the individual's attitude to astrology a matter of conscience. Many orthodox Catholics, especially the more active spirits among them, could take astrology in their stride, whereas others, especially those in the Augustinian tradition, rejected it. Pico della Mirandola's ethical humanism no less than Leonardo da Vinci's sceptical free-thinking could lead to its rejection. Marsilio Ficino's mystical Neoplatonism finally reached a new solution, a somewhat precarious compromise, which was later to degenerate into magic among his successors, such as Agrippa of Nettesheim and Paracelsus.[197]

Western astrology produced texts which generally adhered closely to translations from Arabic authors, and on the whole provided a relatively unoriginal and uniform picture as far as our problem is concerned. If we consult Guido Bonatti and Michael Scot, the writers whom Dante lifted to the rank of "fathers" of the movement, and banished to hell rather for their "magic arts" than for their astrological activity[198]—we find scarcely anything not previously known to us from Arabic sources (or at least deducible from them by a more detailed study), save for an ever more frequent inclusion of individual traits from medicine and humoralism. According to Guido Bonatti,[199] for instance, as in Alcabitius, Saturn is naturally cold and dry and governs all that is heavy and old, especially fathers and forefathers. Owing to his attributes of cold and dryness, Bonatti says of him:

---

[197] For Petrarch's opposition to astrology in which anticipation of modern ironical scepticism and reversion to the arguments of the early Fathers are curiously mixed, cf. WEDEL, M. A. A., pp. 82 sq.; for the polemics of fourteenth-century astronomers, cf. H. PRUCKNER, *Studien zu den astrologischen Schriften des Heinrich von Langenstein* (Studien der Bibliothek Warburg VOL. XIV), Leipzig 1933; for Ficino see below, text pp. 254 sqq.; for Agrippa of Nettesheim, below, text pp. 351 sqq.; for Pico, R. W. REMÉ, *Darstellung des Inhalts der "Disputationes in astrologiam" des Pico della Mirandola* (*Buch I–III*), dissertation Hamburg 1933.

[198] *Inferno*, XX, lines 115 sqq.

[199] *De Astronomia*, I, 3. We quote from the Basle edn. of 1550, col. 97 sqq. Minor emendations of the text were made on the basis of earlier editions.

☞ Ex humoribus significat melancholiam. Et ex complexionibus corporum, significat melancholiam, et fortassis erit illa melancholia cum admixtione phlegmatis et cum ponderositate atque gravedine corporis nati, ita quod non erit levis incessus, nec leviter saliens, nec addiscet natare vel similia quae faciunt ad ostendendum levitatem corporis, et erit foetidus et mali odoris, ac si saporet de foetore hircino, et facit homines multae comestionis.

These are all variations on familiar Arabic texts, especially Johannes Hispalensis's translations of Abû Ma'šar and Alcabitius. The next sentence—

☞ Et si inciperet Saturninus diligere aliquem, quod raro contingit, diliget eum dilectione vera. Et si incoeperit odire aliquem, quod pluries accidit, odiet eum odio ultimato, et vix aut nunquam desistet ab odio illo,

—can be deduced in the main from Alcabitius's "honesty . . . in love", but both in its special emphasis on the lasting quality of Saturnine feelings, and in its choice of words, it corresponds so closely with the characteristics of the melancholic that a connexion seems inevitable.[200] The good and bad qualities of the "children" of Saturn according to the Arabs are then linked with the good and bad positions of the planet.

☞ Et dixit Albumasar, quod si fuerit boni esse, significat profunditatem scientiae, et consilium bonum et profundum, tale quod vix aut nunquam sciet alius meliorare illud. Et ex magisteriis significat res antiquas et laboriosas, et graves et preciosas, et opera aquatica vel quae fiunt prope aquas, sicut sunt molendina . . . aedificationes domorum et maxime domorum religiosorum induentium nigras vestes . . .

At the end of the chapter the unfortunate qualities are listed "Si autem fuerit infortunatus et mali esse, significat res antiqua: et viles. . . ." The description culminates in pointing out the special talent of Saturn's "children" for leatherwork and parchment-working, and in the following chapter this idea is developed in entirely the same way as in Alcabitius. Here Bonatti says that the conjunction of Saturn with one of the other planets determines the special propriety of the finished "coria" and "pergamenta", so that the child of Saturn and Jupiter is gifted for the manufacture and working of parchments for religious, astrological and juridical writings, the child of Saturn and Venus for the manufacture of skins for drums, the child of Saturn and Mercury for the production of parchments for business deeds, and so on.

---

200 See above, p. 131, and p. 71, note 11.

In general one may say that in practical astrological literature of middle and late medieval times, Saturn's redeeming features were more and more buried beneath the mass of his evil qualities, and that he became more of a purely unlucky planet than he had been even according to Vettius Valens or Rhetorius.

This is plain from Michael Scot, Bonatti's companion in Dante's hell. The attribute "cogitatio" is still included, but it appears as a very inorganic part of the series "pavor, timor, guerra, captivitas, carcer, lamentationes, tristitia, cogitatio, pigritia, inimicitia, planctus", and so on. Saturn is "worse than the others"; he is "stella damnabilis, furiosa, odiosa, superba, impia, crudelis, malivola, hebes, tarda, multis nociva, sterilis, nutrix paupertatis, conservans malum, vitans bonum, dura, senex et sine misericordia". He is "strong and powerful in wickedness, always signifying evil and not good" and even when auspicious stars counteract him he finds a means to impose his wicked will.

> Verum est, quod permutatur ab eius influentia secundum potentiam alterius planetae ipsum superantis, et tamen, si non potest operari suam malitiam in alio quantum vellet, nocet omnibus quantum potest.

Hence children born under him are the poorest and most despicable of men, including not only the usual grave-diggers and cleaners of latrines, but also "men who serve writs"—a realistic twist of astrologers' imagination given to the mythical attribute of "imprisonment". The Saturnine man is the worst of all men, and his facial and temperamental peculiarities reflect the vileness of his whole appearance. His skin is dark, brown, yellowish, or almost greenish; his eyes are small and deep-set, but keen-sighted, and seldom blinking; his voice is weak; his regard is bent on the ground; his beard is scanty; his shoulders are bowed; he is sexually weak and inclining to impotence, but has a good memory; his understanding is crude, his mind sluggish, his brain slow of comprehension; moreover, he is timid, depressed, thoughtful, seldom laughing or even cheerful; lazy, envious, negligent in dress, boring in speech, deceitful, rapacious, thievish, ungrateful, miserly and misanthropic.[201]

One can see that astrology was as hard on the notion of Saturn as were medicine and the doctrine of temperaments on the notion of the melancholic; so much so, indeed, that the description of

---

[201] *Liber introductorius*, Oxford, MS Bodley 266, fols. 150ᵛ sqq.

the one corresponds with that of the other even down to the choice of words. It is as though Michael Scot or his source had incorporated whole sections of writings on the theory of the complexions in his own list of Saturn's characteristics, just as his list in turn may have influenced later descriptions of the melancholic. And as, in the case of melancholy, the purely negative conception of it became the general rule, so it was the case of Saturn and his children. Cecco d'Ascoli, who was burnt at the stake in 1327, called Saturn "quella trista stella, tarda di corso e di virtù nemica, che mai suo raggio non fè cosa bella",[202] and (to quote only one more professional astrologer) Bartolomeo da Parma, in a chapter based entirely on Michael Scot, says "omnibus nocet, nemini proficit; quare dicitur esse malus. Nocet enim suis et alienis".[203]

This conception became ever more widespread, despite the more or less meaningless preservation of a few favourable characteristics. Here and there the child of Saturn is still granted riches, wisdom, or the capacity, despite all his evil qualities, to make himself "loved by noble people" and to become "the greatest among his friends".[204] A Latin poem on the planets, of purely literary inspiration, which is found in many late manuscripts, contains sentences which are nothing but a paraphrase, occasionally somewhat free, of Macrobius's list, and of Saturn it even says,

---

[202] Cecco d'Ascoli, *L'Acerba*, I, ed. A. Crespi, Ascoli Piceno 1927, p. 126.

[203] Bartolomeo da Parma, ed. E. Narducci, in *Bulletino di bibliografia e di storia delle scienze matematiche e fisiche*, XVII (1884), p. 178. The author also gives a pictorial description of Saturn: "Picturatur enim senex cum longa barba, macer in carne, brunus in pelle, turpis in facie, displicibilis alteri et infortunatus multum; in manibus habens falcem elevatam ad secandum pratum, sapam, badilem, uangam et zerlam ad cultum terre; scutum ad spallas, helmum in capite, hensem eruginosam ad cincturam, et gladium eruginosum in vagina", which is also based entirely on Scot (see below, p. 208, note 47). How the Florentine factions made use of astrological notions in their propaganda can be seen from one of Coluccio Salutati's letters: "Saturnini et martiales, quales gebellinos volunt, mali, maliciosi, iracundi, superbi, crudeles et irrequieti" (*Epistolario di Coluccio Salutati*, ed. F. Novati, Rome 1893, VOL. II. p. 31).

[204] Thus the MS of the Cassel Landesbibliothek, Cod. astron. I, 20, fol. 62ʳ. The passage is interesting enough to warrant reproduction in an abridged form: "Dise ur Saturni ist . . . nit gut, wann was man wil ubels tun, darzu is sy gerecht. Vnd davon ist darynn nit gut fur chinig und fürsten geen . . . . Aber es ist dann gut gepew grünthen und anheben tzu pawen die da lang sullen weren . . . . Man vindt auch geschriben wer in der ur Saturni geporn wirt, der werd weis vnd geert, und der dann auch an einem tag vnd in seiner ur geporn werd, der werd einer hertten swartzen Complexen die da haisset colica und wirt geittig und begert fremdes gutz und wird ein achter [= Geächteter] und verrätter und wurt doch [!] von edeln lewtten lieb gehabt vnd der mächtigist vnder seinen freunden."

"dat animae virtutem discernendi et ratiocinandi."[205] But it is significant that the verso of the page which is reminiscent of Macrobius contains the following lines:

> Annis viginti currit bis quinque Saturnus,
> et homo, qui nascitur, dum Saturnus dominatur,
> audax, urbanus, malus, antiquus, fur, avarus,
> perfidus, ignarus, iracundus, nequitiosus.

In the later Middle Ages the notion of Saturn was determined by claptrap such as this, and by excerpts from writings of professional astrologers, such as Michael Scot, quoted in debased form in popular almanacs. To such an extent was this the case that even didactic and narrative verse which, in accordance with the dual nature of available sources, used to draw a very clear distinction between Saturn as a mythical figure and Saturn as a planet, based the first of these notions on mythographical texts but the second on that "astrological vulgate", the origin of which we have just traced. In the *Roman de la Rose*, as in Lydgate, Gower and Chaucer, Saturn is on the one hand the god of time, the Ruler of the Golden Age (generally held up as an example to the contemporary age), the King of Crete, the minter of gold, the founder of cities, the inventor of agriculture and so on[206]; on the other hand, he is the cold, leaden, destructive planetary god who says of himself in the Canterbury Tales:

> My cours, that hath so wyde for to turne,
> Hath more power than wot any man.
> Myn is the drenching in the see so wan;
> Myn is the prison in the derke cote;
> Myn is the strangling and hanging by the throte;
> The murmure, and the cherles rebelling;
> The groyning, and the pryvee empoysoning:
> I do vengeance and full correccioun,
> Whyl I dwelle in the signe of the leoun.
> Myn is the ruine of the hye halles,

---

[205] Thus, e.g., the Göttingen Kyeser MS (Cod. philos. 63; cf. A. Hauber, *Planetenkinderbilder und Sternbilder*, Strasbourg 1916, pp. 54 sqq.). Correspondingly Jupiter "Dat magnanimitatem animae"; Mars, "animositatem influit animae"; Sol, "dat animae virtutem meliorandi et reminiscendi"; Venus, "dat animae concupiscentiam et desiderium"; Mercury, "dat animae virtutem gaudendi et delectandi"; Luna, "dat animae virtutem vegetandi, quae dicitur virtus naturalis animalis."

[206] Cf. for instance *Roman de la Rose*, ed. E. Langlois, Paris 1914, lines 5336 sqq. and 20032 sqq.; J. Lydgate, *Reson and Sensuallyte*, ed. E. Sieper, London 1901, lines 1289 sqq. and 3082 sqq.; J. Lydgate, *Fall of Princes*, ed. J. Bergen, Washington 1923, I, lines 1401 sqq., and VII, lines 880 sqq. and 1153 sqq; John Gower, *Confessio amantis*, bk IV, lines 2445 sqq.; and bk V, lines 845 sqq., ed. G. C. Macaulay, vol. I, London 1900.

The fallyng of the toures and of the walles
Up-on the mynour or the carpenter.
I slow Sampsoun in shaking the piler:
And myne be the maladyes colde,
The derke tresons, and the castes olde;
My loking is the fader of pestilence.[207]

Christine de Pisan's *Epître d'Othéa* claims all seven planets as tutors for her "Bon Chevalier", and can therefore attribute only good qualities to them, but it is almost a solitary exception when she holds up Saturn's "slowness" to her hero as a prerequisite for sound judgement and reflection.[208]

How the common man—and not only the common man—regarded the nature and influence of Saturn from the late fifteenth century until relatively modern times, can be illustrated by a small selection from the innumerable "popular" texts.

☞ Quicquid et infaustum, quicquid flagitiosum,
est Saturne tuum: nisi quam cerealia struas.[209]

The child of Saturn is a thief
And in him lieth much mischief;
Saturn is clever, cold and hard,
His child looks on with sad regard.
Faint-hearted and misunderstood
With shame he reaches elderhood.
Thief, spoiler, murderer, untrue
Blasphemer in all manner too,
Never in favour with woman or wife,
In drinking does he spend his life.[210]

---

207 CHAUCER, *Canterbury Tales*, group A, lines 2454 sqq. (The Knightes Tale). Cf. JOHN GOWER, *Confessio amantis*, BK VII, lines 935 sqq., ed. cit., VOL. II, London 1901:

"The heyeste and aboven alle
Stant that planete which men calle
Saturnus, whos complexion
Is cold, and his condicion
Causeth malice and crualte
To him the whos nativite
Is set under his governance.
For alle hise werkes ben grevance
And enemy to mannes hele,
In what degre that he schal dele.
His climat is in Orient,
Wher that he is most violent."

208 Quoted here from Gotha, Landesbibliothek, Cod. I, 119, fol. 22v. The "gloss" repeats the "mythographical vulgate." For the pictorial tradition resulting from this singular interpretation, see below, text p. 205 sq. (PLATE 36).

209 Inscription on a fresco in the Palazzo Trinci at Foligno, dated before 1424, published by M. Salmi, in *Bolletino d'Arte, XIII* (1919), p. 176.

210 From A. HAUBER, *Planetenkinderbilder und Sternbilder*, Strasbourg 1916, p. 75 (translated from the German). Similar verses appear e.g. in Brit. Mus., MS Add. 15697, fol. 27r.

Finally:

The planet Saturn is the highest and the greatest and the most worthless, and is cold and dry and the slowest in his course. The planet is hostile to our nature in every way and stands over to the east, and is a planet of wicked and worthless men who are thin, dark and dry, and is a planet of men who have no beard, and white hair, and who wear unclean garments. Children who are born under Saturn are misshapen of body and dark with black hair, and have hair on the skin, and little hair on the chin, and with a narrow chest, and are malicious and worthless and sad, and like unclean things, and would rather wear dirty linen than fine, and are unchaste and do not like to walk with women and pass the time, and also have all evil things by nature. The hour of Saturn is the hour of evil. In that hour God was betrayed and delivered to death. . . .[211]

[211] *Schönspergerscher Kalender*, Augsburg 1495 (translation from the German). For the corresponding connexion between the traitor Judas and melancholy, see above, p. 121 (text). The connexion of such calendars (cf. e.g. *Kalendarius teütsch Maister Joannis Küngspergers*, Augsburg 1512, fols. Ff ii^v–iii^r) and related texts (e.g. Brit. Mus., MS Add. 17987, from the region of the Lake of Constance, dated 1446, fol. 59^v) with the Michael Scot tradition is unmistakable.

Chapter II

SATURN IN THE PICTORIAL TRADITION

The development of the notion of Saturn as described above is reflected not only in literature but also in figurative art. The pictorial tradition, however, as in all similar cases, follows its own rules.

I. SATURN IN ANCIENT ART AND THE SURVIVAL OF THE TRADITIONAL REPRESENTATION IN MEDIEVAL ART

The late type, developed under eastern influence, of Mithraic Aion–Kronos who, with his wings and other attributes, fulfilled a general cosmic function, in particular as the god of Time, was known to the pre-Renaissance period only from literature and not from art (Plate 9).[1] The "Phoenician Kronos", whose cherubic form bore two wings on the head, and four on the shoulders, and had two eyes open, two shut, survived on coins and in a description by Eusebius.[2] Apart from this, ancient portraits of Saturn, in so far as they concern us, fall into two classes, both of which show the god as an old man and endow him with the attributes of a sickle[3] and a cloak pulled over his head—a trait that Saturn shares only with Asclepius, and one that gives him a strange and somewhat sinister aspect from the start. The first type shows the god in a general hieratical style, either as a bust, usually over his zodiacal symbols (as on Antonine coins),[4] or else at full length,

---

[1] F. Cumont, *Textes et monuments figurés relatifs aux mystères de Mithra*, Brussels 1896/9, vol. i, pp. 74 sqq.; vol. ii, p. 53. The *Mythographus III* (i, 6–8), significantly enough, makes no mention of wings in his description of the Mithraic Aion.

[2] Eusebius, *Praeparatio Evangelica*, i, 10, 39; see below, p. 213 (text). For the Phoenician coins from Byblos, cf. F. Imhoof-Blumer, "Monnaies grecques," in *Verhandelingen d.k. Akademie van Wetenschapen Amsterdam, Afd. Letterkunde*, xiv (1883), p. 442.

[3] See the article "Kronos" in W. H. Roscher, *Ausführliches Lexikon der griechischen und römischen Mythologie*, Leipzig 1890–97, vol. ii, cols. 1549 sqq., by Maximilian Mayer; and M. Pohlenz's article in Pauly-Wissowa, vol. xi, 1922, cols. 2014 sqq. The sickle was variously interpreted even by the ancients; according to some it symbolised Saturn's function as Earth-god, according to others, the myth of Uranus's mutilation by Kronos.

[4] For this type and its oriental derivatives, cf. F. Saxl in *Der Islam*, vol. iii (1912), p. 163. There is an analogous portrait of Venus above her zodiacal sign of the ram on a tessera from Palmyra, published by M. I. Rostovtzeff in the *Journal of Roman Studies*, vol. xxii, p. 113, Plate xxvi, 3 (without explanation of the picture).

standing, but otherwise very similar in conception. The second type shows him in the attitude of a thinker, seated, with his head on his hand.

The first type is exemplified in an impressive mural in the Casa dei Dioscuri at Pompeii (PLATE 10).[5] The god's eyes are frightening. The cloak hides all but the face, the feet, and one hand holding a sickle somewhat awkwardly at one side. This awkwardness is certainly deliberate, for the fresco is the work of a great artist. The implement which the god holds is no ordinary one, but is the symbol of the power of this severe god, and appears to menace the faithful. The unusual rigidity and somehow frenzied quality of the fresco may therefore be regarded as the expression of an individual view on the part of a painter during the golden age of Pompeian painting. For him, Saturn was the awe-inspiring god of the earth.

The second type, as we have said, is characterised by the god's being seated, with his arm resting on some object, a characteristic which seemed so typical of the god that echoes of it survive even in portraits where it is almost wholly out of place. For instance, Saturn's left hand is raised to his head in a picture of the scene where he is given the stone which he is to devour instead of the child.[6] The tomb of Cornutus in the Vatican (PLATE 13) is the most important monument of this type, together with a small bronze in the Museo Gregoriano[7] and a few fragments of monumental statuary. Saturn here appears sadly reflecting, like Attis on other tombs. His right hand does not hold the sickle upright, as in the Pompeian fresco, but lets it rest wearily upon his knee. His head is bent and rests upon his arm. For Cornutus, who ordered this portrait to be placed on his own and his children's tomb, Saturn was symbolic of the sad tranquillity of death. Ancient art therefore gave expression to the two sides of Saturn's nature, on the one hand as the awe-inspiring and beneficent god of the earth, on the other as the destructive but at the same time peace-giving ruler of the underworld. In early medieval art in the west the latter type disappeared; the type of the thinker was at first reserved in Christian art for the evangelists, apostles

---

[5] Now in Naples, Museo Nazionale. P. HERRMANN, *Denkmäler der Malerei des Altertums*, Munich 1904–31, plate 122, text p. 168.

[6] Relief on the Ara Capitolina. G. W. HELBIG, *Führer*, I, 3rd. ed., p. 485. Reproduced in S. REINACH, *Répertoire des reliefs grecs et romains*, VOL. III, Paris 1912, 201.

[7] Reproduced in W. H. ROSCHER, op. cit., VOL. II, col. 1562.

and prophets. Together with the busts, typical of the usual collection of the five planets Saturn, Jupiter, Mars, Mercury and Venus[8] in the Aratea manuscripts, there survived the solemn but non-specific schema that we saw at Pompeii. In a Carolingian picture of the planets (PLATE 15)[9] we find an exact reproduction of Saturn as a full-length figure, with his sickle, and his cloak pulled over his head. We can prove how this type came to be handed down, for ancient manuscripts had already adapted the monumental form to book illustration. The portrait of Saturn in the Calendar of A.D. 354 (PLATE 11) shows the god in walking posture, as at Pompeii[10]; the cloak leaves the upper part of the body free, the right hand holds the weapon. The illustrator of the Carolingian manuscript must have had an example from later antiquity in front of him, bearing in some ways more resemblance to the classical fresco than did the picture in the Calendar. Saturn's outstretched arm with the weapon is a deviation which the Carolingian picture shares with the Calendar, but as in the ancient fresco he turns his head to the side as if looking at the opponent whom he menaces with his weapon.[11]

The illustrations to Rabanus Maurus's encyclopaedia (PLATE 12) are also largely based on the ancient pictorial tradition.[12] Here, Saturn appears in very unmedieval form, half naked and in classical dress, and his attitude in walking also goes back to an ancient model. What, however, is new and surprising is the fact that the god is holding not a sickle but the more modern scythe—a fact

---

[8] The Greek prototype survives in later copies in Vat. graec. 1087 fol. 301 v; for this picture in Latin MSS, cf. GEORG THIELE, *Antike Himmelsbilder*, Berlin 1898, pp. 130 sqq.

[9] Leiden, University Library, Cod. Voss. lat. q. 79.

[10] J. STRZYGOWSKI, "Die Calenderbilder des Chronographen vom Jahre 354," in *Jahrbuch des kaiserlich deutschen archäologischen Instituts*, Ergänzungsheft 1, Berlin 1888, pl. x. More recently (though not convincing with regard to the exclusion of an intermediate Carolingian stage between the post-classical original and the surviving Renaissance copies), cf. C. NORDENFALK, *Der Kalender vom Jahre* 354 *und die lateinische Buchmalerei des* 4. *Jahrhunderts*. (Göteborgs kungl. Vetenskaps- och Vitterhets-Samhälles Handlingar, 5. Földjen, Ser. A., VOL. V, No. 2 (1936), p. 25).

[11] For the Germanicus Codex, Leiden, Voss. lat. q. 79, and the copy in Boulogne, Bibl. Municip., MS 188, see G. THIELE, *Antike Himmelsbilder*, pp. 138 sqq. A similar model was used by the miniaturist of Vat. Reg. lat. 123, reproduced in SAXL, *Verzeichnis*, VOL. I, plate 5, fig. 11. The picture in Reg. lat. 123 which shows Saturn in medieval dress, with covered head and a long scythe, is probably based primarily on descriptions, and not on pictorial tradition. But that does not seem to exclude the possibility of vague reminiscences of ancient models being present even in this portrait.

[12] *Miniature sacre e profane dell'anno* 1023 . . . , ed. A. M. Amelli, Montecassino 1896, plate CVIII; cf. RABANUS MAURUS, *De universo*, BK XV: "Falcem tenet (inquiunt), propter agriculturam significandam" (MIGNE, P. L., VOL. CXI, col. 428).

which owes its existence only to the interpretation of the eleventh-century copyist.[13]

Except in pictures of planets such as that mentioned above,[14] portraits of Saturn appear in Byzantine art only in illustrations to St Gregory of Nazianzus' *Homilies.*

The oldest portrait of Saturn occurs in a ninth-century manuscript in Milan.[15] It illustrates the first homily *Contra Julianum*, and is conceived so exclusively in terms of the text, which vehemently attacks the pagan gods, that the artist has fallen into a ludicrous mistake. St Gregory says ironically that it is an admirable way to make children love their parents, when one reads how Kronos castrated Uranus, and how his son Zeus then lay in wait for him and gave him tit for tat.[16] But the illustrator who took the word Οὔρανος as meaning not the god Uranus but the sky itself, and who understood by τέμνειν not "to castrate" but "to cut" or "to split", shows us Saturn (Ὁ ΚΡΟΝΟΣ ΤΟΝ ΟΥ⟨ΡΑ⟩ΝΟΝ ΤΕΜΝΟ⟨Ν⟩) with a mighty axe cleaving the vaults of heaven, while Zeus (Ὁ ΔΙΑΣ ΚΑΤΑ ΤΟΥ ΚΡΟΝ⟨ΟΥ⟩ 'ΕΠΑΝΙΣΤΑΜΕΝΟΣ) threatens him with a similar axe from behind (PLATE 16).

But a later group of Gregory manuscripts, dating from the eleventh and twelfth centuries (that is, from the peak of the humanist movement starting in the tenth century), shows a substantially different picture. In these manuscripts[17] the illustrations of the pagan gods have been lifted from the homily *Contra Julianum* and added to those of the homily *In sancta lumina.* But the cycle is now much richer and, what is more important, the representations based on literary tradition (such as the "Birth of Venus" from Saturn's genitals thrown into the sea, which appears

---

[13] Cf. E. PANOFSKY and F. SAXL, in *Metropolitan Museum Studies*, VOL. IV, 2 (1933), p. 250, note 3.

[14] Cod. Vat. graec. 1087.

[15] Milan, Biblioteca Ambrosiana, Cod. E. 49/50 inf., in A. MARTINI and D. BASSI, *Cat. Cod. Gr. Bibl. Ambr.*, Milan 1906, VOL. II, pp. 1084 sqq. We owe knowledge of this MS, as well as of the Jerusalem MS mentioned below, to Professor A. M. Friend. The photographs reproduced here were kindly placed at our disposal by Dr Kurt Weitzmann. Cf. A. GRABAR, *Les miniatures du Grégoire de Nazianze de l'Ambrosienne*, Paris 1943, plate 71. K. WEITZMANN, *Greek Mythology in Byzantine Art*, Princeton 1951, p. 38.

[16] MIGNE, P. Gr., VOL. XXXV, col. 660.

[17] Paris, Bibl. Nat. MS Coislin 239 (cf. H. OMONT, *Les miniatures des plus anciens manuscrits grecs de la Bibliothèque Nationale*, 2nd edn., Paris 1929, plate CXVIII, nos. 14 sqq.), Jerusalem Bibl. Graec. Patr. Cod. Taphou 14, Athos Panteleimon, Cod. 6 (PLATES 14 and 17). Of these the Athos MS is the earliest and best, without necessarily being nearest to the original type.

otherwise only in later, western, art) are now reinforced by others which, by contrast, were foreign to western art, and presuppose a pictorial tradition derived from classical antiquity. Of this kind is the "Cunning of Rhea", who gave her spouse a swaddled stone to devour (cf. PLATE 14), and the musical assistance of the Curetes and Corybantes, whose clamour drowned the cries of the infant Zeus and protected him from discovery (PLATE 17). Where Rhea is shown practising her deceit on Saturn we still encounter a type of seated Saturn, similar to the Capitoline relief which we have mentioned above.[18] One can therefore assume that the illustrations to these later Gregory manuscripts arose only partly as translations of the text into pictures; and that in other cases they followed a purely pictorial tradition derived from illustrated texts of a secular nature which did not impinge on the theological cycle till the tenth-century renaissance. This applies not only to the scene of Saturn and Rhea and that of the Corybantes, but also to those illustrating the birth of Athena, Cybele, and Orpheus. This suspicion is made almost a certainty by the fact that the miniatures of the Corybantes in the later Gregory manuscripts obviously derive from the same model as was transmitted in the representations of this scene in the Oppian manuscripts.[19]

2. TEXT-ILLUSTRATION AND ORIENTAL INFLUENCE

The illustrations of Rabanus Maurus's work provided a stepping-stone between representations based on purely pictorial tradition, such as those in the Vossianus manuscript, and a new group of western medieval works destined to be of far greater significance for the general development, because they were not based on any tradition formulated in classical art. In these works new types appeared, partly because the artists started from texts containing descriptions of the ancient gods, which the medieval illustrators could adorn from their own imagination, partly because

---

[18] For the scene of the stone being handed to Saturn, cf. above, p. 197 (text). For the scene with the Corybantes, cf. S. REINACH, *Répertoire des reliefs*, Paris 1912, VOL. II, p. 280, and VOL. III, p. 201. The miniature reproduced in OMONT, op. cit., fig. 14, too, shows the stone being given to Saturn, not the infant Zeus being handed to a maidservant; the figure interpreted by Omont as a maid was originally bearded.

[19] These are: Venice, Biblioteca Marciana, Cod. gr. 479; Paris, Bibl. Nat., MSS gr. 2736 and 2737 (cf. A. W. BYVANCK, *Mededeelingen van het Nederlandsche Histor. Instituut te Rome*, V (1925), pp. 34 sqq.). It is interesting to see that MS gr. 2737, fol. 35, written by Ange Vergèce in 1554, fills the place of the Saturn missing in the Corybantes miniature (Paris Bibl. Nat., MS gr. 2736, fol. 24) with one taken from a western model.

they relied on models emanating from a different culture, that is to say, from that of the east. For both reasons the medieval artist's imagination was free to create really new types, nearer to the contemporary mind. The best example of such an early medieval Saturn is in a manuscript painted in Regensburg[20] (PLATE 18). This has nothing in common with classical models, but is one of those independent illustrations in the learned texts we spoke of in the previous chapter—texts which the Middle Ages took over from late antiquity, where the descriptions of the ancient gods were allegorically interpreted for philosophical and moralistic purposes. In this illustration Saturn is endowed with a multitude of attributes. His head is covered; in his left hand he holds the sickle and—as already encountered in Rabanus's encyclopaedia—the scythe; in his right hand he holds the dragon Time, which is biting its own tail and shows that Kronos must also be interpreted as Chronos. The artist's imagination has given the old description a new, and typically medieval, vitality.[21]

A portrait such as that in the Regensburg manuscript, however, remained for a long time unique, for the Saturn here depicted is at first only a graphic inventory of traits given in the text, made in a general way to resemble contemporary types. It still bore no relation or possibility of relation either to a real person or to the real surroundings of medieval men, for such a purely "transliterating" portrait lacked both the visual force of a pictorial tradition and the vitality of a realistic representation. It is understandable, therefore, that a substantial pictorial revival of the ancient gods could only follow when the obsolete tradition of antiquity had been replaced by a living one, which would make it possible to proceed to a realistic new interpretation of the gods here still represented in a purely "literary" form. This was brought about when the west came into contact with oriental models, which represented the pagan gods admittedly in somewhat exotic costume but none the less in more contemporary form, or at least in a form more capable of assimilation. In the east, perhaps owing to a certain subterranean survival of the old oriental notion of the planets, a series of pictorial types had developed whose particular characteristics had hitherto been foreign to the west, but which could easily be translated into

---

[20] Clm. 14271.

[21] Cf. E. PANOFSKY and F. SAXL, in *Metropolitan Museum Studies*, IV, 2 (1933), pp. 253 sqq. and fig. 39.

contemporary terms. Jupiter and Mercury appeared with a book, Venus with a lute, Mars with a sword and a head without a body, and finally Saturn with spade and pick-axe (PLATES 23–5). From the thirteenth century, at least, these types[22] began to influence western representations, and in certain cases we can even follow the process stage by stage. Here, the most important manuscripts are those containing the illustrations to a text of Abû Ma'šar, which have come down to us in relatively large numbers.[23] The earliest manuscript of this group[24] contains portraits of the planets obviously derived from oriental sources. As in the east, Mercury appears with a book, Venus with a musical instrument, and Mars with a beheaded man, while the Twins are joined to one another, as we find them also in eastern copies. Here also do we find the curious pictures of planets falling headlong downwards[25] (PLATES 19–22); but it is a western characteristic to show the planets as reigning sovereigns (this occurs in manuscripts derived from the Paris MS lat. 7330) and to supplement the two pictures of the rise and the fall as shown in the east (PLATE 23) by a third, representing the "decline". This significant enrichment by a middle stage between the two extremes suggests that the idea of ascent and depression was linked with the western notion of the Wheel of Fortune, a link attested beyond doubt by the typical Wheel of Fortune motif of the falling crowns. It is hardly surprising that at the end of the Paris codex[26] we actually discover a picture of the Wheel of Fortune spread over four leaves, that is to say, dividing the usual sequence "Regnabo, Regno, Regnavi, Sum sine regno" into separate representations corresponding to the different phases of the planets. In these manuscripts we find a curious mixture of eastern and western elements, which alone would indicate that they were first illustrated in southern Italy; and this indication is reinforced, as we shall show elsewhere in a more detailed analysis, by considerations of style.[27]

---

[22] Cf. F. SAXL, in *Der Islam*, III (1912), pp. 151 sqq.

[23] This example of the Abû Ma'šar MSS is not an isolated one. In a geomancy written for King Richard II, Oxford, MS Bodley 581, we also find the oriental Saturn with a pickaxe.

[24] Paris, Bibl. Nat., MS lat. 7330 (mid-thirteenth century, but presupposing an older twelfth-century model).

[25] Cf. BBG, *Sternglaube*, p. 148. The Pierpont Morgan Library owns a Turkish MS of the same group, MS 788.

[26] Fols. 74v sqq.

[27] In F. SAXL, H. MEIER, and H. BOBER, *Catalogue of Astrological and Mythological Illuminated Manuscripts of the Latin Middle Ages*, VOL. III, *Manuscripts in English Libraries*, London 1953, pp. lxiii sqq.

In the Paris codex 7330 Saturn appears in an entirely western form, as a ruler with a sceptre and without any other attributes. His zodiacal signs, too, the Water-Bearer as Ganymede, and the Goat, are conceived in a purely western manner. But if we look at later manuscripts of this group,[28] we find to our surprise that eastern influence has increased to such an extent that Saturn is now given a spade, as in eastern manuscripts, and that the god is shown in a peculiar attitude, standing with one foot on his chair.[29] Here he retains nothing of the calm, regal aspect of the older picture; the figure seems rather to resemble those of eastern manuscripts in which a similarly agitated attitude is found (PLATE 25). After their journeyings in the east the ancient gods could now become far more realistic figures, resembling in their outward appearance late medieval scholars, peasants, or nobles, standing in direct visual relationship to the mortals born under them, and thus for the first time reawakening to powerful vitality. Saturn, in particular, became in later medieval art more and more the leader and representative of the poor and the oppressed, which not only corresponded to the realistic tendencies of late medieval art in general, but also, more specifically, to the social upheaval of the epoch. As early as in the so-called Guariento frescoes in the Church of the Eremitani at Padua[30] he appears as what he was to remain until modern times, despite all humanistic refinements—a ragged peasant, leaning on the tool of his trade. In a North Italian manuscript, too, he appears as a peasant, with a scythe and a water-bottle at his waist, about to go to the fields[31] (PLATE 26). Under eastern influence, the Greek harvest god and the Italian god of husbandry has himself become a peasant. He remains a peasant even in a mythological scene where he appears coupled with Philyra who was turned into a mare, as the Andalus de Nigro manuscripts show him (PLATE 27). He is the representative of the lowest rung of medieval society, to whom all intellectual activity is a closed book, and

---

[28] London, Brit. Mus., Sloane MS 3983 and New York, Pierpont Morgan Library, MS 785 (PLATE 24, painted in Bruges shortly before 1400).

[29] In portraits of Luna, the oriental influence became so strong that while she is still represented as Diana in Paris Bibl. Nat., MS lat. 7330 (fols. 58v sqq.), she appears as a man, like the ancient oriental Sin, in Brit. Mus., Sloane MS 3983 and its derivatives.

[30] For the attribution of this to an assistant of Guariento, cf. L. COLETTI, "Studi sulla pittura del Trecento a Padova," in *Rivista d'Arte*, XII (1930), pp. 376 sqq.

[31] L. DOREZ, *La canzone delle virtù delle scienze di Bartolomeo di Bartoli da Bologna*, Bergamo 1904, p. 84.

who spends his life in wresting a meagre subsistence from the soil. The latter days of life, when man becomes sterile and when his vital warmth diminishes so that he seeks only to crouch by the fire—these days are proper to Saturn.

3. THE PICTURE OF SATURN AND HIS CHILDREN

The east gave to the west entirely new notions of the planetary rulers, notions which no longer had anything in common with the types evolved by classical art. More than that, it brought to the west a hitherto unknown system of complicated designs pictorially representing the relationship of the planets with those men who come under their influence.

Eastern writers inform us that in pagan temples Saturn was represented as an aged Indian, as a man riding on an elephant, as a man meditating on ancient wisdom, as a man drawing a bucket of water from a well, and so on. With few exceptions,[32] these pictures are representations of the occupations attributed to Saturn in the astrological texts dealt with in the previous chapter, and we have therefore every reason to suppose that the murals described by these writers were the predecessors of the designs described by later historians of art as pictures of "planets' children". This belief is strengthened by the fact that such pictures of "planets' children" really are to be found in later eastern manuscripts. In an Arabic manuscript[33] and its later cousins[34] we find the "trades of the planets" represented in eight times seven pictures (PLATE 31). The first picture in each row shows the planet itself, while each of the seven neighbouring pictures shows one of its children. Saturn appears as a man with a pick-axe (as in PLATE 25), with, next to him, trades like leather-working, farming, and so on; Mercury is a scholar with a book, associated with more refined occupations. The west must have met with similar arrangements in the fourteenth century, for that alone would account for the fact that the Salone at Padua[35]

---

[32] The man with the water-bucket is obviously Aquarius, one of the "houses" of Saturn. The fact that he was represented thus in the east can be seen, for instance, from the portrait on the Islamic astronomical instrument in the possession of Prince Öttingen-Wallerstein, reproduced in *Der Islam*, III (1912), plate 7, fig. 13; ib., pp. 156 sq., the texts.

[33] Oxford, Bodl. MS Or. 133.

[34] Such as Paris, Bibl. Nat., suppl. turc. 242, and New York, Pierpont Morgan Library, MS 788.

[35] A. BARZON, *I cieli e la loro influenza negli affreschi del Salone in Padova*, Padua 1924.

contains, arranged in a very similar tabular form, a series of images of "planets' children" which we may describe as a monumental western version of such "tables" as are found, for example, in the Bodleian Oriental manuscript 133. Saturn himself appears PL. 31
in very unclassical form, as a man laying his hand on his mouth to signify either silence or his sinister and ailing nature (PLATES 32–33). The "planets' children", too, underwent an ever greater process of realistic "modernisation" in the west. Later ages found the tabulated series of occupations (such as those which the Salone at Padua had taken over from eastern manuscripts, in the style of the Bodleian Oriental manuscript 133) too monotonous in form, and too heterogeneous in content. They sought a form which should group together the men ruled by the planets in a kind of lively "genre" picture which appeared socially and psychologically more coherent. This involved, in the first place, a reduction of the chaotic variety present in the original "tables" to a limited number of inherently related types; secondly, the assembling of these types in coherent surroundings and in the same perspective. The picture of Jupiter must illustrate the nature and way of life of men blessed with culture and property, Mercury that of scholars and artists, Mars that of warriors, and Saturn that of poor and oppressed peasants, beggars, cripples, prisoners and criminals. At the same time, a wish was felt to make immediately visible the fatal "influence" of each planet on those subject to it, and so it is understandable that after a number of hesitant attempts at modernising the schema in the Salone at Padua, a solution was finally found in a design which had been used in quite another sphere and in quite another sense to show the "influence" of a heavenly power on earthly existence: the design of Christ's Ascension into heaven (or, to be more exact, the risen Christ addressing those left on earth), of Judgement Day, and, above all, of Pentecost and similar mysteries (PLATE 35).[36]

This new design first originated in the northern art of the fifteenth century (PLATES 38, 40), as Kautzsch and Warburg have shown,[37] and later affected Italian art (PLATE 39); despite modification of individual traits, and shifting of emphasis, its composition remained unaltered until the seventeenth and eighteenth centuries (PLATE 53). We first meet with it as a complete series in the illustrations to Christine de Pisan's *Epître*

---

[36] E. PANOFSKY and F. SAXL, in *Metropolitan Museum Studies*, IV, 2 (1933), p. 245.

[37] A. WARBURG, *Gesammelte Schriften*, VOL. I, Leipzig 1932, pp. 86 and 331.

d'Othéa. The planetary god sits on a cloud, a halo of stars about him, like a true heavenly ruler, and beneath, on the earth, live his "children"—in the case of Venus, lovers holding up their hearts as sacrifices, in the case of Saturn, wise men assembled in council (PLATE 36). The phenomenon of such an adaptation of the Pentecostal scene to secular purposes is not unique at this time. In a late fourteenth-century miniature in the Vienna "Oracle Book" (PLATE 37) we find a group of sages and patriarchs assembled under a hemisphere containing the seven planets,[38] and the illustrations drawn about 1400 for Boccaccio's *De claris mulieribus* show Juno as a heavenly apparition hovering above her worshippers, while Minerva forms with her artisan protégés something like a mythology of the "Liberal Arts" (PLATE 34).[39] A fusion of the secularised Pentecostal design with this version of the "Liberal Arts" picture makes further development easily comprehensible.

The use of a religious design in Christine de Pisan's illustrations was made easier by the fact that the planets are here purely of good significance. Each of them represents a particular virtue, so that the assimilation of these pictures to representations such as that of Pentecost seems natural enough. Moreover, once this adaptation was completed by fusion with the "Liberal Arts" motif, the design could also embrace the very different content of the usual astrological texts, and so create the form of the "planets' children" picture which remained in force for several hundred years. Within the framework of this development there were a number of elaborations and modifications. Thus, Saturn was represented as an accountant and arithmetician (PLATE 43); as the god of coffers, holding a key as well as a sickle (PLATE 28); as a labourer digging; and also as a rider bearing not only the grand star but also the humble sickle on his banner (PLATES 29, 41). The scythe which he carries as well as, or instead of, the sickle, may be turned into a spade or mattock, and these in turn can become a crutch (PLATES 30, 38, 57), and finally this god of the humble and oppressed acquires a wooden leg. Perhaps the curious leg posture, which was occasionally copied from certain oriental sources, and even an unconscious memory of the myth of Kronos's

---

[38] Cf. A. STANGE, *Deutsche Malerei der Gotik*, VOL. II, Berlin 1936, fig. 33. The date assumed by Stange seems somewhat too early.

[39] Cf. the portraits of Juno in Paris, Bibl. Nat., MS fr. 598, fol. 12; Paris, Bibl. Nat., MS fr. 12420, fol. 11; Brussels, Bibl. Royale, MS 9509, fol. 12ᵛ; of Minerva in Paris, Bibl. Nat., MS fr. 598, fol. 13; Paris, Bibl. Nat., MS fr. 12420, fol. 13ᵛ; Brussels, Bibl. Royale, MS 9509, fol. 15. For portraits of the arts, see below, pp. 306 sqq. (text).

castration may have played a part in this last disfigurement. But on the other hand, fifteenth-century artists had already begun to paint Saturn in somewhat more heroic colours, especially in Italy, as one would expect. The Florentine series of "planets' children" pictures is in some ways analogous to the pictures of "triumphs", so popular after Petrarch: Saturn appears as King Time with a scythe, in a chariot drawn by the "Dragons of Time" which bite their own tails (PLATE 39). In the north, he appears as a rider, like those in the pictures of tournaments. Finally, in the Florentine *Picture Chronicle* he appears in true humanist fashion as the Latin king who taught the Romans agriculture and founded Sutrium (PLATE 44).[40]

4. SATURN IN MYTHOGRAPHICAL ILLUSTRATIONS OF THE LATE MIDDLE AGES

Meanwhile, however, the mythographical illustrations, of which we saw an early but isolated example in the Munich manuscript,[41] PL. 18 came to life again. With regard to content, the mythographical texts of this time, that is to say, of the fourteenth and fifteenth centuries, seem to have been completely "moralised": their allegorical representation was interpreted in a Christian sense. But their pictorial representation came under the sway of the new "realistic" tendency which favoured a contemporary setting —astrological illustrations, as we saw, had already been affected in this way in relation to their oriental models. Thus the author of *Fulgentius metaforalis*[42] makes Saturn signify wisdom. But in the illustrations to this text (PLATE 45) he appears as a reigning monarch, his queen by his side, in fifteenth-century costume, while about him are depicted the various scenes of his life— which a sensitive mind generally finds offensive. The medieval author could take even disgusting scenes as a subject for moral exhortation, because for him the true significance lay not in the picture itself but in its allegorical meaning.[43]

The most important series of illustrations of this kind are the fourteenth-century picture cycle in the French translation of

[40] SIDNEY COLVIN, *A Florentine Picture-Chronicle*, London 1898, plate 30.

[41] Clm. 14271.

[42] H. LIEBESCHÜTZ, *Fulgentius Metaforalis* (Studien der Bibliothek Warburg, VOL. IV), Leipzig 1926, pp. 71 sqq.

[43] See A. WARBURG, *Gesammelte Schriften*, VOL. II, Leipzig 1932, pp. 627 sqq.

St Augustine's *Civitas Dei*, and also—and these were more fruitful—the illustrations in the *Ovide moralisé*. In both series Saturn is endowed with attributes and brought into contexts which had played, and could play, no part in astrology. In the illustrations to the *Cité de Dieu*, Saturn, in remembrance of his long and difficult voyage to Latium, appears as a dignified old man with a ship or ship's mast in his hand.[44] On the other hand, in the first version of the French *Ovide moralisé*, where portraits of the great pagan gods appear as title vignettes to each book, he is once more connected with the "Dragons of Time"[45]; above all, the scene of Saturn devouring his children, never before represented even in antiquity, is here shown in all its crudity, just as the birth of Venus from the castrated member is shown in the above-mentioned illustrations to *Fulgentius metaforalis*. We see the god putting the child to his lips, sinking his teeth into its arm, or even having already devoured its head (PLATES 46, 49, 52, 144). Here we see the ruthless wickedness of the god, Moloch devouring his own children, and the unbearable starkness of this is softened only by the accompanying text, which endeavours to interpret the picture allegorically.

These motives are elaborated in the illustrations to Berchorius's introduction to the Latin *Ovide moralisé*, and also in those to the *Libellus de imaginibus deorum*,[46] which was taken from the same introduction. The descriptions in this work later won a place in countless representations in both north and south.[47] The

---

[44] Cf. A. DE LABORDE, *Les manuscrits à peintures de la Cité de Dieu*, Paris 1909, VOL. I, pp. 198–9; VOL. II, pp. 322, 367, 385, and plate XXIV b.

[45] As in clm. 14271.

[46] Cf. A. WARBURG, *Gesammelte Schriften*, VOL. II, pp. 453 sqq., 462, 471, 485 sqq.

[47] The fantastic portraits of the planets in the Scotus MSS are a synthesis of astrological and mythological pictorial tradition (the origin of this Saturn type, with shield and helmet, is discussed in E. PANOFSKY and F. SAXL, in *Metropolitan Museum Studies*, IV, 2 (1933), p. 242 sqq.). The Scotus type of planetary portrait becomes the predominant form of illustration in astrological MSS from the fourteenth century onwards, save that in the fifteenth century they become "humanistic" in a remarkable manner by the re-introduction of the style of the Calendar of 354, transmitted by Carolingian models (cf. Darmstadt, Cod. 266, reproduced in PANOFSKY and SAXL (loc. cit.), p. 266; Salzburg, Cod. V 2 G 81/83; and Cod. Vat. Pal. lat. 1370). Similarly, we have the copies of Carolingian Rabanus Maurus MSS made in the fifteenth century, the revival of interest in Carolingian illustrations of Terence (also described by PANOFSKY and SAXL, loc. cit.), the copies of the *Notitia dignitatum*, etc. A certain parallel to this proto-Renaissance in the north can perhaps be discerned in the fact that planetary gods in northern fifteenth-century art appear as a rule as naked standing figures, somewhat reminiscent of the classical type of Roman reliefs representing the Gods of the Week, though no direct influence can be shown. In the high Middle Ages naked planetary gods appear, for special reasons, in the exceptional case of the Provençal illustrations to MATFRE ERMENGAUD'S *Breviari d'Amor* (cf. e.g. the pictures of Saturn in Paris Bibl. Nat., MS fr. 9219, fol. 33, or London, Brit. Mus., Harleian MS 4940, fol. 33).

child-devouring motif passed from mythographical art into the pictures of the planets and their "children" (in PLATE 47, even combined with the castration motif!) and later became a characteristic feature of such representations (PLATES 48 and 49).[48]

5. SATURN IN HUMANISM

The great diversity of types which arose from the fourteenth century onwards shows that, after the almost complete stagnation of the previous epoch, a real revival of the ancient gods had now begun, and that a genuinely humanistic re-creation—that is to say, a consciously "classical" treatment of them—was both possible and to some extent called for. This was especially true of Saturn. We shall see later the significance which this most sinister of the gods was to attain in Italian humanism, but even here we can see how the former portraits of the poor peasant, the wicked devourer of children, the cunning arithmetician, or even the triumphal god of Time or the worthy founder of cities, could not satisfy the requirements of a culture in which the ancient gods again became proper deities. The Italian Renaissance desired a picture of Saturn comprising not only the two aspects of the Saturnine nature, the wicked and the mournful as well as the sublime and the profoundly contemplative, but also revealing that "ideal" form which seemed attainable only by reverting to genuinely classical examples. This humanistic rehabilitation of Saturn was achieved about 1500 in one of the most remarkable centres of Italian culture—the city that was the home of the ageing Bellini, of the young Giorgione, and of Titian.

Humanism took time to reach Venetian art, but after the later years of Jacopo Bellini a distinctly humanistic trend can be observed. In the sketchbooks which Jacopo left to younger generations we find a singular collection of archaeological drawings. Jacopo Bellini not only drew sketches of works of antiquity, which might serve one or another artist as a model or as an inspiration for his own work, but he also preserved inscriptions of no artistic or even historical significance, such as those on the tomb of a seamstress.[49] There was therefore a general archaeo-

---

[48] In the relief on the Campanile in Florence, Saturn, exactly as in the *Ovide moralisé* MS (Paris, Bibl. Nat., MS fr. 19121), holds the child he is about to devour upright, but instead of the dragon of Time he holds a wheel of Time, evidently a humanistic innovation.

[49] C. RICCI, *Jacopo Bellini e i suoi disegni*, VOL. I, Florence 1908, plate 51. *Corpus inscriptionum latinarum*, VOL. V, 2542).

logical and humanist interest in antiquity, which enabled Jacopo's son-in-law, Mantegna, at the beginning of his career, to use one of the drawings in this sketchbook when painting the frescoes of the Eremitani Chapel,[50] and reached the peak of its development in Mantegna's *Triumph of Caesar*. On the other hand, Jacopo Bellini himself, the contemporary of Donatello, seems scarcely to have been touched by classicism in those of his drawings and paintings which do not have antiquity as their subject. He remains a true later-Gothic painter, with a marked and quite unhumanistic interest in the landscapes, trees, rivers, bridges, birds and mountains of his own country. Thus the elder Bellini's work contains the two separate trends whose combination was to give the works of the Venetian renaissance their special character —works such as the young Titian's reconstructions of Philostratic pictures, which showed Bacchic figures and children of Venus in an antique rhythm set in his native landscape, and depicting statues of Venus in noblemen's parks, combined archaeological humanism with the contemporary Venetian manner. Titian's paintings for Alfonso I of Ferrara represent the culmination of this style.

Giulio Campagnola's engraving of Saturn (PLATE 54) is another, though modest, witness to this movement.[51] It is an early work of the artist, who signs it with the scholarly name of "Antenoreus", as a successor to the Antenor who came from Troy to the province of Venice and was said to have founded Padua. Perhaps because this was the work of a less strong personality, it shows the tendencies of the time in many respects particularly clearly.

In the foreground Saturn is lying on the ground, and next to the figure are some curious rocks and the trunk of a tree. In the middle distance to the right there is a small wood with high branches and undergrowth. The background consists of a fortified city by the sea on which a ship is sailing. It is striking how little inner connexion the picture of the god in the foreground has with the "modern" centre and background. Neither the background nor the tree trunk on the left are Campagnola's own invention, but are taken from two different engravings by Dürer. But Campagnola might have been able to take these details from Dürer and yet to relate them to the main figure in such a way

---

[50] See RICCI, op. cit., p. 70.

[51] G. F. HARTLAUB, "Giorgione und der Mythos der Akademien", in *Repertorium für Kunstwissenschaft*, XLVIII (1927), pp. 253 sqq.

that no disunity would be visible in the picture. It looks rather as if he had actually intended a sort of dualism. For it was in the historical tradition of Venetian art after Jacopo Bellini to regard ancient monuments with archaeological detachment, while placing them in a "modern" setting which underlined their remoteness. The figure of the god is strange, so is his name, so is the whole convention, yet he appears in the present, among objects of everyday life. The body on the bare earth looks like a statue, but the left hand reaches gently towards the reed like the hand of a living man, his regard is turned reflectively to one side, his brows are drawn together. There is certainly nothing statuesque about the foot or the reed, but how remote from life the completely rounded folds of the drapery appear, compared with the stones on the ground! Perhaps the impression of this figure can best be explained by saying that it looks like the apparition of a god of antiquity in modern life. In this respect, Campagnola is a typical fifteenth-century Venetian, who studied antiquity from the archaeological point of view and related it to the present without ever quite bringing it to life, as Titian was to do only a little later on. It seems that we can even trace Campagnola's actual model, for his engraving obviously derives from the figure of the river or sea god (the interpretation is not definitely settled) on the triumphal arch at Benevento[52] (PLATE 55). Campagnola's Saturn shares with this god the sidelong glance and bent head, both of which are really only explicable within the whole composition of the arch. Even the tree stump is a visual memory of the somewhat indistinct urn; the attribute of the reed may probably be explained by the fact that in the relief the reeds growing behind the figure merge into the now unrecognisable symbol in the god's right hand, and, more important still, the Benevento god's billowing drapery together with the singular headdress makes it look even to-day as if his cloak were pulled over his head in the classical manner of the "caput velatum". This odd combination of seeming and real peculiarities of the melancholic and Saturnine nature—hand propped up, head apparently concealed by a cloak—might very well have given the archaeologically-minded Campagnola reason to interpret the figure on the Benevento arch as Saturn, or at least to use the figure as Saturn. He certainly considered

[52] The arch may have become known to him through an engraving (or a drawing) like the fifteenth-century engraving published by S. REINACH, "La plus ancienne image gravée de l'arc de Bénévent" in *Mélanges Bertaux*, Paris 1924, pp. 232–235, plate XIV); A. M. HIND, *Early Italian Engraving*, VOL. I, London 1938, p. 285.

Saturn as a divinity who, apart from his other attributes, stood in some special relation to water: this is shown by the symbol of a reed and by the seascape in the background. This conception, moreover, may be based on those texts which describe Saturn as "accidentaliter humidus", call him a voyager over many seas, and attribute to him the patronage of those who live by the sea, and for which the best authority is the famous north Italian astrologer, Guido Bonatti.[53] There was also the fact that since the Middle Ages men had become accustomed to imagine Saturn like this; in the Roman *Mirabilia*, one of the two ancient river gods which stand in front of the Senatorial Palace was taken for a statue of Saturn.[54] The special significance of the engraving whose landscape, as we have said, makes full use of motives in earlier Dürer engravings, lies not so much in its possible influence on Dürer's *Melencolia I*[55] (whose background landscape may well have been inspired by Campagnola) as in the fact that here for the first time, a new, humanist and idealised Saturn has been created—so much so, in fact, that Campagnola's immediate successors reverted to the more usual conception, whether like Girolamo da Santa Croce, forsaking antique motives but retaining the general plan and dressing Saturn as an old peasant (PLATE 56),[56] or like Lorenzo Costa transforming the antique Saturn, in the mournful attitude of a river god, into a Christian St Jerome deep in meditation.[57]

Campagnola's classically idealised form of Kronos, however, could be translated into realms even more remote from reality, in which the classically robed god was equipped with pinions; and thus, as already on Orphic and Mithraic tombstones at the end of classical times, he acquired the special nature of a god of time. Out of Kronos, who possessed the character of a god of time only incidentally, was reborn Chronos, whose main function was the fatal destruction of all earthly things, combined with the rescue of truth and the preservation of fame. In this last metamorphosis he became an almost essential requisite for the marble allegories on tombstones and for the didactic title-pieces

---

[53] See above, p. 189 (text).

[54] *Mirabilia Romae*, ed. G. Parthey, Berlin 1869, p. 24.

[55] See below, p. 288 sq. (text), p. 324, note 135.

[56] G. FIOCCO, "I pittori da Santacroce", in *L'Arte*, XIX (1916), p. 190.

[57] Formerly Berlin, Kaufmann Collection; reproduced in A. VENTURI, *Storia dell'arte italiana*, VOL. VII, 3, Milan 1914, p. 812, fig. 600.

of many works dealing with the ruined and yet remembered past (PLATE 59).[58] In outward appearance, too, portraits of this resurrected Saturn–Chronos often resemble the Chronos, Aion or Kairos of late antiquity[59]; but it is doubtful whether he actually derives from them. The figure of a winged Saturn seems rather to have been formed at a point where a spontaneous connexion could be established between the peasant-deity and the allegory of Time: that is to say, in the illustrations to Petrarch's *Trionfo del Tempo*[60] (PLATE 57). Petrarch makes Time appear in conjunction with the sun, but gives the illustrators no further indications. The latter, therefore, in the representations of this triumph, used Saturn, who is not mentioned in the text, as the personification of Time and endeavoured to make his significance clear by giving to Saturn the attribute of an hour-glass,[61] or, occasionally, of a zodiac. Above all, however, they idealised the traditional, pre-Renaissance form of the peasant god by giving him wings. In this way they equipped him as a true personification of time, completing his portrait by a new and, in medieval opinion, quite un-Saturnine trait taken over from a purely allegorical tradition in art—as seen, for instance, in an allegory of *Temps* of about 1400 (PLATE 58).[62] This process is confirmed by some fifteenth-century Italian illustrations to Petrarch, in which Saturn, personifying time, stands, like the figure in the French miniature, with arms hanging down symmetrically, and is equipped with four wings which are to represent the four seasons.[63] Once completed, this humanist reunion of Saturn and

---

[58] After the reprint made in Amsterdam, entitled *Eigentlyke Afbeeldinge van Hondert der Aldervermaerdste Statuen, of Antique-Beelden, Staande binnen Romen,* of a work by FRANÇOIS PERRIER which had appeared in Rome in 1638 with the remarkable title *Segmenta nobilium signorum et statuarum quae temporis dentem inuidium* [sic] *euasere.*

[59] For this, cf. A. GREIFENHAGEN, *Die Antike,* VOL. XI, Berlin 1935, pp. 67 sqq.

[60] After PRINCE D'ESSLING and E. MÜNTZ, *Pétrarque . . . ,* Paris 1902, plate facing p. 148.

[61] This later found its way into Renaissance and Baroque portrayals of Death, and became a symbol of impermanence and "memento mori" in general.

[62] Cf. E. PANOFSKY, *Hercules am Scheidewege* (Studien der Bibliothek Warburg, VOL. XVIII), Leipzig 1930, p. 4, plate 5.

[63] Reproduced in PRINCE D'ESSLING and E. MÜNTZ, *Pétrarque . . ,* Paris 1902, p. 167. Later the motif of child-devouring or child-menacing penetrated into the illustrations to Petrarch (cf. e.g. a tapestry from Madrid, described by PRINCE D'ESSLING and E. MÜNTZ, op. cit., p. 218, and an engraving by Jörg Pencz, reproduced in the same work, p. 262, as well as a woodcut to *Il Petrarca con l'Espositione d'Alessandro Vellutello,* Venice 1560, fol. 263ᵛ). Only rarely, however, use was made of the idea, suggested by the text, of identifying Time with the sun; cf. PRINCE D'ESSLING and E. MÜNTZ, op. cit., p. 219, or the woodcut to *Il Petrarcha con l'Espositione di M. G. Gesvaldo,* Venice 1581, fol. 407—in which, however, the winged god of time follows behind the sun's chariot.

Chronos led naturally to a reversion, a return to the ancient figures of Chronos, Kairos and Aion. It produced the familiar type of the naked god of Time, an idealised figure of an old man with wings, which, though commonplace enough in later periods, in fact owes its existence to a very complicated and varied series of events.[64]

[64] Sometimes even reviving the winged feet characteristic of the classical Kairos (cf. e.g. F. SAXL, "Veritas filia Temporis", in *Philosophy and History, Essays presented to E. Cassirer*, edd. R. Klibansky and H. J. Paton, Oxford 1936, p. 197, fig. 4). A. GREIFENHAGEN, *Die Antike*, VOL. XI, Berlin 1935, pp. 67 sqq., discusses other Renaissance imitations of the ancient Kairos and Chronos types, occasionally even evolved from the type of Cupid bound and condemned to labour with a pickaxe, as in figs. 13 and 14, which, incidentally, are derived from Cartari. As may be expected, this specifically middle- and late-Renaissance portrayal is based throughout on the two-winged type. The only exception is the figure illustrated in V. CARTARI, *Le Imagini de i dei degli antichi*, Padua 1603, p. 32, and Venice 1674, p. 19, which has four wings on the shoulders and two on the head—and which, as Cartari expressly states, was evolved from a description of the Phoenician Saturn in Eusebius (cf. above, text p. 196).

PART III

''Poetic Melancholy'' and ''Melancholia Generosa''

Chapter I

POETIC MELANCHOLY[1] IN POST-MEDIEVAL POETRY

I. MELANCHOLY AS A SUBJECTIVE MOOD IN LATE MEDIEVAL POETRY

There is a line of development in the history of the word "melancholy" in which it has become a synonym for "sadness without cause". It has come to mean a temporary state of mind, a feeling of depression independent of any pathological or physiological circumstances, a feeling which Burton[2] (while protesting against this extension of the word) calls a "transitory melancholy disposition" as against the "melancholy habit" or the "melancholy disease".

Thus one could say that someone was "melancholy to-day"—something unthinkable in the Middle Ages; moreover, the predicate "melancholy" could be transferred from the person to the object that gave rise to his mood, so that one could speak of melancholy spaces, melancholy light, melancholy notes or melancholy landscapes.[3] Naturally this transformation was accomplished not in medical or scientific writings but in the type of literature which tended essentially to observe and to represent man's sensibility as having value in itself—that is in lyric, in narrative poetry, and also in prose romances. The term "melancholy", ever more widely used in popular late medieval writings, was, specially in France, eagerly adopted by writers of belles-lettres in order to lend colour to mental tendencies and conditions. In doing this they gradually

---

[1] Thus the title of a sonnet by W. Hamilton Reid in *The Gentleman's Magazine*, June 1791, p. 567.

[2] Cf. Robert Burton, *Anatomy of Melancholy*, Partition I, Section I, Member i, sub-section 5: "Melancholy . . . is either in disposition, or habit. In disposition, is that transitory melancholy which goes and comes upon every small occasion of sorrow, need, sickness, trouble, fear, grief, passion or perturbation of the mind . . . . In which equivocal and improper sense we call him melancholy that is dull, sad, sour, lumpish, ill-disposed, solitary, any way moved or displeased. And from these melancholy dispositions no man living is free . . . . This melancholy of which we are to treat is a habit, . . . a chronic or continuate disease, a settled humour, . . . not errant, but fixed." For Burton cf. also Jonathan Wright, in *Medical Journal and Record*, cxxx (1929), pp. 291 sqq. (in several instalments).

[3] Cf. Shakespeare's enumeration in *Henry IV*, pt I, I, ii, 82 sqq.

altered and transferred the originally pathological meaning of this notion in such a way that it became descriptive of a more or less temporary "mood". Parallel with its proper scientific and medical usage, therefore, the word acquired another meaning which we may call a specifically "poetic" one. This use of the word had a history of its own, and, once fixed, was bound to affect everyday usage more strongly than the terms of esoteric science could do.

Not, of course, that the two original notions of melancholy—as a disease and as a temperament—disappeared entirely from literature and common usage. In love lyrics, for instance, "melancholy" was still constantly used as a synonym for madness,[4] and in portraits the description "melancholy" was used entirely in the sense of a permanent disposition. But, except in scientific literature, the traditional usage tended more and more towards the subjective and transitory meaning, until at length it was so overshadowed by the new "poetic" conception that this last became the normal meaning in modern thought and speech.[5]

Even in Boccaccio (especially in his *Ninfale Fiesolano*) we find expressions like

☞ pella maninconia e pel dolore
ch'i' sento, che m'offende dentro il core,

or

ove quel giorno dal padre aspettato
era stato con gran maninconia,

or

malinconoso e mal contento,

or

caendo la sua amante aspra e selvaggia
e che facea lui star malinconoso[6]

---

[4] Cf. the enamoured author's self-portrait in *Les échecs amoureux* (ERNST SIEPER, "Les échecs amoureux", in *Literarhistorische Forschungen*, IX (1898), p. 60):

"Ains me veist on sans demeure
Muer soubdainement coulour,
Muer de froidure en chalour . . .
De sens en parfaitte folie,
De Raison en melancolie . . . ."

Even Ficino reminds us in his commentary on the *Symposium* of the physicians' opinion (see above, text p. 86) that love is "una specie di umore malinconico e di pazzia."

[5] That naturally does not alter the fact that in poetic descriptions of the melancholy mood the typical traits of the "morbus melancholicus" constantly reappear—in fact, this is the rule wherever melancholy appears as a personification, as we shall see later. A particularly instructive example is HANS SACHS's *Gespräch der Philosophia mit einem melancholischen, betrübten Jüngling* (Bibliothek des literarischen Vereins Stuttgart, VOL. CV, 1870), pp. 141 sqq., in which even the medical term "Überschwank nehmen" occurs.

[6] BOCCACCIO, *Ninfale Fiesolano*, ed. B. Wiese, in Sammlung romanischer Elementar- und Handbücher, series V, No. 3, Heidelberg 1913. The examples quoted are from stanza 331, Wiese (ed.) op. cit., p. 75; stanza 71, ibid. p. 18; stanza 70, ibid. p. 17; stanza 55, ibid. p. 14. Also (*inter alia*) stanza 244, ibid. p. 57, and stanza 276, ibid. p. 63.

—all expressions in which melancholy is conceived neither as a disease nor as an habitual disposition, but rather as a purely mental, temporary mood. Only a little later, French literature too began to use the "subjective" notion of melancholy in the same way, and here the noun "mélancolie" signified both the trouble someone had and the trouble he caused others, while the verb "mérencolier" became a synonym for "attrister", and the adjective "mélancolique" or, more commonly, "mélancolieux", could already be transferred from the person experiencing this feeling to the circumstance that caused it. "Quant on s'endort en aucun desplaisir ou mérencolie",[7] for instance, appears in a story by Louis XI, and love literature carried this meaning so far as to speak of "petites mérencolies", in the sense of "lovers' quarrels".[8] "Se mélancolier" meant "to become sad" or "to think sad thoughts",[9] and the adjective "mélancolieux" could describe either the mood of someone sad or out of humour ("on l'a trouvé mélancolieux et iré", or "Alexandre mélancolieusement pensant à ses pertes"[10]) or the look of a mad dog ("le chien enragé regarde de travers et plus mélancholiquement que de coustume"[11]) as well as the impression of night[12] or the mood caused by any "sad" object. "Je suis entrée en grant mérencolie", sings one of Christine de Pisan's women in love, when she thinks that her cavalier has changed his allegiance[13]; and the visionary dream, a very common device in medieval narrative poetry—generally introduced by the narrator finding himself in rural solitude—is

---

[7] Quoted from F. Godefroy, *Dictionnaire de l'ancienne langue française*, vol. v, 8, Paris 1888, pp. 221 sqq.

[8] "Et sachez, qu'elle fait a son amy cent chouses, et monstre des secretz d'amours et fait plusieurs petites merencolies que elle n'ouseroit faire ne montrer a son mary . . . et de tant qu'il l'aura plus chiere, de tant luy fera elle plus de melencolies pour lui donner soussy" (quoted from Godefroy, op. cit.; as early as 1389 we meet with an expression such as "apres plusieurs courroux, desplaisances et mirencoulies"). In a sentence like "vix possumus respirare ex multis quaerimoniis et melancoliis, quibus non cessamus vexari" (according to du Cange, *Glossarium mediae et infimae latinitatis*, vol. v, Niort 1885, p. 329) the word "melancholiae" is almost synonymous with "complaint" or "lament".

[9] "Lorsque le roy vyt que il n'en vendroit point aisieement a son intention, il se melenconia et se party de euls" (taken from Godefroy, op. cit.; ibid.: "et puis il se prenoit a penser sur la table en se merencoliant"). In transitive form: "dont plusieurs fois l'avoient melancoliet et courouciet." It is interesting that German Baroque should have re-introduced the verb "melancholieren" (F. von Spee, *Trutznachtigall*, ed. G. Balke, Leipzig 1879, p. 70).

[10] From Godefroy, op. cit.

[11] From Godefroy, op. cit.

[12] From Godefroy, op. cit.

[13] Christine de Pisan, *Cent Ballades d'Amant et de Dame*, No. 88; (*Oeuvres poétiques*, vol. iii, ed. M. Roy, Société des anciens textes français, Paris 1896, p. 295).

now conjured up not by the writer's fatigue or sorrow, but by his "melancholy". Fifteenth-century poets fly to nature's bosom

> pour oblier merencolie
> et pour faire plus chiere lie.[14]

Thus in all modern European literature the expression "melancholy" (when not in a scientific context) lost the meaning of a quality and acquired instead the meaning of a "mood" which could forthwith be transferred to inanimate objects—sometimes in a simple and serious sense, as when a Florentine patrician's widow speaks of the melancholy of her loneliness,[15] or when a place is described as "lonely and melancholy"[16]; sometimes in a sentimental and emotional sense, as when Sannazzaro makes his shepherds roam with melancholy brow and melancholy speech[17]; sometimes gaily and frivolously, as when Bojardo makes a disappointed lady who has passed an eventless night with her cavalier remain all day "malinconiosa e tacita"[18]; sometimes coarsely and cynically, as when an invalid canon writes to his friend, "But if anyone thinks I am at death's door, let God try me with a young girl, and see how soon with her help I shall drive all melancholy away."[19]

2. "DAME MÉRENCOLYE"

Melancholy's change of meaning was connected with a process generally noticeable in the late Middle Ages when esoteric and

---

[14] ALAIN CHARTIER, *Livre des Quatre Dames*, in *Oeuvres*, ed. A. du Chesne, Paris 1617, p. 594; cf. F. LAMEY, *Romanische Handschriften* (*Die Handschriften der Grossherzoglichen Badischen Landesbibliothek in Karlsruhe*, Beilage II, 1894, pp. 26 sqq.). Very similar, in DIRK POTTER'S *Der Minnen loop*:

> "By wilen so ginghe ic spasieren
> Op eenre lopender rivieren,
> Om te verdriven malancolye,
> Des viel ic in een fantasie . . . ."

(quoted in W. WAETZOLDT, *Das Klassische Land*, Leipzig 1927, p. 8; however, though it has been shown that the poet went to Rome in 1411, there is no reason to assume an inspiration on the bank of the Tiber as the source of this quite conventional introduction to a "dream vision").

[15] ALESSANDRA MACINGHI-STROZZI, *Lettere ai figlioli*, ed. S. Papini, Lanciano 1914, p. 42.

[16] Quoted below, p. 386, note 34.

[17] J. SANNAZARO, *Arcadia*, ed. M. Scherillo, Turin 1888, e.g. p. 15, line 56; p. 131, line 5; p. 154, lines 2 sqq.

[18] M. M. BOJARDO, *Orlando Innamorato*, I, 24, 16.

[19] "Lorenz Beheim an Willibald Pirckheimer", ed. E. Reicke, in *Forschungen zur Geschichte Bayerns*, XVI (1906), p. 34; the above passages are also quoted by O. HAGEN, in *Kunstchronik*, VOL. XXVIII, Leipzig 1917, p. 454.

scientific notions sank down to the level of popular thought and speech. Similar tendencies transformed the seven deadly sins into "follies" or mere characteristics,[20] made townsfolk sentimentally aware of the peasant's toil and the trackless wilds of nature, and led to the attempt at catching the reality of the visible world in the mirage of perspective. Furthermore, melancholy, by acquiring the psychological content of notions originally applying only to mental states, inherited also their pictorial form. In other words, melancholy, understood in this new sense, appears in fifteenth-century poetry both as an expression of speech and as an active and speaking person who was even capable of being portrayed.

Medieval didactic poetry, elaborating the methods inherited from late Roman authors like Prudentius or Martianus Capella, had personified nearly all objects of human thought and feeling. Among these personifications were naturally to be found those embodying mental pain—figures such as "Souci", "Deffiance", "Désespoir", or, above all, "Tristesse". And as common usage tended more and more to describe the content of these notions as "melancholy",[21] it is not surprising that this expression too was personified. In the *Espérance ou Consolation des Trois Vertus* written in 1428 by Maistre Alain Chartier, Royal Notary and Secretary to Charles VI,[22] we find a "Dame Mérencolye" taking over many of the functions, as well as much of the outward appearance, of the "Tristesse" described nearly two hundred years earlier in the *Roman de la Rose*.[23] Like Guillaume de Lorris's "Tristesse", Alain Chartier's "Dame Mérencolye" is of terrifying aspect, pale, lean, wrapped in poor or ragged garments; the same can be said of the "Melencolie" in the romance *Le Cuer d' amours espris*, written by King René of Anjou (who died in 1480), for

[20] See below, pp. 297 sqq. (text).

[21] How greatly the notions of "acedia", "tristitia" and "melancholia" mingled and interpenetrated during the later Middle Ages can be seen, for instance, in the Italian tract *Fiore di Virtù*, in which "maninconia" is introduced as a sub-species of "tristitia" (Rome edn., 1740, p. 28); while on the other hand, in CECCO D'ASCOLI's *Acerba*, "Accedia" appears with all the characteristics of the "Tristesse" of the *Roman de la Rose*. (F. Rougemont kindly informed us that in Florence, Biblioteca Laurenziana Cod. plut. XL, 52, fol. 31ʳ, "Accedia" appears as a woman with torn raiment and flecks of blood on her breast.)

[22] Cf. P. CHAMPION, *Histoire poétique du XVᵉ siècle*, Paris 1923, VOL. I, p. 135, with a list of the more important MSS.

[23] GUILLAUME DE LORRIS and JEAN DE MEUNG, *Le Roman de la Rose*, ed. E. Langlois, VOL. II, Paris 1920, lines 293 sqq.

here she appears as "une grant vielle eschevelee, maigre, et ridee".[24]

Admittedly this "Dame Mérencolye" is not a mere copy of "Tristesse", but has been radically modified. "Tristesse" possessed certain characteristic qualities which "Dame Mérencolye" was denied, and in the same way the latter possessed traits which had been lacking in the former. For instance, the "Tristesse" in the *Roman de la Rose*—a figure by no means dulled and apathetic, but wild and despairing—bears a tear-stained and raddled visage, while King René's "morne et pensive" Melancholy warms herself by a fire which "was so wretched that a cat could barely have burnt its tail at it", and is brooding so deeply that she can scarcely tear herself away from her thoughts. Alain Chartier's "Dame Mérencolye" is distinguished by her "leaden and earthy complexion", "halting speech", "drooping lip" and "downward regard". Needless to say, in both cases the traits which "Melancolie" does not share with "Tristesse" have been taken over from humoral pathology. Even the "wretched fire", which is a familiar touch of calendar illustrations, is nothing but an elaboration of the common attribute of "frigiditas". Common usage had reduced the idea of melancholy to that of a mere mood. But from the moment when this subjective mood became personified, we may say that melancholy regained all its essential characteristics as a visible image of temperament and disease, standing out from mere "Tristesse" (which King René significantly allows next to her as "parente bien prochaine") as something more menacing and at the same time more active. And this corresponds with the dramatic and psychological function henceforth attributed to the personified Melancholy in narrative contexts.

The general character of King René's work (which seeks rather to give life to a given set of allegories than to clothe a personal experience in allegory) is descriptive and unemotional. When

---

[24] Cf. O. SMITAL and E. WINKLER, *Herzog René von Anjou, Livre du Cuer d'amours espris*, Vienna 1926, VOL. II, pp. 23 sqq. and 49 sqq. In fifteenth-century French lyrics, too, it was customary to treat "Melancholie" almost as a living personage:

> "Fermez luy l'uis au visaige,
> Mon cueur, a Merancolye,
> Gardez qu'elle n'entre mye,
> Pour gaster nostre mesnaige . . . ."—

CHARLES D'ORLÉANS, *Poésies*, ed. P. Champion, vol. II, Paris 1927, p. 458. Cf. also a poem by the same author with the refrain

> "Alez-vous-ent, allez, alés,
> Soussy, Soing et Merencolie"—

Champion (ed.) op. cit., p. 320. We owe both these references to Dr A. Heimann.

the hero, "Le Cuer", accompanied by his squire "Désir", strays into Melancholy's wretched hut and asks for food and drink, "Melencolie" contents herself with giving him a beaker of water from the "Fleuve de Larme" and a crust of bread of "Dure Paine" grain, and with pressing the same nourishment on him on a later occasion; whereupon "Le Cuer" falls into "un pensement si tres grief" that he would almost have died of sorrow had not the recollection of his mistress "Espérance" fortified him a little. Melancholy's actions and influence are therefore not particularly dramatic or terrifying, although, within the limitations of a romance where "Dame Tristesse" saddens the hero mainly by the poor quality of her wine, the peculiar nature of a strictly melancholy depression is none the less visible.

Alain Chartier's unfinished poem, however, shows such intensity of emotional experience, and such astounding capacity for finding for this experience dramatic symbols and forms of speech, that here, in complete contrast to King René's work, the poet's verbal images far excel the illustrator's visual ones in power. On account of their unemotional character, the static descriptions of René's romance lent themselves easily to the contemporary style of illustration, and the miniatures of the famous Vienna manuscript with their enchanting lyrical atmosphere were their natural translation into visual terms (PLATE 60).[25] Alain Chartier, on the contrary, described his experience of melancholy with a dramatic force far surpassing the possibilities not only of contemporary or near-contemporary miniaturists (PLATE 64)[26] and wood engravers (PLATE 61),[27] but even of the increased powers of expression

---

[25] O. SMITAL and E. WINKLER, *Herzog René von Anjou, Livre du Cuer d'amours espris*, Vienna 1926, VOL. III, plate VII.

[26] Paris, Bibl. Nat., MS fr. 126, fol. 218, about 1435 (also reproduced in P. CHAMPION, *Histoire poétique du XVe siècle*, Paris 1923, VOL. I, plate VII). The third scene, where the author, overcome by melancholy, lying on his sickbed, has to suffer the invective of "trois femmes espouvantables", "Deffiance", "Indignation", and "Désespérance", as well as receive the consoling words of the ladies "Nature", "Foy", and "Espérance", is closely connected with typical portraits of "Accidia" (see below, text pp. 300 sqq.). Very similar, in that the seat of "Accidia" is here, too, surrounded by personifications of mental faculties, three good and three evil—the "Desperatio" party naturally standing on the left of the main figure, the "Fortitudo" party on the right—is a tapestry in the collection of the Conde de Valencia de Don Juan (*Boletín de la Sociedad Española de Escursiones*, XI (1903), p. 49; our PLATE 66).

[27] Title-page of the printed edition *Fais Maistre Alain Chartier*, Paris 1489, the text of which, unfortunately disfigured by many misprints, we have used for our translation. Even in the title-page woodcut a misunderstanding has crept in, for the word "Entendement" should naturally occur on the blank banner of the youth holding back the bed-curtains, while the reclining man is of course the author. Incidentally it is interesting to find that the

attained in the sixteenth century (PLATE 65).[28] This was because his account is largely a psychiatric self-diagnosis translated into terms of poetry, so that it echoes the often terrifying descriptions of illness given in medical literature. The poet laments the misfortunes of his country. The best are dead, the fields laid waste, the cities ruined, and learning is destroyed; what is there left to live for? The first chapter of this book which was "born of sorrow" ("dont par douleur ay commencé ce livre") begins with the words:

By this sad and painful thought which is ever present in my heart and accompanies me, be it in rising or in going to my bed, making my nights long and my life wearisome, I have so long exerted and tormented my poor brain, so oppressed and encircled it by repugnant images, that I cannot employ it on any matter which might bring me joy or consolation. . . . And in this plight I saw an old woman draw near to me, quite disordered in her clothing and yet indifferent to it, lean, dry, and withered, of a pale, leaden, earthy complexion, with lowered glance, halting speech, and drooping lip. Her head was covered with a soiled and dusty kerchief, her body muffled in a ceremonial cloak. As she drew near, suddenly, in silence, she seized me in her arms and covered me from head to foot with her mantle of misfortune, and she held me so fast in her arms that I felt my heart in my breast crushed as in a vice; and with her hands she blinded my eyes and blocked my ears so that I could neither see nor hear. And so she carried me, unconscious and in a swoon, to the house of Sickness and delivered me into the jaws of Terror and Disease. Even my reason, that young and able attendant[29] who had followed me, sometimes from afar off, sometimes from close at hand, according as God permitted me his company, even him did she intoxicate with such strange and noxious drink, brewed in frenzy and madness, that this good and clever youth, who for this purpose had

---

woodcut is closely connected with a type of representation dating from the beginning of the fifteenth century showing Boethius in bed mourning and being consoled by "Philosophia"—even the curious seat on the left foreground is retained—(PLATE 63, from BOETHIUS, *De consolatione Philosophiae*, New York, Pierpont Morgan Library, MS 332, fol. 4ʳ). The style of this MS probably dating from 1415–1420, resembles that of the workshop of the so-called Master of Boucicaut, and in this circle the same type of picture was used for portraits of rulers showing a prince giving audience from his bed (cf. H. MARTIN, *La miniature française du 13ᵉ au 15ᵉ siècle*, Paris 1923, plate 88, and C. COUDERC, *Album de portraits* . . . , Paris 1927, plates LVIII, 1 and LIX, 2). It is possible that in the idea of such a "levée" as well as of the "lit de justice" (certainly envisaged originally as a real bed) revived by Charles V, the notion of a "lectulum Salomonis" may have played a part, for in the later Middle Ages it was referred to as a "bed of wisdom" (cf. Rome, Cod. Casanat. 1404, fol. 9ᵛ, and F. SAXL, in *Festschrift für Julius Schlosser*, Zürich 1927, p. 118).

[28] New York, Pierpont Morgan Library, MS 438, fols. 1 and 4. One can see that the emotional Renaissance style of this pen drawing, probably dating from 1525–30, seems more appropriate to poetic vision than does the fifteenth-century miniature style. (We have to thank Miss Belle da Costa Green for this photograph.)

[29] "Bachelier".

accompanied me as far as my bed, now stood beside me tranced and as if paralysed by lethargy. And I learned later that this old woman was called Melancholy, who confuses the thought, dries up the body, poisons the humours, weakens the perceptions and leads men to sickness and death. Through her, according to Aristotle, the most sublime minds and understandings of profound and exceptional men were and are often confused and darkened, when they have indulged in thoughts too deep and multifarious.... So, straitly bound in body and soul, I was thrown upon the most wretched couch, where I then lay for several days with stale mouth and without appetite. And after great weakness, long fasting, bitter pain and blankness in my brain, which Dame Melancholy oppressed with her hard hands, I felt the organ located in the middle of the head, in the region of the imagination (called "phantasy" by some) open up and come into flux and movement....[30]

Despite its affinities with the conventional schema of scholastic poetry, this description rises at times almost to a Dantesque level. No more expressive symbol of the darkening of the spirit can be imagined than the mantle of misfortune within whose stifling darkness the unconscious man is "delivered into the jaws of Terror and Disease". This visionary parable of an overwhelming attack of grief has completely absorbed the notion of "Tristesse" expressed in the older poems; but it is also saturated with the power of the traditional psychiatric descriptions of melancholy and therefore preserves the whole of their substance.

Chartier's work comprises, therefore, a compact synthesis of all the traditional or diffused motifs of melancholy that were available to him. The emphatic quotation from Aristotle is particularly remarkable, although here, in accordance with the medical view, the melancholy of "parfons et excellans hommes" is conceived not as a condition of their talent but, on the contrary, as a consequence of their thoughts "too deep and multifarious".

This principle of synthesis continued to be active in contemporary representations of melancholy, by means of literary personification. Wherever "Dame Mérencolye" appears as a person who speaks or is spoken to, she represents, as in the old French romances, the contemporary modification of a notion

[30] There now appear "on the left, dark side of the bed" the three awful figures "Deffiance", "Indignation" and "Désespérance", the last advising the unfortunate man to commit suicide, and quoting the examples of Cato, Mithridates, Hannibal, Jugurtha, Nero, Lucretia and Dido. Alarmed by this thought, "Nature" wakens "Reason" ("Entendement") from his sleep. He opens the "Door of Memory", through which two beautiful women, "Foy" and "Espérance", emerge—the latter shown with an anchor of hope and with a casket of cypress wood, from which, when it is opened, there arises an exquisite perfume of consoling prophecies; and, after a dialogue between "Foy" and "Entendement", everything seems to be turning out well when the poem stops.

formed and transmitted by medical and scientific tradition, and it is to this that she owes her resilient and vivid existence. The beautiful monologue by the German baroque poet, Andreas Tscherning, *Melancholy speaks herself*, is an example of such a synthesis, in which, as in Maistre Alain Chartier, the whole content of scientific tradition—from common fear to the wild hallucinations of a man who thinks he is a glass vessel or fears the heavens will fall; from misanthropy, longing for death, and the ability to write poetry while mad, to the "facies nigra" and the downward gaze—is combined in one coherent picture, except that now a new motif could be added, unfamiliar to a French poet of the early fifteenth century: the humanist idea of divine frenzy or, to use Tscherning's words, "des himmelischen Geistes":

☞ wann der sich in mir reget,
Entzünd ich als ein Gott die Herzen schleunig an,
Da gehn sie ausser sich und suchen eine Bahn,
Die mehr als weltlich ist. . . .[31]

What applies to personifications of melancholy in poetry proper applies no less to those in that peculiar branch of literature which described itself as "iconology", whose aim it was systematically to collect human "imagini di virtù, vitii, affetti, passioni humane" and so on, and to elaborate and classify them so that they could be used by "speakers, preachers, poets, painters, and draughtsmen", for poetic or illustrative purposes. The most famous and influential iconology, that of Cesare Ripa, contains a "Malinconia" which can easily, even without demonstrable proof, be recognised as a "Dame Mérencolye" of the same type as Alain Chartier's or King René's. Naturally it is suitably modified, and is explained down to the last detail:

Donna vecchia, mesta, & dogliosa, di brutti panni vestita, senza alcun' ornamento, starà a sedere sopra un sasso, con gomiti posati sopra i ginocchi, & ambe le mani sotto il mento, & vi sarà a canto un' albero senza fronde, & fra i sassi.[32]

This graphic description, stressing in its interpretation the emotional, moral and intellectual aspects rather than the

---

[31] A. Tscherning, *Vortrab des Sommers deutscher Getichte*, Rostock 1655; printed in W. Unus, *Die Deutsche Lyrik des Barock*, Berlin 1922, p. 101. Cf. the book already mentioned by W. Benjamin, *Ursprung des deutschen Trauerspiels*, Berlin 1928, p. 143, which is of particular interest for this section. For the revival of the notion of divine frenzy, see below, pp. 249 sqq., 355 sqq. (text).

[32] Not illustrated in the editions, Rome 1593 and 1603. For Ripa, cf. E. Mâle, *L'art religieux après le concile de Trente*, Paris 1932, pp. 383 sqq., and E. Mandowsky, "Ricerche intorno all' Iconologia di Cesare Ripa," *La Bibliofilia*, XLI, Florence 1939.

physiological or pathological ones, made a considerable impression on the poets and painters of the seventeenth century, and provided an occasion for a fruitful exchange of ideas between the sister arts. The illustration shows Melancholy as a single figure, and corresponds exactly to the text (below, Fig. 5, p. 405). But for a real "picture", baroque taste demanded some tension either of action or speech, so that a painter such as Abraham Janssens found it best to hark back to the familiar idea of a "syncrisis", and to contrast "Malinconia" with a personification of "Joy".[33] He had only to look up "Allegrezza" in Ripa's *Iconologia* to find the appearance of this protagonist described as exactly as he would wish; and in fact the plump, garlanded maiden with the golden beaker and jug of wine, who in 1623 appears on Janssens's picture (PLATE 69) representing "Allegrezza", answers to Ripa's description even more exactly than Janssens's limping, poorly-dressed old woman with her "leafless tree" does to the description of "Malinconia". For in the latter figure Janssens has departed from Ripa at the one point in which Ripa's description differs from the traditional pictorial type. Here Melancholy rests her head on one hand only, instead of on both, as she does in the text. This is a good example of the obstinate survival of pictorial tradition, for here it persists even in direct contradiction to the very text that the picture purports to illustrate.

The year 1665 provides a poetic counterpart to Janssens's pictorial syncrisis—Filidor's *Debate between Melancholy and Mirth.*[34] Here too, in the introductory description of the two debating personages, we find that their outward appearance is copied as literally from Ripa as it was in Janssens's painting. "One (Melancholy) is an old woman/dressed in filthy rags/with covered

---

[33] This antithesis not only corresponds to general usage (cf. Michelangelo's poem mentioned below, text p. 232), but Ripa himself alludes to it when he contrasts the "giovani allegri" with the "vecchi malinconici" in designing his portrait of "Malinconia". In an illustrated MS of about 1100 (Paris, Bibl. Nat., MS lat. 2077, cf. A. KATZENELLENBOGEN, *Allegories of the Virtues and Vices in Medieval Art*, Studies of The Warburg Institute, VOL. X, London 1939, pp. 11 sqq.), the personifications of the corresponding faculties still appear under the names "Gaudium" and "Tristitia"; in the *Fiore di Virtù*, Rome edn. 1740, we read "Tristizia [which here includes "maninconia," see above, text p. 221 note 21] si é contrario vizio d'Allegrezza." The same pair of opposites appears in the portrayals of "Democritus and Heraclitus", first occurring about 1500, but not really popular till the time of the Baroque (cf. W. WEISBACH, in *Jahrbuch der preussischen Kunstsammlungen*, XLIX (1928), pp. 141 sqq., and H. KAUFFMANN, *Oud Holland*, VOL. XLVIII, Amsterdam 1931, p. 234).

[34] Cf. W. BENJAMIN, *Ursprung des deutschen Trauerspiels*, Berlin 1928, pp. 150 sqq. (though without reference to any connexion with Ripa and Milton).

head/who sits on a stone/under a leafless tree/her head bowed on her knees." The dialogue proper, however, presupposes acquaintance with a far greater work written some thirty years earlier, Milton's poems *L'Allegro* and *Il Penseroso.*

But here we arrive at a subject of such size and intricacy, viz. Melancholy in English literature, that a full account of it would far exceed the scope of this book. A discussion of the School of Night, for instance, would not only have been a vast task in itself but would also have involved us in a history of its antecedents. We are therefore limiting ourselves to a few strokes linking the English development with the tradition traced elsewhere in this book.

3. MELANCHOLY AS HEIGHTENED SELF-AWARENESS

In Milton's poems which, as the titles indicate, show the author's complete familiarity with the Italian tradition, and which, on the other hand, had a far-reaching influence on later writers,[35] "Mirth" and "Melancholy" are apostrophised by the two speakers, the "Joyful" and the "Thoughtful", with such intensity of invective and praise that—although the temperaments are not themselves introduced as speaking characters—their individualities are realised with the utmost vividness.[36]

---

[35] In fact they were the starting point of a literary genus. Cf. the excellent monograph by E. M. Sickels (quoted above, p. 217) and the bibliography given there. The most important books on the subject are: R. D. Havens, *The Influence of Milton in English Poetry*, 1922; A. L. Reed, *The Background of Gray's Elegy*, 1924. In England Milton's poetical companion portraits were also represented in fine art (see Romney, "Mirth and Melancholy", coll. Lady Leconfield, Petworth House, Sussex). In Germany where the contrast was, characteristically, seen more from the point of view of humoral theory, the disputation between "Melancholicus" and "Sanguineus" was even set to music, by Karl Philipp Emmanuel Bach, in a trio whose last movement ended with a reconciliation of the two opponents (cf. H. Meersmann, *Bachjahrbuch* XIV, 1917, pp. 37 sqq.).

[36] For the sake of comparison we quote the first lines of Filidor's disputation side by side with those of Milton's *L'Allegro* (*The Poetical Works*, O.U.P., London 1938):

Milton

"Hence, loathed Melancholy,
Of Cerberus and blackest Midnight born,
In Stygian cave forlorn,
'Mongst horrid shapes, and shrieks, and
sights unholy,
Find out som uncouth cell,
Where brooding Darkness spreads his
jealous wings
And the night-raven sings;
There under ebon shades, and low-brow'd
rocks,
As ragged as thy locks,
In dark Cimmerian desert ever dwell."

Filidor

"Jetzt kenn ich dich/du Feindin
meiner Freuden/Melankoley/
erzeugt im Tartarschlund/
vom dreygeköpfften Hund./
O, sollt ich dich in meiner
Gegend leiden?/Nein, wahrlich, nein!
der kalte Stein/der blätterlose Strauch
muss ausgerottet seyn//und du,
Unholdin, auch".

In spite of the wealth of new and magnificent connotations which this poetry imparts to the descriptions (e.g. when Melancholy is called daughter of Saturn and Vesta, or when she is compared to the *starr'd Ethiope Queen*, Cassiopeia), there are a hundred signs which connect his allegory with the tradition. As in Alain Chartier, Melancholy is accompanied by personifications of secondary rank and she herself recognizably shows features familiar to us from scientific and medical literature: "facies nigra" (*Ore laid with black staid Wisdoms hue*), rigidity (*Forget thy self to Marble . . .*), the leaden eye fixing the ground (*With a sad Leaden downward cast*), the love of lonely nocturnal studies (*Or let my lamp at midnight hour,/Be seen in some high lonely Towr*), the longing for a hermit's life (*And may at last my weary age/Find out the peacefull hermitage, The Hairy Gown and Mossy Cell*). However, all this is filled with new meaning. The name "Penseroso"[37] (not "Melancolico" or Afflitto") by which her advocate is introduced indicates the positive and, as it were, spiritual value ascribed to Melancholy and—according to the old rule governing poetic disputations that "he who has the last word wins"—Melancholy is shown to be superior to the jovial enjoyment of life. While the "Dame Mérencolye" of the French romances, like Ripa's "Malinconia", had been a sort of nightmare, inspiring the reader with even greater fear and repulsion, if that were possible, than her ancestress "Dame Tristesse," Milton's Melancholy is called "divinest", and celebrated as a "goddess sage and holy" and as a "Pensive Nun, devout and pure". While the former appeared in poor and disordered clothing, or even in rags, the latter is clad

All in a robe of darkest grain,
Flowing with majestick train.

While formerly her court was formed of the "grim women Deffiance, Indignation and Désesperance", she is now surrounded by "Peace", "Quiet", "Leisure" and "Silence", and is guided by the "Cherub Contemplation".[38] We shall deal in the next chapter with the

In showing that Milton's work belongs to a separate poetic and iconological tradition we can discard Lord Conway's hypothesis that it had been inspired by Dürer's "Melencolia I" (Festschrift der internationalen Dürerforschung, *Cicerone* 1928, pp. 29 sqq.). If a connection with the visual arts has to be assumed, the influence of a picture imitating Ripa, such as that by A. Janssens, PLATE 69, would be much more likely.

[37] In choosing this title, Milton may also have had in mind Michelangelo's statue of Lorenzo de' Medici, which from the time of Vasari had been known under this name.

[38] It is all the more significant that, in some of the poems on Melancholy from the second quarter of the eighteenth century, in which the aim is again to produce an uncanny and gloomy atmosphere, these pleasant personages are ousted by figures like "Despair" and "Dejection"; cf. SICKELS, op. cit., pp. 43 sq.

consequences of this revaluation. It can also be observed to an astonishing degree in the reinterpretation of Melancholy's symptoms proper. Her "facies nigra" is only an illusion of our weak senses, which cannot stand the brilliance of her true aspect:

> Whose saintly visage is too bright
> To hit the sense of human sight;
> And therfore to our weaker view,
> Ore laid with black staid Wisdoms hue.[39]

Her "Leaden downward cast" is only the sign of complete absorption—nothing but the reverse side of a condition of ecstatic, visionary trance.

> And looks commercing with the skies,
> Thy rapt soul sitting in thine eyes.[40]

The Melancholic in his lonely tower may

> . . . oft out-watch the Bear,
> With thrice great Hermes, or unsphear
> The spirit of Plato . . .
> And of those Daemons that are found
> In fire, air, flood, or under ground . . .

But as well as this, there are echoes of another world, a world of neither prophetic ecstasy nor brooding meditation, but of heightened sensibility where soft notes, sweet perfumes, dreams and landscapes mingle with darkness, solitude and even grief itself, and by this bitter-sweet contradiction serve to heighten self-awareness. The melancholic speaks of the pleasure of the sight of the moon,

> Like one that had bin led astray
> Through the Heav'ns wide pathles way.

or:

> I hear the far-off Curfeu sound,
> Over som wide-water'd shoar,
> Swinging slow with sullen roar;
> Or if the Ayr will not permit,
> Som still removèd place will fit,
> Where glowing embers through the room
> Teach light to counterfeit a gloom,
> Far from all resort of mirth,
> Save the Cricket on the hearth,
> Or the Belmans drousie charm . . .

---

[39] SICKELS, op. cit., p. 42, is obviously mistaken in interpreting these lines in the sense that Milton had described his "Melancholy" "as veiled in black to hide her too awful countenance".

[40] Cf. SICKELS, op. cit., pp. 44 sq., for parallels showing that Milton's formula became conventional. Later poets, however, do not usually combine "downward cast" and "Heav'n-ward eye", but choose the one or the other.

Then there is Old Age, already mentioned, in "Hairy Gown and Mossy Cell", and, above all, the nightingale

> In her sweetest, saddest plight,
> Smoothing the rugged brow of night.

These things are "most musical, most melancholy".

What emerges here is the specifically "poetic" melancholy mood of the modern; a double-edged feeling constantly providing its own nourishment, in which the soul enjoys its own loneliness, but by this very pleasure becomes again more conscious of its solitude, "the joy in grief", "the mournful joy", or "the sad luxury of woe", to use the words of Milton's successors. This modern melancholy mood is essentially an enhanced self-awareness, since the ego is the pivot round which the sphere of joy and grief revolves; and it has also an intimate relationship with music, which is now made subservient to subjective emotions. "I can suck melancholy from a song as a weasel sucks eggs", says Jaques.[41] For music, which used to be a specific against the melancholic disease, was now felt to soothe and at the same time nourish this ambiguous bitter-sweet mood.

Naturally, the fusion of the characters "Melancholy" and "Tristesse" during the fifteenth century brought about not only a modification of the notion of Melancholy, in the sense of giving it a subjective vagueness, but also, *vice versa*, of the notion of grief, giving it the connotations of brooding thoughtfulness and quasi-pathological refinements. The outcome of this interpenetration could only be a singularly complex, affective condition of the soul, in which the subjective and transitory emotion of mere "grief" was combined with brooding withdrawal from the world and with the gloom, verging on sickness, of melancholy in the emphatic sense. During the same period the verbs "attrister" and "s'attrister" tended to be replaced by "mérencolier" and "se mérencolier"; and their derivatives, "mérencoliser" and "mélancomoyer", acquired the sense of "reflecting", or "falling into a brown study".[42] Moreover, all the ideas originally connected with Melancholy and Saturn—unhappy love, and sickness and death—were added to this mixture, so it is not surprising that the new sentiment of Grief, born of a synthesis of "Tristesse" and "Mélancholie", was destined to become a special kind of emotion,

---

[41] *As You Like It*, Act II, sc. 5. The "katharsis" of pain through music also occurs, of course, in earlier writers, cf. e.g. Chaucer's unhappy lover (*Canterbury Tales*, The Knightes Tale, A 1367).

[42] See DU CANGE, loc. cit., p. 330.

tragic through a heightened awareness of the Self (for this awareness is but a correlation to the awareness of Death). This new melancholy could either be didactically anatomized or be poured out in lyrical poetry or in music; it could rise to sublime renunciation of the world, or be dissipated in mere sentimentality.

An early fifteenth-century author had already revealed the link between the notions Death, Melancholy and Self-Awareness in a curious manner. "A la mesure que la cognoissance vient", says Jacques Legrand in his "Observations on Death and Judgement Day", "le soucy croist, et l'omme se mérancolie plus et plus, selon ce qu'il a de sa condicion plus vraie et parfaite cognoissance".[43] Some hundred years later this consciousness became so much a part of self-awareness that there was scarcely a man of distinction who was not either genuinely melancholic or at least considered as such by himself and others. Even Raphael, whom we like to imagine as, above all, a serenely happy man, was described by a contemporary as "inclining to Melancholy, like all men of such exceptional gifts"[44]; while with Michelangelo this feeling is deepened and strengthened to a kind of self-conscious enjoyment, though indeed a bitter one: "La mia allegrezz' è la malinconia."[45]

The point had not yet been reached, however, where anyone could actually revel in the sweet self-sufficiency of the melancholy mood, in the style of Milton's poem, or even say, like Lessing's Knight Templar, half sad and half jesting, "What if I liked to feel thus melancholy?"[46] Under the appalling pressure of the religious conflicts that filled the second half of the sixteenth century, the lines of melancholy were not only graven deep in the

---

[43] Quoted after P. CHAMPION, *Histoire poétique du XVe siècle*, 1923, I, p. 220.

[44] Report of the Ferrarese chargé d'affaires Pauluzzi, of 17 December 1519 (first printed in: CAMPORI, "Documents inédits sur Raphael", *Gazette des Beaux-Arts* 14, 1863, p. 452). But these phenomena are already the result of the fusion of two lines of development: that of "poetic melancholy" and that of the humanists' Neoplatonic theory of melancholy. This latter will be the subject of the following chapter (pp. 249 sqq.).

[45] *Die Dichtungen des Michelangiolo Buonarotti*, ed. CARL FREY, 1897, No. LXXXI. According to Lomazzo, Michelangelo had a "proportione saturnina" (cf. SCHLOSSER, *La letteratura artistica*, 1935, p. 387); above, p. 227 as well as p. 370, note 304 below.

[46] LESSING, *Nathan der Weise*, Act I, scene 5. The self-persiflage of Lessing's Templar is a late ironical echo of the feeling expressed in Michelangelo's passionate outburst. In the same way, the humanists' platonising theory of genius finds a more graceful echo in Goethe's lines:

Zart Gedicht, wie Regenbogen,
Wird nur auf dunkeln Grund gezogen.
Darum behagt dem Dichtergenie
Das Element der Melancholie.

face of poetry—one has only to mention Tasso or Samuel Daniel—but actually determined the physiognomy of men living then, as we can see in the forbidding, reserved, imperious and yet sad features of "mannerist" portraits.[47] In this transitional period the very strength of the emotional pressure made Melancholia a merciless reality, before whom men trembled as before a "cruel plague" or a "melancholy demon", and whom they tried in vain to banish by a thousand antidotes and consolatory treatises.[48] It was as yet impossible for the imagination to transfigure it into an ideal condition, inherently pleasurable, however painful—a condition which by the continually renewed tension between depression and exaltation, unhappiness and "apartness", horror of death and increased awareness of life, could impart a new vitality to drama, poetry and art.

This dynamic liberation first occurred in the Baroque period. Significantly enough, it achieved its fullest and most profound results in the countries where the tension which was to bear fruit in artistic achievement was at its most acute—in Cervantes' Spain, where Baroque developed under the pressure of a particularly harsh Catholicism, and still more in Shakespeare's and Donne's England, where it asserted itself in the teeth of a proudly stressed Protestantism.[49] Both countries were and remained the true

---

[47] E. PANOFSKY, *Idea*, Stud. d. Bibl. Warburg, v, 1924, p. 55 sq.

[48] Cf. above, p. 76. Concerning Germany in particular, abundant material is to be found in: M. PAULUS, *Die Melancholie im 16. Jahrhundert* (Wissenschaftliche Beilage zur "Germania" vom 4. Februar 1879, No. 18). However, this is a definitely tendentious essay. The author is out to prove that the higher incidence of melancholy, both in the sense of depressive tendencies and of an actual mental illness, should be laid at the door of the Reformation and that Protestants were much more liable to suffer from it than Catholics.

[49] As regards Spain, cf. A. FARINELLI, *La Vita è un Sogno*, 1916 (a typical example was Tirso de Molina's play *El Melancolico*, written in 1611, in which the character of the hero Rogerio was generally held to have been drawn after Philip II). As for England, cf., among others, G. B. HARRISON, *Essay on Elizabethan Melancholy* (in the new edition of NICHOLAS BRETON, *Melancholike Humours*, 1929). A book like BURTON's *Anatomy of Melancholy* which, as Harrison rightly remarks, does not stand at the beginning but rather at the end of a whole series of other English writings on melancholy (cf. e.g. the *Treatise of Melancholie* by TIMOTHY BRIGHT, London 1586, which influenced Shakespeare), could only have been written in England, and it is no coincidence that the one extensive poetical description of Dürer's engraving was written by an Englishman—JAMES THOMSON's poetical imitation in *The City of Dreadful Night and Other Poems*, No. XXI:

> "Anear the centre of that northern crest
> Stands out a level upland bleak and bare,
> From which the city east and south and west
> Sinks gently in long waves; and throned there
> An Image sits, stupendous, superhuman,
> The bronze colossus of a winged Woman,
> Upon a graded granite base foursquare.

domain of this specifically modern, consciously cultivated melancholy—for a long time the "melancholy Spaniard" was as proverbial as the "splenetic Englishman".[50] The great poetry in which it found expression was produced during the same period that saw the emergence of the specifically modern type of consciously cultivated humour, an attitude which stands in obvious correlation to melancholy. Melancholic and humorist both feed on the metaphysical contradiction between finite and infinite, time and eternity, or whatever one may choose to call it. Both share the characteristic of achieving at the same time pleasure and sorrow from the consciousness of this contradiction. The melancholic primarily suffers from the contradiction between time and infinity,

---

Low-seated she leans forward massively,
With cheek on clenched left hand, the forearm's might
Erect, its elbow on her rounded knee;
Across a clasped book in her lap the right
Upholds a pair of compasses; she gazes
With full set eyes, but wandering in thick mazes
Of sombre thought beholds no outward sight.

Words cannot picture her; but all men know
That solemn sketch the pure sad artist wrought
Three centuries and threescore years ago,
With phantasies of his peculiar thought:
The instruments of carpentry and science
Scattered about her feet, in strange alliance
With the keen wolf-hound sleeping undistraught;

Scales, hour-glass, bell, and magic-square above;
The grave and solid infant perched beside,
With open winglets that might bear a dove,
Intent upon its tablets, heavy-eyed;
Her folded wings as of a mighty eagle,
But all too impotent to lift the regal
Robustness of her earth-born strength and pride;

And with those wings, and that light wreath which seems
To mock her grand head and the knotted frown
Of forehead charged with baleful thoughts and dreams,
The household bunch of keys, the house-wife's gown
Voluminous, indented and yet rigid,
As if a shell of burnished metal frigid,
The feet thick-shod to tread all weakness down;

The comet hanging o'er the waste dark seas,
The massy rainbow curved in front of it
Beyond the village with the masts and trees;
The snaky imp, dog-headed, from the Pit,
Bearing upon its batlike leathern pinions
Her name unfolded in the sun's dominions,
The "Melencolia" that transcends all wit . . ."

[50] Cf. Fl. KALKÜHLER, *Die Natur des Spleen bei den englischen Schriftstellern des 18 Jahrhunderts*, Diss. Leipzig 1920.

while at the same time giving a positive value to his own sorrow "sub specie aeternitatis", since he feels that through his very melancholy he has a share in eternity. The humorist, however, is primarily amused by the same contradiction, while at the same time deprecating his own amusement "sub specie aeternitatis" since he recognises that he himself is fettered once and for all to the temporal. Hence it can be understood how in modern man "Humour", with its sense of the limitation of the Self, developed alongside that Melancholy which had become a feeling of an enhanced Self. Nay, one could be humorous about Melancholy itself, and by so doing, bring out the tragic elements yet more strongly. But it is also understandable that as soon as this new form of Melancholy had become fixed, the shallow worldling should have used it as a cheap means of concealing his own emptiness, and by so doing have exposed himself to the fundamentally equally cheap ridicule of the mere satirist.

Thus, alongside the tragic melancholic like Hamlet, there stood from the beginning the comic "fashionable melancholic" like Stephen in "Every Man in his Humour", who wanted to "learn" Melancholy as one learns a game or a dance—"Have you a stool to be melancholy upon? . . . Cousin, is it well? Am I melancholy enough?"[51] But the most perfect synthesis of profound thought and poetic wistfulness is achieved when true humour is deepened by melancholy; or, to express it the opposite way, when true melancholy is transfigured by humour—when a man whom at a superficial glance one would judge to be a comic, fashionable melancholic is really a melancholic in the tragic sense, save that he is wise enough to mock at his own *Weltschmerz* in public and thus to forge an armour for his sensitivity.

Compared with Jaques's melancholy, the Miltonic "Penseroso" is at once simpler and richer. Simpler, because Milton renounced the profound and ingenious plan of concealing the tragic face beneath a comic mask; richer, because, as we have seen, he

---

[51] *Every Man in his Humour*, Act III, sc. 1. Cf. C. A. Bieber, *Der Melancholikertypus Shakespeares*, 1913, pp. 34 sqq. Also characteristic is *Every Man out of his Humour*, Act. I, sc. 2, line 55 sq.: "You must endeavour to feed cleanly at your ordinary, sit melancholy, and pick your teeth when you cannot speak." What a long life "fashionable melancholy" had in England, and how faithfully it was attended by the satirists, is shown, e.g. by Churchill's poem (quoted by Sickels, op. cit., p. 39) of 1761:

"If, in these hallowed times, when sober, sad
All gentlemen are melancholically mad,
When 'tis not deemed so great a crime by half
To violate a vestal as to laugh . . ."

combined all the aspects of the melancholic: the ecstatic and the contemplative, the silent and Saturnine no less than the musical and Apollinian, the gloomy prophet and the idyllic lover of nature, and welded their manifoldness into a unified picture, mild on the whole rather than menacing. The portrait could be differentiated further, and this process of differentiation was carried out, more especially in eighteenth-century English literature, with great speed and consistency.[52] The "Odes to Melancholy", the "Elegies" and the poetic glorification of the pleasures of melancholy with all its minor forms and varieties like contemplation, solitude and darkness, increased constantly from Gray to Keats; we can follow step by step how in this type of literature new refinements and distinctions of the melancholic sentiment evolved with regard to both quality and object. Corresponding to the old contrast between natural melancholy and melancholic disease, they distinguished "black melancholy" in the sense of a morbid depression from "white melancholy" in the sense of Goethe's "Selig, wer sich vor der Welt ohne Hass verschliesst". This latter form was expressed sometimes in philosophic resignation, sometimes in elegiac sadness, sometimes in melodramatic passion, finally drowning in a sea of sensibility. The content of the poems varied according to the greater or smaller importance given to the theme of "Withdrawal" or of "Death", or to the "Complaint of Life", though in a work like Gray's "Elegy in a Country Churchyard", where the basic emotion is so singly and expressively sustained, these three themes could very well be combined.[53] Finally, one can see how, in accordance

[52] Outside England, Melancholy was no longer an important poetical subject in the eighteenth century. The reasons for this development are various: in the literature of Italy and France, nations of more extrovert than introvert tendencies, the theme had never taken proper roots; Spanish literature in the first half of the seventeenth century was more or less in abeyance, while in the second half it was under strong French influence; German poets valued melancholy not for its own sake, but only, as it were, as a subsidiary subject, more substantial sorrows or sentiments affording the dominating theme (unhappy love in Goethe's *Werther*, friendship in jeopardy in Klopstock's famous ode *An Ebert*).

[53] In distinguishing these three themes we follow Reed, op. cit., pp. 38 sqq. As regards Gray's *Elegy*, the title already indicates a combination of the three themes, "Elegy" pointing to the general sentiment of *Weltschmerz*, "country" to the "retirement", and "churchyard" to the "death-theme". The connection of these ideas with each other and with the idea of infinity, which makes them more profoundly significant, is beautifully expressed by Balzac in his *Médecin de campagne*: "Pourquoi les hommes ne regardent-ils point sans une émotion profonde toutes les ruines, même les plus humbles? Sans doute elles sont pour eux une image du malheur dont le poids est senti par eux si diversement... un village abandonné fait songer aux peines de la vie; . . . les peines de la vie sont infinies. L'infini n'est-il pas le secret des grandes mélancolies?"

with the new aesthetic theories of "the Sublime", Milton's "smooth shaven Green" and "Waters murmuring" were gradually ousted by a "wild and romantic" landscape with dark forests, caves, abysses and deserts. Thus the Gothic Revival with its love for the Middle Ages enriched the poetic scene with so many Gothic ruins, churchyards, night ravens, cypresses, yew trees, charnel houses and ghosts—mostly of sad virgins—that a certain group of poets was actually described as the "Graveyard School".[54] The "Poetic Calendar" for 1763 contained an anonymous satire entitled "To a Gentleman who Desired Proper Materials for a Monody", in which all these ingredients were amusingly catalogued.[55]

This mockery is understandable, for in English literature of the eighteenth century—a curious age, in which rationalism and sensibility at once denied and evoked one another—poetic expression of the melancholy mood did in fact become more and more of a convention, while the feeling itself became more and more emasculated.[56] And yet, in proportion as the traditional form and content lost their significance, either becoming conventionally insipid or degenerating into sentimentality, so did new and untraditional possibilities of expression arise to rescue the serious and real meaning of melancholy. Therefore, true melancholy, while it fled from the painted backcloths of ruins, vaults and cloisters, is now found, e.g., in the bitter wit of Lessing's later letters, or in the deliberately fragmentary style of Sterne, which was but a symbol of the eternal tragicomic incompleteness of existence as such. It can be perceived in those regions of the mind explored by Watteau and Mozart in which reality and fantasy, fulfilment and renunciation, love and loneliness, desire and death bear so close a likeness that the customary expression of sorrow and pain can scarcely be used save in parody.[57]

---

[54] Cf. Reed, op. cit.; Sickels, op. cit., p. 28 and *passim*. Admittedly, Milton already has "The studious cloister's pale", and "The high embowed roof, With antick pillars massy proof, And storied windows richly dight, Casting a dim religious light." See Kenneth Clark, *The Gothic Revival*, 1928, p. 176, where a passage is quoted from A. Welby Pugin, *An Apology for the revival of Christian Architecture*, London 1843, which is characteristic of the connection between melancholy and gothic style: "It (i.e. the gothic style) is considered suitable for some purposes—*melancholy*, and therefore fit for religious buildings." (Author's italics).

[55] Printed by Sickels, op. cit., p. 67.

[56] Cf. Sickels, op. cit., p. 182 sq.

[57] We are thinking of such passages with comic emphasis on the minor key as those in the suicide aria of Papageno, and in Barbarina's "needle" aria in the *Marriage of Figaro*.

At the beginning of the nineteenth century, however, a new type of melancholy arose out of this strange dualism of a tradition gone stale and the spontaneous and intensely personal utterance of profound individual sorrow—namely, the "romantic" melancholy. This was essentially "boundless" in the sense both of immeasurable and of indefinable, and for that very reason it was not content to bask in self-contemplation, but sought once more the solidity of direct apprehension and the exactness of a precise language in order to "realise" itself. This harsh and alert melancholy, whose very yearning for the eternal brought it in a new sense nearer to reality, might be called a masculine form of romantic *Weltschmerz*, in contrast to the far more common feminine type which had become merely pointless sensibility. It is understandable, therefore, that Keats, in his "Ode on Melancholy", should destroy the whole convention at a blow, rescuing the original meaning of melancholy emotion by discovering it in a sphere where convention had never thought of looking. Just as Shakespeare in his famous sonnet "My Mistress' eyes are nothing like the sun . . ." routs the hyperbolic comparisons of older love-lyrics, to conclude

And yet, by Heaven, I think my love as rare
As any she belied with false compare,

so, with an imperious gesture, Keats too scorns the familiar inventory. Restless and "wakeful",[58] he feeds his melancholy with all his mind and senses, making it embrace all the bright splendour of created things, which he can then truly "discover" and describe in a profusion of rich and varied terms, because the thought of their transitoriness and the feeling of his own pain alone enable him to take possession of their living beauty. It is no coincidence that this new melancholy, which discovers the sanctuary of the Goddess of Melancholy "in the very temple of Delight" returns once more to the antithetic precision[59] and mythological extravagance[60] of the great Elizabethans.

---

[58] Cf. also the wonderful late sonnet (written into his copy of Shakespeare's Poems) in which the poet desires to be immortal as the star, but on condition that immortality does not mean insensibility: "Awake for ever in a sweet unrest, Still, still to hear her tender-taken breath, And so live ever—or else swoon to death". It is consistent with this attitude that Keats in his *Ode on a Grecian Urn* finds pure happiness existing only for the marble figures whose feelings cannot die, just because they are caught for ever in the rigid marble.

[59] One might compare the new form of melancholy which seems to reveal itself in the slow movements of Beethoven's last Quartets and Sonatas, where he returns to a polyphonic style. There is a great contrast between these late works and such movements as that entitled

No, no! go not to Lethe, neither twist
Wolf's-bane, tight-rooted, for its poisonous wine;
Nor suffer thy pale forehead to be kiss'd
By nightshade, ruby grape of Proserpine;
Make not your rosary of yew-berries,
Nor let the beetle nor the death-moth be
Your mournful Psyche, nor the downy owl
A partner in your sorrow's mysteries;
For shade to shade will come too drowsily,
And drown the wakeful anguish of the soul.

But when the melancholy fit shall fall
Sudden from heaven like a weeping cloud,
That fosters the droop-headed flowers all
And hides the green hill in an April shroud;
Then glut thy sorrow on a morning rose,
Or on the rainbow of the salt sand-wave,
Or on the wealth of globed peonies;
Or if thy mistress some rich anger shows,
Emprison her soft hand, and let her rave,
And feed deep, deep, upon her peerless eyes.

She dwells with Beauty—Beauty that must die;
And Joy, whose hand is ever at his lips
Bidding adieu, and aching Pleasure nigh
Turning to poison while the bee-mouth sips.
Ay, in the very temple of Delight
Veil'd Melancholy has her sovran shrine,
Though seen of none save him whose strenuous tongue
Can burst Joy's grape against his palate fine;
His soul shall taste the sadness of her might,
And be among her cloudy trophies hung.

If the *Weltschmerz* at the beginning of the nineteenth century contributed to the great and truly tragic poetry of that time (the work of Hölderlin, for instance), the end of the century brought with it the destructive *Weltschmerz* of the Decadents. This was a morbid *Weltschmerz*, nourished by images taken more

"Malinconia" from the Quartet op. 18, No. 6 and the Largo of the Piano Sonata op. 10, No. 3, explained by Beethoven himself as "description of the state of mind of a melancholic". However beautiful these early works are, they still belong to the eighteenth-century convention of melancholy.

[60] A characteristic phrase is, e.g. "Nightshade, ruby grape of Proserpine" which is not a display of classical erudition, but makes an immediate impact by establishing the connection between the great, distant, and, as it were, "black" goddess of death and the every-day reality of the "little ruby grape". As the same time this reality is in itself a symbol, as the fruit of the vine bringing intoxication and joy is introduced in place of the poisonous lethal berry of the nightshade.

or less consciously from the past as seen with the eye of the historian. In the beautiful poem prefacing Part II of this book,[61] Verlaine explicitly cites the "sages d'autrefois" and "grimoires anciens", and in J. P. Jacobsen we find a *fin-de-siècle*, pleasure-seeking satiety actually attributed to Baroque times. "They have a greater heart and more restless blood", he says of the "secret society" which one might call the Fellowship of Melancholics. "They desire and yearn for more, and their longing is a wilder and more burning one than runs in common veins . . . but the others, what do they know of delight amid grief or despair?" "But why do you call them melancholics, since joys and worldly pleasures are all they think of?" "Because all earthly joy is so fleeting and transitory, so false and incomplete . . . Do you still ask why they are called melancholics, when all delight, as soon as possessed, changes its aspect and turns to disgust . . . when all beauty is a beauty that vanishes, all luck a luck that changes?"[62]

---

[61] See above, p. 126.

[62] J. P. Jacobsen, *Frau Marie Grubbe*, ch. 11. The action of the novel takes place in the seventeenth century, and the author tries to imitate the style and mode of feeling of the baroque period.

Chapter II

"MELANCHOLIA GENEROSA"

The Glorification of Melancholy and Saturn in Florentine Neoplatonism and the Birth of the Modern Notion of Genius

I. THE INTELLECTUAL BACKGROUND OF THE NEW DOCTRINE

The notion of "poetic melancholy" outlined in the previous section developed independently of the notion of melancholy as a condition of creative achievement, and encountered it at only one, though very important, point.

The decisive moment in the development of this notion was reached when the "mérencolie mauvaise", which most fifteenth-century authors and many of their successors had conceived merely as evil, was first reckoned as a positive intellectual force. A new viewpoint fundamentally altering the notions of the nature and value of the melancholy state must have been arrived at, before Raphael's "melancholy" (described in a contemporary account) could be regarded as a natural condition of his genius; before Milton could represent melancholy as a tutelary goddess of poetic and visionary ecstasy as well as of profound contemplation; and before, lastly, the "fashionable melancholic" could arise, who affected the mask not only of melancholy but of profundity.

The elevation of melancholy to the rank of an intellectual force obviously meant something quite different from its interpretation as a subjective emotional condition. Both tendencies may combine, in the sense that the emotional value of the sentimental, pleasurable mood may be enriched by the intellectual value of contemplative or artistically productive melancholy—but the one could never have resulted from the other. They bear the same relation to one another as, say, the tendencies of Italian humanism bore to those of the northern Reformation—tendencies, as has been rightly stressed, which were fundamentally connected[1] but which stood, nevertheless, in marked contrast to one another. Both were results of the desire for emancipation, which sought to free and to stimulate not only the individual personality but also the, allegedly parallel, phenomenon of national personality; both aimed at making this "personality" as far as possible independent of the lashings of tradition and hierarchy by which it had been supported as well as restrained; at enabling it to seek unaided its individual approach to God and the world; and at allowing it to find direct access to its own cultural past instead of relying on the current of traditional opinion—and this was to be achieved by the attempt to uncover the authentic sources of that past. But whereas Protestantism carried out this emancipation and reactivation of personality with an eye on an otherworldly goal and by the employment of irrational faculties, the goal which humanism set itself—in spite of perfect willingness to remain within the bounds of Christian dogma—was an earthly one, and the method of attaining to it was rational. In the one case, the sources of insight and morality to be restored were biblical revelation and Pauline doctrine; in the other, the intellectual culture of classical antiquity and its conception of "virtus".[2] Justification was sought, in the one case, by faith; in the other, by education and knowledge. And freedom was conceived of, in the one case, as a Christian achievement based on a vigorous but transcendent and irrational faith; in the other, as a human privilege, founded on reason and will acting in this world. Humanistic freedom might reveal itself in the virtues of a philosopher, it might find secular expression in the impeccability of the courtier or, finally, it might run wild in the absolute despotism of a prince; but in every case the notion of freedom signified the flowering of the personality into a typical example of

---

1 Cf. K. BORINSKI, *Die Antike in Poetik und Kunsttheorie*, VOL. II, Leipzig 1924, pp. 1 sqq.

2 Cf. E. PANOFSKY, *Hercules am Scheidewege* (Studien der Bibliothek Warburg, VOL. XVIII), Leipzig 1930, pp. 150 sqq. At that time the fact was overlooked that a fourteenth-century author, Francesco Barberini, had noticed the lack of a pictorial type for virtue as such (as against the individual virtues of the Middle Ages), and endeavoured to remedy this state of affairs by an imaginative reconstruction of a portrait of virtue in general (cf. F. EGIDI, *I documenti d'amore di Francesco da Barberino*, VOL. I, Rome 1905, pp. 66 sqq., and in *Arte*, V (1902), pp. 1 sqq. and 78 sqq.). The basis of his invention, however (*Arte* V (1902), p. 89), was still the biblical representative of the original virtue "Fortezza", namely, Samson, for whom the Renaissance then substituted Hercules; it is significant that Francesco's solution, taken up by Ripa, should have been so far forgotten that Filarete (cf. PANOFSKY, op. cit., pp. 192 sqq.) had to formulate the whole problem all over again.

a specific ideal of man, rather than the fulfilment of the individual soul in its uniqueness.

The world of humanism was made to man's measure: that is to say, it was discovered, explored and classified by human reason; at the very least it could be, in theory, discovered, explored and classified in this way. And it provided an occasion for the flowering of an ideal which the epoch described as the "dignity of man", and which might perhaps also be called the sovereignty of the human mind. Yet even long after the wave of the Italian Renaissance had swept over the Alps, the most ardent humanists of the north remained more individualistic and mystical than the most ardent individualists and mystics of the south.

In the north one need only mention Erasmus, Pirckheimer, or, above all, Albrecht Dürer, whose acknowledgement of the incomprehensible God-given nature of artistic achievement revealing itself in unique and incomparable men and works made him constantly call in question the principles of the Italian theory of art which he desired so passionately to make his own.[3] In the south one may mention Marsilio Ficino, among others, whose intellectual life, despite its bias towards the eccentric and irrational, was based fundamentally on classical culture and on the reasoned arguments of philosophical problems, and implied the new awareness of a certain human type rather than the longing of the individual for salvation.

Italian humanism, therefore, reaffirmed an ideal which had arisen in classical antiquity but which became blurred in the Middle Ages; more than that, it exalted it into a criterion for a fundamentally altered way of living. This was the ideal of the speculative life, in which the "sovereignty of the human mind" seemed to be most nearly realised; for only the "vita contemplativa" is based on the self-reliance and self-sufficiency of a process of thought which is its own justification. The Middle Ages, it is true, had never forgotten the joys of the life of searching and knowing,[4] and even the expression "vita contemplativa" continued to be held in regard; but what men meant by it was different from the classical ideal of the "speculative life". It was different in so far as the value of the contemplative life for its

---

[3] See below, pp. 361 sqq. (text).

[4] Cf. F. Boll, "Vita Contemplativa", in *Sitzungsberichte der Heidelberger Akademie der Wissenschaften, phil.-hist. Klasse,* VIII (1920), p. 17.

own sake and without regard to its purpose was questioned. The medieval thinker did not meditate in order to belong to himself, but in order to draw near to God, so that his meditation found meaning and justification not in itself but in the establishment of a relationship with the Deity; and if he was not "contemplating", but using his reason scientifically, he consciously took up his position in the continuity of a tradition which essentially, by its whole method, pointed beyond the individual; his proper function was that of heir and transmitter, of critic and mediator, of pupil and teacher, and he was not meant to be the creator of an intellectual world centred in himself. He was not very different, in fact, from the peasant or craftsman, who also filled the place in the universal order given him by God: the medieval scholar (as distinct from the "exclusive" Renaissance humanist, consciously withdrawn from the "vulgar" mob) did not claim to be a different and superior being.[5] In both cases, therefore, the medieval thinker belonged not to himself but to God, whether directly, as in contemplation of Him, or indirectly, as in the fulfilment of a service ordained by Him and traditionally and hieratically regulated. If he fulfilled neither of these conditions, he belonged to the devil, for whosoever neither meditated, nor worked, fell a victim to the vice of "acedia" or sloth, which led to all manner of other sins. One might say that in the Middle Ages the idea of leisure was lacking.[6] The classical "otium" had a specific value, and could even produce values though (or perhaps because) it was outwardly the same as inactivity; it was therefore contrasted as "different in kind" both with the labour of peasant or soldier and with the useless hedonism of the idler. In the same manner, the life of the classical philosopher whom the Renaissance

---

[5] Hence a relative lack of claims to originality distinguishes medieval from ancient or modern philosophy; cf., among others, JOHANNES HESSEN, *Augustinische und thomistische Erkenntnislehre*, Paderborn 1921, pp. 9 sqq. and 19 sqq.

[6] It is apparently an almost isolated phenomenon when a man like Marbod of Rennes in the twelfth century celebrates the leisure of his country life and closely following Horace, *Ep.*, I, 14, composes a hymn in praise of completely self-sufficient meditation:

"... Herba virens, et silva silens, et spiritus aurae
Lenis et festivus, et fons in gramine vivus
Defessam mentem recreant, et me mihi reddunt,
Et faciunt in me consistere ...
Haec et plura mihi licet atque libet meditari,
Fronde sub agresti dum rure moror patrueli"—

MIGNE, P. L., VOL. CLXXI, col. 1666; cf. W. GANZENMÜLLER, *Das Naturgefühl im Mittelalter*, Leipzig 1914, pp. 224 sqq.

humanist strove to imitate, lay not between "vita activa" and "vita voluptuaria" but beyond either of them. To a certain extent it lay beyond good and evil, very differently from the God-directed course of medieval theologians and mystics, and we can understand how the Renaissance, in order to separate the rediscovered way of life of the classical "philosophus" from that of the medieval "religiosus", abandoned the traditional expression "vita contemplativa" (which had grown with the centuries to mean purely and simply "contemplatio Dei") and coined a new term which, looking back across the Middle Ages, reasserted the ancient notion of self-sufficient thought and research—"vita speculativa sive studiosa", in contrast to "vita contemplativa sive monastica".[7]

The new ideal found concrete expression in a type of man foreign to the Middle Ages, the "homo literatus" or "Musarum sacerdos",[8] who in public and private life was responsible only to himself and to his own mind. A whole branch of literature was devoted to the praises of the "vita speculativa". It received the devotion of Politian and Lorenzo de' Medici and the homage of Landino's *Camaldulensian Conversations*, and was the mainspring of Pico della Mirandola's famous discourse *On the Dignity of Man*. In Dürer's work we can see how the medieval notion of the vicious "accidia" was later overlaid, in *Melencolia I*, by the humanist Pl. 1
idea of a meditation not so much fleeing from activity as leaving it behind.[9]

It is no coincidence that the German Renaissance should have chosen "melancholy", that is to say, awareness of life's menace and sufferings, for its most convincing portrait of contemplation, or that in the *Camaldulensian Conversations* the enthusiastic glorification of the "vita speculativa" and the acknowledgement of Saturn as patron of contemplation[10] were coupled with the sorrowful belief that grief and weariness are the constant companions of profound speculation.[11] For in so far as the mental

---

[7] With this, cf. A. von Martin, *Mittelalterliche Welt- und Lebensanschauung im Spiegel der Schriften Coluccio Salutatis*, Munich 1913, pp. 124 sqq.

[8] Thus Ficino, quoted below, p. 259, note 53.

[9] Cf. E. Panofsky, in *Münchener Jahrbuch der bildenden Kunst*, new series, VIII (1931), pp. 1 sqq.

[10] Disputatio IV; Cristoforo Landino, *Libri Qvattvor* (= *Camaldulensium disput. libri quattuor*), Strasbourg edn. 1508, fol. K ii^r. The passage from Macrobius is quoted *in extenso*.

[11] Pointed out by E. Wolf, in *Neue Jahrbücher für das klassische Altertum*, I (1919), p. 457.

sovereignty desired by humanism sought to fulfil itself within the framework of a Christian culture, it meant danger as much as freedom. A position in the "centre of the universe", such as Pico della Mirandola's discourse had attributed to man, involved the problem of a choice between innumerable directions, and in his new dignity man appeared in an ambiguous light which was soon to show an inherent danger. For in the measure in which human reason insisted on its "god-like" power, it was bound also to become aware of its natural limits. It is significant that the early Renaissance turned with real concern to the theme of ethical choice, which the previous epoch had either ignored entirely, or left to the province of the theological doctrine of grace; it found visible expression in the picture of *Hercules at the Crossroads*. Hercules makes an autonomous choice and thereby becomes involved in the problems resulting from his freedom. And it is equally significant that the early Renaissance began to grasp the problem of astrology as a vital question of the human will affirming its independence even of Providence. The late Middle Ages had slurred over it by compromises such as "inclinant astra, non necessitant" or "sapiens homo dominatur astris". Writers of the fourteenth century had already become curiously uneasy about these questions, and in face of the almost continuous triumphal progress of astrology had to a large extent retreated into a pre-Thomist standpoint of marked intransigence. Even when the burning of Cecco d'Ascoli is left out of account, it must be said that even Chaucer's and Petrarch's polemics, like Luther's later on, were far more "patristic" than "enlightened".[12] In the fifteenth century, which now learned to proceed in a really "enlightened" manner towards a new notion of human dignity, we find neighbouring and crossing currents, the discrepancy between which is due to the very loosening of medieval bonds. There were those who, in the full enjoyment of their freshly found liberty, bitterly disputed against all stellar influence.[13] Next to these there were others who, in a sort of "horror vacui moralis" adopted an almost Islamic fatalism with regard to the stars, or

---

[12] See above, pp. 159 sqq., and in particular WEDEL, M. A. A., esp. pp. 82 sqq. and 148 sqq.

[13] Thus Pico, according to whom the "freedom for good" has its obvious correlative in an equally unlimited "freedom for ill." So, too, in *King Lear*, I, ii, Edmund utterly refuses credence to such stellar fatalism, but he realises that human nature binds a man, even though the stars do not (*King Lear*, I, i), so that he personally, despite his independence of the stars, *must* choose "ill". Nevertheless he is perfectly prepared to take the responsibility for this, because the force moving him comes from within.

practised the most obscure astral magic. There were those, too, who attempted to find a way between that conviction of freedom which was affirmed in theory but could not quite be realised in practice, and that fear of the stars which had not been wholly banished from practice although it was theoretically repudiated.[14] The "bondsman" of the Middle Ages (so to speak) was on the whole immune from astrology, but the "free man" of Renaissance times was obliged either to fight it or to fall its victim.

The birth of this new humanist awareness took place, therefore, in an atmosphere of intellectual contradiction. As he took up his position, the self-sufficient "homo literatus" saw himself torn between the extremes of self-affirmation, sometimes rising to hubris, and self-doubt, sometimes sinking to despair; and the experience of this dualism roused him to discover the new intellectual pattern, which was a reflection of this tragic and heroic disunity—the intellectual pattern of "modern genius". At this point we can see how the self-recognition of "modern genius" could only take place under the sign of Saturn and melancholy; and how, on the other hand, a new intellectual distinction now had to be conferred on the accepted notions of Saturn and melancholy. Only the humanism of the Italian Renaissance was able to recognise in Saturn and in the melancholic this polarity, which was, indeed, implicit from the beginning, but which only 'Aristotle's' brilliant intuition, and St Augustine's eyes, sharpened by hatred, had really seen. And the Italian humanists not only recognised this polarity: they valued it, because they saw in it the main feature of the newly discovered "genius". There was therefore a double renaissance: firstly, of the Neoplatonic notion of Saturn, according to which the highest of the planets embodied, and also bestowed, the highest and noblest faculties of the soul, reason and speculation; and secondly, of the 'Aristotelian' doctrine of melancholy, according to which all great men were melancholics (whence it followed logically that not to be melancholy was a sign of insignificance). But this new acknowledgement of a favourable view of Saturn and melancholy was accompanied—or, as we saw, conditioned—by an unprecedented consciousness of their polarity, which lent a tragic colour to the optimistic view, and thus gave a characteristic tension to the feeling of life experienced by the men of the Renaissance.

---

[14] Thus Ficino, see below, pp. 256 sqq. (text).

Petrarch, perhaps the first of a type of men who are conscious of being men of genius, had himself experienced the contrast between exultation and despair very poignantly indeed, and was so conscious of it that he was able to describe both conditions in literary form:

> Quaedam divina poetis
> vis animi est,

he says in his defence of poetry, which is also a paean on his own coronation.

> Insanire licet, fateor, mens concita; clarum,
> seque super provecta, canet . . .
> . . . subsistere nullum
> censuit ingenium, nisi sit dementia mixta.[15]

The same poet who describes so joyfully his own poetic ecstasies was yet familiar with that state of empty depression and dull grief which made him "see all life in black", and with a sadness which drove him from company to solitude, and from solitude to company once more.[16] But he still is far from describing this sadness—which, to quote Lessing, gives his poems a "voluptuous melancholy"[17] as "melancholy" itself. Rather he calls it by the medieval name of "acedia", which, however, as he uses it, seems to hover half-way between sin and disease[18]; nor does it occur

---

[15] PETRARCH, *Epistola Metrica to Zoilus*, I, line 167 (*Poemata minora*, ed. D. de' Rossetti, VOL. II, Milan 1831, p. 230). The lines

> ". . . subsistere nullum
> Censuit ingenium, nisi sit dementia mixta"

are a quotation from SENECA, *De tranquillitate animi*, 17, 10, which is quoted above, p. 33, note 65.

[16] Cf. A. FARINELLI, "La malinconia del Petrarca," in *Rivista d'Italia*, V, 2 (1902), esp. pp. 12 and 20.

[17] G. E. LESSING, *Briefe die neueste Literatur betreffend*, Letter 332 (conclusion of the whole).

[18] For Petrarch's "acedia", cf. H. COCHIN, *Le frère de Pétrarque*, Paris 1903, pp. 205 sqq., and, more recent, H. NACHOD and P. STERN (edd.), *Briefe des Francesco Petrarca*, Berlin 1931, pp. 385 sqq. P. Stern's polemic against the, as he says, generally held view equating "acedia" with mental disease or "Weltschmerz" (instead of with the sin of sloth) seems to us to miss the salient point; the fluidity or indeterminateness characteristic of every aspect of Petrarch's historical position, which led some authors (e.g. A. VON MARTIN, in *Archiv für Kulturgeschichte*, XVIII (1928), pp. 57 sqq.) to interpret it as the outcome of his own character, permits of no such alternative. When Augustine says to Petrarch in the *Secretum*: "You are tormented by that destructive plague which the moderns [that is Petrarch's contemporaries] call 'acedia' but the ancients 'aegritudo' ", this sentence alone makes it impossible to explain Petrarch's "acedia" in theologico-moral terms. For him, the sin of "acedia" was equivalent to a sickness of the soul, although he had not yet called this sickness by the name of melancholy. Hence, vice versa, FARINELLI (op. cit., p. 11) is not altogether justified in translating "aegritudo" as "malinconia" in the passage just quoted.

to him to describe the divine force of his poetic frenzy—which he still calls "insania" or "dementia"—by the expression "furor", which Cicero had coined, and which he had explicitly distinguished from the two former expressions.[19] The idea that intellectual achievements are determined by the stars was completely foreign to him. And above all, he had not, and indeed could not have had, any notion of conceiving the two opposite conditions, depression and enthusiasm, which he called "acedia" and "dementia", as different aspects of one and the same, essentially bipolar, disposition.[20]

These conceptions matured in the next century during which Petrarch's way of thinking, still half linked with medieval notions, was superseded by something new and different from the Middle Ages, while the opposites that he had perceived without being able to relate them together, were now grasped as an integral unity. Not till the fifteenth century, as far as scholars are concerned, was the still half-theological notion of "acedia" replaced by the purely humanistic "melancholy" in the emphatically 'Aristotelian' sense. Not till then did the expression "furor" receive its solemn rehabilitation in the sense of Platonic "divine frenzy".[21] Not till then was the 'Aristotelian' doctrine of the ambivalence of the melancholy nature summed up in the formula:

> quantum atra bilis, imo candida bilis eiusmodi quaerenda et nutrienda est, tanquam optima, tantum illam, quae contra se habet, ut diximus, tanquam pessimam esse vitandam.[22]

—thus enabling a later writer to say of the melancholic that he

---

[19] CICERO, *Tusculanae disputationes*, III, 5, 2, quoted above, p. 43 (text).

[20] How far Petrarch still was from the notion of "ennobled" melancholy can be seen from a letter to Laelius, in which he excuses his boldness in contradicting Aristotle by a reference to Cicero, who had dared to do as much: "Quale est illud, quod cum Aristoteles omnes ingeniosos melancholicos esse dixisset, Cicero, cui dictum non placebat, iocans ait: gratum sibi quod tardi esset ingenii, clare satis his verbis quid sentiret intimans" (*F. Petrarcae Epistolae*, ed. I. Fracassetti, Florence 1863, VOL. III, p. 50). Petrarch therefore takes Cicero's jest as a serious rebuttal of the Aristotelian notion of melancholy and approves of this criticism.

[21] *Leonardi Bruni Aretini Epistolarum libri VIII*, ed. L. Mehus, Florence 1741, VOL. II, pp. 36 sqq., ep. VI, I. Bruni answers the poet Marrasio's challenge "Indulgere velis nostro Arretine furori?" with the controversial statement: "Id alius forsan aliter, ego certa sic accipio, quasi laudis furor sit, non vituperationis"; and reinforces it with his famous exegesis of the Platonic notion of mania. For the problem of the modern notion of genius see also E. ZILSEL, *Die Entstehung des Geniebegriffs*, Tübingen 1926, and H. THÜME, *Beiträge zur Geschichte des Geniebegriffs in England*, Halle 1927, and their bibliographies. To the particular significance of the notions of Saturn and melancholy in this connexion, however, these authors have not done justice.

[22] FICINO, *De v. tripl.*, I, 6 (*Opera*, p. 499).

was "aut deus aut daemon".[23] Finally, not till then was the equation of the Aristotelian melancholy with Platonic "divine frenzy"—never clearly formulated by the ancients themselves—expressly made.[24] Then—and not till then—did the modern age conceive the modern notion of genius, reviving ancient conceptions indeed, but filling them with a new meaning.

That Petrarch should have felt melancholy before he called himself so, that he should have been conscious of both the "divine" and the "frenzied" nature of his poetic achievements before there had been any revival of the orthodox notion of divine frenzy, and that he found both these aspects in his own experience before he grasped their unity—all this shows most plainly that for the Renaissance the connexion of melancholy with genius was no mere cultural reminiscence, but a reality which was experienced long before its humanistic and literary formulation. Not that the Middle Ages had entirely forgotten the good qualities of the melancholic and Saturn's auspicious influence; the rudiments of such a conception survived even in astrological and medical literature,[25] and scholastic writers like William of Auvergne even made explicit attempts to rescue it, by contrasting the current view with Aristotle's doctrines, and with those of Neoplatonism.[26] But there was a fundamental difference between scholastic attempts to find a theological and moral justification for melancholy and for Saturn's influence, and the humanists' apotheosis of them, rooted and grounded in personal experience. It was one thing, with the permission of supreme authority, to try to find a place in a God-given world order for the connexion between the melancholy disposition and intellectual pre-eminence, and for a similar link between Saturn and "intellectus"; quite another to discover it in one's own experience and, in affirming it, to be driven by one's own personal urge for intellectual self-preservation. The argument was now, so to say, "ad hominem"[27];

---

[23] Cf. T. Walkington, *The Optick Glasse of Humors*, London 1607, p. 64v: "The melancholick man is said of the wise to be 'aut Deus aut Daemon,' either angel of heaven or a fiend of hell: for in whomsoever this humour hath dominion, the soule is either wrapt up into an Elysium and paradise of blesse by a heavenly contemplation, or into a direfull hellish purgatory by a cynicall meditation." This is followed, however, by an entirely unfavourable account both of melancholy and of the influence of Saturn.

[24] Thus Ficino, quoted below, p. 259 (text).

[25] See above, *passim*.

[26] See above, pp. 73 sqq., 169 sqq. (text).

[27] Note a letter from Filelfo to Lodovico Gonzaga, dated 1457, on the method of bringing up his son Federigo (*Epistolae Francisci Philelfi*, Pforzheim 1506, XIV, 1, fol. B8v, kindly

and it finally reached the point where the perception of the dangerous instability of one's own condition, the double awareness of weakness and creative power, and the consciousness of walking on the edge of a precipice, lent to the 'Aristotelian' and Neoplatonic doctrines—hitherto accepted, if at all, merely as theoretical propositions—a pathos which allowed them to merge with the poetic sensation of melancholy.

The change of meaning in the notion of melancholy was by no means confined to a mere revival of the 'Aristotelian' doctrine. No more could the notion of Saturn be endowed with new meaning merely by harking back to Plotinus, Proclus, or Macrobius.[28] Saturn, too, was discovered in a new and personal sense by the intellectual élite, who were indeed beginning to consider their melancholy a jealously guarded privilege, as they became aware both of the sublimity of Saturn's intellectual gifts and the dangers of his ambivalence. At first sight it would seem to refer more to the idea of free will than to Saturn, when a fifteenth-century astrological poet, Matteo Palmieri, attempts to solve the problem of the relationship between free will and astral dependence by fusing together the two contrasting interpretations of the journeyings of the soul into a sort of "choice of Hercules", presenting the soul in its descent with a choice between the ways of good and evil in each planetary sphere, so that it may acquire the fortunate or unfortunate characteristics of each of the planets.[29] But it is of great importance that within this system (which had to be dualistic in order to allow for freedom of choice)[30] the complex

---

pointed out by F. Rougemont): "Fredericus tuus est natura melancholicus. At melancholicos omnes esse ingeniosos docet Aristoteles. Et ne id quidem mirum. . . . Ut igitur opera danda est, ne fervens ingenium nimio ocio defrigescat, ita etiam studendum, ne tristiore consuetudine se atrae omnino bili faciat obnoxium." Here, as in other Renaissance authors (see following notes), the wish to do justice to melancholy at all costs led to the transformation of Cicero's quotation from Aristotle, "omnes ingeniosos melancholicos esse" (see above, text p. 33, note 65), into "omnes melancholicos ingeniosos esse."

[28] The old etymology Saturn = "sacer nus" (see above, p. 177) occurs again e.g. in G. Boccaccio, *Genealogia Deorum*, VIII, I.

[29] Matteo Palmieri, *La Città di Vita*, Florence, Biblioteca Laurenziana, Cod. plut. XL, 53, published (with many misprints) by Margaret Rooke, in *Smith College Studies of Modern Languages*, VOL. VIII, 1926–27; (the sphere of Saturn is described in I, 12; Rooke (ed.) op. cit., pp. 56 sqq.). Cf. B. Soldati, *La poesia astrologica nel Quattrocento*, Florence 1906, pp. 200 sqq.

[30] This idea of the essentially dual influence of the planets (it occurs later e.g. in G. P. Lomazzo, *Idea del tempio della pittura*, Milan 1590, ch. 26, p. 36: here Saturn means either "gravità" or "miseria") occasionally found expression also in the north. Thus a MS by a certain Lazarus Schröter, dated 1497, in Wolfenbüttel, Cod. 29, 14 Aug. 4°, olim 27 Astron., fols. 84 sqq., not only allots corresponding liberal arts, metals and days of the week to the

many-sidedness of Saturn shrinks to a clear antithesis between extreme intellectual disorder and extreme intellectual ability, emphasising strongly the significance and the vulnerability of the latter. The two "valleys" open to the soul's choice—one bright but hard to discover, the other dark, into which "many more spirits can enter", but which "changes and disturbs the mind" by its cold—meet in a wide space where the usual Saturnine professions are assembled, from anonymous peasants, sailors, and rich men, to architects and astronomers. Whosoever decides on one of these Saturnine professions and not on a Jovial or Solar one places himself, as far as his outward life is concerned, under the influence of his chosen patron. His inner life, however, is determined by the road which he has chosen. Whosoever passes through Saturn's sphere by the broad but evil path of the many is inclined to devious thinking, to anger, dullness, rage, sadness, and envy, to a deceitful mind, and to cruelty, and at his worst he can be overtaken by bestial raving; but whosoever chooses ☞ the path of the few, has a mind illuminated by the "intelligenza certa"—

Per darsi a quegli che sapran mostrare
Con ragion vera ben provata e sperta.

All the writers whose interest is directed to Saturn in particular recognise more and more clearly his inherent contradictoriness as his distinctive quality; and the contrast between the negative definitions of current astrology and the laudatory predications of the Neoplatonists becomes more and more acute.[31] An early commentator on Dante, Jacopo della Lana, had contented himself with the idea, based on natural science, that Saturn, through his quality as an earthen, heavy, cold, and dry planet, produced people in whom matter preponderated and who were suited only

---

planets, but systematically endows each of them with one good mental property and one related evil one. Mercury, for instance (the text on Luna is missing), is credited with 'Luterkeit" and "fresserey", Venus with ". . . issikeit" and "Unkuscheit", Mars with "Übung" and "Zorn", the sun with "Gedultikeit" and "Hoffart", Jupiter with "Miltikeit" and "Nid und Hass," and Saturn with "Demut" and "Sittigkeit"—the last attribute, however, which would otherwise upset the whole system, being obviously a misreading or misspelling, perhaps originally of "Geitigkeit" (avarice) or "Hättigkeit" (malice).

[31] It is therefore the more significant that Leon di Pietro Dati's commentary, also preserved in the Laurenziana MS (kindly pointed out by F. Rougemont), should bring in the Neoplatonic theory of the soul's journeyings when entering the sphere of Saturn (terzarima 12): "in qua secundum astrologos anima raciocinationem et intelligentiam acquirit . . . Fulgentius dicit Saturnum quasi Saturnumen, hoc est divinum sensum"; and again terzarima 21 (see note 27) he remarks that "Melanconicos omnes ingeniosos se [sic!] esse scribit Aristoteles . . . ."

to hard work on the land; but through his position, as the highest of the planets, he produced the most spiritual people, such as "religiosi contemplativi", withdrawn from all worldly life.[32] But by the time of Cristoforo Landino the revived Neoplatonism is already well established. In his commentary on Dante, Landino refers to the authority of Macrobius in order to contrast the many base and evil things which astrology had attributed to the influence of Saturn with "quella virtù della mente, la quale i Greci chiamon 'theoreticon'."[33] Finally, a monumental formula was evolved, expressly contrasting Saturn's bipolarity with the influence of the other planets, and, significantly enough, within a few decades it had become a proverb. "Saturn seldom denotes ordinary characters and destinies, but rather men who are set apart from the others, divine or animal, joyous or bowed down by the deepest grief"[34]; or, as Bovillus says in his *Proverbia vulgaria*, "sub Saturno nati aut optimi aut pessimi."[35]

---

[32] LUCIANO SCARABELLI, *Comedia di Dante degli Allagherii, col commento di Jacopo della Lana*, Bologna 1866, VOL. III, p. 316: "sì come si hae per Alcabizio e per gli altri libri d'astrologìa' Saturno universalmente si hae a significare due generazioni di genti, l'una tutta grossa e materiale, sì come sono villani, agricoli e simile gente; l'altra generazione è tutta estratta dalle mondane occupazioni, sì come sono religiosi contemplativi; e provasi di mostrarne ragione in questo modo. La prima gente si è di sua significazione seguendo sua complessione' sì come Saturno freddo e secco, che è complessione materiale e di terra, ... L'altra gente che è sotto sua impressione, si sono contemplanti, com'è detto; questi seguono lo sito di Saturno, che sì come ello è elevato sopra tutti li altri pianeti, così la contemplazione è elevata sopra tutti li altri atti e operazioni."

[33] Fol. cclxvii v in the Venetian edn. of 1491 of Cristoforo Landino's commentary on Dante: "el quale pianeto, quando è ben disposto nella natività dell' huomo, lo fa investigatore delle cose antiche et recondite; et inferisce acuta ratiocinatione et discorso di ragione. Et ancora secondo Macrobio quella virtù della mente, la quale i Greci chiamon 'theoreticon,' i.e. potentia di contemplare et speculare; la qual cosa induxe el poeta che rappresenti in questa sphera l'anime speculatrici."

[34] FICINO, *De v. tripl.* III, 2 (*Opera*, p. 533): "Saturnus non facile communem significat humani generis qualitatem atque sortem, sed hominem ab aliis segregatum, divinum aut brutum, beatum aut extrema miseria pressum. Mars, Luna, Venus, affectus et actus homini cum caeteris animantibus aeque communes."

[35] C. BOVILLUS, *Proverbiorum vulgarium libri tres*, Paris 1531, fol. 109r:

"Sub saturno nati aut optimi aut pessimi.
Qui soubz saturne sont nez sont tout bons ou tout mauluais."

Similarly in LEONARDO DATI's *Sfera* (we quote from MS 721 in the Pierpont Morgan Library, New York):

"Questo pianeta ci fa contemplanti
Et pensativi, casti e bene astuti,
Sottiglieza d'ingegno han tutti quanti,
Sono al ben fare si come al male acuti . . . ."

Again, LEONE EBREO's attempt to combine all the variety of Saturn's traditional traits into a unified black and white picture (*Dialoghi d'Amore*, Venice 1541, fol. 70r–v) is particularly interesting: "fa gli huomini, ne quali domina, malenconici, mesti, graui et tardi, et di color

For that very reason, however, the élite among the Italian humanists turned to Saturn rather than to Jupiter. According to Pico della Mirandola, the very possibility of becoming either a god or a beast was what made man; and the very situation on the narrow ridge between the two "chasms", which was recognised more and more clearly as the main characteristic of the Saturnine and melancholy man, seemed to these elect persons, by its very peril, to raise them above the secure but uneventful level of the commonplace. Thus, out of the intellectual situation of humanism —that is to say out of the awareness of freedom experienced with a sense of tragedy—there arose the notion of a genius which ever more urgently claimed to be emancipated in life and works from the standards of "normal" morality and the common rules of art. This notion arose in close combination with the notion of a melancholy both gracing and afflicting the "Musarum sacerdos" (just as, in ancient belief, the lightning both destroyed and sanctified); and with the notion of a Saturn who despite all his menace, was a "iuvans pater" of men of intellect[36]; because they could honour in him both the ominous demon of destiny and a type of the "insenescibilis intellectus", or even the "intellectualis deus".[37]

2. MARSILIO FICINO

The new view was soon to gain universal acceptance, if by this phrase one means the world of international intellectual aristocracy of the "viri literati", whose notions, naturally, were conceived on a somewhat different level from those of the almanacs and booklets for the use of barbers.[38] It had received a powerful impulse from Dante, who, himself "malinconico e pensoso",[39] had thrown the whole weight of his opinion (constantly operative through his "epigoni" and commentators) on the side of Macrobius,

di terra, inclinati all' agricultura, edificii et officii terreni . . . Da oltra questo grand' ingegno, profonda cogitatione, uera scientia, retti consegli, et constantia d'animo per la mistione della natura del padre celeste con la terrena madre: et finalmente dalla parte del padre dà la diuinità dell' anima, et dalla parte della madre la bruttezza, et ruina del corpo . . ."; the purely mythological reasons for this polarity are also remarkable.

[36] FICINO, *De v. tripl.*, III, 22 (*Opera*, pp. 564 sqq.).

[37] Cf. NICHOLAS OF CUSA's autograph marginal comments on the Latin translation of PROCLUS's *Theologia Platonis* (Cues, Hospital, Cod. 185, fol. 26r and 166r; further passages, fol. 162v).

[38] The new doctrine did not leave even these entirely untouched, however; see above, p. 118 (text), and below, pp. 394 sqq. (text).

[39] BOCCACCIO, *Vita di Dante*, ch. 8.

and had thus from the outset helped the notion of Saturn as a star of sublime contemplation to gain the day. In the twenty-first canto of the *Paradiso*, it is the sphere of Saturn in which the "anime speculatrici", led by Peter Damian and St Benedict, appear to the poet; and from it the shining ladder of contemplation rises to the vision of the Deity, in which Beatrice's smile dies away, and the nearness of the Absolute silences even the music of the spheres—a curious reminiscence of the silence of the ancient god Kronos.[40] The whole conception—here only hinted at and still concealed behind general symbols, although later, as we have seen, it was to include the personal experience of generations of humanists—reached both its full systematic development, and its psychological objectification, in an author from whose work we have already quoted frequently when it was a matter of finding the new doctrine of Saturn and melancholy "classically" formulated. This was Marsilio Ficino, the translator of Plato and Plotinus; or, as he described himself on the title page of his translation of Plato, the "Philosophus Platonicus, Medicus et Theologus". Marsilio went far beyond the scattered remarks of other authors[41] and devoted a complete monograph to the new doctrine. He it was who really gave shape to the idea of the melancholy man of genius and revealed it to the rest of Europe—in particular, to the great Englishmen of the sixteenth and seventeenth centuries—in the magic chiaroscuro of Christian Neoplatonic mysticism.[42] In him the subjective character of the

---

[40] "Tu hai l'udir mortal, sì come il viso,
rispuose a me; onde qui non si canta
per quel che Beatrice non ha riso . . . ."

For this, see the commentaries quoted above, p. 252 sq. (text).

[41] For Guainerio, see above, pp. 95 sqq. (text).

[42] An edition of Ficino's *Libri de vita triplici* was being prepared before the war by Professor E. Weil, Paris, to whom this section of the book owes several additions and rectifications; hence we have limited ourselves here to very brief references and quotations. For other aspects besides the general literature, see F. FIORENTINO, *Il risorgimento filosofico nel Quattrocento*, Naples 1885; A. DELLA TORRE, *Storia dell' Accademia Platonica di Firenze*, Florence 1902; E. CASSIRER, *Individuum und Kosmos* (Studien der Bibliothek Warburg, VOL. X), Leipzig 1927; and GIEHLOW (1903–04); G. SAITTA, *La filosofia di Marsilio Ficino*, Messina 1923; H. BARON, "Willensfreiheit und Astrologie bei Ficino und Pico", in *Kultur- und Universalgeschichte, Walter Götz zu seinem* 60. *Geburtstage dargebracht*. . . , Leipzig 1927; J. PUSINO (with additions by L. THORNDIKE) in *Zeitschrift für Kirchengeschichte*, 1925, pp. 504 sqq.; W. DRESS, *Die Mystik des Marsilio Ficino*, Berlin 1929 (with important remarks on Ficino's secret anthropocratism, esp. p. 79). For Ficino's influence on the Elizabethans, cf. F. S. SCHOELL, "Etudes sur l'humanisme continental en Angleterre à la fin de la Renaissance", in *Bibliothèque de la Revue de littérature comparée*, VOL. XXIX (1926), pp. 2 sqq.; we may add that BURTON too offers a detailed discussion of Ficino's theory of melancholy (Part I, memb. 3, subs. 15).

new doctrine becomes especially pronounced, for he himself was a melancholic and a child of Saturn—the latter, indeed, in particularly unfavourable circumstances, for in his horoscope the dark star in whose influence he so unshakably believed[43] stood in the ascendant, and as it did so, moreover, it was in the sign of the Aquarius, Saturn's "night abode".[44] It is unusually illuminating to see how Ficino's notion of Saturn and melancholy sprang from this personal, psychological foundation, for there is no doubt that fundamentally, despite all his familiarity with Dante and ancient Neoplatonism, he regarded Saturn as an essentially unlucky star, and melancholy as an essentially unhappy fate,[45] so that he attempted to counter it in himself and others by all the means of the medical art which he had learnt from his father, perfected by his own training, and finally firmly based on Neoplatonic astral magic.[46] We can actually determine the moment at which the views of Proclus and Aristotle began to prevail in his mind against the views of Cecco d'Ascoli and Constantinus Africanus. In a letter written between 1470 and

---

[43] Ficino can be counted among the opponents of astrology only with certain qualifications (on this, see below, text pp. 265 sqq.). It is at least understandable that the great astrologer Lucas Gauricus, in a speech in praise and defence of his science, should have quoted him, together with Ptolemy, Picatrix, Pietro d'Abano and the Archduke Leopold of Austria, as one of the main representatives of "astrological magic" (LUCAS GAURICUS, *Oratio de laudibus astrologiae habita in Ferrariensi Achademia*, printed in *Sphere tractatus Joannis de Sacro Busto*, Venice 1531).

[44] For Ficino's horoscope see the letters to Cavalcanti quoted below, pp. 257 sqq. (text), and the passage quoted from his introduction to the commentary on Plotinus; also his letter to Nicholas of Bathor, Bishop of Waitzen in Hungary (*Opera*, VOL. I, p. 884): "Me vero patrias mutare sedes mirum fuerit, sive mutationem prohibeat Saturnus in Aquario nobis ascendens, quod forte iudicabit Astrologus, seu . . . mens contemplationi semper intenta quiescere iubeat." It may be useful to explain that by "ascendant" astrologers meant the point of the ecliptic rising above the horizon at a given moment, and also—not quite correctly—the sign of the zodiac in which this point lay. The first thirty grades of the ecliptic (counting from the ascendant point) are the first "place" (*locus*),—often also equated with the relevant zodiacal sign—which signifies "life". The planet located in this first "locus" is therefore the one governing the life of the man in question, and is really "his" star. When, as in Ficino's case, there is the added fact that the ascendant sign is also one of the "houses" of the planet in question (in which the planet in any case exerts its greatest might), then this act of course increases the planet's influence still further.

[45] See also below, pp. 260 sqq. (text).

[46] For Ficino as a practising physician curing melancholy, see A. CORSINI, "Il 'De vita' di Marsilio Ficino", in *Rivista di storia critica delle scienze mediche e naturali*, VOL. X (1919), pp. 5–13. This is based on Johannes Corsius's biography of Ficino edited by A. M. Bandini, Pisa 1773, which tells us, among other things, how much attention Ficino paid to his own and his friends' health, frequently curing them free of charge; melancholy is mentioned in particular: "Sed quod incredibile cumprimis, nonnullos atra bile vexatos medendi solertia non sine omnium stupore curavit, eosque ad pristinam reduxit valetudinem."

1480 he wrote to his great friend, Giovanni Cavalcanti, as follows:

> Nowadays, I do not know, so to say, what I want, or perhaps I do not want what I know, and want what I do not know. The safety ensured you by the benevolence of your Jupiter standing in the sign of the Fish is denied me by the malevolence of my Saturn retrogressing in the sign of the Lion.[47]

But he received an indignant reply.[48] How could he, as a good Christian Platonist, attribute an evil influence to the stars—he who had every cause to venerate "that highest star" as a good planet?

> Did he not regard you, when you were born in Florence, under the same aspect as he regarded the divine Plato, when he first saw the light in Athens?[49]

---

[47] *Opera omnia*, Basle 1576, VOL. I, pp. 731 (misprinted as 631) sq.; "Ego autem his temporibus quid velim quodammodo nescio. Forte et quod scio nolim, et quod nescio volo. Veruntamen opinor tibi nunc Jovis tui in Piscibus directi benignitate constare, quae mihi Saturni mei his diebus in Leone retrogradi malignitate non constant. Sed quod frequenter praedicare solemus in omnibus agendae illi gratiae sunt, qui infinita bonitate sua omnia convertit in bonum." This conclusion bringing the whole of astrological paganism into harmony with Christian faith is typical of Ficino and his epoch.

[48] *Opera*, p. 732. The translation given here, as elsewhere, is free and considerably abridged. The text runs as follows: "Nunquam ergo mihi amplius, mi Marsili, insimulabis malignitatem Saturni. Nullum Hercle malum facere nobis possunt astra, nequeunt, inquam, nolunt. Velle autem et posse est idem apud superos. Qua ratione autem nos summi boni filios laederent? Cum aliis, qui a summo bono solum originem suam trahunt, ducantur. Atque ea omnino secundum boni ipsius rationem felicissimae illae mentes circumagant. Si tantum quantum videmus et sciunt, qui experti sunt, suos diligit filios secundus et terrestris pater, qui comparatione coelestis Patris, vix dicendus est pater, quantum nos primum et verum Patrem putemus amare? Mirum in modum certe. Nunquam igitur laedemur ab iis, qui convivunt in prospera domo Patris nostri. Cave igitur posthac transferas culpam tuam ad supremum illud astrum, quod te forte innumeris atque maximis beneficiis accumulatum reddidit. Sed ne in singula frustra enumerare coner, nonne te missum ad florentem urbem ornandam, iam per te florentissimam effectam, volui<t> eodem aspicere aspectu, quo divum Platonem aspexit ad Athenas illustrandas euntem? Responde mihi quaeso, unde admirandum ingenium, quo quid si<t> Saturnus intelligis, quod triginta annis suum iter peragat cognoscis, quosve effectus in terris hoc in loco vel illo collocatus producat, non ignoras. Age, dic mihi, unde robustum illud et validum corpus, quo per devios et indomitos saltus universam Graeciam peragrasti, atque in Aegyptum usque penetrasti, ad nos sapientissimos illos senes super tuos humeros allaturus! Audax certe facinus! Pro quo tantum tibi posteri debebunt, quantum solvere difficile erit. Haud te tuum fefellit incoeptum. Tulisti certe eos, quos attingere est nemo, atque Occidentalibus regionibus ostendisti, quorum tantum prius nomina acceperant, eaque tamen magnopere venerabuntur atque ab eis omnem obscuritatem quae circa eos erat, amovisti nostrosque oculos ab omni caligine abstersisti, ita ut etiam cor eorum inspici possit, nisi penitus lippi simus. Denique per te eos inspexit haec aetas, quos nunquam viderat Italia. Haec omnia tibi ab eodem donata sunt. Ad hoc etiam te respondere velim, unde memoria illa tot rerum capacissima, quae adeo tenacissima est, ut quolibet momento sibi omnia adsint quae unquam vidisti aut audisti, nec tantum res tenet, sed quibus eae gestae sunt, meminit temporum atque locorum. Tu ne ergo Saturnum incusabis, qui te tantum ceteros homines superare voluit, quantum ipse ceteros planetas superat. Itaque opus, mihi crede, est palinodia, quam si sapis, quam primum canes."

[49] Cf. the letter to Pico della Mirandola (*Opera*, p. 888): "Sed nonne et magnum aliquid fore decrevit Platonicorum documentorum copulam ab initio supernus ille Saturnus in natali utriusque figura dominus? Dominus et in figura Platonis . . . ." Ficino gives Plato's alleged horoscope in the long letter to Francesco Bandino (*Opera*, p. 763).

. . . . Who gave you the strength to travel through Greece and reach even the land of the Egyptians in order to bring back to us the wisdom of that ancient people? Whence have you that comprehensive memory, in which all things are present in correct time and place? All these things are gifts from Saturn. Therefore, do not complain of him, seeing that he raised you as high above other men as he himself is above the other planets. There is urgent need, believe me, of a palinode, and if you are wise you will sing one as soon as possible.

Marsilio Ficino did sing a palinode. His answer was already a recantation:

Because of that excessive timidity, which you occasionally charge me with, I complain of my melancholy temperament, for to me it seems a very bitter thing, and one that I can only ease and sweeten a little by much lute-playing[!]; . . . Saturn methinks gave it me from the beginning, when in my horoscope he stood in the ascendant in the sign of the Water-Bearer . . . but where have I landed myself? I can see already that you will once more, with some justice, oblige me to embark on a new palinode on Saturn. So what shall I do? I will try to find a way out, and either I will say that melancholy, if you must have it so, does not come from Saturn; or else, if it necessarily comes from him, then I will agree with Aristotle, who described it as a unique and divine gift.[50]

A few years later there appeared the three books *De vita triplici*, on the therapy and symptoms of the Saturnine character.[51]

---

[50] *Opera*, p. 732: "Iubes, mi Ioannes, ut Saturno, de quo superioribus diebus valde quaerebar, palinodiam canam. Et iustissime quidem: nemo enim iubet iustius, quam qui iusta iubens facit ipse, quae iubet . . . . Palinodia igitur Marsilio tuo fuerit epistola tua, in qua laudes illas in eum tuas hac conditione libenter accipit, ut partim ardentissimo amori in eum tuo attribuantur, partim vero Saturni muneribus. Amoris autem, atque Saturni, et denique omnium laudes omnes referantur in Deum, principium omnium atque finem. [Cf. the concluding passage of the letter quoted above, p. 257, note 47.] . . . quod vero circa mala nimis formidolosus sum, quod interdum in me reprehendis, complexionem quandam accuso melancholiam, rem, ut mihi quidem videtur, amarissimam, nisi frequenti usu citharae nobis quodam modo delinita dulcesceret. Quam mihi ab initio videtur impressisse Saturnus in medio ferme Aquario ascendente meo constitutus, et in Aquario eodem recipiens Martem, et Lunam in Capricorno, atque aspiciens ex quadratura Solem Mercuriumque in Scorpio, novam coeli plagam occupantes. Huic forte nonnihil ad naturam melancholiam restiterunt Venus in Libra, Iupiterque in Cancro. Sed quonam temere prolapsus sum? Coges me video rursus non iniuria palinodiam alteram cantare Saturno! Quid igitur faciam? Equidem tergiversabor, ac dicam, vel naturam eiusmodi [sc. melancholicam], si vis, ab illo non proficisci, vel si ab illo proficisci necessarium fuerit, Aristoteli assentiar, hanc ipsam singulare divinumque donum esse dicenti."

[51] This correspondence between Ficino and Cavalcanti cannot be dated with absolute certainty, but as it was printed in Book III of the *Epistolae*, among many letters dated 1474 and 1476 (only the missive to King Matthias of Hungary at the beginning of the book, which occupies a position of its own, bears the date 1480), while the remaining letters of 1480 do not appear until Book VI, and letters after 1480 not until Book VII to XII, it is likely to date from the mid-seventies. The first book of the *De vita triplici*, however, was completed in 1482, the second and third not till 1489 (cf. W. KAHL, *Neue Jahrbücher für das klassische Altertum, Geschichte und deutsche Literatur und für Pädagogik*, VOL. IX, 1906, p. 490). Even the chapters in Book II devoted to the prolongation of life—and therefore, in particular, to dietetics for

In this remarkable work, which embraces all the tendencies which we have hitherto been able to follow only one by one, Ficino chooses the second of the two ways open to him. Melancholy comes from Saturn, but is in fact a "unique and divine gift", even as Saturn is now not only the mightiest star, but also the noblest.[52] As far as we know, Ficino was the first writer to identify what 'Aristotle' had called the melancholy of intellectually outstanding men with Plato's "divine frenzy".[53] It was the black bile which

> obliges thought to penetrate and explore the centre of its objects, because the black bile is itself akin to the centre of the earth. Likewise it raises thought to the comprehension of the highest, because it corresponds to the highest of the planets.

Hence also those thinkers who indulge in the deepest speculation and contemplation suffer most from melancholy.[54] "Planetarum altissimus", Saturn "investigantem evehit ad altissima", and produces those outstanding philosophers whose minds are so far withdrawn from outward stimuli, and even from their own bodies, and so much drawn towards all that is transcendental, that they

---

old men—fit into the subject of the *De vita triplici* as a system of dietetics for, and a phenomenology of, the Saturnine type. For, according to Ficino, old men, because of their age, are as much under Saturn's dominion as the "studiosi" because of their disposition and occupation; and even in his macrobiotic statements he is thinking primarily of scholars: "Desiderant post haec literati non tantum bene quandoque vivere, sed etiam bene valentes diu vivere."

[52] FICINO, *De v. tripl.*, III, 22 (*Opera*, p. 565): "Tu vero potestatem Saturni ne negligas. Hunc enim ferunt Arabes omnium potentissimum . . . . Est enim ipse inter Planetas orbis amplissimi caput". See also the letter to Archbishop Rainald of Florence, quoted below, p. 271, note 100.

[53] FICINO, *De v. tripl.*, I, 5 (*Opera*, p. 497): "Hactenus quam ob causam Musarum sacerdotes melancholici, vel sint ab initio, vel studio fiant, rationibus primo coelestibus, secundo naturalibus, tertio humanis, ostendisse sit satis. Quod quidem confirmat in libro Problematum Aristoteles. Omnes enim, inquit, viros in quavis facultate praestantes melancholicos extitisse. Qua in re Platonicum illud, quod in libro de Scientia scribitur, confirmavit, ingeniosos videlicet plurimum concitatos furiososque esse solere. Democritus quoque nullos, inquit, viros ingenio magnos, praeter illos, qui furore quodam perciti sunt, esse unquam posse. Quod quidem Plato noster in Phaedro probare videtur, dicens poeticas fores frustra absque furore pulsari. Etsi divinum furorem hic forte intelligi vult, tamen neque furor eiusmodi apud Physicos, aliis unquam ullis praeterquam melancholicis incitatur." See also the following note.

[54] FICINO, *De v. tripl.*, I, 4 (*Opera*, p. 497): "Maxime vero literatorum omnium, hi atra bile premuntur, qui sedulo philosophiae studio dediti, mentem a corpore rebusque corporeis sevocant, incorporeisque coniungunt, tum quia difficilius admodum opus maiori quoque indiget mentis intentione, tum quia quatenus mentem incorporeae veritati coniungunt, eatenus a corpore disiungere compelluntur. Hinc corpus eorum nonnunquam, quasi semianimum redditur atque melancholicum. Quod quidem Plato noster in Timaeo significat, dicens: animum divina saepissime, et intensissime contemplantem, alimentis eiusmodi adeo adolescere, potentemque evadere, ut corpus suum supra quam natura corporis patiatur exuperet . . . ."

finally become instruments of things divine.[55] It is Saturn who leads the mind to the contemplation of higher and more hidden matters,[56] and he himself, as Ficino says in more than one place, signifies "divine contemplation".[57]

But Ficino was too much bound up with the established doctrines of medicine and astrology, and had suffered too much

---

[55] Ficino, *De v. tripl.*, I, 6 (*Opera*, p. 498). See quotation in following note.

[56] Ficino, *De v. tripl.*, III, 9 (*Opera*, p. 546, misprint for 545): "Unde ad secretiora et altiora contemplanda conducit." Cf. also III, 24 (*Opera*, p. 568): "Sed qui ad secretissima quaeque curiosius perscrutanda penitus instigatur, sciat se non Mercurialem solum esse, sed Saturnium." As to this latter statement, we may note that Mercury himself—as the Ἑρμῆς λόγιος, identified with the Egyptian Thot and the Babylonian god of scribes, Nebu—had first claim to the patronage of intellectual professions; Vettius Valens (*Anthologiarum libri*, ed. W. Kroll, Berlin 1908, II, 16, p. 74) places geometry as well as philosophy under his care. Neither did Ficino wish to go against the principle that the common nature of all men gifted for the sciences was Mercurial. "Quoniam vero de literarum studiosis loquor, recordari unumquemque volo literarum amore captum inprimis se esse Mercurialem . . . . Atque haec communis his omnibus est conditio." But, within this general assumption, the various types of "viri literati" can be differentiated; thus the pleasant and witty, or dignified and amiable, orator should acknowledge, beside Mercury, Apollo and Venus as his patrons; a man engaged in law or "naturalis communisque philosophia" should acknowledge Jupiter beside Mercury; while—and this is the important point—the thinker rising to the greatest heights and plumbing the greatest depths "sciat se non Mercurialem solum esse, sed Saturnium." Ficino's interest and sympathy, however, is really limited to this Saturnine type of scholar, and moreover he recognises a particularly close relationship between Saturn and Mercury, since the latter too, thanks to his dry nature, corresponds to the black bile (cf. Ficino, *De v. tripl.*, I, 4 and I, 6 (*Opera*, pp. 496 and 498); also Clementius Clementinus, *Lucubrationes*, Basle 1535, p. 15: "Splenque bilem gignit, moestis Mercurius atram"). Mercury too, like Saturn, signified philosophy (letter to Bindacius Recasolanus, *Opera*, p. 943) and, according to Plato, resembled Saturn more than any other planet in light and colouring (letter to Filippo Carducci, *Opera*, pp. 948–949; cf. also the letters to Bernardo Bembo, *Opera*, p. 798, and to Niccolò Valori, *Opera*, p. 952). Thus in the end the Mercurial character gives way completely to the Saturnine in the general picture of the "ingeniosus", and the notion of Mercury is, as it were, absorbed by the notion of Saturn; cf. for instance the characteristic passage in Ficino, *De v. tripl.*, I, 6 (*Opera*, p. 498), which first mentions Saturn and Mercury together, but then refers to Saturn alone: "Congruit insuper [sc. atra bilis] cum Mercurio atque Saturno, quorum alter omnium planetarum altissimus, investigantem evehit ad altissima. Hinc philosophi singulares evadunt, praesertim cum animus sic ab externis motibus, atque corpore proprio sevocatus, et quam proximus divinis, divinorum instrumentum efficiatur. Unde divinis influxibus, oraculisque ex alto repletus nova quaedam inusitataque semper excogitat et futura praedicit."

[57] See the letter to the scholar, Jacopo Antiquario (*Opera*, p. 860): "Sane Platonici, cum animam in tres praecipue distinguant vires, intelligendi videlicet et irascendi atque concupiscendi, primam partiuntur in duas, scilicet in mentem, vel contemplationi vel actioni praecipue deditam. Mentem quidem contemplatricem nomine Saturni significant, mentem vero actionibus occupatam nominant Iovem," etc. Cf. also Ficino, *De v. tripl.*, III, 22 (*Opera*, p. 565), "qui ad divinam contemplationem ab ipso Saturno significatam . . . se conferunt." His sources were of course the Neoplatonists, Plotinus, Macrobius, and, above all, Proclus, whose remarkable influence on the views of Italian humanism is becoming ever more apparent. The general acceptance of this view among Florentine humanists can be seen, for instance, from Cristoforo Landino's *Camaldulensium disputationum libri quattuor* (Strasbourg edn. 1508, fol. K ii^r) or Pico della Mirandola, *Opere di Girolamo Benivieni . . . col Commento dello Ill. S. Conte Gio. Pico Mirandolano*, Venice 1522, I, ch. 7—both referring to the journeyings of the soul in the manner of Macrobius and Proclus.

from his own experience of the bitterness of melancholy and the malevolence of Saturn,[58] to rest content with these praises. The remarks just quoted come from the very books *De vita triplici* in which the extremity of the melancholy humour, and the dangerous bipolarity of Saturn,[59] are so clearly delineated; and the express purpose of his undertaking was to show the Saturnine man some possibility of escaping the baneful influence of his temperament (and its celestial patron), and of enjoying its benefits.[60] Ficino is convinced that not only are children of Saturn qualified for intellectual work but that, vice versa, intellectual work reacts on men and places them under the dominion of Saturn, creating a sort of selective affinity[61] between them:

> Always remember that already by the inclinations and desires of our mind and by the mere capacity of our "spiritus" we can come easily and rapidly under the influence of those stars which denote these inclinations, desires and capacities; hence, by withdrawal from earthly things, by leisure, solitude, constancy, esoteric theology and philosophy, by superstition, magic, agriculture, and grief, we come under the influence of Saturn.[62]

Thus all "studiosi" are predestined to melancholy and subject to Saturn; if not by their horoscope, then by their activity. Obviously, it is only "melancholia naturalis" which can be a

---

[58] Beside the correspondence with Cavalcanti, quoted above, and several passages from the *De vita triplici* (esp. III, 22), cf. esp. the letter to the Archbishop Rainald of Florence (quoted below, p. 271, note 100); the letter to Bernardo Bembo (*Opera*, p. 771) alluding to the "tarditas" of Saturn; the letter to Cardinal Raffael Riario (*Opera*, p. 802: "saevitia Martis atque Saturni"); and, above all, the letter to the Cardinal of Aragon (*Opera*, p. 819): "Duo potissimum inter planetas hominibus assidue pericula machinantur, Mars videlicet et Saturnus."

[59] See above, pp. 33 and 158 sq. (text).

[60] From this alone it is clear that GIEHLOW (1903, p. 36) is not altogether right in interpreting Ficino's main aim as being to harmonise the melancholic's good qualities, as seen by himself and Aristotle, with "the constantly baneful nature of Saturn"; for we have seen how the Neoplatonic notion of Saturn had already won general recognition among Italian humanists.

[61] This notion of elective affinities with the planets, founded on the doctrine of the "concinnity" of certain activities and certain stars, was elsewhere expressed by Ficino in almost exactly the same terms; cf. FICINO, *De v. tripl.*, III, 22 (*Opera*, p. 566): "Expositos, inquam [sc. the souls of men to the influence of heavenly bodies], non tam naturali quodam pacto, quam electione arbitrii liberi, vel affectu." This doctrine for which thinkers like Matteo Palmieri (cf. above, text pp. 251 sqq.) had prepared the way, helped the Renaissance thinkers to bring into harmony astrology and Christian-Neoplatonic ethics. See also FICINO, *De v. tripl.*, III, 12 (*Opera*, p. 548), where " Albertus Magnus in Speculo" is called as main witness for the possibility of such a harmonisation.

[62] This remarkable sentence, which is followed by corresponding statements about the other planets, and which recapitulates in its disparate list the whole confusion of the Saturn complex found in late classical and Arabic writers, comes from FICINO, *De v. tripl.*, III, 2 (*Opera*, p. 534).

danger for the intellectual worker, for "melancholia adusta" can produce only the four well-known forms of weak-wittedness or insanity[63]; but even the former, owing to its instability, is dangerous enough, and Ficino's aim was directed to the practical need of saving the melancholic "literati" from its dangers. *De studiosorum sanitate tuenda, sive eorum, qui literis operam navant, bona valetudine conservanda*: so runs the title of the first of the three books *De vita triplici*. But in the course of development, his work—as so often happens with imaginative writers—goes far beyond its original purpose and intention.[64] It is in itself a remarkable occurrence, and strikingly typical of the spirit of humanism, that, instead of the usual treatises on healthy food and a happy old age, a special work should be written on the health and expectation of life of "viri literati". But what became of this collection of rules of health "for the use of scholars" in Ficino's hands was even more remarkable. In the general introduction to the *De vita triplici*, Ficino, son of a well-known physician, and son by spiritual affinity of the elder Cosimo de' Medici (which provided an occasion for constant puns on "Medici" and "medicus") relates how, thanks to his "two fathers", he was consecrated to the two gods of his existence, to Galen, physician of the body, through his real father, and to Plato, physician of the soul, through his spiritual father. He endeavoured to pay homage to the latter by his commentary on Plato and the eight books of *De immortalitate animarum*, and to the former by the work now under consideration. But in truth even the *De vita triplici* burnt incense at both altars. It expanded and deepened into something which might be ranked with the *Theologia Platonica* as a *Medicina Platonica*, or else, in the words of a somewhat later author, as a "speculum medicinale platonicum".[65] The statements of medical and scientific authorities were constantly compared and measured against the sacrosanct doctrines of Plato and the Platonists—from Hippocrates, Aristotle, and Galen, down to

---

[63] Even the chapter-heading of FICINO, *De v. tripl.*, I, 4, is significant enough: "Quot sint causae, quibus literati melancholici sint, vel fiant."

[64] As mentioned above, p. 258, note 51, there is a lapse of some seven years between the more or less practical dietetics of Book I and the more and more metaphysical and cosmological viewpoint of the succeeding volumes.

[65] Thus SYMPHORIANUS CHAMPERIUS, in the title of his *Symphonia Platonis cum Aristotele, et Galeni cum Hippocrate*; cf. WILLIAM OSLER, *Thomas Linacre*, Cambridge 1908, p. 23. The amusing woodcut on the title-page (Osler, op. cit., plate III) shows the four great men playing a string quartet.

Constantinus Africanus, Avicenna, Pietro d'Abano, and the remarkable Arnaldus de Villanova, who somewhat resembled Ficino in his many-sidedness, and whose work *De conservanda iuventute* was to some extent the pre-humanist forerunner of the *De vita triplici*.[66] Furthermore, the whole of the third book is based, as the author himself admits, on the *Liber de favore coelitus hauriendo* of Plotinus.[67] But, above all, the whole undertaking turned into nothing less than an heroic attempt to reconcile the whole of school medicine, including astrological and purely magical remedies, with Neoplatonism; and, indeed, not only with Neoplatonic cosmology, but—what was considerably harder—with Neoplatonic ethics, which fundamentally denied belief in astrology and magic. This reconciliation was to be no mere outward harmonisation. Rather it was to be an organic synthesis which should not deny the barrier between the realms of freedom and necessity, but should establish it at a significant point. This was made possible by the principle of the series,[68] which Ficino appears to have discovered mainly from a fragment of Proclus known until recently only by his translation.[69]

In accordance with the Platonic and Neoplatonic doctrine, Ficino conceives the cosmos as a completely unified organism,[70] and defends himself hotly against those who see life in the most

---

[66] For ARNALDUS DE VILLANOVA (1234–1311), who, "standing outside the university guild, prepared the way by his medical and chemical labours for a renaissance of medicine" (he was also a prophet, politician, social critic, diplomat, theologian and "clericus uxoratus"), cf. K. BURDACH, *Briefw. des Cola di Rienzo* (*Vom Mittelalter zur Reformation*, II, 1), Berlin 1913, p. 146, with substantial bibliography. His *De conservanda iuventute*, a work of fundamental importance for Ficino, derives, according to E. WITHINGTON (*Roger Bacon. Commemorative Essays*, ed. A. G. Little, Oxford 1914, p. 353), from Roger Bacon.

[67] Cf. the prooemium to Book III. The strange Latin title quoted here by Ficino refers to *Enneads*, IV, 4 (Περὶ ψυχῆς ἀποριῶν B, 30–45) and *Enneads*, II, 3 (Περὶ τοῦ εἰ ποιεῖ τὰ ἄστρα). The difference between Ficino and Plotinus, however, lies in the fact that the latter holds this theory only hypothetically. (Even if all that were so—i.e. even if, as the Stoics believe, all earthly things were determined by cosmic influence—man would still be free to turn to the Ἕν). In fact Plotinus, whom Ficino uses to reconcile free will with iatromathematics, and, even, in a certain sense, astrology, was quoted by the most convinced opponents of astrology as the ancient philosopher who "illius vanitatem falsitatemque deprehendens tandem, eam merito irrisit" (HIERONYMUS SAVONAROLA, *Adversus divinatricem astronomiam*, II, 1, p. 56 in the Florentine edn. of 1581).

[68] See above, pp. 151 sqq. (text).

[69] *De sacrificio et magia*; Ficino's translation edited by W. Kroll, *Analecta graeca*, Wissenschaftliche Beilage zum Vorlesungsverzeichnis der Universität Greifswald, Easter 1901, pp. 6 sqq.; the Greek original was discovered and published by J. Bidez in *Catalogue des manuscrits grecs*, VOL. VI, *Michel Psellus* (Brussels 1928), with an Appendix entitled *Proclus sur l'art hiératique*, Περὶ τῆς κατ' Ἕλληνας ἱερατικῆς τέχνης, pp. 148 sqq.

[70] FICINO, *De v. tripl.*, III, 2 (*Opera*, p. 534); cf. PLATO, *Timaeus*, 30b.

despised creature and lowest plant but refuse to recognise it in the sky and in the cosmos, this "living being".[71] Hence, again still in accordance with 'Platonism', he sees the earthly and heavenly worlds linked by a constant interchange of forces, going far beyond mere correspondences, emanating, through the "rays" or "influences", from the stars[72]:

> Heaven, the bridegroom of Earth, does not touch her, as is commonly thought, nor does he embrace her; he regards [or illuminates?] her by the mere rays of his stars, which are, as it were, his eyes; and in regarding her he fructifies her and so begets life.[73]

Thus all living things and beings in the world are in a peculiar way saturated with the "qualities" of the stars, in which the life force of the universe is concentrated in the same way as that of a man is concentrated in his eyes[74]; nutmeg contains the quality of the sun's rays, peppermint the combined qualities of the sun and of Jupiter.[75] Yet not only inorganic and unconscious things, whose properties are conditioned by the fact that they more or less passively (though for that reason more directly) partake in the "common life of all", but also beings that are alive in the higher sense are connected with the stars, and determined by the universal forces concentrated and differentiated in them. In the latter case, however, the influence of the general cosmic forces has to deal with an individual consciousness, and in man, owing to the special structure of his physical and psychological constitution, an exactly definable limit is set to the scope of the determining power.

As represented by—among others—Nicholas of Cusa and Pico della Mirandola,[76] the anthropological theory held during the Renaissance was that the two basic components of man's nature, "corpus" and "anima", were connected by a third element described as the "medium", the "vinculum", or the "copula",

[71] *Apologia* (*Opera*, p. 573).

[72] This doctrine is developed in Book III of the *De vita triplici*.

[73] *Apologia* (*Opera*, p. 574).

[74] Ficino, *De v. tripl.*, III, 11 (*Opera*, p. 544).

[75] Ficino, *De v. tripl.*, II, 13 (*Opera*, p. 519). The idea that earthly things were to some extent reservoirs for stellar forces and could therefore be used—even in the form of amulets—as instruments of entirely permissible "natural" magic, is already found in Roger Bacon (*Opus Maius*, ed. J. H. Bridges, Oxford 1897, vol. I, pp. 395 sqq., quoted by Wedel, M. A. A., pp. 72 sqq.), whose ideas in this respect come astonishingly close to Ficino's.

[76] Cf. Pico della Mirandola, *Heptaplus*, IV, I (*Opera*, Basle 1572, p. 30). With this, cf. also A. Stöckl, *Geschichte der Philosophie des Mittelalters*, vol. III, Mainz 1866, pp. 71, 176.

between the other two. This was the "spiritus", which was regarded as a highly subtle fluid generated by, or even contained in, the blood, but working only in the brain.[77] Ficino also naturally believed in the "spiritus", which, in accordance with its position between "physis" and "psyche", could influence either part; and since the division of human nature into body, soul and "spiritus humanus" corresponded to a similar division of the universe into universal matter, universal mind and "spiritus mundanus", he imagined the influence of the stars upon men to be of the following kind.

The stars send out rays which confer astral qualities on the "spiritus mundanus" which then passes them on to its counterpart, namely the "spiritus humanus"; the latter, thanks to its central position, can pass them on to both body and soul. These now in their turn—according to the principle of structural "concinnitas" which was the central tenet not only of primitive magic but also of any cosmology based on something other than mechanical causality—were determined by astral qualities. For body and soul either "corresponded" to them from the beginning or else had attuned themselves by special measures. The soul, however—and this is the important consideration—was not quite subordinate to these influences. According to the doctrine held by Ficino, the soul possessed three distinct faculties forming a hierarchically ordered whole: the "imaginatio" or imagination, "ratio" or discursive reason, and "mens" or intuitive reason.[78] Only man's lower

---

[77] FICINO, *De v. tripl.*, III, 11 (*Opera*, p. 544: a characteristic sentence is quoted below, p. 269, note 94). Cf. also the whole of ch. III, 22 (*Opera*, pp. 565 sqq.). For the "spiritus humanus" cf. I, 2 (*Opera*, p. 496): "Instrumentum eiusmodi spiritus ipse est, qui apud medicos vapor quidam sanguinis, purus, subtilis, calidus, et lucidus definitur. Atque ab ipso cordis calore, ex subtiliori sanguine procreatus volat ad cerebrum, ibique animus ipso ad sensus tam interiores, quam exteriores exercendos assidue utitur. Quamobrem sanguis spiritui servit, spiritus sensibus, sensus denique rationi."

[78] This tripartite division, born of a fusion of Platonic and Stoic doctrines, is distinguished from the more or less topographical division of the mental faculties within the brain, "imaginatio", "ratio" and "memoria" (see above, text pp. 91 sqq.), mainly by the fact that "mens" appears in place of "memoria", which results in a rising scale of values in the faculties (see also below, text pp. 350 sqq.). The earliest and most important instance seems to occur in BOETHIUS, *De consolatione Philosophiae*, V, 4 (MIGNE, P. L., VOL. LXIII, col. 849), who includes, however, the "sensus" standing below the "imaginatio" (between the latter and the purely material body a "spiritus" was later assumed), and calls the highest faculty not "mens" but "intelligentia": "Ipsum quoque hominem aliter sensus, aliter imaginatio, aliter ratio, aliter intelligentia contuetur. Sensus enim figuram in subiecta materia constitutam, imaginatio vero solam sine materia iudicat figuram. Ratio vero hanc quoque transcendit speciemque ipsam, quae singularibus inest, universali consideratione perpendit. Intelligentiae vero celsior oculus existit. Supergressa namque universitatis ambitum, ipsam illam simplicem formam pura mentis acie contuetur." After PSEUDO-AUGUSTINUS, *De spiritu*

faculties were to a certain extent subject to the influence of the astral qualities; the faculties of the soul, especially the "mens", were essentially free.

Out of this construction, magnificent of its kind, Ficino evolved a system in which the whole method of traditional therapy could be included—all methods of treatment from sober dietetic prescriptions to the superstitious practices of astral medicine or "iatromathematics" (which had already begun to play a role in the writings of Pietro d'Abano, Arnaldus de Villanova and, especially, in those of Ficino's elder contemporary, Antonio Guainerio).[79] They all were now endowed with a single cosmological significance, and hence with metaphysical justification. It was a system which found room not only for the spells and amulets of late Hellenistic and Arabic conjuring books, but also for free will and freedom of thought; hence it fulfilled the ethical and philosophic needs of the "Philosophus Platonicus et Theologus" just as well as those of the hypersensitive, the introspective or the superstitious.

Corresponding to the three kinds of cause which predisposed the highly gifted to melancholy,[80] the remedies against the disease which Ficino put forward are of three categories. First dietetics, mainly based on the well-tested prescriptions of Arabian and

---

et anima (MIGNE, P. L., VOL. XL, col. 782), "intelligentia" was frequently split into "intelligence" in the narrower sense, and "intellect"; cf. ISAAC DE STELLA (d. 1169), *Epistula de anima* (MIGNE, P. L., VOL. CXCIV, cols. 1180 sqq.); ALANUS AB INSULIS (d. 1202), *Contra haereticos*, I, 28 (MIGNE, P. L., VOL. CCX, col. 330); ALANUS AB INSULIS, *Distinctiones dictionum theologicalium* (MIGNE, P. L., VOL. CCX, cols. 922B, 819D; DOMINICUS GUNDISSALINUS (*c.* 1150), *De processione mundi* (ed. G. Bülow, *C. Baeumkers Beiträge zur Geschichte der Philosophie des Mittelalters*, VOL. XXIV, 3, 1925, p. 259).

[79] Cf. K. SUDHOFF, *Iatromathematiker, vornehmlich im* 15. *und* 16. *Jahrhundert* (Abhandlungen zur Geschichte der Medizin, VOL. II), Breslau 1902, loc. cit.

[80] FICINO, *De v. tripl.*, I, 4 (*Opera*, p. 496): "Ut autem literati sint melancholici, tres potissimum causarum species faciunt, prima coelestis, secunda naturalis, tertia est humana . . . ." The celestial cause lies in the influence of the cold and dry planet Mercury, and, especially, of Saturn. The natural cause lies in the fact that the searching mind concentrates, as it were, inwards ("tanquam a circumferentia quadam ad centrum sese recipere, atque, dum speculatur, in ipso . . . hominis centro stabilissime permanere"), and is therefore analogous to earth ("ad centrum vero a circumferentia se colligere, figique in centro, maxime terrae ipsius est proprium"), which in its turn is related to the black bile; while the black bile, again, "mundi centro similis, ad centrum rerum singularum cogit investigandum, evehitque ad altissima quaeque comprehendenda, quandoquidem cum Saturno maxime congruit altissimo planetarum. Contemplatio quoque ipsa vicissim assidua quadam collectione, et quasi compressione naturam atrae bili persimilem contrahit." Finally, the human cause lies in the purely physiological consequences of the life led by the scholar—drying up of the brain, thickening of the blood, poor digestion, etc.

Salernitan physicians; they were: avoidance of all intemperance,[81] reasonable division of the day,[82] suitable dwelling-place[83] and nourishment,[84] walking,[85] proper digestion,[86] massage of head and body,[87] and, above all, music.[88] Next, medicaments, principally prepared from plants of all kinds, to which may be added fragrant inhalations.[89] Finally, the astral magic of talismans, which evoked the influence of the stars and ensured their most concentrated effect.[90]

The system just described was to be nothing short of epoch-making for medical and scientific thought, especially in the north; without it, for instance, the thought of Paracelsus could never have emerged.[91] But in it, the threefold division into dietetic,

---

[81] FICINO, *De v. tripl.*, I, 3 (*Opera*, p. 496) and, in greater detail, I, 7 (*Opera*, p. 499 sq.). The way to truth and wisdom is "terra marique" beset with peril: "mari," the two mucilaginous humours, "phlegma sive pituita" and "noxia melancholia" lurk like Scylla and Charybdis; "terra," there lower, like three monsters, Venus, Bacchus and Ceres, and finally "dusky Hecate". In less allegorical terms, the intellectual worker must avoid the pleasures of love, excess in eating and drinking, and sleeping until late in the morning. It is remarkable that with regard to "Venerei coitus" the Platonist Ficino departs from the views of the clinicians—to which, in this respect, even Hildegard of Bingen subscribed—and associates himself with the ascetic advice given by authors of a monastic and theological tendency (see above, text p. 77 and *passim*).

[82] FICINO, *De v. tripl.*, I, 7 (*Opera*, p. 500) and I, 8 (*Opera*, p. 501). The day is meant for work, the night for repose; evening or nocturnal work is harmful and unproductive. Therefore the scholar should begin his work of meditation at sunrise, if possible—but not immediately on rising: the first half-hour belongs to "expurgatio"—and continue, with intervals, until noon. The remaining hours of the day are "veteribus alienisque legendis potius, quam novis propiisque excogitandis accommodatae." He should, however, relax once an hour.

[83] FICINO, *De v. tripl.*, I, 9 (*Opera*, p. 501): "Habitatio alta a gravi nubiloque aere remotissima, tum ignis tum calidi odoris usu humiditas expellenda."

[84] FICINO, *De v. tripl.*, I, 10 and 11 (*Opera*, pp. 501 sqq.). Here, Ficino's agreement with school medicine appears particularly clearly; he brought little of his own to the usual prescriptions for eating and drinking (cf. also FICINO, *De v. tripl.*, II, 6 and 7; *Opera*, pp. 513 sqq.).

[85] FICINO, *De v. tripl.*, III, 11 (*Opera*, p. 544).

[86] Cf. esp. FICINO, *De v. tripl.*, I, 7 (*Opera*, p. 500) and I, 22 (*Opera*, p. 507), with the special recommendation of oily clysters.

[87] FICINO, *De v. tripl.*, I, 8 (*Opera*, p. 501): "Sed antequam e lecto surgas, perfrica parumper suaviterque palmis corpus totum primo, deinde caput unguibus"; and "Deinde remittes parumper mentis intentionem, atque interim eburneo pectine diligenter et moderate pectes caput a fronte cervicem versus quadragies pectine ducto. Tum cervicem panno asperiori perfrica . . . ."

[88] For quotations, see above, p. 85 and below, p. 268 (text) and note 93.

[89] FICINO, *De v. tripl.*, I, 9 (*Opera*, p. 502) to I, 25; also II, 8 (*Opera*, p. 516) to II, 19.

[90] Book III (*Opera*, pp. 531 sqq.) is devoted to their use and application.

[91] FRIEDRICH GUNDOLF's fine book on *Paracelsus* (Berlin 1927, pp. 79 sqq.) does not pay enough attention to this background. If Paracelsus "was serious in endeavouring to fathom this presupposed co-operation between the All and Man," and "strove by means of research

pharmaceutic and iatromathematical methods—a division, incidentally, which differed from the threefold classical partition of medicine only in one respect, the substitution of iatromathematics for surgery[92]—was resolved in a higher unity. In the last resort, Ficino considered that the efficacy even of those remedies which were regarded as purely medical was based on the very same cosmic relationship as that which caused the power of amulets or spells. For him there was no clearly-defined line between what people commonly thought they could distinguish as "natural" and "magic" arts. The effects emanating from earthly things, the healing power of drugs, the varied influences of the scents of plants, the psychological effect of colours, and even the power of music—all these are not in reality to be ascribed to the things themselves, but come merely from the fact that the employment of certain materials, or the practice of certain activities, "exposes" us (to use Ficino's words) to those stars with whose qualities the material in question is saturated, or to whose nature the relevant activity is adjusted.

☞ Quoniam vero coelum est harmonica ratione compositum moveturque harmonice, . . . merito per harmoniam solam non solum homines, sed inferiora haec omnia pro viribus ad capienda coelestia praeparantur. Harmoniam vero capacem superiorum per septem rerum gradus in superioribus distribuimus. Per imagines videlicet (ut putant) harmonice constitutas. Per medicinas sua quadam consonantia temperatas. Per vapores odoresque, simili concinnitate confectos. Per cantus musicos, atque sonos. Ad quorum ordinem vimque referri gestus corporis, saltusque, et tripudia volumus, per imaginationis conceptus, motusque concinnos, per congruas rationis discursiones, per tranquillas mentis contemplationes.[93]

Thus, when physicians heal, they are really practising magic, for by means of the remedies they use they are exposing the body

---

and collation to apply the whole breadth of heavenly and earthly forces to the purposes of medicine", this macrocosmic (as Gundolf would say) view of medicine was by no means reactionary or a reversion to the Middle Ages, but, on the contrary, a Renaissance phenomenon —a reversion to Plato, Plotinus and Proclus as against Galen, the Arabs and the medieval physicians, and it was Ficino's *Medicina Platonica* alone which made such a reversion possible for the northerner—transmitted to him as it was, in the main, by Agrippa of Nettesheim (see below, text pp. 351 sqq.).

[92] According to Celsus, medicine includes dietetics, pharmaceutics, and surgery; cf. H. Sigerist, *Antike Heilkunde*, Munich 1927, p. 31.

[93] Ficino, *De v. tripl.*, III, 22 (*Opera*, p. 564). With regard to music we may also mention chapter III, 2 (*Opera*, p. 534); although music in general belongs to Venus, this should strictly speaking only be the case with joyous music; serious music belongs to the Sun and to Jupiter, and neutral (significantly enough) to Mercury; cf. also Ficino, *De v. tripl.*, III, 11. The general law accounting for the healing effect of music on the human organism—which, of course, is also a cosmic law—is explained in a letter to Antonio Canigiani (*Opera*, pp. 650 sqq.).

and soul of the patient to the corresponding occult astral forces. According to Ficino the real point of a walk in the fresh air, which Constantinus Africanus considered a purely dietetic measure, and which to-day we generally regard as essentially an aesthetic experience, lies in the fact that "the rays of the sun and of the stars reach us from all parts in free and unhindered fashion, and fill our soul with the 'spiritus mundanus' which flows more copiously from these rays."[94] And when, in order to obtain a talisman for a long life, magicians choose the hour of Saturn to engrave a picture of an old man with covered head upon a sapphire,[95] they are after all only employing "natural" arts—that is to say, they are only availing themselves of general cosmic laws in order to effect appropriate results, in much the same way as a peasant changes milk into butter by the deliberate use of mechanical force.[96] From this point of view, Ficino is fully justified in clearly distinguishing between the "natural magic" of those who "suitably submit natural substances to natural causes", and the "unholy magic" of the godless conjurers of demons, and in describing the former as no less harmless and legitimate than medicine or agriculture. "Natural magic" was a "link between astrology and medicine".[97]

---

[94] FICINO, *De v. tripl.*, III, 11 (*Opera*, p. 544): "Inter haec diutissime diurno tempore sub divo versaberis, quatenus tuto vel commode fieri potest [!], in regionibus altis et serenis atque temperatis. Sic enim Solis stellarumque radii expeditius puriusque undique te contingunt, spiritumque tuum complent mundi spiritu per radios uberius emicante." The corresponding prescription in CONSTANTINUS AFRICANUS (*Opera*, Basle 1536, p. 295) is: "Melancholici assuescant ad pedum exercitia aliquantulum, apparente aurora, per loca spatiosa, ac plana, arenosa, et saporosa!"

[95] FICINO, *De v. tripl.*, III, 18 (*Opera*, pp. 556 sqq.): "Saturni veteres imaginem ad vitae longitudinem faciebant in lapide Feyrizech, id est Saphyro, hora Saturni, ipso ascendente atque feliciter constituto. Forma erat: homo senex in altiore cathedra sedens, vel dracone, caput tactus panno quodam lineo fusco, manus supra caput erigens, falcem manu tenens aut pisces, fusca indutus veste." This description is derived from the circle of Picatrix.

[96] Cf. H. RITTER, "Picatrix, ein arabisches Handbuch hellenistischer Magie", in *Vorträge der Bibliothek Warburg*, VOL. I (1921–22), *passim*.

[97] *Apologia* (*Opera*, p. 573): "Denique duo sunt magiae genera. Unum quidem eorum, qui certo quodam cultu daemonas sibi conciliant, quorum opera freti fabricant saepe portenta. Hoc autem penitus explosum est, quando princeps huius mundi eiectus est foras. Alterum vero eorum qui naturales materias opportune causis subiiciunt naturalibus, mira quadam ratione formandas." Of the latter, too, there are two sorts, "magia curiosa," which applies these natural magic powers only to unnecessary, or even harmful, ends, and "magia necessaria," with the aid of which cures are brought about, "cum Astrologia copulans Medicinam." Further: "Quae sane facultas tam concedenda videtur ingeniis legitime utentibus, quam medicina et agricultura iure conceditur, tantoque etiam magis, quanto perfectior est industria terrenis coelestia copulans." Only with regard to figurate talismans ("imagines"), Ficino is obviously not certain whether these do not belong to the realm of demonology; he never fails to qualify his statements concerning them by an "ut putant,"

Such was the view contained in Ficino's system, and while it facilitated the recognition of astrological medicine—and in fact attributed an astrological and magical significance to all therapeutic measures—at the same time, it strictly denied astrology the power of determining man's thoughts and actions. Astrological prognostications were regarded as valuable only in so far as the recognition of the constellation at birth, or of the "daemon geniturae", showed the way to iatromathematical treatment of each individual case.[98] Man as an active and thinking being was fundamentally free, and could even, thanks to this freedom, harness the forces of the stars by consciously and willingly exposing himself to the influence of a certain star; he could call such an influence down upon himself not only by employing the manifold outward means, but also (more effectually) by a sort of psychological autotherapy, a deliberate ordering of his own reason and imagination:

☞ Imaginationis conceptus motusque concinnos, congruas rationis discursiones, tranquillas mentis contemplationes.[99]

Thus Ficino's system—and this was perhaps its greatest achievement—contrived to give Saturn's "immanent contradiction" a

"ut opinantur", or "veteres faciebant" (cf. e.g. the passage quoted above, note 95), and formally safeguards himself several times against the views put forward being considered his own discoveries, or even his own serious opinion. Thus, too, in the *Apologia*, loc. cit.: ". . . curiosis ingeniis respondeto, magiam vel imagines non probari quidem a Marsilio, sed narrari"; and again in the introduction to Book III: "Denique si non probas imagines astronomicas, alioquin pro valetudine mortalium adinventas, quas et ego non tam probo, quam narro, has utique me concedente ac etiam si vis consulente dimittito" (*Opera*, p. 530). Despite these reservations which clearly do not come entirely from the heart (and which, as Dr Weil kindly points out, are lacking in the Florence, Biblioteca Laurenziana, Cod. plut. LXXIII, 139, being, for obvious reasons, only added in print), Ficino himself made considerable use of figurate amulets.

[98] FICINO, *De v. tripl.*, III, 23 (*Opera*, p. 567): "Nos autem optare praeterita supervacuum arbitrati, monemus easdem plagas, quas illi pro daemonibus fortunisque optabant, observari pro Planetis et stellis ad opus efficiendum accomodandis . . . ."

[99] Cf. the passage quoted p. 268, FICINO, *De v. tripl.*, III, 22. It is understandable that those who attempted to defend astrology in the traditional or "plebeian" (as the Florentine Platonists scornfully said) sense found the Platonist attitude exceedingly vulnerable. These defenders, naturally ignoring the subtleties of Ficino's doctrine of freedom, could even, with some show of justification, maintain that, in fact, the Florentines rated the influence of the stars higher than did the real astrologers, "quia contendunt omnia in coelo fieri, nedum ad corpus sed ad animam pertinentia." The most interesting polemic of this sort, whence the sentence quoted above is taken, comes from a Milanese, GABRIEL PIROVANUS, *De astronomiae veritate opus absolutissimum* (first edn. 1507, reprinted in Basle, 1554, together with a similar apologia by Lucius Bellantius). According to him, when the Platonists state that the planets influence our souls by their emanations, and call Saturn "intelligentiae ducem" who leads them up to the "intellectus primus" and finally to "Ipsum Bonum", they make the planets the mediators between man and God, and that is a heresy such as not even the most ardent professional astrologer would have dared to propagate.

redemptive power: the highly gifted melancholic—who suffered under Saturn, in so far as the latter tormented the body and the lower faculties with grief, fear and depression—might save himself by the very act of turning voluntarily towards that very same Saturn. The melancholic should, in other words, apply himself of his own accord to that activity which is the particular domain of the sublime star of speculation, and which the planet promotes just as powerfully as it hinders and harms the ordinary functions of body and soul—that is to say, to creative contemplation, which takes place in the "mens", and only there. As enemy and oppressor of all life in any way subject to the present world, Saturn generates melancholy; but as the friend and protector of a higher and purely intellectual existence he can also cure it.

Admittedly, the Saturnine melancholic must take every precaution to counteract the astral danger to his health, and in particular must invoke the influence of Jupiter, who was always reckoned as an auspicious planet, and particularly as an aid against Saturn. ("What Saturn doth wrong", as a popular motto said, "Jove righteth ere long".)[100] But in the last resort Ficino considers all these as mere palliatives.[101] Ultimately the Saturnine man can do nothing else—and certainly nothing better—than embrace his fate, and resign himself heart and soul to the will of his star:

Within the soul ("anima") let us assume there are "imaginatio", "ratio" and "mens". "Imaginatio", whether by the nature or movement of the "spiritus", or by choice, or both, can be so attuned to Mars or the Sun that

---

[100] Cf. GIEHLOW (1904), pp. 10 sqq. For the doctrine of Jupiter as "temperator Saturni", see above, pp. 140; 181, note 173. Beside the main passage in FICINO (*De v. tripl.*, III, 22; *Opera*, p. 564) we may also mention III, 12 (*Opera*, p. 547), and (with an allusion to the mythological connexion) a letter to Archbishop Rainald of Florence (*Opera*, p. 726): "Sed deinde in mentem rediit, quod antiqui sapientes non absque summa ratione de Saturno et Iove, Marteque et Venere fabulantur. Martem videlicet a Venere, Saturnum ab Jove ligari. Hoc autem nihil aliud significat, quam quod Saturni Martisque malignitatem, benignitas Jovis Venerisque coercet . . . . In quo autem omnem Iovis effigiem, vim, dotes agnoscam, praeter te in praesentia Florentiae invenio neminem." In this Florentine circle, belief in the stars was often treated with a certain laughing self-irony, which, however, at east as far as Ficino was concerned, concealed the seriousness of the attitude, rather than questioned it. Thus, in an equally elegant, half jesting form we find a reference to ancient mythology in a letter to Matteo da Forlì (*Opera*, p. 861): "Tradunt poetae Iovem Saturno patri quondam imperium abstulisse, ego vero arbitror Martem his temporibus quasi Saturni vindicem sibi Iovis regnum usurpavisse, etenim (ut aiunt Astronomi) religiosi viri ab Iove significantur atque reguntur . . . ." Later, cf. ANTOINE MIZAULD of Montluçon, *Planetologia*, Lyons 1551, pp. 29 sqq., or LEONE EBREO, *Dialoghi d'Amore*, Venice 1541, fol. 90^r: "Ancora Juppiter con Saturno guardandosi con buono aspetto, fa cose diuine, alte, et buone, lontane dalla sensualità; ancora Juppiter fortunato corregge la durezza di Saturno."

[101] FICINO, *De v. tripl.*, II, 16 (*Opera*, p. 523) is very instructive, enjoining caution in employing anti-Saturnine influences; the greatest contrast exists between Saturn and Venus

it can become in very truth a vessel for solar and Martial influences. In the same way, whether through "imaginatio" and the "spiritus", or through "deliberatio", or both, "ratio" by way of a certain imitation can come so to resemble Jupiter that, being more dignified and more akin, it receives more of Jupiter and his gifts than do "imaginatio" or the "spiritus" (as, for the same reason, "imaginatio" and the "spiritus" receive a greater share of celestial gifts than any lower things or materials). Finally, the contemplative "mens", which withdraws itself not only from what we generally perceive but also from what we generally imagine or express in our human customs and which in desire, ambition and life tends towards the ideas, exposes itself in a certain measure to Saturn. To this faculty alone is Saturn propitious. For just as the sun is hostile to nocturnal animals but friendly to those which are active in daylight, so is Saturn an enemy of those men who overtly lead a commonplace life, or who, though they flee the company of vulgar people, yet do not lay aside their vulgar thoughts. For he resigned common life to Jupiter, but retained the sequestered and divine life for himself. Men whose minds are truly withdrawn from the world are, to some extent, his kin and in him they find a friend. For Saturn himself is (to speak in Platonic terms) a Jupiter to those souls who inhabit the sublime spheres, in the same way as Jupiter is a "iuvans pater" to those who lead an ordinary life. He is most inimical of all, however, to those whose contemplative life is a mere pretence and no reality. Saturn will not acknowledge them as his, neither will Jupiter, tamer of Saturn, support them, because they violate the ordinary customs and morals of men. . . . Jupiter arms us against Saturn's influence, which is generally foreign to, and somehow unsuitable for, mankind: firstly, by his natural properties; then, undoubtedly, by his nourishment and medicines, and also, it is believed, by number-talismans; and finally, by the customs, the occupations, the studies, and all things in general which of their nature belong to him. But those who escape the baneful influence of Saturn, and enjoy his benevolent influence, are not only those who flee to Jupiter but also those who give themselves over with heart and soul to divine contemplation, which gains distinction from the example of Saturn himself.[102] Instead

---

but it would be wrong to endeavour to cure a man labouring under Saturn by Venereal means (or, vice versa, a man too much given over to Venus by Saturnine means): "Hinc rursus efficitur ut si quem Saturnia, vel contemplatione nimium occupatum, vel cura pressum, levare interim et aliter consolari velimus, per venereos actus, ludos, iocos [among which, therefore, according to III, 2, excessively gay music must also be reckoned], tentantes tanquam per remedia longe distantia, frustra atque etiam cum iactura conemur. Atque vicissim si quem venereo vel opere perditum, vel ludo iocoque solutum moderari velimus, per Saturni severitatem emendare non facile valeamus. Optima vero disciplina est, per quaedam Phoebi Iovisque, qui inter Saturnum Veneremque sunt medii, studia similiaque remedia homines ad alterutrum declinantes ad medium revocare."

[102] FICINO, *De v. tripl.*, III, 22 (*Opera*, pp. 564 sqq.). KARL BORINSKI (*Die Rätsel Michelangelos*, Munich 1908, p. 36) mentions a parallel passage in Pico della Mirandola: "Saturno . . . significativo della natura intellettuale . . . fa li huomini contemplativi; Giove che è l'anima del mondo . . . da loro principati, governi . . . perchè la vita attiva è circa le cose inferiori." The subtle thought that Saturn did not harm "his own" (exemplified, further on, by the long-lived Indians, who, according to the Arabs, were under Saturn's dominion, became a firm

of earthly life, from which he is himself cut off, Saturn confers heavenly and eternal life on you.[103]

Thus, despite his lingering fear of the sinister ancient demon,[104] Ficino's work finally culminates in a glorification of Saturn. The aged god who had given up dominion for wisdom, and life in Olympus for an existence divided between the highest sphere of heaven and the innermost depths of the earth, eventually became the chief patron of the Platonic Academy at Florence. Just as the "Platonici" made their eponymous hero a child of Saturn, so, within their own circle, there was a smaller circle of "Saturnines", who felt themselves bound not only to one another, but also to the divine Plato, in a very special relationship—a circle which called Lorenzo himself its head[105] and which included men like Lorenzo's physician, Pierleoni,[106] as well as Ficino. Even the

---

part of Ficino's view of Saturn's relationship to "intellectual workers" after the great change which he underwent in the seventies. Beside the passage just quoted, see also the letter to the Cardinal of Aragon (*Opera*, p. 819, the opening sentence of which has already been quoted): "Duo potissimum inter Planetas hominibus assidue pericula machinantur, Mars videlicet et Saturnus. Uterque tamen, sicut vos docet experientia, plerunque parcit suis, Saturniis inquam Saturnus, Mars similiter Martiis, ut plurimum nescit obesse." Cf., on the contrary, JOHN OF SALISBURY, who says: "Omnibus igitur inimicus, vix suis etiam scolasticis parcit" (*Policraticus*, II, 19, Leyden 1595, p. 76; ed. C. C. I. Webb, Oxford 1909, I, 108).

[103] FICINO, *De v. tripl.*, II, 15 (*Opera*, p. 522): "Saturnus autem pro vita terrena, a qua separatus ipse te denique separat, coelestem reddit atque sempiternam."

[104] The late sixteenth-century "Mascherate" and "Intermezzi" still frequently omitted Saturn from the series of planets as an unlucky star, or replaced him by a more harmless figure. In the Florentine State Archives, for instance (Carteggio Universale, fa. 802, c. 463) Dr Bing found a petition addressed to the Grand Duke Ferdinand I by a certain Baccio Bacelli, dated 20 December, 1588, in which he suggests a masque of the planets, "lasciando indietro Saturno, che per essere di mala constellatione non conviene in cose allegre". In the fourth intermezzo of Guarino's *Pastor Fido* all the planets lay down their gifts in an urn, but Saturn is replaced by a less menacing divinity of wisdom, namely Pallas Athena (VITTORIO ROSSI, *Battista Guarini ed il Pastor Fido*, Turin, 1886, p. 312).

[105] Letter to Pico della Mirandola (*Opera*, p. 888 sq.) ". . . Sed nonne et magnum aliquid fore decrevit Platonicorum documentorum copulam ab initio supernus ille Saturnus in natali utriusque dominus. Dominus et in figura Platonis, horum itaque copulam Saturnii daemones praecipue regunt. Sed hanc interea dissolvere passim Martiales daemones machinantur . . . . Tantum denique copula haec destinata . . . adversarios superabit, quanto Saturnus est Marte superior . . . huc tendit (ut arbitror) Laurentius inter Saturnios praestantissimus, et me tuetur, et Picum ad Florentem revocat urbem . . . ."

[106] Letter to Pierleoni (*Opera*, p. 928): "Vide igitur Pierleone mi alter ego, quam similem in plerisque sortem nacti sumus, disciplinae Medicem [this should clearly read "disciplinam medicam"] in coelestibus eundem, ut coniecto, Saturnum, ducem quoque Platonem, Patronum rursus eundem Laurentium Medicem . . . ." Cf. also *Opera*, II, p. 1537 (introduction to the commentary on Plotinus): "Divinitus profecto videtur effectum, ut dum Plato quasi renasceretur, natur Picus heros sub Saturno Aquarium possidente: sub quo et ego similiter anno prius trigesimo natus fueram, ac perveniens Florentiam, quo die Plato noster est editus, antiquum illud de Plotino herois Cosmi votum mihi prorsus occultum, sed sibi coelitus inspiratum, idem et mihi mirabiliter inspiraverit."

fearless Pico della Mirandola, who often smiled at his good teacher's astrological belief in Saturn,[107] was not displeased when, in reference to the constellation that presided over his birth, and with a typically humanistic play upon his name,[108] he heard himself described as a "son of the sublime Saturn"[109]; nor was he displeased when the elegant jest was directed at him that he devoured "libri" as his divine father did "liberi", even though he did not, like the earthly fire, turn them to ashes, but rather, like the heavenly fire, to light.[110]

---

[107] Letter from Pico to Ficino (*Opera*, p. 889): "Salve pater Platonicae familiae! Iam extra omnem controversiam, et noxium atque infaustum esse Saturni sydus, et te, mi Ficini, et si tuo fortasse bono, meo certe malo Saturnium esse natum. Ut enim ille est plurimum regradarius, sic et tu quoque simili praeditus ingenio iam bis ad me veniens regradarius factus bis retro retulisti pedem . . . . Sed dic, amabo, quid fuit in causa iteratae retrocessionis? An tuus Saturnus? An potius saturi nos? Sed quicquid illud fuit, quod te mihi, id est me mihi abstulit, fac, quaeso, in posterum, ut non seiungat nos, qui nos olim coniunxit [for Pico is also a child of Saturn], nec te unquam credas ad me saturum accessurum, qui te, solatium meae vitae, meae mentis delitias, institutorem morum, disciplinae magistrum, et esurio semper et sitio. Vale et veni, ut tuus Saturnus, id est tuus saturus *νοῦς* me quoque saturum reddat."

[108] According to late classical mythology (Ovid, *Met.* XIV, 320), Picus was the son of Saturn, and grandfather of Latinus.

[109] Letter to Pico della Mirandola (*Opera*, p. 901): "Picum sublimis Saturni filium."

[110] Letter to Francesco Gaddi (*Opera*, p. 892): "Picus Saturno natus, ceu Saturnus ille liberos, sic ipse grandes quotidie libros integros devorat, quos quidem non in cinerem redigat, ut noster ignis, sed ut coelestis in lucem."

PART IV

Dürer

CHAPTER I

MELANCHOLY IN CONRAD CELTES

Dürer's Woodcut on the Title-page of Celtes's "Quattuor Libri Amorum" The Doctrine of Temperaments in Dürer's Writings

Ficino's correspondence, whence the facts just set out were taken, was published in 1497 by Dürer's godfather, Koberger, barely three years after the publication, in Florence, of the first edition; and the *De vita triplici* also had become known in Germany by the end of the fifteenth century.[1] But it would be wrong to assume that the new notion of melancholy forthwith gained unchallenged supremacy. It is obvious that, until well on in modern times, the popular notion of the temperaments was conditioned far more by the medical tradition than by the new revolutionary metaphysical theories, which affected popular ideas only gradually, after the views of the Florentine Neoplatonists had become a part of general culture. But even the humanists themselves were held too fast in the grip of traditional humoralism and astrology for the new doctrine to become established without opposition. Even in Italy, where the rehabilitation of Saturn and melancholy really originated, and where men like Gioviano Pontano, Caelius Rhodiginus, and Francesco Giorgio (for the most part making use of Ficino's own words) unreservedly acknowledged the new

---

[1] Cf. W. KAHL, *Neue Jahrbücher für das klassische Altertum, Geschichte und deutsche Literatur und für Pädagogie*, VOL. IX (1906), p. 490, and GIEHLOW (1903), p. 54 (which contains the information that the young Willibald Pirckheimer had to procure a copy of the *De vita triplici* in Padua for his father), and, more recently, H. RUPPRICH, *Willibald Pirckheimer und die erste Reise Dürers nach Italien*, Vienna 1930, pp. 15 sqq. The first, very faulty, translation (by Adelphus Muelich) appeared in HIERONYMUS BRAUNSCHWEIG's *Liber de arte distillandi simplicia et composita, Das Nüw Buch der rechten Kunst zu distillieren*, fols. cxxxxi sqq., Strasbourg 1505, and contains only the first two books, as do the later reprints. As for the third (fol. clxxiv^v): "Vnd das dritte buch sagt von dem leben von himel herab als von hymelischen Dingen zu vberkommen. Das gar hoch zu verston, ist hie vss gelon."

gospel,[2] the idea still persisted that Saturn was a purely inauspicious planet[3] and could engender great talent only if, like a poison, correctly tempered with other planets. In the north especially, where the third book of the *De vita triplici* first seemed "incomprehensible",[4] it was only Agrippa of Nettesheim who fully adopted Ficino's views. The other German humanists of the first generation occasionally quoted 'Aristotle's' Problem XXX, 1,[5] though without special emphasis, or else made the usual concession that Saturn in combination with Jupiter "excellenter ingenium auget et quarundam artium inventorem facit"[6]; but even Conrad Celtes, generally of so humanistic a turn of mind, seems not to have been influenced at all by the Florentine conceptions. With regard to melancholy, he identified himself completely with the customary views of school medicine,[7] and Saturn was for him nothing but a mischief-maker who produced sad, labouring, and "monkish" men, and who had to be implored to let his "morbosas sagittas" lie idle in the quiver.[8]

---

[2] JOVIANUS PONTANUS, *De rebus coelestibus*, IV ,6, pp. 1261 sqq. in *Opera*, Basle 1556, VOL. III; CAELIUS RHODIGINUS, in *Sicuti antiquarum lectionum commentarios concinnarat olim vindex Ceselius, ita nunc eosdem . . . reparavit . . .* , IX, 29, Venice 1516, p. 455; FRANCISCUS GEORGIUS, *Harmonia mundi totius*, Venice 1525, fols. xlvii^v, xlix^v and cxvi^v.

[3] Also in Dürer's own horoscope, cast by the Bamberg canon, Lorenz Beheim, in 1507, Saturn was mentioned only briefly as a disturbing element against the influence of Venus (E. REICKE in *Festschrift des Vereins für Geschichte der Stadt Nürnberg zur 400jährigen Gedächtnisfeier Albrecht Dürers* 1528–1928, Nuremberg 1928, p. 367). Jovianus Pontanus himself gives elsewhere a description of Saturn (*Urania*, lib. I, p. 2907 in VOL. IV of the Basle edition quoted above) which barely differs from that, say, of Chaucer (see above, text pp. 193 sqq.).

[4] See above, p. 277, note 1.

[5] Thus CONRAD PEUTINGER, in his statement, discovered by GIEHLOW (1903), pp. 29 sqq., about a coin from Thasos with Hercules on it. All the same, Peutinger was familiar with the original text of Ficino's *De vita triplici*, as can be proved, and even made practical use of it when a fall had given him a headache. Cf. clm. 4011, fols. 8^r, 27^v, 36^r–37^v, 38^{r-v}, 39^v, 40^r, 41^r.

[6] Thus JOHANNES AB INDAGINE, *Introd. apotelesmat. in Chyromant.*, VI, quoted in GIEHLOW (1904), p. 10. Moreover, he is convinced that Saturn is the "pessimus planeta" and melancholy the "pessima complexio", and that when the melancholic, already equipped with every bad quality, is in addition subject to a particularly strong influence from Saturn, the latter "omnia haec mala conduplicat"! Similarly JOHANN TAISNIER, *Opus mathematicum*, Cologne 1562, p. 532. For Melanchthon's theory of conjunctions, see below, p. 330, note 158.

[7] See the verses by his pupil Longinus at the beginning of the *Libri amorum* (printed in GIEHLOW (1904), p. 7).

[8] Passages in GIEHLOW (1904), pp. 9 sqq. The most bitter is from *Libri amorum*, I, I: "Saturnus, totiens qui mihi damna tulit". Giehlow endeavoured to interpret the fact that Celtes connected old age with knowledge, wisdom and philosophy as evidence of a fairly favourable attitude to melancholy and Saturn, as Saturn was a "senex" and melancholy was the temperament proper to old age. But one is hardly justified in deducing any such fact merely from the natural respect for the wisdom of old age, least of all here, where it contrasts with such unambiguous statements.

If in the north even the humanists either could not break away from the medieval tradition at all, or only gradually and half reluctantly, we must, a priori, expect as much of a German artist like Dürer, the more so as he first came to grips with the problem of the four complexions in a woodcut which served the same Celtes as title-page to his *Libri amorum*, published in 1502 (PLATE 83); and, in fact, the content of this woodcut shows no influence whatsoever of the new doctrine. He uses a scheme of composition which can be traced from the classical pictures of the four winds, as in the *Tabula Bianchini*, via the medieval representations of Christ surrounded by the symbols of the four evangelists,[9] down to the didactic pictures of the later scholastics, a scheme which others before him had used for the four temperaments.[10] Enthroned in the middle, he represents Philosophy, crowned, and (in accordance with Boethius) equipped with a "scala artium".[11] Philosophy is surrounded by a garland composed of sprays of four different types of plant, which are linked by medallions containing busts of philosophers; while the corners of the page are filled by the heads of the four winds. Each of the four winds is carefully differentiated both in age and in character; and (as may be seen both from older sources and from Celtes's text) each symbolises one of the four elements and one of the four temperaments as well as one of the four seasons. Zephyrus, the west wind, whose youthful, idealised head emerges from the clouds, and from whose mouth flowers blossom forth, signifies air, spring, and the "sanguine" man. Eurus, the east wind, a man's head surrounded by flames, signifies fire, summer, and the "choleric" man. Auster, the south wind, represented by a bloated older man, floating amid waves and showers of rain, signifies water, autumn, and the "phlegmatic" man. Finally Boreas, the north wind, a lean, bald-headed old man, signifies earth, winter (hence the icicles), and the "melancholic" man.

---

[9] Cf., on the one hand, philosophical allegories like that reproduced in L. DOREZ, *La canzone delle virtù e delle scienze* . . . , Bergamo 1904, fol. 6[v] (cf. also SAXL, *Verzeichnis*, VOL. II, p. 34); and, on the other hand, cosmological representations in which the heads of the four winds (sometimes already equated with the seasons, elements, etc.) occupy the corners of the picture. See the numerous plates in E. WICKERSHEIMER, *Janus*, VOL. XIX (1914), pp. 157 sqq.; and, further, the picture of *annus* from Zwiefalten (K. LÖFFLER, *Schwäbische Buchmalerei*, Augsburg 1928, plate 22), or Vienna, Nationalbibliothek, Cod. lat. 364, fol. 4[v]; cf. also C. SINGER, *From Magic to Science*, London 1928, pp. 141 sqq.

[10] For further discussion, see below, pp. 370 sqq. (text).

[11] According to BOETHIUS, *De consolatione Philosophiae*, I, I, the scale should rise from *pi* to *theta* (from practice to theory); Dürer has a *phi* instead of the *pi*. Did he think of an ascent from philosophy to theology?

The cosmological schema underlying this woodcut is as old as the schema of its composition, and comparison with the order given, say, by Antiochus of Athens,[12] shows that it has merely been adapted to suit time and place—Boreas and Auster have exchanged their parts. Autumn, cold and dry in the south and hence allocated in classical sources to Boreas, earth, and the black bile, seemed in the north to suit the cold and damp nature of Auster, water, and the phlegm, far better; while winter, in northern countries more frosty than rainy, as in the south (the "hiems aquosa" cf. *Eclogue* X, 1, 66), seemed to correspond to Boreas, earth, and the melancholic.[13] Thus Boreas, in his new position, has become the senior member of the cycle, and for us he is the first evidence of Dürer's notion of the melancholy state. This notion does not differ at all from that of medieval tradition; in the hollow eyes and wrinkled features of this bald, sharp-nosed, lean, old man, there is more of misanthropic peevishness and petty cunning than of sublime sadness and brooding reflexion; and these qualities are contrasted with the well-nourished good-humour of the phlegmatic man, the hot-blooded strength of the choleric, and the youthful freshness of the sanguine, in a manner familiar to us from hundreds of popular texts on the complexions.

☞

Milencolique a triste face,
conuoiteux et plain d'avarice,
l'on ne luy doit demander grace,
a nul bien faire n'est propice,
barat le bailla a nourrisse
a tricherie et a fallace
de bien dire nul temps n'est chiche
mais querez ailleurs qui le face.[14]

It is not surprising that a doctrine of the four temperaments popularised in so many texts, pictures, and verses, should have seemed as obvious and obligatory to a man of the sixteenth century as, say, the pre-Einstein notion of the universe to men of more recent times; and in fact Dürer never expressly repudiated it. Even in the *Four Books of Human Proportion*, after he had

[12] See above, p. 10 (text).

[13] The equation completed in the last "novenarium" gives the textual explanation of this variant: Melancholicus = Earth = Night = North Wind = Cold = Blueish white = Capricorn = Winter = Old Age (cf. Giehlow (1904), pp. 6 sqq.). Apart from this one variant the schema in Dürer's woodcut is still identical with the ancient system such as it is preserved in, say, Munich, MS graec. 287 (*Cat. astr. Gr.*, vii, p. 104).

[14] Paris, Bibl. Nat., MS fr. 19994, fol. 13r. Cf. also the extracts given above, pp. 113 sqq. text).

long been familiar with the notion of melancholy propounded by Florentine Neoplatonism, he characterised the picture of a Saturnine man as "unfaithful" (whereas the child of Venus "should look sweet and gracious")[15]; and his further remarks on the complexions differ little from what could be deduced from any popular notion of the temperaments, namely that the individual differences between men depended, if not entirely, then at least for the most part, on their belonging to one of the four complexions,[16] and that these for their part were equivalent to a "fiery, airy, watery or earthy" nature, and were conditioned by the influence of the planets. Dürer's remarks go beyond the content of the customary texts only in this, that, although he does not omit descriptive and expressive characteristics, yet, in this theory of proportion he subordinates them to characteristics of proportion, and even goes so far as to say that the whole variety of "elementally" and planetarily conditioned differences can be visibly distinguished by mere measurements:

> So if one should come to you and want a treacherous Saturnine picture or a Martial one or one that indicates the child of Venus that should be sweet and gracious, so you should easily know, from the aforementioned teachings, provided you have practised them, what measure and manner you should use for it. For by outward proportions all conditions of men can be described, whether of a fiery, airy, watery or earthy nature. For the power of art, as we have said, masters all things.[17]

After Dürer's second journey to Italy, he drafted the programme for his comprehensive book on painting, embracing far more than perspective and proportion; but even here we need not presuppose acquaintanceship with Ficino's *De vita triplici*, or with the new notion of melancholy. Formerly such an influence was suspected,[18] because Dürer stipulated that in the choice and education of the painters' apprentices, attention should

---

[15] LF, *Nachlass*, p. 228, 28.

[16] The drafts of 1512–13 actually say: "Wir haben mäncherlei Gestalt der Menschen, Ursach der vier Complexen." LF, *Nachlass*, pp. 299, 23; 303, 9; 306, 12).

[17] Thus the printed version of 1528; LF, *Nachlass*, pp. 228, 25 sqq. For this, see the preliminary drafts, certainly also dating from the 'twenties, LF, *Nachlass*, p. 247, 7: "Item, If thou shouldst diligently make use of the thing of which I have written above, then canst thou very easily portray all manner of men, be they of what complexion they will, melancholics, phlegmatics, cholerics or sanguinics. For one can very well make a picture which is a true image of Saturn or Venus, and especially in painting by means of the colours, but also with other things too"; and LF, *Nachlass*, p. 364, 21 (almost identical with the printed edition).

[18] GIEHLOW (1904), pp. 63 sqq.

be paid to their complexion,[19] and because he specified the general requirements as follows:

First, one must pay attention to the youth's birth, discovering under what sign he was born, with some explanations. Pray God for a fortunate hour. Next, one must observe his figure and limbs, with some explanations. . . . Fifthly, the youth must be kept eager to learn and not be made tired of it. Sixthly, see that the youth does not practise too much, whereby melancholy might get the upper hand of him; see that he learns to distract himself by pleasant airs on the lute, to delight his blood.[20]

But we now know that the view according to which mental exertion caused an ascendancy of black bile[21] and thereby a morbid depressive reluctance to all activity, had, since Rufus of Ephesus, been as universal a principle in medieval school medicine as belief in the healing powers of "pleasant airs on the lute", whose anti-melancholic effect we first find illustrated not in the woodcuts to Muelich's translation of Ficino, but in certain miniatures as early as the thirteenth century (see PLATES 67 and 70).[22] Even the demand that the education of the young pupil be regulated in accordance with his horoscope and his temperament (conditioned by his horoscope) is not as modern as it appears. The *De disciplina scholarium*, attributed to Boethius but really written by an otherwise unknown "Conradus", was known everywhere after the first half of the thirteenth century and translated into French and German; and it describes at great length how the young scholar's lodging, his feeding, and his general way of life should be regulated according to his constitution—sanguine, phlegmatic, choleric, or melancholy—and his constitution should, if necessary, be determined by experts.[23] And Dürer had only to transfer these principles from the sphere of the school and the university to the

---

[19] LF, *Nachlass*, p. 282, 9–12: "Item, the first part shall be of how the boy is to be chosen, and of how attention is to be paid to the aptness of his complexion. This can be done in six ways."

[20] LF, *Nachlass*, pp. 283, 14–284, 2. These six points are nothing but a more detailed elaboration of what was described as the contents of the "first part" of the introduction in the sentence quoted in the previous note. The sentence in LF, *Nachlass*, p. 284, 3–19 bears the same relationship to p. 282, 13–17 and so do pp. 284, 20–285, 6 to p. 282, 18–20.

[21] The expression "überhandnehmen" is a literal translation of the Greek *ὑπερβάλλειν*, or the Latin "superexcedere"; just as "urdrützig" corresponds to the Latin "taedium" or "pertaesus".

[22] Nuremberg, Stadtbibliothek, Cod. Cent. V. 59, fol. 231ʳ; London, Brit. Mus., Sloane MS 2435, fol. 10ᵛ; Paris, Bibl. Nat., MS lat. 11226, fol. 107ʳ.

[23] MIGNE, P. L., VOL. LXIV, col. 1230: "Omnia siquidem superius expedita de scholarium informatione sunt infixa. Nunc de eorum sagaci provisione breviter est tractandum. Cum

painter's workshop—which, it is true, would never have occurred to his teacher Wolgemut—and to combine the notions of the doctrine of complexions with those of astrology in a manner quite familiar to the fifteenth and sixteenth centuries, to have his "iatromathematical" programme of education ready to hand.

---

ergo humani corporis complexio phlegmate, sanguine, cholera et melancholia consistat suffulta, ab aliquo praedictorum necesse est quemlibet elicere praeeminentiam.

"Melancholico vero pigritiei timorique subiecto, locis secretis et angulosis strepituque carentibus, lucisque parum recipientibus, studere est opportunum saturitatemque declivem serasque coenas praecavere, potibusque mediocribus gaudere ad naturae studium, prout studii desiccatio exegerit; plenaria potus receptione ad mensuram confoveri, ne nimii studii protervitas phtisim generet, anhelam thoracisque strictitudinem.

"Phlegmaticus vero licet strepitu vigentibus aedibus, lucisque capacissimis praeceptis studiis potest informari; poculis plenioribus potest sustentari, cibariis omnigenisque confoveri, venereoque accessu, si fas est dicere, mensurnus permolliri deberet.

"Sanguineus autem, cuius complexionis favorabilior est compago, omnibus aedibus vel locis potest adaptari, quem ludendo saepius novimus confoveri gravissima quaestione, quam si obliquantibus hirquis parietes solus occillaret. Tamen in hoc semper non est confidendum, hunc cibariis levioribus potibusque gratissimis decet hilarari.

"Cholericus vero pallidae effigiei plerumque subiectus solitudini supponatur, ne nimii strepitus auditu bilem infundat in totam cohortem, sicque magistratus venerabilem laedat maiestatem. O quam magistratus laesio vitanda est! Hunc coena grandiori novimus sustentari, potuque fortiori deliniri. Cavendum est autem, ne litis horror potus administratione istius rabidis mentibus extrahatur.

"Si autem qualitates assignare ignorans sit societas, theoricos consulat seque sic cognoscat . . . ." For this work, already mentioned in 1247, see PAUL LEHMANN (to whom we owe the discovery of the author's name, Conrad), *Pseudoantike Literatur des Mittelalters* (Studien der Bibliothek Warburg, VOL. XIII) Leipzig 1927, pp. 27 sqq. and 101. ☞

Chapter II

THE ENGRAVING "MELENCOLIA I"

If, despite these negative conclusions, we can still assert that Dürer's elaborately prepared engraving[1] owes a debt to the notion of melancholy propagated by Ficino, and would, in fact, have been quite impossible but for this influence, the proof of this assertion can be based only on internal evidence from the engraving itself.

I. THE HISTORICAL BACKGROUND OF "MELENCOLIA I"

(*a*) Traditional Motifs

(i) *The Purse and the Keys*

All that Dürer tells us of his engraving is an inscription on a sketch of the "putto" (Plate 8) giving the meaning of the purse and bundle of keys which hang from Melancholy's belt: "The key signifies power, the purse riches."[2] This phrase, brief though it is, has some importance in that it establishes one point of what would in any case have been a likely suspicion: namely, that Dürer's engraving was somehow connected with the astrological and humoral tradition of the Middle Ages. It at once reveals two essential traits of the traditional character, which, for Dürer as for all his contemporaries, was typical both of the melancholic man and of the Saturnine.[3]

Among the medieval descriptions of the melancholic there was none in which he did not appear as avaricious and miserly, and hence, implicitly, as rich; according to Nicholas of Cusa, the melancholic's ability to attain "great riches" even by dishonest means was actually a symptom of "avaritiosa melancholia".[4] If,

---

Pl. 2, 3 [1] The preliminary sketches have been discussed by H. Tietze and E. Tietze-Conrat,
4, 5, 6, 7 *Kritisches Verzeichnis der Werke A. Dürers*, vol. ii, i, Basle 1937, Nos. 582–587; cf. also E. Panofsky, *Albrecht Dürer*, Princeton 1943, vol. ii, p. 26.

[2] LF, *Nachlass*, p. 394, 5; cf. also Giehlow (1904), p. 76.

[3] This is obvious, even without the remarks quoted above, text p. 281 (with which cf. Giehlow (1904), p. 67).

[4] See above, p. 120 (text).

in these descriptions of the melancholic, "power"—naturally associated with property, and here symbolised by the keys which we may take to open the treasure-chest—was a mere adjunct to "riches", both characteristics were expressly united in the traditional descriptions of Saturn and his children. For, just as the mythological Kronos–Saturn, who combined with all his other characteristics the attributes of a distributor and guardian of wealth, was in antiquity not only the guardian of the treasury and the inventor of coin-minting, but also the ruler of the Golden Age, so, too, Saturn was worshipped as ruler and as king; and accordingly, not only did he fill the rôle of treasurer, and author of prosperity, in the planetary hierarchy, but also, as in Babylon, he was feared and honoured as the "mightiest"; and then, as always happens in astrology, all these properties were transmitted to those who came under his dominion. In an antithesis worthy of Saturn himself, astrological sources inform us that together with the poor and humble, the slaves, the grave-robbers, Saturn governs not only the wealthy and the avaricious ("Saturnus est significator divitum", says Abû Ma'šar in his *Flores astrologiae*) but also "those who rule and subdue others to their sway"; and we read in the Cassel manuscript that the child of Saturn is a "villain and traitor" but is also "beloved of noble people, and counts the mightiest among his friends".[5]

It is not surprising, therefore, that in turning from the texts to the pictures we find the combination of the two symbols interpreted by Dürer as signs of "power" and "riches" less commonly in pictures of melancholics than in pictures of Saturn. In one early fifteenth-century manuscript (PLATE 28), Saturn not only carries a purse at his waist, but is holding two enormous keys, which obviously belong to the chests, some open, some still closed, on the ground beside his feet.[6] But Dürer's purse appears frequently in pictures of melancholics, for as an age-long symbol of riches and avarice it had become a constant feature of these pictures by the fifteenth century. One of the two corner

[5] See above, p. 192, note 204.

[6] Rome, Bibl. Vat., Cod. Urb. lat. 1398, fol. 11r. Saturn reckoning and counting his gold in Cod. Pal. lat. 1369, fol. 144v (PLATE 43) belongs to this realm of ideas (though this time without the key), and so does the remarkable figure in the top left-hand corner of the portrait of Saturn in Tübingen MS Md. 2 (PLATE 40), a seated king counting gold pieces on top of a large treasure chest with his right hand, but raising a goblet with his left (derived from a combination of the carousing King Janus with the reckoning Saturn, who rules January no less than December).

figures in the picture of Saturn in the Erfurt manuscript (PLATE 42) is reminiscent of the Saturn in manuscripts at Tübingen and the Vatican (PLATES 40 and 43), being placed in front of a coffer covered with large coins; and in the Tübingen manuscript (PLATE 73) the melancholic's similarity to his planetary patron goes so far that he is leaning on his spade in an attitude characteristic of the god of agriculture, about to bury his treasure-chest.[7] But in the second melancholic in the Erfurt manuscript, riches and avarice are symbolised no longer by a treasure-chest, but by a purse, and from now on this attribute becomes so typical that fifteenth-century examples of it are innumerable (PLATES 77, 78, 80 and 81),[8] while Cesare Ripa's *Iconologia*, which was still used in the period of the Baroque, would never have pictured the melancholic without his purse (PLATE 68).[9] This is the motif which induced the worthy Appelius to consider the apostle Judas a melancholic: "Melancholics, whose most noticeable feature is avarice, are well adapted to household matters and management of money. Judas carried the purse."[10]

(ii) *The Motif of the Drooping Head*

A considerable proportion of the above-mentioned portraits of melancholics[11] have a further motif in common with Dürer's *Melencolia*, which, to the modern observer, seems too obvious to require a study of its historical derivation; but Dürer's own preliminary design for the engraving, which deviates in this very particular,[12] shows that it does not simply owe its origin to the observation of the melancholic's attitude but emerges from a pictorial tradition, in this case dating back thousands of years. This is the motif of the cheek resting on one hand. The primary significance of this age-old gesture, which appeared even in the mourners in reliefs on Egyptian sarcophagi, is grief, but it may

---

[7] The caption explains the point of this comparison: "I trust no-one". In K. W. RAMLER's *Kurzgefasste Mythologie* (p. 456 in the 4th edn., Berlin 1820) the melancholic is still equipped with a treasure-chest as well as a dagger, rope and hat (see below, text p. 323).

[8] In one case the purse motif is even combined with the treasure-chest motif.

[9] CESARE RIPA, *Iconologia* (1st edn., Rome 1593), s.v. "Complessioni". The woodcut first appeared in the 1603 edition.

[10] See above, pp. 121 sqq. (text).

[11] J. LIGOZZI's *Allegory of Avarice* (H. Vos, *Die Malerei der Spätrenaissance in Rom und Florenz*, Berlin, 1920, VOL. II, plate 165) with its purse, treasure-chest and hand on chin could equally well stand for "Melancholy" were it not for the remaining motifs.

[12] F. HAACK (in *Zeitschrift für bildende Kunst*, VOL. LX (1926–27), supplement, p. 121) has again shown that it really was a preliminary study.

also mean fatigue or creative thought. To mention medieval types alone, it represents not only St John's grief at the Cross, and the sorrow of the "anima tristis" of the psalmist (PLATE 62),[13] but also the heavy sleep of the apostles on the Mount of Olives, or the dreaming monk in the illustrations to the *Pèlerinage de la Vie Humaine*; the concentrated thought of a statesman,[14] the prophetic contemplation of poets, philosophers, evangelists, and Church Fathers (PLATES 61 and 63)[15]; or even the meditative rest of God the Father on the seventh day.[16] No wonder, then, that such a gesture should spring to the artist's mind when it was a question of representing a configuration which combined in an almost unique fashion the triad grief, fatigue, and meditation; that is to say, when representing Saturn and the melancholy under his dominion. In fact, the veiled head of the classical Kronos[17] (PLATE 13) rests as sadly and as thoughtfully on his hand as does the head of the melancholy Hercules on his in some ancient representations.[18] In medieval portraits of Saturn and melancholy, which had almost lost any direct links with ancient pictorial tradition,[19] this motif frequently receded into the background, but even then it was never quite forgotten[20]; see, for instance, the description of Saturn in King Alfonso's *Book of Chess* as a sad old man, "la mano ala mexiella como omne cuyerdadoso".[21] It was therefore the easier for it to regain its typical significance in the fifteenth and sixteenth centuries, and

---

[13] According to ERNEST T. DE WALD, *The Stuttgart Psalter*, Princeton 1930, fol. 55 (for Psalm 42, 7: "Quare tristis es, anima mea"). Similar types occur in the same work, fol. 58v (for Psalm 45) and fol. 141 (for Psalm 118).

[14] See the examples mentioned above, p. 224, note 27.

[15] The prototype of this extremely widespread design of the "contemplative" person is, of course, the ancient portrait of philosopher or poet, the adoption of which for medieval portraits of the evangelists has been studied in detail by A. M. FRIEND (in *Art Studies*, VOL. V (1927), pp. 115 sqq., plate XVI being particularly instructive).

[16] Paris, Bibl. Mazarine, MS 19, fol. 3r.

[17] See above, pp. 197 sqq. (text).

[18] Reproduced in W. H. ROSCHER, *Ausführliches Lexikon der griechischen und römischen Mythologie*, Leipzig 1884, VOL. I, col. 2160.

[19] For pictures of Saturn, see above, text pp. 200 sqq.; of melancholics, below, pp. 290 sqq. (text).

[20] Cf. e.g. Modena, Biblioteca Estense, Cod. 697; for this MS and the Guariento frescoes in the Eremitani Chapel, Padua, cf. A. VENTURI, in *Arte*, VOL. XVII (1914), pp. 49 sqq., though the connexion between them is not quite correctly stated.

[21] F. SAXL, in *Repertorium für Kunstwissenschaft*, VOL. XLIII (1922), p. 233.

to undergo a renaissance[22] which sprang, indeed, from very different impulses in the north and in the south. In the north, an ever-growing interest in the life-like portraying of certain psychologically distinctive types of men revived this gesture of the drooping head in pictures of melancholics, though it was omitted for the time being from portraits of Saturn. In fifteenth-century Italy, where portraits of the four temperaments were practically unknown (the only example known to us is a copy of a northern cycle, of the type shown in PLATES 77 and 78, but slightly modified in accordance with the classical tradition),[23] it was a desire to characterise distinctive individuals rather than types, and, in particular, a desire to revive the ideal world of classical mythology, that led to the restitution of this classical gesture of Saturn. The melancholic resting his head on his hand, as he appears in German manuscripts and prints, is matched in Italy on the one hand by the figure of Heraclitus in Raphael's *School of Athens*, and on the other by the Saturn in the engraving B4 by Campagnola (PLATE 54)—the majestic embodiment of a god's contemplation, which only later influenced portraits of human contemplation in general.[24]

Whether he was influenced by the northern portraits of Melancholy, or by Italian models such as Campagnola's engraving,[25]

---

[22] How greatly the propped-up head was later considered a specific attitude of the melancholic can be seen, for instance, from the fact that Dürer's drawing L144 (in itself a harmless study for a portrait) appeared in an old inventory as the "Prustpild" of an old melancholy woman (cf. G. GLÜCK, in *Jahrbuch der kunsthistorischen Sammlungen des allerhöchsten Kaiserhauses*, VOL. XXVIII (1909–1910), p. 4). The paper by URSULA HOFF quoted below (p. 392, note 54) contains an interesting collection of "melancholy" portraits with this gesture of the head-on-hand.

[23] The miniatures are illustrations to the above-quoted verses (p. 116, note 148) by LIONARDO DATI in Rome, Bibl. Vat., Cod. Chis. M. VII, 148, fols. 11v sqq. (about 1460–70). Only the choleric is much altered; he has been transformed from a medieval warrior into a Roman one. The sanguinic is carrying a laurel-wreath instead of a hawk's hood.

[24] For Campagnola's engraving of Saturn, cf. HARTLAUB, *Geheimnis*, esp. p. 53 and plate 23; and the same author in *Repertorium für Kunstwissenschaft*, VOL. XLVIII (1927), pp. 233 sqq. For its relation to a river god on the triumphal arch at Benevento, as well as its interesting transformations into (1) a peasant Saturn in a picture by Girolamo da Santa Croce (PLATE 56) and (2) into a St Jerome in a portrait by Lorenzo Costa (published in *Arte*, VOL. V (1902), p. 296) see above, text p. 212. Campagnola himself some years later transformed the philosophical type of Saturn into a purely human, and, so to speak, anonymous type (engraving P12, reproduced in HARTLAUB, *Geheimnis*, p. 24). In the north, the type of Saturn resuscitated by Campagnola was not generally adopted until the late sixteenth century, and even then, significantly enough, not under his mythological name but as a melancholic (PLATE 126, for which cf. text, p. 379).

[25] Hartlaub may be right in stating that pictures such as the engraving B4 may have been directly familiar to Dürer (for a possible connexion between Dürer and Campagnola, see also below, p. 324, note 135), but the supposed dependence of Campagnola's engraving P12 on Giorgione seems to us as little susceptible of proof as the assumption that the engraving B19

Dürer was in any case obeying pictorial tradition when he replaced the lethargically hanging hands which characterise the seated PL. 2 woman in the preliminary study—a typical symptom of melancholy illness, according to medical authorities[26]—by the thoughtful gesture of the hand supporting the cheek in the final engraving.

(iii) *The Clenched Fist and the Black Face*

In one respect, it is true, Dürer's portrait differs fundamentally from those previously mentioned. The hand, which generally lies softly and loosely against the cheek, is here a clenched fist. But even this motif, apparently quite original, was not so much invented by Dürer as given artistic expression by him, for the clenched fist had always been considered a sign of the typical avarice of the melancholy temperament,[27] as well as a specific medical symptom of certain melancholy delusions.[28] In this sense, in fact, it had not been completely foreign to medieval portraits of the melancholic (PLATE 72).[29] But comparison with such a type of medical illustration merely emphasises the fact that similarity of motif and similarity of meaning are two very different things; what Dürer intended to (and did) express by this clenched fist has little more in common with what it meant in the cauterisation charts than the rather elusive nuance of rendering a spasmodic tension. This, however, is not the place to describe what Dürer made of the tradition, but merely to list the elements which he found in it and judged fit to incorporate in his work.[30]

---

by the "master of 1515" represents a figure of Melancholy. The figure inspiring the astrologer is more likely to be the Muse Urania, or, more probably still, a personification of Astrology—of whom, for instance, Ripa expressly states that she is to have wings "per dimostrar che ella sta sempre con il pensiero levata in alto per sapere et intendere le cose celesti."

[26] It is difficult to prove that the drawing L79 was a study of Dürer's wife; but even if it were, the artist could have observed her in a genuinely depressed state.

[27] In DANTE's *Inferno*, for instance (Canto VII, 56), we read of the avaricious man that "Questi resurgeranno del sepulcro, Col pugno chiuso, e questi coi crin mozzi"; according to CAELIUS CALCAGNINUS (*Jahrbuch der kunsthistorischen Sammlungen des allerhöchsten Kaiserhauses*, VOL. XXXII (1915), p. 169), "manus dextra expansa [denotes] liberalitatem, manus sinistra compressa tenacitatem." The originator of this conceit, which still persisted in Sandrart's *Iconology*, seems to have been DIODORUS SICULUS: ἡ δ' εὐώνυμος συνηγμένη τήρησιν καὶ φυλακὴν χρημάτων (III, 4, 3 ed. F. Vogel, Leipzig 1888, p. 272).

[28] For quotations, see above, p. 55 (text).

[29] Erfurt, Wissenschaftliche Bibliothek, Cod. Amplon. Q. 185, fol. 247ʳ (cf. K. SUDHOFF, *Beiträge zur Geschichte der Chirurgie im Mittelalter*, VOL. I, Leipzig 1914, plate XXX).

[30] For the change by Dürer in the expressive value of these traditional motifs, see below, pp. 317 sqq. (text).

One last motif, perhaps of still greater importance for the emotional meaning of the engraving, should be mentioned, in view not of its quite untraditional significance, but of its traditional origin. This is the motif of the shadowed countenance, from which Melencolia gazes forth in an almost ghostly stare. We may remember that this "black face" was a far more frequently cited trait in tradition than was the clenched fist. Both the child of Saturn and the melancholic—whether melancholy through illness or by temperament—were by the ancients reckoned swarthy and black of countenance[31]; and this notion was as common in medieval medical literature as in astrological writings on the planets and in popular treatises on the four complexions. "Facies nigra propter melancholiam",[32] "nigri",[33] "mud-coloured",[34] "corpus niger sicut lutum",[35] "luteique coloris",[36] these are all phrases that Dürer may have read in the traditional texts, as many before him might have done; but, as also in the case of the clenched fist, he was the first to realise that what was there described as a temperamental characteristic, or even as a pathological symptom, could, by an artist, be turned to good account in expressing an emotion or in communicating a mood.

(*b*) Traditional Images in the Composition of the Engraving

Written in his own hand, Dürer's explanation of the symbolism of the purse and keys called our attention to various single motifs. We should now ask ourselves whether the picture as a whole also has its roots in the tradition of pictorial types.

(i) *Illustrations of Disease*

Medical illustrations proper, that is, representations of the melancholic as an insane person, had, as far as we know, neither

---

[31] For quotations, see above, pp. 59 sqq. (text).

[32] Thus Ibn Esra.

[33] Thus Albertus Magnus, quoted on p. 71, note 12.

[34] Thus e.g. the translation of the Salernitan verses in the work *De conservanda bona valetudine*, ed. Johannes Curio, Frankfurt 1559, fol. 237v: "Ir farb fast schwartz vnd erdfarb ist" ("their colour is almost black and earthy"). In view of the contradictory nature of this type of literature, and the contrasts inherent in the notion of melancholy itself, it is not surprising to find the melancholic occasionally described as "pale" in other writings on the complexions, e.g. in the verses on PLATE 81.

[35] Thus Johann von Neuhaus, quoted on p. 115 sq. (text).

[36] Thus the Salernitan verses, quoted on p. 115 (text).

evolved nor attempted to evolve a characteristic melancholy type. When there was an illustration at all, it was more a question of showing certain therapeutic or even surgical measures than of working out a general conception of the psycho-physical state.

The most common illustrations of this kind were the so-called "cauterisation charts", of which one (PLATE 72) has already been mentioned. They were to show how and where the various insane persons were to be cauterised, or trepanned. In the melancholic's case, the grisly operation was to be carried out "in medio vertice". He is shown, therefore, with a round hole in the top of his head, frequently as a single standing figure, sometimes sitting on the operating chair, occasionally, even stretched out on a kind of rack[37]; but only very seldom is some better than average illustrator ambitious enough to characterise the patient psychologically, that is to say, to distinguish him by specifically melancholy gestures.

As well as these cauterisation diagrams, there are also pictures of cures by means of flogging or by music (PLATES 67, 70 and 71)[38]: but even these (some of them quite attractive miniatures) could not be the starting point for a more general line of development, since they created no new types, but endeavoured to treat their theme by adopting forms of composition that were already fully developed (Saul and David, the scourging of Christ, the flogging of martyrs, and so on).

(ii) *Picture Cycles of the Four Temperaments. I: Descriptive Single Figures (the Four Temperaments and the Four Ages of Man)—II: Dramatic Groups: Temperaments and Vices*

On the other hand, an attempt at precise characterisation seems to have been made in portraits of the melancholic in the context of the four temperaments. It is true that here, too, no completely new types were coined; nor was this to be expected, since the problem of illustrating the complexions arose comparatively late. But, through the deliberate use of analogies at relevant points, these pictures grew at length into solid and striking portraits of character types.

---

[37] Cf. K. SUDHOFF, *Beiträge zur Geschichte der Chirurgie im Mittelalter*, VOL. I, plate XXXVI; in some cases the physician operating is also shown, e.g. Rome, Cod. Casanat. 1382 (SUDHOFF, op. cit., plate XXV) and above, pp. 55, 94.

[38] With PLATES 67, 70 cf. e.g. the pictures of Saul and David; with PLATE 71 cf. a miniature like Berlin, Staatsbibliothek, Cod. Hamilton 390, fol. 19ʳ: "Iste verberat uxorem suam" (for this codex, see below, text p. 298).

Some late representations of the temperaments simply adopt the characteristics of the corresponding planet or children of a planet—a striking instance of this is the picture in the Tübingen manuscript of a miser burying his treasure (PLATE 73).[39] In certain isolated cases the melancholic follows the pose—familiar enough in a different context—of a writing evangelist or a scholar, with the mere addition of a treasure-chest[40]; a case in point is a sequence of miniatures dating from about 1480. If we leave these two exceptions aside, the pictures representing the four temperaments in a set or sequence can be divided into two main groups: those showing each temperament as a single figure, more or less inactive and distinguished mainly by age, physique, expression, costume, and attributes; and those in which several figures, preferably a man and a woman, meet in order to enact a scene typical of their particular temperament. Sets of the first group are very numerous; those of the second are fewer in number but more momentous in view of later developments.

The first example of a set of single figures—linked, as it were, with the old schema of the four winds in Dürer's woodcut illustrating Celtes's work—occurs in a crude outline drawing belonging to an eleventh- or twelfth-century treatise on the *Tetrad*, preserved in Cambridge (PLATE 75).[41] The quadrants of a circle contain four seated figures which, according to the caption, represent the "four ages of human life",[42] and are therefore all female. In addition to the caption, however, there are marginal notes which inform us that these figures represent also the four

---

[39] Also the two men with wooden legs, in a woodcut series of the vices (which will be dealt with later, text pp. 300 sqq.) from the Curio edition (quoted above, note 34), fol. 239v, our PLATE 74. For the Swiss drawing on PLATE 139, and the De Gheyn engraving on PLATE 143, where the assimilation of the melancholic to the Saturnine type takes place on a new, humanistic basis, see below, pp. 393, 398 (text).

[40] Berlin, Cod. germ. fol. 1191, fol. 63v, now in Marburg; cf. *Beschreibendes Verzeichnis der Miniatur-Handschriften der Preussischen Staatsbibliothek*, VOL. V, ed. H. Wegener, Berlin 1928, pp. 72 sqq. Here the sanguinics are playing the lute, the cholerics wrestling, and the phlegmatic is seated in a depressed attitude generally characteristic of the melancholic; on this, see below, p. 319, note 117.

[41] Cambridge, Caius College, MS 428, fol. 27v, cf. M. R. JAMES, *Descriptive Catalogue of the Manuscripts in the Library of Gonville and Caius College*, Cambridge 1908, p. 500. Pictures like those discussed here can easily be accounted for as a synthesis of the abstract tetradic
PL. 150 systems occurring from the ninth century onwards, first in Isidore MSS and then in illustrations to cosmological treatises (cf. E. WICKERSHEIMER in *Janus*, VOL. XIX (1914), pp. 157 sqq., and C. SINGER, *From Magic to Science*, London 1928, pp. 211 sqq. and plate XIV), with cognate figure representations from Graeco-Roman times, like the Chebba mosaics, etc.

[42] "Quatuor aetates velut hic patet atque videtur
Humanae vitae spatium conplere iubentur."

complexions, or, more precisely, that they personify the humours preponderating in them. "Childhood" represents also the phlegm, sharing in the elemental qualities cold and damp; warm and moist "Youth" represents the blood; warm and dry "Manhood" represents the yellow bile; and finally, cold and dry, "Decline" represents the black bile.[43] In later centuries there will be sets of pictures representing, primarily, the four temperaments, and only secondarily the four seasons, the four ages of man, and the four points of the compass; but these figures in the Cambridge miniature are meant primarily as portraits of the four ages of man, and in them the representation of the four humours is only of secondary interest.[44]

This is not surprising, at a time when the terms "phlegmaticus" and so on had not yet been coined for the notion of men governed by the phlegm and the various humours.[45] Nevertheless, with this reservation, the Cambridge cycle of four may be considered the earliest known picture of the temperaments; and so the question arises, from which source did the draftsman take the types which he embodies in his design? The answer is that these humorally characterised pictures of the four temperaments evolved from classical representations of the seasons and occupations.[46] But while a connexion made in antiquity was adopted, it was at the same time revised in the sense of its original—in this

---

[43] The series in this list is based (a) on the rule applying almost throughout to all systems, whether they begin with "sanguis", or, as here, with "phlegma"—namely, that the "cholera rubra" precedes the "cholera nigra", and (b) on the verbal usage whereby "decrepitas" denotes a greater age than "senectus". This, however, is contradicted by the pictorial sequence (while, e.g., the cycle of cardinal points shown on fol. 21r of the same MS should be read clockwise starting from the top, the sequence here is irregular), and by the fact that "Decrepitas" is still spinning while "Senectus" is already winding the wool. The ancient tradition following the less customary system beginning with the "phlegma" (see above, text p. 10) was obviously largely eclipsed; fol. 22v shows a circular schema analogous to the two just mentioned, in which the sequence, though normal, begins from the bottom and runs anticlockwise (top, "cholera rubra" = warm and dry; right, "sanguis" = warm and moist; below, "aqua" = cold and moist; left, "terra" = cold and dry). It is also highly unusual to describe the warm and dry "choleric" age as "senectus", and to call the west "cold and dry" as compared with the "warm and moist" east. In the examples collected by Wickersheimer the cycle always runs in the usual sequence: "sanguis", "cholera rubra", "cholera nigra", "phlegma".

[44] Especially in these tetradic cycles it is not uncommon to find a double or even treble significance for each figure. Cf. the examples cited on p. 292, note 41, and the Rivers of Paradise on the Rostock baptismal font of 1291 (which, according to the inscription, also represent the four elements).

[45] See above, p. 103 sq. (text).

[46] Medieval portrayals of the four ages of man seem in fact to have evolved indirectly from representations of the four seasons, these being linked with antiquity by a continuous pictorial tradition.

case, abstract—form. For at first the seasons in classical pictures were distinguished only by attributes; in the mosaics of Lambaesis and Chebba[47] they had become girls and women differentiated according to their ages—and thereby individualized. The Cambridge artist reverts once more from the differentiation by natural, biological, signs of age to the differentiation by conventional attributes. Youth (blood), who in accordance with her youthful age is the only standing figure, is exactly like the well-known figure of the garland-laden Spring; which, in turn, is identical with Maius (May) in the cycles of the months.[48] In contrast with carefree youth, Decline (black bile) has to work, and (in accordance with her advanced age, and the cold season) she is holding a distaff[49]; while Old Age (red bile) is winding the spun wool. Only Childhood (phlegm) has to make do without attributes: she is characterised merely by legs crossed in a typical attitude of rest, which is probably meant to indicate the physical and mental indifference of both the phlegmatic temperament and the age of childhood: εἰς ἠθοποιίαν ἄχρηστος.

This attempt to illustrate the notion of the complexions, hitherto transmitted only in literature, by interpreting certain forms of pictures of seasons and occupations as pictures of the four ages of man, and then including in these the notion of the four humours, set a precedent for the future. By the fifteenth century (unfortunately we have no example of the intermediate period), when what we may call the orthodox pictures of the complexions had been evolved, the combination of the ages of man with his various occupations—a combination unskilfully drafted in the Cambridge miniature—had only to be further modernised in order to produce, as it were, automatically a series of those "single-figure" pictures of the temperaments which form, as we have said, the first and larger group.

---

[47] F. Boll, "Die Lebensalter", in *Neue Jahrbücher für das klassische Altertum*, vol. XVI (1913), p. 103, plate I, 2.

[48] For this type of representation of Spring we need only refer to the above-mentioned Chebba mosaic or the *Chronicon Zwifaltense* mentioned above, p. 279, note 9. The corresponding representations of May are innumerable; the earliest example is the well-known Salzburg calendar of 818 (our Plate 97). That "May" and "Spring" could be used synonymously in literature as well can be seen from the caption to the portrait of the sanguinic in Plate 78: "das wirket mey und Jupiter".

[49] In the fully developed allegory of the ages of man, the distaff denotes the fifth stage in the cycle of seven, and the seventh decade in the hundred-year cycle (W. Molsdorf, *Christliche Symbolik der mittelalterlichen Kunst*, Leipzig 1926, Nos. 1142 and 1143). Apart from this, spinning is the characteristic form of female activity, and the Cambridge miniature is concerned only with feminine occupations.

Since this further development aimed at a transformation of the abstract scientific diagram into the picture of a concrete character, the singularities both of the different ages and of the corresponding temperaments were now depicted with modern realism. Physique, dress and occupation were painted in livelier colours, sometimes almost in the style of a genre picture. The sanguine man generally appears as a fashionably-dressed youth going falconing; the choleric as an armed warrior; the melancholic as a sedate middle-aged gentleman; the phlegmatic as a long-bearded old man, sometimes leaning on a crutch. The psychological attitude is shown partly by the addition of distinguishing attributes but mainly by mimetic means, such as the PL. 75
morose expression and the head-on-hand attitude of the melancholic, or the grimace of rage on the face of the choleric, who draws his sword or even hurls chairs about.[50] If the Cambridge drawing had already represented the four humours in the guise of the four ages of man, it must have been even easier in the fifteenth century for the two sets of illustrations to be more closely associated; for by that time the four ages had preceded the temperaments in the realistic development of single types. A French cycle of about 1300 (PLATE 76)[51] is content to differentiate the various ages by reference rather to physiological than to psychological or occupational characteristics: but in the French miniature (PLATE 58) of the *Wheel of Life* a hundred years later, youth is shown as a young falconer, and the penultimate age of man as a thinker with his head on his hand[52]; and in two closely connected German designs, the older dated 1461 (PLATE 79), the representatives of the middle four of the seven ages are identical with the current types of the four temperaments—a falconer, a knight in armour, an older man counting money or holding a purse, and a frail old man. The only points in which the fifteenth-century pictures of the four complexions—in so far as they belong to the descriptive, single-figure type—differ from the contemporary series of pictures representing the four ages, are the inclusion of

---

[50] Broadsheet, Zürich, Zentralbibliothek (Schreiber 1922 m.); P. HEITZ, *Einblattdrucke des 15. Jahrhunderts*, VOL. IV, No. 4.

[51] London, Brit. Mus., Sloane MS 2435, fol. 31^r.

[52] F. BOLL, "Die Lebensalter", in *Neue Jahrbücher für das klassische Altertum*, VOL. XVI (1913), plate II, 3 and 4. It is obviously an error when, on p. 129, Boll says that the falconer is holding "a dove, the creature sacred to Venus."

the four elements (the sanguine man stands on clouds, the choleric in flames, the melancholic on the earth); and, in certain representations (for example, in PLATE 82), the addition of a symbolic beast, an ape for the sanguine, a lion for the choleric, a boar for the melancholic, and a sheep for the phlegmatic.[53]

Moreover, the form of these pictures shows little variation throughout the fifteenth century; the various types became so well established that, once defined, they intruded upon the illustrations of the "children" of the planets in astrological manuscripts[54]; and could even be included in illustrations to Aristotle's *Problems* (PLATE 77), the fourteenth chapter of which had nothing to do with the late medieval doctrine of the temperaments, but which is headed ὅσα περὶ κράσεις, or, in the French translation, "Qui ont regart a la complexion".[55] Even where the representatives of the four temperaments appear on horseback (PLATE 81), by analogy with a certain planetary type first occurring in the well-known Kyeser manuscripts they remain falconers,

---

[53] For animal symbolism as applied to the four temperaments, see above, text p. 102 sq. The works here in question (*The Shepherds' Calendar* in French and English, the latter edited by O. H. Sommer, 1892, and the printed Books of Hours by Simon Vostre and Thomas Kherver) form a special regional group derived from a single prototype, and distinguished by the fact that the phlegmatic, who occupies the third place, is characterised by a purse, while the melancholic, relegated to fourth place, has a crutch—perhaps because of a mistake which, once made, became traditional. The melancholic is also given fourth place in a few other cycles, though the relevant texts expressly correlate autumn with him (see also above, text p. 280).

[54] Cf. the corner-figures in the picture of Saturn in the Erfurt MS, our PLATE 42; in the picture of the sun in the same MS (A. HAUBER, *Planetenkinderbilder und Sternbilder*, Strasbourg 1916, plate XXIV) the "sanguine" falconer occupies the corresponding position.

[55] Paris, Bibl. Nat., MS nouv. acq. fr. 3371. A special instance, apparently, without analogy, but of some interest because of its early date, appears in a MS dated 1408 by JOHANNES DE FOXTON, *Liber cosmographiae* (Cambridge, Trinity College, MS 943, fols. 12^v sqq.). Here the four temperaments appear as naked men, described as "prima ymago" etc., with the Salernitan couplets as superscriptions, and in the odd sequence sanguinic, phlegmatic, melancholic, choleric, though the phlegmatic is clearly the oldest. The choice of attributes, too, is somewhat singular. The choleric, as usual, is girded with a sword, but this stands out in odd contrast to his nakedness; the sanguinic, too, is brandishing a sword in his right hand, and holding a goblet in his left. The melancholic is holding a raven in his right hand (this, according to the *Fiore di Virtù*, is the companion of "tristizia") while with his left hand—as in portraits of "Ira" or "Desperatio"—he plunges a dagger into his breast (probably a reference to his suicidal leanings); and the phlegmatic, rather drastically shown as 'sputamine plenus", is standing with a book, his head on his hand. Moreover, the sanguinic is further distinguished by a plant across his chest, and a dove sitting on his right arm, and the choleric by a flower emerging from his mouth. No definite interpretation of these details has yet been arrived at—some of them were no doubt taken over from the pictorial types of the deadly sins; nor are the physiognomical descriptions, in each case appearing in the left-hand margin, comprehensible as they stand.

men in armour and so on[56]; and even the series of single figures representing the complexions in the middle and late Renaissance, with which we shall deal later, preserves in many respects a recollection of the fifteenth-century types.

The second group (that in which the different temperaments are represented by means of a scene in which several figures take part) has a very different character. The series so far discussed evolved from, and in combination with, illustrations of the four ages of man, which in their turn could be traced back to classical representations of seasons and occupations. It is therefore understandable that they should emphasise differences of age and occupation, while psychological traits such as the melancholic's avarice and depression, or the choleric's rage, only gradually appear, and then seem to be based as much on the respective ages to which they are allotted as on the respective types of temperament.

In the dramatic representations of the temperaments, on the other hand, difference in age fades as much into the background as difference in occupation or situation. Here, from the beginning, interest is centred so entirely on the humorally-given traits of character that the scene is limited to actions and situations revealing these traits: everything else is neglected; and only the introduction of the four elements (also lacking occasionally) distinguishes works of this type from morality paintings or illustrations to novels.

This difference in artistic intention corresponds to the difference in historical origin. The historical study of pictorial types—which is just as necessary and just as possible for the dramatic compositions as for the static single descriptive figures—takes us, not into the world of "speculum naturale", but into that of "speculum morale", not into the realm of the pictures of the four ages but into that of the illustrations of virtues—or rather, vices; for this realm was almost the only one in which (though under the menacing aspect of ecclesiastical moral theology) the

---

[56] Clm. 4394. PLATE 81, after a broadsheet in the Gotha Museum (Schreiber 1922 o; P. HEITZ, *Einblattdrucke des* 15. *Jahrhunderts*, VOL. LXIV, No. 8). For representations of planets on horseback (probably based on a convention in jousting and tournaments), cf. SAXL, *Verzeichnis*, VOL. I, p. 114. A curious connection between these riders and the Shepherds' Calendars and Books of Hours can be seen in the *Horae B. V. Mariae* printed by Marcus Reinhart, Kirchheim about 1490 (Schreiber 4573, Proctor 3209), fol 1 v. Here the choleric appears as the Wild Huntsman, the sanguinics as a pair of lovers, also on horseback—the phlegmatic, however, as a simple standing figure with a sheep, and the melancholic (in the fourth place) as a standing figure with a pig.

undesirable, and therefore psychologically significant, characteristics of men were shown in brief, sharply defined scenes.

A curiously early example of the dramatic type—which, however, apparently remained quite isolated—may be seen in a famous Hamilton Codex in Berlin, compiled before 1300 in North Italy, which includes also the sayings of Dionysius Cato, the misogynistic outpourings of the "proverbia quae dicuntur super naturam feminarum", a moralised bestiary, and other writings of a similar trend, and endeavours to enliven all of these by innumerable small border miniatures, partly moral, partly didactic. The Salernitan verses on the complexions—with many mistakes in the text—are illustrated in the same style and with the same intention (PLATE 84).[57] The miniaturist introduces auxiliary figures for the purpose of coupling them with the representative of each temperament in a joint action which is designed to reveal the main characteristics listed in each couplet, and in general resembles closely the other illustrations in the manuscript. The sanguine is, above all, the *generous* man ("largus"), and his generosity is shown by his handing a purse to a minor figure kneeling before him.[58] The choleric—*angry* ("irascens")—is giving his partner a blow on the head with a club, which is exactly what the married man on another page, exasperated by contradiction, is doing to his wife.[59] The *sleepy man* ("somnolentus") of the phlegmatic's verses is illustrated by a sleeper being rudely awakened by a second man. Finally, the melancholic—*envious and sad* ("invidus et tristis")—is turning away with a gesture of contempt from a loving couple, and this figure too has its model (and its explanation) in an illustration at the very beginning of the codex, entitled "He shuns love-making" ("Iste fugit meretricem").[60]

These little miniatures are too idiosyncratic and the circumstances which gave them birth too exceptional, for them to have had any influence. In Italy, as already mentioned, no special interest was taken anyhow in pictures of the temperaments and, as far as we know, this was changed only under the influence of

---

[57] Berlin, Staatsbibliothek, Cod. Hamilton 390, fol. 83ᵛ.

[58] For this group, cf. e.g. the illustration on fol. 20ʳ to Cato's epigram "Dilige denarium sed parce".

[59] Fol. 148ᵛ: "Hisque repugnando maior et ira furit".

[60] Fol. 4ʳ. The composition of the pair of lovers reappears in a similar form on fols 104ᵛ and 139ᵛ. The round object which the loving couple are holding up is difficult to interpret. By analogy with fol. 113ʳ, one might think it some sort of ornament.

mannerism, with its northern connotations. North of the Alps—apart from the fact that the Hamilton Codex could hardly have been known there—the conditions for the development and diffusion of scenic and dramatic pictures of the four complexions were not available until the birth of an artistic style which was to be realistic in expression and psychological in intent. The designs in the Hamilton manuscript, therefore, remained an interesting exception. The standard type did not arise until the middle of the fifteenth century, and then apparently in Germany.

The original sequence, which was to become almost canonical, arose in illustrated manuscripts,[61] imposed itself on the majority of almanac illustrations (PLATES 85, 87, 89A, 89B),[62] and underwent its first superficial modernisation as late as about 1500 (PLATES 90A–D).[63] It consisted of the following scenes: "sanguineus"—a pair of lovers embracing; "colericus"—a man beating his wife; "melencolicus"—a woman fallen asleep over her distaff,[64] and a man (in the background) also asleep, generally at a table but occasionally in bed; and "phlegmaticus"—a couple making music. The proverbial indifference of the phlegmatic was made the harder to illustrate by the fact that the motif of exhausted slumber had to be reserved for the melancholics, so that illustrators were forced to be content with a neutral group of musicians.[65] Hence as soon as in the sixteenth century the sleepy melancholic had been replaced by one doing intellectual work the now unemployed slumber-motif naturally reverted to

---

[61] Zürich, Zentralbibliothek, Cod. C 54/719, fols. 34ᵛ–36ʳ.

[62] The first German Calendar, Augsburg, about 1480. The same woodcuts reappear in later ones, e.g. Augsburg, Schönsperger 1490 (published in facsimile by K. Pfister, Munich 1922), 1495, etc.

[63] Strasbourg Calendar about 1500; Rostock Calendar for 1523. As one can see, the sanguine lovers are generally on horseback and going hawking; the representation is derived from a model like the pseudo-Dürer drawing in the Berlin Print Room (*Inv.* 2595, reproduced in H. TIETZE and E. TIETZE-CONRAT, *Der junge Dürer*, Augsburg 1928, p. 229, and elsewhere), while the portrait of the phlegmatics seems based on an engraving by E. S. (Lehrs 203; this observation was made by M. I. Friedländer). The scene of the choleric's cudgelling is now enriched by a horrified female onlooker; and a long-bearded monk, a figure which the average mind would probably still associate with the "vita contemplativa", enters the room of the two melancholics.

[64] Thus the Zürich MS, fol. 35ʳ. Here, as in a few other cases, a weakening of the original idea has resulted in the spinstress, so far from sleeping, being actually engaged in work.

[65] The choice of this motif, which in itself would suit the sanguine temperament far better (cf. PLATES 119 and 124, as well as the usual characteristics of "Voluptas" in the pictures of Hercules at the Crossroads), may have been based on the view that the phlegmatic dullness might be a little animated by "citharae sono" (cf. Melanchthon's account, quoted above, text p. 89 sq.).

the phlegmatic.[66] Apart from the phlegmatics, however, we may say that these scenes are nothing but pictures of vices which, having been taken out of their theological context, have been applied to the profane illustration of the temperaments; and some of these pictures of vices were directly related to the noble tradition of classical Gothic cathedral decoration. In order to see the connexion we need only compare the scene of the sanguine lovers (PLATE 85) with the relief of "Luxuria" in the western porch of Amiens Cathedral (PLATE 86), or the married discord of the choleric with the relief of "Discordia" in the same series (PLATES 87 and 88), or even, because of the knee-motif, with the relief of "Dureté" in the western façade of Notre Dame.[67]

But where is the prototype of the melancholic, who interests us most? (cf. PLATE 89B.) We have several times remarked that the Middle Ages equated melancholy with the sin of "acedia"[68]; but this particular sin was not represented in the great cathedrals. This leads us to a closer examination of the illustrated tracts dealing with the theme of the virtues and vices, of which the best-known example was the *Somme le Roi* of 1279, which was translated into almost every language and gained an extraordinarily wide dissemination.[69] And we do in fact discover "Accide, cest a dire peresce et anui de bien faire," illustrated

---

[66] I.e., in the work *De conservanda bona valetudine* disseminated in many Frankfurt editions, as editors signing, first, Eobanus Hesse and then Curio and Crellius. The complexion-sequence (1551: fols. 118 sqq.; 1553: fols. 116 sqq.; 1554: fols. 152 sqq.) is something of a patchwork. The portraits of the sanguinic and the choleric are taken from older cycles; the melancholic and the phlegmatic, however, are new, and very rough, the former a geo-
FIG. 2 metrician at a writing desk (see text figure 2, cf. text p. 395 sq.), the latter a pot-bellied man asleep in an armchair. A similar instance occurs in the Berlin Cod. germ. fol. 1191, now in Marburg, where the melancholic is shown as a scholar reading (though also, as a miser) while the phlegmatic appears as "homo acediosus". One can see that whenever the portrait of sloth or dullness is not used for the melancholic, it falls to the phlegmatic, as in the Hamilton Codex, PLATE 84, and, *mutatis mutandis*, in the Cambridge Foxton MS.

[67] The Amiens cycle of virtues and vices and the similar ones in Chartres (southern transept) and Paris (base of the western façade and the rose) form, of course, a group of their own. Moreover the complexion-sequences are by no means the only profane cycles derived from the types of vices; the "Luxuria" group, for instance, became a constant part of the astrological picture of Venus, just as, vice versa, the originally courtly picture of the couple hunting on horseback, which occasionally replaces the simple couple embracing, can appear in a moralising connexion (e.g. in a representation of the devotees of "Voluptas" in the Berlin Cassone picture of Hercules at the Crossroads, reproduced in E. PANOFSKY, *Hercules am Scheidewege* (Studien der Bibliothek Warburg, VOL. XVIII), Leipzig 1930.

[68] See above, p. 78 (text) and p. 223, note 26.

[69] Cf. D. C. TINBERGEN, *Des Coninx Summe*, Bibliotheek van Middelnederlandsche Letterkunde, Groningen 1900–03, with bibliography; also H. MARTIN in *Les trésors des bibliothèques de France*, VOL. I, Paris 1926, pp. 43 sqq.

in a manner which proves almost beyond doubt the derivation of our picture of the melancholic from this series. Among the many sins included in the notion of "accidie", it was a question of choosing the one most suited to illustration, and this was the neglect of one's duty to work and to pray. The illustrations to the *Somme le Roi*, therefore, show a ploughman asleep with his head on his hand, having left his plough in the middle of the field, or letting his team graze unwatched in the field; while in contrast to him there is an eager sower—the image of "work" (PLATE 91).[70] And such a human being, "sleeping the sleep of the unjust", (modified in many ways, according to estate and occupation—or rather lack of occupation) became the typical representative of sinful sloth. A pictorial sequence of virtues and vices in the Antwerp Museum, dating from 1480 or 1490 and wrongly attributed to Bosch, represents sloth by a sleeping citizen who, instead of praying before his crucifix, has fallen asleep on his soft pillow ("Ledicheyt is des duivels oorkussen", says a Dutch proverb), and therefore comes under the sway of the devil (PLATE 93, closely similar in type to a tapestry showing "acedia" in person, PLATE 66).[71] The woodcut illustrating the chapter on "Sloth and Idleness" in the 1494 edition of Brant's *Ship of Fools*, retains the diligent sower of the *Somme le Roi* as a virtuous contrast, but for the sleeping ploughman it substitutes the familiar spinning-woman,[72] a figure already used on a broadsheet (probably from Nuremberg) which, thanks to its full text, presents itself, as it were, as a *Somme le Roi* for the plain man (PLATE 92).[73] The figure is here expressly called "Acedia" and can be explained primarily by the wish for a female personification. In the Latin edition of the *Ship of Fools* of 1572 we even find the now traditional spinstress combined in one picture with the sleeping ploughman of the *Somme le Roi* as a double example of the sin of sloth, differing from our pictures of melancholics merely by the circumstance that emphasis is laid on morality rather than on

---

[70] Cf. MARTIN, op. cit., p. 54 and plate XI; later manuscripts, e.g. Brussels, Bibl. Royale, MS 2291 (Van den Gheyn), fol. 88v (dated 1415), repeat this type faithfully. Our reproduction is from Brussels, Bibl. Royale, MS 2294 (Van den Gheyn), fol. 51r.

[71] See above, p. 223, note 26.

[72] Ch. 97, fol. T. iii. The rather inappropriate wood fire amidst the natural landscape is justified by the text:

> "Vnd ist so träg, das jm verbrennt
> Syn schyenbeyn, ee er sich verwennt."

[73] P. HEITZ, *Einblattdrucke des 15. Jahrh.*, VOL. XI, Strasb. 1908, plate 17 (about 1490).

characterisation.[74] It has been stated elsewhere that Dürer's engraving B76, the so-called *Doctor's Dream* (PLATE 96), is nothing but an allegory of sloth, original in conception but as a type clearly derivable from illustrations such as the Antwerp sequence of virtues and vices and the woodcut to the *Ship of Fools* of 1494, and to be interpreted, if one likes, as a moralising and satirical predecessor of *Melencolia I*.[75]

If, therefore, the sanguine pair in the dramatic series of the complexions appeared to be modelled on the "typus Luxuriae" and the choleric pair on the "typus Discordiae" or "Duritiae", the melancholics were nothing but the "Acediosi", whose outward appearance, as was natural, closely resembled that of certain children of Saturn. It may well be no coincidence that the rhymes attached to the pictures of melancholics in the almanacs, in which the type here in question was mainly represented, were also related to the morality tracts and, above all, to the Low German version of the *Somme le Roi*.

☞ Vnser complexion ist von erden reych,
Darumb seyn wir schwaermuetigkeyt gleich.

or:

☞ Dat vierde [i.e. the sin of sloth] is swaerheit, dat een mensce also swaermoedich is, dat hem gheens dinghes en lust, dan te legghen rusten of slapen . . . .[76]

This, then, was the way in which the two main types of illustration of the four temperaments arose. Portraits of characters were created in which either the personifications of certain ages of man, or the representatives of certain sins forbidden by the

---

[74] *Stultifera navis*, Basle (Henricpetri) 1572, p. 194.

[75] Cf. E. PANOFSKY, in *Münchner Jahrbuch der bildenden Kunst*, new series, VOL. VIII (1931), pp. 1 sqq. See also ANDRÉ CHASTEL, "La Tentation de St Antoine, ou le songe du mélancholique", in *Gazette des Beaux-Arts*, VOL. LXXVII (1936), pp. 218 sqq. We may mention that on the title engraving of the *Bericht von der Melancholia Hypochondria*, by Dr JOHANNES FREYTAG (Frankfurt 1644), the "hypochondriac melancholy" successfully overcome by the gallant physician is still shown as a sleeping woman with head propped on hand, into whose brain a bat-winged demon is blowing delusions by means of bellows, the delusions being symbolised by swarming insects.

[76] D. C. TINBERGEN, *Des Coninx Summe*, Bibliotheek van Middelnederlandsche Letterkunde, Groningen 1900–03, p. 253. This passage confirms—if confirmation is needed—the fact that in the Calendar verses the expression "Schwermütigkeit" does not mean the purely mental mood of depression, as it does in modern usage, but a very material heaviness of mind and body which might today be best described as indolence. The choice of the word, too confirms, on the linguistic level, the deeply-rooted connexion between the scenic representations of the temperaments and the portrayals of the vices (as does the term "high-stomached" applied to the sanguinic).

Church, were so far given concrete shape and individuality that they came to represent "real life" and, although still seen in a speculative framework, they tended to become self-sufficient. In the case of the illustrations of the ages of man, this process involved merely a transition from a schematic to a naturalistic type of picture, and an emphasis on the humoral aspect at the expense of the purely biological. In the case of the illustrations of the vices, however—and these of course were the illustrations which produced the infinitely more striking types—it also involved a transition from a moral and theological realm to a profane one. The sculptured or painted sermon against sin became a description of character which not only cancelled the former moral estimate but replaced it in part by another, almost an amoral one—for luxury is at least as immoral as sloth, but the "sanguine" figure which represents the luxurious type has "the noblest complexion". Out of the variety of human sins described in such detail merely as a warning, there emerged a variety of human characteristics worthy of interest purely as such. In this sense the development of the dramatic series acquires an almost symptomatic significance; many other examples could be cited to show how many astonishing achievements of modern realism can be put down to the very fact that medieval morality became secularised. It has, for instance, been suggested that Chaucer's penetrating and subtle characterisation, no less than the modest little illustrations of the complexions, evolved mainly from the descriptions of virtues and vices in sermons of the twelfth and thirteenth centuries.[77]

If from all these pictures depicting temperaments we turn to *Melencolia I*, we receive the strong impression—an impression that is justified, moreover, by the form of wording in the legends—that Dürer's engraving signifies a fundamentally different level of allegory, and one, moreover, fundamentally new to the north. The figure of Decline in the Cambridge miniature, mainly charac- PL. 75
terised by a distaff, is a personification of the "black bile"; the figures of Weariness and Sloth in the fifteenth-century pictures

[77] H. R. PATCH in *Modern Language Notes*, VOL. XL (1925), pp. 1 sqq. The medieval representations of virtues and vices served as a basis for representations of the "Five Senses", so popular in the later sixteenth and, especially, the seventeenth century, as Hans Kauffmann emphasises in his informative review of W. R. Valentiner's book on Pieter de Hooch (*Deutsche Literaturzeitung*, 1930, pp. 801 sqq.). The birth of this type of the "Five Senses" denotes as it were, a second phase in secularisation: the originally moralistic representations, first transformed into objective and cosmological representations of the temperaments, were now drawn into the sphere of the subjective, sensual perception.

are examples of the "melancholic man"; but Dürer's woman, whose wings alone distinguish her from all other representations, is a symbolic realisation of "Melancholia".

To speak more precisely: the Cambridge miniature *embodies* an abstract and impersonal notion in a human figure[78]; the pictures of the complexion-series *exemplify* an abstract and impersonal notion by means of human figures: but Dürer's engraving *is the image of* an abstract and impersonal notion symbolised in a human figure. In the first case, the basic notion fully retains its universal validity; it cannot, however, be identified with the actual picture but can only be equated with it by means of an intellectual process—hence only the legend, or our familiarity with iconographic convention, informs us that the figure in question is meant to represent the "black bile". In the second case, the representation is directly and visibly linked with the basic notion (for any one can see that the choleric is angry, or the melancholic idle or sad), but by this the notion loses its universality, for it is shown in a special example which is only one of many, and can hence be recognised forthwith as the picture of an angry or a sad man, but not as the representation of the choleric or melancholy temperament. Here, too, a caption is necessary, but it no longer says to us, "imagine that this neutral figure *is* black bile," but "in this slothful couple you have a *typical example* of the melancholy temperament". In the third case, on the other hand, the basic idea is translated in its entirety into pictorial terms, without thereby losing its universality and without leaving any doubt as to the allegorical significance of the figure, which is nevertheless entirely concrete. Here, and here alone, can the visible representation completely answer to the invisible notion; here, and here alone, the legend (which at this stage of development begins to be superfluous) says to us neither "this is meant to represent the black bile," nor "this is a typical example of the melancholy temperament," but "melancholy is like this."[79]

---

[78] The function of such human figures in "standing for" a notion can of course be assumed by animals, plants or inanimate objects without the conditions governing the method of personification needing to be altered. In certain circumstances the pomegranate representing the notion of "concord" fulfils the same function as a human "Concordia", while in others it may appear simply as one of her attributes.

[79] The classification of allegorical forms of representation here attempted, which naturally leaves out many mixed or borderline cases, takes the term "allegory" in its literal sense ἄλλα ἀγορεύειν as a generic notion including the "symbolic" as well as the "substituting" (esp. the "personifying") and the "paradigmatic" form of representation. What is generally called allegory (in its narrower sense) is merely a more complicated form of substitution—

Admittedly it was French fifteenth-century art that created the book illustrations in which, instead of the merely paradigmatic melancholic of the temperament-series, or the merely personified figure of the "black bile" in the Cambridge manuscript, the figure of Dame Mérencolye herself first appeared.[80] These French illustrations seem therefore to have anticipated the symbolic representation of Melancholy in Dürer's engraving (PLATES 60, 61, 64). They do certainly surpass any pre-Dürer designs in so far as they combine, to a certain extent, personification with exemplification; for if they share with the Cambridge manuscript the desire to represent the notion of melancholy in all its universality, yet they also share with the temperament-series the power of making an invisible notion visible. The main difference between them and Dürer's work lies in the fact that this combination did not as yet represent a synthesis, but merely a contact of the other two possibilities—in other words, the significance actually visible in these French figures does not really coincide, as yet, with the general notion of melancholy. What we see there, and what are really presented to us with more or less advanced realism, are lean and badly dressed old women in the context of a more or less dramatic scene, from which, at best, we receive the impression of a certain mournful atmosphere; but that these figures are meant to represent melancholy, or indeed anything except mournful old women, is as little expressed visibly, and can hence as little be suspected without knowledge of the literary texts as, say, the fact that we are expected to recognise a knight as "Burning Desire" and the page riding towards him as a messenger of "Love".

The figures in such romance illustrations, therefore, are not in the least degree "symbolic representations", but rather, in the term already used, they are still merely "personifications". In accordance with fifteenth-century style, these personifications are depicted with such a strong sense of reality that they function also as "paradigmata"; but, as yet, the contradiction between paradigm and personification is not resolved by any higher form of allegory. What is actually visible is still a single occurrence:

---

more complicated, in that several personifications (i.e. living beings or objects denoting ideas) meet in a scene or a spatial relationship illustrating the connexion between various abstract notions. A typical example is Dürer's *Triumph of Maximilian*, or Goltzius's allegory (cited below, p. 343, note 202) of the relationship between "Ars" and "Usus".

[80] For the special problems connected with the poetic personification of melancholy (and its pictorial illustration) see above, pp. 221 sqq. (text).

anything that lies beyond remains "in the text". It is, in fact, quite literally in the text, as the curiously indeterminate character of these illustrations shows. It is actually due to the fact that the texts illustrated had already anticipated pictorial art in its function of allegorical translation. In these romances such general psychological notions as "mistrust", "understanding", "honour", "sweet reward", "long hope" and even "melancholy", had already become, in the poet's own mind, so individualised and so concrete—so much progress along the road from the abstract to the visual had already been made—that the illustrator had only to translate the concrete particular figure or event described in the text into pictorial terms; and that there was, in his pictures, not the slightest reason for the spectator to revert in his turn from the particular to the underlying general concept. Situations which in literary form are already well-sustained allegories, that is to say, which provide dramatic connexions between personifications, are bound to become genre or history pictures if the attempt is made to illustrate them literally in all their details.

(iii) *Portraits of the Liberal Arts*

It is therefore a fact that Dürer was the first artist north of the Alps to raise the portrayal of melancholy to the dignity of a symbol, in which there appears a powerfully compelling concordance between the abstract notion and the concrete image. As may be readily understood from the foregoing, truly symbolic forms of representation were evolved by artists of the Italian Renaissance. For it was their achievement to express the ideal in terms of naturalistic art and the transcendental in terms of a rational world order; and (as for instance in Giovanni Bellini's allegories) to discover—or rather, to rediscover in the art of classical antiquity—the means of sublimation which Dürer also used, wings for the chief figure, the "putti", and so on.[81] If we looked for an earlier work of art in which the principle of symbolic

---

[81] On a plaque by Bertoldo, which has not as yet been fully explained, we even find a *putto* taking part with a child's earnestness in the adults' occupation (W. Bode, *Bertoldo und Lorenzo dei Medici*, Freiburg, i.B. 1925, p. 82). The putto seems to be modelling something, while the old man on the left is not, as Bode states, busied with measuring instruments, but is carving an elaborate piece of furniture; Mercury is working with plummet and compasses, the female figure with a triangle. Whether the partly illegible letters should really be interpreted as abbreviations of "Mathematica," = "Ars", "Ludus" and "Usus" remains an open question; such an interpretation would be in consonance with contemporary ideas (see also below, text pp. 339 sqq.).

representation was applied to the subject of melancholy, an analogy would be found, not in the illustrations to French romances, but in a lost painting by Mantegna, which Dürer may possibly have known. Unfortunately we know practically nothing about it: but we do know that it bore the title "Malancolia", and that it contained sixteen putti dancing and making music.[82]

All this naturally does not exclude the possibility that the general conception of *Melencolia I*—as soon as we look at it in the light of the history of pictorial types rather than in the light of a theory of allegorical forms—may also be related to the northern tradition of pictorial allegory; indeed, we may even be led to think that a connexion between the two is absolutely essential to Dürer's engraving. But the first stages are not to be found in the pictures of Dame Mérencolye. Despite their connexion with scientific and medical notions of melancholy, as far as artistic form was concerned, these led, as we have seen, their own life, and they developed according to their own laws. Quite apart from that, they could hardly have become known to Dürer.[83] The first stages are to be sought rather in a group of allegorical pictures representing the "Liberal Arts". These pictures have nothing in common, as regards content, with the pictures representing diseases and temperaments; however, in design they readily lend themselves to Dürer's own particular artistic intentions, the novelty of which they in fact underline. Among them, we are here concerned particularly with those which illustrate the fifth of the "Liberal Arts": that is to say, Geometry.

Art in classical Greece had almost completely neglected the realm of manual labour, and Hellenistic art had dealt with it in the

---

[82] "Un quadro su l'ascia di mano del Mantegna con 16 fanciulli, che suonano e ballano, sopra scrittovi Malancolia, con cornice dorata, alta on. 14, larga on. 20½" (G. CAMPORI, *Raccolta di Cataloghi ed Inventarii inediti*, Modena 1870, p. 328; cf. GIEHLOW (1903), p. 40). Giehlow is no doubt correct in saying that these playing and dancing putti should be interpreted as humanistic symbols of the musical and theatrical entertainments recommended as antidotes to melancholy. But of course it need not have been Ficino who transmitted the knowledge of this (at the time) obvious remedy to Mantegna. Moreover, one can say even less about Mantegna's picture, since from Campori's description it is not even certain that "Melancholy" was there in person. In all essentials we must fall back on Cranach's picture (PLATE 130), which seems to reflect Mantegna's composition (see below, text p. 384); recently the Dürer drawing L623 has come to light, which might confirm Dürer's knowledge of the lost picture (cf. H. TIETZE and E. TIETZE-CONRAT, *Kritisches Verzeichnis der Werke A. Dürers*, VOL. I, Augsburg 1928, p. 21).

[83] The one iconographical trait in which the "Melancolia" of *Melencolia I* agrees with "Dame Mérencolye" (and then only in King René's romance) is in her dishevelled (*eschevelé*) hair, and even this sign of a desolate state of mind is too general a motif to justify the assumption of a connexion.

way of sentimental genre-painting of the pathetic poor or the hard-working peasants, rather than as a factual and natural portrait of reality.[84] Roman antiquity evolved from it, however, an almost inexhaustible variety of pictorial types.[85] Next to the purely descriptive pictures of trades, which remain firmly wedded to reality in a typically Roman manner and show us peasants and artisans at their daily work, there are the Hellenistic representations which playfully mythologise this concrete reality by making putti do the work; and there are, finally, countless tombstones, on which the occupation of the deceased is depicted by showing not the gestures, but, emblematically, the tools, of the trade in question (PLATE 50).[86] Sometimes these emblems of labour can be re-formed into the processes of labour, as is shown by a gilt glass, on which the figure of a ship-owner is surrounded by small scenes from the shipyard.[87] Sometimes, too, though not often, we encounter representations which really "personify" a trade, such as the Etruscan mirror (closely related to the emblematic tomb-stones) which shows a winged Eros surrounded by joiner's tools—as it were, "the spirit of joinery" (PLATE 51).[88]

Only the first of these types, the descriptive pictures of real workaday scenes, were handed down to the Middle Ages by direct pictorial tradition. In the almanacs and encyclopaedias

---

[84] The Hellenistic representations of the life of city populace, peasants, or even beasts are distinguished from the specifically Roman ones by an emotional emphasis arising from a keen sensitivity in regard to the unfamiliar. It may reflect a horror of degradation, as in the case of the *Drunken Old Woman*; or a sentimental interest in fellow-creatures or nature, as in the case of the *Black Boy making Music*, or the *Dam suckling her Young*; or, finally, a longing for the idyllic as in the case of the "peasant type" proper. In exactly the same manner Hellenistic portraiture contrasts with Roman by reason of its excitement and sense of triumph or suffering. The "holy sobriety" of the Latin artistic spirit, which, in educated circles, was often concealed under a mask of Hellenism, but revealed itself the more clearly in popular works, or in what we call provincial art, harked back, despite classicism and Hellenism, to the utter objectivity of the ancient Egyptian occupational portraits.

[85] OTTO JAHN, "Darstellungen des Handwerks und Handelsverkehrs auf Vasenbildern", in *Bericht über die Verhandlungen der sächsischen Gesellschaft der Wissenschaften, phil.-hist. Klasse*, XIX (1867), p. 75–113. Cf. H. GUMMERUS, "Darstellungen aus dem Handwerk auf röm. Grab- und Votivsteinen in Italien", in *Jahrbuch des kaiserlich deutschen archäologischen Instituts*, XXVIII (1913), p. 63–126). More recently P. BRANDT, *Schaffende Arbeit und Bildende Kunst*, Leipzig 1927–1928 (two volumes with numerous plates).

[86] Occupational emblems could either be added to the figure of the deceased (this was the usual pagan custom, as in our PLATE 50), or replace it altogether (this naturally being a particularly popular form in the Christian catacombs).

[87] R. GARUCCI, *Storia dell' Arte cristiana*, VOL. III, 202, 3 = CABROL-LECLERCQ, *Dictionnaire d'archéologie chrétienne et liturgie*, I, 2, col. 2918 (with more detail).

[88] E. GERHARD, *Etruskische Spiegel*, Berlin 1843–67, Plate 330, I.

we can see these scenes from Roman monuments adopted almost without alteration[89]; only in the later course of development were they modified and brought up to date. The personification of the Seven Liberal Arts, however, had still to be created—or rather, translated from Martianus Capella's lively and vivid description[90] into pictorially impressive terms—before they could assume the forms in which we so frequently see them in the great cathedrals and in illustrated manuscripts. There, they are often accompanied by a particular historical figure representing them—just as, in the mosaic pavements of late antiquity, the nine Muses are sometimes accompanied by representative practitioners of the nine arts—Calliope by Homer, Urania by Aratus,[91] and so on. Figures also of the Seven Mechanical Arts, represented mostly by paradigm rather than by personification, still had to be evolved.[92] And, without borrowing from antiquity, by a process of spontaneous re-creation, there arose a type of picture in which the skill of a man or of an allegorical being was indicated merely by the inclusion of a distinctive tool of his trade.

Centuries before the conscious reversion to the Roman type of monument for artisans or architects took place during the Renaissance,[93] the background of the archivolt reliefs showing

---

89 To illustrate the continuity of this tradition we bring together on PLATES 97–99: (*a*) three pictures of the months from the Salzburg Calendar of 818 (G. SWARZENSKI, *Die Salzburger Malerei*, Leipzig 1913, pp. 13 sqq. and plate VII; H. J. HERMANN, *Die illuminierten Handschriften der Nationalbibliothek in Wien*, VOL. I, Leipzig 1923, p. 148), namely May holding flowers, June ploughing, and August reaping; (*b*) the three corresponding pictures from the Rabanus Codex in Monte Cassino, copied in 1023 from a Carolingian model (A. M. AMELLI, *Miniature . . . illustranti l'Enciclopedia medioevale di Rabano Mauro*, Monte Cassino 1896, plate LIII); (*c*) a Roman figure in relief of the type on which August was based (Lateran sarcophagus). The pictures in the Rabanus Codex retain the indications of ground formation which have already lapsed in the Carolingian calendars, though the disposition of the figures would demand them here too. Hence it follows that the Rabanus pictures (for which cf. A. GOLDSCHMIDT, in *Vorträge der Bibliothek Warburg*, VOL. III, 1923–1924, pp. 215 sqq.) are independent of the Salzburg Calendar and are based directly on pictorial sources dating from before the ninth century.

90 *Nuptiae Philologiae et Mercurii*, BK II sqq.; cf. E. MÂLE, "Les arts libéraux", in *Revue archéologique*, 1891, pp. 343 sqq.

91 In these instances, therefore, personifications and paradigmata meet in a dual scene which, a few centuries later, could even be united in a single scene (cf. e.g. the "typus Arithmeticae" in GREGOR REISCH, *Margarita philosophica*, Strasbourg 1504, well reproduced in E. REICKE, *Der Gelehrte in der deutschen Vergangenheit* (Monographien zur deutschen Kunstgeschichte, VOL. VII), Leipzig 1900, plate 45.

92 Cf. E. MÂLE, "Les arts libéraux", in *Revue archéologique*, 1891, pp. 343 sqq., and J. VON SCHLOSSER, in *Jahrbuch der kunsthistorischen Sammlungen des allerhöchsten Kaiserhauses*, VOL. XVII (1896), pp. 13 sqq.

93 Cf. e.g. ANDREA BREGNO's epitaph in Santa Maria sopra Minerva (H. EGGER, in *Festschrift für Julius von Schlosser*, Zürich 1927, plate 57) and the corresponding German examples,

the historical representatives of the seven arts had been furnished with a ruler on a nail and a board with pen, sponge and so on (PLATE 100); and architects' monuments show the profession of the dead master by compasses and set-square.[94] One typical example of this is the monument of the great Hugues de Libergier, which, incidentally, is also a wonderful witness to the veneration which in Late Gothic times (in some ways, at least emotionally, very much like the Renaissance) could be accorded to a brilliant architect. But there can be no doubt that the writing implements in the Chartres archivolts are meant to be realistic, while the tools on the tombstone of the Master of St Nicaise have the same purely emblematic significance as in the Roman monuments.

These were the two roots of the new iconography. It arose when fourteenth-century art—charged with contradiction as always—developed a highly abstract symbolism which was ideographic rather than representational, while at the same time it laid the foundations of naturalistic perspective. Thus, there could develop, on the one hand, those workshop-interiors of the reliefs on the Campanile in Florence which almost look like scenes from ordinary life; on the other, such abstract representations as the miniature of 1376 in which the Aristotelian τέχνη appears surrounded by the tools of the various mechanical arts, with small figures of a farmer and a shepherd at her feet (PLATE 101),[95] or the strange pictures of the "Observance of the Sabbath", in which

---

obviously later in date, discussed in P. BRANDT, *Schaffende Arbeit und Bildende Kunst*, Leipzig
PL. 51 1927–1928, VOL. II, pp. 137 sqq. The type of "Eros Carpenter", too, underwent a revival in the period of humanism, though with an intellectual and satirical refinement of meaning; cf. the putto surrounded by occupational symbols and striving to fly heavenwards, but hindered by terrestrial needs, which often appears in editions by Rivius, but is already influenced by Dürer's *Melencolia I*. That it was so influenced is shown by a comparison with its model in Alciato's *Emblemata*, which is still without any occupational symbols (cf. L. VOLKMANN, *Bilderschriften der Renaissance*, Leipzig 1923, p. 44). Of the use of implements to denote an occupation there are, of course, countless examples in emblem-books; they can replace long narratives or biographies. As a good example, cf. the reverse of the medallion for Tomasso Ruggieri, reproduced in G. HABICH, *Die Medallien der italienischen Renaissance*, Stuttgart 1922, plate LXX, 4.

[94] Cf. E. MOREAU-NÉLATON, *La Cathédrale de Reims*, Paris n.d., p. 33.

[95] The Hague, Mus. Meermanno-Westreenianum, MS 10 D 1 (the "small" Aristotle-Oresme MS of Charles V), fol. 110r (cf. A. BYVANCK, *Les principaux manuscrits à peintures de la Bibliothèque Royale et du Musée Meermanno-Westreenianum à la Haye*, Paris 1924, p. 114; replicas in J. MEURGEY, *Les principaux manuscrits à peintures du Musée Condé à Chantilly*, Publications de la Société française de reproductions de manuscrits à peintures, VOL. XIII–XIV, Paris 1930, plate LII and pp. 46 sqq., with bibliography). On the left, next to "Art", is "Science", reading; on the right is the three-headed "Prudence" (for the motif of the three heads, cf. E. PANOFSKY, *Hercules am Scheidewege* (Studien der Bibliothek Warburg, VOL. XVIII), Leipzig 1930, pp. 1 sqq.; it is remarkable, however, that here the three are

the "arma Christi" of the contemporary representations of the Man of Sorrow are replaced by implements of various crafts.[96]

Thanks to the progress of naturalistic perspective in the course of the fifteenth century, the distinctions observed in portraits of the arts between "personification", "paradigm" and "emblem" became less and less sharp. On the one hand, there were certain historical figures, such as Cicero, Euclid or Pythagoras, who had originally been added to the personifications of the various arts as their "paradigmatic" representatives. These portraits now became so independent, and were at the same time elaborated into pictures of professional activities which seemed so completely realistic, that the personified figure of the art could be dropped, and the individual portrait of a Pythagoras, a Euclid, or a Cicero, could illustrate at one and the same time both an actual activity and the general notion of the art in question. On the other hand, abstract personifications (on the lines of, for example, the Hague miniature) could now become so realistic that they, too, bear the appearance of genre pictures of an occupational activity. In either case the minor figures, and implements that in earlier pictures had been purely emblematic, could be turned into illustrative elements and unite themselves in the three-dimensional space of the picture—both with "Pythagoras" or "Cicero" (now raised to the level of general significance), and with "Rhetoric" or "Music" (now particularised to the extent of resembling a concrete genre scene). PL. 101

Thus, to give an example of the first possibility, a German manuscript of the third quarter of the fifteenth century[97] illustrates the notion "Geometry" by means of a figure of Euclid sitting, accompanied by an assistant, at a table laden with measuring instruments, and holding a pair of compasses and a set-square, while in a special strip along the bottom another assistant is taking soundings (PLATE 102). In this subsidiary scene we have a sort of half-way house between the purely emblematic use of minor figures, as in the Hague miniature, and their inclusion in a common space with the main figure (as in PLATE 104).

---

death's-heads); below are "Entendement" in a pensive attitude, and "Sapience", illumined by the direct vision of God the Father and his angels. Dr B. Martens kindly brought this miniature to our notice. "Ars" as a smith appears in the Brussels Aristotle-Oresme MS 9505, fol. 115ᵛ, which is related to this both in time and manner.

[96] Cf. E. BREITENBACH and T. HILLMANN, *Anzeiger für schweizerische Altertumskunde*, VOL. XXXIX (1937), pp. 23 sqq.

[97] London, Brit. Mus., Add. MS 15692 (*De septem artibus liberalibus*), fol. 29ᵛ.

On the other hand, in a group of somewhat later French manuscripts real personifications appear, representing notions such as "Déduccion loable".[98] These personifications, incidentally, are metaphorical as well as allegorical, since actual working tools could only be attributed to such a sub-division of rhetoric because the text credited it with so strengthening the logical edifice of thought "que rient n'y reste trou ne fente."[99] Armed with a set-square, "Déduccion loable" sits in a room, overlooking two unfinished houses and filled with joists, beams, and carpenter's tools that are entirely realistic. Here we can either interpret the various instruments as emblems around which a room has been built, or regard the whole as a workshop and dwelling-room in which the emblems are distributed (PLATE 103).

After these examples we are in a position to understand a certain portrait of "Geometry" which is of the greatest importance for our subject, namely, a woodcut from Gregor Reisch's *Margarita philosophica*, Strasbourg, 1504 (PLATE 104).[100] "Geometria", once again a real personification, sits at a table full of planimetric and stereometric figures, her hands busied with compasses and a

---

[98] Munich, Staatsbibliothek, Cod. gall. 15. On this, cf. COMTE DE ROSANBO, "Notice sur Les Douze Dames de Rhétorique" (from MS fr. 1174 of the Bibliothèque Nationale), in *Bulletin de la Société française de reproductions de manuscrits à peintures*, VOL. XIII (1929). In the history of types these ladies (and also, for instance "Dame Eloquence") come very near to Dürer's "Melencolia".

[99] A similar "metaphorical" or "double" allegory also occurs in the "Artes" series probably from Alsace (SCHREIBER, *Manuel*, No. 1874, reproduced in P. HEITZ, *Einblattdrucke des 15. Jahrhunderts*, VOL. LXIV, No. 6, and in E. REICKE, *Der Gelehrte in der deutschen Vergangenheit*, Leipzig 1900, figs. 27–29). These portraits, despite their abstract titles such as *Arismetica*, etc. are, regarded as types, fully realistic occupational representations—so much so, indeed, that with one exception they show us not the paradigmatic representatives of the various sciences, but simple peasants and artisans, whose activity refers to the liberal arts either by way of metaphor (as in the case of *Déduccion loable*), or else by alluding to their practical application. Arithmetic alone is represented by a man actually counting; Grammar, Rhetoric and Logic, on the other hand, are represented by a sower, a miller and a baker (for Aristotle made bread out of the seed which Priscian had sown and Cicero ground), and Astronomy by a painter, a figure known from the pictures of the children of Mercury or of Luke's Madonna, except that here he is painting stars in the sky. Geometry, however, is represented not by a geometrician but by an "appareilleur" who is measuring a stone on a site, and the accompanying couplet runs

"Ich kan pawen vnd wol messen,
Darumb will ich Eclides (*sic*) nit vergessen."

The difference, in comparison with *Déduccion loable*, is, as in other cases, that there a lady easily recognisable as a personification is sitting in a carpenter's shop, whereas here ordinary peasants and workmen are really sowing, milling and baking.

[100] Reproduced in O. LAUFFER, *Deutsche Altertümer im Rahmen deutscher Sitte*, Leipzig 1918, plate 5.

sphere.[101] She is surrounded by scenes of activity, of which the smaller scale contrasts sharply both with the perspective of the picture as a whole, and with the size of the main figure. They are subordinated to it as dependent notions rather than co-ordinated with it as objects in a coherent space; that is to say, the relation of the tools to the main figure is something like that of the small occupational scenes in the Hague miniature to the figure of "Art", or those on the gilt glass already mentioned to the figure of the deceased ship-owner. Like these, they may be regarded as dramatised trade emblems. In an organisational sense, the toil of the ship-builders sawing and planing is "governed" by the ship-owner; and in an intellectual sense the activities shown here are "subordinated" to "Geometria"; for all the work that is going on is merely a practical application of her theoretical discoveries. On the ground floor of the house under construction (a huge block of stone is still suspended from a crane) the ceiling is being vaulted; hammer, ruler and moulding plane are lying on the ground; a kneeling man is drawing a plan with the help of a set-square; another is dividing a very naturalistic map into "iugera"; and with the help of a sextant and astrolabe two young astronomers are studying the night sky, in which, despite heavy cloud, the moon and stars are brightly shining.[102]

Pl. 101

No one whose historical sense can bridge the gulf between a didactic picture and a great work of art can deny that this "typus Geometriae"[103] is extraordinarily akin to *Melencolia I*. We must

---

[101] Cf. Martianus Capella, *Nuptiae Philologiae et Mercurii*, vi, 575 sqq., esp. 580–81 (pp. 286 sqq. in A. Dick's edition, Leipzig 1925). Geometry's serving women are here carrying a "mensula" covered with a greenish dust, "depingendis designandisque opportuna formis"; the author describes the lady herself as "feminam luculentam, radium dextera, altera sphaeram solidam gestitantem."

[102] The groundwork for all this had already been laid by Martianus Capella's description. Geometry is wearing a "peplum", "in quo siderum magnitudines et meatus, circulorum mensurae conexionesque vel formae, umbra etiam telluris in caelum quoque perveniens vel lunae orbes ac solis auratos caliganti murice decolorans inter sidera videbatur"; and "in usum germanae ipsius Astronomiae crebrius commodatum, reliqua vero versis illitum diversitatibus numerorum, gnomonum stilis, interstitiorum, ponderum mensurarumque formis diversitate colorum variegata renidebat" (A. Dick (ed.), p. 289). Such a garment could naturally be dispensed with by our artist, as astral phenomena could be directly represented, though the peacock's feather in Geometria's cap is not without allegorical significance; the peacock according to Ripa, under the heading *Notte, seconda parte* (quoting Pierio Valeriano), signifies "la notte chiara, e stellata, vedendosi nella sua coda tanti occhi, come tante stelle nel Cielo".

[103] Already in the 1512 edition of Gregor Reisch's *Margarita philosophica* (fol. o 1ʳ) the portrait is simplified along these lines; Geometria is holding the sextant herself, and is measuring a barrel with a pair of compasses (a remarkable anticipation of Kepler's *Stereometria doliorum*), while a rule lies on the ground, and a ship is sailing in the distance.

not forget that, as has been frequently pointed out, trade tools and trade scenes are constantly interchanged, and, in certain instances, even combined. We are therefore justified in imagining
PL. 104 that the illustrator of Gregor Reisch's book might have represented the tools as emblems instead of showing their application in the minor scenes[104]; and we have then only to add to them the implements that are in fact seen scattered about on the table and on the ground in the woodcut in order to be aware of an astonishing measure of agreement in the inventory of both designs. Dürer, too, still in accordance with Martianus Capella, shows a figure with a sphere and a pair of compasses engaged in construction; here, as in the woodcut, there are hammer, moulding plane and set-square on the ground. In the woodcut, Geometria has writing materials beside her on the table; in Dürer's engraving, also, there are writing materials on the ground near the sphere[105];

---

[104] Thus in the miniature, PLATE 103.

[105] There is no reason to doubt that this object is in reality nothing but a portable writing compendium, consisting of a lockable inkwell with a pen-case attached to it by a leather strap but unfortunately truncated by the left-hand margin of the picture. And yet after I. A. ENDRES (*Die christliche Kunst*, VOL. IX (1913), several instalments), had interpreted it as a spinning top, and F. A. NAGEL (*Der Kristall auf Dürer's Melancholie*, Nuremberg 1922) as a plummet, W. BÜHLER in (*Mitteilungen der Gesellschaft für vervielfältigende Kunst*, 1925, pp. 44 sqq.) called it a paint-jar with a stick and with a thread wound round it in spirals to facilitate the drawing of a straight line (whereas these spiral effects are nothing but plaited leather, such as occurs not only on other pen-cases but even on knife-sheaths, cf. e.g. Breughel's drawing, Tolnai No. 77); while according to P. BRANDT (in *Die Umschau in Wissenschaft und Technik*, VOL. XXXII (1928), pp. 276 sqq.) it was even meant to be a cone-shaped plummet, with a case for the line standing on a saucer! To set all doubt at rest we may mention the analogous cases in Dürer's own works already pointed out by Giehlow and also by F. HONECKER (in *Zeitschrift für christliche Kunst*, VOL. XXVI (1913), col. 323)—the woodcut B60 and the prayer book of Maximilian I, plate 14, both representing St John on Patmos, and the woodcut B113 of St Jerome—and add a few others which might easily be multiplied: (1) the vision of St John by the brothers Limburg in Chantilly (*Les très riches heures de Jean de France*, ed. P. Durrieu, Paris 1904, fol. 17ʳ, plate 14); (2) the vision of St John in the Coburg Bible; (3) Dürer's woodcut B70; (4) the Ruggieri medal already mentioned above, p. 310, note 93; (5) a portrait of St Augustine, dating from *c.* 1450, in a MS at Utrecht of his Confessions (reproduced by A. W. BYVANCK and G. J. HOOGEWERFF, *La miniature hollandaise et les manuscrits illustrés du 14ᵉ au 16ᵉ siècles aux Pays-Bas septentrionaux*, VOL. II, The Hague, 1923, plate 187); (6) a satirical woodcut in GEILER VON KEISERSPERG'S *Sünden des Munds*, Strasbourg 1518 (reproduced in E. REICKE, *Der Gelehrte*, fig. 99); (7) Ghirlandaio's St Jerome in Ognissanti; (8) Hans Döring's woodcut (see below, text p. 335 sq. and PLATE 107) which is all the more important since he took the whole of his instrumentarium directly from Dürer's engraving. Giehlow's explanation (GIEHLOW (1904), p. 76) of the inkwell as a hieroglyph symbolising the sacred writings of the Egyptians does not seem to us tenable because the hieroglyph for the "sacrae litterae Aegyptiorum" (cf. *Jahrbuch der kunsthistorischen Sammlungen des allerhöchsten Kaiserhauses*, VOL. XXXII (1915), p. 195) is not composed merely of the pen or of the inkwell alone, but of inkwell, stilograph and sieve, the accompanying text laying at least as much emphasis on the last component as on the other two: "Aegypciacas ostendentes litteras sacrasve aut finem, atramentum et cribrum calamum quoque effigiant. Litteras

while the relatively simple stereometric objects with which Geometria is busied find their more complicated counterpart in Dürer's much-discussed rhomboid.[106] When one adds that the clouds, the moon and the stars that are shown in the woodcut have their counterpart in Dürer's engraving, and that the putto scribbling on his slate was originally, in the preparatory sketch (PLATE 8), to have been working with a sextant like the boy (!) on the left of Geometria, one is bound to consider the connexion as more than probable. We may even consider as a possibility that the ladder should be interpreted as the implement of a building under construction. The *Margarita philosophica* was one of the most widely known encyclopaedias of the time; it even appeared in an Italian translation as late as 1600: and the connexion with Dürer's engraving is not invalidated by the fact that the latter also took over characteristics from non-allegorical representations of occupations—the less so as they belong to the iconography of portraits of scholars, who were at the same time the liberal arts personified. Thus, regarded historically, the sleeping dog is simply a descendant of the poodle or Pomeranian so often seen in the scholars' studies[107]; the wreath is a constant attribute of the "homo literatus", and Dürer himself (for we think that it was he) had crowned the young Terence with it,[108] while it distinguishes both Jacob Locher the poet,[109] and Marsilio Ficino the philosopher.[110] PL. 7

---

equidem, quoniam apud Aegypcios omnia scripta cum his perficiantur. Calamo etenim ac nulla alia re scribunt. Cribrum vero, quoniam cribrum principale vas conficiendi panis ex calamis fieri soleat. Ostendunt itaque, quemadmodum omnis, cui victus suppeditat, litteras discere potest, qui vero illo caret, alia arte utatur necesse est. Quam ob rem apud ipsos disciplina 'sbo' vocatur, quod interpretari potest victus abundancia. Sacras vero litteras, quoniam cribrum vitam ac mortem discernit." It is highly improbable that anyone who intended making a hieroglyphic translation of certain notions should so arbitrarily have modified the symbols handed down by Horapollo. (From Vienna, Nationalbibl., MS 3255, fol. 47r.)

[106] Appendix I, pp. 400 sqq.

[107] Cf. Dürer's own engraving of St Jerome, the Darmstadt miniature of Petrarch reproduced in J. SCHLOSSER, *Oberitalienische Trecentisten*, Leipzig 1921, plate II), the woodcut in B. Corio's *Chronicle of Milan* of 1503 (reproduced in E. REICKE, *Der Gelehrte in der deutschen Vergangenheit*, Leipzig 1900, fig. 55) or the illustration of medical study in H. BRAUNSCHWEIG's *Liber de arte distillandi*, Strasbourg 1512 (reproduced in REICKE, op. cit., fig. 46).

[108] Cf. E. RÖMER, in *Jahrbuch der preussischen Kunstsammlungen*, VOL. XLVII (1926), plate I, p. 136.

[109] Woodcut in JACOB LOCHER, *Panegyrici ad regem . . .*, Strasbourg 1497 (reissued in H. BRAUNSCHWEIG's *Medicinarius*, 1505, fol. cxxxiv), reproduced in E. REICKE, *Der Gelehrte in der deutschen Vergangenheit*, Leipzig 1900, plate 66.

[110] H. BRAUNSCHWEIG, *Medicinarius*, 1505, fol. cxxxiiv.

With regard to composition, an astronomical picture such as the woodcut on the title page of Johannes Angelus's *Astrolabium planum* may also have had some influence; it was published just at the time of Dürer's first visit to Venice, and in more than one direction it seems generally to prepare the ground for the spatial scheme of the engraving (PLATE 94).[111] However that may be, it cannot possibly be a coincidence that so many of Dürer's occupational symbols correspond with those in the "typus Geometriae", and that, as we shall shortly show, even those details that are lacking in the balder woodcut can be subsumed, almost completely, under the notion of geometry.

Is Dürer's "Melencolia" then really a "Geometria"? Yes and no. For if she shares the circumstances of her occupation with
PL. 104 the lady with the peacock's feather in the woodcut, she shares the manner of her occupation, or, rather of her lack of occupation, with the portraits of melancholics in the German almanacs. While in the Strasbourg illustration all is energetic and joyous activity—the little figures drawing and measuring, observing and experimenting, and the patroness eagerly encompassing her sphere—the essential characteristic of Dürer's "Melencolia" is that she is doing nothing with any of these tools for mind or hand, and that the things on which her eye might rest simply do not exist for her. The saw lies idly at her feet; the grindstone with its chipped edge[112] leans uselessly against the wall; the book lies in her lap with closed clasps; the rhomboid and the astral phenomena are ignored; the sphere has rolled to the ground; and the compasses are "spoiling for want of occupation".[113] There is no doubt that in spite of everything this failure to employ things that are there to be used, this disregard of what is there to be seen, do link *Melencolia I* with the slothful melancholy represented by the spinstress asleep or lost in idle depression. The "Acedia" in the broadsheet (PLATE 92) with her head resting on her left hand, and her spindle lying idle in her lap, is the dull-

---

[111] JOHANNES ANGELUS, *Astrolabium planum*, Venice 1494 (lacking in the 1st edition of 1488). Cf., in a contrary sense, esp. the relationship of the figure to the plane of the picture and the diagonal composition of the whole as conditioned by this; even the attitude of the head, with one eye cut into by the outline of the profile, seems familiar. The same scheme, though with the figure given heightened activity and emotional expression, in typical Renaissance fashion, appears in the woodcut to CECCO D'ASCOLI'S *Acerba*, Venice 1524 (reproduced in HARTLAUB, *Geheimnis*, p. 38).

[112] For the significance of this, see below, p. 329 (text).

[13] H. WÖLFFLIN, *Die Kunst Albrecht Dürers*, 5th edition, Munich 1926, p. 253.

witted sister of Dürer's "Melencolia"; and we know how familiar Dürer was with this lower type of melancholy, from the fact that he accorded it a place in Maximilian I's prayer book.[114]

From the standpoint, therefore, of the history of types alone, Dürer's engraving is made up in its details of certain traditional Melancholy or Saturn motifs (keys and purse, head on hand, dark face, clenched fist): but, taken as a whole, it can only be understood if it is regarded as a symbolic synthesis of the "typus Acediae" (the popular exemplar of melancholy inactivity) with the "typus Geometriae" (the scholastic personification of one of the "liberal arts").

2. THE NEW MEANING OF "MELENCOLIA I"

(*a*) The new Form of Expression

The idea behind Dürer's engraving, defined in terms of the history of types, might be that of Geometria surrendering to melancholy, or of Melancholy with a taste for geometry. But this pictorial union of two figures, one embodying the allegorised ideal of a creative mental faculty, the other a terrifying image of a destructive state of mind, means far more than a mere fusion of two types; in fact, it establishes a completely new meaning, and one that as far as the two starting points are concerned amounts almost to a twofold inversion of meaning. When Dürer fused the portrait of an "ars geometrica" with that of a "homo melancholicus"—an act equal to the merging of two different worlds of thought and feeling—he endowed the one with a soul, the other with a mind. He was bold enough to bring down the timeless knowledge and method of a liberal art into the sphere of human striving and failure, bold enough, too, to raise the animal heaviness of a "sad, earthy" temperament to the height of a struggle with intellectual problems. Geometria's workshop has changed from a cosmos of clearly ranged and purposefully employed tools into a chaos of unused things; their casual distribution reflects a psychological unconcern.[115] But Melancholia's inactivity has changed from the idler's lethargy and the sleeper's unconsciousness to the compulsive preoccupation

---

[114] Prayer Book, fol. 48v. For the presence of the figure in the German *Ship of Fools* to the illustrations of which Dürer probably contributed, see above, p. 301 (text).

[115] H. Wölfflin, *Die Kunst Albrecht Dürers*, p. 255.

of the highly-strung. Both are idle, Dürer's wreathed and ennobled "Melencolia", with her mechanically-held compasses, and the dowdy "Melancholica" of the calendar illustrations with her useless spindle; but the latter is doing nothing because she has fallen asleep out of sloth, the former because her mind is preoccupied with interior visions, so that to toil with practical tools seems meaningless to her. The "idleness" in one case is below the level of outward activity; in the other, above it. If Dürer was the first to raise the allegorical figure of Melancholy to the plane of a symbol,[116] this change appears now as the means—or perhaps the result—of a change in significance: the notion of a "Melencolia" in whose nature the intellectual distinction of a liberal art was combined with a human soul's capacity for suffering could only take the form of a winged genius.

The creative power which generated this new conception naturally informs also the traditional details. Set pieces that seem to be entirely conventional play a curious part in producing that impression of casualness so typical of the engraving; the purse, for instance, instead of being attached to the belt by ribbons, has slipped carelessly to the ground, the keys hang crookedly in their twisted ring—very different from the housewifely chatelaine of the *Madonna at the Wall*. And when even these inanimate details become eloquent, when the sleeping dog (which in the usual picture of scholars is enjoying the quiet of the study and the warmth of the stove) has become a half-starved wretch, curled up, dead-tired, and shivering on the cold earth, then how striking and how new those things appear which have always been significant in a specifically human sense. We know now that the motif of the clenched fist was a traditional one, already used here and there before Dürer (PLATE 72). For a medieval illustrator, the clenched fist was the sign of certain delusions, and he conceived it as an inevitable adjunct of the figure in question, as inevitable as the knife which St Bartholomew always carries. But in Dürer's *Melencolia I* the clenched hand also supports the head; it thereby visibly approaches the seat of thought, and, by ceasing to be an isolated attribute, merges with

---

[116] These stages of development, discussed above from a systematic point of view, can be shown in the example of *Melencolia I* to have been stages in an actual historical process; for the "symbolic" form of the engraving did in fact evolve from the combination of a purely "personifying" representation (i.e. the "typus Geometriae") with a purely "paradigmatic" one (i.e. the portrait of a melancholic as in the calendars).

the thoughtful face into one area of compressed power, containing not only the strongest contrasts of light and shade, but also absorbing all there is, in the otherwise motionless figure, of physical and mental life. Moreover, the clenched left hand is in striking contrast to the lethargically sinking right hand; it is the hand no longer of an unfortunate madman who "thinks", as one text puts it, "that he holds a great treasure, or the whole world, in his hand"; but of a completely reasonable being, intent on creative work—and sharing none the less the same fate as the poor madman in not being able either to grasp or to release an imaginary something. The gesture of the clenched fist, hitherto a mere symptom of disease, now symbolises the fanatical concentration of a mind which has truly grasped a problem, but which at the same moment feels itself incapable either of solving or of dismissing it.

The clenched fist tells the same story as the gaze directed towards an empty distance. How different it is from the downcast eye formerly attributed to the melancholic or child of Saturn![117] Melencolia's eyes stare into the realm of the invisible with the same vain intensity as that with which her hand grasps the impalpable. Her gaze owes its uncanny expressiveness not only to the upward look, the unfocussed eyes typical of hard thinking, but also, above all, to the fact that the whites of her eyes, particularly prominent in such a gaze, shine forth from a dark face, that "dark face" which, as we know, was also a constant trait of the traditional picture of Melancholy, but in Dürer's

---

[117] Cf. Rufus' κατηφεῖς (above, text p. 50), probably to be understood as a psychological term, and numerous later texts, in which certainly the pose is intended as a means of expression: e.g. Raimundus Lullus: "Et naturaliter erga terram respiciunt"; Berlin, Cod. germ. fol. 1191, now in Marburg: "Sin [e.g. the melancholic's] Antlitz czu der Erden gekart"; also the text on Saturn printed in A. HAUBER, *Planetenkinderbilder und Sternbilder*, Strasbourg 1916, p. 23: "Sin [e.g. Saturn's child] angesicht alles geneiget zu der erden." It says something for the power of suggestion of such a tradition that a description of Dürer's engraving (*Pictura Melancholiae*) by Melanchthon—admittedly known to us only at second hand—says in obvious contradiction to the visible fact: "Vultu severo, qui in magna consideratione nusquam aspicit, sed palpebris dejectis humum intuetur." Thus Berlin, MS theol. lat. qu. 97, now in Tübingen, a composite MS which a certain Sebastian Redlich copied from notes by Conrad Cordatus, fol. 290r (rather poorly edited by H. Wrampelmeyer, *Ungedruckte Schriften Philipp Melanchthons*, Beilage zum Jahresbericht des Kgl. Gymnasiums zu Clausthal, Easter 1911, p. 8, No. 62). This description, an illuminating one in many ways ("Albertus Durerus, artificiosissimus pictor, melancholici picturam ita expressit . . .") is a mixture of minute observation and subtle psychological interpretation, and of pure fantasy. At the end, for instance, the author says "Cernere etiam est . . . ad fenestram aranearum tela", although neither a spider's web nor even a window is present. Here Melanchthon was probably thinking of another portrait of melancholy (cf. our PLATE 139 and p. 393 sq.) or of an engraving such as G. Pencz's *Tactus* (B109).

portrait denotes something entirely new. Here too, representing the "dark face" less as dark-skinned than as darkly shadowed,[118] he transformed the physiognomic or pathological fact into an expression, almost an atmosphere. Like the motif of the clenched fist, that of the dark face was taken over from the sphere of medical semeiology; but the discoloration becomes, literally, an overshadowing, which we understand not as the result of a physical condition, but as the expression of a state of mind. In this picture, dusk (signified by a bat)[119] is magically illumined by the glow of heavenly phenomena, which cause the sea in the background to glow with phosphorescence, while the foreground seems to be lit by a moon standing high in the sky and casting deep shadows.[120] This highly fantastic and literal "twilight" of the whole picture is not so much based on the natural conditions of a certain time of day: it denotes the uncanny twilight of a mind, which can neither cast its thoughts away into the darkness nor "bring them to the light". Thus, Dürer's Melencolia (it is unnecessary to add that the upright figure in the preliminary study has been deliberately changed to a drooping one) sits in front of her unfinished building, surrounded by the instruments of creative work, but sadly brooding with a feeling that she is achieving nothing.[121] With hair hanging down unkempt, and her gaze, thoughtful and sad, fixed on a point in the distance, she keeps watch, withdrawn from the world, under a darkening sky, while the bat begins its circling flight. "A genius with wings

---

[118] This fact was questioned by W. Bühler (in *Mitteilungen der Gesellschaft für vervielfältigende Kunst*, 1925, pp. 44 sqq.) as the globe, the fist and the putto's face appear lighter, though they are in the same light. But these objects of comparison seem lighter only because they are merely partly in shadow, while Melancholy's face, turned much further to the left than the putto's, is fully in shadow, and should therefore be compared only with the shadowed portion of the objects named by Bühler (or perhaps with the right half of the collar round her shoulder).

[119] Ripa expressly describes this as an attribute of the "Crepusculo della Sera". Moreover, we know (see above, p. 11, note 24 and *passim*) that the third quarter of the day, i.e. the time between 3 p.m. and 9 p.m., is proper to melancholy.

[120] It seems hitherto to have been ignored that the sun could not possibly stand so high at the time of day indicated by the sky and the bat, as to cast, for instance, the hour-glass's shadow. The scene, therefore, if indeed such a realistic interpretation is desired, was imagined as by moonlight, once more in significant contrast to the sun-drenched interior in the St Jerome engraving (see below, p. 364, note 276).

[121] In Melanchthon's analysis, just quoted, the ladder motif in particular is interpreted in this sense, i.e. as a symbol of an all-embracing but often ineffectual, if not absurd, mental search: "ut autem indicaret nihil non talibus ab ingeniis comprehendi solere, et quam eadem saepe in absurda deferrentur, ante illam scalas in nubes eduxit, per quarum gradus quadratum saxum veluti ascensionem moliri fecit."

that she will not unfold, with a key that she will not use to unlock, with laurels on her brow, but with no smile of victory."[122]

Dürer defined and enhanced this impression of an essentially human tragedy in two ways by the addition of auxiliary figures. The dozing of the tired and hungry dog (the former owner of the preliminary drawing—see PLATE 4—rightly called it "canis dormitans", making use of the intensive form, rather than "canis dormiens") signifies the dull sadness of a creature entirely given over to its unconscious comfort or discomfort[123]; while the industry of the writing putto signifies the careless equanimity of a being that has only just learnt the contentment of activity, even when unproductive, and does not yet know the torment of thought, even when productive; it is not yet capable of sadness, because it has not yet attained human stature. The conscious sorrow of a human being wrestling with problems is enhanced both by the unconscious suffering of the sleeping dog and by the happy unself-consciousness of the busy child.

(*b*) The New Notional Content

The new meaning expressed in Dürer's engraving communicates itself to eye and mind with the same directness as that with which the outward appearance of a man approaching us reveals his character and mood; and it is in fact the distinction of a great work of art, that whether it represents a bunch of asparagus or a subtle allegory it can, on one particular level, be understood by the naïve observer and the scientific analyst alike. Indeed, the impression which we have just attempted to describe will probably be shared, to a certain extent, by almost everybody who looks at the engraving, though in words they may express their feelings differently.

But just as there are works of art whose interpretation is exhausted in the communication of directly experienced impressions, because their intention is satisfied merely by the representation of a "first-order" (in this case purely visual) world of objects,[124] so there are others whose composition embraces a

---

[122] LUDWIG BARTNING, *Worte der Erinnerung an Adolf Bartning*, privately printed, Hamburg 1929.

[123] Thus, too, in Melanchthon's description: "Jacet autem prope hanc ad pedes ipsius, contracta corporis parte, parte etiam porrecta, canis, cuiusmodi solet illa bestia in fastidio esse, languida et sominiculosa et perturbari in quiete."

[124] Cf. E. PANOFSKY, in *Logos*, VOL. XXI (1932), pp. 103 sqq.

"second-order" body of elements, based on a cultural inheritance, and expressing, therefore, a notional content as well. That *Melencolia I* belongs to the latter group is demonstrated not only by Dürer's note, which attributes a definite allegorical meaning even to the innocent appurtenances of a housewife's wardrobe,[125] but, above all, by the evidence—just adduced—that Dürer's engraving is the result of a synthesis of certain allegorical pictures of melancholy and the arts, whose notional content, no less than their expressive significance, did indeed change, but could hardly be altogether lost. It is hence inherently probable that the characteristic motifs of the engraving should be explained either as symbols of Saturn (or Melancholy), or as symbols of Geometry.

(i) *Symbols of Saturn or Melancholy*

We have discussed first the motifs associated with Saturn (or Melancholy)—the propped-up head, the purse and keys, the clenched fist, the dark face[126]—because they belonged to the personal characteristics of the melancholic, and because, with varying degrees of completeness, they had all been evolved in the pre-Dürer tradition. Besides these motifs there are others which are not so much essential properties as extraneous trappings of the figures represented, and some of them are foreign to the older pictorial tradition.

The first of these auxiliary motifs is the dog, which in itself belonged to the typical portraits of scholars. Its inclusion and the inversion of meaning by which it becomes a fellow-sufferer with Melencolia can, however, be justified by several considerations. Not only is it mentioned in several astrological sources as a typical beast of Saturn,[127] but, in the Horapollo (the introduction to the *Mysteries of the Egyptian Alphabet* which the humanists worshipped almost idolatrously), it is associated with the disposition of melancholics in general, and of scholars and prophets in particular. In 1512, Pirckheimer had finished a translation

---

[125] See above, pp. 284 sqq. (text). Among Dürer's unallegorical works showing figures with a purse and keys, we may mention the engravings B40, 84 and 90; the woodcuts B3, 80, 84, 88, 92; and, above all, the costume picture L463 with the caption "also gett man in Hewsern Nörmerck." A purse and keys also characterise the old nurse in the pictures of Danae by Titian (Prado) and Rembrandt (Hermitage).

[126] See above, pp. 289 sqq. (text).

[127] E.g. in Ibn Esra the "canes nigri", and, in a Greek MS, dogs in general (*Cat. astr. Gr.*, v, 1, p. 182, 10; quoted by W. Gundel in *Gnomon*, vol. ii (1926), p. 299, and BBG, *Sternglaube*, p. 114).

of the Horapollo from the Greek, and Dürer himself had supplied it with illustrations; and curiously enough, of this jointly produced codex, there survives the very page (Dürer's drawing L83) on which it is written that the hieroglyph of a dog signifies among other things the spleen, prophets, and "sacras literas"—all notions which, since the time of Aristotle, had been closely linked with the melancholic—, and that the dog, more gifted and sensitive than other beasts, has a very serious nature and can fall a victim to madness, and like deep thinkers is inclined to be always on the hunt, smelling things out, and sticking to them.[128] "The best dog", says a contemporary hieroglyphist, is therefore the one "qui faciem magis, ut vulgo aiunt, melancholicam prae se ferat"[129] —which could be said with all justice of the dog in Dürer's engraving.

The bat motif is quite independent of pictures. In fact, its invention is due purely to a textual tradition; and even in Ramler's *Shorter Mythology* it is still cited as the animal symbolic of melancholics.[130] It is mentioned, too, in the Horapollo as a sign of "homo aegrotans et incontinens".[131] Further, it served the Renaissance humanists (for better or worse) as an example of night vigil or nightly work. According to Agrippa of Nettesheim its outstanding characteristic is "vigilantia"[132]; according to Ficino it is a warning example of the ruinous and destructive effect of night study[133]; and (most remarkable of all, perhaps)

---

[128] On this cf. GIEHLOW from whose works we have frequently quoted, and to whom the credit belongs for having discovered the whole system of Renaissance hieroglyphics and for collecting all the most important material; cf. also L. VOLKMANN, *Bilderschriften der Renaissance*, Leipzig 1923, *passim*. G. LEIDINGER (in *Sitzungsberichte der Bayerischen Akademie der Wissenschaften, philol.-hist. Klasse*, 1929) has shown that Dürer knew, and even owned, the *Hypnerotomachia Poliphili*.

[129] Thus Pierio Valeriano, quoted in GIEHLOW (1904), p. 72.

[130] K. RAMLER, *Kurzgefasste Mythologie*, 4th edn., Berlin 1820, p. 456: "Some make bats flutter about him."

[131] K. GIEHLOW, in *Jahrbuch der kunsthistorischen Sammlungen des allerhöchsten Kaiserhauses*, VOL. XXXII (1915), p. 167.

[132] AGRIPPA OF NETTESHEIM, *Occulta philosophia*, in the autograph of 1510 discovered by Dr Hans Meier, Würzburg, Univ. Bibl., Cod. Q. 50 (for this, see below, text pp. 351 sqq.), fol. 9r. Hence a bat's heart was a talisman against sleepiness.

[133] FICINO, *De v. tripl.*, I, 7 (*Opera*, VOL. I, p. 500): "Spiritus fatigatione diurna, praesertim subtilissimi quique denique resolvuntur. Nocte igitur pauci crassique supersunt . . . , ut non aliter mancis horum fretum alis ingenium volare possit, quam vespertiliones atque bubones." Moreover Agrippa of Nettesheim mentions the bat as among Saturn's beasts: "Saturnalia sunt . . . animalia reptilia segregata, solitaria, nocturna, tristia, contemplativa vel penitus lenta, avara, timida, melancolica, multi laboris et tardi motus, ut bubo, talpa,

in ancient times its membranes were actually used for writing, particularly in setting down spells against sleeplessness.[134]

Finally, the seascape with the little ships can also be fitted into the context of Saturn and Melancholy. By classical and Arabian astrologers the god who fled across the sea to Latium was reckoned "lord of the sea and of seafarers", so that his children liked to live near water and to make a living by such trades.[135] Nor is this all. Saturn—and, more particularly, any comet belonging to him—was also held responsible for floods and high tides; and it can safely be said that any comet which figures in a picture of Melancholy must be one of these "Saturnine comets", of which it is expressly stated that they threaten the world with the "dominium melancholiae".[136] It is, then, scarcely a coincidence that a rainbow shines above Dürer's sea, and that the water has so flooded the flat beach that it is lapping round the trees between the two bright peninsulas; for even in Babylonian cuneiform texts it had been considered a definite fact that a

---

basiliscus, vespertilio" (the Würzburg MS, fol. 17v; from the printed edition also mentioned by W. Gundel, in *Gnomon*, vol. ii (1926), p. 290, and BBG, *Sternglaube*, p. 115). According to this, any incense offered to Saturn should contain bat's blood (the Würzburg MS, fol. 25v; from the printed edition quoted by Gundel, loc. cit.). In addition to these direct mentions there are indirect ones, crediting Saturn with night birds in general (τὰ τῆς νυκτὸς πετεινά, "omnia, quae noctu vagantur"): *Cat. astr. Gr.*, iv, 122 (quoted by Gundel, loc. cit.) and Ranzovius, *Tractatus astrologicus*, Frankfurt 1609, p. 47. The sixty-second emblem in Alciato's famous collection of emblemata is of particular interest:

"Vespertilio.
Vespere quae tantum volitat, quae lumine lusca est,
Quae cum alas gestet, caetera muris habet;
Ad res diversas trahitur: mala nomina primum
Signat, quae latitant, iudiciumque timent.
Inde et Philosophos, qui dum caelestia quaerunt,
Caligant oculis, falsaque sola vident . . . ."

These lines read like a list of the characteristics of the Saturnine and melancholy mind. The reference to a certain type of philosopher is significant.

[134] T. Birt, *Die Buchrolle in der Kunst*, Leipzig 1907, pp. 286 sqq. (with references).

[135] See above, pp. 130, 138, 143 sqq. (text). Leonhard Reynmann's *Nativitet-Kalender* of 1515, too, states that the children of Saturn "deal with watery things" (fol. D. iiv). Campagnola's engraving of Saturn, mentioned above, pp. 210 ff. (text), may have given Dürer the actual impulse to adopt the sea motif. This engraving, influenced in its turn by earlier Dürer engravings, can hardly have been unknown to the mature artist.

[136] Cf. Bartolomeo da Parma, ed. E. Narducci, in *Bulletino di Bibliografia e di Storia delle Scienze Matematiche e Fisiche*, xvii (1884), p. 156. Correlating individual comets to individual planets dates back to Nechepso-Petosiris; cf. BBG, *Sternglaube*, pp. 51 and 129, and W. Gundel in Pauly-Wissowa, s.v. "Kometen", and in *Hessische Blätter für Volkskunde*, vii (1908), pp. 109 sqq. (The planet bequeathes its properties to the comet, "tanquam filio"; cf. A. Mizaldus, *Cometographia*, Paris 1549, p. 91, the same author says (pp. 177 and 180) that Saturn's comet causes "melancholicos morbos" and floods, etc., and is particularly dangerous to the children of Saturn.)

comet with its head towards the earth pointed to high water; and it was the melancholic in particular who was able to foresee such misfortunes.[137]

However, these phenomena, partly sad, partly menacing, are countered by two other motifs[138] signifying palliatives against Saturn and against Melancholy. One is the wreath which the woman has bound round her brow. Although, in the history of types, this wreath is traceable to the adornment of the "homo literatus" and therefore proclaims Melencolia's intellectual powers,[139] nevertheless it must also be reckoned as an antidote to melancholy, because it is made up of the leaves of two plants which are both of a watery nature and therefore counteract the earthy dryness of the melancholy temperament; these plants are water parsley (*Ranunculus aquaticus*)—which Dürer had already associated with the combination of "Auster", "Phlegma" and "Aqua" in his woodcut[140] illustrating the work of Conrad Celtes (PLATE 83)—and the common watercress (*Nasturtium officinale*).[141] The other antidote is the square of the number four, apparently engraved on metal: thanks to Giehlow's pioneer research work there can no longer be any doubt that this is intended not only as a sign of the arithmetical side of the melancholy genius but, above all, as a "magic square" in the original sense of that expression.[142] It is a talisman to attract the healing influence of Jupiter; it is the non-pictorial, mathematical substitute for

---

137 Cf. BBG, *Sternglaube*, p. 114 and below, pp. 357 sqq. (text).

138 For the object which has formerly been interpreted erroneously as a clyster, see below, p. 329, note 151.

139 See above, p. 315 (text).

140 B130.

141 According to Giehlow's unpublished notes, in the sixteenth century the melancholic was expressly advised to place damp (i.e. naturally damp) herbs on his brow, "like a plaster". The identification as water parsley, of the plant appearing in Melencolia's wreath, and in the woodcut B130, is given by W. BÜHLER, in *Mitteilungen der Gesellschaft für vervielfältigende Kunst*, 1925, pp. 44 sqq., and E. BÜCH, in *Die medizinische Welt*, VOL. VII (1933), No. 2, p. 69. Mrs Eleanor Marquand, Princeton, whose help we gratefully acknowledge, points out, however, that Melencolia's wreath consists not of one plant but of two, the second being watercress (cf. e.g. G. BENTHAM, *Handbook of the British Flora*, London 1865). Apart from the fact that it establishes correctly an important detail, the discovery has a methodological significance: if Dürer made up the wreath of two plants having nothing in common save that they are both "watery" plants, this was not mere coincidence or purely aesthetic preference: the choice of these two plants must have been based on a conscious symbolic intention, which justifies our interpreting every detail in the engraving from the point of view of this symbolic intention.

142 GIEHLOW (1904), pp. 16 sqq. W. AHRENS's counter-arguments (in *Zeitschrift für bildende Kunst*, N. S. VOL. XXVI (1915), pp. 291 sqq.) were based on the assumption, which has since been decisively disproved, that the astro-magical significance of the planetary squares cannot be found in western sources before 1531 (see below, text p. 326 sq.). ☞

those images of astral deities which were recommended by Ficino, Agrippa and all the other teachers of white magic. Of this "mensula Jovis", which comprised within itself all the beneficent powers of the "temperator Saturni", one fourteenth-century author wrote: "If a man wears it his bad luck will turn into good, good into better luck"[143]; and in Paracelsus we read: "This symbol makes its bearer fortunate in all his dealings and drives away all cares and fears."[144] Dürer was not an arithmetician, but he was thoroughly familiar with the significance of the magic square in iatromathematics, and that is perhaps the only aspect of this curious combination of numbers which could have attracted his attention and engaged his interest. This indeed is clear, not

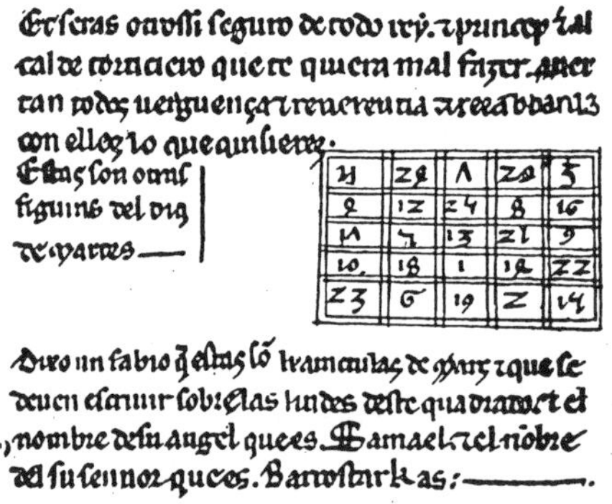

FIGURE I. The magical square of Mars. From a Spanish manuscript of about 1300. Bibl. Vat., Cod. Reg. lat. 1283.

only because the squares had been recognised as symbols of the various planets at a time when the arithmetical problems involved in them had not been gone into at all,[145] but also because, as it was recently discovered, one man with whom Dürer probably

[143] Vienna, Nationalbibliothek, Cod. 5239, fol. 147ᵛ: "Et si quis portauerit eam, qui sit infortunatus fortunabitur, de bono in melius efficiet [*sic*]" quoted in A. WARBURG, *Heidnisch-antike Weissagung in Wort und Bild zu Luthers Zeiten*, in *Gesammelte Schriften*, VOL. II, Leipzig 1932, p. 528).

[144] *Aureoli Philippi Theophrasti Paracelsi Opera omnia*, Geneva 1658, VOL. II, pp. 716. "Sigillum hoc si gestetur, gratiam, amorem et favorem apud universos conciliat . . . gestoremque suum in omnibus negotiis felicem facit, et abigit curas omnes, metumque." It was this constant depression due to worry and ungovernable anxiety (cf. Constantinus Africanus, "timor de re non timenda", and Ficino, "quod circa mala nimis formidolosus sum") that formed one of the worst and most significant symptoms of melancholy.

[145] The planetary squares were shown by A. WARBURG (*Heidnisch-antike Weissagung in Wort und Bild zu Luthers Zeiten*, in *Gesammelte Schriften*, VOL. II, Leipzig 1932, pp. 516 sqq.) to be in evidence as early as Cod. Reg. lat. 1283 (about 1300, from which FIG. I was taken), also in Vienna, Nationalbibliothek, Cod. 5239 (fourteenth century), and Wolfenbüttel, Cod. 17, 8. Aug. 4to. In the East they could no doubt be found considerably earlier.

came into personal contact was familiar with the planetary squares—Luca Pacioli, whom Dürer may easily have met at Bologna, even if he did not go there specially for the sake of meeting him. In 1500, Pacioli had in fact written a short treatise on the symbols of the planets. In it he cites Arabic sources; and a version of Jupiter's square is given which has the same—and by no means the only possible[146]—disposition of numbers as that which appears in Dürer's *Melencolia I*.[147]

But all these antidotes are merely a weak makeshift in the face of the real destiny of the melancholy person. Just as Ficino had already realised that selfless and unconditional surrender to the will of Saturn was after all not only the "ultima" but also the "optima ratio" for the intellectual man, so, too, Dürer (as we can see from the dark face and clenched fist) creates a Melencolia whose sad but sublime destiny cannot, and perhaps should not, be averted by palliatives, whether natural or magical. If the cosmic conflict between Saturn and Jupiter[148] ever came to a final decision, it could for Dürer not end in victory for Jupiter.

(ii) *Geometrical Symbols*

The motifs not yet accounted for are, as we have already hinted, geometrical symbols.

That applies without reservation to the tools and objects shown in the portrait of Geometria in the *Margarita philosophica*

---

[146] The square with 16 cells and the sum 34 can appear in 1232 different variations, cf. K. H. DE HAAS, *Frénicle's* 880 *Basic Magic Squares of* 4 × 4 *cells* . . . , Rotterdam 1935.

[147] LUCA PACIOLI's remarks on the seven planetary squares, written about 1500 (Bologna, Bibl. Univ. Cod. 250, fols. 118–122) were discovered by AMADEO AGOSTINI, who emphasises the likely connexion with Dürer: *Bolletino dell'unione matematica italiana*, II, 2 (1923), p. 2 (cf. W. WIELEITNER, in *Mitteilungen zur Geschichte der Medizin und der Naturwissenschaften*, VOL. XXII (1923), p. 125, and VOL. XXV (1926), p. 8). It is remarkable that Pacioli deals with the squares simply as a mathematical "jeu d'esprit", and merely mentions their astrological and magical significance without going into it: he therefore completely ignores any talismanic virtues of the various squares: "Le quali figure cosi numerose non senza misteri gli l'ano acomodata . . . . Le quali figure in questo nostro compendio ho uoluto inserere acio con epse ale uolte possi formar qualche ligiadro solazo . . . ." Agrippa of Nettesheim's works contain the planetary squares only in the printed edition (II, 22); they were lacking in the original version.

[148] Cf. A. WARBURG, *Heidnisch-antike Weissagung in Wort und Bild zu Luthers Zeiten*, in *Gesammelte Schriften*, VOL. II, Leipzig 1932, p. 529. However, we can associate ourselves with his description only with many reservations, since we cannot imagine the "demoniac conflict" between Saturn and Jupiter ending in a victory for the latter; nor can we accord it that prime significance for the interpretation of Dürer's engraving, which Warburg attributes to it. The "mensula Jovis", after all, is only one of many motifs, and by no means the most important. Despite Giehlow's and Warburg's acute arguments, the relevance of the engraving for Maximilian I cannot be proved; and even if it could, *Melencolia I* would have been a warning rather than a consolation to him.

(PLATE 104)—that is to say, the stars in heaven, the unfinished building, the block of stone, the sphere, the compasses, the moulding plane and set-square, the hammer, the writing materials; for the pictorial history of all these things shows them to be symbols of an occupation which practises "the art of measuring", either as an end in itself, or as a means to other ends, all more or less practical. The compasses in Melencolia's hand symbolise, as it were, the unifying intellectual purpose which governs the great diversity of tools and objects by which she is surrounded; and if we want to subdivide, we may say that, together with the sphere and the writing materials, the compasses signify pure geometry; that the building under construction, the moulding-plane, the set-square, and the hammer signify geometry applied to handicraft and building; that the astral phenomena imply geometry employed for astronomical or meteorological purposes[149]; and then, lastly, that the polyhedron represents descriptive geometry: for here, as in many other contemporary representations, it is both a problem and a symbol of geometrically defined optics—more particularly, of perspective (PLATE 95).[150]

---

[149] The reason why Dürer gave the notion of astrology a meteorological turn is explained below, text pp. 353 sqq. (For the combination of rainbow and stars, cf. e.g. *Denkmäler mittelalterlicher Meteorologie* (Neudrucke von Schriften und Karten über Meteorologie und Erdmagnetismus, ed. G. Hellmann, VOL. XV), Berlin 1904, p. 267.) It may be in connexion with this deviation that the sextant originally allotted to the putto (PLATE 8) was not adopted in the final version, for this was a specific symbol of astronomy; cf. our PLATES 94 and 104, as well as the portrait of Ptolemy in the *Margarita philosophica*, reproduced in E. REICKE, *Der Gelehrte in der deutschen Vergangenheit*, Leipzig 1900, plate 44.

[150] Cf. also the title woodcut to PETRUS APIANUS's *Instrumentbuch*, Ingolstadt 1533, and his *Inscriptiones sacrosanctae Vetustatis*, Ingolstadt 1534, initial fol. A. 1r. PLATE 95 shows Flötner's title woodcut to VITELLIO's Περὶ ὀπτικῆς, Nuremberg 1535 (used again in RIVIUS, *Vitruvius Teutsch*, Nuremberg 1548, fol. cxcviii v). It is well known that the construction of absolutely regular or half-regular polyhedrons formed almost the main problem of practical geometry during the Renaissance. The finest example next to Dürer's own *Unterweisung der Messung* is probably WENZEL JAMNITZER's *Perspectiva corporum regularium*, Nuremberg 1548 and 1568, where the five Platonic bodies are brought into perspective in all possible permutations. Even Jan Boeckhorst's *Geometria* is seated on a polyhedron like Dürer's, which is the more remarkable since for the rest the figure is modelled rather on the woodcut of Doni's *I Marmi*, Venice 1552 (PLATE 131) or its engraved replica (see below); the painting is in the Bonn Landesmuseum, No. 14, our PLATE 132.

The stereometric form of the polyhedron, which Niemann described as a truncated rhomboid (cf. Appendix 1, p. 400), and which is certainly not a truncated cube (thus F. A. NAGEL, *Der Kristall auf Dürers Melancholie*, Nuremberg 1922) gave rise, some time ago, to bitter controversy among Dutch scholars (H. A. NABAR and K. H. DE HAAS, in *Nieuwe Rotterdamsche Courant*, Avondblad, 26 April, 29 April and 5 July 1932). While Nabar confirms Niemann's reconstruction and merely adds that the rhomboids are distinguished by a remarkable regularity (angles 60° and 120°), de Haas considers the surfaces of the polyhedron slightly irregular. This we do not believe, as the perspectival phenomena on which de Haas bases his remarks contradict one another; but we may well leave this question, which for us is of secondary

But all the other objects, too, can be easily associated with the "typus Geometriae" as shown in the Strasbourg woodcut. PL. 104
Plane and saw, nails and pincers, and perhaps the almost hidden object, which is generally called a clyster,[151] but is more likely to be a pair of bellows—all these objects serve simply to swell the inventory of builders, joiners, and carpenters, who use also the grindstone, rounded and smoothed by the stone-mason.[152] Some have even wished to attribute to them the crucible with the little tongs,[153] but we prefer to attribute these to the more delicate art of the goldsmith,[154] or to alchemy, the black art connected, not with geometry, but with Saturnine melancholy.[155] The book

---

importance, to the mathematicians. K. H. DE HAAS's attempt (*Albrecht Dürer's meetkundige bouw van Reuter en Melencolia I*, Rotterdam 1932) to trace the composition of both these engravings back to a detailed system of planimetric surface division is completely outside our sphere of interest. However, it is in any case wrong to say that the rhomboid is a "block still to be chiselled into regularity", and therefore, like the free-masons' "rough block," represents didactically "the human task of moral improvement" (thus HARTLAUB, *Geheimnis*, p. 78). Dürer's polyhedron, whatever its stereometric nature, is as carefully chiselled as possible, with its very exact surfaces, while the "rough block", like Michelangelo's *Pietra alpestra e viva*, must be imagined as a still amorphous mass yet to be shaped (cf. also E. PANOFSKY, *Idea* (Studien der Bibliothek Warburg, VOL. V), Leipzig 1924, pp. 64 and 119).

[151] This interpretation, according to which the instrument in question is to be counted among the antidotes to melancholy ("purgatio ulvi" was to some extent the alpha and omega of anti-melancholy dietetics) has lately been challenged by Bühler, though without very good reason, for the disc- or bulb-like termination also appears in H. S. Beham's well-known woodcut, the *Fountain of Youth* (Pauli 1120; M. GEISBERG, *Der deutsche Einblatt-Holzschnitt*, VOL. XXII, 14) where a clyster is certainly intended. Moreover, though all the attempts at interpretation made so far must be rejected, for the colour spray which Nagel (op. cit.) sees in it occurs nowhere else, and a nail remover such as Bühler (op. cit.) suggests does not occur until the nineteenth century, we too now think that the mysterious object is more likely to belong to the class of occupational tools than to that of antidotes to melancholy. It may be either a glass-blower's pipe (such as is illustrated in G. AGRICOLA's famous work *De re metallica*, Basle 1556, new German edn. 1928, p. 507—this suggestion comes from Dr Schimangk, Hamburg), or, more probably, a pair of bellows: for this latter interpretation could bring to its support a contemporary pictorial statement, namely Hans Döring's woodcut (of which we shall speak in more detail later), which borrows its whole *instrumentarium* from *Melencolia I* and includes, in fact, a pair of bellows (cf. PLATE 107, and our text pp. 335 sqq.).

[152] On former occasions we left the question open as to whether it was a millstone or a knife-grinder's stone, though in view of the Salone frescoes (see above, text p. 204) we inclined to the latter interpretation. We are glad to find that P. BRANDT (in *Die Umschau in Wissenschaft und Technik*, VOL. XXXII (1928), pp. 276 sqq.) and, quite independently of any technical literature, W. BLUMENFELD (in *Idealistische Philologie*, VOL. III (1927–28), pp. 154 sqq.) now accept this.

[153] According to Bühler it served to melt the lead with which the joints were soldered.

[154] Cf. Schongauer's engraving, B91, or JOST AMMAN's *Eygentliche Beschreibung aller Stände auff Erden*, Frankfurt 1568—new edition Munich 1896—fol. H2.

[155] The main argument (originally Giehlow's) in favour of connecting it with alchemical operations is still based on the fact that later masters, such as Beham (PLATE 115), the Master "F. B." (PLATE 116) and M. de Vos (PLATE 140) endowed Melancholy with unmistakably alchemistic attributes, and that later on, the personification of "Alcymia"

expands the symbolism of compasses, sphere, and writing materials, in the sense that it emphasises the theory, rather than the application, of geometry; and it is obvious that, as instruments for measuring time and weight, the scales and the hourglass (with its attendant bell)[156] also belong to the general picture of "Geometria". Macrobius had already defined time as a "certa dimensio, quae ex caeli conversione colligitur" (thus showing its connexion with astronomy)[157]; and with regard to weighing, in a period which had not yet developed the notion of experimental physics, that was so positively accounted as one of geometry's functions that a famous mnemonic for the seven liberal arts quoted "ponderare" as Geometry's main task:

☞ Gram loquitur, Dia vera docet, Rhe verba colorat,
Mus canit, Ar numerat, Geo ponderat, As colit astra.[158]

We know, too, from his own lips, that Dürer himself considered the purely manual activity of the minor crafts to be applied geometry, in exactly the same way as did the tradition represented

---

occasionally held a pair of coal-tongs (e.g. the title woodcut to C. GESNER's *Newe Jewell of Health*, London 1576). The fact that Hermes Trismegistus in De Vries's series of alchemists (reproduced in HARTLAUB, *Geheimnis*, p. 46, text pp. 41 and 81) has a pair of compasses is proof neither for nor against, as he is holding the compasses not in his particular capacity as alchemist but in his general capacity as Hermes Trismegistus, who is also a cosmologer and astrologer, his second attribute being therefore an astrolabe.

156 Thus GIEHLOW (1904), p. 65. In addition the bell, taken in the sense of the hermit's bell with which St Anthony is always endowed, might point to the Saturnine melancholic's leaning towards solitude; in F. PICINELLI's *Mundus symbolicus*, Cologne 1687, XIV, 4, 23, a bell still denotes solitude, and therefore, in remarkable concordance with the usual characteristics of the melancholic, "anima a rebus materialibus, terrenis et diabolicis remota". On the other hand, the belief that the pealing of bells could avert natural disasters (cf. W. GUNDEL, in *Gnomon*, VOL. II (1926), p. 292) implies large church bells.

157 MACROBIUS, *Saturnalia*, I, 8, 7 (for this cf. the passage from Martianus Capella quoted above, p. 313, note 102). A drawing by Lucas van Leyden (Lille, Mus. Wicar) also characterises geometry by an hourglass.

158 Printed e.g. in F. OVERBECK, *Vorgeschichte und Jugend der mittelalterlichen Scholastik*, ed. C. A. Bernoulli, Basle 1917, p. 29. In the face of such evidence and of the fact that the scales are not pictorially differentiated in any way from the other instruments (for after all, Dürer was no longer at the stage of the Tübingen MS brought in for comparison by SIGRID STRAUSS-KLOEBE, in *Münchner Jahrbuch der bildenden Kunst*, new series, II (1925), p. 58, which mixed heavenly and earthly matters with a deliberately humorous intention), it is difficult to interpret the scales astronomically, i.e. as the zodiacal sign of the exaltation of Saturn (thus also W. GUNDEL, in *Gnomon*, VOL. II (1925), p. 293). If one nevertheless wishes to maintain the astrological interpretation, one may quote not only the passage from *Semifora* mentioned by Gundel, but also Melanchthon's view, brought to light by A. WARBURG, *Heidnisch-antike Weissagung in Wort und Bild zu Luthers Zeiten*, in *Gesammelte Schriften*, VOL. II, Leipzig 1932, p. 529, according to which "multo generosior est melancholia, si coniunctione Saturni et Iovis in libra temperetur" (thus also S. Strauss-Kloebe).

in the woodcuts just studied.[159] In the foreword to his *Instructions on Measuring*, on which he was at that time engaged,[160] he wrote:

Accordingly I hope no reasonable person will blame me for my enterprise, for it is done with a good intention and for the sake of all lovers of art; and it may be useful not only for painters but for goldsmiths, sculptors, stone-masons and joiners and all who need measurements.[161]

Perhaps, too, it was not mere chance that in a draft of this same introduction Dürer coupled together "planing and turning", in the same way as the plane and the turned sphere lie together in the engraving.[162]

(iii) *Symbols of Saturn or of Melancholy Combined with Geometrical Symbols: in Relation to Mythology and Astrology—in Relation to Epistemology and Psychology*

So far, in accordance with the corresponding duality in the development of types, we have sought the notional content of *Melencolia I* along two completely separate paths. But it would be surprising, and it would make Dürer's achievement appear as something accidental, or at least arbitrary, if a duality which seems to have been so completely resolved in point of form, should not also be found to possess unity with regard to meaning; or if the bold undertaking to characterise Melancholy as Geometry,

---

[159] We must also mention a highly interesting page out of a Dance of Death dating from about 1430, where the usual groups are at the same time arranged according to the Seven Liberal Arts (Clm. 3941, fol. 17ᵛ). The judge is also subordinated to geometry, and is accompanied by figures with compasses, hammer, shears, etc. The accompanying texts say:

"Gewicht vn mass ler ich dich
des tzyrkels kunst die kenn ich",

and "Rerum mensuras et earum signo figuras",

and "Evclides der meyster an geometrey lert
Der handwerck kunst, zal, wag, hoh, tyeff, leng vn preyt".

[160] Cf. the sketch, dated 1514, for one of the instruments for perspective drawing in book iv, in the Dresden Sketchbook, ed. R. Bruck, Strasb. 1905, plate 135.

[161] LF, *Nachlass*, pp. 181, 30 sqq.

[162] LF. *Nachlass*, p. 268, 12: "Will dorneben anzeigen, waraus die Zierd des Hobels oder Drehwerks, das ist durch die gereden oder runden gemacht werd." Against Bühler's denial that a turned wooden sphere is meant, we may point out that Cranach, who looked at the engraving with the eye of a contemporary, painted the spheres (on PLATES 128 and 129) quite distinctly as brown wooden spheres. We do not wish to insist on this point, but Bühler's statement that Dürer's sphere, which had been to some extent the symbol of geometry ever since Martianus Capella, represents the ball of a church steeple or even the apex of the Temple of the Holy Grail, of which the rhomboid was the base, is simply fantastic. If one insists on such an interpretation, it would have to be shown how such an object was to be fastened.

or Geometry as Melancholy, should not ultimately have revealed an inner affinity between the two themes. And such an affinity does in fact seem to exist.

The earliest (and, at the same time, most complete) western example of the previously mentioned series of pictures representing the "children of the planets"[163] was, as we may remember, the picture cycle in the Salone at Padua. Retaining the scientifically tabulated form of the Islamic manuscripts, but essentially western in style, it shows the occupations and characteristics of all the people whose birth and destiny are governed by a certain planet. Among those ruled by Saturn—who himself is represented as a "silent" king[164]—there are a man plagued with sickness and melancholy, and lame in one leg, with his head resting on his hand; then a scholar, seated, but with his arm in the same typical posture, its double significance—sorrow and reflexion—thus being divided between the two; and further, a tanner, a carpenter, a miser burying treasure, a stonemason, a peasant, a knife-grinder, a gardener, and numerous hermits (PLATES 32–33).

Thus we can see that most of those occupational symbols whose presence in Dürer's engraving of Melencolia has hitherto seemed explicable only in terms of the "art of measurement" find a place also in the world of Saturn; for in so far as they are practical and manual, the trades represented in Dürer's engraving belong not only to that group which we have seen illustrated in the woodcut of "Geometria" in the *Margarita philosophica*, but also to that which the writings on the planets label the "artificia Saturni": namely, the trades of the "carpentarius", the "lapicida", the "cementarius", the "edificator edificiorum"—all trades that are cited by Abû Ma'šar, Alcabitius, Ibn Esra and the rest as typically Saturnine,[165] since they more than others are concerned with wood and stone. Since it is the Salone series that shows not only stonemasons' and woodworkers' tools in action but also the grindstone (elsewhere very rare), it is conceivable that these frescoes exercised a direct influence on the programme of the engraving, especially as we know that Willibald Pirckheimer

---

[163] See above, pp. 204 sqq. (text).

[164] He appears for the second time as an old man with a pick-axe and a mirror, but this figure goes back to a restoration. The original probably occupied the panel now filled by a huge angel.

[165] References quoted above, pp. 130 sqq., 190 sqq. (text, with relevant footnotes).

spent over three years studying in Padua; and Dürer himself also apparently visited the town.[166]

However, it is not only (so to speak) a substantial relationship of materials, based on a preoccupation with stone and wood, which links the Salone's Saturnine trades with the corresponding trades in the non-astrological pictures of different types of work. The intellectual principle, too, the theoretical foundation underlying this practical activity—in other words, geometry itself—has been reckoned part of Saturn's protectorate; and the more scientific instruments and objects, no less than the more ordinary tools in Dürer's engraving, thereby acquire the strange ambivalence which sanctions—as it were—the link between geometry and melancholy.

When the seven liberal arts, which Martianus Capella had still considered the "ministrae" of Mercury, began to be apportioned among the seven planets, Saturn was first given astronomy because, as Dante expressed it, this was the "highest" and "surest" of the liberal arts.[167] This system, almost universally recognised in the Middle Ages, was later modified, so that instead of astronomy, Saturn acquired geometry, which had formerly had other planets for its patrons—Mars, Jupiter, and, especially, Mercury. When and where this occurred, and whether or not certain speculations in scholastic psychology[168] had any influence on it, are questions that cannot be definitely answered; but even without such influence the alteration would be understandable, for the old earth god with whom the measurement of the fields had originally been associated, the god in whose Roman temple the scales hung,[169] the god who, as "auctor temporum" governed the measurement of time[170] no less than of space—this old earth god could the more easily be credited with the patronage of

---

[166] Cf. G. Fiocco, in *L'Arte*, vol. xviii (1915), pp. 147 sqq. (also G. Gronau, in *Pantheon*, vol. ii (1928), p. 533), who points out a portrait of Dürer in Campagnola's frescoes painted between 1505 and 1510 in the Scuola del Carmine, Padua. Recently, however, the frescoes have been given a later date, cf. H. Tietze, *Tizian*, Vienna 1936, pp. 68 sqq. Of course Campagnola may also have drawn Dürer in Venice. Further, cf. H. Rupprich, *Willibald Pirckheimer und die erste Reise Dürers nach Italien*, Vienna 1930, *passim*, whose conclusions, however, are much too sweeping in some cases (cf. the note by Alice Wolf, in *Die graphischen Künste*, new series, i (1936), p. 138).

[167] Dante, *Convivio*, ii, 14, 230. Cf. also J. von Schlosser, in *Jahrbuch der kunsthistorischen Sammlungen des allerhöchsten Kaiserhauses*, xvii (1896), esp. pp. 45 sqq.

[168] See below, pp. 348 sqq. (text).

[169] Varro, *De lingua latina*, v, 183, quoted above p. 135, note 33.

[170] Macrobius, *Saturnalia*, i, 22, 8, quoted above, p. 155, note 96.

geometry in its wider sense, since the translations of Abû Ma'šar available in the West had given to the Arabic author's fairly vague statement, "he signifies the evaluation (or determination) of things", a much more precise meaning by translating it on one occasion, "significat . . . quantitates sive mensuras rerum", and at another time even "eius est . . . rerum dimensio et pondus".

In order to arrive at the point of equating Saturn with Geometry it was only necessary to apply such attributes consciously to the system of the seven liberal arts; and the odd thing is that not long before Dürer this equation had become generally familiar in word and picture, particularly so in Germany. Thus the picture of Saturn in the Tübingen manuscript (PLATE 40)—quite a normal portrait of "Saturn's children", characterising men born under Saturn in the usual way as poor peasants, bakers, cripples and criminals—actually attributes to the god, over and above his shovel and pick, a pair of admittedly somewhat ill-drawn compasses.[171] The same manuscript, in the pictures illustrating the relationship of the seven liberal arts to the planets, credits Saturn with governing geometry[172]; a somewhat later Wolfenbüttel codex actually includes among his followers a begging friar who is unmistakably equipped with a gigantic pair of compasses (PLATE 41).[173] An explanation of this figure is given in the heading. It reads as follows: "the planet Saturn sends us the spirit which teaches us geometry, humility and constancy" (the begging friar represents these three gifts); and an almanac printed in Nuremberg just a year after Dürer's engraving says of Saturn: "Of the arts he signifies geometry."[174]

---

[171] A. HAUBER, *Planetenkinderbilder und Sternbilder*, Strasbourg 1916, plate XIII. Hauber's attempt (p. 93) to interpret the compasses as an ill-drawn snake scarcely needs refuting, as the steel-blue points are in clear contrast to the brown wood.

[172] HAUBER, op. cit., plate VII.

[173] HAUBER, op. cit., plate XVI.

[174] LEONHARD REYNMANN, *Natiuitet-Kalender*, Nuremberg 1515, fol. D ii v. "Saturnus der höchst oberst planet ist mannisch, bös, kalt vnd trucken, ain veind des lebens vnnd der natur. Ain bedeuter der münich, ainsiedel, claussner, der ser alten leut. Melancolici, hafner, ziegler, ledergerber, Schwartzferber, permenter, der ackerleut, klayber, badreyber, Schlot-vnd winckelfeger, vnd alles schnöden volcks, die mit stinnckenden wasserigen vnsaubern dingen vmbgeen. Er bezaichet aus den künsten die Geometrei; die alten köstlichen vesten ding vnd werck der State vesst vnd hewser . . . ." Here too the survival of post-classical notions is remarkable, ranging from the attribution to him of monks—*σχῆμα μοναχικόν*—and the characteristic of hostility to life—Saturn, god of Death!—to the contradiction that he is dry by nature yet signifies people who deal with watery things. This passage is also marked in the notes left by Giehlow.

Thus from an astrological standpoint, too, Dürer (or his adviser) was justified in regarding everything included in the notion of geometry as Saturn's domain; and when he merged the traditional "typus Acediae" with the equally traditional "typus Geometriae" in a new unity, all these symbols of work could, within this unity, be regarded as symbols both of geometry and of melancholy, since it was Saturn who governed them both in their entirety.

Of course there is a vast difference between the occasional appearance of a melancholic or a geometrician among peasants, cripples and criminals in one of the pictures of Saturn's children, and the fusion, by Dürer, of the triad Saturn, Melancholy, and Geometry, in a unified symbolic figure. But once established, this synthesis influenced further development to an extraordinarily high degree, and even retained its force when, formally regarded, it was once more split up. Apart from the direct imitations and elaborations of which we shall speak later,[175] and apart, too, from the effect which an engraving, born of a fusion between portraits of the liberal arts and portraits of the four temperaments, was in its turn to exert on pictures of the arts,[176] the fact remains that even where we cannot prove Dürer's direct influence, we can trace the development of his thought: for instance, in the poor woodcuts to a compendium of the Salernitan rules of health—entirely unoriginal both in its wording and in its illustrations—which show the melancholic at a geometrician's drawing-board (Fig. 2, p. 395).[177] But Dürer's fusion of the notions Melancholy, Saturn and "Artes Geometricae"[178] is endorsed and illustrated in a remarkable way by a large woodcut designed by the Hessian painter Hans Döring and published in 1535 (PLATE 107).[179] This woodcut formed the title page of a book on defence works, and was therefore

---

[175] See also below, pp. 374 sqq. (text).

[176] Cf. Virgil Solis's *Seven Liberal Arts*, B123–129, or H. S. Beham's, B121–127. An etching by Christoff Murer (cf. E. PANOFSKY, *Hercules am Scheidewege* (Studien der Bibliothek Warburg, VOL. XVIII), Leipzig 1930, plate 46, p. 101) shows how even the "virtus" of a Hercules at the Crossroads could be influenced by Dürer's Melancholy.

[177] *De conservanda bona valetudine* (quoted above, p. 300, note 66) fol. 120 v. in the 1551 edn.; fol. 121r in the 1553 edn.; fol. 137r in the 1554 edn.

[178] For Jacob I de Gheyn's and Martin van Heemskerck's sequences of temperaments, in which this fusion is also clearly apparent, see below, text pp. 397 sqq.: PLATES 142–144.

[179] Cf. E. EHLERS, *Hans Döring, ein hessischer Maler des 16. Jahrhunderts*, Darmstadt 1919, pp. 14 sqq., with plates and a reference to the connection with *Melencolia I* as well as to Beham's woodcut of Saturn; for the attribution of this work (Pauli 904) to G. Pencz, cf. H. RÖTTINGER, *Die Holzschnitte des Georg Pencz*, Leipzig 1914, pp. 14 sqq.

intended to glorify the art of "castra moliri" and "loca tuta circumfodere". In order to accomplish his task, however, the artist could think of no better way than to reduce the content of Dürer's *Melencolia I* to a universally comprehensible formula, which involved both compressing and enlarging. His picture, which is expressly described as *Melankolya* on page 4 of the text, collects the tools in Dürer's engraving (omitting the grindstone, the block, the ladder, the magic square, the scales and the hour-glass, but adding a mallet and a soldering lamp)[180] on top of a moulded plinth, which probably represents the "loca tuta"; and on a sphere placed in the centre there sits a small winged figure who, on closer inspection, proves to be a synthesis of Melencolia and her putto—the position and childish air from the latter, the thoughtful gesture, the book and the compasses from the former. The sphere, however, bears the sign of Saturn, and above it all, copied exactly from George Pencz's set of planetary pictures of 1531 (formerly attributed to Hans Sebald Beham), the old child-devourer himself drives furiously past in his dragon chariot. Beneath is a board with an inscription which is intended still further to emphasise the picture's relationship to Saturn:

☞ Grandaeuus ego sum tardus ceu primus in Orbe
omnia consternens quae jam mihi fata dedere
falce mea, ne nunc in me Mavortius heros
bella ciet: loca tuta meis haec artibus usus
circumfossa iacent, sed tu qui castra moliris
valle sub angusta circundare. Respice, quaeso,
ordine quo posset fieri; puer ille docebit:
hoc beo quos genui ingenio, hac uirtute ualebunt.

Martin Luther once said: "Medicine makes men ill, mathematics sad, theology wicked".[181] So far, at least, as mathematics is concerned, this epigram contains a germ of serious and well-authenticated psychology, for whereas Luther's jest against the other two sciences is limited to affirming that they attain the exact opposite of what they intend, he does not say, as one might expect of the schema, that mathematics makes men foolish or confuses them, but that it makes them sad. This striking

---

[180] We have not succeeded in detecting either the borax jar mentioned by Ehlers, or the symbol for lead in the smoke rising from the crucible.

[181] Quoted in W. AHRENS, "Das magische Quadrat", in *Zeitschrift für bildende Kunst*, N.S., VOL. XXVI (1915), p. 301. Vasari, too (see below, text p. 386) says that the instruments shown in Dürer's engraving of Melancholy "riducono l'uomo e chiunque gli adopera, a essere malinconico."

declaration can be explained by the existence of a theory linking mathematics with melancholy—not a myth clothed in astrology, but a psychological theory founded on epistemology. The chief upholders of this thesis were the two great scholastics Raimundus Lullus and Henricus de Gandavo.

Raimundus Lullus, in his *Tractatus novus de astronomia* (1297),[182] drew his information from Arabic compendiums, so that Saturn—both earthy and watery in nature—is therefore essentially malevolent, and endows his children with melancholy through their heavy dispositions. On the other hand, he also gives them a good memory, firm adherence to their principles, deep knowledge, and readiness to undertake great works of construction —in short, everything that Abû Ma'šar and the other kindred astrologers had ascribed to Saturn. Raimundus, however, was familiar with Aristotle, and was not content with quoting these astrological predicates—the truth of which he did not for an instant doubt—but undertook to prove them scientifically down to the last detail. Thus, he attributed the Saturnine man's leaning towards "species fantasticas et matematicas"—as well as his good memory—partly to the fact that water was an impressionable substance, and earth a solid one which long retained all impressions received[183]; and partly to the quite special correspondence ("concordia") between melancholy and the imagination.

They [the children of Saturn] receive strong impressions from their imagination, which is more closely related to melancholy than to any other complexion. And the reason why melancholy has a closer correspondence and relation to imagination than has any other complexion, is that imagination relies on measure, line, form and colour,[184] which are better preserved in water and earth, because those elements possess a denser substance than fire and air.[185]

---

[182] Clm. 10544; the chapter on Saturn, fols. 291ᵛ sqq. With this cf. *Histoire littéraire de la France*, VOL. XXIX, Paris 1885, p. 309; L. THORNDIKE, *A History of Magic and Experimental Science*, VOL. II, London 1923, p. 868, and *Dictionnaire de théologie catholique*, VOL. IX, 1926–27, col. 1107. There is a Catalan translation in a fragment in Brit. Mus. Add. MS 16434, fol. 8ᵛ sqq.

[183] "Et habent bonam memoriam, quia aqua est restrictiva, avara, et impressiva, et species fantasticas diligunt et matematicas. Et terra est subiectum spissum, in quo durat et pressio specierum, que memorate fuerant"; with this cf. the above-quoted passage from Albertus Magnus, and the other passage from Lullus, quoted above, p. 69, note 6.

[184] Cf. the statements from Abû Ma'šar and Alcabitius, quoted above, p. 130 sq.

[185] "Et a longo accipiunt per ymaginacionem, que cum melancolia maiorem habet concordiam quam cum alia compleccione. Et ratio quare melancolia maiorem habet proporcionem et concordiam cum ymaginacione quam alia complecio, est quia ymaginacio considerat mensuras, lineas et figuras et colores, que melius cum aqua et terra imprimi possunt, quoniam habent materiam magis spissam quam ignis et aer."

One of the greatest thinkers in the thirteenth century, Henricus de Gandavo, was inspired by very different and far deeper reflexions. He too sets out from the assumption (dating back originally to the *Nicomachean Ethics*) that there is a substantial relationship between melancholy and imagination.[186] But whereas Lullus, thinking in astrological terms and interpreting melancholy according to the doctrine of the complexions, enquires as to the influence of a certain humoral disposition on an intellectual faculty, Henricus de Gandavo, arguing from purely philosophical premises and conceiving melancholy as a darkening of the intellect, enquires as to the influence of a certain state of the intellectual faculties on emotional life. The former asks why melancholics (in the humoral sense) are particularly imaginative and therefore designed for mathematics. The latter asks why particularly imaginative, and therefore mathematically inclined, men are melancholy; and he finds the answer to this question in the circumstance that a preponderantly imaginative disposition does in fact lead to a marked capacity for mathematics, but at the same time renders the mind incapable of metaphysical speculation. This intellectual limitation and the resultant feeling of imprisonment within enclosing walls, makes people hampered in this way melancholics. According to Henricus de Gandavo, there are two sorts of men, differing in the nature and limitations of their intellectual faculties. There are those endowed with the ability for metaphysical reasoning; their thoughts are not dominated by their imagination. And there are those who can conceive a notion only when it is such that the imagination can keep company with it, when it can be visualised in spatial terms. They are incapable of grasping that there is no space and time beyond the world, nor can they believe that there are incorporeal beings in the world, beings that are neither in space nor in time:

> Their intellect cannot free itself from the dictates of their imagination ... whatever they think of must have extension or, as the geometrical point, occupy a position in space. For this reason such people are melancholy, and are the best mathematicians, but the worst metaphysicians; for they cannot raise their minds above the spatial notions on which mathematics is based.[187]

---

[186] *Eth. Nic.*, 1150 b 25; and esp. *Problem.*, XI, 38; both quoted above, p. 34 (text).

[187] HENRICUS DE GANDAVO, *Quodlibeta*, Paris 1518, fol. xxxiv^r (*Quodl.* II, Quaest. 9): "Qui ergo non possunt angelum intelligere secundum rationem substantiae suae, . . . sunt illi, de quibus dicit Commentator super secundum Metaphysicae: in quibus virtus imaginativa

(iv) *Art and Practice*

Geometry was the science *par excellence* for Dürer, as for his age.[188] Just as one of his friends, probably Pirckheimer, had said that God himself regarded measure so highly that he created all things according to number, weight and measure,[189] so Dürer, consciously echoing the same—platonising—words from Scripture (*Wisdom of Solomon* XI. 21),[190] wrote of himself the proud sentence:

---

dominatur super virtutem cognitivam. Et ideo, ut dicit, videmus istos non credere demonstrationibus, nisi imaginatio concomitet eas. Non enim possunt credere plenum non esse aut vacuum aut tempus extra mundum. Neque possunt credere hic esse entia non corporea, neque in loco neque in tempore. Primum non possunt credere, quod imaginatio eorum non stat in quantitate finita; et ideo mathematicae imaginationes et quod est extra coelum videntur eis infinita. Secundum non possunt credere, quia intellectus eorum non potest transcendere imaginationem . . . et non stat nisi super magnitudinem aut habens situm et positionem in magnitudine. Propter quod, sicut non possunt credere nec concipere extra naturam universi, hoc est extra mundum, nihil esse (neque locum neque tempus, neque plenum neque vacuum) . . . sic non possunt credere neque concipere hic (hoc est inter res et de numero rerum universi, quae sunt in universo) esse aliqua incorporea, quae in sua natura et essentia carerent omni ratione magnitudinis et situs sive positionis in magnitudine. Sed quicquid cogitant, quantum est aut situm habens in quanto (ut punctus). Unde tales melancholici sunt, et optimi fiunt mathematici, sed pessimi metaphysici, quia non possunt intelligentiam suam extendere ultra situm et magnitudinem, in quibus fundantur mathematicalia." The *Commentator super secundum Metaphysicae* (VOL. II, A ἐλάττων, ch. III) is, of course, Averroes, who does in fact literally speak of those "in quibus virtus imaginativa dominatur super virtutem cogitativam, et ideo videmus istos non credere demonstrationibus, nisi imaginatio concomitet eas, non enim possunt credere" etc., down to "incorporea" (VOL. VIII, fol. 17r of the edition of Aristotle with commentary, Venice 1552). But in Averroes this statement does not refer to mathematicians, but to the more poetic variety of the imaginative type, namely those who "quaerunt testimonium Versificatoris" before they believe anything; and there is no mention of melancholy (except for the statement that some become sad over a "sermo perscrutatus" because they cannot retain and digest it). The essential notion in this passage, therefore, must be regarded as belonging to Henricus de Gandavo.

188 It is significant that now the artist, too, likes to portray himself with compasses in his hand; cf. A. ALTDORFER, in *Gazette des Beaux-Arts*, LIII, I (1911), p. 113.

189 LF, *Nachlass*, p. 285, 9.

190 "Omnia in mensura, et numero, et pondere disposuisti." Platonic parallels in *Republic*, 602e, and esp. *Philebus*, 55e: *οἷον πασῶν που τεχνῶν ἄν τις ἀριθμητικὴν χωρίζῃ καὶ μετρικὴν καὶ στατικήν, ὡς ἔπος εἰπεῖν φαῦλον τὸ καταλειπόμενον ἑκάστης ἂν γίγνοιτο.* In illustration of the famous passage from the Bible, God the Father is frequently shown in the Middle Ages as architect of the world, holding a pair of compasses. This type is prefigured in a symbolic and abbreviated form in the Eadwi Gospels in Anglo-Saxon style (Hanover, Kestner-Mus.; beg. of eleventh century; our PLATE 105; cf. H. GRAEVEN, in *Zeitschrift des historischen Vereins für Niedersachsen*, 1901, p. 294, where, however, the compasses are not identified as such); it appears only a little later, and in a very similar form, in the same artistic milieu, as a full-length cosmological figure (London, Brit. Mus., MS Cotton Tiberius C. VI, fol. 7, our PLATE 106). Other pictures of God the Father with compasses and scales are: (1) an English psalter of about 1200, Paris, Bibl. Nat., MS lat. 8846 (reproduced as Italian by A.-N. DIDRON, *Iconographie chrétienne: histoire de Dieu*, Paris 1843, p. 600; (2) Montpellier, Bibliothèque de l'Université MS 298, fol. 300 (unpublished; Dr Hanns Swarzenski kindly brought this miniature to our notice); (3) Piero di Puccio's fresco in the Campo Santo, Pisa (reproduced by L. BAILLET, in *Fondation Eugène Piot, Monuments et Mémoires* VOL. XIX (1911), p. 147,

"And I will take measure, number and weight as my aim."[191]

The "aim" here mentioned was Dürer's book on painting, and the sum of what was to be based on measure, number and weight was what Dürer called "art" in its most significant sense, the "recta ratio faciendorum operum", as Philip Melanchthon, paraphrasing St Thomas Aquinas, had defined the notion of art.[192] After he had returned from his second visit to Italy, Dürer devoted himself to teaching German artists this "ratio", that is, the art of measurement, perspective, and the like; for he regarded it as that in which German artists had hitherto been lacking,[193] and which alone could succeed in excluding "falseness" from a work of art. It alone could give artists mastery over nature and over their own work. It alone saved them from the "approximate"; it alone—next to God's grace—gave that uncompromising quality to the artistic faculty which Dürer called "power". "Item, the other part shows how the youth is to be educated in the fear of the Lord and with care, so that winning grace he may grow strong and powerful in rational art."[194] So says Dürer in the first comprehensive scheme for his book on painting, written at a time when he could still have had no notion how in the course of the years this book was to shrink to two treatises in the strictest sense

---

with a sonnet quoting word for word from the *Wisdom of Solomon*, XI, 21). (4) (here God the Father is replaced by a personification of the cosmos!) the title woodcut to Albertus Magnus's *Philosophia naturalis* in the Brescia and Venice editions of 1493 and 1496 respectively (PRINCE D'ESSLING, *Les livres à figures vénitiens*, VOL. II, PT I, Florence 1908, p. 291). Far more often we encounter God the Father tracing the world with a pair of compasses but without scales, and this is typical of, and probably originated in, the "Bible moralisée": A. DE LABORDE, *Étude sur la Bible moralisée illustrée*, Paris 1911–27, our PLATE 108, after Laborde's plate I; also A. DE LABORDE, *Les manuscrits à peintures de la Cité de Dieu*, Paris 1909, plate VI; H. MARTIN, *La miniature française du 13e au 15e siècle*, Paris 1923, plates 34 and 74; G. RICHERT, *Mittelalterliche Malerei in Spanien*, Berlin 1925, plate 40; London, Royal MS 19. D. III, fol. 3 (dating from 1411–12), reproduced in E. G. MILLAR, *Souvenir de l'exposition de manuscrits français à peintures . . .*, Paris 1933, pl. 43; The Hague, Kgl. Bibl., MS 78 D. 43, fol. 3; Paris, Bibl. Ste-Geneviève, MS 1028, fol. 14, reproduced in *Bulletin de la société française de reproductions de manuscrits à peintures*, VOL. V (1921), plate XXXVII; Brussels, MS 9004, fol. 1; Paris, Arsenal 647, fol. 77; Paris, Bibl. Nat., MS fr. 247, fol. 1 (P. DURRIEU, *Les antiquités judaïques . . .*, Paris 1907, plate 1); and even in single woodcuts like that in P. HEITZ, *Einblattdrucke des 15. Jahrhunderts*, VOL. XL, No. 24. God or the Hand of God, with scales but without compasses, purely as a symbol of justice, appears e.g. in the Stuttgart Psalter, ed. E. De Wald, Princeton 1930, fol. 9^v, 17^v, 166^v, also, with a cosmological meaning, on an apparently unpublished font in the Musée lapidaire in Bordeaux.

[191] LF, *Nachlass*, p. 316, 24.

[192] For this notion of art, cf. E. PANOFSKY, *Dürers Kunsttheorie*, Berlin 1915, pp. 166 sqq., and the same author in *Jahrbuch für Kunstwissenschaft*, 1926, pp. 190 sqq.

[193] LF, *Nachlass*, p. 181, 1 and esp. pp. 207, 35 sqq.

[194] LF, *Nachlass*, p. 282, 13.

mathematical. He never tired of preaching that this creative "power", which he regarded as the essence of artistic genius, was bound up with the possession of "art"—that is to say, with knowledge based ultimately on mathematics.

When you have learnt to measure well . . . it is not necessary always to measure everything, for your acquired art will have trained your eye to measure accurately, and your practised hand will obey you. Thus the power of art will drive error from your work and prevent you from making a mistake . . . and thereby your work will seem artistic and pleasing, powerful, free and good, and will be praised by many, for rightness is made part of it.[195]

"Power", therefore, is what Dürer considered the end and essence of artistic capacity; and thereby the apparently casual sentence "keys signify power" acquires a new and deeper meaning. If, as we have seen, the Melancholy of *Melencolia I* is no ordinary Melancholy but a "geometrical" Melancholy, a "Melancholia artificialis", is it perhaps the case that the "power" attributed to her is not the ordinary power of the Saturnine person, but the special power of the artist based on the "recta ratio faciendorum operum"? Is not Melencolia herself the presiding genius of art? We would like to think so, for it is essentially unlikely that Dürer should have wished to endow a being—clearly recognisable as a personification of geometry—with power in the sense of political might or personal influence. And in thinking so we are the more justified in that Dürer was accustomed also to associate riches—symbolised by the purse, the apparently still more "incidental" attribute of the Saturnine melancholic—with the notion of artistic achievement. Just as the possession of "power" is the ideal goal of the outstanding artist, so are "riches" his legitimate and God-given reward—a reward readily granted many hundreds of years ago to the great masters of the past, and one which artists of his own time should expect, and, in case of necessity, demand:

[195] LF, *Nachlass*, p. 230, 17 (cf. also the sentence, quoted above, from p. 228, 25, and preliminary drafts as in pp. 218, 22 and 356, 20). From these and other passages it is clear that the expressions "Gewalt", "gewaltig", and "gewaltsam" (generally translated as "ingenium", "potentia", and "peritus" in J. Camerarius's Latin translation) are not in opposition to the notions "Verstand", "rechter Grund", "Kunst", etc., stressing the rational aspects of artistic achievement, but include them. In the translation in LF, *Nachlass*, p. 221, 8 the term "gewaltsame Künstler" is rendered as "potentes intellectu et manu". The derivative form, "gewaltiglich" (LF, *Nachlass*, p. 180, 16), however, just because it is a derivative form, has something of the second-hand about it and becomes opposed to the notions of "Besonnenheit" and "rechte Kunst": "Gewaltiglich aber unbedächtlich" is rendered in Latin as "prompte [not "perite"], sed inconsiderate".

For they [mighty kings] made the best artists rich and held them in honour. For they thought that the very wise bore a resemblance to God.[196] . . . Item, that such an excellent artist shall be paid much money for his art, and no money shall be too great, and it is godly and right.[197]

Dürer therefore understood both power and riches in a specifically professional sense, and in a sense inseparably linked with the notion of Art, and therefore with mathematical education; for the true artist—one whose work is based on conscious insight into the theoretical principles of production—power is a goal, and riches a rightful claim.

But art based on measure, weight, and number, as embodied in the figure of Dürer's Melencolia, was for Dürer still only one requisite of artistic achievement, still only one condition of artistic power. However highly he rated "ratio", in true Renaissance fashion, he was no less a man of the Renaissance in affirming that no theoretical perception was useful without mastery of technique, no "good reason" without "freedom of the hand", no "rational art" without "daily practice". "These two must go hand in hand",[198] says Dürer in a preliminary outline of his doctrine of proportion; for although, like all Renaissance thinkers (one has only to remember Leonardo da Vinci's phrase "la scientia è il capitano e la pratica sono i soldati"),[199] Dürer recognised Art as the highest and governing principle of creative endeavour—so that practice without art seemed to him corruption and captivity—yet he had to admit that "without practice"[200] art, as he understood it, "remains hidden", and that theory and practice must go together, "so that the hand can do what the will intends."[201] Now, if the figure of Melencolia signifies Art *generating* power, a question arises whether her non-intellectual counterpart, Practice *revealing* power, has not also, perhaps, received its due in Dürer's engraving?

And so in fact it seems; for if, on the strength of our purely visual impression, we had to interpret the writing putto as a figure contrasted with Melencolia, we may now, so to speak,

---

[196] LF, *Nachlass*, pp. 295, 9, and 297, 19.

[197] LF, *Nachlass*, p. 283, 4; cf. also p. 285, 5.

[198] LF, *Nachlass*, p. 230, 5; cf. also p. 231, 3.

[199] C. Ravaisson-Mollien, *Les manuscrits de Léonard de Vinci*, Paris 1881, MS J. fol. 130r. Cf. also J. P. Richter, *The Literary Works of Leonardo da Vinci*, London 1883, § 19.

[200] LF, *Nachlass*, p. 230, 33.

[201] LF, *Nachlass*, p. 230, 1.

name this contrast and suggest that the child signifies "practice". This child sits in almost the same attitude as the woman, and yet —almost to the point of parody—reverses her appearance in its every detail: eyes not aimlessly gazing on high, but fastened eagerly on the slate, hands not idle or clenched, but actively busy. The putto (also winged, but for all that only a little assistant, offering mere manual activity in exchange for the power of the mind) may well be an example of activity without thought, just as Melencolia herself is an example of thought without activity. He takes no share in intellectual creation, but neither does he share the agony bound up with that creation. If Art feels herself faced with impassable limits, blind Practice notices no limitations. Even when, in Saturn's most inauspicious hour, "Ars" and "Usus" have become separated—such is the hour we see in the picture, for the main figure is too much lost in her own thoughts to heed the child's activity[202]—and even when Art herself is overcome with despondency, Practice still can indulge in pointless and unreasoning activity.[203]

That admirable etcher and engraver, Alexander Friedrich, has shown us that this is no mere arbitrary interpretation[204]; for he

---

[202] *Per contra* Hendrik Goltzius shows a happy and active association between "Ars" and "Usus" in his engraving B111 reproduced in E. PANOFSKY (*in Jahrbuch für Kunstwissenschaft*, 1926, plate 11), where "Ars" appears as teacher and guide to "Usus".

[203] We have now been converted, though for different reasons, to H. Wölfflin's opinion, according to which the putto is not "a thinker in miniature" but "a child scribbling" (*Die Kunst Albrecht Dürers*, 5th edn., Munich 1926, p. 256). In this respect it is also important that Dürer gave a more specifically childish colouring to the putto's activity by replacing the mathematical instruments with the slate. The motif originally intended, like that in the engraving by the Master "A. C." (PLATE 114), would have provided a parallel rather than a contrast. Indeed, there are examples showing that a putto busy with mathematical instruments may mean the very opposite of mere "Usus"; cf. e.g. Hans Döring's woodcut (p. 335 and PLATE 107) as well as an engraving in JOACHIM SANDRART's *Teutsche Akademie* (new edition by A. R. Peltzer, Munich 1925, p. 307), showing a putto with rule and compasses, surrounded by other mathematical instruments, with the inscription "Ars", "Numerus", "Pondus", "Mensura". Hans Döring's "puer docens" provides a sort of *Gegenprobe* for our interpretation of Dürer's putto, in that, although developed from Dürer's, he is holding not a slate but the book and compasses of the main figure, and, instead of eagerly scribbling, has adopted the thoughtful pose of the adult. Dürer's putto could only change from a personification of mere "Practice" to a being embodying "Art" by taking over the attributes and attitudes of Melancholy. On the other hand, the interesting variations on the number four by Paul Flindt (*Quatuor monarchiae, Partes mundi*, etc., ed. Paul Flindt, Nuremberg 1611, No. 12) show the contrast between "Art" and "Practice" by means of two putti, one of whom, eagerly engaged with a chisel, is described as "phlegmaticus", the other, still reminiscent of Dürer, as "melancholicus" (cf. also below, pp. 349, note 217, and 380, note 16).

[204] Another interpretation of the putto, kindly mentioned to us by Dr G. F. Hartlaub, but in our opinion not altogether convincing, will be discussed later on in connexion with Lucas Cranach's portrait of melancholy (see below, text pp. 382 sqq.).

points out that the writing implement which Dürer's putto is plying so eagerly and thoughtlessly is really the artist's own specific tool, namely, a burin, with its own distinctive handle, and its groove for the insertion of the thin square graving point —here applied in a most unsuitable manner. Moreover, there is the fact that the connexion which we discern in Dürer's engraving of theory and practice with ideal and material success, can also be traced in other symbolic or schematic representations of artistic achievement, as for instance in Hendrick Hondius's engraved title-page to his well-known collection of portraits of Dutch painters, which might almost be taken as a more positive version of Dürer's programme (PLATE 109).[205] It shows two naked allegorical figures, one with palette, brushes, and wand of Mercury, signifying "Pictura", the other, with mathematical instruments, signifying "Optica"; though not sunk in depression like Dürer's Melencolia, the two women seem content merely to regard their own excellence, while above them we see two putti eagerly engaged in practical work, and representing "assiduus labor".[206] The two factors of creative achievement which Dürer conceived in the whole complicated tension of their relationship are here shown in friendly accord; but they are still the same two factors, and they still stand in the same relationship of higher and lower: theoretic Art (here split into two forms), and active, eager Practice. The analogy even goes a step further; for just as Dürer showed us the goal and reward of artistic endeavour in the form of keys and purse (an interpretation here reinforced), so Hondius shows us at the bottom of the picture the "fructus laborum". Admittedly there are two significant differences. What men in early baroque times thought the artist's highest goal, next to the riches signified by gold coins, was no longer the power given by God, but fame won in the world, as illustrated by the palm and laurels, and emphasised by Fame with her trumpet.[207] And whereas, in his optimism, Hondius considered the goal as unquestionably attainable, Dürer, in illustrating the unhappy moment when Practice and Art have become separated, questions—and momentarily even

[205] *Pictorum aliquot celebrium . . . effigies*, first published at the Hague about 1610.

[206] The crane allotted to the right-hand putto was a symbol of wakefulness already in late antiquity; the cock on the left (next to the putto), the care or assiduity closely connected with vigilance (cf. e.g. CESARE RIPA, *Iconologia*, 1st edn., Rome 1593, s.v. "Vigilanza" and "Sollecitudine").

[207] An allegory comparable in content is found on the engraved title to *Varie Figure Academiche . . . messe in luce da Pietro de Jode*, Antwerp 1639 (PLATE 110). On the left is "Disegno",

denies—the value of attaining success and being rewarded for it. That is the true significance of a pictorial feature which seems at first to be designed merely to communicate a certain mood—his giving, that is, to both the purse and the bunch of keys ("riches" and "power", as Dürer himself said) an air of confusion and neglect, in other words, of being unused or unattainable.

(c) The Significance of "Melencolia I"

There is no doubt that the idea expressed by Henricus de Gandavo brings us very close to the core of Melencolia's true meaning. She is above all an imaginative Melancholy, whose thoughts and actions all take place within the realms of space and visibility, from pure reflexion upon geometry to activity in the lesser crafts; and here if anywhere we receive the impression of a being to whom her allotted realm seems intolerably restricted—of a being whose thoughts "have reached the limit".

And so we come to one last vital question, namely, the basic attitude towards life underlying Dürer's engraving, with its endlessly complicated ancestry, its fusion of older types, its modification—nay, its inversion—of older forms of expression, and its development of an allegorical schema: the question of the fundamental significance[208] of *Melencolia I.*

The foundations out of which Dürer's idea arose were of course laid by Ficino's doctrine. The revolution which had reinstated the "pessima complexio" and "corruptio animi" as the source of all creative achievement, and made the "most evil planet" into the "iuvans pater" of intellectual men, had, as we have seen, been brought about in the Florence of the Medici. Without it, a northern artist, granted all the astrological likenesses between

---

a handsome youth with a mirror and compasses, on the right, "Labore", a labourer digging; above, "Honore" crowned with the laurel wreath of "Fama", and with "Abondança's" cornucopia. The inscription runs

"Door den arbeyt en door de Teeken-const
Comt menich aen eer en S'princen ionst."

Another equally vivid example of the allegories of Theory and Practice is the engraved title to the *Universa astrosophia naturalis* by A. F. de Bonnattis, Padua 1687: above reigns the victorious "Maiestas Reipublicae Venetae", to the left is an embodiment of "Contemplatione et Iudicio" in the person of an idealised youthful figure with astrolabe and compasses, to the right a personification of "Ratione et Experimento", represented as Mercury.

[208] For this notion cf. K. Mannheim, "Beiträge zur Theorie der Weltanschauungsinterpretation", in *Jahrbuch für Kunstgeschichte* (formerly *Jahrbuch der k.k. Zentralkommission*), I (1921–22), pp. 236 sqq.; for our purposes it seemed necessary to replace the term "representational meaning" inserted by Mannheim between "expressional meaning" and "documentary meaning" by the term "notional meaning".

Saturn and Geometry, would yet have lacked the necessary impulse to demolish the barriers of revulsion and fear which had hidden "Melancholia generosa" from view for hundreds of years, to replace the picture of the idle spinstress by that of the Saturnine art of measurement, and to transform into expressions of feeling and into symbols of abstract ideas all the traditional signs of the melancholy disease and attributes of the melancholy temperament. But beyond this general connexion—one might almost say the "atmospheric" connexion—the *De vita triplici* can hardly have had any influence on the composition of the engraving, for the very idea which is most essential to Dürer's composition, namely the integral interpenetration of the notions of melancholy and geometry (in the widest sense), was not only foreign to Ficino's system, but actually contradicts it.

Ficino had taken an enthusiastic interest in many aspects both of the world of man and of the universe, and had included them in the structure of his doctrine; but there was one realm into which he did not enter and which in fact he really ignored—the realm of "visibility in space", which was the background both of theoretical discoveries in mathematics and of practical achievements in the manual arts. This Florentine, who lived at such close quarters with the art of the Renaissance, and with its theory of art based on mathematics, seems to have taken no part either emotionally or intellectually in the rebuilding of this sphere of culture. His Platonist doctrine of beauty completely ignored the works of human hands, and it was not until a good century later that the doctrine was transformed from a philosophy of beauty in nature to a philosophy of art.[209] His theory of cognition barely glances at mathematical knowledge, and the dietetics and morphology in his *De vita triplici* are the dietetics and morphology of a literary man of genius. As far as Ficino is concerned, the creative intellects—those whose efforts, in their beginning, are protected by Mercury, and, in their development, are guided by Saturn—are the "literarum studiosi", that is to say, the humanists, the seers and poets, and, above all, of course, "those who devote themselves ceaselessly to the study of philosophy, turning their minds from the body and corporeal things towards the incorporeal"[210]—in

---

[209] See below, pp. 360 sqq. (text).

[210] FICINO, *De v. tripl.*, I, 4 (*Opera*, p. 497): "Maxime vero literatorum omnium hi atra bile premuntur, qui sedulo philosophiae studio dediti, mentem a corpore rebusque corporeis sevocant, incorporeisque coniungunt."

other words, certainly not mathematicians, and still less practising artists.[211] Accordingly, in his hierarchy of the intellectual faculties, he does not place the "vis imaginativa" (the lowest faculty, directly attached to the body by the "spiritus")[212] under Saturn. As we read in the third book of the *De vita triplici*, the "imaginatio" tends towards Mars or the sun, the "ratio" towards Jupiter, and only the "mens contemplatrix", which knows intuitively and transcends discursive reasoning, tends towards Saturn.[213] The sublime and sinister nimbus which Ficino weaves about the head of the Saturnine melancholic does not, therefore, have anything to do with "imaginative" men; the latter, whose predominant faculty is merely a vessel to receive solar or Martial influences, do not, in his view, belong to the "melancholy" spirits, to those capable of inspiration; into the illustrious company of the Saturnine he does not admit a being whose thoughts move merely within the sphere of visible, mensurable and ponderable forms; and he would have questioned the right of such a being to be called "Melencolia".

The contrary is the case with Henricus de Gandavo. He considers only imaginative natures—in particular those mathematically gifted—as melancholics; and to that extent his view comes substantially closer to Dürer's. It is also by no means impossible that Dürer was affected by Henricus's ideas, for no less a person than Pico della Mirandola had revived these views in his *Apology*,[214] and thereby reminded many other humanists,

---

[211] In book I, ch. 2 Ficino emphasises explicitly and with considerable pride the fundamental contrast between what he calls the "Musarum sacerdotes" and all other, even artistic professions: "... sollers quilibet artifex instrumenta sua diligentissime curat, penicillos pictor, malleos incudesque faber aerarius, miles equos et arma, venator canes et aves, citharam citharoedus, et sua quisque similiter. Soli vero Musarum sacerdotes, soli summi boni veritatisque venatores, tam negligentes (proh nefas) tamque infortunati sunt, ut instrumentum illud, quo mundum universum metiri quodammodo et capere possunt, negligere penitus videantur. Instrumentum eiusmodi spiritus ipse est, qui apud medicos vapor quidam sanguinis purus, subtilis et lucidus definitur."

[212] See above, pp. 264 sqq. (text).

[213] Quotations above, p. 272 (text).

[214] PICO DELLA MIRANDOLA, *Apologia* (*Opera*, Basle 1572, VOL. I, p. 133): "Qui ergo non possunt angelum intelligere secundum rationem substantiae suae, ut unitatem absque ratione puncti, sunt illi de quibus dicit Commentator super secundo Metaphysicae, in quibus virtus imaginativa dominatur super virtutem cogitativam, et ideo, ut dicit, videmus istos non credere demonstrationibus, nisi imaginatio eos comitetur; et quicquid cogitant, quantum est aut situm habens, in quanto ut punctus; unde tales melancholici sunt, et optimi fiunt mathematici, sed sunt naturales inepti. Haec Henricus ad verbum; ex quibus sequitur, quod secundum Henricum iste magister sit male dispositus ad studium philosophiae naturalis, peius ad studium Metaphysicae, pessime ad studium Theologiae, quae etiam est de abstractioribus: relinquitur ergo ei solum aptitudo ad Mathematica ...." Cf. also M. PALMIERI,

Germans included, of them.[215] But if Ficino's theory does not accord with the trend in Dürer's engraving because his idea of melancholy bears no relation to the notion of mathematics, Henricus de Gandavo's does not accord with it because his idea of melancholy is related too closely to the notion of mathematics. From Ficino's point of view, the description "Melencolia" would not be justified, because he considered that in principle no mathematician had access to the sphere of (inspired) melancholy. From Henricus's point of view, the numeral "I" would seem pointless because he considered that in principle no non-mathematician descended into the sphere of (non-inspired) melancholy. Ficino, who saw in melancholy the highest rung of intellectual life, thought it began where the imaginative faculty left off, so that only contemplation, no longer fettered by the imagination, deserved the title of melancholy. Henricus de Gandavo, who still conceived melancholy as a "modus deficiens", thought that as soon as the mind rises above the level of imagination, melancholy ceases to affect it, so that contemplation no longer fettered by the imaginative faculty could lay claim to the title "philosophia" or "theologia". If an artist really wished to give expression to the feeling of "having reached a limit" which seems to form the basis of the close relationship between Henricus de Gandavo's notions of melancholy and Dürer's, he might certainly have called his picture *Melencolia*, but not *Melencolia I*.

It is assumed implicitly that what is lacking logically to

Città di Vita, I, 12, 48 (ed. M. Rooke, in Smith College Studies in Modern Languages, VOL. VIII, Northampton, Mass., 1926–27, p. 59), where the buildings appearing in Saturn's world and their architects are described as follows:

"Tutto quello è nel mondo ymaginato
per numeri o linee o lor facture
convien che sia da questa impression dato.

Fanno architetti queste creature,
mathematici sono & fanno in terra
& altri in ciel lor forme & lor figure."

Incidentally, the equation "Saturnus" = "Imaginatio", was also made in one of Bovillus's schemata, *Liber de sapiente*, cap. xi (ed. R. Klibansky, in E. CASSIRER, *Individuum und Kosmos in der Philosophie der Renaissance*, Leipzig 1927, pp. 326 sqq.) but this is too individual a construction to be treated here: it consists of an analogy between the seven planets and the mental faculties so that Sol equals "Ratio" while the six other planets correspond each to one instrument of "materialis cognitio".

[215] We know, for instance, that both Conrad Peutinger of Augsburg and Hartmann Schedel of Nuremberg had a copy of Pico's *Apologia* in their libraries (E. KÖNIG, *Peutingerstudien*, Freiburg i.B. 1914, p. 65).

complete the sequence started by *Melencolia I*[216] is neither a representation of the three other temperaments to make up a set of the "four complexions", nor yet a picture of disease contrasting "melancholia adusta" with "melancholia naturalis". What is lacking is, rather, the representation of an intellectual condition signifying the next highest rung of cognition in the scale of melancholy; a *Melencolia II* in contrast to *Melencolia I*, which should reveal not a state of complete derangement, but, on the contrary, a state of relative liberation. Herein lies the greatness of Dürer's achievement; that he overcame the medical distinctions by an image, uniting in a single whole, full of emotional life, the phenomena which the set notions of temperament and disease had robbed of their vitality; that he conceived the melancholy of intellectual men as an indivisible destiny in which the differences of melancholy temperament, disease and mood fade to nothing, and brooding sorrow no less than creative enthusiasm are but the extremes of one and the same disposition. The depression of *Melencolia I*, revealing both the obscure doom and the obscure source of creative genius, lies beyond any contrast between health and disease; and if we would discover its opposite we must look for it in a sphere where such a contrast is equally lacking—in a sphere, therefore, which admits of different forms and degrees within "melancholia generosa".

How then are we to imagine such a gradation?[217] The

---

[216] Interpretations such as "Melencholia, i" ("Go away, Melancholy!") or "Melancolia iacet" ("Melancholy lies on the ground", thus *Mitteilungen des Reichsbundes deutscher Technik*, 1919, No. 47, 6 December) are scarcely worth refuting. More recent but equally untenable is E. BÜCH's view (in *Die medizinische Welt*, VOL. VII (1933), No. 2) that Dürer's engraving was inspired by a prophetic vision of an epidemic of the plague (though nothing is known of one in 1514, at least not in Nuremberg), and that the figure I stood for the first stage of the disease.

[217] Like Allihn, Thausing and Giehlow, we, too, formerly assumed that Dürer's engraving was intended to be the first of a temperament-series. The difficulties involved in such an assumption were not unknown to us, for we realised that it would have been highly unusual to begin the series with Melancholy, and that no fully analogous names would have been available for the other temperaments (cf. *Dürer's "Melencolia I"*, pp. 68 and 142; also H. WÖLFFLIN, *Die Kunst Albrecht Dürers*, 5th edn., Munich 1926, p. 253); we noticed further that artists under Dürer's influence, who did a complete temperament-series, returned for the sake of neatness to the description "melancolicus" and gave this "melancolicus" third or even fourth place in the series (PLATES 122 and 126). Gerard de Jode in his temperament-series after M. de Vos (PLATE 113), which is independent of Dürer, follows a new way of bringing the term "melancholia" into line with those denoting the other temperaments by treating it, by analogy with Greek usage, as the description of an actual humour, as an equivalent for "cholera nigra" or "atra bilis", and thus ranging it alongside "sanguis", "cholera", and "phlegma"; but here too, melancholy occupies third place and not first; cf. our PLATE 126. In these circumstances, however, the other view, postulating a plan for a *Melencolia II* as a picture of disease, or rather insanity (H. WÖLFFLIN, *Die Kunst Albrecht Dürers*, 5th edn., Munich 1926,

Neoplatonist Ficino, as we know, held inspired melancholy in such great honour that in the ascending hierarchy of the faculties of the soul, "imaginatio", "ratio" and "mens contemplatrix", he coupled it only with the highest, the contemplative mind. Henricus de Gandavo, on the other hand, rated uninspired melancholy so low that it could be coupled only with the lowest rank, the imagination. Ficino thought it impossible for the imaginative mind to rise to melancholy, Henricus thought it impossible for the melancholy mind to rise above the imagination. But what if someone were bold enough to expand the notion of inspired melancholy so as to include a rational and an imaginative as well as a contemplative form? A view would then emerge recognising an imaginative, a rational and a contemplative stage within melancholy itself, thus interpreting, as it were, the hierarchy of the three faculties of the soul as three equally inspired forms of melancholy. Then Dürer's *Melencolia I*, as portraying a "melancholia imaginativa", would really represent the first stage in an ascent via *Melencolia II* ("melancholia rationalis") to *Melencolia III* ("melancholia mentalis").

We know now that there was such a theory of gradation,[218] and

---

p. 253, and in *Jahrbuch für Kunstwissenschaft*, 1923, p. 175; also K. BORINSKI, *Die Antike in Poetik und Kunsttheorie*, VOL. I, Leipzig 1914, pp. 165 and 296 sqq.), seem to us still less acceptable and we cannot imagine a representation of "melancholia adusta" such as to constitute a counterpart to Dürer's engraving as it stands. For such a representation, given the generally known doctrine of the "four forms", two possibilities would have lain open. Either all four sub-species of melancholy madness, i.e. melancholy "ex sanguine", "ex cholera", "ex phlegmate" and "ex melancholia naturali", could have been combined in one general picture —which would have resulted in a gruesome collection of madhouse scenes having no point of contact either in content or form with *Melencolia I* (we shall show in appendix II, p. 403, that the much-discussed etching B70 (PLATE 146) may give us an idea of what such a collection of the "quattuor species melancholiae adustae" would have looked like)—or else the one real analogy, i.e. "melancholia ex melancholia naturali", would have had to be chosen from among the four forms of diseases, and in that case it would scarcely have been possible to bring out the intended psychological contrast. Everyone is at least agreed that even the winged woman on the engraving, though she expresses the "melancholia naturalis" of the mentally creative man, has at the moment been overcome by a fit of depression in which the black bile has so far gained the ascendancy that, in Ficino's words, the soul "all too deeply entangled in Saturnine brooding and oppressed by cares" (FICINO, *De v. tripl.*, II, 16, *Opera*, p. 523), "evadit tristis, omnium pertaesa" (*A.P.T. Paracelsi Opera omnia*, Geneva 1658, VOL. II, p. 173); the depression differs from the pathological state of "melancholia ex melancholia naturali adusta" only by its transitory nature (thus, too, H. WÖLFFLIN, *Die Kunst Albrecht Dürers*, 5th edn., Munich 1926, pp. 252 sqq.).

218 Such a possibility was considered by HARTLAUB, *Geheimnis*, pp. 79 sqq. He rightly criticises the interpretation of the *I* as the beginning of a temperament-series, but flies off at a tangent by introducing the freemasonic idea of the grades of apprentice, journeyman and master (the two latter possibly embodied in Dürer's *Knight, Death and the Devil* and *St Jerome*). But what Hartlaub, op. cit., p. 42, says is lacking, i.e. "literary evidence for a regular tripartite division of Saturnine development", appears abundantly in the *Occulta philosophia*, a German source, be it noted, whereas there is no evidence for any connexion with masonic ideas.

that its inventor was none other than Agrippa of Nettesheim, the first German thinker to adopt the teachings of the Florentine Academy in their entirety, and to familiarise his humanistic friends with them. He was, as it were, the predestined mediator between Ficino and Dürer.[219]

Karl Giehlow, in spite of being familiar with all the relevant parts of the printed *Occulta philosophia*,[220] somehow failed to notice what was essentially new in Agrippa's theory, or fully to grasp its special significance for the elucidation of the numeral in *Melencolia I*; in the same way, later interpretations have been equally inadequate by neglecting to follow up the line of research suggested by Giehlow. Admittedly, on Agrippa's own authority, the printed edition of *Occulta philosophia* which appeared in 1531 contained considerably more than the original version completed in 1510,[221] so that it appeared uncertain whether the relevant parts were not later additions: in which case it would be impossible to regard them as sources for Dürer's engraving. But the original version of *Occulta philosophia*, believed lost, did survive, as Hans Meier has proved, in the very manuscript which Agrippa sent to his friend Trithemius in Würzburg in the spring of 1510.[222] We are thus on firm ground; and in this original version the two chapters on the "furor melancholicus" approach the view of life implicit in Dürer's engraving more nearly than any other writing known to us; it was circulated more or less secretly in many manuscript copies[223]; and it was certainly available to Pirckheimer's circle

---

[219] On him, cf. P. ZAMBELLI, "A proposito del 'De vanitate scientiarum et artium' di Cornelio Agrippa," *Riv. Crit. di Storia della Filos.*, 1960, pp. 167–81.

[220] GIEHLOW (1904), pp. 12 sqq.

[221] "Addidimus autem nonnulla capitula, inseruimus etiam pleraque, quae praetermittere incuriosum videbatur."

[222] The dedication, in a slightly altered form, was used in the introduction to the printed edition, as was Trithemius's answer of 8 April 1510. The MS of the original edition (quoted above, p. 323, note 132) bears a seventeenth-century inscription "Mon. S. Jacobi" on the first page (Trithemius, of course, was the abbot of this monastery), and Trithemius himself wrote on the right-hand margin of the top cover: "Heinricus Cornelius Coloniensis de magia". See J. BIELMANN, "Zu einer Hds. der 'Occulta philosophia' des Agrippa von Nettesheim," *Archiv f. Kulturgesch.*, VOL. 27 (1937), pp. 318–24.

[223] "Contigit autum postea, ut interceptum opus, priusquam illi summam manum imposuissem, corruptis exemplaribus truncum et impolitum circumferretur atque in Italia, in Gallia, in Germania per multorum manus volitaret." The delay in issuing a printed edition was probably due mainly to fear of clerical persecution; Trithemius himself advised politely but firmly against publishing it: "Unum hoc tamen te monemus custodire praeceptum, ut vulgaria vulgaribus, altiora vero et arcana altioribus atque secretis tantum communices amicis."

through Trithemius,[224] and can now lay claim to being the main source of *Melencolia I*.

Agrippa's *Occulta philosophia* is, in the printed edition, a highly comprehensive but unwieldy work, encumbered with countless astrological, geomantic and cabbalistic spells, figures and tables, a real book of necromancy in the medieval sorcerer's style. In its original form, however, it was quite different, being rather a neat, homogeneous treatise, from which the cabbalistic element was entirely lacking, and in which there were not so many prescriptions of practical magic as to blur the clear outline of a logical, scientific and philosophical system.[225] This system was presented in a threefold structure,[226] was manifestly based entirely on Neoplatonic, Neopythagorean, and oriental mysticism, and presupposed complete familiarity with Ficino's writings, both as a whole and in detail.[227] It led from earthly matters to the stellar universe, and from the stellar universe to the realm of religious truth and mystic contemplation. Everywhere it reveals the "colligantia et continuitas naturae" according to which each "higher power, in imparting its rays to all lesser things in a long and unbroken chain, flows down to the lowest, while, vice versa, the lowest rises via the higher up to the highest"[228]; and it makes even the wildest manipulations—with snakes's eyes, magic brews, and invocations of the stars—seem less like spells than the deliberate application of natural forces.

After two introductory chapters which try, like Ficino, to distinguish this white magic from necromancy and exorcism,[229] and inform us that as a link between physics, mathematics, and theology, it is the "totius nobilissimae philosophiae absoluta

[224] That Trithemius and Pirckheimer had some connexion with each other during the years in question (1510–1515), in which occult matters also played a part, can be seen from a number of letters, the knowledge of which we owe to the archivist, Dr E. Reicke: P. to T., 1 July 1507, and T. to P., 18 July 1507 (Johannes Trithemius, *Epistolarum familiarium libri duo*, probably Hagenau, 1536, pp. 279–281 and Clm. 4008, fol. 11). P. to T., 13 June 1515 (concerning a work by Trithemius against magic), pointed out by O. CLEMEN in *Zeitschrift für Bibliothekswesen*, VOL. XXXVIII (1921), pp. 101 sqq.

[225] This difference between the two editions of *Occulta philosophia* is of course a vital symptom of the development which northern humanism had undergone between about 1510 and 1530; Dr H. Meier intended to edit the Würzburg MS, which would have facilitated an historical evaluation of his discovery.

[226] The printed edition covers almost three times as much space as the original version even apart from the apocryphal Book IV.

[227] See below, p. 356, note 253; pp. 358 sqq. (text).

[228] I, 29, fol. 22v.

[229] See above, p. 268 (text).

consummatio", the first book lists the manifest and occult powers of earthly things, and then, by means of the "Platonic" doctrine of the pre-formation of individual objects in the sphere of ideas,[230] interprets them as emanations of divine unity transmitted by the stars. As the effects of the "chain" here represented work upwards as well as downwards, metaphysical justification can be found not only for the whole practice of magic with its potions, burnt offerings,[231] sympathetic amulets, healing salves, and poisons, but also for the whole of the old astrological associations[232]; and even the psychological riddles of hypnotism ("fascinatio"), suggestion ("ligatio") and auto-suggestion can be explained by the fact that the influential part can become saturated with the powers of a certain planet and set them in action against other individuals, or even against itself.[233]

The second book deals with "coelestia", the general principles of astrology,[234] and with the manufacture of specific astrological talismans,[235] as well as with the occult significance of numbers (which, remarkably enough, however, are regarded rather from the point of view of mystical correspondence than of practical magic, somewhat in the same way as in the well-known treatises on the numbers seven or four)[236]; it treats also of the astrological and magical character of the stars,[237] and of the effect of music.[238]

---

[230] I, 5. A charming illustration of this doctrine of pre-formation occurs in a miniature in Vienna, Nationalbibliothek, Cod. Phil. graec. 4 (H. J. HERMANN, in *Jahrbuch der kunsthistorischen Sammlungen des allerhöchsten Kaiserhauses*, VOL. XIX (1898), plate VI, text p. 166), where the "ideas" of men and beasts are vividly portrayed linked by rays with their earthly counterparts.

[231] Thus the above-mentioned (p. 323 sq., note 133) burnt-offering to Saturn.

[232] The correlations with the planets (with regard to those referring to Saturn, see the same reference) are given in ch. 16–23 (in ch. 16 add from MS fol. 15^v,"conferunt Saturnalia ad tristitiam et melancoliam, Jovialia ad leticiam et dignitatem"). The localities governed by the different planets are listed in ch. 46, fol. 36^v in astrological terms, but with a new, Ficinesque meaning, while ch. 45, fol. 35^v, contains the mimic and facial characteristics of the children of the planets, whose behaviour both springs from, and evokes, the influence of the star concerned: "Sunt praeterea gestus Saturnum referentes, qui sunt tristes ac moesti, planctus, capitis ictus, item religiosi, ut genuflexio aspectu deorsum fixo, pectoris ictus vultusque consimiles et austeri, et ut scribit satyricus:

> 'Obstipo capite et figentes lumina terra,
> Murmura cum secum et rabiosa silentia rodunt
> Atque exporrecto trutinantur verba palato'. "

[233] Thus, for instance, a man can calm or sadden others by suggestion, because he is the stronger "in ordine Saturnali" (I, 43, fol. 33^v), or by auto-suggestion evoke Saturn's aid against love, or Jupiter's against the fear of death (I, 43, fol. 44^r).

[234] II, 1–3.

[235] II, 4–16.

[236] II, 17–29. Ch. 30 briefly mentions geometric figures, ascribing their efficacy to numerical relationships; we have already stated (p. 327, note 147) that planetary squares are still lacking.

[237] II, 31.

[238] II, 32–33.

Next, it deals in great detail with incantations and invocations, among which those invoking the aid of Saturn are once again distinguished by series of antitheses more numerous than anywhere else[239]; and finally it comes to the casting of spells by means of light and shadows,[240] and the different sorts of "divinatio"—from the flight of birds, astral phenomena, or prodigies, and by sortilege, geomancy, hydromancy, pyromancy, aeromancy, necromancy (much despised), and the interpretation of dreams.[241]

The work reaches its climax in the third book, which, as the introduction says, leads us "to higher things", and teaches us "how to know accurately the laws of religion; how, thanks to divine religion, we must participate in the truth; and how we must properly develop our minds and spirits, by which alone we can grasp the truth".[242] With this third book we leave the lower realm of practical magic and divination by outward aids, and come to that of "vaticinium", direct revelation, in which the soul, inspired by higher powers, "recognises the last fundamentals of things in this world and the next" and miraculously sees "everything that is, has been, or will be in the most distant future".[243] After some introductory remarks on the intellectual and spiritual virtues required to obtain such grace, and a detailed argument designed to prove that this form of mysticism is compatible with Christian dogma, especially with the doctrine of the Trinity,[244] this book enquires into the transmitters of higher inspiration, who are the "daemons", incorporeal intelligences, who "have their light from God" and transmit it to men for purposes of revelation or seduction. They are divided into three orders: the higher or "super-celestial", who circle about the divine unity above the cosmos; the middle or "mundane", who inhabit the heavenly spheres; and the lower or elemental spirits, among whom are also reckoned woodland and domestic gods, the "daemons" of the four quarters of the world, guardian spirits

---

[239] II, 34–38. The prayer to Saturn (ch. 37, fol. 70ᵛ–71ʳ) runs as follows: "Dominus altus magnus sapiens intelligens ingeniosus revolutor longi spatii, senex magne profunditatis, arcane contemplationis auctor, in cordibus hominum cogitationes magnas deprimens et vel imprimens, vim et potestatem subuertens, omnia destruens et conseruans, secretorum et absconditorum ostensor et inuentor, faciens amittere et inuenire, auctor vite et mortis." In the printed edition (II, 59, p. 205) this polarity, which we found affecting even Alanus ab Insulis (cf. text p. 186), appears equally clearly ("vim et potestatem subvertentem et constituentem, absconditorum custodem et ostensorem").

[240] II, 49.

[241] II, 50–58.

[242] III, 1, fol. 84ʳ.

[243] III, 29, fol. 103ʳ⁻ᵛ.

[244] III, 1–6.

and so on.[245] As these "daemons" fulfil the same function in the universal soul as the different faculties of the soul fulfil in the individual, it is understandable that the human soul, "burning with divine love, raised up by hope and led on by faith", should be able to associate itself directly with them and, as in a mirror of eternity, should be able to experience and achieve all that it could never have experienced and achieved by itself.[246] This makes possible "vaticinium", the power of "perceiving the principles ("causae") of things and foreseeing the future, in that higher inspiration descends on us from the daemons, and spiritual influences are transmitted to us"; this, however, can only happen when the soul is not busied with any other matters but is free ("vacat").[247] Such a "vacatio animae" could take three forms, namely true dreams ("somnia"),[248] elevation of the soul by means of contemplation ("raptus")[249] and illumination of the soul ("furor") by the daemons (in this case acting without mediators)[250]; and we are told, in terms unmistakably reminiscent of Plato's *Phaedrus*, that this "furor" could come from the Muses, or Dionysus, or Apollo, or Venus,[251]—or else from melancholy.[252]

As physical cause of this frenzy [says Agrippa in effect], the philosophers give the "humor melancholicus", not, however, that which is called the black bile, which is something so evil and terrible that its onset, according to the view of scientists and physicians, results not only in madness but in possession by evil spirits as well. By "humor melancholicus" I mean rather that which is called "candida bilis et naturalis". Now this, when it takes fire and glows, generates the frenzy which leads us to wisdom and revelation, especially when it is combined with a heavenly influence, above all with

---

[245] III, 7–10. The "daemones medii" inhabiting the spheres correspond on the one hand to the nine Muses (cf. MARTIANUS CAPELLA, *Nuptiae Philologiae et Mercurii*, I, 27–28, ed. A. Dick, Leipzig 1925, p. 19); on the other, to certain angels; it is typical of the survival of ancient mythology that the spirit of Mercury was identified with Michael, who had taken over so many of the functions of Hermes Psychopompus, while the spirit of the virginal goddess of birth, Luna-Artemis, was identified with Gabriel, angel of the Annunciation. We cannot here enter into Agrippa's demonology or evaluate the cosmology and highly interesting psychology contained in ch. III, 16–29.

[246] III, 29, fol. 103^{r-v}.

[247] III, 30, fol. 104^{r}. "Illapsiones vero eiusmodi . . . non transeunt in animam nostram, quando illa in aliud quiddam attentius inhians est occupata, sed transeunt, quando vacat."

[248] III, 38.

[249] III, 37.

[250] III, 31–36.

[251] III, 33–36.

[252] For the doctrine of "vacatio animae" and the possibility of its being caused by melancholy, see e.g. FICINO, *Theologia Platonica de immortalitate animorum*, BK XIII, 2 (*Opera*, VOL. I, p. 292).

that of Saturn. For, since, like the "humor melancholicus", he is cold and dry, he influences it constantly, increases it and sustains it. And as moreover, he is the lord of secret contemplation, foreign to all public affairs, and the highest among the planets, so he constantly recalls the soul from outward matters towards the innermost, enables it to rise from lower things to the highest, and sends it knowledge and perception of the future. Therefore Aristotle says in the *Problemata* that through melancholy some men have become divine beings, foretelling the future like the Sibyls and the inspired prophets of ancient Greece, while others have become poets like Maracus of Syracuse; and he says further that all men who have been distinguished in any branch of knowledge have generally been melancholics: to which Democritus and Plato, as well as Aristotle, bear witness, for according to their assurance some melancholics were so outstanding by their genius that they seemed gods rather than men. We often see uneducated, foolish, irresponsible melancholics (such as Hesiod, Ion, Tynnichus of Chalcis, Homer, and Lucretius are said to have been) suddenly seized by this frenzy, when they change into great poets and invent marvellous and divine songs which they themselves scarcely understand. . . .[253]

Moreover, this "humor melancholicus" has such power that they say it attracts certain daemons into our bodies, through whose presence and activity men fall into ecstasies and pronounce many wonderful things. The whole of antiquity bears witness that this occurs in three different forms, corresponding to the threefold capacity of our soul, namely the imaginative,

---

[253] III, 31, fols. 104r sqq. (proper names corrected in the translation): "Furor est illustratio anime a diis vel a demonibus proveniens. Unde Nasonis hoc carmen:

'Est deus in nobis, sunt et commercia celi;
Sedibus ethereis spiritus ille venit.'

Huius itaque furoris causam, que intra humanum corpus est, dicunt philosophi esse humorem melancolicum, non quidem illum, qui atra bilis vocatur, qui adeo prava horribilisque res est, ut impetus eius a phisicis ac medicis ultra maniam quam inducit, eciam malorum demonum obsessiones afferre confirmatur. Humorem igitur dico melancolicum, qui candida bilis vocatur et naturalis. Hic enim quando accenditur atque ardet, furorem concitat ad sapientiam nobis vaticiniumque conducentem, maxime quatenus consentit cum influxu aliquo celesti, precipue Saturni. Hic enim cum ipse sit frigidus atque siccus, qualis est humor melancolicus, ipsum quotidie influit, auget et conservat; preterea cum sit arcane contemplationis auctor ab omni publico negocio alienus ac planetarum altissimus, animam ipsam tum ab externis officiis ad intima semper revocat, tum ab inferioribus ascendere facit, trahendo ad altissima scientiasque ac futurorum presagia largitur. Unde inquit Aristoteles in libro problematum ex melancolia quidam facti sunt sicut diuini predicentes futura ut Sibille et Bachides, quidam facti sunt poete ut Malanchius Siracusanus; ait preterea omnes viros in quauis scientia prestantes ut plurimum extitisse melancolicos, quod etiam Democritus et Plato cum Aristotele testantur confirmantes nonnullos melancolicos in tantum prestare ingenio, ut diuini potius quam humani videantur. Plerunque etiam videmus homines melancolicos rudes, ineptos, insanos, quales legimus extitisse Hesiodum, Jonem, Tymnicum Calcidensem, Homerum et Lucretium, sepe furore subito corripi ac in poetas bonos euadere et miranda quedam diuinaque canere etiam que ipsimet vix intelligant. Unde diuus Plato in Jone, ubi de furore poetico tractat: 'Plerique, inquit, vates, postquam furoris remissus est impetus, que scripserunt non satis intelligunt, cum tamen recte de singulis artibus in furore tractauerunt, quod singuli harum artifices legendo diiudicant'." It is evident throughout that Agrippa follows Ficino.

the rational, and the mental. For when set free by the "humor melancholicus", the soul is fully concentrated in the imagination, and it immediately becomes an habitation for the lower spirits, from whom it often receives wonderful instruction in the manual arts; thus we see a quite unskilled man suddenly become a painter or an architect, or a quite outstanding master in another art of the same kind; but if the spirits of this species reveal the future to us, they show us matters related to natural catastrophes and disasters—for instance, approaching storms, earthquakes, cloudbursts, or threats of plague, famine, devastation, and so on. But when the soul is fully concentrated in the reason, it becomes the home of the middle spirits; thereby it attains knowledge and cognition of natural and human things; thus we see a man suddenly become a [natural] philosopher, a physician or a [political] orator; and of future events they show us what concerns the overthrow of kingdoms and the return of epochs, prophesying in the same way as the Sibyl prophesied to the Romans. . . . But when the soul soars completely to the intellect ("mens"), it becomes the home of the higher spirits, from whom it learns the secrets of divine matters, as, for instance, the law of God, the angelic hierarchy, and that which pertains to the knowledge of eternal things and the soul's salvation; of future events they show us, for instance, approaching prodigies, wonders, a prophet to come, or the emergence of a new religion, just as the Sibyls prophesied Jesus Christ long before he appeared. . . .[254]

This theory of melancholy frenzy occupied a central position in the original version of *Occulta philosophia*, for the "furor

---

[254] III, 32, fol. 105r: "Tantum preterea est huius humoris imperium ut ferant suo impetu eciam demones quosdam in nostra corpora rapi quorum presentia et instinctu homines debachari et mirabilia multa effari. Omnis testatur antiquitas et hoc sub triplici differentia iuxta triplicem anime apprehensionem, scilicet imaginatiuam, rationalem et mentalem; quando enim anima melancolico humore vacans tota in imaginationem transfertur, subito efficitur inferiorum demonum habitaculum, a quibus manualium artium sepe miras accipit rationes; sic videmus rudissimum aliquem hominem sepe in pictorem vel architectorem vel alterius cuiusque artificii subtilissimum subito euadere magistrum; quando vero eiusmodi demones futura nobis portendunt, ostendunt que ad elementorum turbationes temporumque vicissitudines attinent, ut videlicet futuram tempestatem, terremotum vel pluuiam, item futuram mortalitatem, famem, vel stragem et eiusmodi. Sic legimus apud Aulum Gellium Cornelium sacerdotem castissimum eo tempore quo Cesar et Pompeius in Thessalia confligebant, Pataui furore correptum fuisse, ita quod et tempus et ordinem et exitum pugne viderat. Quando vero anima tota in rationem conuertitur, mediorum demonum efficitur domicilium. Hinc naturalium rerum humanarumque nanciscitur scientiam atque prudentiam. Sic videmus aliquando hominem aliquem subito in philosophum vel medicum vel oratorem egregium evadere; ex futuris autem ostendunt nobis que ad regnorum mutationes et seculorum restitutiones pertinent, quemadmodum Sibilla Romanis vaticinata fuit. Cum vero anima tota assurgit in mentem, sublimium demonum efficitur domicilium, a quibus arcana ediscit divinorum, ut videlicet Dei legem, ordines angelorum et ea que ad eternarum rerum cognitionem animarumque salutem pertinent; ex futuris vero ostendunt nobis, ut futura prodigia, miracula, futurum prophetam vel legis mutationem, quemadmodum Sibille de Jesu Christo longo tempore ante aduentum eius vaticinate sunt, quem quidem Vergilius spiritu consimili iam propinquum intelligendo Sibille Cumane reminiscens cecinit:

'Ultima Cumei venit iam carminis etas;
Magnus ab integro seculorum nascitur ordo,
Iam redit et virgo, redeunt Saturnia regna;
Iam noua progenies celo dimittitur alto'. "

melancholicus" was the first and most important form of "vacatio animae", and thereby a specific source of inspired creative achievement. It therefore signified the exact point at which the process whose goal was the "vaticinium" reached its climax[255]; and this theory of melancholy enthusiasm reveals the whole variety of the sources merging in Agrippa's magical system. The 'Aristotelian' theory of melancholy, which had already been given an astrological turn by Ficino, was now also coupled with a theory of "daemons" which a late antique mystic like Iamblichus had considered incompatible with astrology[256]; and when Agrippa converted the hierarchy of the three faculties "imaginatio", "ratio" and "mens" into a hierarchy of melancholy illumination and of the achievements based on it, he also went back partly to Ficino,[257] partly to a very ancient gradation of human careers into mechanical, political and philosophical.[258] Again, in part, he was also indebted to the theory widely known after Averroes, in which various effects of the "humor melancholicus" were distinguished, not only as differing in kind, but also as affecting different qualities of the soul. It is true that this purely psychiatric theory had contemplated merely the destructive effect of melancholy and that in place of the ascending scale "imaginatio"—"ratio"—"mens" it had posited "imaginatio", "ratio", and "memoria" all on a footing of equality.[259] To this extent, Agrippa's view represents a fusion of Ficino's theory with other elements. This

---

[255] Ch. III, 39–56, following the "somnium" section, sets out and explains what is required of the magician in respect of purity, operational rites, "nomina sacra", etc., while the last chapter (III, 57) attempts to define the distinction between "religio" and unlawful "superstitio"—the latter, logically, being limited to the application of the sacraments to improper objects, e.g. the excommunication of noxious worms or the baptism of statues. Ch. III, 30–38, therefore really forms the core of the whole. How greatly this whole structure was dismembered in the printed edition can be seen from the fact that the two chapters on melancholy have, with minor alterations, been compressed into one section and placed in Book I (60), following ch. 59, on "somnium", which is preceded in turn by a chapter on cases of alleged resurrection from the dead and phenomena of stigmatization as well as by the chapter on geomancy formerly in Book II.

[256] See above, p. 152 (text).

[257] See the parallel passage quoted above, p. 271 sq. (text).

[258] Perhaps the most striking example is in the *Disciplina scholarium*, see above p. 282 sq., ☞ ch. V (P. L., VOL. LXIV, col. 1233): "Cum ad magistratus excellentiam bonae indolis adolescens velit ascendere, necessarium est ut tria genera statuum, quae in assignatione probabilitatis innuit Aristoteles, diligenter intelligat. Sunt autem quidam vehementer obtusi, alii mediocres, tertii excellenter acuti. Nullum vero vehementer obtusorum vidimus unquam philosophico nectare vehementer inebriari. Istis autem mechanica gaudet maritari, mediocribus politica."

[259] See above, pp. 92 sqq. (text).

very fusion, however, was what was most fruitful and impressive in Agrippa's achievement; the notion of melancholy and of Saturnine genius was no longer restricted to the "homines literati", but was expanded to include—in three ascending grades—the geniuses of action and of artistic vision, so that no less than the great politician or religious genius, the "subtle" architect or painter was now reckoned among the "vates" and "Saturnines". Agrippa expanded the self-glorification of the exclusive circle of the humanists into a universal doctrine of genius long before the Italian theorists of art did the same; and he varied the theme of the gifts of melancholy by distinguishing their subjective aspects from their objective effects; that is to say, by placing side by side the gift of prophecy and creative power, vision and achievement.

The three grades and the two ways in which, according to Agrippa, Saturnine and melancholy inspiration works is summarised in the following table.

Level	Instru-ments	Psychological Habitat	Realm of Creative Achievement	Realm of Prophecy
I	Lower Spirits	"Imaginatio"	Mechanical arts, especially architecture, painting, etc.	Natural events, especially cloudbursts, famine, etc.
II	Middle Spirits	"Ratio"	Knowledge of natural and human things, especially natural science, medicine, politics, etc.	Political events, overthrow of rulers, restoration, etc.
III	Higher Spirits	"Mens"	Knowledge of divine secrets, especially cognition of divine law, angelology and theology	Religious events, especially the advent of new prophets or the birth of new religions

Let us now imagine the task of an artist who wishes to undertake a portrait of the first or imaginative form of melancholy talent and "frenzy", in accordance with this theory of Agrippa of Nettesheim. What would he have to represent? A being under a cloud, for his mind is melancholy; a being creative as well as prophetic, for his mind has a share of inspired "furor";

a being whose powers of invention are limited to the realms of visibility in space—that is to say, to the realm of the mechanical arts—and whose prophetic gaze can see only menacing catastrophes of nature, for his mind is wholly conditioned by the faculty of "imaginatio"; a being, finally, who is darkly aware of the inadequacy of his powers of knowledge, for his mind lacks the capacity either to allow the higher faculties to take effect or to receive other than the lower spirits. In other words, what the artist would have to represent would be what Albrecht Dürer did in *Melencolia I*.

There is no work of art which corresponds more nearly to Agrippa's notion of melancholy than Dürer's engraving, and there is no text with which Dürer's engraving accords more nearly than Agrippa's chapters on melancholy.

If we now assume the *Occulta philosophia* to be the ultimate source of Dürer's inspiration, and there is nothing against such an assumption, then we can understand why Dürer's portrait of Melancholy—the melancholy of an imaginative being, as distinct from that of the rational or the speculative, the melancholy of the artist and of the artistic thinker, as distinct from that which is political and scientific, or metaphysical and religious—is called *Melencolia I*[260]; we can also understand why the background contains no sun, moon or stars, but the sea flooding the beach, a comet and a rainbow (for what could better denote the "pluviae, fames et strages" which imaginative melancholy foretells?), and why Melancholy is creative, and, at the same time, sunk in depression; prophetic, and, at the same time, confined within her own limits.

Dürer, more than anyone, could identify himself with Agrippa's conception; contemporary in thought with Agrippa, and opposed to the older Italian art-theorists such as Alberti or Leonardo, he, more than anyone, was convinced that the imaginative achievements of painters and architects were derived from higher and ultimately divine inspiration. While fifteenth- and early sixteenth-century Italians had waged war for the recognition of pictorial art as a liberal art purely in the name of a "ratio" which should enable the artist to master reality by means of his rational insight into natural laws, and thereby to raise his activity to the rank

---

260 In itself the *I* does not necessarily mean that Dürer actually intended to draw the other two forms of melancholy; it is possible that in engraving this one he merely imagined the other two, and expected the educated spectator to imagine them as well.

of an exact science,[261] Dürer, despite his passionate championship of this very "ratio",[262] was aware of the fact that the deepest source of creative power was to be sought elsewhere, in that purely irrational and individual gift or inspiration[263] which Italian belief granted, if at all, only to the "literarum studiosi" and the "Musarum sacerdotes". Alberti's and Leonardo's speculations on the theory of art were totally unaffected by the Florentine Neoplatonists,[264] and laid the foundations of an "exact" science, as defined by Galileo. They assigned to pictorial art that place in culture as a whole which we to-day are accustomed to allocate to "sober science", and none of the classical art-theorists would ever have thought of considering the architect, painter or sculptor as divinely inspired; that did not happen until the birth of that mannerist school which inclined to northern conceptions in all things; which saturated the theory of art (until then wholly objective and rational) with the spirit of mystic individualism[265]; which conferred the adjective "divine" on the artist; and which tried—significantly enough—to imitate *Melencolia I*, which until then had been almost ignored in Italy.[266] But Dürer had known, by instinct, what the Italians learnt only later, and then as a matter of secondary importance: the tension between "ratio" and "non-ratio", between general rules and individual gifts; as early as 1512 or 1513 he had written the famous words in which he

---

[261] Cf. E. PANOFSKY, *Idea* (Studien der Bibliothek Warburg VOL. V), Leipzig 1924, pp. 25 sqq.

[262] See above, pp. 339 sqq. (text).

[263] For Dürer's individualism, cf. E. PANOFSKY, *Hercules am Scheidewege* (Studien der Bibliothek Warburg, VOL. XVIII), Leipzig 1930, pp. 167 sqq.

[264] Cf. E. PANOFSKY, *Idea* (Studien der Bibliothek Warburg, VOL. V), Leipzig 1924, pp. 25 sqq.

[265] For the transformation of Ficino's doctrine of beauty into a metaphysics of mannerist art, cf. E. PANOFSKY, *Idea*, pp. 52 sqq. For the protests against mathematical rules which had been the pride of the classical theory of art, cf. ibid. pp. 42 sqq.

[266] See below, pp. 385 sqq. (text). From this point of view it is understandable that, in spite of the remarks on Raphael quoted above, p. 232, note 44, a fundamental connexion between melancholy and figurative art, such as Agrippa had established at the beginning of the sixteenth century, did not appear in Italy until the mannerist epoch, though it was then used at once as an argument for the nobility of artistic activity. ROMANO ALBERTI's *Trattato della nobiltà della pittura*, Rome 1585, says (p. 17): "Et a confirmazione di ciò [i.e. the statement that painting deserved to be ranked as a liberal art] vediamo che li Pittori divengono malencolici, perchè volendo loro imitare bisogna, che ritenghino li fantasmati fissi nell'Intelletto: a ciò dipoi li esprimeno in quel modo, che prima li havean visti in presentia; Et questo non solo una volta, ma continuamente, essendo questo il loro essercitio: per il che talmente tengono la mente astratta et separata dalla materia, che conseguentemente ne vien la Malencolia; la quale però dice Aristotile, che significa ingegno et prudentia, perchè, come l'istesso dice, quasi tutti gl'ingegnosi et prudenti son stati malencolici."

elevated the "species fantastica" of the imagination to the rank of those "interior images" which are connected with Platonic ideas, and attributed the artist's powers of imagination to those "influences from above" that enable a good painter "always to pour forth something new in his work"[267] and "every day to have fresh figures of men and other creatures to make and pour out which no one has seen or thought of ever before".[268]

Here, in terms of German mysticism, and in phrases which are sometimes direct echoes of Ficino and Seneca,[269] a view is expressed which claims for the creative artist what the German mystics had claimed for the religiously illuminated man, Ficino for the philosophers, and Seneca for God. For this reason it harmonises with Agrippa's new doctrine. It is by no means impossible that it was the *Occulta philosophia* itself which brought the Florentine Neoplatonist doctrine of genius in a specifically German interpretation to Dürer who was not only the creator of *Melencolia I* but also the author of the *Four Books of Human Proportion*,[270] and thereby made it possible for him to formulate, in concepts and in words, the irrational and individualistic elements of his own views on art.

Both in his mind and in words—for there is no doubt that Dürer's words just quoted represent the personal experience of

---

[267] LF, *Nachlass*, p. 295, 13 (cf. p. 299, 1), and p. 297, 16.

[268] LF, *Nachlass*, p. 218, 16. The theory of genius held by Ficino and his circle, despite all the emphasis laid on increased self-awareness, is not really an individualistic one, in so far as the "Musarum sacerdotes" or "viri literati" are always conceived of as a class, and men of genius appear, as it were, in flocks. Recognition of an individual as original and unrepeatable ("desgleichen ihm zu seinen Seiten Keiner Gleich erfunden wirdet und etwan lang Keiner vor ihm gwest und nach ihm nit bald Einer kummt," LF, *Nachlass*, p. 221, 16) or of a work as original and unrepeatable ("das man vor nit gesehen noch ein Ander gedacht hätt") occurs in Dürer earlier than in the South. This also accounts for Dürer's deep aversion to self-repetition in his work. The man whose "economical habits" (Wölfflin) disposed him to re-use sketches or studies made many years earlier, did not once repeat himself in any of the works which actually left his studio, i.e. engravings, pictures or woodcuts; the monkey and the man with the gimlet, taken over from the engraving B42 or the woodcut B117 into the Dresden series of the Seven Sorrows of the Virgin, merely bear witness against the authenticity of the paintings; for the connexion between the St Paul at Munich and the engraving B46, see above, p. 302, note 75, the paper in the *Münchner Jahrbuch der bildenden Kunst.*

[269] References in E. PANOFSKY, *Idea* (Studien der Bibliothek Warburg, VOL. V), Leipzig 1924, p. 70. The sentence concerning the "*oberen Eingiessungen*" was already mentioned in this connexion by GIEHLOW (1904).

[270] We have already mentioned (text p. 353) that Agrippa refers also to the Platonic doctrine of Ideas. We may further note in connexion with the specifically northern notion of the inspired artist that it was in late Gothic art in the north that "the Mother of God portrayed by St Luke" was first represented as a visionary image in the clouds; (cf. DOROTHEA KLEIN, *St Lukas als Maler der Maria. Ikonographie der Lukas-Madonna*, dissertation, Hamburg 1933, which, however, leaves unnoticed several important examples).

the creative artist—Dürer himself was a melancholic.[271] It is no coincidence that, clearly understanding his own nature (and anticipating an eighteenth-century custom in portraiture),[272] he painted his own portrait, even in youth, in the attitude of the melancholy thinker and visionary.[273] Just as he had his share of the inspired gifts of imaginative melancholy, so, too, he was familiar with the terrors of the dreams that it could bring; for it was the vision of a flood which so shattered him by its "speed, wind, and roaring" that, as he said, "all my body trembled and I came not to my right senses for a long time."[274] Then, again, an "all too stern judge of himself",[275] he recognised the insuperable

---

[271] We know this through Melanchthon's expression discovered by A. WARBURG (*Heidnisch-antike Weissagung in Wort und Bild zu Luthers Zeiten*, in *Gesammelte Schriften*, VOL. II, Leipzig 1932, p. 529) concerning the "melancholia generosissima Dureri". Independently of this discovery, M. J. FRIEDLÄNDER, in the course of a fine and judicious account of *Melencolia I*, had already posed the question whether Dürer himself had not been a melancholic (*Albrecht Dürer*, Leipzig 1921, pp. 146 sqq.), and the question can the more readily be answered in the affirmative as Dürer suffered from an illness which the physicians of his time reckoned definitely among the "morbi melancholici": the famous Bremen drawing L130, with the superscription "Do der gelb fleck ist vnd mit dem finger drawff dewt, do ist mir we", indicates an affection of the spleen. This drawing (PLATE 145) is usually associated with Dürer's last illness. But in this connexion we may point out that this view cannot be substantiated. The style of the faintly coloured drawing recalls the studies in proportion of 1512–13 much more than later drawings, while the writing—an important aid to chronology in Dürer's case—is very different from the superb regularity—manifest even in the slightest notes—of the 'twenties, and is only a little more developed than in the letters to Pirckheimer, the closest analogy being once again the theoretical drafts of 1512–13. Moreover, the body is that of a man in his prime, the hair is still fair, and the whole appearance of the head is closest to the self-portrait in the picture of *All Saints*. There is everything to be said for assigning the Bremen drawing to the third lustrum of the sixteenth century, i.e. to the years immediately preceding the composition of *Melencolia I*, and for regarding it as yet further evidence of Dürer's eminently personal interest in the subject. There is the less reason to refer the Bremen drawing to his last illness as he had frequently been ill earlier; in 1519 Pirckheimer wrote "Turer male stat" (E. REICKE in *Mitteilungen des Vereins für Geschichte der Stadt Nürnberg*, VOL. XXVIII (1928), p. 373), and in 1503 Dürer himself wrote on the drawing L231 that he had made it "in his illness". Since noting this, we find that two other scholars are inclined to give a new date to the Bremen drawing—H. A. VAN BAKEL in an essay called "Melancholia generosissima Dureri" in *Nieuw Theologisch Tijdschrift*, VOL. XVII, 4 (1928), p. 332; and E. FLECHSIG, in *Albrecht Dürer*, VOL. II, Berlin 1931, pp. 296, sqq., who for some reason wants to date it as far back as 1509.

[272] For this, cf. URSULA HOFF, *Rembrandt und England*, dissertation, Hamburg 1935.

[273] L429.

[274] LF, *Nachlass*, p. 17, 5. It is very typical of Dürer's nature that even in the disturbance attendant on this visionary dream he notices at what distance the waters meet the land and even attempts to infer from the rapidity of the rainfall the height from which it falls ("und sie kamen so hoch hèrab, dass sie im Gedunken gleich langsam fieln").

[275] Cf. Kant's account of the melancholic, quoted above, p. 123 (text), which was anticipated, to a considerable extent, by Camerarius's fine description of Albrecht Dürer: "Erat autem, si quid omnium in illo viro quod vitii simile videretur, unica infinita diligentia et in se quoque inquisitrix saepe parum aequa." (Introduction to the Latin translation of the *Theory of Proportion*, Nuremberg 1532.)

limits set by destiny to the possessor of the melancholy of *Melencolia I*, the melancholy of a mind conditioned solely by the imagination.

In mathematics, above all, to which he devoted half a lifetime of work, Dürer had to learn that it would never give men the satisfaction they could find in metaphysical and religious revelation,[276] and that not even mathematics—or rather mathematics least of all—could lead men to the discovery of the absolute, that absolute by which, of course, he meant in the first place absolute beauty. At thirty, intoxicated by the sight of the "new kingdom" of art-theory revealed to him by Jacopo de' Barbari, he thought he could define the one universal beauty with compasses and set-square; at forty he had to admit that this hope had deceived him[277]; and it was in the years immediately preceding the engraving of *Melencolia I* that he became fully aware of this new insight, for about 1512 he wrote "but what beauty is, I do not know,"[278] and in the same draft he said "there is no man living on earth who can say or prove what the most beautiful figure of man may be. None but God can judge of beauty."[279] In the face of such an admission, even belief in the power of mathematics was bound to falter. "With regard to geometry," wrote Dürer some ten years later, "one can prove that certain things are true. But certain things one must leave to the opinion and judgement of

[276] Only in this one respect is *Melencolia I* in fact a counterpart to the engraving of *St Jerome*. A. WEIXLGÄRTNER (in *Mitteilungen der Gesellschaft für vervielfältigende Kunst*, 1901, pp. 47 sqq.) shows that the idea of an external, formal *pendant* is here entirely out of place. Still less can one assume, as R. WUSTMANN does (in *Zeitschrift für bildende Kunst*, new series, VOL. XXII (1911), p. 116), that the gourd hanging from the ceiling in the *St Jerome* engraving was originally intended to receive the inscription "Melencolia II". Nevertheless, Dürer almost always gave away these two engravings together (LF, *Nachlass*, pp. 120, 16; 121, 6; 125, 12; 127, 13, 17; 128, 17); and they have frequently been inspected and discussed together (cf. the letter to John Cochlaeus of 5 April 1520 printed, with others, by E. REICKE in *Mitteilungen des Vereins für Geschichte der Stadt Nürnberg*, VOL. XXVIII (1928), p. 375).

[277] For this change in Dürer's view of art, cf. esp. LUDWIG JUSTI, *Konstruierte Figuren und Köpfe unter den Werken Albrecht Dürers*, Leipzig 1902, pp. 21 sqq., and the same author in *Repertorium*, VOL. XXVIII (1905), pp. 368 sqq. Also E. PANOFSKY, *Dürers Kunsttheorie*, pp. 113, 127 sqq., and the same author in *Jahrbuch für Kunstwissenschaft*, VOL. III, Leipzig 1926, pp. 136 sqq.

[278] LF, *Nachlass*, p. 288, 27. Dürer's ignorance naturally refers not to the idea of beauty, but to the visible conditions, esp. proportion, determining beauty (thus also H. WÖLFFLIN, *Die Kunst Albrecht Dürers*, 5th edn., Munich 1926, p. 368). So much is clear from what follows: "Idoch will ich hie die Schonheit also für mich nehmen: Was zu den menschlichen Zeiten van dem meinsten Theil schön geachtt würd, des soll wir uns fleissen zu machen." The sentence "was aber die Schönheit sei, das weis ich nit" is equivalent, therefore, to the statements quoted below, LF, *Nachlass*, p. 222, 7, or p. 359, 16.

[279] LF, *Nachlass*, pp. 290, 23 sqq. This is identical almost word for word with a draft dated 1512 (LF, *Nachlass*, p. 300, 9).

men"[280]; and his scepticism had now reached such a pitch that not even an approximation to the highest beauty seemed possible to him any longer.

For I believe that there is no man living who can contemplate to the very end what is most beautiful even in a small creature, much less in man. . . . It enters not into man's soul. But God knows such things, and if He wishes to reveal it to someone, that person too knows it. . . . But I know not how to show any particular measure that approximates to the greatest beauty.[281]

And so finally, when his affectionate veneration for mathematics once more finds powerful and moving expression, he pays homage to mathematics as confined within, and resigned to, its limits, and the sentence "Whosoever proves his case and reveals the underlying truth of it by geometry, he is to be believed by all the world; for there one is held fast" is preceded by a sentence which might almost serve as a caption to *Melencolia I*: "For there is falsehood in our knowledge, and darkness is so firmly planted in us that even our groping fails."[282]

Thus, having established its connexions with astrology and medicine, with the pictorial representations of the vices or the arts, and with Henricus de Gandavo and Agrippa of Nettesheim, we hold none the less that those, too, are justified in their opinion who wish to consider the engraving *Melencolia I* as something other than a picture of a temperament or a disease, however much ennobled. It is a confession and an expression of Faust's "insuperable ignorance".[283] It is Saturn's face which regards us; but in it we may recognise also the features of Dürer.

---

[280] LF, *Nachlass*, p. 363, 5.

[281] LF, *Nachlass*, p. 359, 3. The printed edition of the *Theory of Proportion* continues: "Das gib ich nach, dass Einer ein hübschers Bild . . . mach . . . dann der Ander. Aber nit bis zu dem Ende, dass es nit noch hübscher möcht sein. Dann Solchs steigt nit in des Menschen Gemüt. Aber Gott weiss Solichs allein, wem ers offenbarte, der wesst es auch. Die Wahrheit hält allein innen, welch der Menschen schönste Gestalt und Mass kinnte sein und kein andre . . . In solichem Irrtum, den wir jetzt zumal bei uns haben, weis ich nit statthaft zu beschreiben endlich, was Mass sich zu der rechten Hübsche nachnen möcht." (LF, *Nachlass*, p. 221, 30).

[282] LF, *Nachlass*, p. 222, 25 (from the printed *Theory of Proportion*).

[283] It was of course the Romantics who interpreted Dürer's "Melancholy" as a direct portrait of the Faustian character. Dr Hermann Blumenthal kindly pointed out the source in KARL GUSTAV CARUS'S *Briefe über Goethes Faust*, VOL. I, Leipzig 1835, letter II, pp. 40 sqq. This remarkably fine analysis, which also strikingly emphasises the "contrast of the eagerly writing child with the idly meditating and sadly gazing larger figure", is the more admirable since the picture of a Dürer torn by Faust's emotions was—as Carus himself clearly felt and several times stated—in complete contradiction to the conception, originated by Wackenroder and at that time generally accepted, of the "otherwise so quiet and pious" master. It is especially significant that Carus, fascinated by the analogy with Faust which he had discovered, speaks of the main figure in the engraving as male.

(*d*) The "Four Apostles"[284]

"Further," says Joachim Sandrart of Dürer's so-called *Four Apostles* (PLATE III), which he had admired in the Electoral Gallery at Munich, "there are the four evangelists in the form of the four complexions, painted in oils in the very best and most masterly fashion."[285] This information, which earlier writers on Dürer had considered absolutely reliable,[286] fell into an ill-founded discredit among later historians. With the sole exception of Karl Neumann (who, however, drew no conclusions from it,[287]) it was spoken of merely as an "old tradition", which was sometimes denied completely, because Dürer "took the apostles far too seriously to use them merely as an opportunity for representing the temperaments"[288]; sometimes it was modified so arbitrarily that the whole point of the theory of the four complexions was lost,[289] and sometimes it was admitted only in so far as Dürer "in the course of his work made use of his view of the four

---

[284] In connexion with this section, see the essay already cited on p. 302, note 75, in the *Münchner Jahrbuch der bildenden Kunst*, new series, VOL. VIII (1931), pp. 1 sqq. As both accounts deal with the same subject matter, though from a different viewpoint, it has been difficult to avoid overlapping; some phrases and even whole paragraphs have had to be repeated almost word for word for the sake of clarity and coherence.

[285] JOACHIM SANDRART, *Teutsche Akademie*, ed. A. R. Peltzer, Munich 1925, p. 67.

[286] Cf. e.g. J. HELLER, *Das Leben und die Werke Albrecht Dürers*, Leipzig 1827, VOL. II, I, pp. 205 sqq.; F. KUGLER, *Geschichte der Malerei*, 3rd edn., Leipzig 1867, BK IV, § 240 (VOL. II, p. 498); A. VON EYE, *Leben und Wirken Albrecht Dürers*, Nördlingen 1860, p. 452; M. THAUSING, *Dürer*, Leipzig 1884, VOL. II, pp. 278 sqq.

[87] "Die vier Apostel von Albrecht Dürer in ihrer ursprünglichen Gestalt", *Zeitschrift für deutsche Bildung*, IX (1930), pp. 450 sqq., with reproductions of the inscriptions now reunited with the pictures and a detailed account of Dürer's relationship with Neudörffer. H. A. VAN BAKEL ("Melancholia generosissima Dureri", in *Nieuw Theologisch Tijdschrift*, 1928) has also returned to the old, traditional interpretation of these pictures of the Apostles as portrayals of the temperaments, but wrongly regards St John as the melancholic, which makes his conclusions as to the spiritual complexion of *Melencolia I* somewhat questionable.

[288] Thus H. WÖLFFLIN, *Die Kunst Albrecht Dürers*, Munich 1926, p. 348 (and later T. HAMPE in *Festchrift des Vereins für die Geschichte der Stadt Nürnberg zur 400 jährigen Gedächtnisfeier Albrecht Dürers*, 1528–1928, Nuremberg 1928, p. 58). A similar note is sounded when a man of the eighteenth century rejects any attempt to classify the historical figures of the Apostles according to the complexions with the remark that he does not like it "when men of God, who are directly inspired by the Holy Ghost, are judged so completely with a philosophical yardstick like ordinary people, and when not only their temperaments but also the degree, usefulness and God knows what else of the smallest parts of them are detailed and precisely determined". (J. W. APPELIUS, *Historisch-moralischer Entwurff der Temperamenten*, Preface to the 2nd edn., 1737, fol. C. 42ᵛ).

[289] H. KAUFMANN, *Albrecht Dürers rhythmische Kunst*, Leipzig 1924, pp. 60 and 135 sqq. According to Kaufmann the descriptions of the four Apostles as the four types of complexion originally referred not to the difference in their humoral constitution but to the difference in their attitudes and gestures, and it was only from this that "the opinion gradually arose that these four complexions were the four temperaments". Kaufmann apparently did not notice that it was actually the oldest source which expressly described them as "sanguinicus, cholericus, phlegmaticus et melancholicus".

temperaments as well as of his other special artistic experience, as a help in his representation".[290] This "old tradition", however, goes back in fact to such a reliable witness that, had it been a question of authorship rather than an iconographical problem, it would never have been treated so disdainfully. This witness is Johann Neudörffer, who did the lettering of the subscriptions to the picture of the apostles in Dürer's own workshop, and stated, not without pride, that he often had the honour of confidential talks with the master.[291] Now Neudörffer says quite unequivocally that Dürer presented the counsellors of Nuremberg with four life-size "pictures" (that is, figures) "in oils . . . wherein one may recognise a sanguinic, a choleric, a phlegmatic, and a melancholic"[292]; and we cannot simply ignore such evidence.

There can, of course, be no question of Dürer's "using the apostles merely as an opportunity for representing the temperaments"; but that does not exclude the possibility that he may have regarded the temperaments as a basis for his characterisation of the apostles. He did not, of course, consider the nature of the apostles exhaustively expressed by the fact that each of them belonged to one of the four humoral types, but he could, to use Sandrart's admirable expression, have represented them "in the form of the four temperaments". They are sanguine or choleric in precisely the same sense and to precisely the same degree as they are young or old, gentle or violent: in short, inasmuch as they are individual personalities.

Dürer differentiated the most significant variants of religious behaviour according to the most significant variants of human (or, for him, temperamental) character; and far from lowering the apostles to mere examples of complexional types, he gave the complexions a higher meaning, which they were altogether fitted to acquire. Men had always been accustomed to couple the four temperaments with the seasons, the rivers of Paradise, the four winds, the four ages of man, the points of the compass, the elements, and, in short, with everything determined by the "sacred tetrad". In the fifteenth century artists ventured to

---

[290] E. Heidrich, *Dürer und die Reformation*, Leipzig 1909, p. 57.

[291] He says of Daniel Engelhart, the armorial sculptor and sealcutter, that he was so excellent "that Albrecht Dürer told me here in his room, as I was writing at the foot of the aforementioned four pictures and entering various sentences from Holy Writ, that he had not seen a mightier or more skilful armorial sculptor." (Johann Neudörffer, *Nachrichten von Künstlern u. Werkleuten Nürnbergs*, 1547, newly edited by G. W. K. Lochner in *Quellenschriften für Kunstgeschichte*, vol. x, Vienna 1875, pp. 158 sqq.).

[292] Neudörffer, op. cit. (ed. Lochner), pp. 132 sqq.

place the Divine Face in the centre between the figures of the four temperaments, thereby showing the four humours as the fourfold reflexion of a single divine ray (PLATE 80).[293] It was the change from this schematic manner of representation to the particularising tendency of Dürer's time which made it possible to fuse the varieties of religious characters with the four temperaments in the persons of the apostles, thus combining veneration for the bearers of the "divine word"[294] with veneration for the variety of God's creatures.[295]

How then are the four temperaments to be apportioned among the four apostles? The order suggested by earlier writers (John melancholy, Peter phlegmatic, Mark sanguine, and Paul choleric)[296] derives from a specifically modern psychology not based on any historical sources, and a sixteenth-century copy which gives each figure its complexion is of no value because it mechanically follows the order given in Neudörffer's account.[297] Fortunately, however, we have numerous texts describing the four complexions according to their physical and mental characteristics, and positively connecting each of them with one of the four ages of man; and these texts enable us to put the order on an historical basis.

Anyone regarding the Munich portraits must be struck by the fact that the four apostles are shown as the most heterogeneous types possible—as compared, for instance, with Giovanni Bellini's four apostles (whose grouping Dürer may perhaps have remembered),[298] or even as compared with Dürer's own series of engravings of the apostles.[299] Each figure is as different as possible from the others, not only in age and in physical and mental disposition,[300] but more especially, in colouring, which played so important a

---

[293] London, Brit. Mus., Egerton MS 2572, fol. 51 v.

[294] LF, *Nachlass*, p. 382, 2.

[295] LF, *Nachlass*, p. 227, 4.

[296] Thus A. VON EYE, *Leben und Wirken Albrecht Dürers*, Nördlingen 1860; M. THAUSING, *Dürer*, Leipzig 1884; F. KUGLER, *Geschichte der Malerei*, 3rd edn., Leipzig 1867.

[297] According to this St John was the sanguinic, St Peter the choleric, St Mark the phlegmatic (!) and St Paul the melancholic. Prof. Mayer-Bamberg kindly informed us of the whereabouts of the picture mentioned by J. HELLER, *Das Leben und die Werke Albrecht Dürers*, Leipzig 1827 (Sacristy of St James in Bamberg), and obtained a photograph for us.

[298] Triptych of 1488 in the Church of the Frari; cf. KARL VOLL, in *Süddeutsche Monatshefte*, VOL. III (1906), pp. 74 sqq., and G. PAULI, in *Vorträge der Bibliothek Warburg*, VOL. I (1921–22), p. 67.

[299] The Apostles in the engravings B48, 49 and 50 are approximately of the same age.

[300] Thus also H. BEEKEN, in *Logos*, VOL. XIX (1930), p. 225, although he denies any connexion with the doctrine of temperaments.

role in the doctrine of temperaments that the word "complexion" is now limited to that sense. The reserved John, a fine example of youthful sobriety, is a nobly-built young man some twenty-five years of age, in whose blooming complexion red and white are mingled. Mark, who is showing his teeth and rolling his eyes, is a man of about forty, whose bloodless hue carries almost greenish overtones. Paul, with his earnest and menacing yet calm regard, is fifty-five or sixty years of age, and the colour of his clear-cut features—he is the leanest of the four—despite a few reddish tinges, can only be described as dark brown. Finally, the somewhat apathetic Peter is an old man of at least seventy, whose weary and relatively fleshy face is yellowish, and in general decidedly pale.[301]

Whether we have recourse to post-classical or early scholastic texts, popular treatises on the complexions, or, above all, to the Salernitan verses,[302] we always find a substantially uniform system of apportioning the various characteristics and attributes, which can be summed up in the following schema:

1. Youth = Spring; well-proportioned body, harmoniously balanced nature, ruddy complexion ("rubeique coloris"); sanguine.
2. Prime = Summer; graceful body, irascible nature, yellow complexion ("croceique coloris," "citrinitas coloris")[303]; choleric.
3. Middle Age = Autumn; lean body, gloomy nature, dark complexion ("luteique coloris", "facies nigra"); melancholic.
4. Old Age = Winter; plump body, lethargic nature, pale complexion ("pinguis facies", "color albus"); phlegmatic.

From this summary it is clear that the complexions can only be apportioned as follows: John is the sanguine, Mark (whose symbol, moreover, is the lion, the beast symbolic of the "cholera rubra") is the choleric, Paul the melancholic, and Peter the phlegmatic.[304]

---

[301] The authors' remarks on the colouring have been compared with a description made independently by Dr Erwin Rosenthal, to whom we owe our thanks.

[302] See above, pp. 3; 10; 114 sqq. (text).

[303] Thus Constantinus Africanus, *Theorica Pantegni* (*Opera*, vol. ii, Basle 1539, p. 249).

[304] Incidentally Rubens, so far as comparison with Dürer's figures is possible (for only two of these are evangelists), followed the same sequence of age or, if one likes, of temperaments, in his picture of the four evangelists at Sanssouci (*Klassiker der Kunst*, ed. R. Oldenbourg, Stuttgart 1921, p. 68). St John is represented as a youth (sanguinic), St Mark as a youngish man (choleric), St Luke as an older man (melancholic), and St Matthew as an old man (phlegmatic). Here we may also remark that Steinmann's suggestion of equating Michelangelo's Hours of the Day with the temperaments can only be maintained, if at all, by following the traditional literary correlation of the hours of the day with the four humours (see above, p. 11, note 24). Thus we could not say: Dawn = melancholy, Day = cholera,

If further evidence is needed we have only to recall the woodcut illustrating the book by Conrad Celtes (PLATE 83). Here, it is true, since Celtes had transposed the qualities of two seasons,[305] the phlegmatic has—exceptionally—become the representative of autumn, and therefore is younger than the melancholic; but apart from this modification, which is required by the text, the division of the dispositions and ages corresponds throughout with that in Dürer's picture of the apostles, save that in the latter the biological characteristics have acquired a human or superhuman significance. In the woodcut, too, the "sanguine" person is the handsome youth; the "choleric" is the irascible man in the prime of life; the "phlegmatic" is the well-nourished man with the "pinguis facies"; and the "melancholic" is the bony bald-headed man with the long beard. Indeed, the "melancholic" of 1502 is positively an anticipatory caricature of the St Paul of 1526; or, vice versa, the St Paul of 1526 is the subsequent ennobling of the "melancholic" of 1502.[306] And if we enquire into the artistic means which Dürer employed in order to transform the representative of the "least noble complexion" (for so the melancholic still was in the Celtes woodcut) into one of the noblest figures in European art, we find that they were the means used in *Melencolia I*. Not only does the pure proportion of the features—which, in an artist such as Dürer, is also an expression of inner greatness—link the head of St Paul with that of Melencolia; but the two most essential elements of facial expression are the same

---

Dusk = phlegma and Night = sanguis, but "Aurora" = sanguis, "Giorno" = cholera, "Crepuscolo" = melancholy (E. Zola in his *L'oeuvre* happens to say "pénétré par la mélancolie du crépuscule") and "Notte" = phlegma. It is not impossible that such notions played a part in the artistic conception even of Michelangelo (particularly since there was no iconographical tradition for the hours of the day); and "Giorno's" ire, which is not intelligible in itself, could quite well be associated with the notion of choler. One must, however, remember that Michelangelo's world as a whole was far too much conditioned by melancholy to have room for a purely phlegmatic, let alone a purely sanguine nature. If one wished to draw a parallel between the temperaments and Michelangelo's Hours of the Day, one would have to consider the latter as a series of melancholy natures superimposed on a sanguine, choleric, natural melancholic and phlegmatic basis.

305 See above, p. 279 (text).

306 The melancholic's head of 1502 and St Paul's head of 1526 represent, of course, merely the two extremes of a series, the main intermediate figures of which are the Barberini picture, the Heller altar (esp. L510), the drawing L18, the woodcut B38 and the engraving B50. But when one compares all these, related in principle as they are, the Munich St Paul seems specially close, at least physiognomically, to the head of the melancholic in B132, despite all the differences of "ethos"—closer, at any rate, than to the head of the engraved St Paul on B50 with which F. HAACK wishes to connect it all too closely (*Mitteilungen des Vereins für Geschichte der Stadt Nürnberg*, VOL. XXVIII (1928), p. 313).

here as there: the "facies nigra" and, standing out in strong contrast to it, the glowing brilliance of the eyes. St Paul as a type is, so to speak, the melancholy type of the Celtes woodcut, but shot through with the colouring of *Melencolia I*. 1502, 1514 and 1526—these are three stages in the development of the notion of melancholy, three stages in the development of Dürer himself.

An attempt has been made elsewhere to prove that his portraits of the four apostles, long suspected of being the wings of an uncompleted altarpiece,[307] were in fact undertaken in 1523 as the wings of a triptych; that each of these panels was originally intended to include only one figure; and that the pair originally envisaged were not Paul and John, but Philip and (probably) James. It was not until 1525, the year of his drawing of John,[308] that Dürer decided to make the side-pieces independent, and worked out the new, final scheme, in the execution of which Philip, already complete, had to be changed into Paul. The left wing seems not to have been far enough advanced for there to be any signs of the original idea remaining.[309]

It was therefore one and the same act of creative transformation that gave birth to the idea of these four particular saints and of the four complexions in Dürer's mind. The ideas "John, Peter, Mark, and Paul", and "sanguine, phlegmatic, choleric, and melancholic", must have formed an inseparable union in his mind, finding expression the moment the plan arose of changing the original two figures into the present four: in particular, the moment Philip became Paul, he became also a melancholic. In other words—not until the former Philip had become a melancholic could he correspond to what Dürer understood by Paul. And from now on we have an answer to the problem of Dürer's later attitude to the problem of melancholy.

The four apostles, as we see them to-day, express a creed, and, as Heidrich's research has established beyond doubt, the polemical side of this creed (which is none the less a creed for having been prompted by a mere historical coincidence) is directed against the fanatics and Anabaptists, in whose minds "Christian

---

[307] M. THAUSING, *Dürer*, VOL. II, Leipzig 1884, p. 288, and (with the illuminating suggestion that the centrepiece was to have been a "Santa Conversazione" in the style of the drawing L363) G. PAULI, in *Vorträge der Bibliothek Warburg*, VOL. I (1921–22), p. 67.

[308] L368.

[309] For details cf. E. PANOFSKY, in *Münchner Jahrbuch der bildenden Kunst*, new series, VOL. VIII (1931), pp. 1 sqq.

freedom" seemed to have degenerated into unlimited sectarianism. This rebuttal of fanaticism, however, as Heidrich has clearly proved, is based as a matter of course on an acceptance of the Reformation. Dürer explains that he is against Hans Denck and the "three godless painters"; and for that very reason he need not explain that he is in favour of Luther. Hence he had been certain since 1525 that of the four men bearing witness for him, two must occupy a dominant position: Paul, in whose doctrine of justification by faith the whole structure of Protestant doctrine was based, and John, Christ's beloved disciple, who was also Luther's "beloved evangelist".[310] And in the same way as these two figures, grown to majestic size, occupy the dominant positions in the composition of the picture (and the relegation of Peter to the background signifies something of an illustrative protest against the "primatus Petri" so strongly defended by the Catholics),[311] so, too, they are representative both of the most profound religious experience and of the most excellent temperaments. Compared with John's quiet but unshakable devotion, Peter's weary resignation represents a "too little", to use an Aristotelian term; while, compared with Paul's steely calm, Mark's fanaticism represents a "too much"; and so, compared with the other two complexions, the phlegmatic is inferior in power, the choleric in nobility. The sanguine temperament, which the whole of the Middle Ages had considered the noblest, indeed the only worthy one, and which of course even in Dürer's time was regarded as an enviably healthy and harmonious disposition, had been joined since the days of Ficino and Agrippa of Nettesheim by a disposition admittedly less happy, but spiritually more sublime, the "complexio melancholica", the rehabilitation of which was as much a work of the new humanism as the rediscovery of Pauline Christianity was a work of the Reformation.

Hence it is understandable, from several angles, that Dürer thought the best way of characterising the tutelary genius of Protestantism was to represent him as a melancholic. In making the apostle of the new faith a representative of the new ideal

---

[310] M. THAUSING, *Dürer*, VOL. II, Leipzig 1884, p. 279.

[311] Cf. JOHANN ECK, *De primatu Petri libri tres*, Paris 1521, and later. St Paul's prominence compared with St Peter may the more readily be interpreted as the result of an anti-papal attitude, as an iconographical tradition, established in early Christian times and never interrupted until the Reformation, required that the two apostolic leaders be placed on an exactly equal footing—a tradition which the Dürer of 1510 had followed as a matter of course on the outer wings of the Heller altar, and in the woodcut B38.

expressed by the notion of "melancholia generosa", he not only emphasised the asceticism so characteristic of the historical Paul, but endowed him with a noble sublimity denied to the other temperaments. In doing so, however, Dürer also affirmed that for his own part melancholy still remained such as it had been revealed to him through contact with the Neoplatonic doctrine of genius, the mark of the true elect, the mark of those illuminated by "higher influences". But the Dürer of 1526 no longer illustrated this inspiration by an allegorical figure of the Spirit of Art whose power flows from the imagination, but by the holy person of a "spiritual man"; he now painted the "furor", not of the artist and thinker, but of a hero of the faith, and thus expressed the fact that his notion of melancholy had, by this time, undergone a profound change. This change might, to use Agrippa of Nettesheim's classification, be described as an advance from the painting of *Melencolia I* to the painting of a *Melencolia III*, and was, in the last resort, a change in Dürer himself. In his youth he had striven after the heroic and erotic enthusiasm of classicising Italian art; in the second decade of the sixteenth century he had found the way to the great symbolical forms of *Melencolia I* and *The Knight, Death and the Devil*; in the last and greatest years of his life he applied his gifts almost entirely to religious subjects. In the years when Cranach, Altdorfer, Aldegrever, Vischer and Beham were drawing strength from the classicism which Dürer had brought to German art, and were never tired of "Judgements of Paris", "Labours of Hercules", and scenes of centaurs and satyrs—in these very years the aged Dürer was employing all the force left to him by his theoretical work and his portrait commissions, on holy subjects, and primarily on the Passion of our Lord. And we can understand that for the late Dürer, who had been deeply stirred by Luther's mission, and who, feeling himself mortally sick, had seen himself as the suffering Christ and had even dared to paint himself as such[312]—we can understand that for the late Dürer even *Melencolia I* no longer seemed an adequate expression of human grandeur.

[312] Cf. the fine Bremen drawing, L131, of the Man of Sorrows.

Chapter III

THE ARTISTIC LEGACY OF "MELENCOLIA I"

Dürer's *Melencolia I* belongs, like his *Apocalypse*, to those works of art which seem to have exercised an almost compulsive power over the imagination of posterity. Exceptions to this influence are relatively few. On the one hand, there are illustrations to almanacs and popular treatises on health, in which the old types of the various temperaments survive, modified only outwardly in accordance with the needs of the time[1]; on the other hand, there are illustrations conditioned by the requirements of the text, such as the title-engravings of scientific treatises—the richest example of which (Plate 112) is in Burton's *Anatomy of Melancholy*[2]—, the frontispiece to a set of pictures of planets after Marten de Vos (Plate 113),[3] the pictures in Cesare Ripa's *Iconology* (Plate 68),[4] or the illustrations to a poem such as Alain Chartier's (Plates 61, 64 and 65).[5] Apart from these, nearly all portraits of melancholy in the strict sense, as well as many pictures on

[1] See above, pp. 115 sqq. (text). As late as 1861, for instance, an *École de Salerne* appeared in Paris, translated by C. Meaux St-Marc and containing a poor lithograph (p. 131) of the four temperaments in the shape of four fashionably dressed gentlemen round a table. Karl Arnold published, as late as 1928, in the *Münchener Illustrierte Presse* (p. 133), a series of the "Four Dancing Temperaments", ultimately derived from the old Calendar schema of the psychologically differentiated couples.

[2] First in the 3rd edn. of 1628. This engraving, by Le Blon, shows the various main forms of melancholy: the melancholy lover, the hypochondriac, the maniac, and (representing the "superstitiosus") the monk reciting his rosary. Le Blon's engraving also contains a portrait of the author as Democritus iunior, and his ancient predecessor, Democritus Abderites, as well as two allegorical figures of the causes or peculiarities of the melancholy temperament in the background ("Zelotypia" = envy, and "Solitudo" = loneliness); and finally two remedies, borage and hellebore, which are recommended at length as antidotes to melancholy in the Peutinger codex (Clm. 4011, fol. 23). Another example is the titlepiece, mentioned above (p. 302, note 75), to Johannes Freytag's *Bericht von der Melancholia Hypochondria* which, in addition to the already described group of melancholy being worsted by a doctor, shows Asclepius with cock and book ("Confortat") and a personification of Truth with lyre and sun ("Illustrat").

[3] See above, p. 349, note 217, and below, p. 396 (text).

[4] The "Malenconico" of the temperament-series in Cesare Ripa's *Complessioni* is a man standing, in dark clothing, a book in one hand to show his inclination to study, a miser's purse in the other, a bandage across his mouth to show his silence, and a sparrow on his head to show his predilection for solitude. For melancholy as a single personification (Plate 68), which also occurs in Ripa, see above, pp. 226 sqq. (text).

[5] See above, pp. 223 sqq. (text).

similar themes, right down to the middle of the nineteenth century, owe a debt to the model set by Dürer, either direct, through conscious imitation, or by virtue of the unconscious pressure that is called "tradition".

To classify these portraits of melancholy, which are "after Dürer" in more than the temporal sense, one might divide them into those which, like their great model, are allegories complete in themselves, and those which are once more embodied in the usual sequence of the four temperaments. The groups resulting from this quite mechanical method of classification, moreover, broadly coincide with the groups resulting from regional or chronological classification. As far as any connexion with Dürer's engraving exists, portraits of melancholy as one of the four complexions are limited almost entirely to the sixteenth century, whereas later periods favoured the single and independent allegory; moreover, one can see that even during the sixteenth century, when portraits of melancholy after Dürer's engraving were most frequently included in the complexion-sequences, not every country participated in this development to the same extent. In Italy, where even during the fifteenth century there was a dearth of regular temperament-sequences, they are also in the sixteenth century less numerous than single allegories. The reverse is the case in the Netherlands, while in Germany the two types are more or less equally balanced.[6]

Nevertheless, it seemed better to us to classify the portraits of melancholy[7] deriving from Dürer's engraving not iconographically, but according to their inherent composition. That is to say, to divide them thus:

1. Those essentially retaining the formula of their model—that is, representing melancholy, either independently or in connexion with a complexion-sequence, as a single, more or less idealised female figure, sometimes even (when

[6] France, "encombrée par sa tradition", to use Henri Focillon's words, seems to have escaped the influence of Dürer's engraving almost completely during the sixteenth century, and to have been affected by it only in the seventeenth via Italian baroque art (cf. PLATE 136, and text p. 390 sq.).

[7] It would take a separate study to collect all the representations in which the endless wealth of motifs in the Dürer engraving was drawn upon for the depiction of other themes, especially the personifications of "Contemplatio", "Meditatio", "Penitentia", etc., and of the Liberal and Mechanical Arts; especially characteristic of these is Virgil Solis's *Artes* series, B183–189, and that of H. S. Beham, B121–127. As the types of both the meditating author, etc., and of the *Artes* formed the basis of Dürer's engraving, it could now influence the development of both.

agreeing particularly closely with Dürer) accompanied by a putto.

2. Those which revert to the dramatic two-figure type of late medieval calendar illustrations and betray their indebtedness to Dürer only by certain details.

3. Those whose composition derives from the portraits of Saturn or his 'Children' rather than from the complexion-sequences, so that their relation to Dürer is merely conceptual.

1. PORTRAITS OF MELANCHOLY AS A SINGLE FEMALE FIGURE IN THE MANNER OF DÜRER

We have to record the remarkable fact that apparently the earliest portrait of melancholy in Dürer's manner did not originate in his own circle, but came from an artist who was earlier regarded definitely as a Netherlander and who, even if this was not the case, can only have flourished in north-west Germany, perhaps Westphalia; this was the master with the monogram "A.C." (Pass. 112, our PLATE 114). As an engraving similar in style and probably also inspired by Dürer's engraving of Melancholy, the *Geometria* (Pass. 113), bears the date 1526, we should no doubt place his *Melancholy*, too, not later than the third decade of the sixteenth century, and even, since his *Geometria* seems somewhat more advanced in style, before rather than after 1526. The style of this engraving of melancholy is markedly Italianate. The movement of the chief figure, naked and without wings, reminds one of Michelangelo's slaves in the Sistine Chapel—particularly those to the left above Joel and to the right above the Libyan Sibyl—and also of the Donatellesque roundels in the courtyard of the Palazzo Riccardi, which influenced Michelangelo and are themselves copies of works of antiquity. The putto reminds one not only of Dürer but also of Raphael: see for instance the Michelangelesque pose of the genius in the fresco of the Sibyls in Santa Maria della Pace. The master A.C.'s putto, however, is holding a sextant in his right hand, and this is remarkable not only because mathematical attributes are otherwise largely neglected, but also, above all, because the motif of a putto holding a sextant has only been encountered once before in this connexion, and that was in Dürer's original sketch, in London (PLATE 8). We can hardly assume that an engraver otherwise so different from the great master arrived at this by no means obvious motif unaided, and since it would also explain the relatively early date of the engraving in question, it would perhaps not be too much to look for the master A.C. (whose signature appears on engravings as early as 1520) among the large number of artists fortunate enough to make Dürer's personal acquaintance during his stay in the Netherlands.[8]

Apart from the title woodcut to Egenolff's *Book of Formulae*,[9] which is almost a mechanical copy of Dürer and therefore of no interest to us, the next, and unmistakably German, imitation of Dürer's engraving was Beham's engraving B144, dated 1539 (PLATE 115). Here, too, the chief figure has become more classical both in dress and attitude, while the composition shows the new "manneristic" tendency of the time[10] in being designed rather to fill a flat surface than to make use of values of volume and space. Putto and dog are lacking, like most of the other attributes, while on the other hand two bottles are added, probably in connexion with the crucible, and obviously indicating alchemistic studies. Jost Amman's woodcut in the armorial of 1589 (PLATE 118) also belongs to this group. He, too, shows Melancholy

---

[8] Nothing definite is yet known as to the identity of the artist "A.C." The earlier, generally accepted opinion that the initials stood for Allart Claesz has been sharply attacked by M. J. FRIEDLÄNDER (U. THIEME and F. BECKER, *Allgemeines Lexikon der bildenden Künstler*, VII, p. 36); Friedländer concludes from the stylistic differences in the various designs that the signature "A.C." may signify only a goldsmith's workshop in which different engravers were at work, and is inclined to identify this goldsmith with a certain "Aleart", surname unknown, mentioned by Scorel. Recently, however, as Dr Winkler kindly informs us, even the Netherlandish origin of the engravings has been doubted (for their connexion with Gossart, however, cf. E. WEISS, *J. Gossart*, Parchim 1913, p. 42), while the opinion held prior to the Allart Claesz hypothesis, namely that the master "A.C." was identical with Adrian Collaert senior, an Antwerp engraver and art dealer active "about 1540", seems now to have been quite abandoned; according to B. LINNIG, *La gravure en Belgique*, Antwerp 1911, p. 76, Collaert was not born until 1520, which would exclude this identification, but, to our knowledge, there is no evidence for this date. We dare not plunge into this controversy, but might mention that in September 1520 Dürer gave a certain "Master Adrian" prints to the value of two guilders (LF, *Nachlass*, p. 131, 8), and that this Adrian can therefore hardly be identified with A. Herbouts or Horebouts, the Recorder of Antwerp: for the latter was always respectfully addressed by some title (LF, *Nachlass*, pp. 154, 4 and 151, 22), and moreover, as emerges from the passage just quoted, Dürer later presented him with a "whole impression."

[9] PLATE 117. The variations consist merely in the Greek version of the legend and in the bowdlerisation of the magic square. Iconographically, the design is a patchwork of the most varied motifs. The top part links Melancholy with the Amymone in B71, the lower part shows the exploit of M. Curtius, on the left there is a portrait of Fortitudo, on the right the "Miles christianus", whom the powers of darkness are attempting to hinder in his ascent to God. For the artist, cf. H. RÖTTINGER, *Der Frankfurter Buchholzschnitt* 1530–1550, Strasbourg 1933, p. 62.

[10] Cf. S. STRAUSS-KLÖBE, in *Münchner Jahrbuch der bildenden Kunst*, new series, VOL. II (1925), p. 58.

in classical attire, but gives her no wings, and reduces the symbolic implements of her profession still further, the only addition being the bellows, familiar to us from Hans Döring's woodcut (PLATE 107).[11] The stump of a column seems to indicate that Amman made use of an engraving by Virgil Solis, as well as of Dürer's.

This engraving by Virgil Solis (B 181, PLATE 122), in contrast to the pictures hitherto mentioned, is one of a set of the four temperaments, where it takes fourth place, with the significant alteration of the title to *Melancolicus*. The same applies to a small set of drawings in Wolfegg attributed to Jost Amman (PLATES 124–127), except that in this case the "melancolicus" takes third place. Solis's engraving is considerably nearer in essentials to Dürer, in so far as he lets the chief figure retain the compasses, whereas the drawing in Wolfegg exchanges them for a roll of parchment, thereby generalising the specifically mathematical idea in Dürer's engraving to a wider notion of creative meditation. Both pictures, however, have this much in common with the ones previously mentioned that, although they retain several of Dürer's attributes, they replace the contemporary middle-class costume depicted in *Melencolia I* by one that is idealised and classical; in the Wolfegg drawing, the attitude of the main figure also suggests the typical posture of a classical Muse. On the other hand, both pictures endeavour to compromise with medieval tradition, not only by denying wings to the main figure, but also, in more or less modern and humanistic form, by returning to the use of beasts as symbols, such as we saw in
PL. 82 the Shepherds' Calendar and the Books of Hours. In Solis's engraving, the sanguine temperament is represented by horse and peacock, the choleric by lion and eagle, the phlegmatic by owl and ass, and the melancholic by the gloomy elk (apparently taken over from Dürer's engraving *Adam and Eve*), and by the swan which, as the bird sacred to Apollo, may refer to the "praesagium atque divinum" which is proper to the melancholic.[12] In the Wolfegg drawings the monkey belongs to the sanguine, the bear to the choleric, the pig to the phlegmatic and the lamb

---

[11] There is a copy of Amman's woodcut on the façade of the inn "Zum roten Ochsen" in Stein am Rhein.

[12] Thus, GIEHLOW (1904), p. 66. CICERO, *De divinatione*, I, 81, is the classical passage for this correlation.

to the melancholic—all of which largely agrees with the distribution in the Shepherds' Calendar and Books of Hours.[13]

Apart from anything else, two characteristics of fundamental importance distinguish all these portraits from their original. In the first place, they fail to represent any antidote to melancholy, and, in particular, they lose sight of the profound cosmological connexion between melancholy and Saturn; secondly, the dark, meditative aspect of the chief figure is expressed by quite different physiognomic means and is therefore to some extent differently interpreted. The heavy pose of the figure seated on its low stone
ledge has become, in Beham, an attitude of negligence and apathy; Pl. 115
in the Wolfegg drawings, one of classical balance; in Amman and 124–127
A.C., one of anguished contortion; and in Virgil Solis one of 118, 114
mannered elegance. The clenched fist is replaced by a loosely 119–122
opened hand. So, too, the eyes no longer gaze into the distance with that uncanny wakefulness, but are lowered wearily and sleepily to the ground. There is no doubt that these post-Dürer pictures still attempt to show the noble melancholy of the man thinking and working; so much can be seen from the retention of the occupational symbols, as well as from the distich beneath Solis's engraving[14] (clearly reminiscent of 'Aristotle's' Problem XXX, 1) and the somewhat homely verses explaining Amman's engraving. Yet the inward temper expressed in them resembles the inactive sloth of medieval "acedia" rather than the intellectuality of melancholy as ennobled by the humanists—still alert and wakeful despite its overclouding. However much these artists adopt the outward features of Dürer's picture, and however much they endeavour to surpass him in classical idealisation, yet

---

[13] On these, see above, p. 295 sq. (text). The differences are merely that the Wolfegg series exchanges the lamb with the pig—either an instance of the frequent confusion of melancholy with phlegm, or a consequence of the humanist sublimation of the notion of melancholy, the pig being excluded on grounds of incongruousness—while the choleric's lion is replaced by a bear, the traditional symbol of wrath; also in Cesare Ripa (*Iconologia*, 1st edn., Rome 1593, s.v. "Ira"). A Dutch stained-glass portrait of melancholy, dating from about 1530, in the Victoria and Albert Museum (Murray Bequest, No. C.1380–1924), shows a grotesque mixture of animal symbols, emblems of death, and an image of the monastic rule such as could have originated only during the struggles of the Reformation, with their "Popish asses" and "monkish calves": Saturn as a warrior in half-oriental clothing, with one leg still propped up, is dismissing the melancholic from the doors of his palace to a farmyard; the melancholic himself, nervously shrinking back, appears in a monk's habit with a gigantic rosary, and a skull under his left arm, but has a boar's head instead of a human one on his shoulders. The pane seems to have belonged to a sequence, but whether it was one representing the temperaments has not as yet been determined.

[14] "Omne Melancholici studium sine fine pererrant,
Hac generis celebres parte fuere viri."

as far as the inner meaning of their works is concerned they relapse into the conception of the older representations of the temperaments.[15] The mind behind the classical drapery is at bottom nearer to the spirit of the fifteenth century than to Dürer's.[16]

Beham, Amman, Solis and similar masters present as little difficulty to the purely factual exegesis of content, as does the master "F.B." (now generally identified as Franz Brun) in his engraving, which, though reduced to a genre picture, has a certain originality, and is quite impressive in its dungeon-like gloom (B78, PLATE 116).[17] Paintings are a very different matter. As far as those by German masters are concerned, we have so far discovered only five, the picture dated 1558, formerly in the Trau collection in Vienna, which M. J. Friedländer has conjecturally attributed to the painter Matthias Gerung from Lauingen,[18] and four paintings which emerged in quick succession (1528, 1532, 1533, 1534) from Lucas Cranach's workshop.

Matthias Gerung's picture of 1558 (PLATE 123) shows in the centre Melancholia winged, and seated, in a typical attitude of "elbow on knee", but full face and without any attributes. The compasses are not held by her, but by a man crouching at the bottom of the picture, and apparently busy measuring a globe, not unlike God the Father in the *Bibles Moralisées*; we see in him a cosmographer,[19] a perfect example of the possessor of the cast

---

[15] See above, pp. 295 sqq. (text) and p. 319, note 117.

[16] This also applies to the portrait of melancholy in the temperament-series by Paul Flindt, 1611, mentioned above, p. 343, note 203, which occupies a special position in so far as the four complexions are all represented by putti, stylised *à la* Spranger, "Sanguineus" playing the lute, "Cholericus" in armour, "Phlegmaticus" carving and "Melancholicus" brooding in the midst of the usual tools.

[17] Dated 1560 and showing melancholy as a nun-like woman, the surroundings stretching endlessly away, completely empty, and the few attributes arranged with such regularity and geometrical order that it looks as if they could never leave their places again. The dark shading of walls and ceiling, and the sharp contrast between light and shade are particularly effective, while the pedantic execution of the close-view perspective achieves great power of psychological expression.

[18] *Katalog der Erfurter Leihausstellung*, 1893, No. 173, reproduced in O. DOERING and G. VOSS, *Meisterwerke der Kunst aus Sachsen und Thüringen*, Magdeburg n.d., Plate 35; cf. also U. THIEME and F. BECKER, op. cit., XIII, p. 488; auction catalogue of the collector F. Trau, Gilhofer and Ranschburg, Vienna, 26–30 April 1937, No. 551.

[19] G. Hellmann kindly pointed out to us that a gem reproduced in C. DAREMBERG and E. SAGLIO, *Dictionnaire des antiquités*, I, I, Paris 1877, No. 587, shows a very similar figure, although appearing in profile. If this type of picture is really classical, a question on which we dare not pronounce, the portrait of God the Father in the *Bibles moralisées* might also be traced back to this origin; so that a classical type of astronomer or cosmographer was deified in the Middle Ages, to become human once more in the Renaissance. The model for the "Cosmographer", which Matthias Gerung copied almost exactly, has meanwhile been recognised in Campagnola's *Astrologer* (HARTLAUB, *Geheimnis*, plates 25–27), save that the latter is busy measuring the heavens and not the earth.

of mind symbolised by the chief figure. About these two figures there winds a bright garland of miniature scenes. In a richly variegated and undulating landscape we see every possible activity of urban, rural, and military life: but, though realistically conceived, these representations appear to have no connexion of any kind either with each other or with the notion of melancholy. The astral phenomena, however, point the way to a possible interpretation. Apart from the motifs of the rainbow and the comet, which have been taken over from Dürer, we see the sun and the two planetary deities Luna and Mars, and between them a cherub apparently beckoning to Mars. (That angels guided the planets in their courses was a notion very familiar to Christian astrology, which survived even in Raphael's mosaic in the Chigi Chapel in Santa Maria del Popolo.)

It is uncertain whether the planets of this triad are to be interpreted as the ruling planets of the year,[20] as a conjunction, or as a mere sign of the general state of affairs, but it is certain that their presence is not accidental. One has the impression that there is a certain actuality inherent in the picture, and that it is a picture of melancholy not merely painted in the year 1558 but somehow conditioned by it. (This was the year of the death of Charles V.) In actual fact, the three planets are so obviously connected with the scenes in the lower half of the picture (up to about the scroll), that one can divide the scenes almost out of hand into the typical occupations of the "children" of the sun, the moon and Mars. Banquets, games, baths, jugglers—note the dancing bear—belong to the moon; music, wrestling, fencing and archery to the sun; warfare and metalwork—note the mine—belong of course to Mars. The scenes in the upper part of the picture, however, seem to represent the seasons, or the months, and probably signify the course of that ominous year: tilling, harvesting, pasturing, pig-slaughtering, hunting and sleighing. Sleighing, indeed, since it appears in a landscape not otherwise wintry, is scarcely explicable save by an intention to characterise the different parts of the year. The picture is by no means without charm, but the artistic effect of it as a whole is achieved by the fact that neither Melancholia nor the human representative of

[20] The list of the reigning planets of the year seems to vary considerably in the relevant literature. G. Hellmann kindly informed us of two lists for the year 1558, giving respectively Mars and Venus, and Mars, Saturn and Jupiter. Mars, therefore, is mentioned in both cases, Luna and Sol in neither. But in G. Hellmann's opinion a third source might equally well list this trio.

this temperament, the cosmographer, appear to take any part in all this gay or perilous round of daily life. They are unmoved by the misery of war, they take no pleasure in the games, banquets or other amusements, no part in the joys and sorrows of the countryside. The homely verses in Amman's armorial sum up this quality of the melancholy disposition:

Children's prattle joys me not
Nor laying hens, nor capons fat.
Let me alone, to think my mind,
Small profit else in me you'll find.

This opposition between worldly gaiety and melancholy earnestness, in contrast to the splendid unity regulating the mood of Dürer's engraving, applies to Cranach's paintings also. The first, dated 1528[21] and now in the possession of the Earl of Crawford, shows Melancholy in contemporary dress (though she was originally winged), seated on an airy terrace (PLATE 128). Compasses, sphere, chisel and gimlet are lying on the ground; a plate of fruit and two glasses are standing on the table; beyond, one looks into a joyous landscape. Four naked children, probably derived from a modification and elaboration of Dürer's putto,[22] are romping with each other and with a dog who somewhat resents it, while the

---

[21] CHRISTIAN SCHUCHARDT, *Lucas Cranach d. Ä. Leben und Werke*, VOL. II, Leipzig 1851, p. 103 mentions this copy as being in the Campe Collection, Nuremberg: cf. now M. J. ☞ FRIEDLÄNDER and J. ROSENBERG, *Die Gemälde von Lucas Cranach*, Berlin 1932, No. 228, which also mentions a copy "in the possession of Dr Paul Weber of Jena". Subsequently owned by Consul Moslé in Leipzig, this copy was sold in New York, at the Parke-Bernet sale ☞ of 22 April, 1948; its present location is unknown to us. Mr Moslé pointed out to us that in the Earl of Crawford's picture Melancholy was not wingless, as stated in *Dürers Melencolia I*, but that traces can be seen of wings which disappeared almost completely when part of the picture was cut off. A further picture, of the same subject (probably only a workshop product), knowledge of which we owe to M. J. Friedländer, is dated 1534 but reverts, in the ☞ main, to the 1528 conception. But the elements of magic are reduced to the indispensable wand-peeling, while the connexion with geometry, emphasised by Dürer's set-square, is stronger than either in the Copenhagen or even in the Hague composition, where the sphere is lacking as well.

[22] Dr G. E. Hartlaub kindly informs us that he believes that he has found the explanation for the group of putti in Cranach's pictures, and perhaps even for the child scribbling in Dürer's engraving, in a treatise on alchemy dated 1530 and beautifully illustrated, namely, *Splendor Solis* (Nuremberg, Germanisches Museum), where a group of children playing represents a certain stage in alchemical transformation, i.e. "coagulatio", because this "wirdet zugeleichet dem Spil der Kinder, die so spylen, das so oben gelegen, ligt yetzt unndten." The putti accompanying Melancholy should therefore be interpreted as symbols of alchemy. We must confess that this interpretation could only convince us if the alternating positions of above and below, on which the whole comparison is based, were shown as unequivocally as they are in the Nuremberg MS miniature. This, however, is not the case even in Cranach's pictures, let alone Dürer's engraving, where the putto, solitary and very much in earnest, is busy with his slate.

real "dog of Melancholy"[23] is curled up on a bench right at the back. So far the interpretation of the picture presents little difficulty. Two powerful motifs, however, can only be accounted for by the same increase in superstitious and magical beliefs as caused the fundamental difference between the two versions of Agrippa of Nettesheim's *Occulta philosophia*. One is the chief figure's occupation, for she appears to be sharpening or peeling a twig with a knife. The other is the emergence of a horde of witches under Satan's command, who, in the midst of a dark cloud, are careering across the clear sky. Now the Saturnine melancholic is connected with all sorts of magic and devilish arts, and his dark and sinister cast of mind, averse from thoughts of daily life, inclines him to harmful magic[24] as easily as it raises him to religious or scientific contemplation. The motif of the cutting or peeling of the stick (it certainly is not a real divining-rod, as it is not forked),[25] taken together with the witches' sabbath, could therefore be interpreted as the preparation of a magic wand, which according to ancient belief had to be peeled so that "no spirits nest twixt wood and bark".[26]

Cranach's next picture (PLATE 129), dated 1532 and now in Copenhagen,[27] contains little fresh matter. The occupational symbols are lacking, save for the sphere, with which the children, now three in number, are playing a noisy game. The only new item is the pair of partridges, which, however, is probably intended to enrich the scene of happy worldly activity. Here, too, we see the witches' sabbath, and the chief figure is busy cutting a stick.

---

[23] A closer copy of the dog in Dürer's engraving, but in reverse, and enriched by a comically outstretched foreleg, appears in Cranach's picture of *Paradise*, 1530: Vienna, Kunsthist. Mus. No. 1462 (cf. M. J. FRIEDLÄNDER and J. ROSENBERG, *Die Gemälde von Lucas Cranach*, Berlin 1932, plate 167).

[24] Cf., for instance, Ibn Esra: "Et in eius parte [sc. Saturni] sunt diabolici"; and Abû Ma'šar: "Omneque magice omnisque malefici studium". The connexion appears particularly clearly in an engraved series of the planets by Henri Leroy (1579–c. 1651; G. K. NAGLER, *Künstlerlexikon*, VOL. VIII, p. 399), where witches and magicians are almost the sole representatives of the "children of Saturn" (PLATE 53); the inscription reads: "Saturnus . . . magis et sagis, fodinis et plumbo praeest".

[25] What appears to be a bifurcation of the twig on the Copenhagen picture is really only two chips of the peeled bark.

[26] Cf. C. BORCHLING, in *Vorträge der Bibliothek Warburg*, VOL. III (1923–4), p. 229. According to G. C. HORST, in *Zauberbibliothek*, VOL. VI (1826), p. 210, the rod on which the witch is swearing allegiance to the devil is "a white stick which looks as if it had been cut from a willow and then peeled".

[27] Cf. now M. J. FRIEDLÄNDER and J. ROSENBERG, *Die Gemälde von Lucas Cranach*, Berlin 1932, fig. 227.

Even the third of these pictures (PLATE 130),[28] dated 1533 and now in Dr Volz's collection in the Hague, retains these two motifs apparently peculiar to Cranach. For the rest, however, it departs fundamentally from the two earlier works. The main figure is squeezed right into a corner of the foreground, the view reduced to a minimum, and all accessories, animate or inanimate, omitted, save for the head of an old man (Saturn himself, or some other spirit?) appearing in the sky, and no less than fifteen putti, most of them dancing, some sleeping and two making music with pipe and drum. A new influence seems therefore to have been at work on this latest picture, and it would be odd if it did not come from Mantegna. There was his painting almost exactly similar in form, which had represented "Malancolia" with sixteen putti dancing and making music, and which, as we have seen, may have been not without significance for Dürer's engraving.[29] But whereas in the latter case the accord was only vague and general, in the former, where the putti are present in almost as great a number and engaged in the same dancing and musical activities, it seems to go comparatively far; and since we know of no other similar picture, we are unlikely to be at fault in connecting Cranach's work with the now lost picture by Mantegna. Cranach need not even have seen a copy or sketch of it, for news of it by, word of mouth or by letter might have been enough to influence his interpretation, original as it was in style and composition, in Mantegna's direction.

The fact that Cranach used only fifteen putti instead of sixteen does not appear to be of any particular significance, and would be very easily explicable by his not having seen his model.[30] The exact number mattered little to the German master, whereas Mantegna probably chose it for some good reason; for this master who was so interested in archaeology that he occasionally even signed his name in Greek, can certainly be credited with the knowledge that one of the most famous works of antiquity, the statue of the Nile, had grouped the allegorical figure of a man with sixteen playing children.[31]

---

[28] Cf. now FRIEDLÄNDER and ROSENBERG, op. cit., fig. 228.

[29] See above, p. 307 (text).

[30] Moreover, as Consul Moslé kindly pointed out, this picture, like that in the possession of the Earl of Crawford, seems to have been cut, and it is not improbable that, here too, the main figure was originally winged.

[31] Pliny, *Nat. Hist.*, XXXVI, 58: "Numquam hic [sc. basanites] maior repertus est, quam in templo Pacis ab imperatore Vespasiano Augusto dicatus argumento *Nili, sedecim liberis*

Historically, if not artistically, the most important imitation of Dürer's engraving produced in Germany during the sixteenth century has been that discovered by L. Volkmann.[32] The altar in the east chancel of Naumburg cathedral, dated 1567, is adorned with—among other things—eight reliefs, seven of which represent the familiar cycle of the "Liberal Arts". The encyclopaedic cycles of monumental art, or the illustrations to Boethius, would lead one to expect this train of seven female figures to be led by a personification of philosophy or theology. In this case, however, the role of leader is taken over by a Melancholia obviously derived from the Dürer tradition.[33] It is indeed a remarkable historical occurrence when, in a church, and in the framework of a tradition going back for over a thousand years, the figure representing the unifying principle of all intellectual achievements is no longer that of philosophy, the discipline providing the systematic foundation of them all, but that of a subjective psychological force, *viz.* of the disposition which makes intellectual activity possible—a distinction of which the north had become aware through Dürer's engraving.

A more modest monument, pointed out to us by Dr Erdmann, may perhaps be cited as witness of a similar intention. This is a clock (made by a Nuremberg master "F.F.L." in 1599), shaped like a turret, which shows Astronomy on one side and Melancholy on the other, and is equipped with the whole symbolism of Dürer's engraving, save that the magic square has been simplified to a board with ordinary numbers, and the putto appears to have been reduced to a mere infant-school pupil. On this modest object too, therefore, Melancholy appears as a comprehensive symbol of intellectual capacities; but since on clocks, especially, there is often a warning reference to the transience of all earthly things (like the famous "una ex illis ultima"), it is not impossible that even here there may be mingled a thought of the futility of all intellectual endeavour, however noble.

The inheritance left by Dürer's engraving was naturally less extensive in sixteenth-century Italy than in the north, but it was

---

circa ludentibus . . . ." For replicas of the group (the Vatican copy, of course, was not discovered until Leo XIII's time), cf. W. AMELUNG, *Die Skulpturen des Vatikanischen Museums*, Berlin 1903, p. 130.

[32] *Zeitschrift für bildende Kunst*, VOL. LIX (1925–6), pp. 298 sqq.

[33] Elsheimer, on the contrary, in a delicate small picture in the Fitzwilliam Museum, Cambridge, showed the goddess Minerva as the patroness of art and science in an attitude typical of Melancholy (W. DROST, in *Belvedere*, VOLS. IX–X (1926), pp. 96 sqq., plate 2).

of more consequence there, in so far as a development decisive for posterity began soon to take place—a development from the intellectually contemplative to the emotionally pathetic.

There do indeed seem to have been imitations founded on an intellectual attitude not essentially different from that which prevailed in the north; we may mention Vasari's Melancholy, surrounded by a number of mathematical instruments, on a fresco done in 1553 in the Palazzo Vecchio, Florence,[34] as well as the allegory of Sculpture described in Antonio Francesco Doni's *Disegno*, which seems almost a double of *Melencolia I*.[35] The Melancholy painted by Francesco Morandini, called Poppi, as one of four temperaments on the wall of the "studiolo" in the Palazzo Vecchio, Florence—incidentally, neither particularly attractive nor original—is distinguished from her northern sisters by her markedly pathetic expression of sorrow, agitated almost to weeping point[36]; and in *Marmi*, another work by the above-mentioned Doni, which appeared in 1552, we find a woodcut which, though very ordinary, exercised a most powerful influence, and shows the sublime profundity of the main figure of *Melencolia I* (Doni mentions that he owned a copy of Dürer's engraving) transformed into the elegiac sadness of a "feminetta tutta malinconosa, sola, abandonata, mesta et aflitta" mourning on a lonely rock (PLATE 131).[37] We can understand how Italian art, with a native inclination to pathos, and lacking a firm pictorial

---

[34] Cf. L. VOLKMANN, in *Werden und Wirken, Festschrift für K. W. Hiersemann*, Leipzig 1924, p. 417, and *Zeitschrift für bildende Kunst*, VOL. LXIII (1929–30), pp. 119 sqq. The fresco which was destroyed during the transformation of the "Sala di Saturno" into the "Loggia di Saturno" showed the foundation of the city "Saturnia", which, as G. Vasari says in his *Raggionamenti*, was built in a "lonely and melancholy spot". Melancholy herself was shown "with craftsman's tools, compasses, quadrants and measuring rods".

[35] Cf. J. SCHLOSSER, *La letteratura artistica*, Florence 1935, p. 213. Doni's description (fol. 8f. in the Venice edn., 1549) runs as follows: "Nell' aspetto la fecero grave, nel mirar severa, e d'habito intero vestita: puro et honorato, equale così alla testa come a tutto il corpo. Il quale habito mostrava non meno d'esser da temere, che da esser honorato. Et così ferma e stabile, solitaria e pensosa, si stava a sedere con le sue masseritie, e artifitiosi stromenti intorno; si come a tal arte si conviene."

[36] Cf. L. VOLKMANN, in *Zeitschrift für bildende Kunst*, VOL. LXIII (1929–30), pp. 119 sqq., with plates. Melancholy, as in Dürer's original, appears as a winged female, whereas the other three temperaments, significantly enough, lack wings; her chin is resting on her right hand, and she is leaning against a table, one foot raised, while in her right hand she is holding a pair of scales. At her feet a boy is crouching with a book, and on a projection from one of the walls is another book, an hour-glass, and an astrolabe.

[37] A. F. DONI, *I Marmi*, VOL. II, Venice 1552, p. 87. The verses put in the mouth of this mourning woman are attuned to the elegiac character of the picture:

tradition in the field of complexion-sequences proper,[38] should give preference to the subjective and poetic conception of melancholy, as also represented some twenty years later in Ripa's *Iconologia*,[39] rather than to the objective and scientific conception, even when, as in Poppi and Doni, one can assume direct knowledge of Dürer's engraving. Thus by the sixteenth century the groundwork was laid for what was to occur in the period of the Baroque, namely, the fusion of the portrait of Melancholy with the picture representing Vanity.

A monograph on "Vanity pictures" has yet to be written, though H. Janson has made a good beginning in his essay "The Putto with the Death's Head" (*Art Bulletin*, VOL. XIX, 1937). It might begin with the late medieval tomb monuments and allegories of Death, which so often show a beholder facing a picture of transience or even of decay, and urge him to repentance with the warning "tales vos eritis, fueram quandoque quod estis", or something of the sort. It would then go on to the works of the fifteenth and sixteenth centuries, in which the

---

"Che pena si può dire
  Più grande che morire?
Maggior è la mia pena
  E passa ogn' aspra sorte,
  Che mai punto raffrena
  Ma cresce ogn'hor più forte;
  Io vivo, et ogni dì provo la morte,
Dunque è maggior martire
  Chi vive in doglia, et mai non può morire."

Doni's woodcut, with its title altered in all sorts of ways (e.g. to *Sibylla Albunea*) was reissued in a whole series of Venetian prints, and therefore became widely known and extremely influential in Italy (see also below, text pp. 389 sqq.). A series of forty-two *Emblemata*, traditionally attributed to Cornelis Massys, also contained a copy in reverse of Doni's woodcut; the heading is "Melancholia", the caption: "Hanc caveas, moneo, si alacrem vis ducere vitam". The other parts of the series dealt with themes such as "Pertinacia", "Punitio", "Dolor", etc. The inclusion of Doni's picture in the series explains why the Italian woodcut also influenced later Dutch art. For instance, a temperament-series engraved by Cornelis Bloemaert after Abraham Bloemaert (PLATE 133), contains a Melancholy which, though in most respects a lineal descendant of Dürer's engraving, owes her posture, a gentle *Kontrapost*, and her elegiac character unmistakably to Doni. The same can be said of the "Dialectic" ☞ in the famous Turin allegory of *The Liberal Arts slumbering during the war* by Frans Floris. For J. Boeckhorst's "Geometria" (PLATE 132), see above, p. 328, note 150.

[38] See above, pp. 287 sqq., 299 (text).

[39] It is no coincidence that Ripa's *Malinconia* (Fig. 5), discussed above (pp. 226 sqq.), FIG. 5
resembles the generally established type of Melancholy less than his personifications of "Accidia" and "Meditatione", and it is very understandable that the text should make no reference to Dürer's engraving. Hence it is all the more remarkable that the Flemish edition corrects the omission (Amsterdam 1644, p. 500). For a picture by Abraham Janssens, which, following Ripa, contrasted "Malinconia" with "Allegrezza" (PLATE 69), see above, p. 227 (text).

presence of Death himself is replaced by a meditation on death. Finally it would have to show how the idea of such a "Meditazione della Morte"[40] gradually freed itself from the notion of a significant individual personality, and developed into a personification complete in itself; and how, in the course of this process, the fascinating contrast between the grisly content of the meditation and the youthful beauty of the meditating subject was increasingly stressed, so that the St Jerome was frequently replaced by a Mary Magdalen. This Vanity picture, impressive alike by its sensuous charm and by the chill of death lurking within it, could clearly accord in many respects with other pictorial notions, with subjects in the sphere of Arcadian idylls no less than in the sphere of ascetic moral philosophy.[41] It is therefore understandable that even Dürer's picture of contemplative melancholy, whose dark nature had always been associated with thought of night and Death, and which after the Counter-Reformation had been interpreted more than ever in a religious sense,[42] could be combined with the type of the Vanity picture.

The earliest and most important example of this kind, and perhaps the most important work of art resulting from the influence of Dürer's *Melencolia I*, is Domenico Feti's composition,[43] of which several copies have been preserved. Significantly enough, they

---

[40] Ripa made a special personification of this describing it as "donna scapigliata, con vesti lugubre, appoggiata col braccio à qualche sepoltura, tenendo ambi l'occhi fissi in una testa di morto . . . ." As earlier examples of this sort we mention merely Campagnola's youth meditating on a skull (HARTLAUB, *Geheimnis*, plate 24), and the beautiful etching of "Vanitas" (B15) by Parmigianino.

[41] Cf. W. WEISBACH in *Die Antike*, VOL. VI (1930), pp. 127 sqq.

[42] Significant in this respect is the title-piece to Marten de Vos's series of the Planets, 1581 (see above, p. 349, note 217 and PLATE 113). Here the "Phlegma" appears as Diana, "Sanguis" as Venus, and "Cholera" as Minerva armed, but "Melancholia" as a nun with a scroll, making an admonitory gesture; the engraved title to J. GUILLEMEAU's *Tables anatomiques*, Paris 1586, is derived from this, but here "Melancholia" once more appears seated, with her head propped on her hand. In the series itself, too, the religious element takes a prominent place; the seven planets and the seven ages of man are correlated with the seven works of mercy, and the aged "Saturnian" is being urged to repent by "Conscientia", pointing heavenwards. Milton and many of his successors apostrophise Melancholy as "pensive nun, devout and pure".

[43] Copies in the Louvre, in the Accademia, Venice, and in the Ferdinandeum, Innsbruck. We see no ground for doubting, with Wölfflin, the connexion between Feti and Dürer, in view of the wide circulation of Dürer's engraving, and of the presence of so many similar attributes (dog, compasses, sphere, set-square, hour-glass, plane); but of course Feti, too, must have been familiar with the more sentimental Doni type. The objects lacking in Dürer's engraving (sculptor's model and astrolabe) are present, for instance, in an etching of "Vanitas" by Jacob Matham, which, like so many Dutch representations of this type (cf. H. WICHMANN, *Leonaert Bramer*, Leipzig 1923, pp. 45 sqq.), dispenses with human figures altogether, and is content to contrast the symbols of secular arts and sciences with a religious still-life made up of skull, bible, crucifix and rosary.

are known under the names both of *Melancholy* and of *Meditation* (PLATE 134). Before a wall revealing, to the left, a cheerful landscape, a woman of voluptuous figure is kneeling; all the portraits hitherto seen have shown Melancholy sitting, or, rarely, standing. The upper part of her body is reclining against a stone block on which are lying a closed book and—in the Venetian copy—a pair of compasses. Her hair is loosely plaited, her head is resting on her left hand, while the right, unmistakably reminiscent of the motif in Vanity pictures, is clasping a skull on which her veiled regard is fixed.[44] About her are the most varied symbols of activity, in the background a celestial globe, books and an hour glass, in the foreground an open volume, a huge sphere, a set-square, plane, palette and brushes, and, finally, a sculptor's model which (not unintentionally) represents a satyr and is regarded by a large and handsome dog. The meaning of this picture is obvious at first glance: all human activity, practical no less than theoretical, theoretical no less than artistic, is vain, in view of the vanity of all earthly things.

However great the difference between Domenico Feti's fine composition and the modest woodcut in *Marmi*, they have one thing in common as compared with the northern pictures: they conceive melancholy as a state of the emotions, and refine the original melancholy disposition down to the acute despair arising out of a melancholy emotion. But Feti's work is in many ways the more profound, and in fact one may say that, starting from the very different concepts of the Counter-Reformation, it met Dürer's engraving on common ground. The skull with its "memento mori" now gives the aimless grief of Dürer's Melancholy a definite object, and what had been a vague and hardly explicit doubt as to whether human thought and activity has any meaning when faced with eternity, is now condensed into a plain question, which had to be answered by a decisive and unambiguous "No". Melancholy now resembles the type of the repentant Magdalen.[45]

---

[44] Cf. Domenico Feti's own *Magdalena* reproduced in R. OLDENBOURG, *Domenico Feti*, Biblioteca d'Arte Illustrate, 1, 2, Rome 1921, plate XII. A similar representation of Vanitas, but this time again with wings, is reproduced in *Jahrbuch der kunsthistorischen Sammlungen des allerhöchsten Kaiserhauses*, VOL. XXVI (1906–07). plate XII. During the seventeenth century these types merged to such a degree that in many cases (e.g. in that of Chaperon's drawing, PLATE 136) either title, *Melancholy* or *Vanitas*, would be equally justified.

[45] In point of fact the Paris copy of Feti's work was catalogued as a "Magdalene" in the seventeenth century, and not until the eighteenth century (when its connexion with Dürer was perhaps recognised) was the name *Melancholie* given to it. (Cf. M. ENDRES-SOLTMANN, *Domenico Fetti*, dissertation, Munich 1914, pp. 28 sqq.).

For 'Aristotle', the value of the melancholy disposition had been its capacity for great creative achievements in all possible fields; the blessing which the Middle Ages had seen in the "melancholy disease" had been a moral good rather than a practical one, in that it shielded one from worldly temptation. In the Renaissance, and with Dürer in particular, consciousness of human creative power became merged for the first time with a longing for religious fulfilment. But now the period of Italian Baroque reverted to the conception of the Middle Ages, save that it turned to the emotional rather than the metaphysical. What Domenico Feti had expressed only by visible, though hardly ambiguous signs, was expressed in words a generation later, in an etching by Benedetto Castiglione (PLATE 135), indebted to both Feti and Dürer. "Ubi inletabilitas," runs the legend, "ibi virtus"—"where there is grief, there is virtue."[46]

In Domenico Feti's picture, and, much more, in Castiglione's etching, the general notion of impermanence is given a specific turn by the introduction of crumbling walls and broken pillars; this corresponds with a tendency that had grown steadily stronger since the fifteenth century, and reached one of its recurrent peaks about or just after 1600—the romantic cult of ruins.[47] Guercino's famous *Notte* is another example,[48] and derives historically not from the "Day-and-Night" series but from the formula of "Melancholy" or "Vanity" pictures. Two drawings by Nicholas Chaperon (one of which is illustrated in PLATE 136) show this "Vanity–Melancholy", sorrowful, and in a veritable open-air museum: one represents her without wings and still betraying her traditional heritage by the unused tools of work (books, rolls of parchment, lamps, and globe); the other one shows her with wings, and so intent upon the perishability of ancient beauty that of the whole inventory only a small indistinct pile of papers and

---

[46] We would reiterate here our sincere thanks to Dr Ludwig Münz, who drew our attention to this etching (B22) by Castiglione. In this connexion we may also mention another etching of Melancholy (B26, a horizontal oblong) by the same artist.

[47] For the interpretation of ruins see e.g. C. HUSSEY, *The Picturesque. Studies in a Point of View*, London and New York 1927; K. CLARK, *Landscape into Art*, London 1949.

[48] It was J. HESS (*Agostino Tassi*, Munich 1935, p. 22) who pointed out the connexion between Guercino's *Notte* and Dürer's engraving. It must, however, be emphasised that Guercino's composition presupposes not only the Dürer original but also its sentimental modifications in the manner of Doni's woodcut, indeed in general conception primarily the latter.

an hour-glass survive, the latter a symbol of death rather than an indication of intellectual activity.[49]

During the eighteenth century, the "typus Melancholiae" suffered a fate common to all traditional forms at this time—that is to say, it was conventionalised to such a degree that the true reality of the melancholy mood could only find expression in other spheres.[50] In poetry, Melancholy's typical attitude had degenerated to a mere pose with mournful glance and cheek propped on hand:

> Say in what deep-sequester'd vale,
> Thy head upon thy hand reclin'd
> Sitt'st thou to watch the last faint gleams of light

—as John Whitehouse, for instance, says in an ode dating from the 1780's, in which Ripa's familiar rocks are wrapped in the grey mist or illumined by the blue flashes of the Gothic school.[51] In painting, too, Melancholy's typical attitude had become a mere flourish, and so noncommittal that, for instance, the Frenchman Langrenée the elder was able to take any mourning female figure out of a "tableau de grande histoire" and copy it as a personification of melancholy.[52] English art either sentimentalised Milton's "pious nun"—witness an engraving by J. Hopwood after J. Thurston, with Melancholy as a heavenward-gazing nun, cypresses in the background, and a verse by Collins underneath:

> With Eyes up-rais'd, as one inspir'd,
> Pale Melancholy sat retir'd[53]

—or even made the melancholic's saturnine attitude into a desirable pose for the lady of fashion, as, for instance, to take a telling example, Angelica Kauffmann's portrait of Lady Louisa

---

[49] Louvre, Inv. Nos. 25196 and 25198. Cf. the etching of *Vanitas* by J. H. Schönfeldt, 1654 (reproduced in W. Drost, *Barockmalerei in den germanischen Ländern*, Handbuch der Kunstwissenschaft, Wildpark-Potsdam 1926, plate XV) which differs iconographically from the Chaperon drawings only in that the main figure is male, and that there is the typically German insistence on the idea of death.

[50] See above, p. 237 (text).

[51] John Whitehouse, quoted in E. M. Sickels, *The Gloomy Egoist*, New York 1932.

[52] Louvre, Catal. No. 450. The figure is identical with one of the female mourners in the *Death of Darius's Wife* in the Nantes Museum. Of the representations of Melancholy produced by the so-called "classicism of milieu", which came into fashion about 1760, we may mention the *Douce Mélancholie* by Joseph Marie Vien (engraved by Beauvarlet), personified by a meditative young woman in a richly decorated room, and a *Mélancholie* by his pupil François André Vincent, dated 1801, which, according to Nagler, represents "a marvellous female figure beneath cypress trees".

[53] See above, p. 236 (text).

Macdonald, whose grieving attitude is rendered completely meaningless by the addition of an anchor of hope.[54]

Nineteenth-century romanticism, on the contrary, endeavoured to endow the traditional expression of melancholy once more with its original meaning, and in so doing it sometimes consciously reverted to Dürer. But in various ways it broke up the typical Renaissance compactness of Dürer's creation, which, for all its personal overtones, had been objective, and, for all its philosophical profundity, easy to grasp visually. Whereas we saw how literary exegesis, in marked contrast to the conception of Dürer then current, raised the emotion expressed in *Melencolia I* to the realms of Faustian metaphysics, the pictorial derivations softened it to—so to speak—a "private" feeling of loneliness. In both cases, however, sorrow turns to longing, grief for mankind to a flight from reality; and, independently of their objective significance, the romantic portraits of melancholy move us, accordingly, in an entirely new way. Thanks to this nostalgia, sorrow gains possession of a fresh range of objects: instead of being, as hitherto, limited to present existence, it embraces all time within the span of imagination. Hence the impression which the romantic pictures give us, that the longing, whether for a past beyond recall or for a future without hope of attainment, now for the first time enables the theme of the melancholy mood, so often and so closely linked with music, to be expressed "musically" also.

Thus the modest Steinle, striving after an "old German" effect in orthography, lettering and ornament, while at the same time combining this with the attempt, common to Nazarene painters, to emulate the sweetness of Umbrian art, transforms the sublime brooding of the Melancholy of *Melencolia I* into the humble, quiet grief of a forsaken maiden, in words that read like a folksong (PLATE 137):

☞ Jhe lenger jhe lieber ich bin allein,
denn treu und wahrheit ist worden klein.[55]

---

[54] See Reynolds's portraits discussed and reproduced (plates 79, 80 and 85) by EDGAR WIND ("Humanitätsidee und heroisiertes Porträt in der englischen Kultur des 18. Jahrhunderts", in *Vorträge der Bibliothek Warburg*, VOL. IX (1930–31), pp. 156 sqq.). Lady Macdonald's portrait, to which Dr Wind kindly drew our attention, is reproduced in V. MANNERS and G. G. WILLIAMSON, *Angelica Kauffmann*, London 1924, p. 97; see also URSULA HOFF, *Rembrandt und England*, dissertation, Hamburg 1935.

[55] Water-colour in the Städelsches Kunstinstitut, Frankfurt; cf. P. WEBER, *Beiträge zu Dürers Weltanschauung; eine Studie über die drei Stiche, Ritter Tod und Teufel, Melancholie und Hieronymus im Gehäus*, Strasbourg 1900, p. 82. This picture cannot, of course, be adduced for the interpretation of Dürer's engraving, because the wreath on the head of *Melencolia I* is not made of honeysuckle (Teucrium). See above, p. 325 (text).

Caspar David Friedrich[56] broadens, and, at the same time, dilutes the feeling to a profound longing, without aim or direction, for something unknown. The form of his picture anticipated the *Iphigenia auf Tauris* by Anselm Feuerbach, who, however, replaced the unknown distance towards which the romantic painter's "lonely maiden" is looking nostalgically, by the all too literary notion of the "land of the Greeks" (PLATE 138).

2. TYPICAL PORTRAITS OF MELANCHOLY IN LATE MEDIEVAL ALMANACS

The ambiguous subjectivity of so markedly romantic a work as Caspar David Friedrich's naturally forbade as precise a use of symbols as that which we so far encountered in earlier treatment of this theme. That does not, however, exclude the possibility that certain single motifs, originally regarded as notional symbols, may have survived as emotional symbols or, equally probably, have been recreated independently of tradition. Thus the wilderness, whence Caspar David Friedrich's Melancholy is desolately gazing, is characterised not only by flowerless, tangled leaves and harsh thistles, but by the "barren tree" which had been one of her constant attributes in Ripa's illustration and in German baroque poetry, while her lonely captivity is indicated by a spider's web, which, curiously enough, also appeared in a sixteenth-century German portrait of Melancholy (PLATE 139). This latter composition, known to us in a South German, or possibly Swiss, pen-and-ink drawing of about 1530–40,[57] seems to belong to a

---

[56] Drawing in Dresden, 1801; woodcut after it by the artist's brother, Christian, about 1818; cf. W. KURTH, *Amtliche Berichte aus den königlichen Kunstsammlungen*, VOL. XXXVI (1914–15), pp. 229 sqq. The pose of the figure very much resembles that of the well-known *St Helena* (London), by Paolo Veronese who, in turn, made considerable use of the engraving B460, formerly wrongly attributed to Marcantonio and perhaps derived from a composition by Parmigianino. This engraving, with some modification of the upper part of the body, was also used as a model for Barthel Beham's *Madonna*, B8 (cf. A. OBERHEIDE, *Der Einfluss Marcantonio Raimondis auf die nordische Kunst des 16. Jahrhunderts*, dissertation, Hamburg 1933, pp. 104, 113, plate XLI), which, again, was used in Rembrandt's drawing H.d.G.877. It is therefore an error when J. L. A. A. M. VAN RIJCKEVORSEL, *Rembrandt en de Traditie*, Rotterdam 1932, pp. 121 sqq., unfamiliar with the Pseudo-Marcantonio engraving, treats Veronese's *St Helena* as also deriving from Beham. A drawing by Bartolomeo Passarotti in the Mond Collection, published by T. BORENIUS and R. WITTKOWER, *Catalogue of the collection of drawings by the old masters, formed by Sir Robert Mond*, London 1937, p. 44, plate 30, is also derived from this engraving.

[57] The drawing in the École des Beaux-Arts was published as French by P. LAVALLÉE in *Les Trésors des Bibliothèques de France*, VOL. II, Paris 1929, p. 88, though the author admitted that "sujet et style sont plutôt allemands que français." The German origin of the drawing, however, is established by the artist's inscription "Sametkäplin", specifying the head-covering of the male figure, whereas the French title "Un mélancolique spéculatif" must date from a later owner of the drawing.

set of the four temperaments.[58] It has obviously come under Dürer's influence, even if only indirectly, for without it the speculative content of the picture, already emphasised by the French owner in the caption, would be as little intelligible as the numerous symbols of mensuration, or the compasses with which the meditative melancholic is vainly endeavouring to measure his globe (for so Dürer's sphere is occasionally interpreted, as, for instance, on the clock mentioned above). But the fact that this embodiment of deep reflexion no longer appears as an idealised female figure, but in the very realistic form of a ragged and barefooted man accompanied by a similar old woman, clearly shows that the manner of illustrating the meaning inherent in Dürer's engraving has reverted to the late medieval type of almanac illustrations—to pairs of figures realistically portrayed in a dramatic relationship. On the other hand, this realistic pair is surrounded by a quantity of symbols, the meaning of which goes as far beyond the range of the medieval almanacs as it differs from that of Dürer's engraving. The barren tree already mentioned can still, of course, be taken merely as an indication of winter, the season which corresponds to the melancholy humour and to the earth; and also the three zodiacal signs seem to point to the time of year[59]; in Ripa, the motif of the barren tree was explained by saying that melancholy produced the same effect on men as winter on vegetation. But the brazier beside which the old woman is warming herself is an implement of magic,[60] as well as of practical use, and the parchment on the ground beside her with its six-rayed star and other magic characters[61] obviously shows that she, like Lucas Cranach's "Melancholies", is concerned with devilment and wizardry. The owl, too, indicates not only night, misfortune and loneliness in general, but, in particular, the "studio d'una vana

---

[58] The sign 🜃, the alchemical symbol of the earth, clearly points to the three corresponding symbols (△ = fire, ▽ = water, 🜁 ≐ air; cf. G. Carbonelli, *Sulle fonti storiche della Chimica e dell'Alchimia in Italia*, Rome 1925, p. 23). An additional proof of its being part of a sequence of four is the presence of the three zodiacal signs, for which, however, see the following note.

[59] The third zodiacal sign for winter, Capricorn, has been replaced by Virgo, but this may be due merely to an error, unless, as in the engraved series after Heemskerck, Plate 144, which we discuss on p. 397 sq. in the text, the combination of the zodiacal signs is meant to take into account the pathology of the humours as well.

[60] Cf. P. d'Abano's *Elementa magica*, added to Agrippa's *Occulta philosophia* (Lyons edition, p. 561) "Habeat [sc. operans] vas fictile novum igne plenum."

[61] P. d'Abano, op. cit. p. 560: "Deinde sumat hoc pentaculum [the illustration is identical with the star in the Paris drawing] factum . . . in charta membrana hoedi."

sapienza" with which the polemics of the Fathers had reproached the bird of the heathen Minerva.[62] The same can also be said of the spider's web. The Renaissance considered it an emblem of "vain toil",[63] so that it seems to refer to the fruitless distraction into which the equally ill-fated companion of the melancholy witch has fallen. We do not venture to decide why this partner is sitting on a barrel; perhaps his bare feet and raggedness suggest Diogenes,[64] or it may be merely the modification of an earlier model showing a globe instead of a barrel.[65] The hedgehog, however, which has made its nest in this barrel, has only one explanation. It is an ancient symbol of hesitation, but as applied to the special case of the toiling thinker it signifies the melancholic's destiny of being subject to such strong inhibitions that he can only achieve his labours, if at all, at the cost of great agony—in the same way as the female hedgehog delays giving birth to her young for fear of its prickles, thereby making the birth yet more painful.[66]

FIGURE 2. From Eobanus Hesse, *De conservanda bona valetudine*, Frankfurt, 1551.

Indirectly influenced by Dürer, then, this South German drawing undertook to intellectualise the late medieval almanac illustrations, as had already been more crudely attempted in

---

[62] Cf. GIOVANNI PIERIO VALERIANO, *Ieroglifici*, Venice 1625, p. 256, with references to St Basil and Hesychius of Jerusalem. Ripa still gives the owl as a symbol of superstition.

[63] Cf. GIOVANNI PIERIO VALERIANO, op. cit., pp. 342–3; the spider's web denotes "opera vana".

[64] Cf. E. PANOFSKY, *Hercules am Scheidewege* (Studien der Bibliothek Warburg, VOL. XVIII), Leipzig 1930, pp. 51 and 110.

[65] Jacob I de Gheyn's engraving, shown in PLATE 143, seems to suggest this possibility.

[66] Cf. GIOVANNI PIERIO VALERIANO, *Ieroglifici*, Venice 1625, p. 104. The hedgehog denotes "Danni che si sentono per l'indugio", because "questo animale quando la femina sente lo stimolo del partorire, che il ventre le duole, differisce, et indugia à partorire quanto più può; onde avviene, che il suo parto sempre più crescendo, maggior dolore poi nel partorire le arreca."

the woodcut illustrating Eobanus Hesse's *De conservanda bona valetudine*.[67] We have here an increase in the hieroglyphic and emblematic elements, and an added interest, present also in Cranach, in magic and the demonic. The same development occurred in later Dutch mannerist paintings, but for quite different reasons—namely, the tendency, characteristic of this style, to emulate, as to form, the artistic ideals of the Italian successors of Michelangelo and Raphael, while at the same time expounding the imagery in the light of contemporary manners so far as story and scenery were concerned.

Thus, for instance, in a set of the four temperaments engraved by Pieter de Jode after Marten de Vos, we find the traditional pairs of figures both idealised in Italian fashion and brought up to date in Dutch style. Differentiated according to type, rank and dress, they fulfil every requirement of manneristic "grazia" and "grandezza", but they are placed in surroundings which, though containing the elements and seasons traditionally associated with the complexions and retaining their characteristic significance,[68] yet produce the effect of pure landscapes. The behaviour of the figures themselves is shown sociologically rather than psychologically, so that an illustration of human dispositions has been transformed to a certain extent into an illustration of different social ways of life. The picture of the phlegmatics might have the title "The Fishmongers", that of the cholerics "Soldier and Sutler", and that of the sanguine pair "Open-air Duet". The portrait of the melancholics shows a woman endowed with all the charms of mannered beauty, but so lost in deep, if slightly apathetic, meditation over her alchemical problems (an echo of Dürer's inspiration) that she cannot be cheered even by the gold and jewelry which a prosperous merchant is offering her. This group, too, corresponds to a well-known type of Dutch morality picture (generally called "The ill-matched Couple"), except that in this case the woman has inherited something of the meditative depth of "melancholia generosa" (PLATES 140, 141).[69]

FIG. 2 [67] Cf. p. 330, Fig. 2.

[68] Cf. e.g. the windmill in the picture of the "volatile" sanguinic, the castle in flames in that of the "fiery" choleric, the seascape in that of the "watery" phlegmatic.

[69] The quatrain beneath it is a variation of the Salernitan verses, though eliminating all the melancholic's good qualities. The same applies to another sequence of temperaments, engraved by J. Sadeler after Marten de Vos, in which Melancholy is represented by an almost

3. MELANCHOLY IN PORTRAITS OF SATURN OR OF HIS CHILDREN

The type of portrait of the "children" of the various planets that was formed in the fifteenth century (PLATE 38), remained relatively unaltered until well on in the eighteenth century. In a sequence of the planets engraved by Muller after Marten van Heemskerck, for instance, the mortals ruled by Saturn are grouped and characterised in exactly the same way as the corresponding pictures in the *Hausbuch* or the Tübingen manuscript as peasants, woodmen, beggars, cripples, prisoners and condemned criminals (PLATE 144).[70] The same master also designed a set of the four temperaments distinguished by the fact that, as types, they keep entirely within the framework of the portraits of the "children of the planets".[71] PL. 52 The representatives of the four humours, too, are collected in numerous small-scale groups in Heemskerck's picture, arranged in a unified landscape, and once more characterised according to elements and seasons; they also appear as representatives of certain trades and sociological strata. In addition, they are visibly under the domination of their planetary patrons, who hover in the clouds, each accompanied by three zodiacal signs,[72] the phlegmatic subject to the moon, the choleric to Mars, the sanguine to Jupiter and Venus, and the melancholic, of course, to Saturn. Were it not for the titles and the explanatory couplets, the observer would scarcely think it anything other than a mere sequence of the "children of the planets".

It is, therefore, the more remarkable that the conservatism of these—in every sense—traditional pictures should have been breached at one point. It was the point at which the traditional view of Saturn's nature came into conflict with Dürer's view of Melancholy. Whereas we see only the representatives of the usual planetary trades in the other three pictures—the dancing, hunting,

---

naked woman wringing her hands, and a man who has fallen asleep amidst a variety of broken implements. Here too the connexion with the couples in the Calendar pictures is unmistakeable.

[70] Cf. T. KERRICH, *A Catalogue of the prints which have been engraved after M. Heemskerck*, Cambridge 1829, p. 98.

[71] Cf. T. KERRICH, op. cit., pp. 98 sqq. Dr Bella Martens kindly drew our attention to this series.

[72] The signs of the zodiac are those in which, according to old Calendar lore, the moon must be if one wishes to bleed successfully a melancholic, a sanguinic, etc. "Quando Luna est in thauro, in virgine et in capricorno, tunc minutio valet melancholicis", we read, for instance, in MARCUS REINHART, *Horae B. V. Mariae*, Kirchheim about 1490, quoted above, p. 297, note 56.

fencing, and love-making worldlings in the sanguine picture, and soldiers, armourers, and so forth, in the choleric—in the melancholy portrait we find the traditional repertory of Saturn's children reduced to a hanged man (or a suicide) and two hermits strolling in the background. Beggars, peasants, cripples, woodmen, and prisoners have given place to builders, opticians, and scholars preoccupied with problems of geometry and astrology. Here, even more unequivocally than in Dürer, in whose *Melencolia I* the skeleton of merely suggested relationships lies hidden within the living body of the visible picture, the nexus Saturn–Melancholy–Geometry comes to light[73]; and the fact that this should occur in a series of engravings which is otherwise so traditional, and which, even when forsaking tradition, had yielded only to the notional and not to the formal influence of Dürer, gives yet more impressive proof of his power of intellectual suggestion.

A complexion-sequence by Jacob I de Gheyn ("illustrated" with remarkably witty Latin couplets) seems at first sight to be merely a parallel to the above-mentioned engravings after Marten de Vos. Both are modernisations of late medieval types, leading to genre pictures idealised in the Italian manner and placed in landscapes distinguished in accordance with the temperament to which they belong. But Jacob I de Gheyn follows the single-figure type of the almanac illustrations instead of the dramatically associated pairs of figures.[74] The choleric, for instance, is a savage, bewhiskered soldier, surrounded by weapons of war, a guttering torch at his side, a burning town at his back, sitting on a drum and swinging his weapon in a heroically distorted posture. The phlegmatic is an old fisherman with bleary eyes and dripping hair, shaking all sorts of sea-beasts into a wooden tub on a rainy shore. But even these two figures show themselves on closer inspection to be something more than idealised figures from contemporary daily life. De Gheyn's exalted ambition goes one rung higher than that of Marten de Vos: he reaches out to antiquity and mythology. For instance, despite his contemporary costume, the

---

[73] The same tendency can already be observed in the woodcut by Hans Döring reproduced in PLATE 107.

[74] The coarsely humorous metamorphosis of such a series, which apparently occurred about the beginning of the seventeenth century in the Netherlands, can be seen in a lithograph dating from 1845. This shows the effects of drunkenness on the four temperaments. The characters are accompanied by their traditional beasts, the sanguinic by a lamb, the choleric by a bear, and the phlegmatic by a pig, except for the melancholic who is given an ape because when drunk he is credited with the ability to "invent a thousand tricks".

choleric does not wield the modern swords or firearms—they stand or lie uselessly about him—but an ancient short-bladed sword, and a round shield completely unserviceable in 1600; he is designed to remind one of the warriors of classical antiquity or even of Mars himself. And the "piscis homo"[75] in the portrait of the phlegmatic, both in type and pose, reveals himself as a reincarnation of a classical sea- or river-god, whose urn, while retaining its form and function, has been transformed into a gigantic straw-plaited fisherman's basket (PLATE 142).

In these two pictures, as well as in that of the sanguine man, it is rather a question of suggesting mythological associations than of achieving a mythological identification. But in the melancholic's portrait, which here again occupies a special place, there is a real fusion of the "black bile" with the classical divinity guiding and protecting it (PLATE 143). This heroic naked figure of a thinker, with his veiled head, is none but the ancient Saturn himself, such as we know him from the statuette in the Museo Gregoriano or from the fresco in the Casa dei Dioscuri, save that, with compass in hand and sphere on knee, closed eyes, and weary, lined face, he takes a share in all the problems of the human spirit that suffers from melancholy.[76] And whereas the representatives of the other three temperaments were placed in landscapes which, though allusive and symbolic in character, yet appeared temporal and unmysterious, this melancholy Saturn is seated on a globe poised in the universe beneath a starry heaven.

In Heemskerck's melancholic, as in Jacob I de Gheyn's, what could only be inferred from Dürer's *Melencolia I* was made fully explicit: that is to say, the essential unity of Melancholy, Saturn and Mathematics. But while Heemskerck makes his point at the price of showing his melancholic in a scene of prosaic everyday life, Gheyn pushes the allegory even farther than Dürer had done. He not only represents the nature of the melancholic symbolically but raises him to the stature of a semi-divine being, remote from all contact with the world of men, who yet carries his human sorrow with him into the spaces of the heavens.

---

[75] So the humorous formula in the explanatory couplet calls him.

[76] "Atra, animaeque animique lues aterrima, bilis
Saepe premit vires ingenii et genii."

In point of fact, Jacob I de Gheyn's Saturn is so closely related in motif to the *Mélancolique spéculatif* in the Paris pen-drawing, PLATE 139, that one might almost imagine that they were based on the same model. If such an original did exist, the suggestion put forward (text p. 395) that the barrel in the pen-drawing was a modification of a sphere would have some support.

APPENDIX I

THE POLYHEDRON IN "MELENCOLIA I"

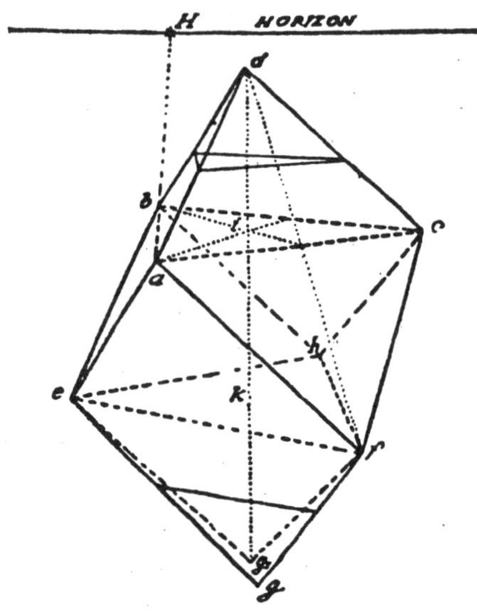

FIGURE 3. Reconstruction of the polyhedron on Dürer's engraving.

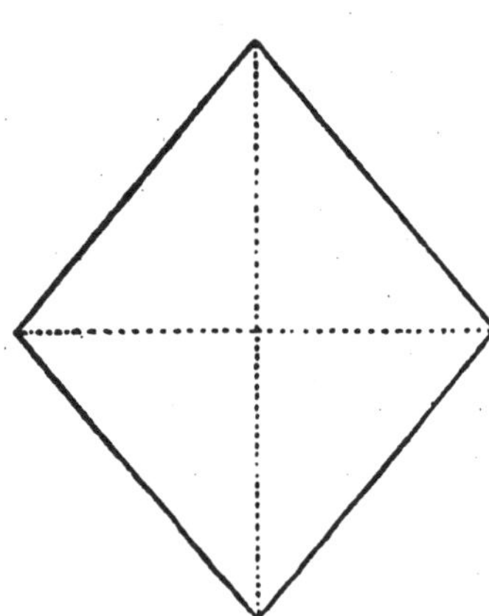

FIGURE 4.

The large block in the middle ground of Dürer's engraving being made of stone, it seemed to us to indicate the trade of a "lapicida", especially as there is also a stonecutter in the Salone at Padua, engaged in cutting an admittedly simpler stone (PLATES 32, 33). Further, since the block was in the form of a polyhedron, it seemed to represent descriptive, that is to say, optical, geometry, the chief task of which was at that time considered to be the mathematical and perspectival construction of such many-sided figures.[1]

With regard to the stereometric nature of this polyhedron, it has generally been looked upon as a truncated rhomboid, a figure formed of six rhomboids which, owing to the cutting off of two opposite points (those in which the sharp angles of the rhomboid meet), has been transformed into an octahedron. Other authors have thought it a cube off which pieces have been cut. Others again have quite wrongly described this octahedron

[1] See text p. 328.

as an icosahedron. Dürer's engraving of Melancholy is very carefully constructed with regard to perspective. The focal point is on the sea horizon, approximately underneath the C in "MELENCOLIA", and exactly matches the focal point given in the preliminary study D134 (PLATE 7); and the polyhedron's stereometric form is easily ascertainable. At Giehlow's request, the late Professor G. Niemann, one of the foremost experts in this field, undertook a reconstruction of the figure, and we here reproduce his opinion (cf. Figures 3 and 4).

The figure is a polyhedron with two truncated corners, to all appearances a rhomboid rather than a cube. It rests on one of the triangular surfaces made by truncating the corners, so that one diagonal of the figure is perpendicular. FIGURE 3 shows the figure completed.

The perpendicular axis is *DIKG*. If we draw the diagonals *AC*, *AB* and *BC* in the three upper surfaces of the figure, we make a horizontal equilateral triangle. The perspective vanishing-point of the side *AB* is *H*, which is also the focal point of the drawing and the vanishing-point of the side cornices on the house shown in the picture.

The vanishing-point of the line *AC* lies about 0.39 m. from the focal point of the engraving. As the angle *BAC* is known (= 60°) we can determine the distance from the eye at 0.225 m.

Further research into the perspective shows that the point *D* lies exactly above the centre (*I*) of the triangle; it shows, moreover, that the triangle *EFH* is also equilateral, and that its centre lies exactly on the axis *DG*, and that $KI = ID$.

The figure is correctly drawn in perspective except for the point *G*, which should be shifted to G_1; and the lines of the top horizontal plane are not drawn exactly. This plane lies somewhat below the middle of the line *DI*; a definite relationship cannot be observed between the cut off parts and the length of the edge.

If we measure the lines *AC* and *DF* with the usual aids to perspective, we see that they are of different lengths, and that *ADCF* is therefore not a square. Figure 4 shows the true form of the surface.

On the whole, the precision in the drawing of the figure is astonishing, since in Dürer's time the theory of perspective was not sufficiently developed for the depicting of the figure in this position. Several other objects in the engraving are not in correct perspective.

Professor Niemann, then, does allow the possibility of Dürer's having intended to draw a truncated cube rather than a truncated rhomboid, but in our opinion it would do injustice to Dürer's powers of perspective, as well as to his illustrative and artistic powers, to attribute to him such an obvious failure to make good his intentions, when he had so much experience in the construction of asymmetrical stereometric bodies. In any case, the polyhedron in *Melencolia I*, as it now appears, seems both to the innocent eye and to exact reconstruction in perspective, to be a truncated rhomboid, in whose completed surfaces the diagonals are related not as 1 : 1 but as, say, 10 : 12, the angles being not 90° each but, ☞ say, 80° and 100°.

Appendix II

THE MEANING OF THE ENGRAVING B70

The engraving B70 (PLATE 146), generally, for want of a better title, called *The Despairing Man*, has hitherto withstood any attempts at convincing interpretation. It is often stated that the picture is connected with Michelangelo,[2] but this does not help anybody except those who believe it to be a portrait of "the artist with his work".[3] And, in any case, the London *Cupido*, from which the motif of the despairing man was supposed to be taken, has been proved to be a much later work,[4] and the likeness to Michelangelo in the profile developed from the drawing L532 is, as we shall shortly show, pure coincidence. An attempt to interpret the picture as a vision in a dream[5] is ultimately as unsatisfactory as the old opinion that it was merely a "technical experiment".[6] Whichever interpretation one chooses—the latter being the more probable, since there is no signature—the artist would have imagined something sufficiently definite to be reproduced, and which sufficiently occupied his mind to flow into the etching needle of its own accord, so to speak, or even, alternatively, to appear to him in a dream. Now we can prove that the profile portrait can be excluded from the picture as a whole, and ignored in any interpretation, for it is obvious that it was originally considerably larger, a substantial portion of the cap and a small piece of the nose having been later removed—and only thus did the likeness to Michelangelo arise. We can hence conclude that

[2] C. EPHRUSSI, *Albert Dürer et ses dessins*, Paris 1882, p. 179; M. THAUSING, *Dürer*, Leipzig 1884, p. 67; the strongest advocate is G. GRONAU, in *Belvedere*, VOL. III (1923), pp. 1 sqq.

[3] F. WINKLER (following A. E. Popp) in "Albrecht Dürer", in *Klassiker der Kunst*, 4th edn., Berlin 1928, p. 426.

[4] F. KRIEGBAUM, in *Jahrbuch der kunsthistorischen Sammlungen in Wien*, new series, VOL. III (1929), pp. 247 sqq. The connexion with Michelangelo of the *Écorché*, recently suggested as a substitute (E. TIETZE-CONRAT in *Burlington Magazine*, LXVIII (1936), pp. 163 sqq.), is just as loose as that of the London Cupid.

[5] O. SCHNEID, in *Belvedere*, VOL. VIII (1929), pp. 334 sqq.

[6] Revived, with great conviction, by E. FLECHSIG, *Albrecht Dürer*, VOL. I, Berlin 1928, pp. 249 sqq.

this profile portrait was originally alone on the plate, and was reduced in size later when the other four figures were added. Now these four figures (though we advance this theory with reserve) could be connected with notions especially preoccupying Dürer in 1514 (the year of *Melencolia I* and the drawing L532) —notions, that is to say, of the morbid states characteristic of the four forms of "melancholia adusta".[7] Anyone can sense the gruesome abnormality informing these somehow sub-human beings, and when we call in the aid of any of the universally known medical texts describing the four species of "melancholia adusta", the agreement with them seems too close for it to be merely a strange coincidence. The vacantly smiling youth with the cannikin in his hand, who is making an awkward attempt at approaching the sleeping woman, and whose animal-shaped leg shows him to be a sort of satyr (though the head shows no signs of it), corresponds to descriptions of the sanguine melancholic who, "ridicule laetans", endeavours to enjoy the pleasures of Bacchus and Venus. "Hos Venus et Bacchus delectat," "Et placet ebrietas et male sanus amor," say the usual rhymes, and the sanguine man in the series of illustrations *De conservanda bona valetudine* mentioned above (p. 300, note 66) is also handing his lady a goblet.[8] In the same way, the "despairing man" tearing the wild, thick hair that covers his whole head,[9] corresponds to the clinical picture of the choleric melancholic who, "terribilis in aspectu", tormented by terrifying "furores et maniae", "se et alios percutit", "cum agitatione et laesione" as Avicenna says; and even to-day this form of illness is described as "melancholia agitata". The staring head of the old man emerging in so ghostly and isolated a fashion from the background, could then be the "melancholicus ex melancholia naturali", characterised by "tristitia, moeror, plurima cogitatio, fuga hominum, corruptae imaginationes". Finally, the fat sleeping woman could be the phlegmatic melancholic, with her unhealthy bloatedness and equally unhealthy desire for sleep; "qui fere perpetuo dormiebat", says Melanchthon, for instance, of a patient of this type. There are also two good

---

[7] See above, pp. 86–90; the quotations following are taken mainly from Avicenna, Platearius, Guainerio and Melanchthon.

[8] Fol. 213v of the 1559 edition contains the same woodcut as a portrait of Spring in a representation of the four seasons!

[9] The head is not, however, seen from behind, as Flechsig thinks, but is convulsively bent forward and seen foreshortened, from the crown downwards.

reasons for the fact that this type, and only this type, of melancholy madness is exemplified by a woman. First, there was Dürer's intention to provide an object for the sanguine melancholic's characteristic sexual excitement. The combination of a smiling youth with a reclining woman is unmistakably reminiscent of the famous group of a satyr with a sleeping nymph, as Dürer may have recognised in a copy of Marcantonio's engraving B319, or in the woodcut to *Hypnerotomachia*[10]; and this seems further indicated by the goat-like leg. Secondly, there was the doctrine held by all physicians and natural philosophers that woman was by nature "cold and moist" and therefore phlegmatic. "Calidissima mulier frigidior est frigidissimo viro," says William of Conches,[11] and in Johann von Neuhaus we read: "Phlegmaticus est frigidus et humidus, sicut sunt omnes mulieres naturaliter."[12]

MALINCONIA.

FIGURE 5. Malinconia.
From Cesare Ripa's *Iconologia*, Padua, 1611

---

[10] Fol. E. 1r.

[11] See p. 105, note 122.

[12] See text p. 115 sq.

Appendix III

LUCAS CRANACH'S DEPICTIONS OF MELANCHOLY (1990)

Studies made of Cranach's work over the last decade have led to new results that complement and update our text on some points. We shall sum them up briefly here.

While for Dürer the ancient world of gods and astrological motifs is central, Cranach seems clearly to be influenced by Luther, with whom he was close during his years in Wittenberg. Time and again Luther emphasizes, in his *Table Talk*, that those "plagued with sadness" are full of fear, and that sadness, diseases and melancholy come from Satan, the very "spirit of sadness" (*spiritus tristitiae*).[1] He is adapting the old monks' saying: melancholy is "the bath prepared for the devil".[2] Where Dürer finds Saturn's influence, Cranach—following Luther—sees Satan's doing. Notwithstanding the similarities in several details that Cranach obviously borrows from Dürer in his paintings, his understanding of melancholy is fundamentally different from Dürer's. However one interprets Dürer's engraving, the sublime sobriety and mysterious tension expressed by the image cannot be denied. Cranach's figure of Melancholy, on the other hand, and in whichever version, has something witchy and seductive about her. The whittling of the stick next to the children playing games in the foreground, the objects lying about in no obvious connection, the frenzied band of demons in the background—together these give the work an eerie, sinister feeling.

The strength of Cranach's fascination with melancholy is evident in the numerous versions he made on the theme during the five years between 1528 and 1533 [see Plates 128, 129, 130 and 147].

To say, in relation to the differences between these female figures in the work of Dürer and Cranach, that Cranach's figure "is not protected by Christian Cabbala from demonic powers"[3] and is therefore a witch is, to our mind, a misunderstanding of both Dürer and Cranach. The derogatory attitude toward melancholy, plain in all of Cranach's versions, can only be explained by his relationship to Luther, as noted by Koepplin and also by Heck (see below). Hence the absence of astrological elements.

Translated from the 1990 German edition by Elisabeth Otto and Jillian Tomm. Footnotes and translations are the editors' unless otherwise specified.

[1] Cf. a. o. M. Luther, *Tischreden* 2. Band, No. 1349, Kritische Gesamtausgabe, Weimar, 1913, p. 64.

[2] For a more specific attribution, see H. Peacham, *The Compleat Gentleman*, ch. 11 (London, 1622; facs. Amsterdam/New York, 1989, p. 98): "The exercise of singing openeth the breast and pipes; it is an enemy to melancholy and dejection of the mind, which S. Chysostome truly calleth '*The Deuels Bath*' (In lib. *De Angore animi*)." [Note from the original German Appendix.]

[3] F. Yates, *The Occult Philosophy in the Elizabethan Age*, London, 2004 [1979], p. 70.

Melanchthon compares the work of Dürer and Cranach in formal terms in the numerous late editions of his rhetoric.[4] He wants to show, no doubt based on Quintilian, that the classical differentiation of the three styles in rhetoric is also true for painting: "For example, Dürer painted everything in the Grand style, variegated with a great number of traits. The paintings of Lucas are simple; although they are charming, a comparison will show how distinct they are from the works of Dürer. Matthias [Grünewald] remained more or less in the Middle style."[5] Melanchthon's special interest in melancholy both as temperament and as illness is visible in several ways in his book *De anima* (1540). There he provides an extensive explanation of *Problem* XXX, 1 ("in order to invite the many to read those pages of Aristotle, which contain a most comforting doctrine").[6] To the great heroes and poets of antiquity mentioned there, Melanchthon adds several others, such as Heraclitus and Democritus, Archimedes, Scipio and Augustus. In earlier editions of his text—e.g. Wittenberg 1540, fol. 150v (Rabelais's copy can be found at the Bodleian Library, Oxford)—he speaks about Dürer's "generosissima melancholia"; yet at the same time he shows that he is acquainted with the possibility of deleterious effects from melancholy. That Dürer's and Cranach's representations of melancholy caught his interest seems certain, but whether he had these in mind particularly when characterising their differences as artists, remains a matter of speculation.

The list of Cranach's works on depictions of Melancholy in the final edition of Friedländer and Rosenberg's catalogue (*The Paintings of Lucas Cranach*, rev. ed., Ithaca, N.Y., 1978 [*FR*]) is incomplete and contains at one point an error. It seems therefore necessary to provide the following summary, referring where possible in each case to the numbers both in *FR* and in the excellent catalogue to the exhibition at the Kunstmuseum Basel of 1974 by Dieter Koepplin and Tilman Falk, *Lucas Cranach*, Basel and Stuttgart 1974 [*KF*].

Of the five works attributed to Cranach the elder, the following four are authentic:

1. [*An Allegory of*] *Melancholy*, dated 1528 (Plate 128, see text p. 382), formerly in the collection of the Earl of Crawford and Balcarres, now in a Swiss

4 See *Elementa rhetorices*, Paris, 1532, fol. 63v; and Wittenberg, 1539. [Reference from the original German Appendix.]

5 P. Melanchthon, *Elementorum rhetorices libri duo*, in *Opera quae supersunt omnia*, ed. K. G. Bretschneider, Halle, 1846 (Corpus Reformatorum, vol. XIII), col. 504; facsimile in J. Knape, *Philipp Melanchthons "Rhetorik"*, Tübingen, 1993 [Reference from the original German Appendix]: "Durerus enim pingebat omnia grandiora, et frequentissimis lineis variata. Lucae picturae graciles sunt, quae et si blandae sunt, tamen quantum distent a Dureri operibus, collatio ostendit. Matthias quasi mediocritatem servabat." Cf. "De rhetorica. Libri tres", in *Schriften zur Dialektik und Rhetorik / Principal Writings on Dialectic and Rhetoric*, ed. W. P. Weaver, S. Strohm and W. Wels, Berlin, de Gruyter (Opera philosophica, 2.2), 2017, p. 373.

6 Melanchthon, *De anima*, in *Opera quae supersunt omnia*, ed. K. G. Bretschneider, Halle 1846 (Corpus Reformatorum, vol. XIII), col. 85: "...ut multi invitentur ad illas ipsas Aristotelis paginas legendas, quae doctrinam dulcissimam continent."

private collection (*FR* 277A; *KF* Nr. 171, Fig. 133).[7] Beatus Rhenanus reports that among several other paintings by Cranach that he viewed in 1530 in the house of Raimund Fugger (d. 1535) in Augsburg, he noticed what he described as "a long panel with children playing hide and seek, joking and chasing each other and other things more, Lucas of Nuremberg [!] Melancholy."[8] Whether this is the painting mentioned above or a slightly different one cannot be determined with certainty.

2. *Melancholy*, dated 1532 (Plate 129, see text p. 383), Statens Museum for Kunst, Copenhagen (*FR* 276). Once owned by Queen Christina of Sweden (probably previously part of the collection of Emperor Rudolph II in Prague, looted by the Swedes).

3. *Melancholy*, dated 1532 (Plate 147), Musée d'Unterlinden, Colmar (not in *FR*; *KF* Nr. 172, with coloured plate 13), formerly in a series of private collections of Swedish nobles (also part of the seventeenth-century spoils of war), subsequently deposited in Switzerland, where it was shown in the Baseler Kunstmuseum in 1974, and then acquired in New York by the Musée d'Unterlinden in Colmar in 1983. Christian Heck's identification, in his instructive essay "Entre Humanisme et Réforme. La Mélancolie de Lucas Cranach l'Ancien",[9] of a painting dated "1534", learned of by word of mouth from Friedländer, as that in the Colmar collection, is an error (see p. 382, n. 21 of this volume); neither do the geometrical symbols stand out more prominently than in the Copenhagen painting nor are the magical elements less pronounced than in other versions of the same master. In the revised edition of Friedländer's catalogue there is no mention of a painting of 1534. It can be assumed, therefore, that the information given in footnote 21 of page 382 is based on a mistake.

The winged female figure here has a slightly coarser expression than those of the figures mentioned in versions 1, 2 and 4. But principally, she differs from these in her attitude towards the spectator, her deep cleavage, the seductive position of her legs, the bold coquetry of the crown of thorns on her long curls, and an invitingly knowing, lascivious smile. The resemblance of her expression with the Venus of the same year (held in the Städelsches Kunstinstitut, Frankfurt) is unmistakable. Four naked children play with a rope swing, whose upper attachment remains invisible; a chalice and a plate with fruit are untouched. In the foreground lies an inactive hound, curled up and looking sadly at the spectator, in contrast to two lively partridges further back; between them lies a large ball. In the distance can be seen a fortified

---

7 Now held by the Scottish National Gallery, Edinburgh.

8 D. Koepplin and T. Falk, *Lucas Cranach* [*KF*], Basel and Stuttgart, 1974, p. 96: "eine ablange Tafel, wie die Kindlein fangen und scherzen und andere mehr Sachen, Lukas von Nürnberg [!], Melancholey."

9 C. Heck, "Entre Humanisme et Réforme. La Mélancolie de Lucas Cranach l'Ancien", in *La Revue du Louvre et des Musées de France* No. 4/5 (October 1986), pp. 257–264.

castle. Clearly separated from the rest is a dark cloud in the upper left corner, dominated by the devil's menacing realm, in which two human figures are abducted by witches.

The question has been raised (*KF*, p. 283) as to whether the nineteen-year-old Hans Cranach may have collaborated on this painting; if so, this could explain why it is not quite on a level with similar paintings by Cranach the Elder. A thorough and enthusiastic description of the Colmar painting is offered by Yves Hersant in "Le regard oblique. Note sur une Mélancolie de Lucas Cranach."[10]

4. *Melancholy*. [ca] 1533 (PLATE 130, see text page 384), previously in a private collection (Dr Volz) in The Hague, now in private possession in the United States (*FR* 277).[11]

Furthermore, the following versions have a relationship with Cranach:

5. *Melancholy*, once in the possession of the Consul Moslé in Leipzig (see above, p. 382, n. 21), has been, since 1949, in the Museum of Fine Arts, Columbus, Ohio, by bequest of Fred M. Schumacher (*FR* 277B). As *FR* and C. Heck (op. cit., pp. 259f.) have shown, this painting is not by Cranach. It is a copy from the second half of the sixteenth century.

6. A (questionable) *Melancholy* dated 1524 (PLATE 148), so far only known from a black and white photograph signalled by Maxime Préaud in "Objets de Mélancolie", *Revue de la Bibliothèque Nationale de France* 22, Winter 1986. (The original was in the hands of a Parisian art dealer some twenty years ago, presumably P. Delaroff.) It shows a female figure richly dressed, turned toward the spectator with her gaze on the ground, holding in her left hand a wooden stick that she works with a knife. At her feet are three putti, one holding a ring while two others play at pushing a ball through the hoop with a pair of sticks. The terrace on which the woman sits is separated from the background by a wall, against which leans a long thin object. Comparing this object with the instruments in Hans Burgkmair's woodcut *Maximilian und seine Musikanten* in *Der Weisskunig*,[12] it can be identified with confidence as a *tromba marina*,[13] a stringed instrument described in depth by Heinrich Glarean (or Henricus Loritus Glareanus), in *Dodecachordon*, Basel 1547 (the instrument is known in German by the names *Trumscheit*, *Marientrompete* and *Nonnengeige*). The

---

10 *LMS – Littérature, Médecine, Société* 9 (1988), pp. 157–164. [Reference from the original German Appendix.]

11 Subsequent sales of this work are indicated by Christie's London auction house to an unnamed buyer in 2006, and again in 2014.

12 *Der Weisskunig* or *The White King* is an illustrated fictionalised biography of Maximilian I, Holy Roman Emperor.

13 See D. MUNROW, *Instruments of the Middle Ages and Renaissance*, London, 1974, pp. 30f., 37. [Reference from the original German Appendix.]

background is a landscape of Italian style, divided in the middle by a classical column on a base; on the right hand side is a highly stylized façade with two arched windows, beyond which stands a fruit tree; to the left of the column, a fantastically formed rock protrudes from behind a wall in ruins; a structure between the rock and the wall cannot be identified from the photograph.

A connection with Cranach is unmistakable despite the considerable differences (the wings are missing; the feet of the female figure are covered by her dress; and, especially, the demonic creatures in the background are absent). The year 1524 inscribed on a socle in the foreground is puzzling: Could it in fact be the first version, earlier by several years, of the work by Cranach? Préaud keeps this possibility open, but the inferior quality of the execution and the character of the overall composition exclude the possibility. The following options remain:

a) It is the work of a later painter who, knowing the painting held today in Copenhagen (see no. 2, above), omitted most of the dramatic characteristics and back-dated his own creation for a reason unknown to us—a very unlikely conjecture.
b) It is the work of an unknown predecessor of Cranach who—judging from the landscape, and the form of the rocks and house—was familiar not only with Dürer but also with some Italian models. Some years later, Cranach was inspired by this work; he kept the motif of the stick-chipping woman, gave her a more charming appearance, left aside the music instrument, fundamentally altered the whole composition and, most notably, introduced the dimension of the satanic horde. To accept this interpretation, one would need to find an explanation as to why Cranach's first representation of Melancholy from 1528 (PLATE 128) differs more from this 1524 version than does his later depiction of the same subject, the 1532 Copenhagen painting (PLATE 129), with the three putti, the ball, and the ring.
c) Both Cranach and the painter of the 1524 painting draw from the same unknown model. Cranach rearranges the elements in four fundamentally different ways—each one a masterpiece. In comparison, the 1524 painting seems to be the product of a lesser draughtsman whose putti fail and who, not hesitating to mix different styles, puts a Flemish female figure in an Italian landscape. Whether this is actually so—and how the original may have related to the lost *Malancolia* by Mantegna—is impossible to determine.

A sound judgement can only be made once the painting is accessible to the public and can be closely examined.[14]

14 The editors did not find evidence of a change in the accessibility of this work.

Additions to the Notes from the 1990 German Edition

WITH SUPPLEMENTAL TRANSLATIONS OF QUOTATIONS

Page 3, note 4
ANON., *De mundi caelestis terrestrisque constitutione* (BEDE, in MIGNE, *Patrologia Latina*, vol. XC, col. 881 D).

☞ *Sunt enim quattuor humores in homine …*
There exist namely four humours in man, which imitate the different elements; they grow in different seasons, and reign in different ages of life. Blood imitates air, it grows during spring and reigns during childhood. Yellow bile (*cholera*) imitates fire; it grows during summer and reigns during adolescence. Black bile (*melancholia*) imitates earth; it grows during autumn and reigns during adulthood. Phlegm imitates water; it grows during winter and reigns during old age. When these humours are abundant, not more, not less, then man is in full vigour.

☞ The text is newly available as PSEUDO-BEDE, *De mundi celestis terrestrisque constitutione: A Treatise on the Universe and the Soul*, ed. and trans. C. Burnett (Warburg Institute Surveys and Texts, Vol. XI), London, 1985. There, no connection is drawn to the late antique text, Περὶ τῆς τοῦ κόσμου καταοκευῆς καὶ τοῦ ἀνθρώπου (*Of the Constitution of the Universe and of Man*, in J. L. Ideler, *Physici et medici graeci minores*, Vol. I, Berlin, 1841, pp. 303–304; reprinted Amsterdam, 1963).

p. 31, note 62
M. FICINO, *De vita triplici*, I, 5, in *Opera Omnia*, Basel, 1576; vol. I, p. 498.

☞ *Bilis enim atra ferri instar, quando …*
Black bile is indeed like steel: when it turns cold, it becomes extremely cold, but when it turns hot, it becomes extremely hot.

Cf. FICINO, *Three Books on Life. A Critical Edition and Translation with Introduction and Notes*, ed. and trans. C. V. Kaske and J. R. Clark (Medieval & Renaissance Texts & Studies, vol. 57), Binghampton, Center for Medieval and Early Renaissance Studies, State University of New York at Binghampton, 1989.

Additions to the notes are translated from the 1990 German edition by Elisabeth Otto and Jillian Tomm. Translations of Latin, Greek, Italian, French, Flemish and German quotations from the main text are the editors' unless otherwise specified.

p. 33, note 64
Ficino, *De vita triplici*, I, 5, in *Opera Omnia*, Basel, 1576; vol. I, p. 498.

> ☞ *Ad utrumque extremum melancholia vim habet …*
> It is at both extremes that black bile (*melancholia*) is powerful, as if it got its stability from a sort of unity of its fixed nature. This extreme character doesn't happen for the other humours.

Cf. Ficino, *Three Books on Life* (ed. and trans. Kaske and Clark, 1989).

p. 46, note 120

> ☞ We agree with M. Wellmann and O. Temkin and their masterly study "Geschichte des Hippokratismus im ausgehenden Altertum" (*Kyklos* IV, Leipzig, 1932), whereupon Areatus recites the teachings of the physician Archigenes, who was highly praised by Galen. Fridolf Kudliens argues, to the contrary, that it was Aretaeus who influenced Archigenes ("Untersuchungen zu Aretaios von Kappádokien", *Mainzer Akademie der Wissenschaften und der Literatur, Abhandlungen der Geistes- und Sozialwissenschaftlichen Klasse*, 1963, no. 11).

p. 48, note 127
Cælius Aurelianus, *De morbis acutis et chronicis*, Libri VIII, I, 6, Amsterdam, 1709.

> ☞ *Melancholia dicta, quod nigra fella ægrotantibus …*
> It is called melancholy, because black biles often come to sick people when they vomit … and not, contrary to what many people think, because the cause or the development of the sickness would be these black biles; this is the case for those who cast opinions on the truth, more than for those who see it; or rather it is the case of those who cast opinions on what is false, as we show elsewhere.

Cf. Cælius Aurelianus, *De morbis acutis et chronicis, Libri VIII*, soli ex Methodicorum scriptis superstites, Jo. Conradus Amman M.D. recensuit, emaculavit, notulasque adjecit … Cum indicibus locupletissimis, Editio Nova, Amsterdam, Ex officina Wetsteniana, 1722.

p. 49, note 130
Rufus of Ephesus = *Œuvres de Rufus D'Éphèse*, texte collationné sur les manuscrits, traduit pour la première fois en français, avec une introduction. Publication commencée par Ch. Daremberg, continuée et terminée par C.-É. Ruelle, Paris, Imprimerie Nationale, 1879, p. 457, 18.

☞ *Illi qui sunt subtilis ingenii et multae perspicationis …*
Those who are endowed with a subtle mind and great perspicacity fall easily into melancholy, due to the fact that they act swiftly and with great premeditation and imagination.

Cf. Rufus, *On Melancholy*, ed. P. E. Pormann, Tübingen, Mohr Siebeck (Sapere, vol. 12), 2008.

p. 50, note 131
Rufus = *Œuvres de Rufus D'Éphèse*, texte collationné sur les manuscrits, traduit pour la première fois en français, avec une introduction. Publication commencée par Ch. Daremberg, continuée et terminée par C.-É. Ruelle, Paris, Imprimerie Nationale, 1879, p. 455, 31.

☞ *dixit, quod multa cogitatio et tristitia …*
He said that much reflection and sadness produces melancholy.

Cf. Rufus, *On Melancholy* (ed. Pormann, 2008).

p. 55, note 150
Alexander of Tralles = *Alexandri Tralliani præcellentis medici, De singularium corporis partium, ab hominis coronide ad imum usque calcaneum, vitiis, ægritudinibus & injuriis, libri ad unguem facti quinque, per Albanum Torinum Vitodurensem recens latinitate donati*, Basileae, Henricus Petrus [Heinrich Peter], 1533, liber I, p. 50. [Translated from the Greek into Latin by Albanus Torinus.]

☞ *Novimus quippe foeminam ipsi eiusmodi phantasia …*
As a matter of fact, we know of a woman afflicted with an imagination of that sort, who would contract her thumb with such force that nobody could straighten it easily; she declared that she supported the whole universe.

p. 66, note 180
Isidore of Seville, *Etymologiarum sive originum libri XX*, recognovit brevique adnotatione critica instruxit W. M. Lindsay, Oxford, Clarendon Press (Scriptorum classicorum bibliotheca Oxoniensis), 1911, X, 176.

☞ *malus appellatur a nigro felle, quod Graeci …*
It is named "malus" from the black bile, that the Greeks call μέλαν; this is the reason why we call melancholic those men who not only avoid human contact, but even remain suspicious of their close friends.

Cf. ISIDORE, *The Etymologies*, trans. S. A. Barney, et al., with the collaboration of M. Hall, Cambridge, Cambridge University Press, 2006.

p. 69, note 6

ALEXANDER NECKHAM, *De Naturis rerum libri duo,* ed. T. Wright, London (*Rerum Britannicarum medii aevi Scriptores,* vol. XXIV), 1863, p. 42.

> ☞ *Videtur autem nobis contrarius esse Aristoteles, qui dicit solos melancholicos ingeniosos esse. Sed hoc dictum est ab Aristotele propter felicitatem memoriae, quae frigida est et sicca, aut propter eorum* astutiam.*
> In our opinion, Aristotle holds the opposite doctrine; he says that only the melancholics are intelligent. But Aristotle says that either on account of the fecundity of their memory, which is cold and dry, or because of their being wise.
> * correction of the Latin text, introduced in the French translation, p. 125.

Cf. NECKHAM, *De Naturis rerum libri duo, with the poem of the same author, De laudibus divinae sapientiae,* ed. T. Wright, London and Cambridge, Cambridge University Press, 2012; online publication, 2013.

p. 79, note 30

HILDEGARD VON BINGEN, *Hildegardis Causae et curae*, ed. P. Kaiser, Leipzig, 1903, p. 145, 35.

> ☞ *Cum autem Adam transgressus est …*
> However, when Adam fell … bile transformed itself into bitterness, and melancholy into the blackness of impiety.

Cf. HILDEGARD VON BINGEN, *Beate Hildegardis Cause et cure*, ed. L. Moulinier and R. Berndt, Berlin, Akademie-Verlag (Rarissima Mediaevalia, vol. 1), 2003.

p. 80, note 36

G. OFFHUYS, "Beitræge zur Biographie Hugos van der Goes und zur Chronologie seiner Werke", ed. H. G. Sander, in *Repertorium für Kunstwissenschaft*, XXXV (1912), pp. 519 sqq.

> ☞ … *quo incessanter dicebat se esse dampnatum* …
> … by the effect of which he repeated constantly that he was damned and condemned to eternal damnation, and by which he wanted to do harm to his body and even kill himself (if he hadn't been stopped by force with the help of people around him).

p. 90, note 70
HOMER (translated into Latin by CICERO), in MELANCHTON, *De anima*, *Opera quae supersunt omnia*, in C. G. Bretschneider, ed., Halle, Schwetschke (Corpus Reformatorum, vol. XIII), 1846, col. 85.

☞ *Qui miser in campis errabat solus Aleis, …*
Who wandered miserably, alone, in the Aleian fields, / Eating his own heart, and fleeing the traces of men.

p. 91, note 73
A. ABYNZOHAR, *Colliget Averroys*, Venice, 1514, fol. 65, v°.

☞ *Quando fuerit causa in prora cerebri …*
When the cause is in the prow of the brain, then it is the imagination that will be injured; and when it is in the middle part, then it is reason and thought that will be injured; and when it is in the posterior part, then it will be memory and the faculty of conservation.

p. 97
A. GUAINERIUS, *Practica, seu Opera medica*, Venice, Octaviani Scoti, 1517, tract. 15, fol. 22, v°.

☞ *… et hoc de problemate, cuius assignatae causae …*
… and regarding this problem, of which the causes assigned [to solve it] bring with them difficulties of great weight, I abandon it to those who rely on speculation. And it is by turning back to glorious practice that I bring this chapter to an end.

p. 98, note 96
GERALDO OF SOLO, *Practica super nonos Almanzoris*, in *Almansori liber nonus cum expositione Geraldi de Solo*, Lyon, 1504, chap. XIII, fol. 34, v°.

☞ *Nota primo, quod melancolia potest sumi dupliciter …*
Note first that melancholy can be understood in two ways. The first way is by considering it as a humour distinct from other humours, and this is not the way we understand it here. The other way is to consider it as a certain affection of the brain, and this is the way considered here.

p. 98, note 97
VALESCUS OF TARENTA, *Aureum ac perutile*, seu *Opus Philonium*, I, 13, Venice, 1521, fol. 12, r°.

☞ *Melancholia est nomen humoris unius de quattuor …*
Melancholy is the name of one humour amongst four that are present in our body: and this is the name of a sickness originating in that humour.

p. 112, note 143
Johannes de Sancto Paulo, *Flores diaetarum, eine Salernitanische Nahrungsmitteldiätetik aus dem 12. Jahrhundert, verfasst von Johannes de Sancto Paulo,* ed. H. J. Ostermuth, Dissertation, Leipzig, 1919.

☞ *… nam si aegritudo fuerit nata ex sanguine …*
… yet, if the sickness came about from the blood, which is sweet, humid and warm, it will be cured by bitter, dry and cold elements.

On this medieval treatise, see M. Nicoud, *Les régimes de santé au Moyen Âge. Naissance et diffusion d'une écriture médicale en Italie et en France (XIIIe–XVe siècles),* Rome, Publications de l'École française de Rome, 2007.

p. 114 & p. 115, note 146
Regimen sanitatis Salernitanum, apud Th. Meyer-Steineg und K. Sudhoff, *Geschichte der Medizin im überblick*, II. durchgesehene Auflage, Jena, Fischer, 1922, p. 185.

(p. 114)
☞ *Invidus et tristis, cupidus, dextraeque tenacis …*
Envious and sad, cupidinous and with strenuous hands,
And not devoid of fraud, they remain timid and their complexion resembles clay.

(p. 115)
☞ *Restat adhuc tristis colerae substantia nigra …*
We must now talk about the black substance of the sad bile
Which renders men base, gloomy and taciturn.
These men stay awake studying, and their mind doesn't yield to sleep.
They serve one purpose, they think that nothing will remain out of their keep.
Envious and sad, cupidinous and with strenuous hands,
And not devoid of fraud, they remain timid and their complexion resembles clay.

Cf. J. Ordronaux, ed., *Regimen sanitatis Salernitatum. Code of health of the school of Salernum,* trans. into English verse, with an introduction, notes and appendix, Philadelphia, J. B. Lippincott, 1870.

p. 136, note 35

☞ See also M. J. Bottéro's recent study *Mésopotamie: L'écriture, la raison et les dieux* (Paris, 1987), which enables us to correct some assumptions that were based on the earlier research of Cumont (see also, p. 140, n. 47). According to Bottéro, the planets were not, at least in the Babylonian period, identified with gods as such; Venus was not Ishtar, but Ishtar's star.

p. 140, note 47

☞ As M. J. Bottéro, *Mésopotamie* (see, p. 136, n. 35), has shown, the Babylonians did not conceive of planets as "good" or "bad." The differentiation of days as "convenient" or "inconvenient" was based not on astrological influences but on hemerological or menological criteria—that is, considering the numeric position of the day or month within the calendar.

p. 180, note 170

☞ The manuscripts, including one from the library of Cardinal Bessarion, are listed in *The Continuity of the Platonic Tradition*, London, 1939, p. 30 (more recent edition: Munich, 1981; Millwood, N.Y., 1982), and in "The School of Chartres," in *Twelfth-Century Europe and the Foundations of Modern Society*, ed. M. Clagett, G. Post and R. Reynolds, Madison, 1961, p. 11. The text of William of Conches is now available in the edition by E. Jeauneau of *Glosae Super Platonem*, [first published] Paris, 1965.

p. 186, note 193
Alanus ab Insulis, *Anticlaudianus*, IV, 8 (Migne, Patrologia Latina, vol. CCX, col. 528).

☞ *Ulterius progressa suos Prudentia gressus …*
Progressing further on, Prudence carries her steps
Towards the superior spheres, even higher than the domain of Jupiter
And to the dwellings of Saturn, which are of a wider magnitude.
She gets inside, and she trembles from the winter cold and the frosts of the solstice
And she wonders at the paralyzing cold in summer.
There, winter is boiling, and summer gets colder, and the heat
Becomes icy, the splendour is extravagant while the flame fades away.
Here, darkness become lucent, here light darkens, and in this place

Night exists in full light, and light appears within the night.
In that place, Saturn walks his way rapidly through the space,
And with a heavy movement, pacing slowly his walk,
Here he spoils with his coldness the joys of spring
And he robs the adornment of the fields and the brightness of flowers
He freezes while burning, and he boils while freezing; he floods
He who is dry; he, who is obscure, he illuminates; while young, he grows old.
But the sound of his voice doesn't alter, and doesn't differ from song,
Quite the contrary, his voice is heard before the voices of his companions,
With a male tone, that his song doesn't render
Insipid, its own sweetness gives his voice all its flavour.
Here, suffering and moaning, tears, discord, terror,
Sadness, pallidness, blows and wounds, all these reign.

Cf. Alanus de Insulis [Alan of Lille], *Anticlaudianus*, ed. R. Bossuat, Paris, J. Vrin (Textes philosophiques du Moyen Âge), 2003.

p. 187
Bartholomeus Anglicus, *De proprietatibus rerum*, VIII, 23, Strasbourg, 1485, fol. O 2, v°.

☞ *Saturnus est a saturando dictus. Cuius uxor Ops …*
Saturn gets his name from being satisfied. His wife, Ops, is named after opulence, which she granted to mortals, according to Isidorus and Martianus. On this subject there are legends that depict him as deeply sad, because he is represented being castrated by his own son, his male organs thrown into the sea to become Venus. According to Misael, Saturn is a malign planet, cold and dry, nocturnal and heavy, and therefore depicted as an old man. This circle is the farthest from earth, and nevertheless the most harmful to earth. As to colour, he is pallid and livid like lead, because he possesses two mortal qualities, coldness and dryness. And this is the reason why the fœtus conceived and born under his domination either dies or is born with the worst qualities to follow. As a matter of fact, according to Ptolemaeus, in his book on the judgement of celestial bodies, he endows man with a dark complexion, he makes him ugly, author of abominable acts, lazy, heavy, sad, rarely joyous or smiling. This is why, says the same Ptolemaeus: "Men subjected to Saturn have a stern complexion, they have bluish hair, their whole body is covered with asperities and their appearance is entirely neglected; they do not dislike ugly and stinking clothes, they care for stinking and squalid

animals. They have a taste for acidic and astringent food, because in their complexion the melancholic humour dominates."

See, for introductory material, R. James Long, ed., *Bartholomeus Anglicus on the Properties of Soul and Body* (*De proprietatibus rerum libri III & IV*, edited from the Bibliothèque Nationale MS Latin 16098, at Toronto, Publications of the Centre for Medieval Studies of the Pontifical Institute of Mediaeval Studies (Toronto Medieval Latin Texts, vol. 9), 1979.

p. 190
G. Bonatti, *De Astronomia*, I, 3, Basel, 1550, col. 97, sqq.

☞ *Ex humoribus significat melancholiam …*
Among the humours, he signifies melancholy. And within the complexions of the bodies, he signifies melancholy, and perhaps this melancholy comes with a mixture of phlegm and a certain heaviness and gravity of the body born with it, in such a way that he will not walk with lightness, he will not jump swiftly, and will not learn to swim or other things of that sort that display the lightness of the body; he will be disgusting and stinking, as if he smelled of the odour of the goat, and this produces men who eat a lot.

☞ *Et si inciperet Saturninus diligere aliquem …*
And if the Saturnine would begin loving someone, which happens rarely, he would love them with a true affection. And if he would begin to hate someone, which happens often, he hates them with an extreme hate, and he will with difficulty, or even never, detach himself from that hate.

☞ *Et dixit Albumasar, quod si fuerit boni esse …*
And Abū Maʿshar says that if there should exist a good man, that would refer to the profundity of his science, as to a wise and profound judgement, in such a measure that another man would with difficulty, or even never, know how to make him better. And among the disciplines, this would refer to things antique and which require labour, things that are valued and precious, labours accomplished either on water or near it, such as watermills … constructions of houses, and for the most part, buildings for the religious, wearing black clothes.

Cf. G. Bonatti, *Liber astronomiae, Part I*, trans. R. Zoller and ed. R. Hand, (Project Hindsight, Latin Track, vol. VII), Berkeley Springs, Golden Hind Press, 1994. This edition, sponsored by the astrological community, is not part of a scholarly project, but it is the only complete English translation available and contains interesting introductory material. It is available online.

p. 191, note 201
M. Scot, *Liber introductorius*, Oxford, MS Bodley 266, f° 2150 v° sqq.

> ☞ *Verum est, quod permutatur ab eius influentia …*
> It is true that he is drawn away from using his influence by relying on the power of another planet that dominates him, and yet, if he cannot carry out his malignant work on another, as much as he would want, he harms everyone as much as he can.

See, on this text, G. M. Roberts, *The Liber Introductorius of Michael Scot*, PhD Dissertation, University of Southern California, 1978. Full text available online.

p. 193
[Anon.]

> ☞ *Annis viginti currit bis quinque Saturnus …*
> In twenty years, Saturn accomplishes ten times his cycle,
> And a man born when Saturn is dominating,
> Will be audacious, civilized, naughty, old, a thief, greedy,
> Perfidious, ignorant, irritable and indolent.

p. 194, note 209
Inscription on a fresco in the Palazzo Trinci at Foligno, dated before 1424, published by M. Salmi, in *Bolletino d'Arte*, XIII (1919), p. 176.

> ☞ *Quicquid et infaustum, quicquid flagitiosum …*
> Everything that is disastrous, everything that is scandalous,
> That is yours, Saturn: except the cereals that you harvest.

p. 218, note 6
Boccaccio, *Ninfale Fiesolano*, ed. B. Wiese, Heidelberg, Winter, 1913.

> ☞ *pella maninconia e pel dolore / ch'i' sento …*
> for the pain and melancholy / that assail my heart (stanza 331)
> there, this day, full of melancholy, / his father awaited him (stanza 71)
> melancholic and unhappy (stanza 70)
> he sought his pitiless, untamed beloved, / the cause of his melancholy (stanza 55)

Modified translation from Giovanni Boccaccio, *The Nymph of Fiesole*, trans. D. J. Donno, New York, Columbia University Press, 1960, pp. 93, 22 and 18.

p. 226, note 31
A. Tscherning, *Vortrab des Sommers deutscher Getichte*, Rostock, 1655; printed in W. Unus, *Die deutsche Lyrik des Barock*, Berlin, 1922, p. 101 (also mentioned by Walter Benjamin, *Ursprung des deutschen Trauerspiels*, Berlin, 1928, p. 143).

> ☞ *wann der sich in mir reget, / Entzünd ich* …
> when the heavenly spirit moves me / I swiftly enflame hearts like a god, / they are then beside themselves, and seek a path / which transcends the earthly…

This English translation from Walter Benjamin, *The Origin of German Tragic Drama,* trans. J. Osborne, London and New York, Verso, 1998, p. 148.

p. 248, note 15
Petrarch, *Epistola Metrica to Zoilus*, I, line 167 (*Poemata minora*, ed. D. de Rossetti, vol. II, Milan, 1831, p. 230).

> ☞ *Quaedam divina poetis / vis animi est* …
> There exists in poets a certain divine power of the mind

> ☞ *Insanire licet, fateor, mens concita* …
> To be mad, I must confess, the emotion of the soul allows it;
> when it transcends itself, she sings a noble song …
> he [Aristotle] thought that no genius exists, unless it is mixed with madness.

On this collection of letters, see E. H. Wilkins, *The Epistolae Metricae of Petrarch. A Manua*l, Rome, Edizioni di Storia e Letteratura (Sussi eruditi, 8), 1956.

p. 249, note 22
Ficino, *De vita triplici*, I, 6, in *Opera Omnia*, Basel, 1576; vol. I, p. 499.

> ☞ *quantum atra bilis, imo candida bilis eiusmodi* …
> Inasmuch as we must seek and nurture black bile, and even a certain bright bile of this sort, as it is the best sort, in the same measure we should avoid this (black) bile, that works against itself, as we said, as it is the worst kind.

Cf. Ficino, *Three Books on Life* (ed. and trans. Kaske and Clark, 1989).

p. 252
M. Palmieri, *La Città di Vita*, Florence, Biblioteca Laurenziana, Cod. plut. XL, 53.

> ☞ *[la intelligenza certa …] / Per darsi a quegli che sapran mostrare …*
> [the trustworthy intelligence …] / Which gives itself to those able to demonstrate / With true reason, well proven, and competent.

p. 268, note 93
Ficino, *De vita triplici*, III, 22 (in *Opera Omnia*, Basel, 1576; vol. I, p. 564).

> ☞ *Quoniam vero coelum est harmonica ratione compositum …*
> Because indeed heaven is composed according to a harmonic reason, and because it is moved in harmony, […] it is right to think that through that harmony alone not only men, but also all inferior beings before men are disposed to receive celestial harmony. As for the powerful harmony of the superior beings, we have ranged it into seven grades of beings. That is, into images (as they think) constituted harmonically, and into medicines tempered according to a certain consonance; vapours and odours, prepared following a similar rule of proportion. Also into musical songs, and sonorities. To this order and structure, we must add the movements of the body, the steps and ritual exercises, the conceptions and measured movements of imagination, the coherent rational discourses, and the serene contemplations of the mind.

Cf. Ficino, *Three Books on Life* (ed. and trans. Kaske and Clark, 1989).

p. 270, note 99
Ficino, *De vita triplici*, III, 23 (in *Opera Omnia*, Basel, 1576; vol. I, p. 567).

> ☞ *Imaginationis conceptus motusque concinnos …*
> The conceptions and measured movements of imagination, the coherent rational discourses, and the serene contemplations of the mind.

Cf. Ficino, *Three Books on Life* (ed. and trans. Kaske and Clark, 1989).

p. 280, note 14
Paris, Bibliothèque Nationale, MS fr. 19994 fol. 13^{r}.

> ☞ *Milencolique a triste face, / conuoiteux et plain d'avarice*
> The melancholic's face is sadness / All twisted and full of avarice / We must not ask his favour / He offers not his succour / Deception had for

nanny / Guile and chicanery / Nor can he speak of good / Seek elsewhere for one who would.

p. 283, note 23

☞ There is also now a critical text edition by Olga Weijers of Pseudo-Boethius, *De disciplina scholarium*, Leiden and Cologne, 1967, where the passage cited by us (ch. 4, 1–2) can be located on p. 108. According to Weijers, the author of this work, written between 1230 and 1240, cannot be identified. It should be noted that the critical edition states that the "humana conditio" is based on the four humours, while the text in the Latin patrology only mentions the "humani corporis complexion."

p. 302
See Plate 89b: *Melancholics*, woodcut, First German Calendar, Augsburg, ca 1480.

☞ *Vnser complexion ist von erden reych …*
Our complexion is full of earth / That's why we are so like indolence.

p. 302, note 76
C. Tinbergen, *Des Coninx Summe*, Bibliotheek van Middelnederlandsche Letterkunde (Groningen, Wolters, 1900–03), p. 253.

☞ *Dat vierde […] is swaerheit, dat een mensce …*
The ferthe is right hevynesse, whan a man is so hevy that he loveth not but to lyn and reste & slepe …

Middle English translation from *The Book of Vices and Virtues: A Fourteenth Century English Translation of the* Somme le roi *of Lorens d'Orléans*, ed. from the three extant manuscripts by W. Nelson Francis, London: Published for the Early English Text Society by Milford, Oxford University Press, 1942, p. 27.

p. 319, note 117

☞ This description, commonly but erroneously attributed to Melanchthon (as also in our edition from 1964), is found in *Elementa rhetoricae* (Basel, 1541, p. 138; reproduced in Dürer, *Schriftlicher Nachlass*, vol. I, ed. H. Rupprich, Berlin, 1956, p. 319), by Joachim Camerarius (1500–1576). This famous scholar and close friend of Melanchthon was from 1526 headmaster of the Nürnberger Gymnasium and was close to Dürer; he mentions the artist often in his writings and translated his *Vier Bücher von menschlicher Proportion* (*Four Books of Human Proportion*) into Latin. On Camerarius's description, see now the article by W. S. Heckscher, "The Unconventional Index and its Merits", in *Art and Literature: Studies in Relationship* [Festschrift for Heckscher on his 80th birthday], *Saecula spiritalia*, vol.17, ed. E. Verheyen, Baden-Baden, 1985, pp. 503–521.

p. 323, note 132

☞ A published facsimile of this manuscript is now available. See p. 351, n. 222.

p. 325, note 142

☞ The magic square in the top right corner of the engraving remains the subject of numerous new interpretations; for more on this, including an alchemical interpretation, see the section on Dürer in the Supplemental Bibliography below, p. 433–435.

p. 330, note 158
[Anon.]

☞ *Gram loquitur, Dia vera docet, Rhe …*
Gram[matica] speaks, Dia[lectica] teaches the truth, Rhe[torica] adds colour to words,
Mus[ica] sings, Ar[ithmetica] counts, Geo[metria] weighs and measures,
As[tronomia] studies the stars.

p. 336
[Anon.], Inscription on a woodcut of H. Döring, published 1535; see also p. 335 note 179 and Plate 107.

☞ *Grandaeuus ego sum tardus ceu primus in Orbe…*
I am old, and slow, as I am the first being in the World
I cut down everything that destiny offers me
With my sickle, to make sure that a hero born from Mars
Doesn't fare war against me: these places are safe, thanks to my arts
They are circled by a ditch, but you who builds a fortress
Make sure to surround it with a narrow mound. Make sure, I pray you,
To do it in good order; this child will show you the way:

Indeed, I have endowed those children that I fathered with this gift,
[and by this virtue they will excel.

p. 351, note 222

☞ A facsimile of the Würzburg manuscript is included in appendix to K. A. Nowotny's edition of AGRIPPA OF NETTESHEIM's *De occulta philosophia*, Graz, 1967, pp. 519–586. Nowotny was unaware that the discovery of this first edition was made by Hans Meier; see above, p. 323, n. 132.

p. 358, note 258

☞ See also the more recent O. WEIJERS, ed. cit. (see above, p. 282–283, n. 23) [*alternative terms in square brackets are from the cited Weijers edition*]: "Cum ad magistratus excellentiam bonae indolis adolescens [W: iuvenis] velit ascendere [W: accedere], necessarium est ut tria genera statuum, quae [W: quos] in assignatione probabilitatis innuit Aristotcles, diligenter intelligat. Sunt autem quidam vehementer obtusi, alii mediocres, tertii excellenter acuti. Nullum vero vehementer obtusorum vidimus unquam philosophico nectare vehementer inebriari [W: debriari]. Istis autem mechanica gaudet maritari, mediocribus politica."

p. 382, note 21

☞ (see now M. J. FRIEDLÄNDER and J. ROSENBERG, *The Paintings of Lucas Cranach*, rev. ed. Ithaca, N.Y., 1978, Nr. 277A) …

☞ (the copy is now held by the Museum of Fine Arts in Columbus, Ohio; see Appendix III, p. 410) …

☞ (see, however, Appendix III, p. 409–410) …

p. 387, note 37

☞ (about this engraving see now M. PRÉAUD, "Objets de Mélancolie", in *Revue de la Bibliothèque Nationale* 22 (Winter 1986), pp. 25–35).

p. 392, note 55
See PLATE 137: E. von STEINLE, *Melancholy*, pen and water-colour, 1867 (Städelsches Kunstinstitut, Frankfurt).

☞ *Jhe lenger jhe lieber ich bin allein …*
The longer I am alone the better / as fidelity and truth have become tiny.

p. 402

☞ Terence LYNCH provides us with a new interpretation ("The Geometric Body in Dürer's Engraving Melencolia I", in *Journal of the Warburg and Courtauld Institute* 45, 1982, pp. 226–232) by highlighting a perspectival relation of the magic square to the geometrical object. To this end, Lynch shows the relationship between the plane and the form, the incline at the fore and the perspectival view. He then identifies the ways in which Dürer deviates from an exact construction of the object.

His ingenious study succeeds in shedding new light on the problem. He concludes, however, without critical caution, that the entire engraving was conceived so as to present this complex geometric form while hiding the method by which it was constructed. According to Lynch, the bizarrely shaped block and its magic square are not simply two iconographical elements among many others, "but perhaps even the *raison d'être* of the whole work." In short, the erudition attested by this iconography, as well as the geometric knowledge and ability demonstrated in the representation of this form indicate for Lynch that *Melencolia I* is not so much "a spiritual self-portrait" as "a summary of Dürer's intellectual achievements."

Supplemental Bibliography for the German Edition (1990)

The following offers a limited selection of the rich literary treatment of the topic. Titles named in the text and notes are not repeated here.

In order to do justice to the numerous publications on modern Spanish literature, the French authors of the eighteenth (such as Diderot and Rousseau) and nineteenth centuries (from Chateaubriand to Baudelaire, Flaubert, and Verlaine), as well as titles on German Romanticism, a separate bibliography would be required; yet another would be needed to take into account topics such as "*Weltschmerz*", "*mal du siècle*", and "*ennui*".

General Works

Bandmann, Günter. *Melancholie und Musik. Ikonographische Studien.* Wissenschaftliche Abbandlungen der Arbeitsgemeinschaft für Forschung des Landes Nordrhein-Westfalen 12. Cologne/Opladen: Westdeutscher Verlag, 1960.

Jackson, Stanley W. *Melancholy and Depression: From Hippocratic Times to Modem Times.* New Haven: Yale University Press, 1986.

Kristeva, Julia. *Soleil noir. Dépression et mélancolie.* Paris: Gallimard, 1987. Translated into English by Leon S. Roudiez as *Black Sun: Depression and Melancholia.* New York: Columbia University Press, 1989.

Lambotte, Marie-Claude. *Esthétique de la mélancolie.* Paris: Aubier, 1984.

Lepenies, Wolf. *Melancholie und Gesellschaft.* 2nd ed. Frankfurt am Main: Suhrkamp, 1972 (1969). Translated into English by Jeremy Gaines and Doris Jones as *Melancholy and Society*, with a foreword by Judith N. Shklar. Cambridge, Mass.: Harvard University Press, 1992.

Neaman, Judith S. *Suggestion of the Devil: The Origins of Madness.* Garden City, N.Y.: Anchor Press/Doubleday, 1975.

Préaud, Maxime. *Mélancolies.* Paris: Herscher, 1982.

—"Objets de mélancolie." *Revue de la Bibliothèque Nationale* 22 (1986), 25–35.

Sena, John F. *A Bibliography of Melancholy: 1660–1800.* London: Nether Press, 1970.

Starobinski, Jean. "L'Encre de la mélancolie." *Nouvelle Revue française* 11 (1963), 410–423.

—*Histoire du traitement de la mélancolie des origines à 1900.* Documenta Geigy, Acta Psychosomatica 4. Basel: Geigy, 1960. Appears in the same series in English as *History of the Treatment of Melancholy from the Earliest Times to 1900.* Basel: Geigy, 1962.

Reproduced from Raymond Klibansky's bibliography for the German edition, with additions and minor corrections introduced by the editors. Additions are either English versions of titles listed in the German edition or recognized updated editions since 1990.

—*Trois fureurs*. Paris: Gallimard, 1974.

Tradition de la mélancolie. Special issue of *Le Débat* 29 (1984), 44–138. Paris: Gallimard. Includes: Yves Hersant, "Acedia"; Jean Starobinski, "Démocrite parle: L'utopie mélancolique de Robert Burton"; Marc Fumaroli, "Classicisme français et maladie de l'âme"; Krzysztof Pomian, "Raymond Klibansky, Erwin Panofsky, Fritz Saxl: Saturne et la mélancolie."

Völker, Ludwig, ed. *"Komm heilige Melancholie." Eine Anthologie deutscher Melancholie-Gedichte; mit Ausblicken auf die europäische Melancholie-Tradition in Literatur- und Kunstgeschichte*. Stuttgart: Reclam, 1983.

Wittkower, Rudolf and Margot. *Born Under Saturn: The Character and Conduct of Artists; A Documented History from Antiquity to the French Revolution*. New York: Random House, 1963.

Antiquity

Actes du Colloque Hippocratique. Corpus Hippocraticum: Actes du Colloque Hippocratique de Mons, Sept. 1975. Edited by Robert Joly. Mons: Université de Mons, 1977.

—*Formes de pensée dans la Collection Hippocratique: Actes du IVe Colloque International Hippocratique,* Lausanne 1981. Edited by François Lasserre and Philippe Mudry. Geneva: Université de Lausanne, Faculté des Lettres, 1983.

Deichgräber, Karl. *Hippokrates' De humoribus in der Geschichte der griechischen Medizin*. Abhandlungen der Geistes- und Sozialwissenschaftliche Klasse, Jahrgang 1972, no. 14. Mainz: Akademie der Wissenschaften und der Literatur, 1972.

Flashar, Hellmut. *Melancholie und Melancholiker in den medizinischen Theorien der Antike*. Berlin: de Gruyter, 1966.

Gensemann, Hermann. *Der Arzt Polybos als Verfasser hippokratischer Schriften*. Abhandlungen der Geistes- und Sozialwissenchaftl. Klasse, Jahrgang 1968, no. 2. Mainz: Akademie der Wissenschaften und der Literatur, 1968.

Gundel, Wilhelm. "Individualschicksal, Menschentypen und Berufe in der antiken Astrologie." *Jahrbuch der Charakterologie*, edited by Emil Utitz, 4:135–193. Berlin: Pan Verlag, 1927.

Kudlien, Fridolf. *Der Beginn des medizinischen Denkens bei den Griechen von Homer bis Hippokrates*. Zürich: Artemis, 1967.

—"Dialektik und Medizin in der Antike." *Medizinhistorisches Journal* 9 (1974), 187–200.

—"Galen's Religious Belief." In *Galen: Problems and Prospects; A Collection of Papers Submitted at the 1979 Cambridge Conference*, edited by Vivian Nutton. London: Wellcome Institute of Medicine, 1981.

—"Schwärzliche Organe im frühgriechischen Denken." *Medizinhistorisches Journal* 8 (1973), 53–58.

Kümmel, Werner. "Melancholie und die Macht der Musik. Die Krankheit König Sauls in der historischen Diskussion." *Medizinhistorisches Journal* 4 (1969), 189–209.

MÜRI, Walter. "Melancholie und schwarze Galle." *Museum Helveticum* 10 (1953), 21–38. Reprinted in Müri, *Griechische Studien*, edited by Eduard Vischer, 139–164. Basel: F. Reinhardt, 1976.

PIGEAUD, Jackie. *La maladie de l'âme: Étude sur la relation de l'âme et du corps dans la tradition médico-philosophique antique*. Paris: Belles Lettres, 1981.

—*Folie et cures de 1a folie chez les médecins de l'Antiquité gréco-romaine: la manie*. Paris: Belles Lettres, 1987.

SCHÖNER, Erich. *Das Viererschema in der antiken Humoralpathologie*. Sudhoffs Archiv für Geschichte der Medizin und der Naturwissenschaften, Supplement 4. Wiesbaden: Franz Steiner, 1964.

SCHUMACHER, Joseph. *Die naturphilosophischen Grundlagen der Medizin in der griechischen Antike*. 2nd ed, revised. Berlin: de Gruyter, 1963.

SIMON, Bennett. *Mind and Madness in Ancient Greece: The Classical Roots of Modern Psychiatry*. lthaca, N.Y.: Cornell University Press, 1978.

TEMKIN, Owsei. *The Double Face of Janus and other Essays in the History of Medicine*. Baltimore: Johns Hopkins University Press, 1977.

ULLMANN, Manfred. "Neues zu den diätetischen Schriften des Rufus von Ephesos." *Medizinhistorisches Journal* 9 (1974), 23–40.

Middle Ages

ARNALDUS DE VILLANOVA. *Tractatus de amore heroico*. In *Opera medica Omnia*, vol. 3, edited with an introduction and commentary in English by Michael R. McVaugh. Barcelona: Edicions de la Universitat de Barcelona, 1985.

AVICENNA. [*Canon of Medicine (al-Qānūn fī l-ṭibb)*] *Praesens maximus codex est totius scientie medicine principis Aboali Abinsene cum expositionibus omnium principalium et illustrium interpretum eius*, 1–5. Venice: P. Pincius, 1523.

BAADER, Gerhard. "Zur Terminologie des Constantinus Africanus." *Medizinhistorisches Journal* 2 (1967), 36–53.

BECCARIA, Augusto. *I codici di medicina del periodo presalernitano (seccoli IX, X, XI)*. Rome: Edizioni di Storia e Letteratura, 1956.

BRANN, Noel L. "Alchemy and Melancholy in Medieval and Renaissance Thought: A Query into the Mystical Basis of their Relationship." *Ambix* 32 (1985), 127–148.

CHASTEL, André. "La mélancolie de Pétrarque." *Cahiers du Sud* 38 (1953), 25–34.

CIAVOLELLA, Massimo. *La "malattia d'amore" dall'Antichità al Medioevo*. Rome: Bulzoni, 1976.

DINANTO, David de. *Quaternulorum fragmenta*. Primum ed. Marianus Kurdzialek. Studia mediewistyczne 3, Polska Akademia Nauk, Instytut Filozofii i Sociologii. Warsaw: Panstwowe wydawnictwo naukowe, 1963.

GERSON, Jean. *De passionibus animae*. In *Œuvres complètes*, vol. 9, *L' œuvre doctrinale*, edited by Palémon Glorieux. Paris: Desclée, 1973.

—*Enumeratio peccatorum ab Alberto posita*. In *Œuvres complètes*, vol. 9, *L'œuvre doctrinale*, edited by Palémon Glorieux. Paris: Desclée, 1973.

HEGER, Henrik. *Die Melancholie bei den französischen Lyrikern des Spätmittelalters.* Romanistische Versuche und Vorarbeiten 21. Bonn: Romanisches Seminar der Universität Bonn, 1967.

HILDEGARD VON BINGEN. *Cause et cure* [*Causae et curae*]. Edited by Laurence Moulinier, with an introduction in French. Rarissima mediaevalia. Opera latina 1. Berlin: Akademie Verlag, 2003. Translated from Latin into English by Priscilla Throop as *Causes and Cures: The Complete English Translation of Hildegardis Causae et Curae Libri VI.* 2nd ed. Charlotte, Vermont: Medieval MS, 2008.

—*Liber divinorum operum.* Edited by Albert Derolez and Peter Dronke. Corpus Christianorum Continuatio Mediaevalis 92. Turnhout: Brepols, 1996. Translated from the Latin into English by Priscilla Throop as *Book of Divine Works: The Complete English Translation of Hildegardis Bingensis Liber Divinorum Operum.* Charlotte, Vermont: Medieval MS, 2009.

JEHL, Rainer. *Melancholie und Acedia. Ein Beitrag zur Anthropologie und Ethik Bonaventuras.* Paderborn/Munich: Schöningh, 1984.

KLOSTERMANN, Wolf-Günter. "Acedia und schwarze Galle." *Romanische Forschungen* 74, no. 1/2 (1964), 183–193.

KUKSEWICZ, Zdzislaw. "Les Problemata de Pietro d'Abano et leur rédaction par Jean de Jandun." *Medioevo* 11 (1985), 113–185.

LITT, Thomas. *Les Corps célestes dans l'univers de Saint Thomas d'Aquin.* Philosophes médiévaux 7. Louvain: Publications universitaires; Paris: Béatrice-Nauwelaerts, 1963.

LOWES, John Livingstone. "The Loveres Maladye of Hereos." *Modern Philology* 11, no. 4 (1914), 491–546.

NORPOTH, Leo. "Zur Bio-, Bibliographie und Wissenschaftslehre des Pietro d'Abano, Mediziners, Philosophen und Astronomen in Padua." *Kyklos. Jahrbuch des Instituts für Geschichte der Medizin* 3 (1930), 292–353.

OTTOSSON, Per-Gunnar. *Scholastic Medicine and Philosophy: A Study of Commentaries on Galen's Tegni (ca. 1300–1450).* Naples: Bibliopolis, 1984.

PETRUS DE ABANO. *Conciliator differentiarum philosophorum et precipue medicorum.* Venice: Johannes Herbort, 1483.

RHAZES. *Continens... qui omnia fere que ad rem medicam pertinent... compleaitur.* Venice, 1509.

SCHIPPERGES, Heinrich. *Arabische Medizin im lateinischen Mittelalter.* Sitzungsberichte der Heidelberger Akademie der Wissenschaften. Berlin/Heidelberg/New York: Springer, 1976.

—*Die Assimilation der arabischen Medizin durch das lateinische Mittelalter.* Sudhoffs Archiv, Supplement 3. Wiesbaden: F. Steiner, 1964.

—*Der Garten der Gesundheit. Medizin im Mittelalter.* Munich/Zurich: Artemis, 1985.

—"Melancolia als ein mittelalterlicher Sammelbegriff für Wahnvorstellungen." *Studium Generale* 20 (1967), 723–736. Reprinted in *Melancholie*, edited by Lutz Walther, 49–76. Leipzig: Reclam, 1999.

SCHNEIDER, Ilse. "Die Schule von Salerno als Erbin der antiken Medizin und ihre Bedeutung für das Mittelalter." *Philologus* 115 (1971), 278–291.

WENZEL, Siegfried. "Petrarch's Accidia." *Studies in the Renaissance* 8 (1961), 36–48.

Late Fifteenth Century

BENESCH, Dieter. *Marsilio Ficino's "De triplici vita" (Florenz 1489) in deutschen Bearbeitungen und Übersetzungen.* Europäische Hochschulschriften: Series 1, Deutsche Literatur und Germanistik 207. Frankfurt am Main: Lang, 1977.

CHASTEL, André. *Marsile Ficin et l'art.* Travaux d'humanisme et renaissance 14. Geneva: Droz, 1975.

—"Melancholia in the Sonnets of Lorenzo de Medici." *Journal of the Warburg and Courtauld Institutes* 8 (1945), 61–67.

CRISTALDI, Rosario Vittorio. "Homo ille melancholicus. II 'Trentasettenne' di Lorenzo Lotto." *Synaxis* 2 (1984), 201–238.

FICINO, Marsilio. *De triplici vita.* Basel: Johannes Amerbach, [not after 1498]. *De vita Libri tres* [Venice, 1498]. Reprint of the Venice edition, with a critical apparatus, notes and afterword by Martin Plessner, edited by Felix Klein-Franke. Hildesheim/New York: Olms, 1978. Translated into English by Charles Boer as *The Book of Life.* A translation of *Liber de vita* (or *De vita triplici*). Irving, Texas: Spring Publications, 1980.

—*Epistolae.* Nuremberg: Anton Koberger, 1497. Selected letters published in English as *Meditations on the Soul.* Translated from the Latin by members of the Language Department of the School of Economic Science, London. London: Shepheard-Walwyn, 2002.

SCHÖNFELDT, Klaus. "Die Temperamentenlehre in deutschsprachigen Handschriften des 15. Jahrhunderts." Diss. Heidelberg University, 1962.

Dürer

ANZELEWSKY, Fedja. *Dürer. Werk und Wirkung.* Stuttgart: Elecca-Klett-Cotta, 1980. Translated into English by Heide Grieve as *Dürer: His Art and Life.* New York: Alpine Fine Arts, 1980.

—*Dürer-Studien. Untersuchungen zu den ikonographischen und geistesgeschichtlichen Grundlagen seiner Werke zwischen den beiden Italienreisen.* Berlin: Deutscher Verlag für Kunstwissenschaft, 1983.

AREND, Henrich Conrad. *Das Gedächtnis der Ehren … Albrecht Dürers, um eben die Zeit, als er vor 200 Jahren die Welt verlassen.* Goslar: König, 1728. Reproduced in a facsimile edition with an afterword by Matthias Mende. Unterschneidheim: Alfons Uhl, 1978.

BIALOSTOCKI, Jan. *Dürer and his Critics: 1500–1971.* Saecula spiritalia 7. Baden-Baden: Valentin Koerner, 1986.

BÖHME, Hartmut. *Albrecht Dürer, Melencolia I. Im Labyrinth der Deutung.* Kunststück. Frankfurt am Main: Fischer Taschenbuch, 1989.

BONICATTI, Maurizio. "Dürer nella storia delle idee umanistiche fra Quattrocento e Cinquecento." *Journal of Medieval and Renaissance Studies* 1 (1971), 131–250. See also 268–269 in the English review of this title from Wolfgang Stechow, "Recent Dürer Studies," *The Art Bulletin* 56 no. 2 (1974) 259–270.

CALVESI, Maurizio. "A noir (Melencolia I)." *Storia dell'Arte* 1–2 (1969), 37–96.

CELTES, Conrad. *Oratio in gymnasio in lngelstadio publice recitata.* [Augsburg, 1492 (Ratdolt)]. Bibliotheca scriptorum Medii Recentisque Aevorum, Saecula XV–XVI. Edited by Hans Rupprich. Leipzig: Teubner, 1932. Reprinted in Rupprich's *Humanismus und Renaissance in den deutschen Städten und Universitäten*, 226–238. Leipzig: Reclam, 1935. Translated into English by Leonard Forster in *Selections from Conrad Celtis 1459–1508*, edited by Forster, 36–65. Cambridge: Cambridge University Press, 1948.

DÜRER, Albrecht. *Schriftlicher Nachlass.* 3 vols. Edited by Hans Rupprich. Berlin: Deutscher Verein für Kunstwissenschaft, 1956–1969.

FINKE, Ulrich, "Dürers Melancholie in der französischen und englischen Literatur und Kunst des 19. Jahrhunderts." *Zeitschrift des deutschen Vereins für Kunstwissenschaft* 30 (1976), 63–81.

FISCHER, Ludolph. "Zur Deutung de magischen Quadrates in Dürers *Melencolia I.*" *Zeitschrift der Deutschen Morgenländischen Gesellschaft* 103, n.s. 28, no. 2 (1953), 308–314.

HECKSCHER, William S. "Melancholia (1541): An Essay in the Rhetoric of Description by Joachim Camerarius." In *Joachim Camerarius (1500–1574): Beiträge zur Geschichte des Humanismus im Zeitalter der Reformation*, edited by Frank Baron, 32–120. Munich: Wilhelm Fink, 1978.

HEYER, Gustav-Richard. "Dürer's Melancolia und ihre Symbolik." *Eranos-Jahrbuch* 2 (1934), 231–261. Zurich: Rhein-Verlag, 1935.

HOFFMANN, Konrad. "Dürers 'Melencolia.'" In *Kunst als Bedeutungsträger. Gedenkschrift für Günter Bandmann*, edited by W. Busch, R. Haussherr, and E. Trier, 251–277. Berlin: Gebr. Mann, 1978.

La Gloire de Dürer. Colloque international Albrecht Dürer dans l'art et la pensée européens, organisé par l'Université de Nice, Faculté des Lettres et des Sciences Humaines, 1972. Actes et colloques 13. Edited by Jean Richer. Paris: Klincksieck, 1974.

MACKAY, Alan L. "Dürer's technique." *Nature* 301 (February 1983), 652.

MANN, Thomas. "Dürer." [1928] In *Altes und Neues. Kleine Prosa aus fünf Jahrzehnten*, 715–718. Frankfurt am Main: S. Fischer, 1953.

MENDE, Mathias. *Dürer-Bibliographie. Zur 500. Wiederkehr des Geburtstages von Albrecht Dürer, 21 Mai 1971.* Wiesbaden: Harrassowitz, 1971.

MEYERS, Jeffrey. "Dürer and Manns Doctor Faustus." *Art International* (Lugano) 17, no. 8 (October 1973), 56–60; 63–64.

PANOFSKY, Erwin. *The Life and Art of Albrecht Dürer.* 4th ed. Princeton, N.J.: Princeton University Press, 1955. Republished with a new introduction by Jeffrey Chipps Smith in the Princeton Classic Editions series, 2005.

PFEIFFER, Elisabeth. "Zahlen und Zahlenverhältnisse im magischen Quadrat Dürers." *Mitteilungen des Vereins für Geschichte der Stadt Nürnberg* 58 (1971), 168–207.

RITTERBUSH, Philip C. "Dürer and Geometry: Symmetry in an Enigma." *Nature* 301 (January 1983), 197–198.

RÖSCH, Siegfried. "Gedanken eines Naturforschers zu Dürers 'Melancholie.'" *Mitteilungen des Vereins für Geschichte der Stadt Nürnberg* 58 (1971), 161–167.

ROSSMANN, Kurt. "Wert und Grenze der Wissenschaft. Zur Symbolik von Dürers Kupferstich 'Melencolia I.'" In *Offener Horizont: Festschrift für Karl Jaspers*, edited by Klaus Piper, 126–146. Munich: Piper, 1953.

SAFFARO, Lucio. "Analisi delle strutture nascoste nella Malinconia di Dürer." *Nuova Scienza. Rivista mensile di ricerca e di scoperte* (September 1984), 36–50.

SEHAAL, Hermann. "Geometrische Studien zu Dürers Melencolia." *Der Mathematikunterricht* 28 (1982), 66–83.

SCHRÖDER, Eberhard. *Dürer: Kunst und Geometrie. Dürers künstlerisches Schaffen aus der Sicht seiner "Underweysung."* Berlin: Akademie-Verlag, 1980. Also published as vol. 37 in the series Wissenschaft und Kultur. Basel/Boston: Birkhäuser, 1980.

SCHUSTER, Peter Klaus. "Das Bild der Bilder. Zur Wirkungsgeschichte von Dürers Melancholiekupferstich." *Idea. Jahrbuch der Hamburger Kunsthalle* 1 (1982), 72–134.

—*Melencolia I. Dürers Denkbild*. 2 vol. Berlin: Gebr. Mann Verlag, 1991.

SOHM, Philip L. "Dürer's *Melencolia I*: The Limits of Knowledge." *Studies in the History of Art*. 9 (1980), 13–32.

STECHOW, Wolfgang. "Recent Dürer Studies." *The Art Bulletin* 56 no. 2 (June 1974), 259–270.

WÖLFFLIN, Heinrich. "Zur Interpretation von Dürers 'Melancholie.'" In *Gedanken zur Kunstgeschichte. Gedrucktes und Ungedrucktes*, 96–105. 3rd ed. Basel: Schwabe, 1941.

WUTTKE, Dieter. "Dürer und Celtis: Von der Bedeutung des Jahres 1500 für den deutschen Humanismus; 'Jahrhundertfeier als symbolische Form.'" *Journal of Medieval and Renaissance Studies* 10 (1980), 73–129.

Sixteenth and Early Seventeenth Century

ADAMS, Thomas. *Diseases of the Soule*. London: G. Purslowe for J. Budge, 1616.

[ARISTOTLE]. *Le Miroir des Melancholicques: descript en la XXXe section des Problemes D'aristote concernant ce qui appartient à Prudence, Entendement & Sapience, traduict de Grec en Francoys par Meury Riflant.* Paris [Rouen?]: pour N. de Burges; Jehan Petit, 1543.

BOAISTUAU, Pierre [also known as Pierre Launay]. *Le Theatre du monde, ou il est faict un ample discours des miseres humaines. Avec un brief discours de*

l'excellence & dignité de l'homme. Paris: V. Sertenas, 1561. Translated into English by John Alday as *Theatrum mundi, the theatre or rule of the world, wherein may be sene the running race and course of euerye mans life, as touching miserie and felicity … wherevnto is added a learned, and maruellous worke of the excellencie of mankinde. Written in the Frenche & Latin tongues by Peter Boaystuau, and translated into English by Iohn Alday*. London: H. D. for Thomas Hacket, [1566?].

Böhme, Jacob. *Christosophia oder der Weg zu Christo verfasset in Neun Büchlein. Das Achte Büchlein: De Quatuor Complexionibus oder Trost-Schrift von vier Complexionen* … Geschrieben im Martio Anno 1624 … Gedruckt im Jahre des ausgebornen grossen Heils 1730. Reproduced in *Jakob Böhme. Sämtliche Schriften*, facsimile reprint of the 1730 edition in eleven volumes, vol. 4, edited by Will-Erich Peuckert. Stuttgart: Frommann, 1957. Translated into English by Peter Erb as *The Way to Christ*, with an introduction by Erb and preface by Winfried Zeller. New York: Paulist Press, 1978.

Breton, Nicholas. *Melancholike Humours, in verses of diuerse natures*. London: R. Bradocke, 1600. *Melancholike Humours*. Edited with an "Essay on Elizabethan Melancholy" by George Bagshawe Harrison. Elizabethan Gallery 2. London: Scholartis Press, 1929.

Bright, Timothy. *A Treatise of Melancholie. Containing the causes thereof … with the phisicke cure, and spirituall consolation for such as haue thereto adioyned an afflicted conscience*. London: Thomas Vaucrollier, 1586. Reproduced with an introduction by Hardin Craig. Facsimile Text Society 50. New York: Columbia University Press, 1940. Reprinted Amsterdam: Theatrum Orbis Terrarum, 1969.

Burton, Robert. *The Anatomy of Melancholy, what it is, with all the kindes, causes, symptomes, prognostickes, and severall cures of it. Philosophically, medicinally, historically opened and cut up. By Democritus Iunior*. Oxford: Iohn Lichfield and Iames Short for Henry Cripps, 1621. *The Anatomy of Melancholy*. Edited by Thomas C. Faulkner, Nicolas K. Kiessling, Rhonda L. Blair, with an introduction by J. B. Bamborough. Commentary by J. B. Bamborough with Martin Dodsworth. 6 vols: text vols 1–3; commentary vols. 4–6. Oxford English Texts. Oxford: Clarendon Press, 1989–2001.

Du Laurens, André. *Discours de la conservation de la veve: des maladies melancholiques: des catarrhes: & de la vieillesse… Reveuz et augmentez de plusieurs chapitres*. Paris: J. Mettayer, 1597. Translated into English by Richard Surphlet [Surflet] as *A Discourse of the Preservation of the Sight, of melancholike Diseases, of Rheumes, and of old age* … London: F. Kingston, 1599. Reproduced with an introduction by Sanford V. Larkey. Shakespeare Association Facsimiles 15. London: Oxford University Press for the Shakespeare Association, 1938.

Ferrand, Jacques. *Traité de l'essence et guérison de l'amour, ou De La mélancholie érotique*. Toulouse: Vve J. et R. Colomiez, 1610. Also appeared as *De La Maladie d'amour ou mélancholie érotique. Discours curieux qui enseigne à cognoistre l'essence, les causes, les signes, et les remèdes de ce mal fantastique.*

Paris: D. Moreau, 1623. Translated into English by Edmund Chilmead as *Erōtomania or A treatise discoursing of the essence, causes, symptomes, prognosticks, and cure of love, or erotique melancholy.* Oxford: L. Lichfield, 1640.

GUIBELET, Jourdain. *Trois discours philosophiques: Le I. de la comparaison de l'homme avec le monde; ... Le lll. de l'humeur mélancolique, mis de nouveau en lumière.* Évreux: Antoine Le Marié, 1603.

—*Examen de l'Examen des esprits.* Paris: Michel Soly, 1631.

HEYD, Michael. "Robert Burton's Sources on Enthusiasm and Melancholy: From a Medical Tradition to Religious Controversy." *History of European ldeas* 5 (1984), 17–44.

[HIPPOCRATES]. *Epistola ad Damagetum.* In Laurent Joubert, *Traité du ris ... Item, La cause morale du ris de Démocrite, expliquée & temognée par le divin Hippocras en ses épîtres.* Translated from the Latin into French by Jean Guichard. Paris: N. Chesneau, 1579.

—*La Conference et entrevue d'Hippocrate et de Démocrite tirée du grec et commentée par Marcelin Bompart.* Paris: Vve P. Gaultier, 1631.

HUARTE DE SAN JUAN, Juan. *Examen de ingenios para las sciencias.* Baeza, 1575; Valencia, 1580. Published in English as *Examen de ingenios. The Examination of mens Wits ... Translated out of the Spanish tongue by M. Camillo Camili. Englished out of his Italian, by R[ichard] C[rew]. Esquire.* London: Adam Islip, for R. Watkins, 1594.

LA PRIMAUDAYE, Pierre de. *Académie Françoise. En laquelle il est traicté de l'institution des moeurs, & de ce qui concerne le bien & heureuseme[n]t viure en tous estats & conditions.* Paris: Guillaume Chaudiere, 1577. Translated into English by Thomas Bowes as *The French Academie, wherein is discoursed the institution of manners.* London: Edmund Bollifant for G. Bishop and R. Newbery, 1586.

—*Suite de l'Académie Françoise, en laquelle u est traicté de l'homme ...* Paris: Guillaume Chaudiere, 1583. Translated into English by Thomas Bowes as *The Second Part of the French Academie.* London: [Printed by George Bishop, Ralph Newbery, and R. Barker,] 1594.

—*L'Académie Francoise, distinguée en quatre volumes, traitans I. de la Philosophie Morale. II. de la Philosophie Humaine. III. de la Philosophie Naturelle. IV. de la Philosophie Chrestienne ... Revue et corrigée de nouveau.* 4 vols. [Geneva?], 1608–1609. Translated into English by Thomas Bowes, Richard Dolman (Bk. 3) and W. P. (William Phillip?, Bk. 4) as *The French Academie. Fully discoursed and finished in Foure Workes. 1. Institution of manners and callings of all estates. 2. Concerning the soule and body of man. 3. A notable description of the whole world, &c. 4. Christian philosophie, instructing the true and onely meanes to eternal life; this fourth part neuer before published in English.* London: Thomas Adams, 1618.

LEMNIUS, Levinus. *The Touchstone of Complexions ... contayning ... rules ... whereby euery one may ... knowe, as well, the exact state ... of his Body outwardly, as also the inclinations ... of his Mynde inwardly. First wrytten in*

Latine, by Leuine Lemnic, and now Englished by Thomas Newton. London: Thomas Marsh, 1576; 1581.

PARACELSUS. Das Buch Paragranum [1530]. In *Sämtliche Werke. Medizinische, naturwissenschaftliche und philosophische Schriften*, vol. 8, edited by Karl Sudhoff, 142 f. Munich: Barth, 1924. Translated and edited with a commentary and introduction, by Andrew Weeks as *Paracelsus (Theophrastus Bombastus von Hohenheim, 1494–1541): Essential Theoretical Writings*. Leiden/Boston: Brill, 2008.

PLATERUS, Felix [Felix Platter] *Observationum in hominis affectibus plerisque, corpori et animo, functionum laesione, dolore, aliave molestia et vitia incommodantibus, libri tres*. Basel: C. Waldkirch, 1614.

R.S. [Samuel ROWLANDS]. *Democritus, or Doctor Merry-Man his Medicines, against Melancholy Humors*. London: Printed for John Deane, 1607.

TIRSO DE MOLINA [Fray Gabriel Tellez]. *El Melancólico* [1611]. In *Obras Dramaticas Completas*, edited by Blanca de los Rios, I:107–165. 3rd ed. Madrid: Aguilar, 1969.

WALKINGTON, Thomas. *The Optick Glasse of Humors or, The touchstone of a golden temperature: or the Philosophers stone to make a golden temper… Lately pend by T. W. Master of Artes*. London: Imprinted by Iohn Windet for Martin Clerke, 1607.

WRIGHT, Thomas. *The Passions of the Minde*. London: V. Simmes for W. B. [Walter Burre], 1601. Also published as *The Passions of the Minde in Generall. Corrected, and … augmented*, 1604. Reprinted (1604 edition) with an introduction by Thomas O. Sloan at Urbana: University of Illinois Press, 1971.

Modern Representations

BABB, Lawrence. *The Elizabethan Malady: A Study of Melancholia in English Literature from 1580 to 1642*. Studies in Language and Literature. East Lansing: Michigan State College Press, 1951.

—*Sanity in Bedlam: A Study of Robert Burton's Anatomy of Melancholy*. East Lansing: Michigan State University Press, 1959.

BIEBER, Gustav Arthur. *Der Melancholikertypus Shakespeares und sein Ursprung*. Anglistische Arbeiten 3. Heidelberg: Winter, 1913.

JORDAN-SMITH, Paul. *Bibliographia Burtoniana: A Study of Robert Burton's The Anatomy of Melancholy; With a Bibliography of Burton's Writings*. Stanford: Stanford University Press, 1931.

LYONS, Bridget Gellert. *Voices of Melancholy: Studies in Literary Treatments of Melancholy in Renaissance England*. Ideas and Forms in English Literature. London: Routledge & Kegan Paul, 1971.

SCHALK, Fritz. "Melancholie im Theater von Tirso de Molina." In *Ideen und Formen. Festschrift für Hugo Friedrich zum 24. XII. 1964*, edited by F. Schalk, 215–238. Frankfurt am Main: Klosternann, 1965.

SCREECH, Michael Andrew. *Montaigne and Melancholy: The Wisdom of the Essays*. London: Duckworth, 1983.

WEINRICH, Harald. *Das Ingenium Don Quijotes. Ein Beitrag zur literarischen Charakterkunde*. Forschungen zur romanischen Philologie 1. Münster: Aschendorff, 1956.

YATES, Frances. *The Occult Philosophy in the Elizabethan Age*. London: Routledge & Kegan Paul, 1979.

Seventeenth Century, after Böhme and Burton

BENJAMIN, Walter. *Ursprung des deutschen Trauerspiels*. Berlin: Rowohlt, 1928. Reprinted in Benjamin, *Gesammelte Schriften* 1.1, edited by Rolf Tiedemann and Hermann Schweppenhäuser. Frankfurt am Main: Suhrkamp, 1974. Translated into English by John Osborne as *The Origin of German Tragic Drama*. New York: Verso, 1977.

CARDANUS, Hieronymus [Girolamo Cardano]. *Opera Omnia II*. Lyon, 1663. Reproduced in *Opera Omnia*, vol. 2, *Moralia quaedam et Physica*. Facsimile of the Lyon 1663 edition [10 vols], with an introduction by August Buck. Stuttgart-Bad Cannstatt: Frommann, 1966.

OBERMÜLLER, Klara. *Zur Melancholie in der deutschen Lyrik des Barock*. Studien zur Germanistik, Anglistik und Komparatistik 19. Bonn: Bouvier, 1974.

PEUCKERT, Will-Erich. *Gabalia. Ein Versuch zur Geschichte der magia naituralis im 16. bis 18. Jahrhundert*. Vol. 2 of *Pansophie. Ein Versuch zur Geschichte der weissen und schwarzen Magie*. Berlin: Erich Schmidt, 1967.

SCHMITZ, Heinz-Günter. "Das Melancholieproblem in Wissenschaft und Kunst der frühen Neuzeit." *Sudhoffs Archiv* 60 (1976), 135–162.

SEPTALIUS, Ludovicus [Lodovico Settala]. *In Aristotelis Problemata commentaria* … 3 vols. Lyon: Claude Landry, 1632.

WATANABE-O'KELLY, Helen. *Melancholie und die melancholische Landschaft. Ein Beitrag zur Geistesgeschichte des 17 Jahrhunderts*. Basler Studien zur deutschen Sprache und Literatur 54. Bern: Francke, 1978.

Eighteenth and Nineteenth Centuries

BAUDELAIRE, Charles. "Épigraphe pour un Œuvre condamné" [1861]. In *Œuvres complètes*, 2 vols., edited by Claude Pichois, 1: 137. Bibliothèque de la Pléiade. Paris: Gallimard, 1975.

BORCHMEYER, Dieter. *Macht und Melancholie. Schillers Wallenstein*. Frankfurt am Main: Athenäum, 1988.

BUSCHENDORF, Bernhard. *Goethes mythische Denkform. Zur Ikonographie der "Wahlverwandtschaften."* Frankfurt am Main: Suhrkamp, 1986.

CASTORINA, Giuseppe Gaetano. *Le forme della malinconia; ricerche sul sonetto in lnghilterra (1747–1800)*. Saggi di letterature moderne. Sezione di letteratura inglese, angloamericana, e letterature anglofone 2. Bologna: Patron, 1978.

DÍAZ-PLAJA, Guillerrno. *Tratado de las melancolias españolas*. Madrid: Sala, 1975.

Diderot, Denis. "Mélancolie." In *Encyclopédie, ou Dictionnaire raisonné des sciences, des arts et des métiers*, par une société de gens de lettres. 10: 307–310. Neufchastel (sic), 1765.

Kuhn, Reinhard. *The Demon of Noontide: Ennui in Western Literature*. Princeton, N.J.: Princeton University Press, 1976.

Loquai, Fritz. *Künstler und Melancholie in der Romantik*. Helicon 4. Frankfurt am Main/Bern: Lang, 1984.

Mattenklott, Gert. *Melancholie in der Dramatik des Sturm und Drang*. Augmented and revised edition. Königstein im Taunus: Athenäum, 1985.

McCarthy, Vincent A. "'Melancholy' and 'Religious Melancholy' in Kierkegaard." *Kierkegaardiana. Journal of the Kierkegaard Society* 10 (1977), 152–165.

Mehnert, Henning. *Melancholie und Inspiration. Begriffs- und wissenschaftsgeschichtliche Untersuchungen zur poetischen Psychologie Baudelaires, Flauberts und Mallarmés, mit einer Studie über Rabelais*. Heidelberg: Carl Winter, 1978.

Nordström, Folke. *Goya, Saturn and Melancholy: Studies in the Art of Goya*. Acta Universitatis Upsaliensis. Stockholm: Almquist and Wiskell, 1962.

—"Baudelaire and Dürer's Melencolia I: A Study of a Portrait of Baudelaire by Manet." In *Contributions to the History and Theory of Art*, edited by Rudolf Zeitler. Acta Universitatis Upsaliensis; Figura 6. 148–160. Upsala: Universitatis Upsalienisis, 1967.

Redon, Odilon. *À soi-même, journal (1887–1915): notes sur la vie, l'art et les artistes*. Paris: José Corti, 1979. First published Paris: H. Floury, 1922.

Schalk, Fritz. "Der Artikel 'Mélancolie' in der Diderotschen Enzyklopädie." In *Studien zur französischen Aufklärung*, 206–220. Frankfurt am Main: Klostermann, 1977.

Schings, Hans-Jürgen. *Melancholie und Aufklärung. Melancholiker und ihre Kritiker in Erfahrungsseelenkunde und Literatur des 18. Jahrhunderts*. Stuttgart: Metzler, 1977.

Schmitz, Heinz-Günter. "Phantasie und Melancholie. Barocke Dichtung im Dienst der Diätetik." *Medizinhistorisches Journal* 4 (1969), 210–230.

Völker, Ludwig. *Muse Melancholie, Therapeutikum Poesie. Studien zum Melancholie-Problem in der deutschen Lyrik von Hölty bis Benn*. Munich: Fink, 1978.

—ed. "*Komm, heilige Melancholie.*" *Eine Anthologie deutscher Melancholie Gedichte; mit Ausblicken auf die europäische Melancholie-Tradition in Literatur- und Kunstgeschichte*. Stuttgart: Reclam, 1983.

Twentieth Century

Bauer, Markus. *Melancholie in den Schriften Walter Benjamins*. Magister-Arbeit, Germanist. Seminar, Universität Marburg, 1985.

Benjamin, Walter. "Linke Melancholie. Zu Erich Kästners neuem Gedichtbuch." In *Gesammelte Schriften*, vol. 3, *Kritiken und Rezensionen*, 279–283. Frankfurt am Main: Suhrkamp, 1972. Originally published in *Die Gesellschaft* 8, no. 1,

1931. Translated into English in *Selected Writings, vol. 2, 1927–1934*, edited by Michael W. Jennings, Howard Eiland and Gary Smith, with translations by Rodney Livingstone and others, 423–427. Cambridge, Mass./London: Belknap Press, 1999.

BERGSTEN, Gunilla. *Thomas Manns Doktor Faustus. Untersuchungen zu den Quellen und zur Struktur des Romans*. Studia litterarum Upsaliensia 3. Stockholm: Svenska Bokförlaget, 1963.

BLAMBERGER, Günter. *Versuch über den deutschen Gegenwartsroman. Krisenbewußtsein und Neubegründung im Zeichen der Melancholie*. Stuttgart: Metzler, 1985.

CLAIR, Jean. "'Sous le signe de Saturne': Ordre visuel et ordre politique; notes sur l'allégorie de la Mélancolie dans l'art de l'entre-deux-guerres en Allemagne et en ltalie." *Cahiers du Musée national d'art moderne* 7/8 (1981), 177–207.

GRASS, Günter. "Vom Stillstand im Fortschritt. Variationen zu Albrecht Dürers Kupferstich 'Melencolia I.'" Appended to *Aus dem Tagebuch einer Schnecke*, 340–369. Neuwied/ Darmstadt: Luchterhand, 1972. Translated into English by Ralph Manheim as "On Stasis in Progress: Variations on Albrecht Dürer's Engraving *Melencolia I*," in *The Diary of a Snail*. New York: Harcourt Brace Jovanovich, 1973. Also in the exhibition catalogue *Albrecht Dürer and his Legacy: The Graphic Work of a Renaissance Artist*, ed. Giulia Bartrum, 61–76. Princeton, N.J.: Princeton University Press, 2002.

GUARDINI, Romano. *Vom Sinn der Schwermut*. Zürich: Die Arche, 1949. Translated into English by Gregory Roettger as "The Meaning of Melancholy," in *The Focus of Freedom*, 55–94. Baltimore: Helicon, 1966.

SAUERLAND, Karol, ed. *Melancholie und Enthusiasmus. Studien zur Literatur- und Geistesgeschichte der Jahrhundertwende; Eine internationale Tagung veranstaltet vom Österreichischen Kulturinstitut in Bachotek, Oktober 1985*. Frankfurt am Main/Bem: Lang, 1988.

SONTAG, Susan. *Under the Sign of Saturn*. New York: Farrar, Straus & Giroux, 1980.

Psychiatry and Psychoanalysis

ESQUIROL, Jean Étienne Dominique. *Des passions considérées comme causes, symptômes et moyens curatifs de l'aliénation mentale*. Paris: Didot Jeune, 1805.

—"Mélancolie." In *Dictionnaire des sciences médicales par une société de médecins et de chirurgiens*, vol. 32, 147–183. Paris: Panckoucke, 1819.

—*Des maladies mentales, considérées sous les rapports médical, hygiénique et médico-légal*. Paris: J. B. Bailliere, 1838. Published in German as *Von den Geisteskrankheiten*, edited by Erwin. H. Ackerknecht. Hubers Klassiker der Medizin und der Naturwissenschaften 11. Bern: H. Huber, 1968. Translated into English, with additions, by Ebenezer Kingsbury Hunt as *Mental Maladies: A Treatise on Insanity*. Philadelphia: Lea and Blanchard, 1845.

FREUD, Sigmund. "Trauer und Melancholie" (1917 [1915]). In *Gesammelte Werke* 10, 428–446. Frankfurt am Main: S. Fischer, 1967. Translated into English as "Mourning and Melancholia," in *The Standard Edition of the Complete*

Psychological Works of Sigmund Freud, vol.14, *1914–1916: On the History of the Psycho-Analytic Movement, Papers on Metapsychology and Other Works*, 237–258, edited by James Strachey. London: Hogarth Press, 1957.

SCHMIDT-DEGENHARD, Michael. *Melancholie und Depression. Zur Problemgeschichte der depressiven Erkrankungen seit Beginn des 19. Jahrhunderts*. Stuttgart/Berlin: Kohlhammer, 1983.

TELLENBACH, Hubert. *Melancholie. Problemgeschichte, Endogenität, Typologie, Pathogenese, Klinik*. With a foreword by V. E. von Gebsattel IV and expanded ed. Berlin/Heidelberg/New York: Springer, 1983.

—*Psychiatrie als geistige Medizin*. Munich: Verlag für Angewandte Wissenschaften, 1987.

WHITE, John. *The Masks of Melancholy*. Downers Grove, Ill.: InterVarsity Press, 1982.

Addendum

ON THE TEXT HISTORY OF [PS-] ARISTOTLE, *PROBLEM* XXX, 1

The importance of the *Problem* XXX, 1 for the history of the concept of melancholy has long been recognised in the scholarly tradition. Although many editions of the Greek text were published since the mid-nineteenth century, some accompanied by a complete translation and commentary, others limited to a critical edition of the text, or as a part of the *Corpus aristotelicum*, no scholarly consensus has been reached regarding its author, nor the exact date of its composition. The philological history of this *Problem* is of course part of the greater discussion on Aristotle's *Problems* and it is therefore important to consider the general context of this discussion in order to get a clearer idea of the significance of this particular *Problem*.

Most scholars today agree about the fact that the collection of *Problems* (*Problemata physica)* attributed to Aristotle, of which *Problem* XXX, 1 is a part, has been neglected from the start. The reason often alleged for this neglect is the fragmentary composition of these texts, which stands in strong contrast to the architecture of the Aristotelian treatises. This difference in style has been put forward as an argument against Aristotelian authorship, but it is today considered as perfectly compatible with Aristotle's research methods on many different topics of inquiry. But this doesn't settle the discussion. A majority of scholars would agree with István Bodnár, who describes it as a "peripatetic compilation, often dependent on Theophrastan and even later material."[1] This collection contains nearly 890 texts, arranged in 38 sections or chapters devoted to particular subjects and edited under the common category of *Problems*. That it is considered as a collection of shorter treatises concerning physical matters or questions is, in itself, a problem, since the collection in fact presents *Problems* on a wide variety of topics, from philology to music, mathematics, biology, anthropology, law and many others.[2] What would have been the unifying principle, if not precisely this form of fragmentary inquiry serving a more general purpose? The literary form of the *Problems* is also worth careful study, if only for the influence of these texts, during the Middle Ages and Renaissance, on the formation of an entire literature of *Problems*, which became at that time almost a genre.

The manuscript tradition of about sixty manuscripts has often been mixed, and therefore confused, with the tradition of later collections of *Problems*, as

---

1 I. Bodnár, "The *Problemata physica*: An Introduction", in *The Aristotelian* Problemata Physica: *Philosophical and Scientific Investigations*, ed. R. Mayhew, Leiden and Boston, Brill (Philosophia antiqua, vol. 139), 2015, pp. 1–9.

2 For a complete survey of the *Problems*, including modern editions, manuscripts, modern translations and special editions of individual *Problems*, see the contribution of J. Bertier, "Aristote de Stagire. *Problemata physica*", in *Dictionnaire des philosophes antiques. Supplément*, ed. R. Goulet, Paris, CNRS Éditions, 2003, pp. 574–593. This study concentrates on the Greek tradition and it is completed by a section on the oriental tradition by L. S. Filius.

in the case of the widely circulated collection of Alexander of Aphrodisias.[3] The fact that modern editors of the text had to untangle all these mixed traditions might explain why a satisfactory edition in English has been long in preparation. Such an edition is now available thanks to the excellent work of Robert Mayhew,[4] to which we will return after a short overview of the treatment of *Problem* XXX, 1 in a series of studies leading up to the 1964 edition of the study of melancholy by Erwin Panofsky, Fritz Saxl and Raymond Klibansky.

In his 1903–04 pioneering work on Dürer's engraving, Karl Giehlow had already pointed to the importance of *Problem* XXX, 1, but he did not include an edition of the text;[5] nor did he discuss the doctrine of the *Problem*. He mentioned the richness of the Aristotelian tradition of the *Problemata physica* and referred to an important essay by the German historian Carl Prantl on this tradition.[6] In their study on *Melencolia I*, published in 1923, Erwin Panofsky and Fritz Saxl were the first to give the *Problem* XXX, 1 greater attention.[7] The section devoted to the ancient doctrines of melancholy refers to this text as a writing of Aristotle[8] and presents it as a thoroughly original discussion of the question. In an appendix to their book (Anhang III, p. 93–104), the authors offer a Greek text and a German translation prepared with the help of Heinz Cassirer, who was at the time a student in Hamburg. They refer to the 1922 edition prepared by Charles-Émile Ruelle for the Bibliotheca Teubneriana.[9] The Ruelle edition presents a good survey of prior scholarship on the text, with a bibliographical apparatus and indexes. It was considered to have replaced both the edition prepared by Immanuel Bekker for the standard Aristotle complete edition (Berlin 1831) and the edition published by U. C. Bussemaker for the French edition of Aristotle's works (Paris 1857). A comparison between these three older editions of *Problem* XXX, 1 highlights important philological progress, and this may explain why the edition of Ruelle was also retained by a later editor, W. S. Hett, for his two-volume edition in the Loeb Classical Library in 1936–37.[10] Because of its defective editorial procedures, this edition is today considered faulty.

---

3 For a series of studies on this collection, see PSEUDO ARISTOTELES (Pseudo-Alexander), *Supplementa Problematorum*, ed. and trans. S. Karetanaki and R. W. Sharples, Berlin and New York, Walter de Gruyter, (Peripatoi, vol. 20), 2006.

4 See ARISTOTLE, *Problems*, ed. R. Mayhew, Cambridge, Mass., Harvard University Press (Loeb Classical Library), 2 vols., 2011.

5 K. GIEHLOW, «Dürers Stich 'Melencolia I' und der maximilianische Humanistenkreis», in *Mitteilungen der Gesellschaft für vervielfältigende Kunst* 2 (1903), pp. 29–41; 4 (1904), pp. 6–18 and 57–78; see (1903), p. 30.

6 C. PRANTL, "Über die *Probleme* des Arisloteles", in *Abhandlungen der philos. - philol. Classe der kgl. Bayerischen Akademie der Wissenschaften*, München, 1852, vol. VI, p. 5.

7 See E. PANOFSKY and F. SAXL, *Dürers 'Melencolia I'. Eine Quellen- und Typengeschichtliche Untersuchung*, Leipzig-Berlin, Teubner, 1923.

8 Ibid., p. 15.

9 C.-É. RUELLE, H. KNOELLINGER and J. KLEK (eds.), *Aristotelis quae feruntur Problemata physica*, Leipzig-Berlin, Teubner (Bibliotheca scriptorum graecorum et romanorum Teubneriana), 1922.

10 ARISTOTLE, *Problems*, ed. and trans. A. S. Hett, London, Heinemann (Loeb Classical Library, 2 volumes), 1953–1957.

This leads us to the preparation of the edition of *Saturn and Melancholy* by Erwin Panofsky, Fritz Saxl and Raymond Klibansky, finally published in London and New York in 1964. As the now-available history of this book makes clear,[11] the original German edition of this book, of which the 1938–39 proofs are preserved at the Warburg Institute Archive, was never published.[12] For that edition, the authors had decided to reproduce the Greek text of Ruelle, and had acknowledged the help, for the criticism of the Greek text and for the German translation, of the English translation of E. S. Forster, published in 1927.[13] As several notes on the text illustrate, the authors retained some emendations proposed by Forster. This decision was maintained for the 1964 edition, where we find the full Greek text, for which the help of Dr Lotte Labowsky is acknowledged in the Preface signed by R. Klibansky and E. Panofsky (Fritz Saxl not having survived to see it published).[14] The English translation of *Problem* XXX, 1 found in this edition has also, most certainly, benefited from the textual observations of Dr Labowsky. It is interesting to note that here the text of *Problem* XXX, 1 is mentioned as "attributed to Aristotle".

This edition, which is re-edited here, offers a reproduction of the Greek text of Ruelle (1922), with some corrections by the authors. Some of these are credited to Forster, others to the work of H. P. Richards[15] and others. Except for an important note on a passage showing evident corruption,[16] the improvement on the edition of Ruelle seems limited. However, one must note a remark by the authors, quoting an essay already referred to by Giehlow, on the possibility often alluded to in modern scholarship that the author of *Problem* XXX, 1 could be Theophrastus, a close disciple of Aristotle. They write: "As we know from the list of his writings given in Diogenes Laertius (V, 44) that Theophrastus wrote a book *On Melancholy*, the inference that our *Problem* is connected with this book seems safe."[17] In their analysis of the *Problem* in the subsequent pages, Klibansky and Panofsky still cast some doubt on the authorship; they recall the fact that both Cicero and Plutarch considered the work authentic, but this attribution seems to them quite uncertain.[18] An argument against Aristotelian authorship is later drawn from the contradiction between "the picture of the melancholic as a complete and expressive whole, shown in

---

[11] See the Afterword to the present edition, p. 457

[12] See the unpublished proofs of E. Panofsky, F. Saxl, unter Mitarbeit von R. Klibansky, *Melancholie und Saturn. Studien zur Geschichte der Naturphilosophie, Charakterlehre und Bildenden Kunst*, London, The Warburg Institute, 1939, pp. 17–29, and see note p. 17.

[13] As part of *The Works of Aristotle Translated into English*, ed. W. D. Ross, Oxford, Clarendon Press, 1927, vol. VII.

[14] See this edition, p. xxx.

[15] H. P. Richards, *Aristotelica*, London, Grant Richards, 1915.

[16] See p. 24, note 58 in the present edition. Cf. *Problem* XXX, 1, 954a39–b2 in Ruelle, *Aristotelis quae feruntur Problemata physica*.

[17] See the present edition, p. 23, note 57.

[18] They write: "From this it is clear at least that it bore Aristotle's name even before the edition of his complete works, which appeared probably not earlier than the first or second century A.D. But had it any right to bear that name?"; present edition p. 33, note 65.

Problem XXX, 1, and that which we can piece together, mosaic-wise, from statements made by Aristotle elsewhere."[19] But this statement is followed by the conclusion that "the *Problem* links up with genuine Aristotelian themes."[20]

The next step in the edition of *Problem* XXX, 1, in relation to *Saturn and Melancholy*, is the post-1964 work done by Raymond Klibansky in the preparation of the German and French translations of the book. Now working alone, after the death of Erwin Panofsky, Klibansky decided to thoroughly revise the entire text. In the preface of the German translation, completed in 1988 and published in 1990 (and translated in the present re-edition), he writes that this revision, presented as a "critical edition", takes into account the literature published since the 1964 edition.[21] The result is of utmost importance, especially when one considers the work undertaken for the French translation and notes in collaboration with the French editor, Louis Évrard, and published in 1989. The philological notes in the apparatus allow for a much better text (see for instance the note on 954a in the French edition),[22] and the systematic comparison among modern translations for difficult passages, prepared for the French edition, is of great help. This comparison is not present in the German edition.

On the question of the authorship of *Problem* XXX, 1, our authors, although refraining from a clear attribution to Aristotle, had pointed in the 1964 edition to the complexity of the tradition. After much reflection, Klibansky, in the preface written for the German translation published in 1990,[23] speaks of a writer close to his teacher, and "certainly a student of Aristotle's." This opinion is quite similar to that of the shorter discussion found in the preface to the French translation. The 1990 preface to the German edition offers thus the clearest affirmation of the close relation between the text of *Problem* XXX, 1 and—based on the allusion to the treatise on fire attributed to Theophrastus—Theophrastus himself. Being the "first philosopher to have written a treatise on melancholy," a fact attested to by the presence of this treatise in the list of his works transmitted by Diogenes Laertius, Theophrastus is singled out as the most plausible hypothesis for the authorship of *Problem* XXX, 1. This attribution cannot be confirmed, however, and Klibansky concludes his discussion with a more historical and general framework—that of a compilation augmented through the centuries but consistently ascribed to Aristotle until the attribution was disputed in modern times.[24]

Recent scholarship has drawn considerable attention to the *Problemata physica*. First and foremost, the critical edition with an English translation

---

19 Ibid., p. 36, and note 82, referring to the opinion of Albertus Magnus.

20 Ibid., p. 39.

21 See the translated Preface to the German Edition (1990) in the present edition, p. xiii.

22 Klibansky, Panofsky and Saxl, *Saturne et la Mélancolie. Études historiques et philosophiques: nature, religion, médecine et art*, Paris, Gallimard, 1989, p. 65, note 58 and "Notes du traducteur" (for Greek text p. 64).

23 See the translated Preface in the present edition, p. xviii.

24 Ibid., p. xix sq.

prepared by Robert Mayhew for the Loeb Library,[25] accompanied by an edited collection of studies on various aspects of the work,[26] now offers important improvements on the text and provides very useful discussions on particular topics, among which is an interesting study on *Problem* XXX, 1.[27] But this edition does not completely supersede the critical edition, in three volumes, prepared for the Budé series by Pierre Louis, which offers a more comprehensive and detailed discussion of the text.[28] The German translation of the *Problemata physica*, published by Helmut Flashar with a comprehensive bibliographical study and extensive notes, stands out as the nearly encyclopaedic commentary on these texts.[29] Italian scholarship is also well represented, with Bruno Centrone's studies on *Problem* XXX, 1.[30] Finally, one must mention the studies assembled by Pieter de Leemans and Michèle Goyens on the medieval tradition of the *Problemata*. This collection highlights the richness of this tradition, nurtured by a variety of translations and commentaries. The corpus of the *Problems* went through translations in several languages, mainly Latin (David of Dinant and Bartholomew of Messina), but also Arabic and Middle French, creating a complex web of texts, translations and commentaries, which developed under the authority of Aristotelian authorship.[31]

G. L.

---

25 Aristotle. *Problems*, ed. R. Mayhew.

26 R. Mayhew (ed.), *The Aristotelian* Problemata Physica. *Philosophical and Scientific Investigations*, Leiden and Boston, Brill (Philosophia antiqua, vol. 139), 2015, pp. 1–9.

27 E. Schütrumpf, "Black Bile as the Cause of Human Accomplishments and Behaviors in *Problem, 30, 1*: Is the Concept Aristotelian?", in R. Mayhew (ed.), *The Aristotelian* Problemata Physica, pp. 357–380, with a bibliography.

28 [Aristotle] *Aristote. Problèmes*, ed. and trans., P. Louis, Paris, Belles Lettres (Collection des Universités de France), 3 vols., 1991–1994.

29 [Aristotle] *Aristoteles* Problemata Physica, ed. and trans. H. Flashar, Berlin, Akademie Verlag, (Aristoteles Werke in deutscher Übersetzung, vol. 19), 1962; 4th ed., 1990. See also the important study of Flashar, *Melancholie und Melancholiker in der medizinischen Theorien der Antike*, Berlin, De Gruyter, 1966.

30 See B. Centrone (ed.), *Studi sui* Problemata physica *aristotelici*, Naples, Bibliopolis (Elenchos, vol. 58), 2011, with an important essay by Centrone on *Problem* XXX,1, "*Melancholikos* in Aristotele e il *Problema* XXX,1", pp. 309–339. See also his edition of [Aristotle], *Problema XXX, 1, Perché tutti gli uomini straordinari sono melancolici*, Pisa, Edizioni ETS, 2018.

31 See P. de Leemans and M. Goyens (eds.), *Aristotle's* Problemata *in different Times and Tongues*, Leuven, Leuven University Press, (Mediaevalia Lovaniensa, se. 1, studia 39), 2006.

Afterword

THE LONG AND COMPLEX HISTORY OF A WARBURGIAN PUBLICATION PROJECT (1913–1990)

Rare are the learned monographs whose gestation has been so complex and difficult. An eminent emblem of the collective productions of the Warburg Library and Institute, the publication of *Saturn and Melancholy* by Raymond Klibansky, Erwin Panofsky, and Fritz Saxl in 1964 is testimony, in its way, of the history and heritage of this unique institution. More than half a century after its first publication it becomes possible, by summoning a history particular to the Warburgian tradition that is not only intellectual but also disciplinary and institutional, to sketch from the archives a reconstruction of the major phases and challenges of this project.

I. THE GENESIS OF PANOFSKY AND SAXL'S DÜRERS 'MELENCOLIA I' *(1923)*

The 1964 preface to *Saturn and Melancholy* mentions the 1923 publication of *Dürers 'Melencolia I'* by Erwin Panofsky and Fritz Saxl as the beginning of the project that would eventually become the famed augmented three-authored tome. It is, however, not the publication but rather the genesis of this earlier volume that gives the project its real scope as a collective undertaking of the Kulturwissenschaftliche Bibliothek Warburg (KBW), one that included Aby Warburg himself, founder of the KBW.

The preliminary stage of this long publication project reaches back in fact to 1913, when Warburg learned of the abrupt death of Karl Giehlow. As an art historian Giehlow had been the first to investigate, in his pioneering essay series "Dürers Stich 'Melencolia I' und der maximilianische Humanistenkreis" (Dürer's Engraving "Melencolia I" and Maximilian's Humanist Circle, 1903–04), the link between the iconographic program of the 1514 artwork and Florentine Neoplatonic conceptions of melancholy related to Ficino.[1] His sudden passing had left incomplete an important monograph on Dürer's famous master print.

Giehlow's work was highly esteemed by Warburg, for whose research Dürer was also a key figure, and the two had corresponded after a first meeting in 1908.[2] Upon hearing of his death, the Hamburg scholar enquired about the state of Giehlow's late book project and bought parts of the collection of

---

[1] K. GIEHLOW, "Dürers Stich 'Melencolia I' und der maximilianische Humanistenkreis", in *Mitteilungen der Gesellschaft für vervielfältigende Kunst*, 2 (1903), pp. 29–41; and 4 (1904), pp. 6–18 and 57–78.

[2] See C. WEDEPOHL, "The Genesis, Writing, and Re-Writing of Erwin Panofsky and Fritz Saxl's *Dürers 'Melencolia I'*", in *Raymond Klibansky and the Warburg Library Network: Intellectual Peregrinations from Hamburg to London and Montreal*, ed. P. Despoix and J. Tomm with the collaboration of E. Méchoulan and G. Leroux, Montreal, McGill-Queen's University Press, 2018, pp. 201–235: here 213 sqq.

reproductions relevant to the study. He then also contacted Giehlow's literary executor, Arpád Weixlgärtner, and proposed to put his own research at the latter's disposition and to help complete and publish the unfinished volume on *Melencolia I*.[3]

Giehlow's genuine iconographical method was for Warburg a welcome alternative to the dominant formalism in art studies and intersected with his own approach to the history of astrology.[4] During the Hamburg Academic Summer School of 1913, a few months after Giehlow's death, he would himself explore the transference of astral representations from antiquity to the Renaissance, with particular attention to its importance for Dürer's *Melencolia I*. Warburg concluded his slide lecture there, "Die Planetenbilder auf der Wanderung von Süd nach Nord und ihre Rückkehr nach Italien" (The Planetary Images in their Migration from South to North and Their Return to Italy), with a detailed analysis of the engraving as a singular point of inflexion in the "afterlife" of ancient planetary divinities. Critically relying on Giehlow, he focused especially on three details: the peculiar holding of the compass, being a visual transposition of the concentration exercises proposed by Ficino against melancholy; the numeric magic square—itself a testimony of Arab astrological influence, plausibly mediated by Cornelius Agrippa—symbolising Jupiter's protective power against Saturn's potentially destructive qualities; and the stone polyhedron, underlining the decisive turning point in Dürer's close study of geometric forms and perspective with Italian masters.[5] These traces of transmission from ancient medical art, astrological magics, and mathematical representation illuminated for Warburg Dürer's "humanization" of the fearsome Saturnine figure and its metamorphosis into a new emblem of the artist's genius.

In 1917 the Hamburg scholar returned shortly to Dürer's engraving in what would be published as his now classic *Pagan-Antique Prophecy in Words and Images in the Age of Luther* (1920). There, he coined the formula characterising *Melencolia I* as a "humanistic comfort against the fear inspired by Saturn" (*humanistisches Trostblatt wider Saturnfürchtigkeit*), highlighting its difference of orientation with other contemporary conceptions such as the popular illustrated astrological predictions of Johannes Lichtenberger, or Luther's anathema against belief in the power of the stars, seen as diabolical idolatry.[6] Warburg's reflections on how to approach Dürer's art had in fact already

---

3 See P. Despoix, "*Melancholie und Saturn*: A Long-Term Collective Project of the Warburg Library", ibid., pp. 236–268: here 237; and Warburg Institute Archive, General Correspondence (henceforth WIA, GC): Aby Warburg to Gustav Glück, 15 December 1913; Warburg to Arpád Weixlgärtner, 23 March 1915 and 12 January 1916.

4 See Wedepohl, "The Genesis, Writing, and Re-Writing ...", p. 216.

5 A. Warburg, "Die Planetenbilder auf der Wanderung von Süd nach Nord und ihre Rückkehr nach Italien" (1913), in Warburg, *Werke in einem Band*, ed. M. Treml, S. Weigel and P. Ladwig, Berlin, Suhrkamp, 2010, pp. 366–370.

6 Cf. Warburg, *Heidnisch-antike Weissagung in Wort und Bild zu Luthers Zeiten*, ed. F. Boll, Heidelberg, Winter, 1920, pp. 54–65; trans. by David Britt as "Pagan-Antique Prophecy in Words and Images in the Age of Luther", in A. Warburg, *The Renewal of Pagan Antiquity. Contributions to the*

articulated the programmatic research of the KBW, conceived in the 1920s as an interdisciplinary laboratory for a cultural history of images, with a specific focus on representations symbolising human fate as related to the powers of the cosmos.

Warburg's desire to see Giehlow's work on Dürer into print was steady but, becoming ill after the war, he was unable to contribute to its publication. This role fell to Fritz Saxl, who was left in charge of the Library. Receiving Giehlow's material in 1921, Saxl concluded that the late scholar had, in searching for a specific hieroglyphic dimension in *Melencolia I*, ultimately taken a wrong path, but nonetheless intended to complete the work. Following a lecture by Saxl on Dürer's print in a KBW seminar given by Erwin Panofsky, the two decided to join efforts towards a double volume: the first part would contain Giehlow's studies, and the second Saxl and Panofsky's complementary interpretation of the engraving.[7] However, after it was discovered that the typeset proofs of Giehlow's book had been pulped at the Viennese *Staatsdruckerei* where it was initially to be printed, this plan was discarded.[8]

The single volume, which was finally published in Leipzig by Teubner in 1923 as the second of the *Warburg Studien* series under the title *Dürers 'Melencolia I'. Eine Quellen- und Typengeschichtliche Untersuchung* (Dürer's 'Melencolia I': A Historical Investigation of Sources and Types), is authored by Panofsky and Saxl alone. The preface contributed by Arpád Weixlgärtner paid homage to Giehlow, retracing the story of the obstacles to publication of his study, and forty of the volume's sixty-eight illustrations were taken over from the latter's estate; but, aside from references in the footnotes, Giehlow's text is absent from the book.[9] In order to explore the long historical genesis of Dürer's depiction, Panofsky and Saxl returned to the different textual and visual sources on the melancholic affect surviving since ancient times. The book's imposing appendices of material on melancholy and its later association with Saturn—from pseudo-Aristotle to Abū Ma'shar, and from the astrological representations of planetary gods to Ficino—take up as much space (approximately seventy-five pages) as does the main account covering the periods of antiquity, the Middle Ages, and the Florentine Renaissance, before focusing on Dürer and his master engraving.

The collaboration between Saxl, with his expertise in astrological manuscripts, and Panofsky, a *Privatdozent* at the Hamburg University whose dissertation (from 1914) focused on Dürer's theory of art, was well balanced and

Cultural History of the European Renaissance, Los Angeles, Getty Institute, 1999, pp. 641–647: here 644 (modified translation).

7 See WEDEPOHL, "The Genesis, Writing, and Re-Writing …", pp. 218–220; and WIA, GC: Saxl to Warburg, 21 November 1921, and Saxl to Weixlgärtner, 7 January 1922.

8 See D. STIMILLI, "The Melancholy of the (Co-)Author", in *Raymond Klibansky and the Warburg Library Network*, pp. 269–288: here 276 sqq.; and WIA, GC: Weixlgärtner to Saxl, 29 January 1922, and Saxl to Weixlgärtner, 7 March 1922.

9 E. PANOFSKY and F. SAXL, *Dürers 'Melencolia I'. Eine Quellen- und Typengeschichtliche Untersuchung*, Leipzig–Berlin, Teubner, 1923; and A. WEIXLGÄRTNER, "Zum Geleite," I–XV. See also STIMILLI, ibid., pp. 277–279.

the book's chapters reflect the complementary specializations of the two scholars. The remarkable erudition of the relatively thin volume is indeed a testimony to the environment—both material and intellectual—of the KBW: the four-handed study enlarges on Warburg's previous work, not only exploiting the ancient and oriental sources on the figuration of Saturn, but also drawing from both popular and learned iconography of melancholy up to the fifteenth century, adopted essentially from Giehlow.

The crucial chapter on Dürer is likewise informed by Warburg's 1920 essay but differs in its evaluation of the astrological dimension of the engraving. This dimension, linked to the function of the "magic square", is slightly downplayed, implying that *Melencolia I* should be understood more as a "warning than as a comfort" (*Warnungsblatt denn als Trostblatt*) against Saturn's power and his ambivalent moods.[10] New, too, is the hypothesis explaining the numeral "*I*" of the work's title. The authors saw in this number the first stage of an ascending series pointing to an eventual surpassing of the limitations of the saturnine artist. The source of this conception of melancholy (for Dürer) could, they thought, be found in Pico della Mirandola's *Apologia* (1489). There, Pico quotes Henry of Ghent's ideas regarding a split relation between two human types under Saturn's influence: those, like artists, whose power of representation remain linked to imagination in space, on the one hand, and those with pure metaphysical and theological minds who can free themselves from spatial representation on the other.[11] Set against a second, higher state—for which the print *Saint Jerome in His Study* (also 1514), depicting the translator of Holy Scripture, could have been a counterpart for Dürer—*Melencolia I* would symbolise the first step in this twofold series: namely *resignation* in the face of the limits of an art primarily based on spatial geometry and mathematical measurement.[12] Here emerges firmly the interpretation of the engraving—which we can attribute with certainty to Panofsky—as a self-confession of the artist and Faustian expression of the impossibility of his attaining the highest knowledge.

II. THE MAKING OF A SECOND EDITION: TOWARDS SATURN AND MELANCHOLY

Still in the sanatorium at Kreuzlingen, Warburg read the proofs and praised the forthcoming book on Dürer's *Melencolia I*, but he regretted the lack of discussion on the complementary types of Hamlet and Faust. His criticism

[10] See PANOFSKY and SAXL, *Dürers 'Melencolia I'*, p. 54, n.1: when for Warburg assuaging Saturn's ambivalence by combining his influx with the protection of Jupiter (the magic square) was one of the preconditions for the humanising metamorphosis at work in Dürer.

[11] See PICO, *Apologia* (*Opera omnia*, Basel, 1572, vol. 1, 133), ibid., pp. 72–73, n.3.

[12] Ibid., pp. 73–74, and n.1; Heinrich Wölfflin, author of an important monograph on Dürer (1904), would imagine in the same year a (lost) *Melencolia II* representing a victory over his depressive and morbid side; see WÖLFFLIN, "Zur Interpretation von Dürers 'Melancholie'" (1923), in *Gedanken zur Kunstgeschichte. Gedrucktes und Ungedrucktes*, Basel, Benno Schwabe, 1941, pp. 96–105.

was insistent and when the volume came out in early 1924, he would again comment that he was "missing the emphasis on the reason for a reformation of Saturn in Panofsky's and Saxl's study."[13]

It is not known whether Warburg's critiques contributed to the planning decisions for a new edition of *Dürers 'Melencolia I'*—a book that nonetheless had been successful and was rapidly out of print—but Saxl and Panofksy began to consider the need for a revised edition.[14] What is certain is that discussion with Raymond Klibansky in 1926, then a graduate student in philosophy, in Hamburg at Cassirer's invitation and working at the Library, was crucial for that step.[15] Asked to comment on the KBW publications, Klibansky "took the liberty of criticising the volume, since … it did not take sufficient account of the philosophical and theological roots of the various concepts of melancholy."[16] Saxl and Panofsky did basically agree with the critique, and for an enlarged edition invited Klibansky's collaboration on the chapters he had expertise on; that is, ancient and medieval sources.

Saxl then collected and commented new sources while Panofsky took responsibility for the overall redaction of expanded chapters. Klibansky worked, from the end of 1927, on providing critical notes and materials related to ancient and medieval concepts of melancholy. He regularly sent handwritten notes by topic and chapter to Saxl, most often from Heidelberg where he was still completing his thesis on Proclus.[17] Saxl relied on Klibansky's assistance not only for the history of the system of the temperaments but also for sources on ideas and representations related to Saturn. In 1930, after three years of collaborative work, the riddle of the discursive context in which the planetary gods had been associated with the temperaments was solved, and Ptolemy was discerned as the first author to have made a connection between melancholy and people born under the sign of Saturn.[18] The following years were challenging, however, for the advance of the expanded edition: the KBW was launching the large collective project of a *Bibliography of the Survival of the Classics*; Klibansky, still in Heidelberg, began in the meantime to work with Ernst Hoffmann on

---

13 See WEDEPOHL, "Warburg, Saxl, Panofsky and Dürer's *Melencolia I*", in *Schifanoia* 48/49, 2015, pp. 27–44: here 34 sqq.; and WIA, FC: Aby to Mary Warburg, 26/27 January 1924 for the quote.

14 See WEDEPOHL, "The Genesis, Writing, and Re-Writing …", pp. 201–235: here 221.

15 Klibansky was also tasked with editing the *Liber de sapiente* by C. BOVILLUS for E. CASSIRER's book *Individuum und Kosmos in der Philosophie der Renaissance*, which appeared in 1927. For an overview of Klibansky's role within the Warburg network, see DESPOIX, G. LEROUX and J. TOMM, "Raymond Klibansky and the Warburg Library Network; from Hamburg to London to Montreal", the introduction to *Raymond Klibansky and the Warburg Library Network*, pp. 3–25: here 8.

16 KLIBANSKY, *Le philosophe et la mémoire du siècle. Tolérance, liberté et philosophie. Entretiens avec Georges Leroux*, Paris, Belles Lettres, 1998, p. 35; see further: D. MCEWAN, *Fritz Saxl: Eine Biografie. Aby Warburgs Bibliothekar und erster Direktor des Londoner Warburg Institutes*, Vienna, Böhlau, 2012, p. 178.

17 See DESPOIX, "*Melancholie und Saturn*", p. 249; WIA holds in the Saxl Papers more than twenty so-called *Zettel* in Klibansky's hand (about eighty pages of quotations from and commentaries on different sources.)

18 See WEDEPOHL, "The Genesis, Writing, and Re-Writing …", pp. 224–226; and WIA, GC: Klibansky to Panofsky, 8 May 1930.

a newly planned Cusanus critical edition; and in 1931–32 Panofsky was invited to teach at New York University.

Wider KBW involvement in the project included librarian Hans Meier, who in 1928 contributed one of its main findings: the first and unpublished version of Cornelius Agrippa's *De occulta philosophia,* a manuscript dated around 1510, quite different from the printed edition of 1533. The manuscript, without the many later references to astrology, could have been determining for Dürer's conception of *Melencolia I.* Warburg himself—who, having returned in 1924 to the Library, was following the collective work in progress—informed Panofsky that the interpretation of melancholy in this codex was divided into "*imaginativa, rationalis* and *mentalis*," but also that the controversial magical squares were missing from it.[19] This manuscript would decide Panofsky to reconsider his Dürer chapter and to coin Agrippa's text as *the* decisive programmatic source of the 1514 print. (Warburg's death in 1929 prevented a continuation of this dialogue.)

It is also worth noting that the *Melencolia* study in preparation represented an important research area in which Panofsky matured his specific iconological method. His seminal essay "On the Problem of Describing and Interpreting Works of the Visual Arts", published in *Logos* in 1932, was the first systematic attempt to distinguish three levels of interpretation: phenomenal meaning (factual and expressive); meaning of the notional content (linked to literary knowledge); and the documentary or intrinsic meaning of an artwork.[20] Panofsky's text concluded with the first exposition of what would became his "scheme" of iconological interpretation: taking the example of *Melencolia I* and referring to the artist's "world vision" to exemplify the last interpretive stage of his formalised approach, it also referred to the forthcoming "second edition … of the study compiled together with Fritz Saxl" in 1923.[21] The bulk of the remaining reworking for the expanded edition would, however, only be completed with Panofsky's short return to Germany in 1933, just before the Library moved to Britain, fleeing Nazi power.

The KBW left Hamburg for London in December 1933 and the subsequent years were difficult for what would become the Warburg Institute.[22] Saxl remained its director and, with Gertrud Bing, Edgar Wind, Klibansky and Meier, would ensure a continuity with the Warburgian research impetus. When it became possible, after 1935, for Saxl and Klibansky to resume work on the *Melencolia I* volume and prepare the proofs, Panofsky had received an appointment at

---

19 See WIA, GC: Warburg to Panofsky, 9 August 1928.

20 Phänomen-, Bedeutungs-, Dokument- or Wesenssinn: see PANOFSKY, "Zum Problem der Beschreibung und Inhaltsdeutung von Werken der bildenden Kunst", in *Logos* vol. 21 (1932), pp. 103–119; in English: "On the Problem of Describing and Interpreting Works of the Visual Arts", trans. J. Elsner and K. Lorenz, in *Critical Inquiry*, vol. 38, no.3 (Spring 2012), pp. 467–482.

21 Ibid., pp. 117 and 118, n.1; transl. pp. 480 and 481, n.21.

22 See SAXL, "The History of Warburg's Library", in E. GOMBRICH, *Aby Warburg: An Intellectual Biography,* 2nd ed., Chicago, University of Chicago Press, 1986, pp. 325–338 at 336 sqq.

Princeton University and would stay in America. The process of completion became even more challenging when, after 1938, a disagreement broke out among the three contributors about the title of the new edition.

At the end of the summer of 1938, Klibansky, who had taken primary charge of the proofs in London, pointed to the need for a new subtitle to the planned volume. But his suggestion to Saxl, which was *Studien zur Geschichte der Naturphilosophie, Medizin, Astrologie und deren Einwirkung auf die darstellende Kunst* (Studies on the History of Natural Philosophy, Medicine, Astrology and their Impact on Visual Art),[23] would be flatly rejected by Panofsky. In his answer, Panofsky stuck strongly to the conception of the first edition, proposing instead to rephrase the title entirely as: *Melancholia. Eine quellen- und bildgeschichtliche Studie über den Typus des saturnischen Melancholikers* (Melancholia: A Study on the Literary and Visual Sources of the Saturnian Melancholic Type).[24]

This argument about the title and possible subtitle, which was meant to clarify the aim of the new work, disclosed an issue concerning method and disciplinary anchoring. Panofsky not only disapproved of Klibansky and Saxl's proposition but refused any reference to natural philosophy or intellectual history. He preferred to locate the enterprise primarily within art history. This disagreement in fact revealed questions about disciplinary frontiers—the place of astrology and Saturn was particularly telling—with conceptual implications for the relation of art to medical, religious, magical, or scientific representations, relations at the heart of the Warburgian approach that were obviously difficult to transpose in Panofsky's new American context.

Controversy also surrounded the naming of the authors for the forthcoming volume. Saxl had proposed that Klibansky appear on the title page; however, even though Klibansky had been the main editor in charge of the final phase, Panofsky did not consider that he had earned the status of full co-author of the volume.[25] The forthcoming book was nonetheless announced in the Warburg publication prospectus of 1939 under the title: *Melancholie und Saturn. Studien zur Geschichte der Naturphilosophie, Charakterlehre und bildenden Kunst* (Melancholy and Saturn. Studies in the History of Natural Philosophy, of the Theory of Character Types and of the Visual Arts), and with the three co-authors' names, even if it was presented explicitly as a "second edition of

23 See R. Weber, "Aktivitäten der Warburg-Bibliothek, gespiegelt im Marbacher Nachlass Raymond Klibansky", in *Exilforschung*, vol. 29 (2011), pp. 107–108; see also, in the Raymond Klibansky papers at the Deutsches Literaturarchiv Marbach (henceforth DLA, A, KLIBANSKY): Klibansky to Saxl, 17 August 1938.

24 On Panofsky's answer to Saxl from 2 September 1938, see Stimilli, "The Melancholy of the (Co-) Author", p. 279.

25 See Weber, "Aktivitäten der Warburg-Bibliothek …", 108; compare to Saxl's letter to Klibansky, 8 December 1937, in the Raymond Klibansky Collection, at McGill University Library's Rare Books and Special Collections (RKC).

Erwin Panofsky's and Fritz Saxl's *Dürers 'Melencolia I'*, enlarged and entirely rewritten, with 146 illustrations."[26]

The Saxl Papers at the Warburg Institute Archive and Klibansky's estate at Deutsches Literaturarchiv Marbach contain different sets of proofs of the volume in preparation, dating from 1937 to 1939, which document a profound transformation of the 1923 project.[27] If the subtitle of this new volume made no explicit mention of medicine and astrology, the presence of "Saturn" in the title alongside "Melancholy" made up the balance.[28] With the exception of the introduction, appendices and index, the book was in fact completed—with the last set of proofs stamped by the German printer J. J. Augustin at Glückstadt on 2 August 1939—one month before the outbreak of the war. We know that the book never went to print, and that the plates were to disappear in the Nazi war effort.[29]

This new version had further developed and integrated into its main text the numerous sources and documents that had been presented in the appendices of the 1923 edition. The text had almost tripled in volume, and the number of visual documents nearly doubled, displaying an extensive atlas of melancholy of about 150 images.[30] Yet the shift was also a qualitative one: the expanded edition moved well beyond the original focus on Dürer's art to include a broad cultural history of the relations between discourses on the affect of melancholy and beliefs and images attached to the planetary god Saturn. An entire chapter was added to cover post-medieval poetic melancholy. Dürer's *Melencolia I* did not appear until the fourth section of the book, some three hundred pages into the text. A fifth section, which mapped the engraving's impact on the visual arts of its time ("Die künstlerische Nachfolge der 'Melencolia I'") had also been added.[31]

As a history of ideas and representations of melancholy in medicine, theology, astrology, and literature, the first three parts of the book were fairly autonomous from the last sections of the work. The fourth part, on Dürer, had remained relatively stable, even if the sub-chapter devoted to the "new meaning" of *Melencolia I* differed somewhat in its interpretative context from the 1923 edition. In its method, this section is clearly informed by Panofsky's scheme of iconological interpretation—its three stages providing the structure of the corresponding subdivisions in the 1939 proofs: the new form of expression (*Ausdruckssinn*); the new notional content (*Begriffsgehalt*); and the significance

---

26 "Warburg Institute Prospect of Publications", London, 1939, in Stimilli, "The Melancholy of the (Co-)Author", pp. 271 and Fig. 11.1; compare with WIA, Saxl Papers, "Draft of Title-page" of 30 June 1939, which would be rejected by Klibansky on August 10 (also in the Saxl Papers).

27 Claudia Wedepohl at the WIA in London and Regina Weber at the DLA Marbach were determinant in tracing the different proofs.

28 "Melancholie und Saturn", see WIA, Fritz Saxl Papers, boxes "Saturn und Melancholie": "Titelzeug und neues Vorwort"; and Despoix, "*Melancholie und Saturn* ...", p. 251, Fig. 10.9.

29 See Klibansky, *Le Philosophe et la mémoire du siècle*, p. 151.

30 See WIA, Saxl Papers, boxes "Saturn und Melancholie", proofs [1939]: the text was extended from 154 to 424 pages, and the number of illustrations from 68 to 146 (plus 5 figures).

31 See the reconstruction of the Contents in Despoix, "*Melancholie und Saturn* ...", p. 252.

(*Dokumentsinn*) of the artwork.[32] This last subsection returned to the philosophical sources of melancholy in order to modify the hypothesis on the enigmatic "*I*" of the print's title. It was the German author Agrippa of Nettesheim who now became the main programmatic mediator via the first manuscript version (ca 1510) of his *De occulta philosophia*, which contained in fact a specific compilation of Ficino's ideas on melancholy without the many later references to astrology.

The elucidation of Agrippa's early doctrine for the new significance of Dürer's engraving culminated in the presentation of the gradation *imaginatio – ratio – mens* of the related three stages of melancholy, dividing those affected by it into: artists; scholars and politicians; theologians and prophets. Enumerated in the conclusion are the elements characterising the "Agrippian" first stage of melancholic imagination as exactly corresponding to the depiction of Dürer's allegorical figure.[33] Again, then, though relying on a different textual intermediary than that considered in the 1923 interpretation, *Melencolia I* was presented as an expression of the Faustian resignation of the artist who realises the inevitable failure of his skills.[34]

The outbreak of war postponed *sine die* the prospect of publication for the collective work, which should have been printed at the end of 1939. In London, Saxl was struggling to ensure long-term support for the Warburg Institute. As a new British citizen, Klibansky enlisted and became active within the Political Warfare Executive. At Princeton, Panofsky had brought out in 1939 his *Studies in Iconology*—introducing in English the new method that would become famous in art history. The United States was not yet at war and Panofsky was also preparing his important monograph, *Albrecht Dürer*, the first edition of which appeared in 1943.[35]

In this book on Dürer, a large part of the chapter on the three "master engravings" was again devoted to *Melencolia I*, transposing into the new English framework the main elements of the corresponding chapter in the unpublished German collective volume. Panofsky, who probably no longer expected to see the co-authored book in print, acknowledged in his preface that for this section "half of the credit … goes to Dr. Saxl and his associates."[36] Taking up the early manuscript of Agrippa's *De occulta philosophia* as the main interpretative key, the signification of the engraving was reaffirmed as the first *limited* stage of melancholic inspiration.

Only with the end of the war could the idea of publishing the collective book on Melancholy and Saturn be relaunched. At the Warburg Institute it

---

32 Ibid., p. 253 sqq.

33 See "Saturn und Melancholie", proofs [1939], p. 381, and Despoix, ibid. p. 256, Fig. 10.10.

34 See "Saturn und Melancholie", proofs [1939], p. 382 sqq.

35 See Panofsky, *Studies in Iconology: Humanistic Themes in the Art of the Renaissance*, Oxford and New York, Oxford University Press, 1939; and *Albrecht Dürer*, Princeton, N.J.: Princeton University Press, 1943, later editions of which will be published under the title *The Life and Art of Albrecht Dürer*.

36 See Panofsky, "Preface to the first edition", in *The Life and Art of Albrecht Dürer*, 4th ed., 1955, p. xi.

was decided to publish the text in English, and after Saxl's death in 1948 Klibansky continued alone with the preparations and final editing. He had just been appointed to McGill University in Montreal, and had relocated to Canada, but was at the same time involved in two other major Warburg projects—as co-editor of the journal *Mediaeval and Renaissance Studies* (1941–1968), and as main editor of the multi-volume edition of the Latin and Arabic *Corpus Platonicum Medii Aevi* (1940–1962).[37] Panofsky's reservations about publishing the now somehow dated volume, on the other hand, persisted. The tension between Saxl's Warburgian concept of an interdiscursive transmission history of the melancholy affect and Panofsky's stronger accent on a formalised interpretative iconology was an unresolved one; but Klibansky, who stood for the philological-philosophical tradition, still wished to see the collective work in print.

After Saxl's death, Gertrud Bing did take on the task of sustaining, from London, this difficult edition project which eventually became double: while moving ahead toward an English edition, Bing also reached an agreement in 1949 with the publisher Einaudi, who undertook to produce an Italian translation based on the proofs of the unpublished German text. Still in 1954, in a letter to André Chastel, who had been following the Melancholy project from Paris since the 1930s, she wrote of the Italian translation being prepared by Einaudi.[38] But after examination by Bing and Klibansky, the Italian translation was found unsatisfactory and it was agreed to leave it aside until the English edition in preparation would be published.[39]

What Gertrud Bing had called, in a 1949 letter to Panofsky, "the long argument which passed between [him] and Saxl"[40] was finally resolved when Klibansky visited the art historian in Princeton in 1955. After the meeting Panofsky communicated to Bing, who had just become director of the Warburg Institute, that he had now come to see that "Klibansky did in fact much more for the English edition than he had done for the German version, and the former thus seems to differ more emphatically from the latter than [he] knew."[41] He therefore withdrew his "original objection" and let her formulate the new by-line for the book. After nine more years, the book appeared in 1964 from Thomas Nelson and Sons as *Saturn and Melancholy: Studies in the History of Natural Philosophy, Religion and Art*, carrying the three authors' names. A comparison shows that the published English edition differs relatively little in terms of contents from the proofs of 1939. The most notable difference in structure is that the fifth and last part of the German version on "The Artistic

37 *Mediaeval and Renaissance Studies*, co-edited with R. Hunt and, for the last volumes, L. Labowsky, published by The Warburg Institute, 1940–1968; Klibansky also taught for several years at the Institut d'études médiévales (Université de Montréal), 1947–68.

38 See WIA, GC: Gertrud Bing to André Chastel, 15 December 1954.

39 See E. OTTO, "Editing the 'Melancholy Project'", in *Raymond Klibansky and the Warburg Library Network*, p. 208 n.19.

40 See Bing to Panofsky, 12 April 1949, in PANOFSKY, *Korrespondenz 1910 bis 1968*, vol. 2, p. 1071.

41 Panofsky to Bing, 20 June 1955, ibid., vol. 3, pp. 779–780.

Legacy of *Melencolia I*" was integrated into the fourth, imposing section on Dürer as its final chapter. The iconographic material is unchanged, and the English text turns out be a revision—by Bing among others—of the original German translated into English by Frances Lobb.[42] (Lotte Labowsky had also been involved in establishing the Greek text of pseudo-Aristotelian *Problem* XXX, 1.) The central role given in the section on *Melencolia I* to the conception of saturnine melancholy from Agrippa's early manuscript was preserved, and the conclusions about the intrinsic meaning of the engraving did not change. But Dürer's masterpiece was now tightly embedded in a long transmission history of the representations of melancholy since the ancient times.

III. THE POST-HISTORY OF THE 1964 THREE-AUTHORED EDITION

In spite of the delays in its publication, *Saturn and Melancholy*, which would probably have attracted only a highly specialised readership if published in German in the 1930s or 1940s, enjoyed a relatively wide response in the mid-1960s.[43] Panofsky's reticence to publish it with references not updated since the forties appeared in fact unjustified and it detracted little from its reception.[44] One of the first reviews, published in the journal of history of science *Isis*, not only stressed "the gain of scope" in comparison to the 1923 study, but explicitly noticed that, even if the bibliography of the volume was two decades out of date, the scholarship was "so largely based on original sources that nothing of importance would have been altered if the manuscript had been fresh."[45] In specialised journals the book likewise found a positive response, *The Classical Review* underlining, for instance, "the surpassing interest of the book for historians of Greek thought and of the later growth of science, including psychology."[46]

Yet probably the most comprehensive review of the volume came from art historian and philosopher Robert Klein, who worked with André Chastel and had just been on a research stay at the Warburg Institute. "I think the 'Warburgian spirit' has never been better illustrated," Klein wrote in *Mercure de France*, 1964, pointing to the work as a joint project from the Warburg Library and Institute and to its tangled history since Giehlow.[47] The review is

42 See "Preface to the First English Edition (1964)," p. vi, in which L. Labowsky's collaboration is also acknowledged for helping in establishing the Greek text of pseudo-Aristotelian *Problem* XXX,1, and p. xx of this edition.

43 See STIMILLI, "The Melancholy of the (Co-)Author", p. 282.

44 Ibid., p. 274 sqq. and also Panofsky to Robert Klein, 27 September, 1965, in PANOFSKY, *Korrespondenz*, vol. 5, p. 701.

45 "Lynn White on Black Bile, and Other Comments", *Isis*, vol. 56, no. 4 (Winter, 1965), pp. 458–459: here 458.

46 E. D. PHILLIPS, review of *Saturn and Melancholy* in *The Classical Review*, vol. 16, no. 2 (Jun., 1966), pp. 239–240: here 239.

47 R. KLEIN, "Saturne: croyances et symboles (1964)", reprinted in *La Forme et l'intelligible*, Paris, Gallimard, 1970, pp. 224–230: here 224. The English translation of the book, *Form and Meaning* (New

a long, detailed and enthusiastic appraisal of the erudite collaboration among the three authors and of their findings. It ends, however, with a note of new critical interpretation of a significant detail in Dürer's engraving: the identification of the putto near Melancholy as a representation of Practice (*Usus*). For Klein, the putto appears rather as a personification of the genius of inspiration: "Its attribute, the chisel, characterises it more precisely as the spirit of *disegno* … no other detail of the engraving tells us that the Melancholy has anything whatever to do with this art."[48] Panofsky, who corresponded with Klein during these years, was apparently convinced by the statement of a self-reflexive dimension in the engraving, reacting quite positively to Klein's critiques and writing to him, after reading the review: "In point of fact, you may be quite right in interpreting the busy putto as a personification of *Disegno* rather than *Usus*."[49]

Panofsky's death in 1968 meant that Klibansky alone lived to see the publication of the delayed Italian edition, now based on the English version of the book.[50] *Saturno e la melanconia* appeared in 1983, thus completing the series of Italian editions planned decades earlier by Gertrud Bing of three major Warburg Institute productions,[51] which together partly explain the Warburgian renaissance that first developed in Italy beginning at the end of the sixties. Contributing to the prolonged delay of the Italian publication was that the original plates, this time of the 1964 edition, had once again been lost, and Einaudi had to retrace the entire series of 150 images. Enrica Melossi, later a renowned designer of literature and art books, headed this challenging task for Einaudi, and all subsequent editions would be based on her iconographic work.[52]

Klibansky continued to conduct research on melancholy in the following years, especially in philosophical and literary fields. Attending, for instance, a conference on "Genius" as an historical idea in 1987 at the University of

York, Viking Press, 1979), does not include this essay. See also Jean-Philippe UZEL, "The Theme of Melancholy …", in *Raymond Klibansky and the Warburg Library Network*, p. 296.

48 KLEIN, ibid., p. 229: "Son attribut, le burin, le caractérise plus précisément comme esprit du *disegno*, inspirateur des artistes… nul autre détail de la gravure ne nous dit que la Mélancolie ait quoi que ce soit à faire avec cet art."

49 See the Smithsonian Archives of American Art, Erwin Panofsky Papers, Box 7, Folder 11: Panofsky to Klein, 7 October 1965: "We are still faced with a little dilemna: can we assume that *Disegno* was exceptionally deprived of his compass or that *Usus* was, equally exceptionally, equipped with wings? I grant that the first of these alternatives might well be preferable." The discussion referred to Cesare Ripa and Plates 109 and 110 of the volume.

50 See Klibansky's letter to Gerda Panofsky from 1974 (DLA, A, KLIBANSKY XX–XXI, 2, "Warburg Institute"), in OTTO, "Editing the 'Melancholy Project'", p. 208, n.19.

51 These editions appeared after Bing's death in 1964, see: SAXL, *La storia delle immagini*, Bari, Laterza, 1965; A. WARBURG, *La rinascità del paganesimo antico*, Firenze, La Nuova Italia, 1966; and KLIBANSKY, SAXL, and PANOFSKY, *Saturno e la melanconia*, Torino, Einaudi, 1983.

52 See Klibansky's acknowledgements to Melossi in the French edition *Saturne et la Mélancolie. Études historiques et philosophiques: nature, religion, médecine et art*, Paris, Gallimard, 1989, p. 26; it is the Italian edition of the book that has thus far enjoyed—with a third edition in 2010—the most successful reception, see also OTTO, "Editing the 'Melancholy Project'", p. 208, n.17.

Warwick, he gave a keynote address entitled "Saturn and Melancholy revisited."[53] Two years later, the augmented French edition, *Saturne et la Mélancolie* appeared from Gallimard, followed in 1990—fifty years after it had been planned—by the German Suhrkamp publication of *Saturn und Melancholie*. The two editions, although slightly different in layout, shared a new and longer preface added by Klibansky which broadens the scope of the collective study with an overview of melancholy in philosophy and literature after Dürer. Once again recalling in Warburgian manner the significance of the pagan and astrological dimensions in *Melencolia I*, Klibansky nonetheless rejected the idea of an artist drifting towards occult magic, reminding us of the complex Christian constellation of Dürer's context—particularly explicit in his other contemporary master engraving, *Saint Jerome in His Study*.[54] This preface is also something of a call for methodological circumspection and an acknowledgement of the limits of the volume in view of the gigantic task undertaken by the three authors. Moreover, Klibansky contributed a few new elements to both editions: a critically revised Greek text for *Problem* XXX, 1, a further appendix on Cranach's depictions of Melancholy, four new images, and some expansions to the notes.[55] The German publication also offered a supplemental and updated selected bibliography, covering text editions and research by period of focus or topic, reaching from antiquity to the Renaissance and from Dürer's art up to the twentieth century, including philosophy, literature, psychoanalysis and psychiatry.[56]

The reputation of the book was established in the French-speaking world through Chastel's and Klein's references to it even before it was published in French in 1989.[57] The German publication came out at a time of renewed interest in the topic, partly due to the late but intense discussion around Walter Benjamin's *Ursprung des deutschen Trauerspiels* (*The Origin of the German Tragic Drama* had first been published in 1928) whose chapter on melancholy relied on Giehlow and Warburg, and quoted Panofsky and Saxl's 1923 study. Martin Warnke's important 1991 review of the three-authored book in *Die Zeit* underscored the differences between its accent on the limits of the artist's melancholic inspiration and Warburg's enlightened and positively open evaluation of Dürer's engraving. But Warnke also relocated the discussion within the contemporary context, linking the possible response to this challenging

53 See DLA, A, KLIBANSKY: VI, 2: Conference Program. The corresponding publication, *Genius: The History of an Idea*, ed. Penelope MURRAY (Oxford, Basil Blackwell, 1989) has the following dedication: "For Raymond Klibansky / Democritus Senior". On Klibansky's persistent interest in melancholy, see UZEL, "The Theme of Melancholy ...," pp. 290–292.

54 See *Saturn und Melancholie.Studien zur Geschichte der Naturphilosophie und Medizin, der Religion und der Kunst*, Frankfurt am Main, Suhrkamp, 1990, p. 27 sqq., now in this volume, Preface to the German Edition (1990) p. xxvii.

55 See here Appendix III on Lucas Cranach's depiction of Melancholy; Addendum on the text history of *Problem* XXX,1; and Additions to the Notes from the 1990 German Edition, p. 407 sqq.

56 See here Supplemental Bibliography for the 1990 German Edition, p. 429 sqq.

57 See also K. POMIAN, "Livre-montage: *Saturne et la mélancolie*, de Raymond Klibansky, Erwin Panofsky et Fritz Saxl", special issue ("Tradition de la mélancolie") of *Le Débat* 29 (1984), pp. 115–138.

book to the question of whether one "could be freed of this troubling artist-type, whose task involves a departure from the societal normalcy occasioning his melancholy."[58] The erudite volume continued, then, to contribute indirectly to contemporary conversation on the state of the arts. The French and German enlarged editions opened the way to a long series of further translations into several other languages.[59] With the English version of *Saturn and Melancholy* long out of print, Klibansky also discussed its republication with Yale University Press in 1993. But although a contract was dispatched for a new edition, it was never signed.[60] The then senior Canadian scholar nonetheless continued into the mid-1990s to give lectures on the history of melancholy—in particular when honoured at the universities of Bologna and Heidelberg.[61]

A review of the supplemental bibliography of the last updated edition of 1990 shows, apart from the continuous scholarly re-editing of primary texts, an impressive extension of specialised research in the areas covered by the study since its first English publication. It shows at the same time that no other learned publication fully compares in scope and approach to the interdisciplinary three-authored work originating from the Warburg Library. In the preamble of his bibliographical addition, Klibansky noted that "in order to do justice to the numerous publications on modern literature a new separate bibliography would be required." An extensive actualization of the 1990 research references until today would face the same problem, within an even larger arena.

It is only possible to mention here a small selection of recent publications whose subject directly intersects with the materials and questions connected to *Saturn and Melancholy* (see below). Notwithstanding the strong tendency towards increasing specialisation in the last quarter century, one can observe in the recent literature a broadening of the range within which the historical phenomenon of melancholy has been treated. Moreover, if *Melencolia I* remains the most commented work by Dürer, a differentiation in the disciplinary spectrum and methodical approaches to the famous engraving—from art history to psychology and psychoanalysis, from the history of philosophy to that of mathematics or medicine—is also becoming perceptible.

A number of recent studies offer precious and potentially extremely productive complements to the investigations of this three-authored book, thus opening new perspectives. But with, perhaps, the sole exception of Jean Starobinski's late *summa* of his medicinal and literary historical studies on

58 M. Warnke, "Die traurige Muse. Ein grundlegendes Werk über die Melancholie", in *Die Zeit*, no.18/1991; Warnke would become the first director of the restored Warburg Haus in Hamburg.

59 For the Spanish (1991), Japanese (1991), Romanian (2002), Polish (2009) and Slovenian (2013) editions, see Otto, "Editing the 'Melancholy Project'", p. 209, n. 22.

60 See DLA, A, Klibansky: VI, 2: Letter of Agreement from 12 April 1993,

61 See Klibansky, "Le avventure della malinconia", in *Dianoia*, I, 1996, pp. 11–27, and *Tradition antique et tolérance moderne*, ed. P. Despoix and G. Leroux, Montreal, Presses de l'Université de Montréal, pp. 187–209.

melancholy,[62] the relative scarcity of genuine multidisciplinary conceptualization is still manifest. It reminds us once again that it was the unique framework of KBW and the Warburg Institute that made up the material and intellectual preconditions of an enterprise like *Saturn and Melancholy*. A critical rethinking—even if in confrontation with the present work—of the intertwined historical research in philosophy, medicine, astrological magics, religion, literature and the arts that might parallel the study collectively articulated in this book has not been initiated. Yet, the current renewal of studies on Warburg and the Library will establish a broader understanding and evaluation of the specific *kulturwissenschaftliche* approach to the long-term transmission of ideas and representations that this volume echoes. A renewed dissemination of *Saturn and Melancholy* will certainly open a productive dialogue with actual research tendencies; republishing it today should be at the same time seen as a critical contribution to the history of the humanist disciplines in the last century, a historical configuration the Warburg Library network definitively shaped and advanced.

P. D.

SELECTED BIBLIOGRAPHY SINCE THE GERMAN 1990 EDITION

On Melancholy and Saturn

AGAMBEN, Giorgio. *Stanzas: Word and Phantasm in Western Culture*. Part 1. Translated by Ronald L. Martinez. Minneapolis: University of Minnesota Press, 1993.

BLAMBERGER, Günter, Sidonie KELLERER, Tanja KLEMM, Jan SÖFFNER, eds. *Sind alle Denker traurig? Fallstudien zum melancholischen Grund des Schöpferischen in Asien und Europa*. Paderborn: Fink, 2015.

DIXON, Laurinda S. *The Dark Side of Genius: The Melancholic Persona in Art, ca. 1500–1700*. University Park: Pennsylvania State University Press, 2013.

HERSANT, Yves, ed. Mélancolies. *De l'antiquité au XXe siècle*. Paris: Robert Laffont, 2005.

HOLLY, Michael Ann. *The Melancholy Art*. Princeton: Princeton University Press, 2013.

LUND, Mary A. *Melancholy, Medicine and Religion in Early Modern England: Reading the* Anatomy of Melancholy. Cambridge: Cambridge University Press, 2010.

[62] Klibansky had already noted in his preface to the 1989 French edition the exception of STAROBINSKI's work without knowing *L'Encre de la mélancolie* (Paris, Seuil, 2012), an expanded collection of his numerous medical and literary studies on the subject.

Mélancolie: génie et folie en Occident. Edited by Jean Clair. Paris: Réunion des musées nationaux/Gallimard, 2005.

Pigeaud, Jackie. *Melancholia: le malaise de l'individu*. Paris: Payot & Rivages, 2008.

Sillem, Peter. *Saturns Spuren: Aspekte des Wechselspiels von Melancholie und Volkskultur in der frühen Neuzeit*. Frankfurt am Main: Klostermann, 2001.

Saturne en Europe. Edited by Roland Recht. Strasbourg: Éditions Musées de la Ville de Strasbourg, 1998.

Starobinski, Jean. *L'Encre de la mélancolie*. Paris: Seuil, 2012.

Theunissen, Michael. *Vorentwürfe der moderne. Antike Melancholie und die Acedia des Mittelalters*. Berlin: de Gruyter, 1996.

Wittstock, Antje. *Melancholia translata: Marsilio Ficinos Melancholie-Begriff im deutschsprachigen Raum des 16. Jahrhunderts*. Göttingen: V&R unipress, 2011.

On Dürer and the Melencolia I *Engraving*

Albrecht Dürer and His Legacy: The Graphic Work of a Renaissance Artist. Edited by Giulia Bartrum. Princeton, N.J.: Princeton University Press, 2002.

Albrecht Dürer: His Art in Context. Exhibition Dürer. Kunst-Künstler-Kontext at Frankfurt's Städel Museum. Edited by Jochen Sander. Munich: Prestel, 2013.

Bertozzi, Marco and Andrea Pinott, eds. *La "Melencolia" di Albrecht Dürer cinquecento anni dopo (1514–2014)*. Special issue of *Schifanoia* 48–49 (2015), Roma: Fabrizio Serra Editore, 2016.

Bizzi, Giancarlo. *Il poliedro della Melencolia I di Dürer*. Firenze: Cadmo, 2003.

Bubenik, Andrea. *Reframing Albrecht Dürer: The Appropriation of Art, 1528–1700*. Farnham: Ashgate, 2013.

Büchsel, Martin. *Albrecht Dürers Stich "Melencolia, I". Zeichen und Emotion. Die Logik einer kunsthistorischen Debatte*. Munich: Wilhelm Fink, 2010.

Calvesi, Maurizio. *La Melanconia di Albrecht Dürer*. Torino: Einaudi, 1993.

Eichberger, Dagmar and Charles Zika, eds. *Dürer and His Culture*. Cambridge and New York: Cambridge University Press, 1998.

Filippi, Elena. *Inesauribile Melencolia, chiavi e ricchezza del capolavoro düreriano*. Venice: Marsilio, 2018.

Heubach, Friedrich Wolfram. *Ein Bild und sein Schatten. Zwei randständige Betrachtungen zum Bild der Melancholie und zur Erscheinung der Depression*. Bonn: Bouvier, 1997.

Hoffmann, Rainer. *Im Zwielicht. Zu Albrecht Dürers Meisterstich Melencolia I*. Cologne, Weimar and Vienna: Böhlau, 2014.

Hutchison, Jane Campbell. *Albrecht Dürer: A Biography*. Princeton, N.J.: Princeton University Press 1990; see also Hutchison's *Albrecht Dürer: A Guide to Research*. New York: Garland, 2000.

Merback, Mitchell B. *Perfection's Therapy: An Essay on Albrecht Dürer's Melencolia I*. New York: Zone Books, 2017.

RICHTER, Leonhard G. *Dürer-Code. Albrecht Dürers entschlüsselte Meisterstiche.* Dettelbach: J. H. Röll, 2014.

SILVER, Larry and Jeffrey Chipps Smith, eds. *The Essential Dürer.* Philadelphia: University of Pennsylvania Press, 2010.

Index of Manuscripts

Index (1964)

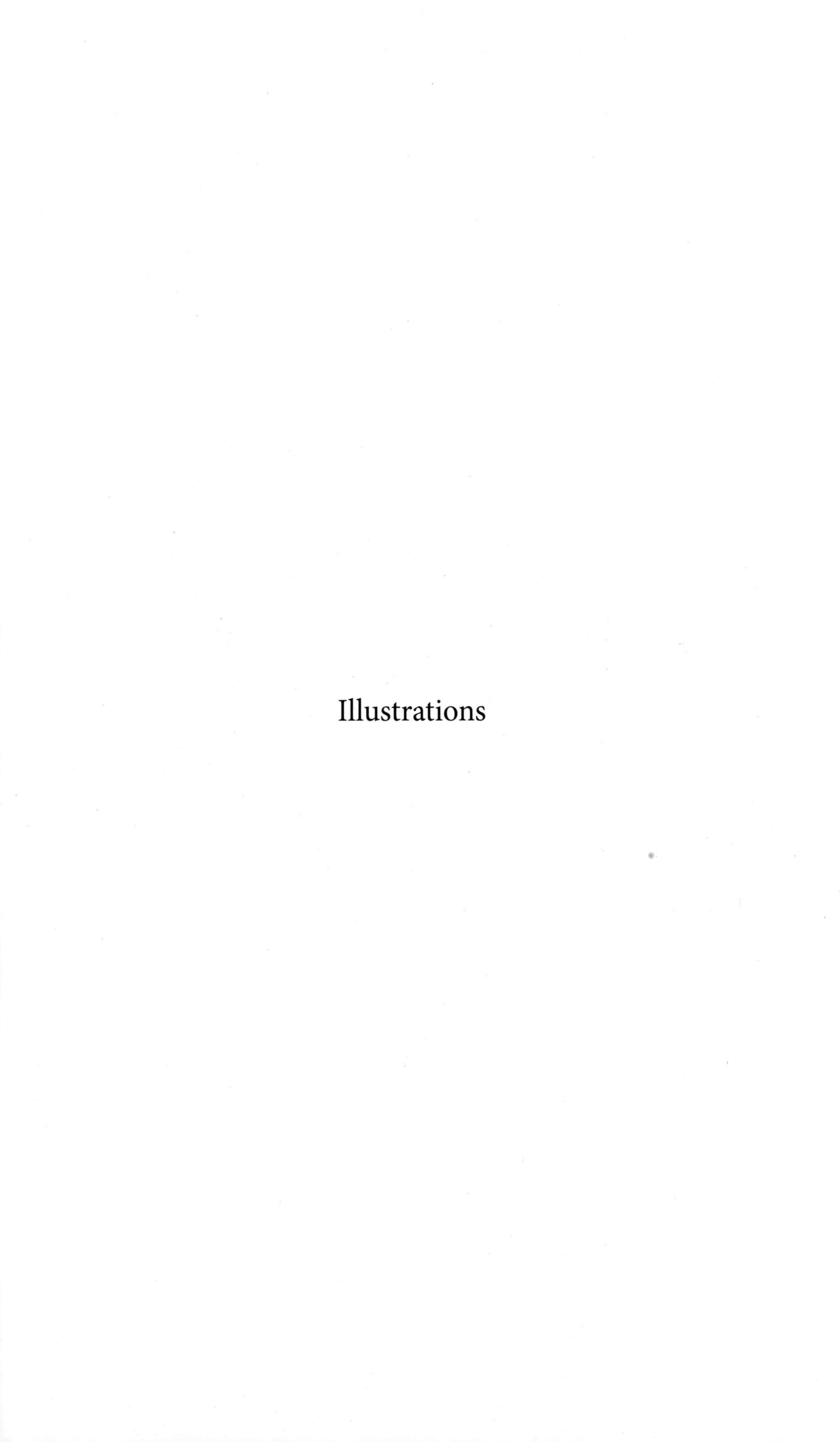

Illustrations

1. Albrecht Dürer, *Melencolia I*. Engraving. 1514

2. Dürer, Study for *Melencolia I*. Pen drawing. 1514

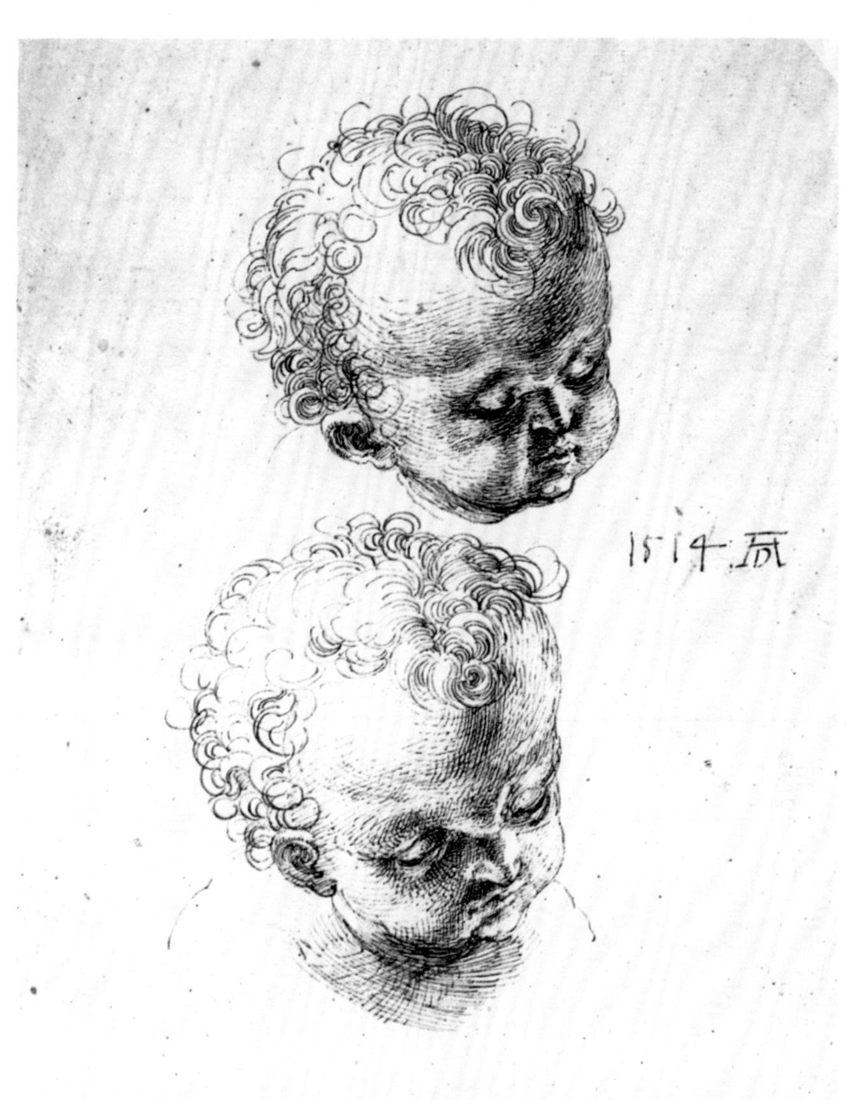

3. Dürer, Studies for the putto's head.
Pen drawing. 1514

4. Copy of a lost sketch by Dürer. Study for the dog.
Pen drawing

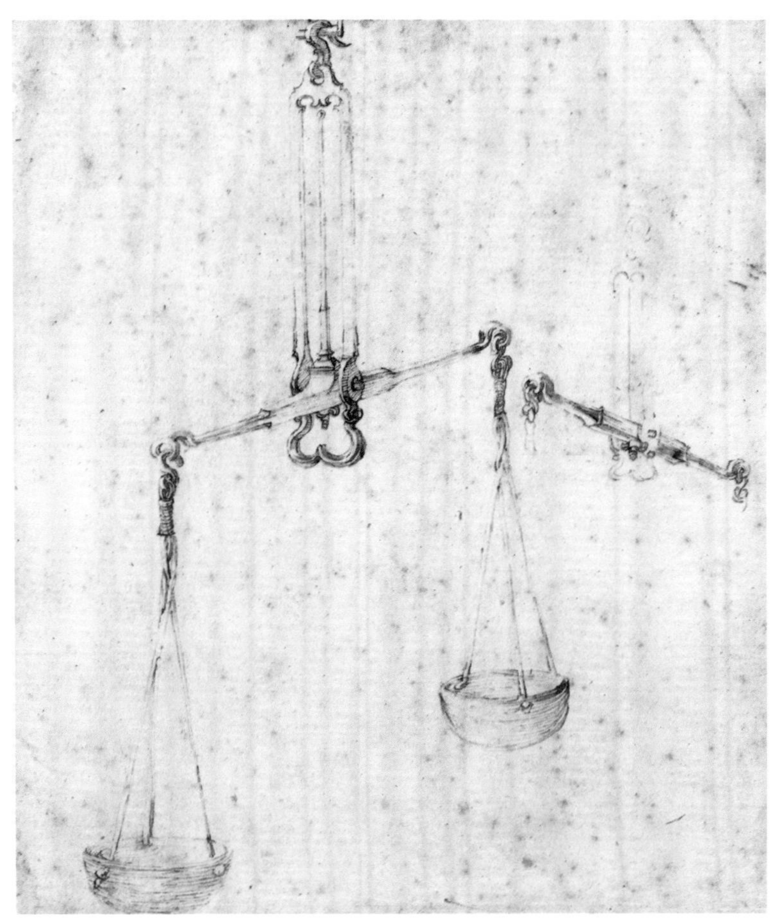

5. Dürer, Preliminary studies for the scales.
Pen drawing. 1514

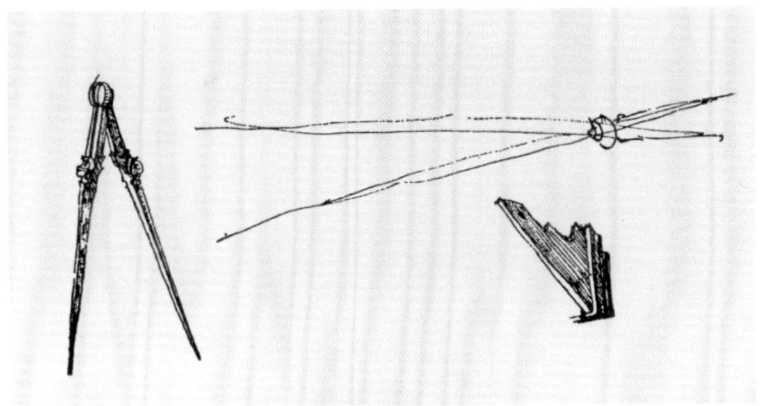

6. Dürer, Studies for the compasses and the moulding plane.
Pen drawing. 1514

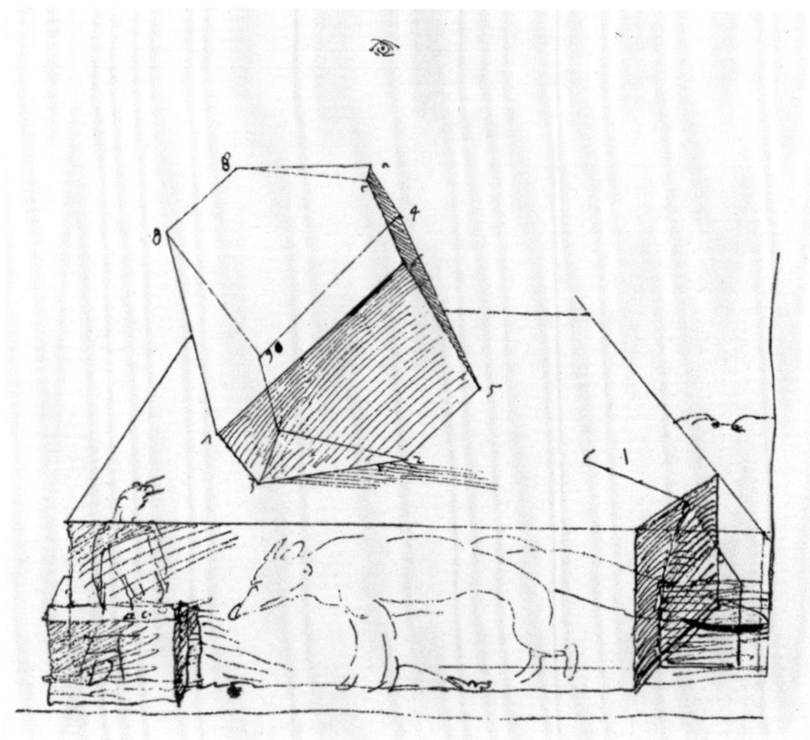

7. Dürer, Preliminary studies for the polyhedron.
Pen drawing. 1514

8. Dürer, Putto.
Pen drawing. 1514

9. Mithraic Aion. Relief.
2nd century A.D.

10. Saturn. Mural painting.
Pompeii, Casa dei Dioscuri. ca 63 A.D.

11. Saturn. Calendar of 354

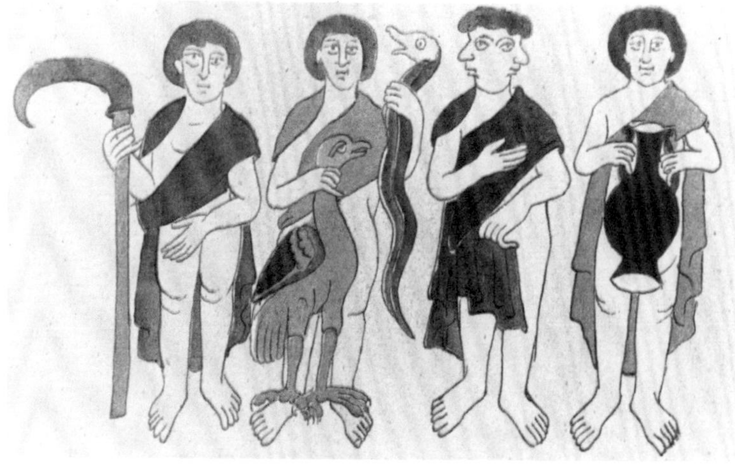

12. Saturn, Jupiter, Janus and Neptune.
R. Maurus, *De Universo*. ca 1023

13. Saturn. Tomb of Cornutus.
3rd century A.D.

14. Kronos devouring the swaddled stone.
G. of Nazianzus, *Orationes*. 11th century

15. Saturn. Germanicus, *Aratea*. 9th century

17. Corybantes and Curetes protecting Zeus. G. of Nazianzus, *Orationes*. 11th century

16. Kronos and Zeus. G. of Nazianzus, *Orationes*. 9th century

18. The Pagan Gods. Remigius of Auxerre.
Commentary on M. Capella's *Nuptiae Philologiae*. ca 1100

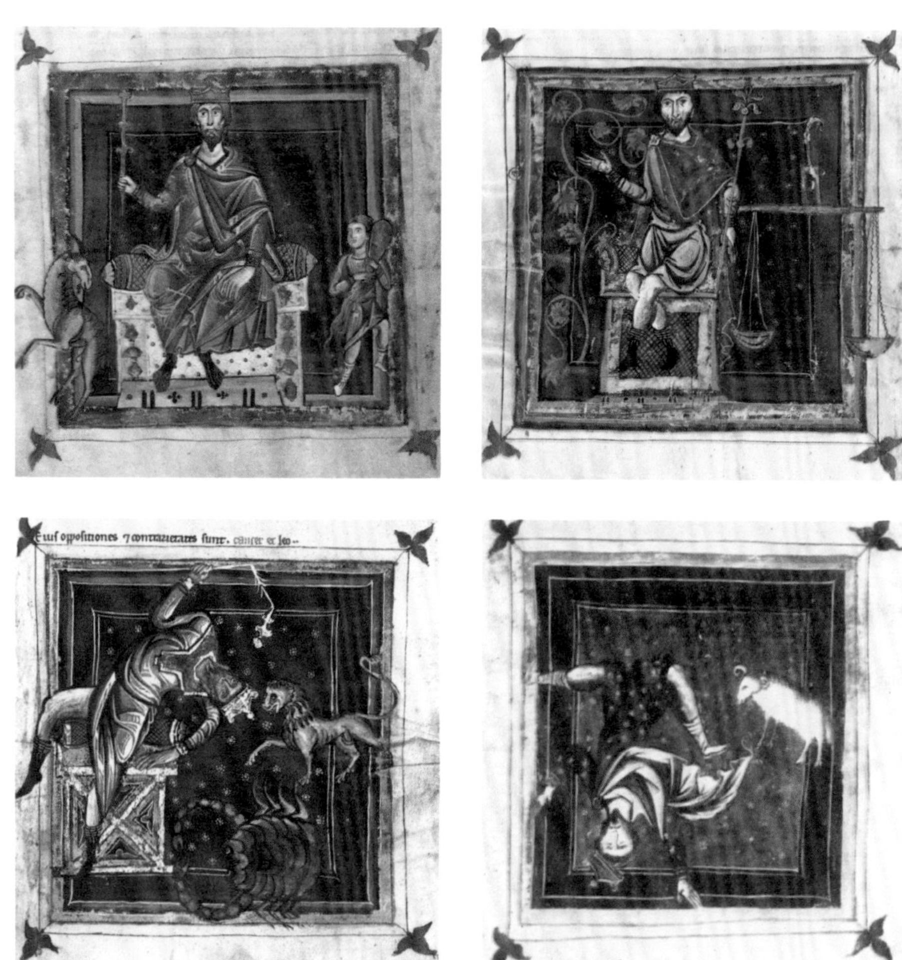

19–22. Saturn's exaltation and decline.
Albumasar, *Introductio in astrologiam*. Mid-13th century

23. Saturn's and Jupiter's exaltation and decline.
Albumasar, *Kitab al-Bulhan*. 1399

24. Saturn and his zodiacal signs.
Albumasar, *Introductio in astrologiam*. ca 1400

25. Saturn. al-Qazwīnī,
Wonders of Creation. 1366

26. Saturn and his zodiacal signs.
B. di Bartoli, *Canzone delle virtù e delle scienze*. 14th century

27. Saturn and Philyra. A. de Nigro, *Introductorius ad iudicia astrologie....* ca 1352

28. Saturn. *Sphaera armillaris cum XII signis.* 15th century

29. Saturn on horseback.
Liber de septem signis. ca 1400

30. Saturn and his zodiacal signs.
Von den XII Zeichen des Gestirns. 1470

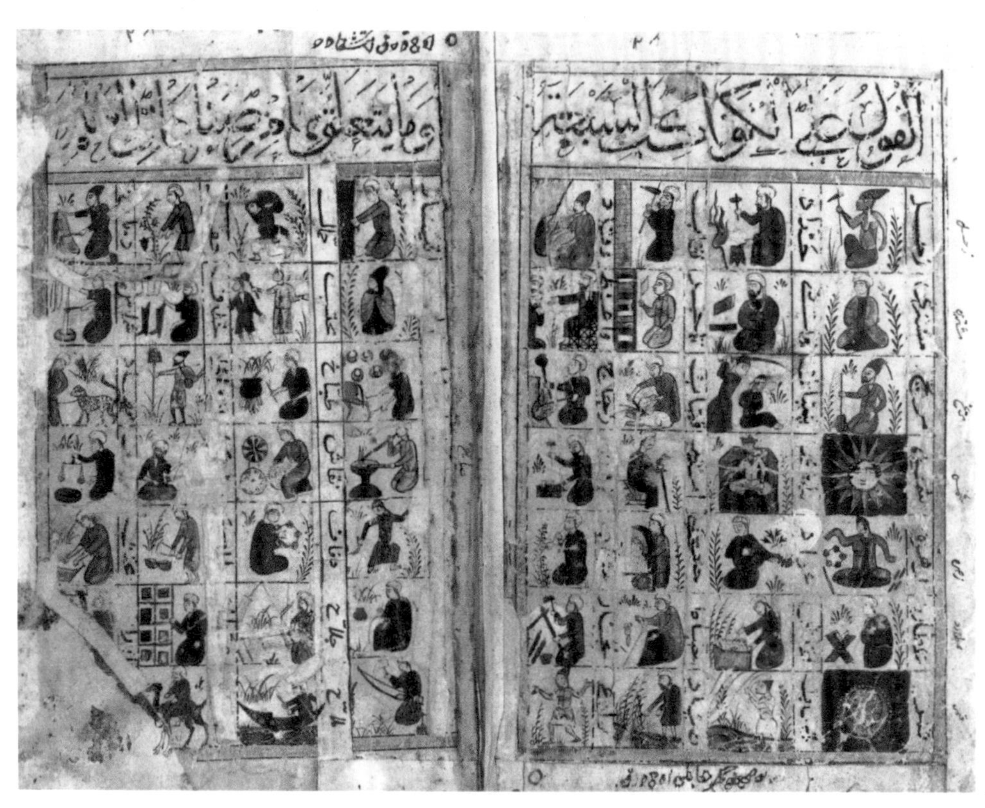

31. Children of the planets.
Albumasar, *Kitab al-Bulhan*. 1399

32–33. Children of Saturn. Fresco.
Padua, Sala della Ragione. 14th century

34. Minerva and her children.
Boccaccio, *Cas des nobles femmes*. 1402

35. Community of the faithful.
Troparium and *Sequentiarium*.
ca 1000

36. Saturn and his children.
C. de Pisan, *Épître d'Othéa*. Beginning 15th century

37. Influences of the planets.
Losbuch in Reimpaaren. End 14th century

38. Saturn and his children. Blockbook. ca 1470

39. Saturn and his children.
Engraving. [B. Baldini.] ca 1464

40. Saturn and his children.
German manuscript. Early 15th century

41. Saturn and his followers.
German manuscript. End 15th century

42. The children of Saturn.
Single leaf from an astrological manuscript. 1458

43. Saturn counting money.
Über die Planeten. 1444

44. Saturn as founder of Sutrium.
Cronica figurata. ca 1460

45. Saturn as Wisdom.
Fulgentius metaforalis. Mid-15th century

46. Saturn and the Dragon of Time.
Ovide moralisé. Second half 14th century

47. The castration of Saturn.
Silverpoint drawing. First third 15th century

48. Saturn devouring a child. Engraving.
After M. de Vos, *Septem Planetae*. 1581

49. Saturn. Studio of A. di Duccio. Relief.
Rimini, Tempio Malatestiano. 1454

50. Roman tomb of a master mason. Relief.
2nd century

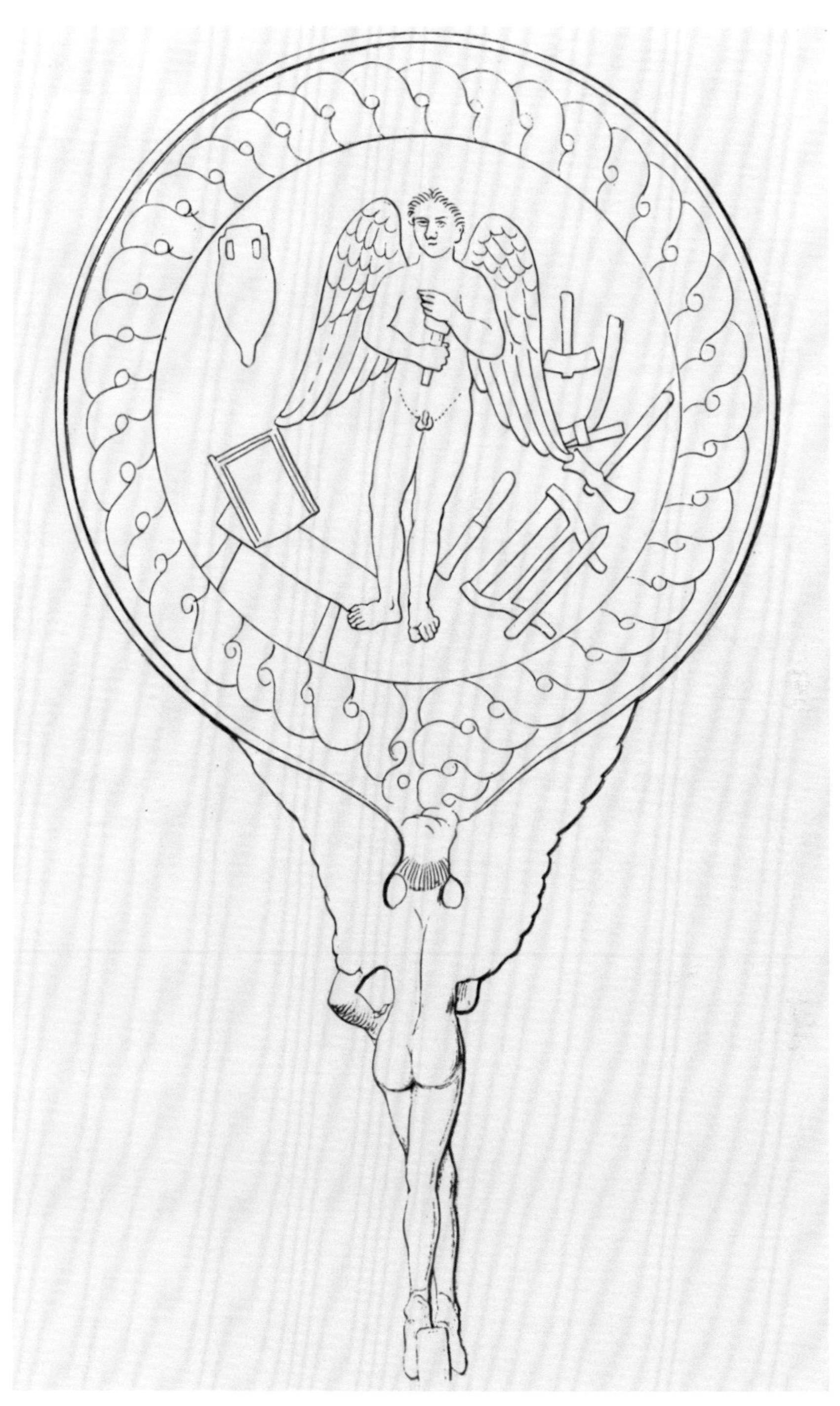

51. Eros as a carpenter. Etruscan Mirror

52. Children of Saturn. Engraving.
After M. van Heemskerck. [1566]

53. Saturn and his children. Engraving.
H. Leroy. 16th century

54. G. Campagnola, *Saturn*. 15th century

55. River God. Relief.
Triumphal Arch of Benevento. 114 A.D.

56. G. da Santa Croce, *Saturn*. 16th century

57. F. Pesellino, *The Triumph of Time, Fame, and Eternity*. Detail. ca 1450

58. The Wheel of Life dominated by Time.
French illuminated manuscript. ca 1400

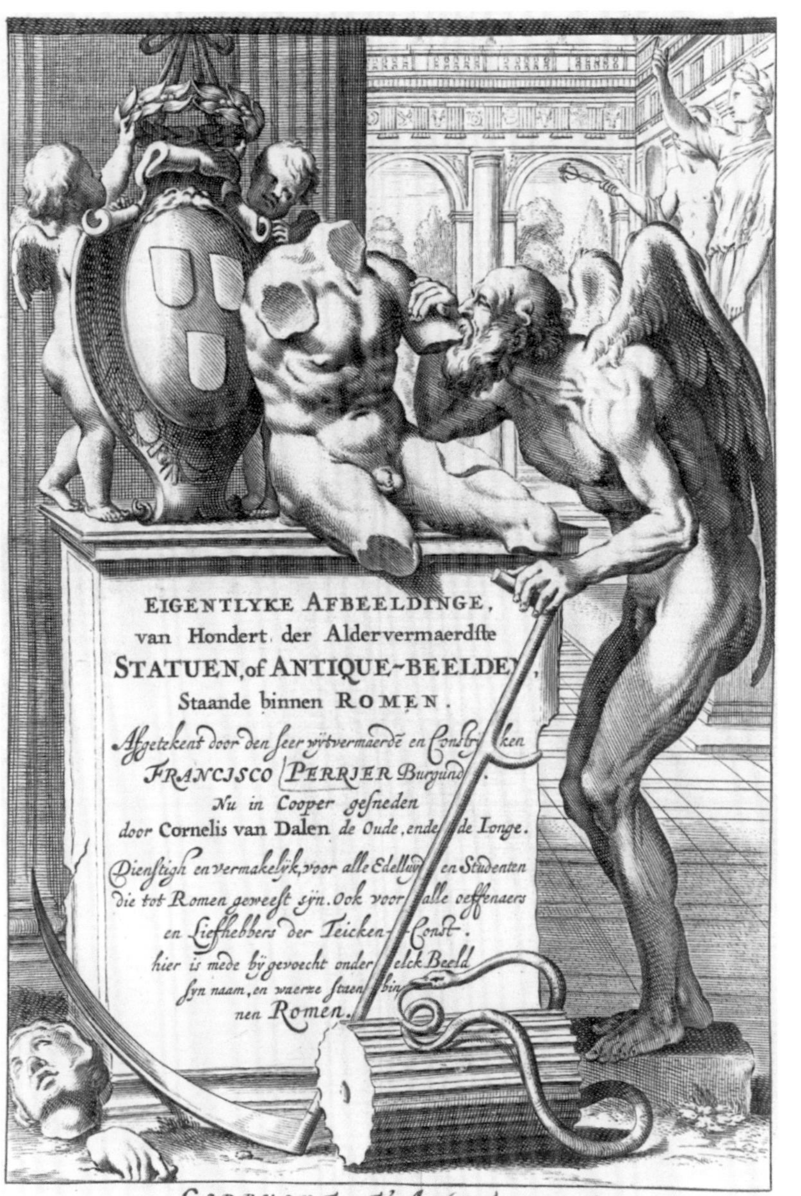

59. Time gnawing at the torso of the Apollo Belvedere.
F. Perrier, *Eigentlyke afbeeldinge van 100
der aldervermaerdste statuen....* 1702

60. Le Cuer et Melencolie.
R. d'Anjou, *Le cuer d'amours espris*. ca 1475

61. Mérencolye and Entendement visiting the Poet.
Les Fais Maistre Alain Chartier. 1489

62. Anima and the Psalmist.
Psalter. Early 9th century

63. The Author and Philosophy. Boethius,
De Consolation de phylosophie, ca 1415–20

64. The Author on his sickbed.
A. Chartier, *L'Espérance ou consolation des trois vertus*. 1428

65. The Author, Melancholy and Reason.
A. Chartier, *Le triomphe de l'Espérance*. ca 1530

66. Acedia. Tapestry.
End 15th century

67. Consolation through music.
Livres pour la santé garder.
Late 13th century

68. The Melancholic.
C. Ripa, *Iconologia*. 1603

69. A. Janssens,
Melancholy and Joy. 1623

70. Healing by Music. Aristotle, *De somno et vigilia*. 13th century

71. Healing by Scourging. T. dei Borgognoni, *Chirurgia*. ca 1300

72. The Melancholic.
Prescriptions for cauterisation. 13th century

73. The Melancholic as a miser.
Von den vier Complexion der Menschen. 15th century

74. Melancholics.
De conservanda bona valetudine. 1557

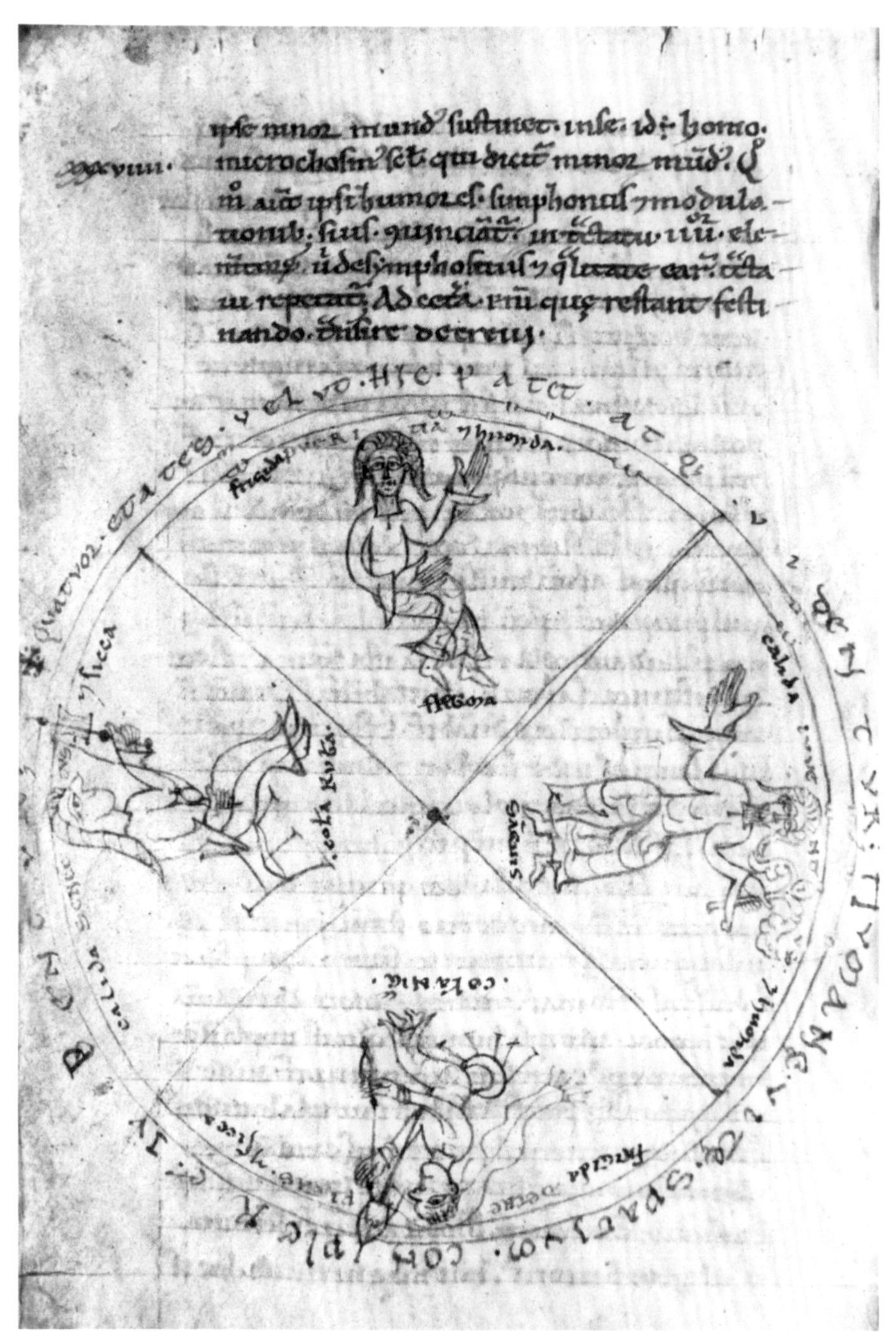

75. The Age of Man and the Temperaments.
Tractatus de quaternario. ca 1100

76. The Four Ages of Man. *Livres pour la santé garder.* Late 15th century

77. The Four Temperaments. *Problèmes d'Aristote.* First half 15th century

78. The Four Temperaments. Broadsheet. Mid-15th century

79. The Wheel of Life. German *Losbuch*. 1461

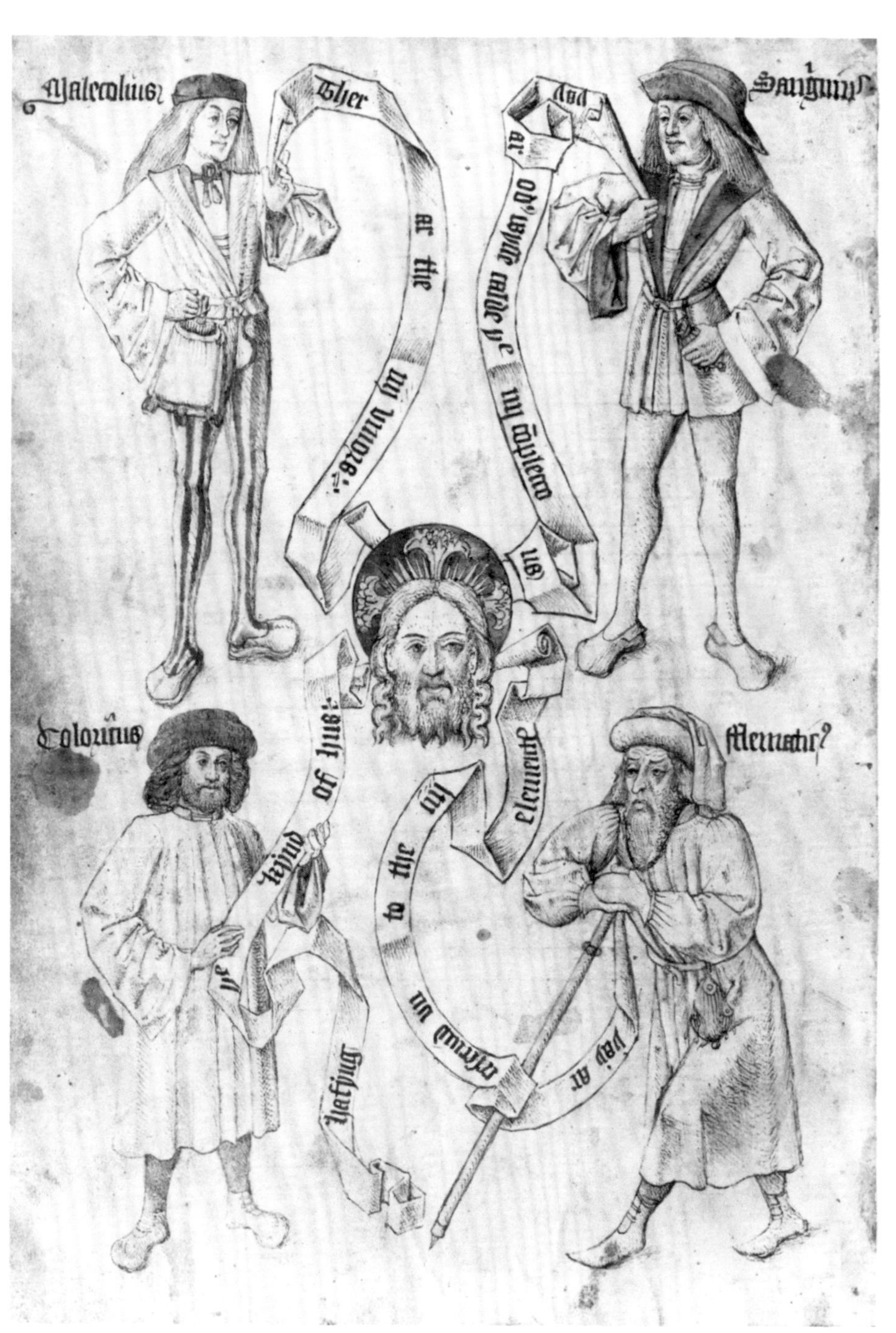

80. The Four Temperaments. Guild-book of the Barber-Surgeons of the City of York. End 15th century

81. The Four Temperaments as riders. Broadsheet. Second half 15th century

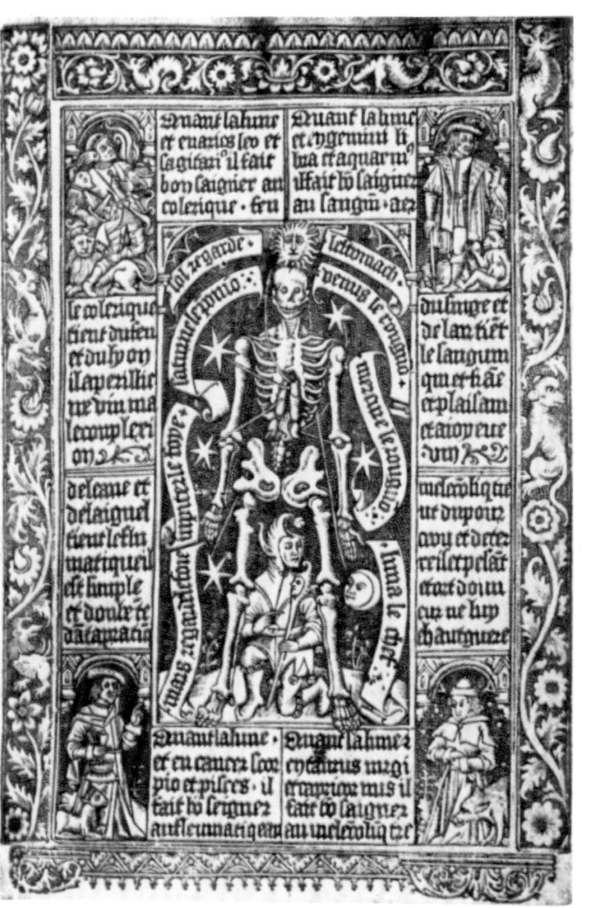

82. The Four Temperaments.
S. Vostre, *Book of Hours*. 1502

83. Dürer, Philosophia. Woodcut.
C. Celtes, *Quattuor Libri Amorum*. 1502

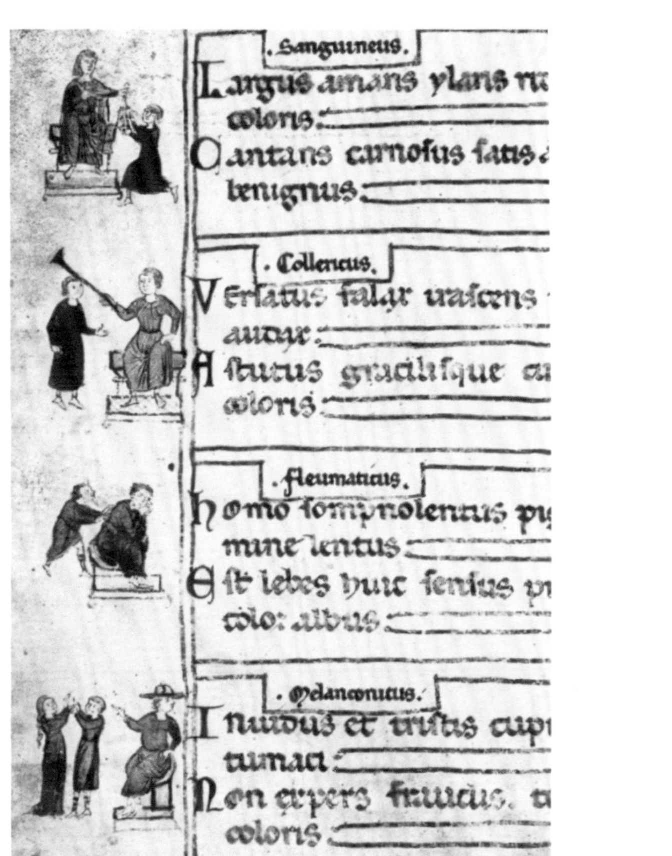

84. The Four Temperaments.
Italian miscellany. Second half 13th century

85. Sanguinics. Woodcut.
Augsburg Calendar. ca 1480

87. Cholerics. Woodcut.
Augsburg Calendar. ca 1480

86. Luxuria. Relief.
Amiens Cathedral. ca 1225–36

88. Discordia. Relief.
Amiens Cathedral. ca 1225–36

Flegmaticus.
Vnser complex ist mit wasser mer getan
Darum̄ wir subtilikeit nit mügen lan.

Melencolicus.
Vnser complexion ist von erden reÿch
Darūb seÿ wir schwärmütigkeyt gleich

89a–b. Phlegmatics and Melancholics.
Woodcut. Augsburg Calendar. ca 1480

90a–d. Sanguinics, Phlegmatics, Cholerics, Melancholics.
Woodcut. Strasbourg Calendar. ca 1550

91. Paresse, Labeur and Prouesse with David and Goliath.
Fr. Laurent, *La Somme le Roi.* Beginning 15th century

92. Acedia.
Franconian Broadsheet. ca 1490

93. Envy and Sloth. Antwerp Master. ca 1490–1500

94. The Astronomer.
J. Angelus, *Astrolabium planum*. 1494

95. P. Flötner. The Opticians.
Witelo, *Perspectiva*. 1535

96. Dürer, *The Doctor's Dream*.
Engraving. 1497–98

97. Pictures of the Months.
De signis XII mensium. 818

98. Pictures of the Seasons.
R. Maurus, *De Universo.* ca 1023

99. Peasants. Sarcophagus of L. A. O. Valerianus.
Detail. 3rd century A.D.

100. Aristotle.
Chartres Cathedral, West Porch. ca 1145

101. Science, Art, Prudence, Entendement, Sapience. Aristotle, *Ethics*. 1376

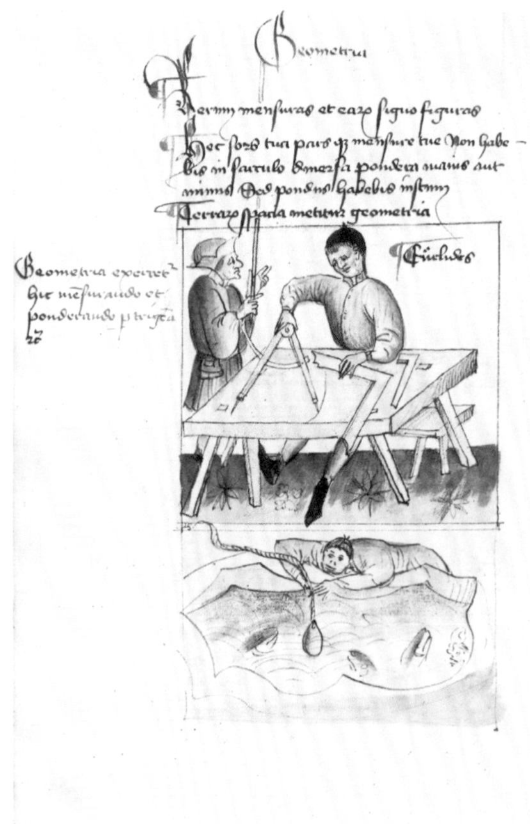

102. Geometry. *De septem artibus liberalibus*. Second half 15th century

103. Deduccion loable. *Douze Dames de rhétorique.*
Late 15th century

104. Geometry. G. Reisch, *Margarita philosophica.* 1504

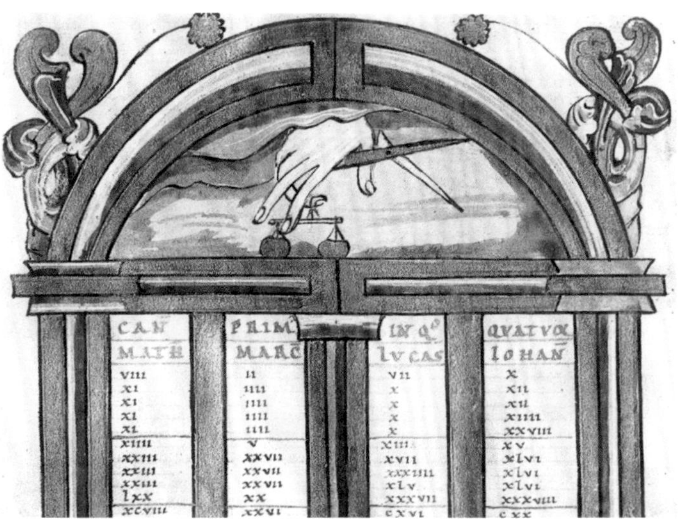

105. The Hand of God with scales and compasses. Eadwi Gospels. Beginning 11th century

106. God the Father with scales and compasses.
Psalter. First half 11th century

107. Saturn with putto as Geometer.
H. Döring, *Eyn gesprech....* 1535

108. God the Father measuring the world.
Bible moralisée. ca 1250

109. Fructus Laborum. H. Hondius, *Pictorum aliquot celebrium*. ca 1610

110. Honore, Disegno, Labore.
P. de Jode, *Varie Figure Academiche*. 1639

111. Dürer, *The Four Apostles*. 1526

Zelotypia

Democritus Abderites

Solitudo

THE ANATOMY OF MELANCHOLY.
What it is, With all the kinds causes, Symptomes, Prognostickes, & Severall cures of it.
In three Partitions, with their severall Sections, members & subsections.
Philosophically, Medicinally, Historically, opened & cut up.
By
Democritus Junior.
With a Satyricall Preface, Conducing to the following Discourse.
The third Edition, corrected and augmented by the Author.
Omne tulit punctum, qui miscuit utile dulci.

Inamorato

Hypocondriacus

Superstitiosus

Democritus Junior

Maniacus

Oxford Printed for Henry Cripps 1628

Borago

C. le Blon fe:

Helleborus

112. Title page by C. Le Blon to R. Burton's book. *The Anatomy of Melancholy.* 1638

113. Temperaments and Elements.
After M. de Vos. *Septem Planetae*. 1581

114. Melancholy. Engraving.
Master A. C. ca 1525

115. Melancholy. Engraving.
H. S. Beham. 1539

116. Melancholy. Engraving.
Master F. B. ca 1560

New Formu-
lar/Teutsch/Allerlei
Schreibenn/Als Instrument/
Sendbrieff/Anlaß/Compaß/Testa-
ment rc. vñ dergleichen andere Schriff
ten/In vnd ausserhalb Gericht zubrauchen/In
Fürsten Cantzleien/vnd sunst üblich/belangend.
Vorhin im Truck nie außgangen. Allen vnd ieden/so sich
Schreibens gebrauchen/fast nutzlich vnd dienlich.

Mit einem vorgehnden gûtten vnd
vnderschidlichen Register.

Cum Gratia, & Priuilegio.

Zû Franckenfurt/Bei Christian Egenolff.

117. [Figure of Melancholia sitting], after Dürer.
New Formular. 1545

MELANCHOLIA.

Hienauß/dortnauß/mein sinn sich lenckt/ Vnd manche seltzam Kunst erdenckt.
Bist du mein freundt/thu mich nicht jrren/ Sonst wirstu mir mein Hirn verwirren.

Mir bringt kein freuwd der Kinder schreyen/ Der Hüner getzen/Eyer legen.
Laß mich nur bleiben bey meim sinn/ Sonst wirstus haben klein gewin.

***

118. Melancholy. Engraving.
J. Amman, *Wappen- und Stammbuch*. 1589

119–122. The Four Temperaments. Engraving.
V. Solis. 16th century

123. M. Gerung, *Melancholy*. 1558

124–127. The Four Temperaments. Engraving.
South German Master (Jost Amman?). ca 1570

128. Lucas Cranach, *An Allegory of Melancholy*. 1528

129. Cranach, *Melancholy*. 1532

130. Cranach, *Melancholy*. ca 1533

131. Melancholic Maiden. Woodcut.
A. F. Doni. *I marmi.* 1552

132. J. Boeckhorst. *Geometria*. ca 1650

133. Melancholy. Engraving.
After A. Bloemaert. 17th century

134. D. Feti, *Melancholy*. ca 1614

135. G. B. Castiglione, *Melancholy*.
Etching. 17th century

136. Melancholy. Red chalk drawing.
N. Chaperon. 17th century

137. E. von Steinle, *Melancholy*.
Pen and water-colour. 1867

138. C. Friedrich, *Melancholy*. 1818.
Woodcut after C. D. Friedrich. 1801

139. Melancholics. Pen drawing.
Second quarter 16th century

140. Melancholics. Engraving.
After M. de Vos. ca 1590

141. Phlegmatics. Engraving.
After M. de Vos. ca 1590

142. Phlegma. Engraving.
After J. de Gheyn [II]. [1596–97]

143. Melancholy. Engraving.
After J. de Gheyn [II]. [1596–98]

144. Saturn and his children. Engraving.
After M. van Heemskerck. 16th century

145. Dürer, *Self-portrait with the yellow spot*.
Drawing. 1509–11

146. Dürer, *Man in despair.*
Etching. 1515–16

147. Cranach, *Melancholy*. 1532

148. Cranach (?), *Melancholy*. 1524

149. Formae Saturni, *Picatrix*. trad. latina

150. Correspondence between Microcosm and Macrocosm.
Isidore of Seville, *De natura rerum*. 1472